Dewey Decimal Classification

Devised by Melvil Dewey

January 2019

Volume 2

Edited by

Julianne Beall, Consulting Senior Editor

Violet Fox, Editor

Alex Kyrios, Editor

Winton E. Matthews, Jr., Consulting Senior Editor

OCLC
OCLC, Inc.
Dublin, Ohio
2019

OCLC, Inc.
6565 Kilgour Place
Dublin, OH 43017-3395 USA
www.oclc.org/dewey

ISBN: (set) 978-1-55653-088-3
ISBN: (vol. 2) 978-1-55653-082-1

200   Religion

Beliefs, attitudes, practices of individuals and groups with respect to the ultimate nature of existences and relationships within the context of revelation, deity, worship

Including public relations for religion

Class here comparative religion; religions other than Christianity; works dealing with various religions, with religious topics not applied to specific religions; syncretistic religious writings of individuals expressing personal views and not claiming to establish a new religion or to represent an old one

Class a specific topic in comparative religion, religions other than Christianity in 201–209. Class public relations for a specific religion or aspect of a religion with the religion or aspect, e.g., public relations for a local Christian church 254.4

> *For government policy on religion, see 322.1*

> *See also 306.6 for sociology of religion*

> *See Manual at T1—0882 and 200; also at 130 vs. 200; also at 200 vs. 100; also at 201–209 and 292–299*

(Option: To give preferred treatment or shorter numbers to a specific religion other than Christianity, use one of the two options described at 290)

SUMMARY

200.1–.9	Standard subdivisions
201	Religious mythology, general classes of religion, interreligious relations and attitudes, social theology
202	Doctrines
203	Public worship and other practices
204	Religious experience, life, practice
205	Religious ethics
206	Leaders and organization
207	Missions and religious education
208	Sources
209	Sects and reform movements
210	Philosophy and theory of religion
.1	Theory of philosophy of religion
211	Concepts of God
212	Existence of God, ways of knowing God, attributes of God
213	Creation
214	Theodicy
215	Science and religion
218	Humankind

220	**Bible**
.01–.09	Standard subdivisions and special topics of Bible
.1–.9	Generalities
221	**Old Testament (Tanakh)**
222	**Historical books of Old Testament**
223	**Poetic books of Old Testament**
224	**Prophetic books of Old Testament**
225	**New Testament**
226	**Gospels and Acts**
227	**Epistles**
228	**Revelation (Apocalypse)**
229	**Apocrypha, pseudepigrapha, intertestamental works**
230	**Christianity**
.002–.007	Standard subdivisions of Christianity
.01–.09	Standard subdivisions and specific types of Christian theology
.1–.9	Doctrines of specific denominations and sects
231	**God**
232	**Jesus Christ and his family**
233	**Humankind**
234	**Salvation and grace**
235	**Spiritual beings**
236	**Eschatology**
238	**Creeds, confessions of faith, covenants, catechisms**
239	**Apologetics and polemics**
240	**Christian moral and devotional theology**
241	**Christian ethics**
242	**Devotional literature**
243	**Evangelistic writings for individuals and families**
246	**Use of art in Christianity**
247	**Church furnishings and related articles**
248	**Christian experience, practice, life**
249	**Christian observances in family life**
250	**Local Christian church and Christian religious orders**
.9	History, geographic treatment, biography
251	**Preaching (Homiletics)**
252	**Texts of sermons**
253	**Pastoral office and work (Pastoral theology)**
254	**Local church administration**
255	**Religious congregations and orders**
259	**Pastoral care of families, of specific groups of people**
260	**Christian social and ecclesiastical theology**
.9	History, geographic treatment, biography
261	**Social theology and interreligious relations and attitudes**
262	**Ecclesiology**
263	**Days, times, places of religious observance**
264	**Public worship**
265	**Sacraments, other rites and acts**
266	**Missions**
267	**Associations for religious work**
268	**Religious education**
269	**Spiritual renewal**
270	**History, geographic treatment, biography of Christianity**
.01–.09	Standard subdivisions
.1–.8	Historical periods
271	**Religious congregations and orders in church history**
272	**Persecutions in general church history**
273	**Doctrinal controversies and heresies in general church history**
274–279	**Christianity by specific continents, countries, localities in modern world**

280	**Denominations and sects of Christian church**
.01–.09	**Standard subdivisions and special topics**
.2–.4	**Branches**
281	**Early church and Eastern churches**
282	**Roman Catholic Church**
283	**Anglican churches**
284	**Protestant denominations of Continental origin and related bodies**
285	**Presbyterian churches, Reformed churches centered in America, Congregational churches, Puritanism**
286	**Baptist, Restoration movement, Adventist churches**
287	**Methodist churches; churches related to Methodism**
289	**Other denominations and sects**
290	**Other religions**
292	**Classical religion (Greek and Roman religion)**
293	**Germanic religion**
294	**Religions of Indic origin**
295	**Zoroastrianism (Mazdaism, Parseeism)**
296	**Judaism**
297	**Islam, Babism, Bahai Faith**
299	**Religions not provided for elsewhere**

> **200.1–200.9 Standard subdivisions**

Limited to comparative religion, religion in general

.1 Systems, scientific principles, psychology of religion

Do not use for philosophy and theory; class in 210

.11 Systems

[.12] Classification

Do not use; class in 201.4

[.14] Communication

Do not use; class in 210.14

.15 Scientific principles

Class philosophic treatment of the relation of science and religion in 215

.19 Psychological principles

Class here psychology of religion

.2–.5 Standard subdivisions

[.6] Organizations and management

Do not use; class in 206

.7 Education, research, related topics

.71   Education

Class here religion as an academic subject

Class religious education to inculcate religious life and practice, comprehensive works on religious education in 207.5

See also 379.28 for place of religion in public schools

See Manual at 207.5, 268 vs. 200.71, 230.071, 292–299

.8   **Groups of people**

Class here attitudes of religions to social groups; discrimination, equality, inequality, prejudice

.9   **History, geographic treatment, biography**

See Manual at 200.9 vs. 294, 299.5

.901 2   To 4000 B.C.

Do not use for prehistoric religions; class in 201.42

.92   Biography

See Manual at 200.92 and 201–209, 292–299

.93   Ancient world

Class here religions of antiquity

For Christianity to 325, see 270.1. For a specific religion of antiquity other than Christianity, see the religion in 290, e.g., classical religion 292, Celtic religion 299.16

> **201–209 Specific aspects of religion**

Class treatment of religious topics with respect to philosophy of religion, natural theology in 210; class treatment with respect to Christianity in 230–280; class treatment with respect to a specific religion other than Christianity in 292–299; class comprehensive works on comparative religion in 200

See Manual at 200.92 and 201–209, 292–299; also at 201–209 and 292–299

201   **Religious mythology, general classes of religion, interreligious relations and attitudes, social theology**

SUMMARY

201.3	**Mythology and mythological foundations**
.4	**General classes of religion**
.5	**Interreligious relations**
.6	**Religions and secular disciplines**
.7	**Attitudes of religions toward social issues**

[.012]   Classification

Do not use; class in 201.4

.3 **Mythology and mythological foundations**

Stories of primeval history, beings, origins, and customs archetypally significant in the sacred life, doctrine, and ritual of religions

Class myths on a specific subject with the subject, e.g., creation myths 202.4

See Manual at 398.2 vs. 201.3, 230, 270, 292–299

.4 **General classes of religion**

Including monotheistic, nontheistic, pantheistic, polytheistic religions

Class here classification of religions

Class concepts of God or the gods in world religions in 202.11; class philosophic treatment of concepts of God in 211

.42 Prehistoric religions

.43 Goddess religions

See also 202.114 for female goddesses

.44 Shamanism

Class shamanism in a specific religion with the religion, e.g., shamanism in religions of North American native origin 299.71144

.5 **Interreligious relations**

Class here relations between three or more religions

A work on relations between two religions is classed with the religion of the author's viewpoint, e.g., a work on relations between Christianity and Islam from a Christian viewpoint 261.27, a work on relations between Christianity and Islam from a Muslim viewpoint 297.283. If viewpoint cannot be determined, give priority to the religion coming first, e.g., a work on relations between Christianity and Islam from an undetermined viewpoint 261.27

.51 Relations of religions with irreligion

Class here relations of religions with atheism

.52 Relations with Christianity

Use this number only for building other numbers, e.g., relations of Buddhism with Christianity 294.3352; never use it by itself

.53 Relations with classical religion (Greek and Roman religion) and Germanic religion

Use this number only for building other numbers, e.g., relations of Zoroastrianism with Greek religion 295.153; never use it by itself

.54–.59 Relations with other religions

Add to base number 201.5 the numbers following 29 in 294–299, e.g., relations with Hinduism 201.545

Use these numbers only for building other numbers, e.g., relations of Buddhism with Hinduism 294.33545; never use them by themselves

.6   **Religions and secular disciplines**

> Class guides to religious life and practice on specific topics in secular disciplines in 204.4
>
> *For attitudes of religions toward social sciences, see 201.7*

.600 01–.600 09   Standard subdivisions

.600 1–.619 9   Computer science, information, philosophy, parapsychology and occultism, psychology

> Add to base number 201.6 notation 001–199, e.g., religions and psychology 201.615

.64–.69   Language, natural sciences, mathematics, technology, arts, literature, rhetoric, geography, history

> Add to base number 201.6 notation 400–900, e.g., religions and science 201.65; however, for ecology, see 201.77

.7   **Attitudes of religions toward social issues**

> Attitudes of religions toward and influences on secular matters
>
> Class here religion and culture, social theology
>
> Class human ecology in 201.77; class guides to religious life and practice on specific topics in the social sciences in 204.4; class sociology of religion in 306.6
>
> *For attitudes toward social groups, see 200.8; for attitudes toward various religions, see 201.5*
>
> *See also 205 for religious ethics*

.72   Political affairs

> Attitudes toward and influences on political activities and ideologies
>
> Including civil war and revolution
>
> Class secular view of religiously oriented political theories and ideologies in 320.55; class secular view of relation of state to religious organizations and groups in 322.1
>
> *See Manual at 322.1 vs. 201.72, 261.7, 292–299*

.721   Theocracy

> Supremacy of organized religion over civil government

.723   Civil rights

> Including citizenship, religious freedom

.727   International affairs

.727 3   War and peace

> Including conscientious objectors, disarmament, pacifism
>
> *For nuclear weapons and nuclear war, see 201.7275*

.727 5   Nuclear weapons and nuclear war

.73	Economics

Class socioeconomic problems in 201.76

For environment, natural resources, see 201.77

.76	Social problems and services

Class here socioeconomic problems

See also 361.75 for welfare work of religious organizations

.762–.763	Specific social problems

Add to base number 201.76 the numbers following 36 in 362–363, e.g., poor people 201.7625, hunger 201.7638; however, for population problems, see 201.7; for environmental problems, see 201.77

.764	Crime and punishment

.77	Environment

Class here ecology, human ecology, environmental problems, natural resources, pollution

Class environmental ethics in 205.691

202 Doctrines

Class here beliefs, apologetics, polemics; comprehensive works on theology

For social theologies, see 201.7; for religious ethics, see 205

.1	**Objects of worship and veneration**

Class here animism, spiritism

.11	God, gods, goddesses, divinities and deities

Class here supernatural beings

Class concepts of God in philosophy of religion in 211

.112	Attributes of God, of the gods

For attributes of male gods, see 202.113; for attributes of female goddesses, see 202.114

.113	Male gods

.114	Female goddesses

See also 201.43 for goddess religions

.117	Relation to the world

Including miracles, prophecy, providence, revelation, relation to and action in history

For creation and cosmology, see 202.4

.118	Theodicy

Vindication of God's justice and goodness in permitting existence of evil and suffering

.12	Nature

Including fire, sex, sun, trees, water

See also 203.5 for sacred places

.13	Persons

Including ancestors, the dead, heroes, monarchs, saints

.14	Personified abstractions
.15	Good spirits

Class here angels

.16	Evil spirits

Class here demons, devils

.18	Images
.2	**Humankind**

Including atonement, creation of humankind, repentance, salvation, sin, soul

Class here comprehensive works on karma

Class creation of the world in 202.4

For eschatology, see 202.3. For a specific aspect of karma, see the aspect, e.g., karma as a concept in Buddhist ethics 294.35

.3	**Eschatology**

Including death, end of the world, heaven, hell, immortality, other worlds, punishments, purgatory, resurrection, rewards

.37	Reincarnation
.4	**Creation and cosmology**

For creation of humankind, see 202.2

203	**Public worship and other practices**

Practices predominantly public or collective in character

Unless other instructions are given, class a subject with aspects in two or more subdivisions of 203 in the number coming first, e.g., religious healing and ceremonies connected with it 203.1 (*not* 203.8)

Class leaders and organization in 206; class missions and religious education in 207; class comprehensive works on worship in 204.3

.1	**Religious healing**

See Manual at 615.852 vs. 203.1, 234.131, 292–299

.2	**Divination**

Including omens, oracles, prophecies

Class comprehensive works on divination in 133.3

.3	**Witchcraft**

Class religions based on modern revivals of witchcraft in 299.94; class comprehensive works on witchcraft in 133.43

.4	**Offerings, sacrifices, penances**
.42	Human sacrifice

.5	**Sacred places and pilgrimages**

Standard subdivisions are added for sacred places and pilgrimages together, for sacred places alone

Class here grottoes, holy buildings, pagodas, shrines, temples

Class monasteries in 206.57

.509 3–.509 9	Specific continents, countries, localities

Class here pilgrimages to specific sacred places

.51	Pilgrimages
[.510 93–.510 99]	Specific continents, countries, localities

Do not use; class in 203.5093–203.5099

.6	**Sacred times**

Including holy days, religious calendar, religious festivals

See Manual at 203.6, 263.9, 292–299 vs. 394.265–394.267

.7	**Symbolism, symbolic objects, sounds**

Including mandalas, mantras

Class here religious use, significance, purpose of the arts

See also 201.67 for attitudes of religions toward the arts

.8	**Rites and ceremonies**

Conduct and texts

Including liturgy, music, processions, public feasts and fasts, public prayer

Class interdisciplinary works on sacred music in 781.7; class interdisciplinary works on sacred vocal music in 782.22

.81	Birth rites
.82	Initiation rites
.85	Marriage rites
.88	Funeral and mourning rites

Standard subdivisions are added for either or both topics in heading

204   Religious experience, life, practice

> Practices predominantly private or individual in character
>
> Class here spirituality
>
> Class religious ethics in 205

.2   Religious experience

> Including conversion, enlightenment

.22   Mysticism

.3   Worship, meditation, yoga

> Class here practical works on prayer, on contemplation; comprehensive works on worship
>
> *For public worship, see 203*

.32   Devotional literature

> Including meditations

.33   Prayer books

.35   Meditation

.36   Yoga

> Religious and spiritual discipline
>
> Including kundalini yoga
>
> Class interdisciplinary works on yoga in 181.45
>
> *For Hindu kundalini yoga, see 294.5436*
>
> *See also 613.7046 for hatha yoga, physical yoga*

.4   Religious life and practice

> Class here guides to religious life and practice
>
> *For worship, meditation, yoga, see 204.3*

[.408 5]   Relatives

> Do not use; class in 204.41

.408 6   People by miscellaneous social attributes

[.408 655]   Married people

> Do not use; class in 204.41

.408 7   Gifted people

> Do not use for people with disabilities and illnesses; class in 204.42

.41 Marriage and family life

> Including divorce, interreligious marriage; adoption, child rearing, religious training of children in the home, single-parent family

> Class here comprehensive works on marriage

> Class comprehensive works on religious training in 207.5

> > *For abuse within the family, see 201.7628292; for marriage rites, see 203.85; for ethics of marriage, see 205.63*

.42 People experiencing illness, trouble, addiction, bereavement

> *See Manual at 616.86 vs. 158.1, 204.42, 248.8629, 292–299, 362.29*

.46 Individual observances

> Not provided for elsewhere

> Including almsgiving, ceremonial and ritual observances, dietary limitations, observance of restrictions and limitations

.47 Asceticism

> Including practice of celibacy, fasting and abstinence, poverty, solitude

205 Religious ethics

> Including conscience, sin

.6 Specific moral issues, sins, vices, virtues

> Add to base number 205.6 the numbers following 17 in 172–179, e.g., sexual relations 205.66, morality of discriminatory practices 205.675

206 Leaders and organization

> Class here management

.1 Leaders and their work

> Variant names: clergy, gurus, messiahs, priests, prophets, shamans

> Role, function, duties

> Including pastoral counseling and preaching

> Class theologians in 202. Class a specific activity of a leader with the activity, e.g., religious healing by shamans 203.1

> > *For founders of religions, see 206.3*

> > *See Manual at 200.92 and 201–209, 292–299*

[.109 2] Biography

> Do not use; class as instructed in Manual at 200.92 and 292–299

.3 Founders of religions

[.309 2] Biography

> Do not use; class as instructed in Manual at 200.92 and 292–299

.5   **Organizations and organization**

> Including associations, congregations, institutions, orders, parties; exercise of religious authority
>
> Class laws and decisions in 208.4

.57   Monasticism and monasteries

> Class here religious orders

207   Missions and religious education

.2   **Missions**

.5   **Religious education**

> Class here comprehensive works on religious education and religion as an academic subject
>
> > *For education in and teaching of comparative religion, religion as an academic subject, see 200.71; for religious training of children in the home, see 204.41*
>
> > *See Manual at 207.5, 268 vs. 200.71, 230.071, 292–299*

208   Sources

> Class theology based on sacred sources in 202

.2   **Sacred books and scriptures**

> > *For sacred books and scriptures of sects and reform movements, see 208.5*

.3   **Oral traditions**

> > *For oral traditions of sects and reform movements, see 208.5*

.4   **Laws and decisions**

> Class civil law relating to religious matters in 340
>
> > *For laws and decisions of sects and reform movements, see 208.5*
>
> > *See also 364.188 for offenses against religion as defined and penalized by the state*

.5   **Sources of sects and reform movements**

209   Sects and reform movements

> Class here new religious movements
>
> Class specific aspects of sects and reform movements in 201–208
>
> > *For specific sects and reform movements, see 280–290*
>
> > *See Manual at 299.93*

210   Philosophy and theory of religion

Class here natural theology, philosophical theology; works that use observation and interpretation of evidence in nature, speculation, and reasoning, but not revelation or appeal to authoritative scriptures, to examine religious beliefs

Class a specific topic treated with respect to religions based on revelation or authority with the topic in 201–209, e.g., concepts of God in world religions 202.11; class a specific topic with respect to a specific religion with the religion, e.g., Christian concepts of God 231

(Option: To give local emphasis and a shorter number to a specific religion other than Christianity, class it in this number, and add to base number 21 the numbers following the base number for that religion in 292–299, e.g., Hinduism 210, Mahabharata 219.23; in that case class philosophy and theory of religion in 200, its subdivisions 211–218 in 200.1. Another option is described at 290)

.1   **Theory of philosophy of religion**

Including methodology of the philosophy of religion

[.11]   Systems

Do not use; class in 200.11

[.12]   Classification

Do not use; class in 201.4

.14   Communication

[.15]   Scientific principles

Do not use; class in 200.15

[.19]   Psychological principles

Do not use; class in 200.19

211   Concepts of God

Including anthropomorphism

Class here comprehensive works on God, on The Holy

Class God, gods and goddesses in comparative religion in 202.11

For existence of God, ways of knowing God, attributes of God, miracles, see 212

.2   **Pantheism**

Class comprehensive works on viewpoints based on belief in the existence of God in 211.3

.3   **Theism**

Class here comprehensive works on viewpoints based on belief in the existence of God

For pantheism, see 211.2; for deism, see 211.5

.32   Polytheism

.33   Dualism

.34   Monotheism

.4   **Free thought**

Class here rationalism

Class comprehensive works on viewpoints based on lack of belief in, doubt about, or rejection of the existence of God in 211.8

.5   **Deism**

Class comprehensive works on viewpoints based on belief in the existence of God in 211.3

.6   **Humanism and secularism**

Standard subdivisions are added for either or both topics in heading

Class here secular humanism

Class comprehensive works on viewpoints based on lack of belief in, doubt about, or rejection of the existence of God in 211.8

.7   **Agnosticism and skepticism**

Standard subdivisions are added for either or both topics in heading

Class comprehensive works on viewpoints based on lack of belief in, doubt about, or rejection of the existence of God in 211.8

.8   **Atheism**

Class here comprehensive works on viewpoints based on lack of belief in, doubt about, or rejection of the existence of God

For free thought, see 211.4; for humanism and secularism, see 211.6; for agnosticism and skepticism, see 211.7

212   **Existence of God, ways of knowing God, attributes of God**

Including miracles

.1   **Existence of God**

Including proofs

.6   **Ways of knowing God**

Including role of faith, reason and revelation

Class proofs in 212.1

.7   **Attributes of God**

Including love, omniscience

213   **Creation**

Including creation of life and human life, evolution versus creation, evolution as method of creation

See Manual at 231.7652 vs. 213, 500, 576.8

214   **Theodicy**

> Vindication of God's justice and goodness in permitting existence of evil and suffering

> Class here good and evil

   .8   **Providence**

215   **Science and religion**

> Including technology and religion

> Class religion and scientific theories of creation in 213

> > *See also 201.65 for various religions and science; also 261.55 for Christianity and science*

   .2   **Astronomy**

> Including cosmology

   .3   **Physics**

   .7   **Life sciences**

> Including natural history, paleontology

> Class evolution versus creation, evolution as method of creation in 213; class anthropology and religion, ethnology and religion in 218

[216]   **[Unassigned]**

> Most recently used in Edition 21

[217]   **[Unassigned]**

> Most recently used in Edition 18

218   **Humankind**

> Including anthropology and religion, ethnology and religion, immortality

> *For creation of humankind, human evolution, see 213*

[219]   **[Unassigned]**

> Most recently used in Edition 19

>   # 220–290   Bible and specific religions

> *See Manual at 220–290*

> (Option: To provide a chronological/regional arrangement for the Bible and specific religions use the optional arrangement of 220–290 given in the Manual at 220–290)

220   Bible

Holy Scriptures of Judaism and Christianity

Class Christian Biblical theology in 230.041; class Biblical precepts in Christian codes of conduct in 241.52–241.54; class Jewish Biblical theology in 296.3; class Biblical precepts in Jewish codes of conduct in 296.36

(If option A under 290 is chosen, class here sources of the specified religion; class Bible in 298)

SUMMARY

220.01–.09	**Standard subdivisions and special topics of Bible**
.1–.9	**Generalities**
221	**Old Testament (Tanakh)**
222	**Historical books of Old Testament**
223	**Poetic books of Old Testament**
224	**Prophetic books of Old Testament**
225	**New Testament**
226	**Gospels and Acts**
227	**Epistles**
228	**Revelation (Apocalypse)**
229	**Apocrypha, pseudepigrapha, intertestamental works**

.01–.02   Standard subdivisions

[.03]   Dictionaries, encyclopedias, concordances

> Do not use for dictionaries and encyclopedias; class in 220.3. Do not use for concordances; class in 220.4–220.5

.04   Special topics of Bible

.046   Apocalyptic passages

> Class apocalyptic passages in a book or group of books with the book or group of books, plus notation 0046 from table under 221–229, e.g., apocalyptic passages in the prophets 224.0046, in Book of Daniel 224.50046

> *For Revelation (Apocalypse), see 228*

.05–.08   Standard subdivisions

.09   History, geographic treatment, biography

> Do not use for geography, history, chronology, persons of Bible lands in Bible times; class in 220.9

> Class the canon in 220.12

SUMMARY

220.1	**Origins and authenticity**
.3	**Encyclopedias and topical dictionaries**
.4	**Original texts, early versions, early translations**
.5	**Modern versions and translations**
.6	**Interpretation and criticism (Exegesis)**
.7	**Commentaries**
.8	**Nonreligious subjects treated in Bible**
.9	**Geography, history, chronology, persons of Bible lands in Bible times**

> ### 220.1–220.9 Generalities

Class comprehensive works in 220. Class generalities applied to a specific part of the Bible with the part, plus notation 01–09 from table under 221–229, e.g., a commentary on Job 223.107

.1   Origins and authenticity

.12   Canon

Class here selection of the books accepted as Holy Scripture

.13   Inspiration

The Bible as revelation (word of God)

Including authority of Bible

.132   Inerrancy

.15   Biblical prophecy and prophecies

Class Christian messianic prophecies in 232.12; class Christian eschatological prophecies in 236; class Jewish messianic and eschatological prophecies in 296.33

See also 224 for prophetic books of Old Testament

.3   Encyclopedias and topical dictionaries

For dictionaries of specific texts, see 220.4–220.5

> ### 220.4–220.5 Texts, versions, translations

Class here critical appraisal of language and style; concordances, indexes, dictionaries of specific texts; complete texts; selections from more than one part; paraphrases

Class texts accompanied by commentaries in 220.77; class comprehensive works in 220.4. Class selections compiled for a specific purpose with the purpose, e.g., selections for daily meditations 242.2

.4   Original texts, early versions, early translations

Class here original texts accompanied by modern translations, comprehensive works on texts and versions

For modern versions and translations, see 220.5

.404   Textual criticism and word studies

.404 6   Textual criticism (Lower criticism)

Use of scientific means to ascertain the actual original texts

.404 7   Theological studies of words or phrases

> 220.42–220.49 Texts in specific languages

> Add to each subdivision identified by † the numbers following 220.404 in 220.4046–220.4047, regardless of specific version, e.g., textual criticism of Bible in Latin, of Vulgate 220.476, of Old Testament in Greek, of Septuagint 221.486

> Class comprehensive works in 220.4

.42	†Aramaic versions
.43	†Syriac versions
.44	†Hebrew version
.45	†Samaritan versions
.46	Other Semitic language versions

> Including Arabic, Geʻez

.47	†Latin versions
.48	†Greek versions
.49	Other early versions

> Including Armenian, Coptic

.5	**Modern versions and translations**
.51	Polyglot
.52	Versions in English and Anglo-Saxon

> Standard subdivisions are added for versions in English and Anglo-Saxon, for English alone

> Class works containing translations in English and one other modern language with the other language, e.g., the Bible in English and German 220.531

.520 01–.520 09	Standard subdivisions

---

†Add as instructed under 220.42–220.49

> 220.520 1–220.520 9 English

Add to each subdivision identified by * as follows:
01–02   Standard subdivisions
[03]   Dictionaries, encyclopedias, concordances
         Do not use; class in notation 3 from this table
05–08   Standard subdivisions
09   Geographic treatment and biography
         Do not use for history of the translation; class in notation 8 from this table
2   Standard editions
3   Concordances, indexes, dictionaries
4   Special editions
         Including annotated editions, study editions, editions notable for illustrations
6   Selections
7   Paraphrases
8   History, criticism, explanation of the translation

Class comprehensive works in 220.52

.520 1   English versions before 1582

Including Coverdale, Tyndale, Wycliffe versions

.520 2   *Douay version

Class here Rheims-Douay, Rheims-Douay-Challoner versions

See also 220.5205 for Confraternity-Douay-Challoner version

.520 3   *Authorized version (King James version)

.520 4   Revised version

Including English Revised (1881–1885), American Revised (American Standard) (1901) versions

.520 42   *Revised Standard version (1946–1957)

.520 43   *New Revised Standard version (1990)

.520 5   *Confraternity Bible and New American Bible

Class here Confraternity-Douay-Challoner version

Subdivisions are added for either or both topics in heading

See also 220.5202 for Rheims-Douay, Rheims-Douay-Challoner versions

.520 6   *New English Bible and Revised English Bible

Subdivisions are added for either or both topics in heading

.520 7   *Jerusalem Bible and New Jerusalem Bible

Subdivisions are added for either or both topics in heading

*Add as instructed under 220.5201–220.5209

.520 8	Other English translations since 1582
	Including New King James, New Century versions
	For translations by individuals, see 220.5209
.520 81	*New International Version
.520 82	*Today's English Bible (Good News Bible)
.520 83	*Living Bible and New Living Translation
	Subdivisions are added for either or both topics in heading
.520 9	Translations by individuals
	Including Goodspeed, Knox, Moffatt, Phillips
.529	Anglo-Saxon
.53–.59	Versions in other languages

Add to base number 220.5 notation 3–9 from Table 6, e.g., the Bible in German 220.531

Works containing translations in two modern languages other than English are classed with the language coming later in Table 6; in more than two modern languages in 220.51

.6   Interpretation and criticism (Exegesis)

Class Christian meditations based on Biblical passages and intended for devotional use in 242.5; class material about the Bible intended for use in preparing Christian sermons in 251; class Christian sermons based on Biblical passages in 252; class material about the Bible for preparation of Jewish sermons and texts of Jewish sermons in 296.47; class Jewish meditations based on Biblical passages and intended for devotional use in 296.72

For textual criticism, see 220.4046; for commentaries, see 220.7

.601	Philosophy and theory
	Class here hermeneutics
.61	General introductions to the Bible
	Including isagogics (introductory studies prior to actual exegesis)
.64	Symbolism and typology
	Standard subdivisions are added for either or both topics in heading
	Class here interpretation of specific symbols
.65	Harmonies

*Add as instructed under 220.5201–220.5209

.66	Literary criticism

Literary examination of the text in order to reach conclusions about its meaning, structure, authorship, date

Class here higher criticism, internal criticism, redaction criticism

Class language and style of specific texts in 220.4–220.5

See also 809.93522 for the Bible as literature

.663	Form criticism

Analysis of preliterary or oral forms and traditions in Biblical text

.67	Historical criticism

Interpretation of texts in light of the cultural, historical, religious, social milieu in which written

Class form criticism in 220.663

.68	Mythological, allegorical, numerical, astronomical interpretations

Including mythology in the Bible, demythologizing

.7	**Commentaries**

Criticism and interpretation arranged in textual order

.77	Commentaries with text

.8	**Nonreligious subjects treated in Bible**

Class a religious subject treated in Bible with the specific religion and topic, e.g., Christian theology 230, Jewish theology 296.3

.800 01–.800 09	Standard subdivisions
.800 1–.899 9	Specific nonreligious subjects

Add to base number 220.8 notation 001–999, e.g., natural sciences in Bible 220.85; however, for geography, history, chronology, persons of Bible lands in Bible times, see 220.9

.9	**Geography, history, chronology, persons of Bible lands in Bible times**

Class general history of Bible lands in ancient world in 930

.91	Geography

Class here description and civilization

Class civilization treated separately from geography in 220.95

.92	Collected biography

Class an individual person with the part of the Bible in which the person is chiefly considered, e.g., Abraham 222.11092

See Manual at 220.92; also at 230–280

.93	Archaeology (Material remains)

.95   History

Including civilization treated separately from geography

Class geographic description and civilization treated together in 220.91

.950 01–.950 09   Standard subdivisions

.950 5   Bible stories retold

Including picture books

> ## 221–229 Specific parts of Bible, Apocrypha, pseudepigrapha, intertestamental works

Add to each subdivision identified by * as follows (subdivisions from this table may be added for a part of any work that has its own number):
001–009   Standard subdivisions
            Add to 0 the numbers following 220 in 220.01–220.09, e.g., apocalyptic passages in a book or group of books 0046
01–08   Generalities
            Add to 0 the numbers following 220 in 220.1–220.8, e.g., interpretation of the work or of a part of the work 06
09   Geography, history, chronology, persons
            Add to 09 the numbers following 221.9 in 221.91–221.95, e.g., biography 092
Class comprehensive works in 220

221   Old Testament (Tanakh)

Holy Scriptures of Judaism, Old Testament of Christianity

Class Jewish Biblical theology in 296.3; class Biblical precepts in Jewish codes of conduct in 296.36

For historical books, see 222; for Torah, see 222.1; for poetic books, Ketuvim, see 223; for prophetic books, Nevi'im, see 224

See Manual at 221

[.03]   Dictionaries, encyclopedias, concordances

Do not use for dictionaries and encyclopedias; class in 221.3. Do not use for concordances; class in 221.4–221.5

.04   Special topics of Old Testament

.044   Megillot (Five scrolls)

For a specific book of Megillot, see the book, e.g., Ruth 222.35

.046   Apocalyptic passages

Class apocalyptic passages in a book or group of books with the book or group of books, plus notation 0046 from table under 221–229, e.g., apocalyptic passages in the prophets 224.0046, in Book of Daniel 224.50046

.09   History, geographic treatment, biography

> Do not use for geography, history, chronology, persons of Bible lands in Bible times; class in 221.9

> Class the canon in 221.12

.1–.8   **Generalities**

> Add to base number 221 the numbers following 220 in 220.1–220.8, e.g., Targums 221.42, commentaries 221.7

.9   **Geography, history, chronology, persons of Old Testament lands in Old Testament times**

> Class general history of ancient areas in 930

.91   Geography

>> Class here description and civilization

>> Class civilization treated separately from geography in 221.95

.92   Persons

>> *See Manual at 220.92; also at 230–280*

.922   Collected treatment

.93   Archaeology (Material remains)

.95   History

>> Including civilization treated separately from geography

>> Class geographic description and civilization treated together in 221.91

.950 01–.950 09   Standard subdivisions

.950 5   Old Testament stories retold

>> Including picture books

> **222–224 Books of Old Testament**

> Class comprehensive works in 221

> *See Manual at 221*

> (Option: To arrange the books of the Old Testament (Tanakh) as found in Jewish Bibles, use one of the following:
> (Option A: Use the optional arrangement of 222–224 given in the Manual at 221
> (Option B: Class in 296.11

> (A table giving the three numbers for each book is given in the Manual at 221)

222   ***Historical books of Old Testament**

---

*Add as instructed under 221–229

.1   ***Pentateuch (Torah)**

         Class here Hexateuch

         For Joshua, see 222.2

.11   *Genesis

.12   *Exodus

         For Ten Commandments, see 222.16

.13   *Leviticus

.14   *Numbers

.15   *Deuteronomy

         For Ten Commandments, see 222.16

.16   *Ten Commandments (Decalogue)

         Class Ten Commandments as code of conduct in Christianity in 241.52; class Ten Commandments as code of conduct in Judaism in 296.36

.2   ***Joshua (Josue)**

.3   ***Judges and Ruth**

.32   *Judges

.35   *Ruth

.4   ***Samuel**

.43   *Samuel 1

         Variant name: Kings 1

.44   *Samuel 2

         Variant name: Kings 2

.5   ***Kings**

.53   *Kings 1

         Variant name: Kings 3

.54   *Kings 2

         Variant name: Kings 4

.6   ***Chronicles (Paralipomena)**

.63   *Chronicles 1 (Paralipomenon 1)

.64   *Chronicles 2 (Paralipomenon 2)

.7   ***Ezra (Esdras 1)**

         See also 229.1 for Esdras 1 (also called Esdras 3) of the Apocrypha

---

*Add as instructed under 221–229

.8   ***Nehemiah (Esdras 2, Nehemias)**

> *See also 229.1 for Esdras 2 (also called Esdras 4) of the Apocrypha*

(.86)   *Tobit (Tobias)

> (Optional number; prefer 229.22)

(.88)   *Judith

> (Optional number; prefer 229.24)

.9   ***Esther**

> (Option: Class here deuterocanonical part of Esther; prefer 229.27)

223   *Poetic books of Old Testament

> Class here Ketuvim (Hagiographa, Writings), wisdom literature

> *For Apocryphal wisdom literature, see 229.3. For a specific book of Ketuvim not provided for here, see the book, e.g., Ruth 222.35*

.1   ***Job**

.2   ***Psalms**

.7   ***Proverbs**

.8   ***Ecclesiastes (Qohelet)**

.9   ***Song of Solomon (Canticle of Canticles, Song of Songs)**

(.96)   *Wisdom of Solomon (Wisdom)

> (Optional number; prefer 229.3)

(.98)   *Ecclesiasticus (Sirach)

> (Optional number; prefer 229.4)

224   *Prophetic books of Old Testament

> Class here Major Prophets, Nevi'im

> *For a specific book of Nevi'im not provided for here, see the book, e.g., Joshua 222.2*

.1   ***Isaiah (Isaias)**

.2   ***Jeremiah (Jeremias)**

.3   ***Lamentations**

(.37)   *Baruch

> (Optional number; prefer 229.5)

.4   ***Ezekiel (Ezechiel)**

---

*Add as instructed under 221–229

.5	***Daniel**

> (Option: Class here Song of the Three Children, Susanna, Bel and the Dragon; prefer 229.6)

.6	***Hosea (Osee)**
.7	***Joel**
.8	***Amos**
.9	***Minor Prophets**

> *For Hosea, see 224.6; for Joel, see 224.7; for Amos, see 224.8*

.91	*Obadiah (Abdias)
.92	*Jonah (Jonas)
.93	*Micah (Micheas)
.94	*Nahum
.95	*Habakkuk (Habacuc)
.96	*Zephaniah (Sophonias)
.97	*Haggai (Aggeus)
.98	*Zechariah (Zacharias)
.99	*Malachi (Malachias)
(.997)	*Maccabees 1 and 2 (Machabees 1 and 2)

> (Optional number; prefer 229.73)

225   New Testament

> *For Gospels and Acts, see 226; for Epistles, see 227; for Revelation, see 228*

[.03]	Dictionaries, encyclopedias, concordances

> Do not use for dictionaries and encyclopedias; class in 225.3. Do not use for concordances; class in 225.4–225.5

.04	Special topics of New Testament
.046	Apocalyptic passages

> Class apocalyptic passages in a book or group of books with the book or group of books, plus notation 0046 from table under 221–229, e.g., apocalyptic passages in Gospels 226.0046, in Gospel of Mark 226.30046

> *For Revelation (Apocalypse), see 228* ⁕

.09	History, geographic treatment, biography

> Do not use for geography, history, chronology, persons of Bible lands in Bible times; class in 225.9

> Class the canon in 225.12

---

*Add as instructed under 221–229

.1–.8   Generalities

> Add to base number 225 the numbers following 220 in 220.1–220.8, e.g., Authorized Version 225.5203

.9   Geography, history, chronology, persons of New Testament lands in New Testament times

> Add to base number 225.9 the numbers following 221.9 in 221.91–221.95, e.g., individual persons 225.92; however, for Jesus Christ, Mary, Joseph, Joachim, Anne, John the Baptist, see 232
>
> *See Manual at 220.92; also at 230–280*

226   *Gospels and Acts

> Class here synoptic Gospels
>
> Subdivisions are added for Gospels and Acts together, for Gospels alone
>
> *See Manual at 230–280*

.095 05   Gospel stories retold

> Number built according to instructions under 221–229
>
> Class Jesus as a historical figure, biography and specific events in life of Jesus in 232.9

.1   Harmonies of Gospels

> **226.2–226.5 Specific Gospels**

> Class comprehensive works in 226
>
> *For miracles, see 226.7; for parables, see 226.8*

.2   *Matthew

> Class Golden Rule as code of conduct in 241.54
>
> *For Sermon on the Mount, see 226.9*

.3   *Mark

.4   *Luke

> Class Golden Rule as code of conduct in 241.54
>
> *For Sermon on the Mount, see 226.9*

.5   *John

> Class here comprehensive works on Johannine literature
>
> *For Epistles of John, see 227.94; for Revelation (Apocalypse), see 228*

.6   *Acts of the Apostles

---

*Add as instructed under 221–229

.7   ***Miracles**

> Class miracles in context of Jesus' life in 232.955

.8   ***Parables**

> Class parables in context of Jesus' life in 232.954

.9   ***Sermon on the Mount**

> Class Sermon on the Mount as code of conduct in 241.53

.93   *Beatitudes

.96   *Lord's Prayer

227   ***Epistles**

> Class here Pauline epistles

.1   ***Romans**

.2   ***Corinthians 1**

> Class here comprehensive works on Epistles to Corinthians
>
> *For Corinthians 2, see 227.3*

.3   ***Corinthians 2**

.4   ***Galatians**

.5   ***Ephesians**

.6   ***Philippians**

.7   ***Colossians**

.8   ***Other Pauline epistles**

.81   *Thessalonians 1

> Class here comprehensive works on Epistles to Thessalonians
>
> *For Thessalonians 2, see 227.82*

.82   *Thessalonians 2

.83   *Timothy 1

> Class here comprehensive works on Epistles to Timothy, on Pastoral Epistles
>
> *For Timothy 2, see 227.84; for Titus, see 227.85*

.84   *Timothy 2

.85   *Titus

.86   *Philemon

*Add as instructed under 221–229

.87	*Hebrews
.9	***Catholic epistles**
.91	*James
.92	*Peter 1

Class here comprehensive works on Epistles of Peter

For Peter 2, see 227.93

.93	*Peter 2
.94	*John 1

Class here comprehensive works on Epistles of John

For John 2, see 227.95; for John 3, see 227.96

.95	*John 2
.96	*John 3
.97	*Jude

228   *Revelation (Apocalypse)

229   *Apocrypha, pseudepigrapha, intertestamental works

Apocrypha: works accepted as deuterocanonical in some Bibles

Pseudepigrapha, intertestamental works: works from intertestamental times connected with the Bible but not accepted as canonical

Subdivisions are added for Apocrypha, pseudepigrapha, intertestamental works together; for Apocrypha alone

---

>   **229.1–229.7 Specific books and works of Apocrypha**

Class comprehensive works in 229

.1	***Esdras 1 and 2**

Variant names: Esdras 3 and 4

See also 222.7 for Ezra; also 222.8 for Nehemiah

.2	***Tobit, Judith, deuterocanonical part of Esther**
.22	*Tobit (Tobias)

(Option: Class in 222.86)

.24	*Judith

(Option: Class in 222.88)

---

*Add as instructed under 221–229

.27   *Deuterocanonical part of Esther

           (Option: Class in 222.9)

.3   ***Wisdom of Solomon (Wisdom)**

           Class here Apocryphal wisdom literature

           For Ecclesiasticus, see 229.4

           (Option: Class in 223.96)

.4   ***Ecclesiasticus (Sirach)**

           (Option: Class in 223.98)

.5   ***Baruch and Epistle of Jeremiah**

           (Option: Class Baruch in 224.37)

.6   ***Song of the Three Children, Susanna, Bel and the Dragon, Prayer of Manasseh**

           (Option: Class Song of the Three Children, Susanna, Bel and the Dragon in 224.5)

.7   ***Maccabees (Machabees)**

.73   *Maccabees 1 and 2 (Machabees 1 and 2)

           (Option: Class in 224.997)

.75   *Maccabees 3 and 4 (Machabees 3 and 4)

>   **229.8–229.9 Pseudepigrapha, intertestamental works**

           Class comprehensive works in 229.9

           For Maccabees 3 and 4, see 229.75

.8   ***Pseudo gospels**

           Including agrapha (Jesus' words not appearing in canonical Gospels), Gospel of Thomas

           Class comprehensive works on New Testament pseudepigrapha in 229.92

.9   ***Pseudepigrapha**

           For pseudo gospels, see 229.8

.91   *Old Testament

           For Maccabees 3 and 4, see 229.75

.911   *Historical books

.912   *Poetic books

           Including Odes of Solomon

---

*Add as instructed under 221–229

.913	*Prophetic books

Including Apocalypse of Elijah, Ascension of Isaiah, Assumption of Moses, Books of Enoch, Jewish apocalypses

.914	*Testaments

Including Testament of the Twelve Patriarchs

.92	*New Testament

For pseudo gospels, see 229.8; for Epistles, see 229.93; for Apocalypses, see 229.94

.925	*Acts of the Apostles
.93	*Epistles
.94	*Apocalypses

230–280 Christianity

Unless other instructions are given, observe the following table of preference for the history of Christianity and the Christian church (*except* for biography, explained in Manual at 230–280: Biography), e.g., Jesuit missions in India 266.254 (*not* 271.53054); persecution of Jesuits by Elizabeth I 272.7 (*not* 271.53042, 274.206, or 282.42):

Specific topics	220–260
Persecutions in general church history	272
Doctrinal controversies and heresies in general church history	273
Religious congregations and orders in church history	271
Denominations and sects of Christian church	280
Christianity by continent, country, locality	274–279
History, geographic treatment, biography of Christianity (*except* 271–279)	270

Class comprehensive works in 230

For Bible, see 220

See Manual at 230–280

(Option: To give local emphasis and shorter numbers to a specific religion other than Christianity, e.g., Buddhism, class it in these numbers, its sources in 220, comprehensive works in 230; in that case class the Bible and Christianity in 298. Another option is described at 290)

230–270 Specific elements of Christianity

Class here specific elements of specific denominations and sects
(Option: Class specific elements of specific denominations and sects in 280)

Class comprehensive works in 230

*Add as instructed under 221–229

230   Christianity

Including Christian mythology

Class here Christian theology, Christian doctrinal theology, contextual theology

Class doctrinal controversies in general church history in 273

> *For Christian moral and devotional theology, see 240; for local Christian church and Christian religious orders, see 250; for Christian social and ecclesiastical theology, see 260; for history, geographic treatment, biography of Christianity, see 270; for denominations and sects of Christian church, see 280*

See Manual at 398.2 vs. 201.3, 230, 270, 292–299

SUMMARY

230.002–.007	**Standard subdivisions of Christianity**
.01–.09	**Standard subdivisions and specific types of Christian theology**
.1–.9	**Doctrines of specific denominations and sects**
231	**God**
232	**Jesus Christ and his family**
233	**Humankind**
234	**Salvation and grace**
235	**Spiritual beings**
236	**Eschatology**
238	**Creeds, confessions of faith, covenants, catechisms**
239	**Apologetics and polemics**

[.001]   Philosophy and theory of Christianity

> Do not use; class in 230.01

.002–.003   Standard subdivisions of Christianity

.005   Serial publications of Christianity

[.006]   Organizations and management of Christianity

> Do not use; class in 260

.007   Education, research, related topics of Christianity

[.007 1]   Education

> Do not use; class in 230.071

[.008]   Groups of people in Christianity

> Do not use; class in 270.08

[.009]   History, geographic treatment, biography of Christianity

> Do not use; class in 270

.01   Philosophy and theory of Christianity, of Christian theology

.02–.03   Standard subdivisions of Christian theology

.04   Specific types of Christian theology

> Class theology of specific denominations and sects in 230.1–230.9

See Manual at 230–280

[.040 1–.040 9]	Standard subdivisions

Do not use; class in 230.01–230.09

.041   Biblical theology

Class theology of a specific part of Old or New Testament with the part, e.g., theology of Pauline epistles 227.06; class biblical theology of a specific topic in doctrinal theology with the topic in 231–239, e.g., Old Testament minor prophets' view of repentance and forgiveness 234.509014; class biblical theology of a specific topic in moral and devotional theology, local Christian church and Christian religious orders, social and ecclesiastical theology with the topic in 240–260, e.g., New Testament writers' view of war and peace 261.87309015

.041 1   Christian theology of Old Testament

.041 5   Christian theology of New Testament

.042   Theology of Eastern and Roman Catholic churches

Class specific schools and systems of theology in 230.046

.044   Protestant theology

Class specific schools of Protestant theology in 230.046

.046   Specific schools and systems of theology

Including dominion, existentialist, liberal, neo-orthodox, process theologies

[.046 01–.046 09]   Standard subdivisions

Do not use; class in 230.01–230.09

.046 2   Evangelical and fundamentalist theology

.046 24   Evangelical theology

.046 26   Fundamentalist theology

.046 3   Dispensationalist theology

.046 4   Liberation theology

.05–.06   Standard subdivisions of Christian theology

.07   Education, research, related topics of Christian theology

.071   Education in Christianity, in Christian theology

Class here Christianity as an academic subject

Class comprehensive works on Christian religious education, religious education to inculcate Christian faith and practice, catechetics in 268

See Manual at 207.5, 268 vs. 200.71, 230.071, 292–299

.071 1   Higher education in Christianity, in Christian theology

> Class here Bible colleges, divinity schools, theological seminaries, graduate and undergraduate faculties of theology; education of ministers, pastors, priests, theologians

> Class training for clergy in a specialized subject with the subject, plus notation 0711 from Table 1, e.g., education in pastoral counseling 253.50711

> *For higher education for specific denominations and sects, see 230.073*

> *See Manual at 207.5, 268 vs. 200.71, 230.071, 292–299*

.071 14–.071 19   Higher education in specific continents, countries, localities

> Class here nondenominational and interdenominational schools and courses

.073   Higher education for specific denominations and sects

> Add to base number 230.073 the numbers following 28 in 281–289, e.g., Roman Catholic seminaries 230.0732, a Roman Catholic seminary in Dublin 230.073241835

.08–.09   Standard subdivisions of Christian theology

> *See Manual at 230–280*

.1–.9   Doctrines of specific denominations and sects

Add to base number 230 the numbers following 28 in 281–289, e.g., Methodist doctrines 230.7

> *See Manual at 230–280; also at 270, 230.11–230.14 vs. 230.15–230.2, 281.5–281.9, 282*

(Option: Class here specific doctrines of specific denominations and sects; prefer 231–236. If option is chosen, add as above, then add 0* and to the result add the numbers following 23 in 231–236, e.g., Methodist doctrines on salvation 230.704)

> ## 231–239 Christian doctrinal theology

Class here antagonism between and reconciliation of a specific Christian doctrine and a secular discipline

Class specific types of Christian doctrinal theology in 230.042–230.046; class comprehensive works on Christian doctrinal theology in 230; class comprehensive works on doctrines of specific denominations and sects in 230.1–230.9; class comprehensive works on antagonism between and reconciliation of Christian belief and a secular discipline in 261.5

---

*Add 00 for standard subdivisions; see instructions at beginning of Table 1

> ## 231–236 Specific topics in Christian doctrinal theology

Class here specific doctrines of specific denominations and sects
(Option: Class specific doctrines of specific denominations and sects in
230.1–230.9)

Class comprehensive works in 230

231 God

.04 Special topics of God

.042 Ways of knowing God

Including faith, reason, tradition

Class proofs of existence of God based on reason alone in 212.1; class
revelation in 231.74

.044 General concepts of God

Including non-Trinitarian concepts

Class here comprehensive works on Holy Trinity

> ### 231.1–231.3 Holy Trinity

Class comprehensive works in 231.044

.1 **God the Father**

.2 **God the Son**

For Jesus Christ, see 232

.3 **God the Holy Spirit**

For gifts of and baptism in the Holy Spirit, see 234.13

.4 **Attributes**

Including omnipotence, omnipresence, omniscience, transcendence

*For love and wisdom, see 231.6; for sovereignty, see 231.7; for justice and
goodness, see 231.8*

.5 **Providence**

.6 **Love and wisdom**

.7 **Relation to the world**

Including relation to nature, sovereignty

Class here God's relation to individual believers

Class redemption in 234.3; class divine law in 241.2; class believers' experience
of God in 248.2; class God's relation to the church in 262.7

For Providence, see 231.5

.72	Kingdom of God

Class Kingdom of God to come in 236

.73	Miracles

Class here miracles associated with saints, comprehensive works on miracles

For miracles associated with Mary, see 232.917; for miracles of Jesus, see 232.955; for stigmata, see 248.29

.74	Revelation

For private visions, see 248.29

.745	Prophecy

For Biblical prophecy and prophecies, see 220.15; for messianic prophecies, see 232.12; for eschatological prophecies, see 236

.76	Relation to and action in history

Including covenant relationship, relationship to the Jewish people

.765	Creation

For creation of humankind, see 233.11

.765 2	Relation of scientific and Christian viewpoints of origin of universe

Class here creationism, creation science, evolution versus creation, reconciliation of evolution and creation

See also 379.28 for teaching creationism in public schools

See Manual at 231.7652 vs. 213, 500, 576.8

.8	**Justice and goodness**

Including good and evil

Class here theodicy (vindication of God's justice and goodness in permitting existence of evil and suffering)

For providence, see 231.5; for Christian ethics, see 241

232   Jesus Christ and his family

Class here Christology

> ### 232.1–232.8 Christology

Class here doctrines and theories about Jesus Christ, e.g., doctrine of the resurrection 232.5

Class events in the life of Jesus in 232.9, e.g., historicity and narration of events surrounding the resurrection 232.97; class comprehensive works in 232

.1	**Incarnation and messiahship of Christ**

Including typology

.12	Messianic prophecies

.2   **Christ as Logos (Word of God)**

.3   **Christ as Redeemer**

Including atonement

Class comprehensive works on the doctrine of redemption in 234.3

For sacrifice of Christ, see 232.4

.4   **Sacrifice of Christ**

.5   **Resurrection of Christ**

.8   **Divinity and humanity of Christ**

Standard subdivisions are added for divinity and humanity of Christ together, for divinity of Christ alone

Including Person; offices as Prophet, Priest, King; intercession

Class here hypostatic union

For incarnation, see 232.1; for Christ as Logos, see 232.2; for Christ as Redeemer, see 232.3; for humanity of Christ, see 232.9

.9   **Family and life of Jesus**

Class here rationalistic interpretations of Jesus; humanity of Christ

For Islamic doctrines about Jesus, see 297.2465

See Manual at 230–280

.900 1–.900 9   Standard subdivisions

.901   Life of Jesus

For birth, infancy, childhood of Jesus, see 232.92; for adulthood of Jesus, see 232.95–232.97

.903   Character and personality of Jesus

.904   Jesus as teacher and exemplar

Including influence

Class teachings in 232.954

.906   Jewish interpretations of Jesus

.908   Historicity of Jesus

.91   Mary, mother of Jesus

Class here Mariology

Class Mary's husband and parents in 232.93

.911   Immaculate Conception

.912   Annunciation

.913   Virginity

.914	Assumption (Ascent to heaven)
.917	Miracles and apparitions
.92	Birth, infancy, childhood of Jesus

> Including Holy Family, circumcision, massacre of innocents, flight into Egypt

> Class here Christmas story

> *For Mary, see 232.91; for Joseph, see 232.932*

.921	Virgin birth
.922	Adoration of shepherds
.923	Wise men (Magi)
.927	Childhood of Jesus

> *For presentation in temple, see 232.928; for Jesus among doctors in temple, see 232.929*

.928	Presentation in temple
.929	Jesus among doctors in temple
.93	Mary's husband and parents
.932	Joseph
.933	Joachim and Anne
.94	John the Baptist
.95	Public life of Jesus

> Including baptism, temptation, calling of apostles

.954	Teachings

> Class texts and interpretations of New Testament passages narrating parables in 226.8

.955	Miracles

> Class texts and interpretations of New Testament passages narrating miracles in 226.7

.956	Transfiguration
.957	Last Supper
.958	Last words to disciples
.96	Passion and death of Jesus
.961	Betrayal by Judas

> Class comprehensive works on Judas Iscariot in 226.092

.962	Trial and condemnation
.963	Crucifixion and death

.963 5		Seven last words on cross
.964		Burial
.966		Relics of Passion
.967		Descent into hell
.97		Resurrection, appearances, ascension of Jesus

233 Humankind

Class salvation in 234

.1 Creation and fall

.11 Creation

Including relation of human creation and human evolution

Class comprehensive works on creation in 231.765

.14 Original sin and fall

Class sins in 241.3

.4 Accountability

Including guilt

.5 Nature

Including body, soul, spirit, sexuality; humankind as image and likeness of God, as child of God

Class free will in 233.7

For original sin, see 233.14; for death, see 236.1; for immortality, see 236.22

.7 Freedom of choice between good and evil

Class predestination and free will in relation to salvation in 234.9

For accountability, see 233.4

234 Salvation and grace

Variant name for salvation: soteriology

Including election, innate virtues, merit, universal priesthood

.1 Kinds and means of grace

Including actual and sanctifying grace

.13 Spiritual gifts

Including interpretation of tongues, prophecy, working of miracles, helps, governments, apostleship, teaching, exhortation, speaking words of wisdom and knowledge

Class here gifts of and baptism in the Holy Spirit

For faith, see 234.23

.131		Healing

Spiritual, emotional, or physical

For discussion of whether cures are miracles, see 231.73

See Manual at 615.852 vs. 203.1, 234.131, 292–299

.132   Speaking in tongues (Glossolalia)

.16   Sacraments

Class liturgy and ritual of sacraments in 265

.161   Baptism

.161 2   Infant baptism

.161 3   Adult baptism

.162   Confirmation (Chrismation)

.163   Eucharist (Holy Communion, Lord's Supper)

.164   Holy Orders

.165   Matrimony

.166   Penance

Including confession

.167   Anointing of the sick

.2   Faith and hope

See also 236 for eschatology; also 241.4 for virtues

.23   Faith

.25   Hope

.3   Redemption

.4   Regeneration

.5   Repentance and forgiveness

Including atonement, reconciliation

.6   Obedience

.7   Justification

.8   Sanctification and holiness

Class here deification (theosis)

.9   Predestination and free will

235   Spiritual beings

For Mariology, see 232.91

.2	**Saints**

Class miracles associated with saints in 231.73

For Joseph, see 232.932; for Joachim and Anne, see 232.933; for John the Baptist, see 232.94

See Manual at 230–280

.24 Beatification and canonization

> **235.3–235.4 Pure spirits**

Class comprehensive works in 235

For God, see 231

.3 **Angels**

Including archangels, celestial hierarchy, cherubim, seraphim

.4 **Devils (Demons)**

Class here spiritual warfare

.47 Satan (Lucifer)

236 **Eschatology**

Including Antichrist

Class here Kingdom of God to come

.1 **Death**

.2 **Future state (Life after death)**

Class resurrection of the dead in 236.8

For intermediate state, see 236.4

.21 Eternity

.22 Immortality

For conditional immortality, see 236.23

.23 Conditional immortality (Annihilationism)

.24 Heaven

.25 Hell

.4 **Intermediate state**

Probation after death

Including limbo of fathers (limbus patrum), limbo of infants (limbus infantium)

For purgatory, see 236.5

.5 **Purgatory**

.8   **Resurrection of the dead**

.9   **Last Judgment and related events**

Including Armageddon, Day of the Lord, end of the world, Judgment of Christ, millennium, rapture, Second Coming of Christ, tribulation

Class interdisciplinary works on end of the world in 001.9

[237]   [Unassigned]

Most recently used in Edition 16

238   Creeds, confessions of faith, covenants, catechisms

Class catechetics in 268. Class creeds and catechisms on a specific doctrine with the doctrine, e.g., attributes of God 231.4

.1   **Early and Eastern creeds**

.11–.19   Creeds of early church and Eastern churches

Add to base number 238.1 the numbers following 281 in 281.1–281.9, e.g., creeds of Eastern churches 238.15, creeds of Orthodox Church 238.19

.11   Creeds of Apostolic Church to the time of the great schism, 1054

Number built according to instructions under 238.11–238.19

Class here Apostles' Creed

For creeds of Post-Nicene church, 325–1054, see 238.14

.14   Creeds of Post-Nicene church, 325–1054

Number built according to instructions under 238.11–238.19

.142   Nicene Creed

Class here Niceno-Constantinopolitan Creed

.144   Athanasian Creed

.19   Creeds of Orthodox Church

Number built according to instructions under 238.11–238.19

Class Nicene Creed, Niceno-Constantinopolitan Creed in 238.142

.2–.9   **Other denominations**

Add to base number 238 the numbers following 28 in 282–289, e.g., Lutheran catechisms 238.41

239   Apologetics and polemics

Apologetics: systematic argumentation in defense of the divine origin and authority of Christianity

Standard subdivisions are added for either or both topics in heading

Class apologetics of specific denominations in 230.1–230.9; class comprehensive works on the attitude of Christianity toward other religions in 261.2. Class apologetics and polemics on a specific doctrine with the doctrine, e.g., on doctrine of Holy Trinity 231.044

See also 273 for doctrinal controversies and heresies in general church history

.1   **Apologetics and polemics in apostolic times**

For polemics against doctrines of specific groups in apostolic times, see 239.2–239.4

>

239.2–239.4 Polemics against doctrines of specific groups in apostolic times

Class comprehensive works in 239.1

.2   **Polemics against Judaism in apostolic times**

.3   **Polemics against paganism in apostolic times**

.4   **Polemics against Neoplatonism in apostolic times**

.7   **Polemics against free thought, humanism, secularism, agnosticism, skepticism, atheism in postapostolic times**

Including polemics against secular humanism

.9   **Polemics against other doctrines in postapostolic times**

Class comprehensive postapostolic defenses of and attacks on doctrines of specific denominations or sects in 230.1–230.9. Class attacks on doctrines of a specific religion with the religion, e.g., doctrines of Judaism 296.3

.93   Polemics against doctrines associated with New Age religions

.94   Polemics against doctrines associated with modern paganism, neopaganism, wicca

240   Christian moral and devotional theology

SUMMARY

241   Christian ethics

Variant name: Moral theology

See Manual at 241 vs. 261.8

.04	Specific branches, denominations, sects

.040 2   Eastern and Roman Catholic churches

For ethics of Eastern churches, see 241.0415; for ethics of Roman Catholic Church, see 241.042

.040 4   Protestant churches and Protestantism

For ethics of specific Protestant denominations and sects, see 241.043–241.049

.041–.049   Specific denominations or sects

Add to base number 241.04 the numbers following 28 in 281–289, e.g., Lutheran ethics 241.0441

.1   Conscience

.2   Laws and bases of morality

Including divine law, natural law

Class here relation of law and gospel

For codes of conduct, see 241.5

.3   Sin and vices

Standard subdivisions are added for either or both topics in heading

Including specific vices

Class original sin in 233.14

For specific moral issues, see 241.6

.31   Mortal and venial sin

.4   Virtues

Including specific virtues

Class faith and hope as means of salvation in 234.2

For specific moral issues, see 241.6

.5   Codes of conduct

For specific moral issues, see 241.6

.52   Ten Commandments

.53   Sermon on the Mount

.54   Golden Rule

.6   Specific moral issues

> Add to base number 241.6 the numbers following 17 in 172–179, e.g., morality of warfare 241.6242, of abortion 241.6976; however, for specific vices, see 241.3; for specific virtues, see 241.4

242   Devotional literature

> Class here texts of meditations, contemplations, prayers for individuals and families, religious poetry intended for devotional use

> Unless other instructions are given, observe the following table of preference, e.g., prayers and meditations for daily use based on passages from the Bible 242.2 (*not* 242.5):

> | | |
> |---|---|
> | Prayers and meditations for use in times of illness, trouble, bereavement | 242.4 |
> | Prayers and meditations for specific groups of people | 242.6 |
> | Prayers and meditations for daily use | 242.2 |
> | Prayers and meditations for church year, other Christian feast and fast days | 242.3 |
> | Prayers and meditations based on passages from the Bible | 242.5 |
> | Specific prayers and groups of prayers | 242.7 |
> | Collections of prayers | 242.8 |

> Class devotional literature on a specific subject with the subject, e.g., meditations on passion and death of Jesus 232.96

> *For evangelistic writings, see 243; for hymns, see 264.23*

.08   Groups of people

> Do not use for devotional literature for specific groups of people; class in 242.6

> Class here devotional literature by specific groups of people

.2   Prayers and meditations for daily use

> Not limited to saints' days or specific parts of the church year

> Including meditations and prayers for Sunday, Sabbath

> Class prayers and meditations for daily use for specific groups of people in 242.6

.3   Prayers and meditations for church year, other Christian feast and fast days

> Class prayers and meditations for church year, other Christian feast and fast days for specific groups of people in 242.6

\>   242.33–242.36 Church year

> Class comprehensive works in 242.3

> *For Pentecost and time after Pentecost (Ordinary time), see 242.38*

.33   Advent and Christmas

.332	Advent
.335	Christmas season

                 Class here Christmas day

.34	Lent

                 For Holy Week, see 242.35

.35	Holy Week
.36	Easter season

                 Including Ascension Day

                 Class here Easter Sunday

.37	Other Christian feast and fast days

                 Including saints' days

.38	Pentecost and time after Pentecost (Ordinary time)
.4	**Prayers and meditations for use in times of illness, trouble, bereavement**
.5	**Prayers and meditations based on passages from the Bible**

                 Class interpretation and criticism of Bible passages for other than devotional use in 220.6; class Bible prayers in 242.722

.6	**Prayers and meditations for specific groups of people**

                 Class here prayers and meditations for daily use, church year, other Christian feast and fast days for specific groups of people

                 Add to base number 242.6 the numbers following 248.8 in 248.82–248.89, e.g., prayers and meditations for college students 242.634; however, for prayers and meditations for use in times of illness, trouble, bereavement, see 242.4

                 Class collections of prayers for specific groups of people in 242.82–242.89

.7	**Specific prayers and groups of prayers**
.72	Specific types of prayers

                 Including doxologies

                 Class here prayers to Father, Son, Holy Spirit

.722	Bible prayers

  >   242.74–242.76   Prayers addressed to spiritual beings other than God

                 Class comprehensive works in 242.7

.74	Prayers to Mary

                 Including Ave Maria (Hail Mary), Rosary

.75	Prayers to Joseph, Joachim, Anne

.76   Prayers to saints and angels

> *For Joseph, Joachim, Anne, see 242.75*

.8   **Collections of prayers**

> Class here prayer books
>
> *For specific prayers and groups of prayers, see 242.7*

.800 1–.800 7   Standard subdivisions

.800 8   Groups of people

> Do not use for collections of prayers for specific groups of people; class in 242.82–242.89
>
> Class here collections of prayers by specific groups of people

.800 9   History, geographic treatment, biography

.801–.809   Collections of prayers by adherents of specific denominations and sects

> Add to base number 242.80 the numbers following 28 in 281–289, e.g., collections of private prayers by Methodists 242.807

.82–.89   Collections of prayers for specific groups of people

> Add to base number 242.8 the numbers following 248.8 in 248.82–248.89, e.g., collections of private prayers for college students 242.834
>
> *For collections of prayers by adherents of specific denominations and sects, see 242.801–242.809*

243   **Evangelistic writings for individuals and families**

> Works designed to convert readers, promote repentance
>
> Class evangelistic sermons in 252.3

[244]   **[Unassigned]**

> Most recently used in Edition 15

[245]   **[Unassigned]**

> Most recently used in Edition 21

246   **Use of art in Christianity**

> Religious meaning, significance, purpose
>
> Class attitude of Christianity and Christian church toward secular art, the arts in 261.57; class creation, description, critical appraisal as art in 700
>
> *For church furnishings and related articles, see 247*

>   **246.1–246.4 Schools and styles**

Class specific elements by school and style in 246.5–246.9; class comprehensive works in 246. Class interdisciplinary works on schools and styles of Christian art with the school or style in 709, e.g., interdisciplinary works on early Christian art 709.0212

.1   **Byzantine and Gothic art**

.2   **Early Christian and Romanesque art**

.4   **Renaissance and modern art**

Including Protestant art

>   **246.5–246.9 Specific elements**

Class comprehensive works in 246

.5   **Icons, symbols, insignia**

.53   Icons

.55   Symbols

Including banners, emblems, incense, votive offerings

Class here Christian symbolism

For colors and lights, see 246.6

.558   Crosses and crucifixes

Standard subdivisions are added for either or both topics in heading

.56   Insignia

Including insignia of rank

.6   **Colors and lights**

.7   **Dramatic, musical, rhythmic arts**

Including dance, liturgical dance

.72   Dramatic arts

.723   Passion plays

.725   Puppetry

.75   Music

Class here comprehensive works on music in Christianity

Class attitude of Christianity and Christian church toward secular music in 261.578; class interdisciplinary works on Christian sacred music in 781.71

For music in public worship, see 264.2

.9　　　**Architecture**

> Add to base number 246.9 the numbers following 726 in 726.4–726.9, e.g., cathedral church buildings 246.96; however, for church furnishings, see 247

247　Church furnishings and related articles

> Including paintings, plastic arts, sculpture, structural decoration, textiles

.1　　　**Furniture**

248　Christian experience, practice, life

> Class here spirituality
>
> *See Manual at 230–280*

SUMMARY

248.06	**Organizations and management**
.2	**Religious experience**
.3	**Worship**
.4	**Christian life and practice**
.5	**Witness bearing**
.6	**Stewardship**
.8	**Guides to Christian life for specific groups of people**

.06　　　Organizations and management

> Class pious societies, sodalities, confraternities in 267

.2　　　**Religious experience**

.22　　　Mysticism

.24　　　Conversion

> *For moral renewal and commitment, see 248.25*

> 248.241–248.246　Conversion from one system of belief to another
>
> Class comprehensive works in 248.24
>
> *For conversion of Christians to another religion, see the religion, e.g., conversion of Christians to Judaism 296.714*

.241   Conversion from within Christianity to specific denominations and
                sects

                Class here comprehensive works on conversion to specific
                denominations and sects

                Add to base number 248.241 the numbers following 28 in 281–289, e.g.,
                conversion to Seventh-Day Adventist Church 248.2416732; then, for
                conversion from another specific denomination or sect, add 0* and to the
                result add the numbers following 28 in 281–289, e.g., conversion from
                Roman Catholicism to Seventh-Day Adventist Church 248.241673202;
                however, for conversion from within Christianity to Roman Catholicism,
                see 248.242

                For conversion from non-Christianity to Christianity, see 248.246

                *See also 248.244 for conversion from Roman Catholicism to
                unspecified Protestant denominations and sects*

.242   Conversion from within Christianity to Roman Catholicism

                Class here conversion from Protestantism to Roman Catholicism,
                comprehensive works on conversion to Roman Catholicism

                Add to base number 248.242 the numbers following 28 in 281–289,
                e.g., conversion to Roman Catholic Church from Mennonite churches
                248.24297

                *For conversion from non-Christianity to Roman Catholicism, see
                248.246*

.244   Conversion from Roman Catholicism to Protestantism

                *For conversion from Roman Catholicism to specific Protestant
                denominations and sects, see 248.241*

.246   Conversion from non-Christianity to Christianity

                Add to base number 248.246 the numbers following 29 in 292–299
                for conversion from a specific religion, e.g., conversion from Judaism
                248.2466; then, for conversion to a specific Christian denomination or
                sect, add 0* and to the result add the numbers following 28 in 281–289,
                e.g., conversion from Judaism to Roman Catholic Church 248.246602

                Class comprehensive works on conversion to specific denominations and
                sects in 248.241

.25   Moral renewal and commitment

.29   Other religious experiences

                Including stigmata, private visions

                Class spiritual gifts in 234.13; class speaking in tongues (glossolalia) in
                234.132

---

*Add 00 for standard subdivisions; see instructions at beginning of Table 1

.3   **Worship**

Class here comprehensive works on worship

Class texts of prayers and devotions in 242

For observances in family life, see 249; for public worship, see 264

.32   Prayer

.34   Meditation and contemplation

Standard subdivisions are added for either or both topics in heading

.4   **Christian life and practice**

Class here Christian marriage and family

For Christian ethics, see 241; for worship, see 248.3; for witness bearing, see 248.5; for stewardship, see 248.6; for Christian observances in family life, see 249

.408   Groups of people

Do not use for guides to Christian life for specific groups of people; class in 248.8

Class here guides to Christian life by specific groups of people

.46   Individual observances

Including ceremonial and ritual observances, observance of restrictions and limitations

For asceticism, see 248.47; for pilgrimages, see 263.041

.47   Asceticism

Attitudes and practices aside from and beyond normal moral duties adopted as aids to moral and spiritual development

Including practice of celibacy, fasting and abstinence, poverty, solitude, other physical austerities, e.g., flagellation

For clerical celibacy, see 262.140865; for practices of religious congregations and orders, see 255

.48   Guides to Christian life by or for adherents of specific branches, denominations, sects

Class guides to Christian life for specific groups of people who are adherents of specific denominations and sects in 248.8

.480 2   Eastern and Roman Catholic churches

For guides to Christian life by or for adherents of Eastern churches, see 248.4815; for guides to Christian life by or for adherents of Roman Catholic Church, see 248.482

.480 4   Protestant churches and Protestantism

For guides to Christian life by or for adherents of specific Protestant denominations and sects, see 248.483–248.489

.481–.489   Specific denominations or sects

> Add to base number 248.48 the numbers following 28 in 281–289, e.g., guides for Roman Catholics 248.482

.5   **Witness bearing**

.6   **Stewardship**

.8   **Guides to Christian life for specific groups of people**

> Limited to groups provided for below

> Class here guides to Christian life for specific groups of people who are adherents of specific denominations and sects

> Class guides to a specific aspect of Christian life with the aspect, e.g., prayer 248.32

.808   Groups of people

.808 1   People by gender or sex

[.808 11]   Men

> Do not use; class in 248.842

[.808 2]   Women

> Do not use; class in 248.843

[.808 3]   Young people

> Do not use for children; class in 248.82. Do not use for young people twelve to twenty; class in 248.83

[.808 4]   People in specific stages of adulthood

> Do not use; class in 248.84

.808 5   Relatives

> Do not use for parents; class in 248.845

.808 6   People by miscellaneous social attributes

.808 65   People by marital status

> Do not use for men by marital status; class in 248.8422–248.8429. Do not use for women by marital status; class in 248.8432–248.8439

[.808 653]   Separated and divorced people

> Do not use; class in 248.846

[.808 655]   Married people

> Do not use; class in 248.844

.808 7   Gifted people

> Do not use for people with disabilities or illnesses; class in 248.86

[.808 8]   Occupational and religious groups

> Do not use for adherents of specific denominations or sects; class in 248.48. Do not use for occupational groups; class in 248.88. Do not use for clergy or people in religious orders; class in 248.89

> 248.82–248.85 Guides to Christian life for specific age groups

> Class people of specific ages in specific occupational groups or experiencing illness, trouble, bereavement in 248.86–248.89; class comprehensive works in 248.8

.82   Children

> Through age eleven

.83   Young people twelve to twenty and college students

> Standard subdivisions are added for young people twelve to twenty and college students together, for young people twelve to twenty alone

.832   Males twelve to twenty

.833   Females twelve to twenty

.834   College students

> Male and female

.84   Adults

> *For people in late adulthood, see 248.85*

.842   Men

.842 1   Fathers

> Regardless of marital status

.842 2–.842 9   Men by marital status

> Add to base number 248.842 the numbers following —0865 in notation 08652–08659 from Table 1, e.g., guides for husbands 248.8425

> Class fathers in 248.8421

.843   Women

.843 1   Mothers

> Regardless of marital status

.843 2–.843 9   Women by marital status

> Add to base number 248.843 the numbers following —0865 in notation 08652–08659 from Table 1, e.g., guides for wives 248.8435

> Class mothers in 248.8431

.844   Married people

> Class husbands in 248.8425; class wives in 248.8435

.845		Parents

Class here child rearing, religious training of children in the home

Class comprehensive works on Christian religious training of children in 268.432

For fathers, see 248.8421; for mothers, see 248.8431

.846	Separated and divorced people

For separated and divorced men, see 248.8423; for separated and divorced women, see 248.8433

.85	People in late adulthood

> 248.86–248.89 Guides to Christian life for occupational classes; people experiencing illness, trouble, bereavement

Class comprehensive works in 248.8

.86	People experiencing illness, trouble, bereavement
.861–.864	People experiencing specific illnesses and disabilities

Add to base number 248.86 the numbers following 362 in 362.1–362.4, e.g., people experiencing addiction 248.8629

See Manual at 616.86 vs. 158.1, 204.42, 248.8629, 292–299, 362.29

.866	People experiencing bereavement
.88	Occupational groups

For religious groups, see 248.89

.89	Religious groups
.892	Clergy

For people in religious orders, see 248.894

.894	People in religious orders
.894 2	Men
.894 22	Vocation
.894 25	Selection and novitiate
.894 3	Women
.894 32	Vocation
.894 35	Selection and novitiate

249 Christian observances in family life

Class here family prayer; family observance of religious restrictions, rites, ceremonies

> ## 250–280 Christian church

Class comprehensive works in 260

250 Local Christian church and Christian religious orders

Standard subdivisions are added for local Christian church and Christian religious orders together, for local Christian church alone

Class church renewal in 262.0017; class public worship in 264; class missions in 266; class religious education in 268

SUMMARY

250.9	History, geographic treatment, biography
251	Preaching (Homiletics)
252	Texts of sermons
253	Pastoral office and work (Pastoral theology)
254	Local church administration
255	Religious congregations and orders
259	Pastoral care of families, of specific groups of people

[.68] Management

Do not use for management of local Christian church and Christian religious orders together; class in 250. Do not use for management of local Christian church; class in 254

.9 **History, geographic treatment, biography**

Class general history of local church in specific continents, countries, localities in 274–279; class history, geographic treatment, biography of specific denominations in 280

> ## 251–254 Local church

Class here local churches in church organization, basic Christian communities

Class comprehensive works in 250

For pastoral care of families, of specific groups of people, see 259

See Manual at 260 vs. 250

251 Preaching (Homiletics)

Class texts of sermons in 252; class pastoral methods in 253.7

.001–.009 Standard subdivisions

.01 Preparation

.02 Sermon outlines

.03 Delivery

Class here voice, expression, gesture

.07   Radio and television preaching

> Class specific aspects of radio and television preaching in 251.01–251.03

.08   Homiletic illustrations

.1–.9   **Material for preparation of sermons for specific occasions, for specific groups of people**

> Add to base number 251 the numbers following 252 in 252.1–252.9, e.g., material for preparation of sermons arranged for the church year 251.6

252   Texts of sermons

> Class sermons on a specific subject with the subject, e.g., God's Providence 231.5

.001–.009   Standard subdivisions

.01–.09   Texts of sermons by specific denominations and sects

> Add to base number 252.0 the numbers following 28 in 281–289, e.g., Anglican sermons 252.03

.1   **Texts of sermons for baptisms, confirmations, funerals, weddings**

> Class sermons for memorial occasions in 252.9

.3   **Texts of sermons for evangelistic meetings**

.5   **Texts of sermons for specific groups of people**

.53   Children

> Through age eleven

.55   Young people twelve to twenty and college students

> Including academic, chapel, convocation, commencement sermons

.56   People in late adulthood, and people experiencing illness, trouble, bereavement

.58   Occupational groups

> *For religious groups, see 252.59*

.59   Religious groups

.592   Clergy

> *For people in religious orders, see 252.594*

.594   People in religious orders

.6   **Texts of sermons for church year and public occasions**

> Standard subdivisions are added for texts of sermons for church year and public occasions together, for church year alone

---

\>   252.61–252.64 Church year

> Class comprehensive works in 252.6

.61	Advent and Christmas
.612	Advent
.615	Christmas season

> Class here Christmas day

.62	Lent
.625	Holy Week
.63	Easter season

> Including Ascension Day
>
> Class here Easter Sunday

| .64 | Pentecost and time after Pentecost (Ordinary time) |
| .67 | Other feast and fast days |

> Including saints' days

| .68 | Secular occasions |

> Including elections, holidays, thanksgivings

| .7 | **Texts of sermons for consecrations, ordinations, installations** |
| .9 | **Texts of sermons for memorial occasions** |

253   Pastoral work (Pastoral theology)

Class here the work of priests, ministers, pastors, rectors, vicars, curates, chaplains, elders, deacons, assistants, laity in relation to the work of the church at the local level

Class local clergy and laity in relation to the government, organization and nature of the church as a whole in 262.1; class the role of clergy in religious education in 268

| .08 | Groups of people |

> Do not use for pastoral care of specific groups of people; class in 259
>
> Class here pastoral care performed by groups of people

| .082 | Women |

> Do not use for ordination of women not limited to its effect on the local church; class in 262.14082. Do not use for ordination of women to a specific office; class with the office in 262.1, plus notation 082 from Table 1, e.g., ordination of women as Anglican bishops 262.123082

| .086 | People by miscellaneous social attributes |
| .086 5 | People by marital status |

> Do not use for clerical celibacy not limited to its effect on the local church; class in 262.140865

| .09 | History, geographic treatment, biography |

.092   Biography

> Do not use for biography of clergy in the period prior to 1054; class in 270.1–270.3. Do not use for biography of clergy in the period subsequent to 1054; class in 280

> *See Manual at 230–280*

.2   **Life and person**

> Including professional and personal qualifications

> Class education of clergy in 230.0711; class guides to Christian life for clergy in 248.892

> *For qualifications for clerical ordination for groups of people, see 262.1408*

.22   Families of clergy

.3   **Pastoral work (Pastoral theology) by denomination**

> Add to base number 253.3 the numbers following 28 in 281–289, e.g., pastoral work in Methodist churches 253.37

> **253.5–253.7 Pastoral duties and responsibilities**

> Class methods for services to families, to specific groups of people in 259; class comprehensive works in 253

> *For preaching, see 251; for local church administration, see 254*

.5   **Counseling and spiritual direction**

> Standard subdivisions are added for counseling and spiritual direction together, for counseling alone

> Class pastoral counseling, spiritual direction of specific groups of people in 259; class premarital, marriage, family counseling in 259.12–259.14

.52   Pastoral psychology

.53   Spiritual direction

.7   **Pastoral methods**

> Including group work, telephone work

.76   Pastoral methods in homes

.78   Use of radio and television

254   Local church administration

> Class here parish administration

.001–.009   Standard subdivisions

.01–.09   Local church administration by specific denominations and sects

> Add to base number 254.0 the numbers following 28 in 281–289, e.g., administration of Roman Catholic parishes 254.02

.1   **Initiation of new churches**

.2   **Local church administration in specific kinds of communities**

> Class a specific activity in a specific kind of community with the activity, e.g., membership promotion 254.5

.22   Urban communities

.23   Suburban communities

.24   Rural communities

.3   **Use of communications media**

> Including use of audiovisual materials

.4   **Public relations and publicity**

> *For use of communications media, see 254.3*

.5   **Membership**

> Promotion and growth

.6   **Programs**

> Planning and execution

.7   **Buildings, equipment, grounds**

.8   **Finance**

> Including budget, expenditures, income, methods of raising money

255   **Religious congregations and orders**

> Class here religious congregations and orders in church organization; monasticism, comprehensive works on Christian religious congregations and orders

> When adding from 271 to indicate kinds of orders or specific orders, add only the notation for the kind or order. Do not use the footnote instruction to add as instructed under 271, but add notation from the table under 255.1–255.7 if it applies, or add notation 01–09 from Table 1. For example, the correct number for contemplative orders in the United Kingdom is 255.010941 (*not* 255.01041); for Benedictines in the United Kingdom 255.100941 (*not* 255.1041)

> *For guides to Christian life for people in religious orders, see 248.894; for religious congregations and orders, monasticism in church history, see 271. For specific types of activity of religious congregations and orders, see the activity, e.g., pastoral counseling 253.5, missionary work 266*

.001–.009   Standard subdivisions

.01–.09   Specific kinds of congregations and orders

> Add to base number 255.0 the numbers following 271.0 in 271.01–271.09 for the kind only, e.g., contemplative orders 255.01; then, for each kind having its own number, add notation 01–09 from Table 1 (*not* as instructed under 271), e.g., contemplative orders in the United Kingdom 255.010941

.1–.7   **Roman Catholic orders of men**

> Add to base number 255 the numbers following 271 in 271.1–271.7 for the order only, e.g., Benedictines 255.1; then, for each order having its own number, add further as follows (*not* as instructed at 271), e.g., Benedictines in the United Kingdom 255.100941, the rule of St. Benedict 255.106:
>
> 001–009   Standard subdivisions
> 02   Constitutions
> 04   Statutes, ordinances, customs
> 06   Rule

.8   **Non-Roman Catholic orders of men**

.81   Monasticism of Eastern churches

> Add to base number 255.81 the numbers following 281 in 281.5–281.9, e.g., Orthodox monasticism 255.819

.83   Anglican orders of men

.9   **Congregations and orders of women**

.900 1–.900 9   Standard subdivisions

.901–.909   Specific kinds of congregations and orders

> Add to base number 255.90 the numbers following 271.0 in 271.01–271.09 for the kind only, e.g., contemplative orders 255.901; then, for each kind having its own number, add notation 01–09 from Table 1 (*not* as instructed under 271), e.g., contemplative orders in the United Kingdom 255.9010941

.91–.97   Roman Catholic orders of women

> Add to base number 255.9 the numbers following 271.9 in 271.91–271.97 for the order only, e.g., Dominican sisters 255.972; then, for each order having its own number, add further as instructed under 255.1–255.7 (*not* as instructed at 271), e.g., Dominicans in the United Kingdom 255.97200941, the rule of the Dominicans 255.97206

.98   Non-Roman Catholic orders of women

.981   Monasticism of women of Eastern churches

> Add to base number 255.981 the numbers following 281 in 281.5–281.9, e.g., Orthodox monasticism of women 255.9819

.983   Anglican orders of women

[256]   **[Unassigned]**

> Most recently used in Edition 14

[257]   **[Unassigned]**

> Most recently used in Edition 14

[258]   **[Unassigned]**

> Most recently used in Edition 17

259   Pastoral care of families, of specific groups of people

Performed by clergy or laity

Class here pastoral counseling of specific groups of people

Unless other instructions are given, observe the following table of preference, e.g., pastoral care of bereaved young people 259.6 (*not* 259.2):

Pastoral care of the bereaved	259.6
Pastoral care of antisocial and asocial people	259.5
Pastoral care of people with disabilities, with physical or mental illnesses	259.4
Pastoral care of families	259.1
Pastoral care of young people	259.2
Pastoral care of people in late adulthood	259.3

Class comprehensive works on pastoral care of more than one kind of person in 253

See also 253.08 for pastoral care performed by groups of people; also 261.83 for response the church or Christian community should make to alleviate a social problem; also 361.75 for works limited to social welfare work by religious organizations

See Manual at 260 vs. 250

[.01–.07]   Standard subdivisions

Do not use; class in 253.01–253.07

.08   Groups of people

Do not use for bereaved people; class in 259.6

[.083]   Young people

Do not use; class in 259.2

.084   People in specific stages of adulthood

[.084 2]   People in early adulthood

Do not use; class in 259.25

[.084 6]   People in late adulthood

Do not use; class in 259.3

.086   People by miscellaneous social attributes

[.086 92]   Antisocial and asocial people

Do not use; class in 259.5

.087   Gifted people

Do not use for people with disabilities and illnesses; class in 259.4

.088   Occupational and religious groups

[.088 378 198]   College students

Do not use; class in 259.24

[.09]	History, geographic treatment, biography

Do not use; class in 253.09

.1   **Pastoral care of families**

.12   Family counseling

For premarital counseling, see 259.13; for marriage counseling, see 259.14

.13   Premarital counseling

.14   Marriage counseling

.2   **Pastoral care of young people**

.22   Pastoral care of children

Through age eleven

.23   Pastoral care of young people twelve to twenty

Class here comprehensive works on pastoral care of young adults

For pastoral care of young adults over twenty-one, see 259.25

.24   Pastoral care of college students

Class here campus ministry

.25   Pastoral care of people in early adulthood

Class here young adults over twenty-one

For pastoral care of college students, see 259.24

.3   **Pastoral care of people in late adulthood**

.4   **Pastoral care of people with disabilities, with physical or mental illnesses**

Class here programs for visiting the sick

Add to base number 259.4 the numbers following 362 in 362.1–362.4, e.g., pastoral care of those who have attempted suicide 259.428

.5   **Pastoral care of antisocial and asocial people**

Class here prison chaplaincy; pastoral care of juvenile delinquents and predelinquents, of offenders

.6   **Pastoral care of the bereaved**

260   Christian social and ecclesiastical theology

Institutions, services, observances, disciplines, work of Christianity and Christian church

Class here comprehensive works on Christian church, on practical theology

For moral and devotional theology, see 240; for local church and religious orders, see 250; for denominations and sects, see 280

See Manual at 260 vs. 250

SUMMARY

.9   History, geographic treatment, biography

Do not use for history, geographic treatment, biography of Christian church; class in 270

261   Social theology and interreligious relations and attitudes

Attitude of Christianity and Christian church toward and influence on secular matters, attitude toward other religions, interreligious relations

Class here Christianity and culture

Class sociology of religion in 306.6

.1   Role of Christian church in society

Class specific socioeconomic problems in 261.8

.2   Christianity and other systems of belief

For polemics against other systems of belief, see 239

.21   Christianity and irreligion

Including Christianity and communism, Christianity and the apostate and indifferent

.22–.29   Christianity and other religions

Add to base number 261.2 the numbers following 29 in 292–299, e.g., Christianity and Islam 261.27

.5   **Christianity and secular disciplines**

Class here antagonism between and reconciliation of Christian belief and a secular discipline

For antagonism between and reconciliation of a specific Christian doctrine and a secular discipline, see the doctrine in 231–239, e.g., relation between Christian doctrine on the soul and modern biology 233.5

See Manual at 261.5

.51   Philosophy, logic, related disciplines

.513   Parapsychology and occultism

.515   Psychology

.52   Communications media

Class here comprehensive works on attitude toward and use of communications media

For a specific use of communications media by the church, see the use, e.g., use in local church administration 254.3

.55   Science

Class the relation of scientific and Christian views on creation in 231.765; class ecology in 261.88

.56   Technology

.561   Medicine

.57   The arts

.578   Music

.58   Literature

.7   **Christianity and political affairs**

Including civil war and revolution

Class here Christianity and civil rights

For Christianity and international affairs, see 261.87

See Manual at 322.1 vs. 201.72, 261.7, 292–299

.72   Religious freedom

.73   Theocracy

Supremacy of church over civil government

.8 **Christianity and socioeconomic problems**

Class here comprehensive works on the Christian view of socioeconomic and political affairs

For Christianity and political affairs, see 261.7

See also 361.75 for welfare services of religious organizations

See Manual at 241 vs. 261.8

.83 Social problems and services

.832 Social welfare problems and services

.832 1–.832 5 Problems of and services to people with illnesses and disabilities, the poor

Add to base number 261.832 the numbers following 362 in 362.1–362.5, e.g., Christian attitude toward alcoholism 261.832292, toward poor people 261.8325

.832 6 Hunger

.832 7 Abuse within the family

.832 71 Child abuse and neglect

For sexual abuse, see 261.83272

.832 72 Sexual abuse

.832 73 Adults who were victims of abuse as children

.832 8 Refugees and victims of political oppression

.833 Crime

Add to base number 261.833 the numbers following 364 in 364.1–364.8, e.g., Christian attitude toward treason 261.833131, toward capital punishment 261.83366

.835 Sexual relations, marriage, family

Add to base number 261.835 the numbers following 306 in 306.7–306.8, e.g., Christian attitude toward divorce 261.83589

Class abuse within the family in 261.8327

.836 Population

Including abortion, family planning

Class ecology in 261.88

.85 Economics

Including management of business enterprises

For environment, natural resources, see 261.88

.87 International affairs

.873 War and peace

For civil war and revolution, see 261.7

| .873 2 | Nuclear weapons and nuclear war |
| .88 | Environment |

Class here ecology, environmental problems, natural resources, pollution

Class environmental ethics in 241.691

262   Ecclesiology

Church government, organization, nature

Class here ecclesiastical polity

See Manual at 260 vs. 250

SUMMARY

262.001–.009	Standard subdivisions, ecumenism, church renewal
.01–.09	Government and organization, ecclesiology of specific denominations and sects
.1	Governing leaders of churches
.2	Local church and religious congregations and orders in church organization
.3	Government and organization of systems governed by papacy and episcopacy
.4	Government and organization of systems governed by election
.5	General councils
.7	Nature of the church
.8	Church and ministerial authority and its denial
.9	Church law and discipline

| .001 | Philosophy and theory, ecumenism, church renewal |

Notation 01 from Table 1 as modified below

| .001 1 | Ecumenism |

Do not use for systems; class in 262.001

See Manual at 280.042 vs. 262.0011

| .001 109 | History, geographic treatment, biography |

Do not use for history of the ecumenical movement; class in 280.042

| .001 7 | Church renewal |

Class here renewal of the church as a whole, renewal of local churches

.002–.005	Standard subdivisions
.006	Organizations
.006 8	Particular aspects of administration

Do not use for management without subdivision; class in 262

Add notation 0681–0688 as appropriate for particular aspects of administration, e.g., financial administration of United Methodist Church 262.0760681

.007–.009 Standard subdivisions

.01–.09 Government and organization, ecclesiology of specific denominations and sects

> Add to base number 262.0 the numbers following 28 in 281–289, e.g., government and organization of the United Methodist Church 262.076

.1 Governing leaders of churches

Authority, function, role

[.108 82] Religious groups

> Do not use; class in 262.12–262.16

[.109 2] Biography

> Do not use for biography of church leaders; class in 270. Do not use for biography of leaders of specific denominations; class in 280

See Manual at 230–280

.11 Apostolic succession

.12 *Episcopacy

> Class here bishops, archbishops, national conferences of bishops

> Add to base number 262.12 the numbers following 28 in 281–289, e.g., episcopacy of Anglican churches 262.123, of Church of England 262.12342, ordination of women as bishops in Church of England 262.12342082

> *For papacy and patriarchate, see 262.13*

> *See also 262.14 for local clergy with the title of bishop*

.13 *Papacy and patriarchate

> Standard subdivisions are added for papacy and patriarchate together, for Roman Catholic papacy alone

———————

> 262.131–262.136 Specific aspects of Roman Catholic papacy

Class comprehensive works in 262.13

.131 Papal infallibility

.132 Temporal power of the pope

.135 College of Cardinals

.136 Administration

> Including congregations, offices of Curia Romana, Synod of Bishops, tribunals

> *For national conferences of bishops, see 262.12; for College of Cardinals, see 262.135*

*Use notation 08 from Table 1 as modified at 262.1408

.14   **Local clergy**

Persons who lead a local church, regardless of degree, ordination, or pay status

Add to base number 262.14 the numbers following 28 in 281–289, e.g., local Methodist clergy 262.147

.140 8   Groups of people

Class here comprehensive works on qualifications for clerical ordination

.140 82   Women

Class here comprehensive works on ordination of women

Class works that treat the ordination of women only in relation to its effect on the local church in 253. Class ordination of women at a specific rank with the rank, plus notation 082 from Table 1, e.g., ordination of women as Anglican bishops 262.123082

.140 86   People by miscellaneous social attributes

.140 865   People by marital status

Class here comprehensive works on clerical celibacy

Class works that treat clerical celibacy only in relation to its effect on the local church in 253. Class clerical celibacy at a specific rank with the rank, plus notation 0865 from Table 1, e.g., marital status of priests in Orthodox church 262.14190865

.15   **Laity**

Body of church members

Add to base number 262.15 the numbers following 28 in 281–289, e.g., laity of Lutheran church 262.1541, in United States 262.154173

.16   **Other governing leaders**

Add to base number 262.16 the numbers following 28 in 281–289, e.g., apostleship of Church of Jesus Christ of Latter-day Saints 262.169332

>   **262.3–262.4 Specific forms of church government**

Class works on government and organization of specific denominations and sects using forms of government not provided for below, comprehensive works on government and organization of specific denominations and sects regardless of form of government in 262.01–262.09; class comprehensive works in 262. Class a specific aspect of government and organization with the aspect, e.g., role of bishops in an episcopal form of church government 262.12 (*not* 262.3)

.3   **Episcopal forms of church government (Episcopal polity)**

Including sees, dioceses, cathedral systems

Class here specific episcopal forms of church government, e.g., connexionalism

.4   **Presbyterian and congregational forms of church government**

.42	Presbyterian forms of church government (Presbyterian polity)

        Including presbyteries, synods, general assemblies

.44	Congregational forms of church government (Congregational polity)
.5	**General councils**

        Add to base number 262.5 the numbers following 28 in 281–289, e.g., ecumenical councils of Roman Catholic Church 262.52

        Class legal acts of general councils in 262.9. Class nonlegal decrees on a specific subject with the subject, e.g., statements on original sin 233.14

.7	**Nature of the church**

        Including God's relation to the church

.72	Attributes, marks, notes

        Including apostolicity, catholicity, credibility, holiness, infallibility, necessity, unity, visibility and invisibility

.73	Communion of saints
.77	Mystical body of Christ
.8	**Church and ministerial authority and its denial**

        Including heresy, schism

.9	**Church law and discipline**

        Class here canon (ecclesiastical) law

        Class civil law relating to church or religious matters in 340

        See also 364.188 for offenses against religion as defined and penalized by the state

---

>   262.91–262.94 Roman Catholic law

        Class comprehensive works in 262.9

.91	Acts of the Holy See

        Including apostolic letters, briefs, encyclicals, papal bulls and decrees

        Class acts on a specific subject with the subject, e.g., on the nature of the church 262.7

.92	Early Roman Catholic codes
.922	Early codes to Gratian, ca. 1140
.923	Corpus iuris canonici
.924	Quinque compilationes antiquae
.93	Codex iuris canonici (1917)
.931	General principles (Canons 1–86)

.932   Persons (Canons 87–725)

> Clergy, religious, laity

.933   Things (Canons 726–1551)

> Including benefices, sacraments, sacred times and places, teaching office, temporal goods, worship

.934   Procedure (Canons 1552–2194)

> Including trials, causes of beatification and canonization

.935   Crimes and penalties (Canons 2195–2414)

.94   Codex iuris canonici (1983)

> Unless other instructions are given, class a subject with aspects in two or more subdivisions of 262.94 in the number coming last, e.g., annulment of marriage 262.947 (*not* 262.944)

.941   General norms (Canons 1–203)

.942   The people of God (Canons 204–746)

> Including clergy, laity; hierarchical organization of the Church; religious congregations and orders

.943   Teaching mission of the Church (Canons 747–833)

> Including Catholic education, catechetical instruction

.944   Function of the Church (Canons 834–1253)

> Class here worship, sacred places and times; comprehensive works on canon law on sacraments
>
>> For a specific aspect of canon law on sacraments provided elsewhere, see the aspect, e.g., annulment of marriage 262.947

.945   Church temporal goods (Canons 1254–1310)

.946   Sanctions (Canons 1311–1399)

> Class here crimes, penalties, delicts

.947   Processes (Canons 1400–1752)

> Class here trials, judgments, procedures

.98   Branches and other denominations and sects

.980 2   Eastern and Roman Catholic churches

> For church law of Eastern churches, see 262.9815; for church law of Roman Catholic Church, see 262.982

.980 4   Protestant churches and Protestantism

> For church law of specific Protestant denominations and sects, see 262.983–262.989

.981–.989   Other specific denominations or sects

> Add to base number 262.98 the numbers following 28 in 281–289, e.g., Anglican ecclesiastical law 262.983

263 Days, times, places of religious observance

.04　　　　　Special topics of days, times, places of religious observance

.041　　　　　Pilgrimages

[.041 093–.041 099]　　　　Specific continents, countries, localities

> Do not use; class in 263.0423–263.0429

.042　　　　Holy places

> Class here pilgrimages to holy places in specific continents, countries, localities
>
> *For works treating miracles and shrines associated with them, see 231.73; for miracles associated with Mary and shrines associated with them, see 232.917; for miracles of Jesus and shrines associated with them, see 232.955*

[.042 093–.042 099]　　　　Specific continents, countries, localities

> Do not use; class in 263.0423–263.0429

.042 3–.042 9　　　Specific continents, countries, localities

> Add to base number 263.042 notation 3–9 from Table 2, e.g., Santiago de Compostela 263.0424611

> ### 263.1–263.3 Sabbath and Sunday
>
> Class comprehensive works in 263.3

.1　　　**Biblical Sabbath**

.2　　　**Observance of the seventh day**

.3　　　**Sunday**

> Class here Sunday observance, comprehensive works on Sabbath and Sunday
>
> *For Biblical Sabbath, see 263.1; for observance of the seventh day, see 263.2*

.9　　　**Church year and other days and times**

> Standard subdivisions are added for church year and other days and times together, for church year alone
>
> *See Manual at 203.6, 263.9, 292–299 vs. 394.265–394.267*

> ### 263.91–263.94 Church year
>
> Class comprehensive works in 263.9

.91　　　Advent and Christmas

.912　　　　Advent

.915	Christmas season

> Class here Christmas day

.92	Lent
.925	Holy Week
.93	Easter season

> Including Ascension Day
>
> Class here Easter Sunday

.94	Pentecost and time after Pentecost (Ordinary time)
.97	Other feast and fast days

> *For saints' days, see 263.98*

.98	Saints' days

> Standard subdivisions are added for individual saint's days

264   Public worship

Ceremonies, rites, services (liturgy and ritual)

Class works not limited by denomination or sect about sacraments, other rites and acts in 265; class Sunday school services in 268.7; class comprehensive works on worship in 248.3

SUMMARY

264.001–.009	**Standard subdivisions**
.01–.09	**Public worship by denominations and sects**
.1	**Prayer**
.2	**Music**
.3	**Scripture readings and communion sacrament**
.4	**Responsive readings**
.7	**Prayer meetings, Holy Hours, novenas**
.9	**Sacramentals**

.001	Philosophy and theory

> Class here liturgical renewal

.002–.009	Standard subdivisions

>	264.01–264.09 Public worship by denominations and sects

> Class here works limited by denomination or sect about sacraments, other rites and acts
>
> Class comprehensive works in 264; class comprehensive works on sacraments, other rites and acts in 265

.01	Early and Eastern churches

> Add to base number 264.01 the numbers following 281 in 281.1–281.9, e.g., liturgy and ritual of Orthodox churches 264.019; then add further as instructed under 264.04–264.09, e.g., Orthodox Divine Liturgy 264.019036

.02	Roman Catholic Church
.020 01–.020 09	Standard subdivisions
.020 1–.020 9	History, meaning, place of liturgy, ritual, prayers in public worship

> Add to base number 264.02 notation 01–09 from the table under 264.04–264.09, e.g., the Mass 264.02036; however, for texts, see 264.021–264.029

>   264.021–264.029 Texts of liturgy, ritual, prayers

Class comprehensive works in 264.02

.021	Texts of calendars and ordos
.022	Texts of ceremonials

> Ceremonials: canonization of saints, election and coronation of popes, creation of cardinals, other papal functions and services; instructions for bishops

.023	Texts of missals

> Class here sacramentaries
>
> *For lectionary, see 264.029*

.024	Texts of breviaries

> *For psalters, see 264.028*

.025	Texts of ritual

> Class here Pontificale Romanum, Rituale Romanum
>
> Add to base number 264.025 the numbers following 265 in 265.1–265.7, e.g., texts of baptism 264.0251

.027	Texts of special books
.027 2	Texts for special times of year

> Including Holy Week

.027 4	Texts for special liturgical services

> Including funeral services outside the Mass, litanies, novenas, stations of the cross

.028	Texts of psalters
.029	Texts of lectionary
.03	Anglican churches

> Including rubrics
>
> Class here Book of Common Prayer; Common Worship

.030 01–.030 09	Standard subdivisions

.030 1–.030 9   History, meaning, place of liturgy, ritual, prayers in public worship

> Add to base number 264.03 notation 01–09 from the table under 264.04–264.09, e.g., prayer 264.0301; however, for texts, see 264.031–264.038

> 264.031–264.038   Texts of liturgy, ritual, prayers

Class comprehensive works in 264.03

.031   Texts of calendars, festivals, fasts

.032   Texts of lectionary

> Including texts of epistles, Gospels

.033   Texts of morning prayer and litany

.034   Texts of evening prayer and vespers

.035   Texts of sacraments, ordinances, services

> Add to base number 264.035 the numbers following 265 in 265.1–265.9, e.g., texts of baptism 264.0351

> Class texts of morning prayer and litany in 264.033; class texts of evening prayer and vespers in 264.034

.036   Texts of collects

.038   Texts of psalters

.04–.09   Other specific denominations and sects

> Add to base number 264.0 the numbers following 28 in 284–289, e.g., United Methodist services 264.076; then add further as follows:
> 001–009   Standard subdivisions
> 01–07   Specific elements
>   History, meaning, place in public worship, texts
>   Add to 0 the numbers following 264 in 264.1–264.7, e.g., the Lord's Supper 036, the Lord's Supper in the United Methodist Church 264.076036
> 08   Sacraments
>   History, meaning, place in public worship, texts
>   Add to 08 the numbers following 265 in 265.1–265.7, e.g., the ceremony of baptism 081, the ceremony of baptism in the United Methodist Church 264.076081; however, for Holy Communion (Eucharist, Lord's Supper, Mass), see 036
> 09   Sacramentals, other rites and acts
>   History, meaning, place in public worship, texts
> 091   Sacramentals
> 098–099   Other rites and acts
>   Add to 09 the numbers following 265 in 265.8–265.9, e.g., funeral services 0985, United Methodist funerals 264.0760985

> ## 264.1–264.9 Specific elements

History, meaning, place in public worship, texts

Class specific elements in public worship of specific denominations and sects in 264.01–264.09; class use of the arts (*except* music), of color in public worship in 246; class liturgical year in 263.9; class comprehensive works in 264

Specific elements as part of the Mass are classed in 264.36, e.g., Eucharistic prayers (*not* 264.1)

.1 Prayer

Class prayers for a specific ceremony with the ceremony, e.g., prayers for funerals 265.85

.13 Texts of prayers

Including litanies

Class comprehensive collections of public and private prayers in 242.8

.15 Liturgy of the hours (Divine office)

Including psalters

Class here breviaries

.2 Music

Class comprehensive works on music in Christianity in 246.75; class interdisciplinary works on Christian sacred music in 781.71; class interdisciplinary works on sacred vocal music in 782.22

.23 Hymns

Class here texts of hymns for devotional use of individuals and families

Class hymnals containing both text and music, interdisciplinary works on hymns in 782.27

.3 Scripture readings and communion sacrament

.34 Scripture readings

Class here common lectionary

.36 Holy Communion (Eucharist, Lord's Supper, Mass)

Including specific elements when part of the Mass

For viaticum, see 265.7

.4 Responsive readings

.7 Prayer meetings, Holy Hours, novenas

.9 Sacramentals

For consecrations and dedications, see 265.92

265   Sacraments, other rites and acts

> Standard subdivisions are added for sacraments and other rites and acts together, for sacraments alone
>
> Not limited by denomination or sect
>
> Class works limited by denomination or sect about sacraments, other rites and acts in 264.01–264.09

> **265.1–265.7 Sacraments**
>
> Class comprehensive works in 265
>
> *For Holy Communion (Eucharist, Lord's Supper, Mass), see 264.36*

.1	**Baptism**
.12	Infant baptism
.13	Adult baptism

> Class here Christian initiation (baptism and confirmation) of adults, catechumenate
>
> *For confirmation, see 265.2; for religious education for catechumens, see 268.434*

.2	**Confirmation (Chrismation)**
.4	**Holy Orders**
.5	**Matrimony**
.6	**Penance**
.61	Contrition

> Examination of conscience, prayers preparatory to confession

.62	Confession
.63	Satisfaction

> Penitential prayers and acts for the remission of sin

.64	Absolution
.66	Indulgences
.7	**Viaticum and anointing of the sick**
.8	**Rites in illness and death**
.82	Religious ceremonies for the afflicted

> *For viaticum and anointing of the sick, see 265.7*

.85	Religious ceremonies for the dead

> Class here funeral services
>
> *For requiem Mass, see 264.36*

.9   **Other acts**

> Including ceremonies of joining a church, foot washing, laying on of hands, love feasts (agapes)

.92   Consecrations and dedications

.94   Exorcism

266   Missions

> Class here missionary societies, religious aspects of medical missions

> Class medical services of medical missions in 362.1

> *For mission schools, see 371.071*

.001–.008   Standard subdivisions

.009   History, geographic treatment, biography

> Do not use for foreign missions originating in specific continents, countries, localities; class in 266.023. Do not use for history, geographic treatment, biography of missions of specific denominations and sects; class in 266.1–266.9

> Class here joint and interdenominational missions; foreign missions by continent, country, locality served

.02   Kinds of missions

.022   Home missions

.023   Foreign missions

[.023 091–.023 099]   Geographic treatment and biography

> Do not use for foreign missions characterized only by place served; class in 266.009. Do not use for foreign missions originating in specific areas; class in 266.0231–266.0239

.023 1–.023 9   Biography; foreign missions originating in specific areas

> Add to base number 266.023 notation 1–9 from Table 2, e.g., missions originating in France 266.02344; then add 0* and again add notation 1–9 from Table 2 for place served, e.g., French missions to Africa 266.0234406

.1–.9   **Missions of specific denominations and sects**

> Add to base number 266 the numbers following 28 in 281–289, e.g., Anglican missions 266.3; Anglican missions serving Africa 266.36

267   Associations for religious work

> Class here pious societies, sodalities, confraternities

> *For religious congregations and orders, see 255; for missionary societies, see 266*

> *See Manual at 230–280*

---

*Add 00 for standard subdivisions; see instructions at beginning of Table 1

.1	**Associations for religious work for both men and women**
.13	Interdenominational and nondenominational associations

> *For Moral Rearmament, see 267.16*

.16	Moral Rearmament
.18	Specific branches, denominations, sects
.180 2	Eastern and Roman Catholic churches

> *For religious associations of Eastern churches, see 267.1815; for religious associations of Roman Catholic Church, see 267.182*

.180 4	Protestant churches and Protestantism

> *For religious associations of specific Protestant denominations and sects, see 267.183–267.189*

.181–.189	Specific denominations or sects

Add to base number 267.18 the numbers following 28 in 281–289, e.g., Baptist Adult Union 267.186132

.2	**Men's associations**
.23	Interdenominational and nondenominational associations

> *For Young Men's Christian Associations, see 267.3*

.24	Specific branches, denominations, sects
.240 2	Eastern and Roman Catholic churches

> *For men's religious associations of Eastern churches, see 267.2415; for men's religious associations of Roman Catholic Church, see 267.242*

.240 4	Protestant churches and Protestantism

> *For men's religious associations of specific Protestant denominations and sects, see 267.243–267.249*

.241–.249	Specific denominations or sects

Add to base number 267.24 the numbers following 28 in 281–289, e.g., Baptist societies 267.246

.3	**Young Men's Christian Associations**
[.309]	History, geographic treatment, biography

Do not use; class in 267.39

.39	History, geographic treatment, biography
.390 1–.390 5	Historical periods

Add to base number 267.39 notation 01–05 from Table 2, e.g., Young Men's Christian Association in 21st century 267.3905

.391–.399   Geographic treatment, biography

> Add to base number 267.39 notation 1–9 from Table 2, e.g., Young Men's Christian Association in New York City 267.397471

.4   **Women's associations**

.43   Interdenominational and nondenominational associations

> *For Young Women's Christian Associations, see 267.5*

.44   Specific branches, denominations, sects

.440 2   Eastern and Roman Catholic churches

> *For women's religious associations of Eastern churches, see 267.4415; for women's religious associations of Roman Catholic Church, see 267.442*

.440 4   Protestant churches and Protestantism

> *For women's religious associations of specific Protestant denominations and sects, see 267.443–267.449*

.441–.449   Specific denominations or sects

> Add to base number 267.44 the numbers following 28 in 281–289, e.g., Baptist societies 267.446

.5   **Young Women's Christian Associations**

[.509]   History, geographic treatment, biography

> Do not use; class in 267.59

.59   History, geographic treatment, biography

.590 1–.590 5   Historical periods

> Add to base number 267.59 notation 01–05 from Table 2, e.g., Young Women's Christian Association in 21st century 267.5905

.591–.599   Geographic treatment, biography

> Add to base number 267.59 notation 1–9 from Table 2, e.g., Young Women's Christian Association in New York City 267.597471

.6   **Young adults' associations**

.61   Interdenominational and nondenominational associations

> *For Young Men's Christian Associations, see 267.3; for Young Women's Christian Associations, see 267.5*

.62   Specific branches, denominations, sects

.620 2   Eastern and Roman Catholic churches

> *For young adults' religious associations of Eastern churches, see 267.6215; for young adults' religious associations of Roman Catholic Church, see 267.622*

.620 4   Protestant churches and Protestantism

> *For young adults' religious associations of specific Protestant denominations and sects, see 267.623–267.629*

.621–.629   Specific denominations or sects

> Add to base number 267.62 the numbers following 28 in 281–289, e.g., Baptist Young People's Union 267.626132

.7   **Boys' associations**

> *For Young Men's Christian Associations, see 267.3*

.8   **Girls' associations**

> *For Young Women's Christian Associations, see 267.5*

268   Religious education

> Class here catechetics (the science or art devoted to organizing the principles of religious teaching), curricula, comprehensive works on Christian religious education
>
> Class Christian religious schools providing general education in 371.071; class place of religion in public schools in 379.28. Class textbooks on a specific subject with the subject, e.g., textbooks on missions 266
>
> *For religious education at the university level, see 230.0711; for study of Christianity in secular secondary schools, see 230.0712*
>
> *See Manual at 207.5, 268 vs. 200.71, 230.071, 292–299*

[.068]   Management

> Do not use; class in 268.1

.08   Groups of people

> Do not use for education of specific groups of people; class in 268.4
>
> Class here education, teaching performed by groups of people

[.088 2]   Religious groups

> Do not use; class in 268.8

.1   **Administration**

> *For plant management, see 268.2; for personnel management, see 268.3*

.2   **Buildings and equipment**

.3   **Personnel**

> Class here preparation, role, training, personnel management
>
> *See Manual at 230–280*

.4   **Religious education of specific groups of people**

> Class here curricula, records and rules, teaching methods, services for specific groups

[.408 3–.408 4]	Age groups

Do not use; class in 268.43

.43	Age groups
.432	Children

Through age eleven

For religious training of children in the home, see 248.845

See also 372.84 for religion courses in secular primary schools

(.432 04)	Special topics of children
(.432 045)	Textbooks

(Option: Class here religious education textbooks; prefer the specific subject, e.g., textbooks on Christianity 230, textbooks on missions 266)

.433	Young people twelve to twenty
(.433 04)	Special topics of young people twelve to twenty
(.433 045)	Textbooks

(Option: Class here religious education textbooks; prefer the specific subject, e.g., textbooks on Christianity 230, textbooks on missions 266)

.434	Adults
(.434 04)	Special topics of adults
(.434 045)	Textbooks

(Option: Class here religious education textbooks; prefer the specific subject, e.g., textbooks on Christianity 230, textbooks on missions 266)

.5	**Records and rules**

Including attendance, decorations, honor rolls, prizes, promotion

Class records and rules for specific groups in 268.4

.6	**Methods of instruction and study**

Class methods for a specific group with the group, e.g., methods for instruction of children 268.432071

.63	Lecture and audiovisual methods
.632	Lecture method
.635	Audiovisual methods
.67	Dramatic method

Class use of dramatic arts for religious purposes not limited to religious education in 246.72

.7   **Services**

> Including anniversaries, festivals, music, rallies, special days

> Class services for specific groups in 268.4

.8   **Specific branches, denominations, sects**

.802   Eastern and Roman Catholic churches

> *For religious education of Eastern churches, see 268.815; for religious education of Roman Catholic Church, see 268.82*

.804   Protestant churches and Protestantism

> *For religious education of specific Protestant denominations and sects, see 268.83–268.89*

.81–.89   Specific denominations or sects

> Add to base number 268.8 the numbers following 28 in 281–289, e.g., Presbyterian religious education 268.85

> Class a specific element in religious education by specific denominations and sects with the element in 268.1–268.7, e.g., religious education of children in Baptist churches 268.432088286

269   Spiritual renewal

> Class history of the pentecostal movement in 270.82

.2   **Evangelism**

> *See also 243 for evangelistic writings for individuals and families; also 248.5 for witness bearing by individual lay Christians; also 252.3 for texts of evangelistic sermons; also 266 for missionary evangelization*

.24   Revival and camp meetings

.26   Evangelism by radio and television

.6   **Retreats**

> Add to base number 269.6 the numbers following 248.8 in 248.82–248.89, e.g., retreats for men 269.642

> ## 270–280 History, geographic treatment, biography of Christianity; Church history; Christian denominations and sects

Unless other instructions are given, observe the following table of preference for the history of Christianity and the Christian church (*except* for biography, explained in Manual at 230–280), e.g., persecution of Jesuits by Elizabeth I 272.7 (*not* 271.53042, 274.206, or 282.42):

Persecutions in general church history	272
Doctrinal controversies and heresies in general church history	273
Religious congregations and orders in church history	271
Denominations and sects of Christian church	280
Christianity and Christian church by continent, country, locality	274–279
General history, geographic treatment, biography of Christianity and Christian church (*except* 271–279)	270

Class comprehensive works in 270

See Manual at 230–280

270 History, geographic treatment, biography of Christianity

Class here Church history, collected writings of apostolic and church fathers (patristics)

Observe table of preference under 230–280

For history, geographic treatment, biography of specific denominations and sects, see 280

See Manual at 230–280; also at 270, 230.11–230.14 vs. 230.15–230.2, 281.5–281.9, 282; also at 398.2 vs. 201.3, 230, 270, 292–299

SUMMARY

270.01–.09	**Standard subdivisions**
.1–.8	**Historical periods**
271	**Religious congregations and orders in church history**
272	**Persecutions in general church history**
273	**Doctrinal controversies and heresies in general church history**
274–279	**Christianity by specific continents, countries, localities in modern world**

.01–.07   Standard subdivisions

.08   Groups of people

Class here Christian attitudes toward social groups; discrimination, equality, inequality, prejudice

.09   Areas, regions, places in general; biography

.092 2

[.093–.099]   Specific continents, countries, localities

> Do not use; class in 274–279

>   **270.1–270.8 Historical periods**

> Class historical periods in specific continents, countries, localities in 274–279; class comprehensive works in 270

.1   **Apostolic period to 325**

.2   **Period of ecumenical councils, 325–787**

.3   **787–1054**

> Class here comprehensive works on Middle Ages

> *For a specific part of Middle Ages, see the part, e.g., late Middle Ages 270.5*

.38   Great schism, 1054

.4   **1054–1200**

.5   **Late Middle Ages through Renaissance, 1200–1517**

.6   **Period of Reformation and Counter-Reformation, 1517–1648**

> Including 17th century

> *For 1648–1699, see 270.7*

.7   **Period from Peace of Westphalia to French Revolution, 1648–1789**

.8   **Modern period, 1789–**

.81   1789–1900

.82   1900–1999

> Class here comprehensive works on evangelicalism, fundamentalism, pentecostalism, charismatic movement

> Add to base number 270.82 the numbers following —0904 in notation 09041–09049 from Table 1, e.g., 1960–1969 in church history 270.826

> Class ecumenical movement in 280.042; class pentecostal churches that are independent denominations in 289.94; class evangelical churches, fundamentalist churches that are independent denominations in 289.95

> *For evangelicalism, fundamentalism, pentecostalism, charismatic movement in the period 2000 to present, see 270.83. For evangelicalism, fundamentalism, pentecostalism, charismatic movement in a specific branch or denomination, see the branch or denomination, e.g., Protestant fundamentalism 280.4*

.83   2000–

>   **271–273 Special topics of church history**

> Class comprehensive works in 270

271 Religious congregations and orders in church history

Class here history of monasticism, history of specific monasteries and convents even if not connected with a specific order

Add to each subdivision identified by * as follows:

001–008   Standard subdivisions
[009]   History
              Do not use; class in base number without further addition
[0091–0099]   Geographic treatment and biography
              Do not use; class in notation 01–09 from this table
01–09   Geographic treatment and biography
              Add to 0 notation 1–9 from Table 2, e.g., collected biography 022, collected biography of Benedictines 271.1022, Benedictines in the United Kingdom 271.1041

Class persecutions involving religious congregations and orders in 272; class doctrinal controversies and heresies involving congregations and orders in 273

SUMMARY

271.001–.009	**Standard subdivisions**
.01–.09	**Specific kinds of congregations and orders**
.1	**Benedictines**
.2	**Dominicans (Friars Preachers, Black Friars)**
.3	**Franciscans (Gray Friars)**
.4	**Augustinians**
.5	**Regular clerics**
.6	**Passionists and Redemptorists**
.7	**Roman Catholic orders of men not otherwise provided for**
.8	**Non-Roman Catholic orders of men**
.9	**Congregations and orders of women**

.001–.009   Standard subdivisions

> 271.01–271.09 Specific kinds of congregations and orders

Class comprehensive works in 271

.01   *Contemplative religious orders

.02   *Eremitical religious orders

.03   *Teaching orders

.04   *Preaching orders

.06   *Mendicant religious orders

.07   *Nursing orders

.08   *Canons regular

.09   Other specific kinds

.092   *Brothers

See also 271.093 for lay brothers

*Add as instructed under 271

.093	*Lay brothers
.094	*Third orders
	Secular and regular
.095	*Secular institutes

> **271.1–271.8 Specific orders of men**

Class comprehensive works in 271

> **271.1–271.7 Roman Catholic orders of men**

Class comprehensive works in 271

.1	***Benedictines**
.11	*Confederated Benedictines
	For Olivetans, see 271.13
.12	*Cistercians (Bernardines)
.125	*Trappists
.13	*Olivetans
.14	*Cluniacs
	Including Camaldolese, Silvestrians, Monks of Saint Paul the Hermit
	For Carthusians, see 271.71
.16	*Celestines
.17	Mechitarists and Basilians
.18	Antonines (Antonians), Maronites, Chaldeans, Syrians
.19	*Canons
	Including Crosier Fathers, Crosiers of the Red Star, Premonstratensians
	Class Augustinians in 271.4
.2	***Dominicans (Friars Preachers, Black Friars)**
.3	***Franciscans (Gray Friars)**
	Including Alcantarines, Observants, Recollects
	See also 271.4 for Augustinian Recollects
.36	*Capuchins
.37	*Conventuals
.38	*Third Order Regular

*Add as instructed under 271

.4	***Augustinians**

Including Augustinian Recollects

.42	*Trinitarians
.45	*Mercedarians
.47	*Servites
.49	Other Augustinians

Including Brothers Hospitallers of St. John of God, Minims

.5	***Regular clerics**
.51	*Theatines
.52	*Barnabites
.53	*Jesuits (Society of Jesus)
.54	*Somaschi
.55	*Camillians
.56	*Minor Clerks Regular (Caracciolini)
.57	*Clerks Regular of the Mother of God
.58	*Piarists

.6	***Passionists and Redemptorists**
.62	*Passionists
.64	*Redemptorists

.7	**Roman Catholic orders of men not otherwise provided for**
.71	*Carthusians
.73	*Carmelites (White Friars)
.75	*Sulpicians
.76	*Oblates
.77	*Lazarists (Vincentians)
.78	*Christian Brothers (Brothers of the Christian Schools)
.79	Other Roman Catholic orders of men
.791	*Orders of knighthood

Class here military orders

.791 2	*Knights of Malta (Knights Hospitalers of St. John of Jerusalem)
.791 3	*Knights Templars
.791 4	*Teutonic Knights

*Add as instructed under 271

.8 **Non-Roman Catholic orders of men**

.81 Monasteries of Eastern churches

> Add to base number 271.81 the numbers following 281 in 281.5–281.9, e.g., Orthodox monasteries 271.819, on Mount Athos 271.8190949565

.83 Anglican orders of men

.9 **Congregations and orders of women**

.900 01–.900 08 Standard subdivisions

.900 09 History

[.900 091–.900 099] Geographic treatment and biography

> Do not use; class in 271.9001–271.9009

.900 1–.900 9 Geographic treatment and biography

> Add to base number 271.900 notation 1–9 from Table 2, e.g., collected biography of women religious 271.90022, congregations and orders of women in France 271.90044

.901–.909 Specific kinds of congregations and orders

> Add to base number 271.90 the numbers following 271.0 in 271.01–271.09, e.g., contemplative orders 271.901

> 271.91–271.98 Specific orders of women

Class comprehensive works in 271.9

> 271.91–271.97 Roman Catholic orders of women

Class comprehensive works in 271.9

.91 *Sisters of Charity orders

.92 *Sisters of Mercy orders

.93 *Sacred Heart orders

.94 *Sisters of Bon Secours

.95 *Little Sisters of the Poor

.97 Other Roman Catholic orders of women

.971 *Carmelites

.972 *Dominicans

.973 *Franciscan orders

> Class here Poor Clares

.974 *Ursulines

*Add as instructed under 271

.975	*Visitation orders
.976	*Saint Joseph orders
.977	*Presentation orders
.98	Non-Roman Catholic orders of women
.981	Women's convents of Eastern churches

> Add to base number 271.981 the numbers following 281 in 281.5–281.9, e.g., Orthodox convents of women 271.9819

.983	Anglican orders of women

272 Persecutions in general church history

Regardless of denomination

Class here martyrs

Class relation of state to church in 322.1

> *See also 364.188 for offenses against religion as defined and penalized by the state*

.1	**Persecutions of Apostolic Church by imperial Rome**
.2	**Persecutions by Inquisition**
.3	**Persecutions of Waldenses and Albigenses**
.4	**Persecutions of Huguenots**
.5	**Persecutions of Molinists and Quietists**
.6	**Persecutions of Anglican reformers by Mary I**
.7	**Persecutions of Roman Church by Elizabeth I and Anglicans**
.8	**Persecutions of Quakers, Baptists, witches by Puritans and others of Puritan times**
.9	**Modern persecutions and martyrs**

273 Doctrinal controversies and heresies in general church history

Class persecutions resulting from controversies and heresies in 272; class churches founded on specific doctrines in 280

> *See also 239 for apologetics and polemics*

.1	**1st-2nd centuries**

Class here Christian gnosticism

Class comprehensive works and non-Christian Gnosticism in 299.932

> *For gnosticism of 3rd century, see 273.2*

---

*Add as instructed under 271

.2 **3rd century**

    Including Christian Manicheism

    Class comprehensive works and non-Christian Manicheism in 299.932

    For Sabellianism, see 273.3

.3 **Sabellianism**

.4 **4th century**

    Including Arianism, Donatism

.5 **5th century**

    Including Pelagianism

.6 **6th-16th centuries**

    Including Albigensianism, Catharism, Waldensianism

    Class here antinomianism

     For later antinomianism, see 273.7–273.9; for Albigensian, Catharist, Waldensian churches, see 284.4

.7 **17th century**

    Including Molinism, Pietism; comprehensive works on Jansenism

    For Jansenist churches, see 284.84

.8 **18th century**

.9 **19th century and later centuries**

    Including modernism

274–279 Christianity by specific continents, countries, localities in modern world

    Class here Christian church history by continent, country, locality

    Add to base number 27 notation 4–9 from Table 2, e.g., Christianity, Christian church in Europe 274, in France 274.4; then add further as follows:

    001–008 Standard subdivisions
    009   History, geographic treatment, biography
          Do not use for historical periods; class in notation 01–08 from this table
    01–08 Historical periods
          Add the numbers following 27 in 270.1–270.8, e.g., Christian church in France during the Reformation 274.406

    Class geographic treatment of a specific subject with the subject, plus notation 09 from Table 1, e.g., persecutions in France 272.0944

274 Christianity in Europe

    Number built according to instructions under 274–279

275   **Christianity in Asia**

> Number built according to instructions under 274–279

276   **Christianity in Africa**

> Number built according to instructions under 274–279

277   **Christianity in North America**

> Number built according to instructions under 274–279

278   **Christianity in South America**

> Number built according to instructions under 274–279

279   **Christianity in Australasia, Pacific Ocean islands, Atlantic Ocean islands, Arctic islands, Antarctica**

> Number built according to instructions under 274–279

280   Denominations and sects of Christian church

> Including nondenominational and interdenominational churches

> Class here general history and geographic treatment of, comprehensive works on specific denominations and sects and their individual local churches

> Class a denomination or sect not explicitly provided for here with the religion, denomination, or movement to which its own members say it belongs

> Class persecution of or by specific churches in 272

> *For a specific element of specific denominations and sects, see the element, e.g., doctrines 230*

> *See also 273 for doctrines of specific churches considered as heresies*

> *See Manual at 201–209 and 292–299; also at 230–280*

(Option: Class here specific elements of specific denominations and sects; prefer 230–270. If option is chosen, add to the number for each specific denomination, sect, group as follows:

001–008	Standard subdivisions
[009]	History, geographic treatment, biography
	Do not use; class in notation 07 from this table
02	Basic textual sources
	Class Bible in 220
03–06	Doctrinal, moral, devotional, social, ecclesiastical theology
	Add to 0 the numbers following 2 in 230–260, e.g., the denomination and international affairs 06187
07	History, geographic treatment, biography
0701–0708	Historical periods
	Add to 07 the numbers following 27 in 270.1–270.8, e.g., 20th century 07082
071–079	Special topics of church history; Christianity by continent, country, locality
	Add to 07 the numbers following 27 in 271–279, e.g., Africa 076)

SUMMARY

280.01–.09	Standard subdivisions and special topics of denominations and sects of Christian church
.2–.4	Branches
281	Early church and Eastern churches
282	Roman Catholic Church
283	Anglican churches
284	Protestant denominations of Continental origin and related bodies
285	Presbyterian churches, Reformed churches centered in America, Congregational churches, Puritanism
286	Baptist, Restoration movement, Adventist churches
287	Methodist churches; churches related to Methodism
289	Other denominations and sects

.01–.03   Standard subdivisions

.04   Special topics of denominations and sects of Christian church

.042   Relations between denominations

         Class here ecumenical movement

         See Manual at 280.042 vs. 262.0011

.05–.09   Standard subdivisions

>   **280.2–280.4 Branches**

         Class specific denominations and sects in 281–289; class comprehensive works in 280

.2   **Eastern and Roman Catholic churches**

         Class comprehensive works on Roman Catholic Church and Eastern churches in communion with Rome in 282

         For Eastern churches, see 281.5; for Roman Catholic Church, see 282

.4   **Protestant churches and Protestantism**

         Standard subdivisions are added for either or both topics in heading

         Class here dissenters, free churches, nonconformists (British context); works on Protestant evangelicalism, fundamentalism, pentecostalism, charismatic movement

         Class comprehensive works on evangelicalism, fundamentalism, pentecostalism, charismatic movement in general church history in 270.82

         For specific Protestant denominations, see 283–289

>   # 281–289 Specific denomination or sect

         Class comprehensive works in 280

         (Option: Class a specific denomination or sect requiring local emphasis in 289.2)

281   Early church and Eastern churches

>   **281.1–281.4 Early church**

Use these subdivisions only for building other numbers in 230–260, e.g., theology in the Ante-Nicene church 230.13; never use these subdivisions by themselves. When building numbers in 230–260 using these subdivisions, use 281.1 for comprehensive works

Class collected writings of apostolic and church fathers (patristics) in 270; class all works on early church in 270.1–270.3. Class a specific work of an apostolic or church father on a specific subject with the subject, e.g., philosophy 189.2

See Manual at 270, 230.11–230.14 vs. 230.15–230.2, 281.5–281.9, 282

.1   **Apostolic Church to the time of the great schism, 1054**

For Apostolic Church to 100, see 281.2; for Ante-Nicene church, see 281.3; for Post-Nicene church, see 281.4

.2   **Apostolic Church to 100**

.3   **Ante-Nicene church, 100–325**

.4   **Post-Nicene church, 325–1054**

.5   **Eastern churches**

For Oriental Orthodox churches, see 281.6; for Assyrian Church of the East (Church of the East), see 281.8; for Orthodox churches, see 281.9

See Manual at 230–280; also at 270, 230.11–230.14 vs. 230.15–230.2, 281.5–281.9, 282

.52   Eastern Catholic churches (Eastern rite churches in communion with Rome)

Including Saint Thomas Christian churches in communion with Rome

Class comprehensive works on Saint Thomas Christian churches in 281.54

.54   Saint Thomas Christian churches

Including Mar Thoma Syrian Church, Malabar Independent Syrian Church, St. Thomas Evangelical Church of India

For a specific church within the Saint Thomas Christian tradition not provided for here, see the church, e.g., Syriac Orthodox Church 281.63

.6   **Oriental Orthodox churches**

Including Eritrean Orthodox Church, Indian Orthodox Church

Class here non-Chalcedonian churches

For Coptic and Ethiopian churches, see 281.7

See Manual at 230–280; also at 270, 230.11–230.14 vs. 230.15–230.2, 281.5–281.9, 282

.62   Armenian Church

.63   Syriac Church

        Class here Syriac Orthodox Church, Jacobite Patriarchate of Antioch

        See also 281.95691 for Orthodox Church in Syria

.7   **Coptic and Ethiopian churches**

        See Manual at 270, 230.11–230.14 vs. 230.15–230.2, 281.5–281.9, 282

.72   Coptic Church (Coptic Orthodox Church)

.75   Ethiopian Church (Ethiopian Orthodox Tewahedo Church)

.8   **Assyrian Church of the East (Church of the East)**

        See Manual at 270, 230.11–230.14 vs. 230.15–230.2, 281.5–281.9, 282

.9   **Orthodox churches**

        See Manual at 230–280; also at 270, 230.11–230.14 vs. 230.15–230.2, 281.5–281.9, 282

.909   History, geographic treatment, biography

[.909 3]   Ancient world

        Do not use for early church; class in 270

.909 4–.909 9   Specific continents, countries, localities in modern world

        Do not use for specific autocephalous, arbitrary autocephalous, autonomous, independent churches; class in 281.94–281.99

        See Manual at 281.9094–281.9099 and 281.94–281.99

.94–.99   Specific autocephalous, arbitrary autocephalous, autonomous, independent churches

        Add to base number 281.9 notation 4–9 from Table 2 for the country of the seat of the church, e.g., Russian Orthodox Church, Russian Orthodox Church Outside Russia 281.947, Orthodox Church in America 281.973; then, for geographic treatment, add 0* and to the result add notation 4–9 from Table 2, e.g., Russian Orthodox Church Outside Russia in United States 281.947073
        Subdivisions are added for any or all topics in heading

        See Manual at 281.9094–281.9099 and 281.94–281.99

.947   Russia

        Number built according to instructions under 281.94–281.99

        Class here Moscow Patriarchate, Russian Orthodox Church

.947 7   Ukraine

        Number built according to instructions under 281.94–281.99

        Class here Ukrainian Autocephalous Orthodox Church, Ukrainian Orthodox Church (Kyivan Patriarchate), Ukrainian Orthodox Church (Moscow Patriarchate)

---

*Add 00 for standard subdivisions; see instructions at beginning of Table 1

.949 5	Greece
	Number built according to instructions under 281.94–281.99
	Class here Orthodox Church of Greece
.949 6	Balkan Peninsula
	Number built according to instructions under 281.94–281.99
.949 61	Turkey in Eastern Europe
	Number built according to instructions under 281.94–281.99
	Class here Ecumenical Patriarchate of Constantinople (Church of Constantinople)
.949 71	Serbia
	Number built according to instructions under 281.94–281.99
	Class here Serbian Orthodox Church
.949 8	Romania
	Number built according to instructions under 281.94–281.99
	Class here Romanian Orthodox Church
.973	United States
	Number built according to instructions under 281.94–281.99
	Class here Orthodox Church in America (OCA)

282   Roman Catholic Church

Class here the Catholic traditionalist movement, comprehensive works on Roman Catholic Church and Eastern rite churches in communion with Rome

Class modern schisms in Roman Catholic Church in 284.8

For Eastern rite churches in communion with Rome, see 281.52

See Manual at 270, 230.11–230.14 vs. 230.15–230.2, 281.5–281.9, 282

.09	History, geographic treatment, biography
	See Manual at 270, 230.11–230.14 vs. 230.15–230.2, 281.5–281.9, 282
[.093]	Ancient world
	Do not use for early church; class in 270
[.094–.099]	Specific continents, countries, localities in modern world
	Do not use; class in 282.4–282.9

.4–.9   Specific continents, countries, localities in modern world

Add to base number 282 notation 4–9 from Table 2, e.g., Roman Catholic Church in Latin America 282.8

> ### 283–289 Protestant and other denominations

Class comprehensive works on Protestant churches in 280.4; class comprehensive works on Protestant and other denominations in 280

See Manual at 283–289

283   Anglican churches

[.094–.099]   Specific continents, countries, localities in modern world

Do not use; class in 283.4–283.9

.3   **Branches not in communion with the See of Canterbury**

Including Reformed Episcopal Church and its affiliates

See Manual at 230–280; also at 283–289

.4–.9   **Specific continents, countries, localities in modern world**

Class here national churches in communion with the See of Canterbury

Add to base number 283 notation 4–9 from Table 2, e.g., Church of England 283.42, Episcopal Diocese of Long Island 283.74721

284   Protestant denominations of Continental origin and related bodies

For Protestant denominations of Continental origin not provided for here, see the denomination, e.g., Baptists 286

.094 3   Germany and neighboring central European countries

Class here Evangelische Kirche in Deutschland

.1   **Lutheran churches**

[.109 4–.109 9]   Specific continents, countries, localities in modern world

Do not use; class in 284.14–284.19

(.12)   (Permanently unassigned)

(Optional number used to provide local emphasis or a shorter number for Lutheran church in a specific country other than the United States; prefer 284.14–284.19)

.13   Specific denominations, branches, synods centered in the United States

See Manual at 230–280; also at 283–289

[.130 1–.130 9]   Standard subdivisions

Do not use; class in 284.101–284.109

.131   *The American Lutheran Church

.131 2   *The Evangelical Lutheran Church

---

*Do not use notation 094–099 from Table 1; class in 284.14–284.19

.131 3	*United Evangelical Lutheran Church
.131 4	*The Lutheran Free Church
.132	*The Evangelical Lutheran Synodical Conference of North America

For Wisconsin Evangelical Lutheran Synod, see 284.134

.132 2	*The Lutheran Church—Missouri Synod

For Synod of Evangelical Lutheran Churches, see 284.1323

.132 3	*Synod of Evangelical Lutheran Churches (Slovak)
.133	*The Lutheran Church in America
.133 2	*American Evangelical Lutheran Church
.133 3	*Augustana Evangelical Lutheran Church
.133 4	*Finnish Evangelical Lutheran Church
.133 5	*The United Lutheran Church in America
.134	*Wisconsin Evangelical Lutheran Synod
.135	*Evangelical Lutheran Church in America
.14–.19	Specific continents, countries, localities in modern world

Add to base number 284.1 notation 4–9 from Table 2, e.g., Lutheran Church of Sweden 284.1485, Memorial Evangelical Lutheran Church of Washington, D.C. 284.1753

(Option: Class Lutheran churches in a specific country other than the United States in 284.12)

.2   Calvinistic and Reformed churches of European origin

Standard subdivisions are added for either or both topics in heading

Class here comprehensive works on Calvinistic churches, on Reformed churches

For Huguenot churches, see 284.5; for Presbyterian churches, see 285; for Reformed churches centered in America, see 285.7

See also 285.9 for Puritanism

[.209 4–.209 9]	Specific continents, countries, localities in modern world

Do not use; class in 284.24–284.29

.24–.29	Specific continents, countries, localities in modern world

Add to base number 284.2 notation 4–9 from Table 2, e.g., Reformed churches in Holland 284.2492, in South Africa 284.268

.3   Hussite and Anabaptist churches

Including Lollards, Wycliffites

See also 289.7 for Mennonite churches

*Do not use notation 094–099 from Table 1; class in 284.14–284.19

.4   **Albigensian, Catharist, Waldensian churches**

.5   **Huguenot churches**

.6   **Moravian churches**

> *For Hussite churches, see 284.3*

[.609 4–.609 9]   Specific continents, countries, localities in modern world

> Do not use; class in 284.64–284.69

.64–.69   Specific continents, countries, localities in modern world

> Add to base number 284.6 notation 4–9 from Table 2, e.g., Moravian churches in Germany 284.643

.8   **Modern schisms in Roman Catholic Church**

> Including Constitutional Church, Gallican schismatic churches, Liberal Catholic Church, Little Church of France, Old Catholic churches, Philippine Independent Church

.84   Jansenist churches

.9   **Arminian and Remonstrant churches**

285   **Presbyterian churches, Reformed churches centered in America, Congregational churches, Puritanism**

> Standard subdivisions are added for Presbyterian churches, Reformed churches centered in America, Congregational churches together; for Presbyterian churches alone

---

>   **285.1–285.2 Presbyterian churches of United States, of British Commonwealth origin**

> Class comprehensive works on Presbyterian churches, Presbyterian churches of other origin in 285

> (If option under 280 is followed, use 285.001–285.008 for standard subdivisions, 285.02–285.07 for specific elements of Presbyterian churches)

.1   **Presbyterian churches of United States origin**

[.109 4–.109 9]   Specific continents, countries, localities in modern world

> Do not use; class in 285.14–285.19

.13   Specific denominations

> *See Manual at 230–280; also at 283–289*

[.130 1–.130 9]   Standard subdivisions

> Do not use; class in 285.101–285.109

.131   *United Presbyterian Church in the U.S.A.

---

*Do not use notation 094–099 from Table 1; class in 285.14–285.19

.132	*Presbyterian Church in the United States of America
.133	*Presbyterian Church in the United States
.134	*United Presbyterian Church of North America
.135	*Cumberland Presbyterian Church
.136	*Reformed Presbyterian churches
.137	*Presbyterian Church (U.S.A.)
.14–.19	Specific continents, countries, localities in modern world

> Add to base number 285.1 notation 4–9 from Table 2, e.g., the Hudson River Presbytery 285.17473

.2   Presbyterian churches of British Commonwealth origin

[.209 4–.209 9]	Specific continents, countries, localities in modern world

> Do not use; class in 285.24–285.29

.23	Specific denominations

> Including Countess of Huntingdon's Connexion
>
> *See Manual at 230–280; also at 283–289*

[.230 1–.230 9]	Standard subdivisions

> Do not use; class in 285.201–285.209

.232	†United Reformed Church in the United Kingdom

> Class Congregational Church of England and Wales in 285.842

.233	†Church of Scotland
.234	†Free Church of Scotland
.235	†Presbyterian Church of Wales (Welsh Calvinistic Methodist Church)
.24–.29	Specific continents, countries, localities in modern world

> Add to base number 285.2 notation 4–9 from Table 2, e.g., Presbyterianism in Ireland 285.2415, a Church of Scotland parish in Edinburgh 285.24134
>
> Class United Church of Canada in 287.92; class Uniting Church in Australia in 287.93

.7   Reformed churches centered in America

[.709 4–.709 9]	Specific continents, countries, localities in modern world

> Do not use; class in 285.74–285.79

.73	Specific denominations

> *See Manual at 230–280; also at 283–289*

---

*Do not use notation 094–099 from Table 1; class in 285.14–285.19
†Do not use notation 094–099 from Table 1; class in 285.24–285.29

[.730 1–.730 9]	Standard subdivisions

                Do not use; class in 285.701–285.709

.731   *Christian Reformed Church

.732   *Reformed Church in America (Dutch)

.733   *Reformed Church in the United States (German)

.734   *Evangelical and Reformed Church

.74–.79   Specific continents, countries, localities in modern world

                Add to base number 285.7 notation 4–9 from Table 2, e.g., First Reformed Church of Schenectady, N.Y. 285.774744

.8   **Congregationalism**

[.809 4–.809 9]   Specific continents, countries, localities in modern world

                Do not use; class in 285.84–285.89

(.82)   (Permanently unassigned)

                (Optional number used to provide local emphasis or a shorter number for Congregational churches in a specific country other than the United States; prefer 285.84–285.89)

.83   Specific denominations centered in the United States

                See Manual at 230–280; also at 283–289

[.830 1–.830 9]   Standard subdivisions

                Do not use; class in 285.801–285.809

.832   †Congregational Churches of the United States

.833   †Congregational Christian Churches

.834   †United Church of Christ

                For Evangelical and Reformed Church, see 285.734

.84–.89   Specific continents, countries, localities in modern world

                Class here specific denominations centered outside the United States

                Add to base number 285.8 notation 4–9 from Table 2, e.g., Congregational Church of England and Wales 285.842, Congregational churches in New England 285.874

                Class United Church of Canada in 287.92; class Uniting Church in Australia in 287.93

                (Option: Class Congregational churches in a specific country other than the United States in 285.82)

.9   **Puritanism**

---

*Do not use notation 094–099 from Table 1; class in 285.74–285.79
†Do not use notation 094–099 from Table 1; class in 285.84–285.89

286   Baptist, Restoration movement, Adventist churches

> Standard subdivisions are added for Baptist, Restoration movement, Adventist churches together; for Baptist churches alone

---

> ### 286.1–286.5 Baptist churches

Class comprehensive works in 286

(If option under 280 is followed, use 286.001–286.008 for standard subdivisions, 286.02–286.07 for specific elements of Baptist churches)

.1   Regular Baptists (Calvinistic Baptists)

[.109 4–.109 9]   Specific continents, countries, localities in modern world

Do not use; class in 286.14–286.19

(.12)   (Permanently unassigned)

(Optional number used to provide local emphasis or a shorter number for Regular Baptist churches in a specific country other than the United States; prefer 286.14–286.19)

.13   Specific denominations centered in the United States

See Manual at 230–280; also at 283–289

[.130 1–.130 9]   Standard subdivisions

Do not use; class in 286.101–286.109

.131   *American Baptist Churches in the U.S.A.

Former name: American (Northern) Baptist Convention

.132   *Southern Baptist Convention

.133   *National Baptist Convention of the United States of America

.134   *National Baptist Convention of America

.135   *Progressive National Baptist Convention

.136   *American Baptist Association

.14–.19   Specific continents, countries, localities in modern world

Class here specific denominations centered outside the United States

Add to base number 286.1 notation 4–9 from Table 2, e.g., Association of Regular Baptist Churches of Canada 286.171, a Southern Baptist association in Tennessee 286.1768

(Option: Class Regular Baptist churches in a specific country other than the United States in 286.12)

.2   Freewill Baptists

.3   Seventh-Day Baptists

---

*Do not use notation 094–099 from Table 1; class in 286.14–286.19

.4   **Old School Baptists**

> Including Antimission, Primitive Baptists

.5   **Other Baptist churches and denominations**

> Including Baptist General Conference, Church of the Brethren, Dunkers

.6   **Restoration movement**

[.609 4–.609 9]   Specific continents, countries, localities in modern world

> Do not use; class in 286.64–286.69

.63   Specific denominations

> Including Christian Church (Disciples of Christ), Christian Churches and Churches of Christ, Churches of Christ

> Class a specific denomination in a specific geographic area with the area in 286.64–286.69

> *See Manual at 230–280; also at 283–289*

[.630 1–.630 9]   Standard subdivisions

> Do not use; class in 286.601–286.609

.64–.69   Specific continents, countries, localities in modern world

> Class here specific denominations and specific churches in specific geographic areas

> Add to base number 286.6 notation 4–9 from Table 2, e.g., the Christian Church (Disciples of Christ) in Florida 286.6759

.7   **Adventist churches**

[.709 4–.709 9]   Specific continents, countries, localities in modern world

> Do not use; class in 286.74–286.79

.73   Specific denominations

> Including Advent Christian Church, Church of God General Conference

> Class a specific denomination in a specific geographic area with the area in 286.74–286.79

> *See Manual at 230–280; also at 283–289*

[.730 1–.730 9]   Standard subdivisions

> Do not use; class in 286.701–286.709

.732   Seventh-Day Adventist Church

[.732 094–.732 099]   Specific continents, countries, localities in modern world

> Do not use; class in 286.74–286.79

.74–.79   Specific continents, countries, localities in modern world

> Class here specific denominations and specific churches in specific geographic areas

> Add to base number 286.7 notation 4–9 from Table 2, e.g., Seventh-Day Adventists in South America 286.78

287   Methodist churches; churches related to Methodism

> Standard subdivisions are added for Methodist churches and churches related to Methodism together; for Methodist churches alone

.1   Wesleyan Methodist Church

[.109 4–.109 9]   Specific continents, countries, localities in modern world

> Do not use; class in 287.14–287.19

.14–.19   Specific continents, countries, localities in modern world

> Add to base number 287.1 notation 4–9 from Table 2, e.g., Wesleyan Methodist Church in British Isles 287.141, Wesleyan Methodist Church in New South Wales 287.1944

.2   Miscellaneous Methodist churches

> Including Congregational Methodist Church, Free Methodist Church of North America

.4   Primitive Methodist Church

[.409 4–.409 9]   Specific continents, countries, localities in modern world

> Do not use; class in 287.44–287.49

.44–.49   Specific continents, countries, localities in modern world

> Add to base number 287.4 notation 4–9 from Table 2, e.g., Primitive Methodist Church in British Isles 287.441

.5   Methodist churches in British Isles

[.509 41–.509 42]   British Isles

> Do not use; class in 287.54

.53   Specific denominations

> Including Bible Christians, Methodist New Connexion, Protestant Methodists, United Methodist Church (Great Britain), United Methodist Free Churches, Wesleyan Conference, Wesleyan Reformers, Yearly Conference of People Called Methodists

> Class a specific denomination in a specific geographic area with the area in 287.54

> *For Wesleyan Methodist Church in British Isles, see 287.141; for Primitive Methodist Church in British Isles, see 287.441*

> *See also 285.23 for Countess of Huntingdon's Connexion; also 285.235 for Welsh Calvinistic Methodist Church*

> *See Manual at 230–280; also at 283–289*

[.530 1–.530 9]	Standard subdivisions

> Do not use; class in 287.501–287.509

.532	*United Conference of Methodist Churches
.533	*Independent Methodists
.534	*Wesleyan Reform Union
.536	*Methodist Church of Great Britain
.54	Country and locality

> Class here specific denominations and specific churches in specific geographic areas
>
> Add to base number 287.54 the numbers following —4 in notation 41–42 from Table 2, e.g., Methodist Church of Great Britain in Wales 287.5429

.6   United Methodist Church

> *See also 287.53 for United Methodist Church (Great Britain)*

[.609 4–.609 9]	Specific continents, countries, localities in modern world

> Do not use; class in 287.64–287.69

.63	Specific antecedent denominations

> *For Methodist Protestant Church, see 287.7; for Evangelical United Brethren Church, see 289.9*
>
> *See Manual at 230–280; also at 283–289*

[.630 1–.630 9]	Standard subdivisions

> Do not use; class in 287.601–287.609

.631	†The Methodist Church (1939–1968)
.632	†Methodist Episcopal Church
.633	†Methodist Episcopal Church, South
.64–.69	Specific continents, countries, localities in modern world

> Add to base number 287.6 notation 4–9 from Table 2, e.g., United Methodist churches in Ohio 287.6771

.7   Methodist Protestant Church

.8   Black Methodist churches of United States origin

[.809 4–.809 9]	Specific continents, countries, localities in modern world

> Do not use; class in 287.84–287.89

---

*Do not use notation 0941–0942 from Table 1; class in 287.54
†Do not use notation 094–099 from Table 1; class in 287.64–287.69

.83   Specific denominations

> Including African Methodist Episcopal Church, African Methodist Episcopal Zion Church, Christian Methodist Episcopal Church

> Class a specific denomination in a specific geographic area with the area in 287.84–287.89

> *See Manual at 230–280; also at 283–289*

[.830 1–.830 9]   Standard subdivisions

> Do not use; class in 287.801–287.809

.84–.89   Specific continents, countries, localities in modern world

> Class here specific denominations and specific churches in specific geographic areas

> Add to base number 287.8 notation 4–9 from Table 2, e.g., Black Methodist churches in Georgia 287.8758, in Liberia 287.86662

.9   **Churches related to Methodism**

> Limited to those listed below

.92   United Church of Canada

.93   Uniting Church in Australia

.94   Church of South India

.95   Church of North India

.96   Salvation Army

.99   Church of the Nazarene

[288]   [Unassigned]

> Most recently used in Edition 19

289   Other denominations and sects

SUMMARY

289.1	**Unitarian and Universalist churches**
.3	**Latter-Day Saints (Mormons)**
.4	**Church of the New Jerusalem (Swedenborgianism)**
.5	**Church of Christ, Scientist (Christian Science)**
.6	**Society of Friends (Quakers)**
.7	**Mennonite churches**
.8	**Shakers (United Society of Believers in Christ's Second Appearing)**
.9	**Denominations and sects not provided for elsewhere**

.1   **Unitarian and Universalist churches**

> Class here Anti-Trinitarianism, Socinianism, Unitarianism

[.109 4–.109 9]   Specific continents, countries, localities in modern world

> Do not use; class in 289.14–289.19

.13 Specific denominations

> *See Manual at 230–280; also at 283–289*

[.130 1–.130 9] Standard subdivisions

> Do not use; class in 289.101–289.109

.132 *Unitarian Universalist Association

.133 *Unitarian churches

.134 *Universalist churches

.14–.19 Specific continents, countries, localities in modern world

> Add to base number 289.1 notation 4–9 from Table 2, e.g., Unitarianism in Boston 289.174461

(.2) **(Permanently unassigned)**

> (Optional number used to provide local emphasis or a shorter number for a specific denomination or sect; prefer the number for the specific denomination or sect in 281–289)

.3 **Churches of Latter Day Saint movement origin**

[.309 4–.309 9] Specific continents, countries, localities in modern world

> Do not use; class in 289.34–289.39

.32 Sources (Sacred books)

.322 Book of Mormon

.323 Doctrine and Covenants

.324 Pearl of Great Price

.33 Specific branches

> Class sources of specific branches in 289.32

> *See Manual at 230–280; also at 283–289*

[.330 1–.330 9] Standard subdivisions

> Do not use; class in 289.301–289.309

.332 Church of Jesus Christ of Latter-day Saints

[.332 094–.332 099] Specific continents, countries, localities in modern world

> Do not use; class in 289.34–289.39

.333 Community of Christ

> Former name: Reorganized Church of Jesus Christ of Latter-Day Saints

[.333 094–.333 099] Specific continents, countries, localities in modern world

> Do not use; class in 289.34–289.39

---

*Do not use notation 094–099 from Table 1; class in 289.14–289.19

.334   Fundamentalist Church of Jesus Christ of Latter-Day Saints

[.334 094–.334 099]   Specific continents, countries, localities in modern world

                Do not use; class in 289.34–289.39

.34–.39   Specific continents, countries, localities in modern world

      Add to base number 289.3 notation 4–9 from Table 2, e.g., Latter Day Saints in Utah 289.3792

.4   Church of the New Jerusalem (Swedenborgianism)

[.409 4–.409 9]   Specific continents, countries, localities in modern world

                Do not use; class in 289.44–289.49

.44–.49   Specific continents, countries, localities in modern world

      Add to base number 289.4 notation 4–9 from Table 2, e.g., Swedenborgianism in Europe 289.44

.5   Church of Christ, Scientist (Christian Science)

[.509 4–.509 9]   Specific continents, countries, localities in modern world

                Do not use; class in 289.54–289.59

.52   Sources

      Writings by Mary Baker Eddy

.54–.59   Specific continents, countries, localities in modern world

      Add to base number 289.5 notation 4–9 from Table 2, e.g., First Church of Christ, Scientist, Boston 289.574461

.6   Society of Friends (Quakers)

[.609 4–.609 9]   Specific continents, countries, localities in modern world

                Do not use; class in 289.64–289.69

.63   Specific denominations

      See Manual at 230–280; also at 283–289

[.630 1–.630 9]   Standard subdivisions

                Do not use; class in 289.601–289.609

.64–.69   Specific continents, countries, localities in modern world

      Add to base number 289.6 notation 4–9 from Table 2, e.g., Quakers in England 289.642

.7   Mennonite churches

[.709 4–.709 9]   Specific continents, countries, localities in modern world

                Do not use; class in 289.74–289.79

.73   Specific branches

> Including Amish, Church of God in Christ, Defenseless Mennonites, General Conference Mennonites, Hutterian Brethren
>
> Class a specific denomination in a specific geographic area with the area in 289.74–289.79
>
> *See Manual at 230–280; also at 283–289*

[.730 1–.730 9]   Standard subdivisions

> Do not use; class in 289.701–289.709

.74–.79   Specific continents, countries, localities in modern world

> Class here specific denominations and specific churches in specific geographic areas
>
> Add to base number 289.7 notation 4–9 from Table 2, e.g., Amish churches in Lancaster County, Pennsylvania 289.774815

.8   **Shakers (United Society of Believers in Christ's Second Appearing)**

.9   **Denominations and sects not provided for elsewhere**

> Including Christadelphians, Christian and Missionary Alliance, Christian Israelite Church, Churches of God, Dukhobors, Evangelical Congregational Church, Evangelical United Brethren Church, Messianic Judaism (Jewish Christians), Plymouth Brethren, United Brethren in Christ
>
> Class nondenominational and interdenominational churches in 280; class Protestant nondenominational and interdenominational churches in 280.4
>
> *See Manual at 201–209 and 292–299*
>
> (Option: Class a specific denomination or sect requiring local emphasis in 289.2)

.92   Jehovah's Witnesses

.93   African independent churches

> Independent denominations originating in Africa and not connected to another denomination
>
> Including Celestial Church of Christ, Cherubim and Seraphim Church, Eglise de Jésus-Christ sur la terre par le prophète Simon Kimbangu

.94   Pentecostal churches

> Including Assemblies of God, United Pentecostal Church
>
> Class comprehensive works on the pentecostal movement in general church history in 270.82

.95   Independent fundamentalist and evangelical churches

> Including Evangelical Free Church of America, Independent Fundamental Churches of America
>
> Class comprehensive works on fundamentalist, evangelical movements in general church history in 270.82

.96   Unification Church

.97   Unity School of Christianity

.98   New Thought

> Class eclectic New Thought, comprehensive works in 299.93

290   Other religions

> Limited to specific religions other than Christianity

> Except for modifications shown under specific entries, add to each subdivision identified by † as follows:

01–05	Standard subdivisions
[06]	Organizations and management
	Do not use; class in notation 6 from this table
07	Education, research, related topics
071	Education

> Class here the religion as an academic subject
> Class comprehensive works on religious education, religious education to inculcate religious faith and practice in notation 75 from this table
> *See Manual at 207.5, 268 vs. 200.71, 230.071, 292–299*

08–09	Standard subdivisions
1–9	Specific elements

> Add the numbers following 20 in 201–209, e.g., organizations 65

> Class a denomination or sect not explicitly provided for here with the religion, denomination, or movement to which its own members say it belongs

> Class religion in general, comprehensive works on religions other than Christianity in 200; class specific aspects of religion in 201–209

> (Options: To give preferred treatment or shorter numbers to a specific religion, use one of the following:

> (Option A: Class the sources of the religion in 220, other specific aspects of the religion in 230–280, comprehensive works on the religion in 230; in that case class the Bible and Christianity in 298

> (Option B: Class in 210, and add to base number 21 the numbers following the base number for the religion in 292–299, e.g., Hinduism 210, Mahabharata 219.23; in that case class philosophy and theory of religion in 200, its subdivisions 211–218 in 200.1)

SUMMARY

292	**Classical religion (Greek and Roman religion)**
.001–.009	**Standard subdivisions**
.07–.08	**Classical religion by specific culture**
.1–.9	**Specific elements**
293	**Germanic religion**
294	**Religions of Indic origin**
.3	**Buddhism**
.4	**Jainism**
.5	**Hinduism**
.6	**Sikhism**

295	Zoroastrianism (Mazdaism, Parseeism)
296	Judaism
.01–.09	Standard subdivisions
.1	Sources
.3	Theology, ethics, views of social issues
.4	Traditions, rites, public services
.6	Leaders, organization, religious education, outreach activity
.7	Religious experience, life, practice
.8	Denominations and movements
297	Islam, Babism, Bahai Faith
.01–.09	Standard subdivisions
.1	Sources of Islam
.2	Islamic doctrinal theology ('Aqā'id and Kalām); Islam and secular disciplines; Islam and other systems of belief
.3	Islamic worship
.4	Sufism (Islamic mysticism)
.5	Islamic ethics and religious experience, life, practice
.6	Islamic leaders and organization
.7	Protection and propagation of Islam
.8	Islamic sects and reform movements
.9	Babism and Bahai Faith
299	Religions not provided for elsewhere
.1–.4	Religions of Indo-European, Semitic, Non-Semitic Afro-Asiatic, North and West Asian, Dravidian origin
.5	Religions of East and Southeast Asian origin
.6	Religions originating among Black Africans and people of Black African descent
.7	Religions of North American native origin
.8	Religions of South American native origin
.9	Religions of other origin

[291]   [Unassigned]

Most recently used in Edition 21

292   Classical religion (Greek and Roman religion)

See also 299 for modern revivals of classical religions

See Manual at 200.92 and 201–209, 292–299; also at 201–209 and 292–299; also at 203.6, 263.9, 292–299 vs. 394.265–394.267; also at 322.1 vs. 201.72, 261.7, 292–299; also at 398.2 vs. 201.3, 230, 270, 292–299; also at 615.852 vs. 203.1, 234.131, 292–299; also at 616.86 vs. 158.1, 204.42, 248.8629, 292–299, 362.29

.001–.005   Standard subdivisions

[.006]   Organizations and management

Do not use; class in 292.6

.007   Education, research, related topics

.007 1   Education

Class here classical religion as an academic subject

Class comprehensive works on religious education, religious education to inculcate religious faith and practice in 292.75

See Manual at 207.5, 268 vs. 200.71, 230.071, 292–299

.008–.009   Standard subdivisions

> 292.07–292.08 Classical religion by specific culture

Class specific elements regardless of culture in 292.1–292.9; class comprehensive works in 292

.07   Roman religion

.08   Greek religion

.1–.9   Specific elements

Add to base number 292 the numbers following 20 in 201–209, e.g., mythology 292.13, organizations 292.65

Class classical religion as an academic subject in 292.0071

293   †Germanic religion

Class here Scandinavian religion, Norse religion

See also 299 for modern revivals of Germanic religion

See Manual at 200.92 and 201–209, 292–299; also at 201–209 and 292–299; also at 203.6, 263.9, 292–299 vs. 394.265–394.267; also at 207.5, 268 vs. 200.71, 230.071, 292–299; also at 322.1 vs. 201.72, 261.7, 292–299; also at 398.2 vs. 201.3, 230, 270, 292–299; also at 615.852 vs. 203.1, 234.131, 292–299; also at 616.86 vs. 158.1, 204.42, 248.8629, 292–299, 362.29

294   Religions of Indic origin

Including Divine Light Mission, Radha Soami Satsang

See Manual at 200.9 vs. 294, 299.5; also at 200.92 and 201–209, 292–299; also at 201–209 and 292–299; also at 203.6, 263.9, 292–299 vs. 394.265–394.267; also at 207.5, 268 vs. 200.71, 230.071, 292–299; also at 322.1 vs. 201.72, 261.7, 292–299; also at 398.2 vs. 201.3, 230, 270, 292–299; also at 615.852 vs. 203.1, 234.131, 292–299; also at 616.86 vs. 158.1, 204.42, 248.8629, 292–299, 362.29

SUMMARY

294.3	**Buddhism**	
.4	**Jainism**	
.5	**Hinduism**	
.6	**Sikhism**	

.3   Buddhism

[.306]   Organizations and management

Do not use; class in 294.36

.307   Education, research, related topics

---

†Add as instructed under 290

.307 1	Education

Class here Buddhism as an academic subject

Class comprehensive works on religious education, religious education to inculcate religious faith and practice in 294.375

See Manual at 207.5, 268 vs. 200.71, 230.071, 292–299

.33	Religious mythology, interreligious relations and attitudes, and social theology

Add to base number 294.33 the numbers following 201 in 201.3–201.7, e.g., social theology 294.337

.34	Doctrines and practices
.342	Doctrines

For social theology, see 294.337; for Buddhist ethics, see 294.35

.342 04	Doctrines of specific branches, sects, reform movements

Add to base number 294.34204 the numbers following 294.39 in 294.391–294.392, e.g., Zen doctrines 294.3420427

.342 1–.342 4	Specific doctrines

Add to base number 294.342 the numbers following 202 in 202.1–202.4, e.g., reincarnation 294.34237

.343–.344	Public worship and other practices; religious experience, life, practice

Add to base number 294.34 the numbers following 20 in 203–204, e.g., religious experience 294.3442

.35–.37	Religious ethics, leaders and organization, missions, religious education

Add to base number 294.3 the numbers following 20 in 205–207, e.g., the Buddha 294.363, organizations 294.365

See Manual at 207.5, 268 vs. 200.71, 230.071, 292–299

.38	Sources
.382	Sacred books and scriptures (Tripiṭaka, Tipiṭaka)

Works sacred to both Theravadins and Mahayanists

Class here comprehensive treatment of Theravadin and Mahayanist sacred texts

For works sacred only to Mahayanists, see 294.385

.382 2	Vinayapiṭaka
.382 3	Sūtrapiṭaka (Suttapiṭaka)
.382 32	Khuddakanikāya
.382 322	Dhammapada
.382 325	Jatakas
.382 4	Abhidharmapiṭaka (Abhidhammapiṭaka)

.383	Oral traditions
.384	Laws and decisions
.385	Sources of branches, sects, reform movements
	Including Buddhist Tantras, Mahayanist sacred works
.39	Branches, sects, reform movements
	Class specific aspects of branches, sects, reform movements in 294.33–294.38
.391	Theravada Buddhism
	Variant names: Southern, Hinayana Buddhism
	Including Mahasanghika, Saravastivada, Sautrantika schools
.392	Mahayana Buddhism (Northern Buddhism)
	Including Madhyamika, Yogacara (Vijnana) schools
.392 3	Tibetan Buddhism (Lamaism)
	See also 299.54 for Bon
.392 5	Tantric Buddhism
.392 6	Pure Land sects
.392 7	Zen (Ch'an)
	Including Rinzai, Soto
.392 8	Nichiren Shoshu and Sōka Gakkai
.4	**†Jainism**
.49	Sects and reform movements
	Number built according to instructions under 290
	Class specific aspects of sects and reform movements in 294.41–294.48
.492	Svetambara
.493	Digambara
.5	**Hinduism**
	Class here Brahmanism

SUMMARY

294.501–.509	**Standard subdivisions**
.51–.53	**Mythology, relations, doctrines, public worship and other practices**
.54	**Religious experience, life, practice, religious ethics**
.55	**Sects and reform movements**
.56–.57	**Leaders, organization, missions, religious education**
.59	**Sources**

†Add as instructed under 290

[.506]	Organizations and management
	Do not use; class in 294.56
.507	Education, research, related topics
.507 1	Education
	Class here Hinduism as an academic subject
	Class comprehensive works on religious education, religious education to inculcate religious faith and practice in 294.575
	See Manual at 207.5, 268 vs. 200.71, 230.071, 292–299
.509	History, geographic treatment, biography
.509 013	3999–1000 B.C.
	Class here religion of Vedic period
.51–.53	Mythology, relations, doctrines, public worship and other practices
	Add to base number 294.5 the numbers following 20 in 201–203, e.g., gods and goddesses 294.5211
.54	Religious experience, life, practice, religious ethics
	Practices predominantly private or individual in character
	Class here spirituality
.542	Religious experience
	Including conversion, enlightenment
.542 2	Mysticism
.543	Worship, meditation, yoga
	Class here description, interpretation, criticism, history, practical works on prayer, on contemplation; comprehensive works on worship
	For public worship, see 294.538
.543 2	Devotional literature
	Including meditations
.543 3	Prayer books
.543 5	Meditation
.543 6	Yoga
	Religious and spiritual discipline
	Including bhakti yoga, jnana yoga, karma yoga, kundalini yoga, raja yoga
	Class yoga philosophy, raja yoga philosophy, interdisciplinary works on yoga in 181.45
	See also 613.7046 for hatha yoga, physical yoga

.544	Religious life and practice

Add to base number 294.544 the numbers following 204.4 in 204.41–204.47, e.g., asceticism 294.5447

.548	Religious ethics

Including conscience, dharma, sin, vice

.548 6	Specific moral issues, sins, vices, virtues

Add to base number 294.5486 the numbers following 17 in 172–179, e.g., morality of family relationships 294.54863

.55	Sects and reform movements

Class Buddhism in 294.3; class Jainism in 294.4; class Sikhism in 294.6. Class a specific aspect of a Hindu sect or reform movement with the subject, e.g., doctrines of Vishnuism 294.52

.551	Early Hindu sects
.551 2	Vishnuism

Including International Society for Krishna Consciousness

.551 3	Shivaism

Including Lingayats

.551 4	Shaktaism

Class here Tantric Hinduism

.551 5	Ganapataism
.551 6	Shanmukaism
.551 7	Sauraism
.555	Ramakrishna movement
.556	Reformed Hinduism
.556 2	Brahma Samaj
.556 3	Arya-Samaj
.56–.57	Leaders, organization, missions, religious education

Add to base number 294.5 the numbers following 20 in 206–207, e.g., the role of the guru 294.561

Class Hinduism as an academic subject in 294.5071

See Manual at 207.5, 268 vs. 200.71, 230.071, 292–299

.59	Sources

.592   Sacred books and scriptures

          Add to each subdivision identified by * as follows:
          04   Special topics
          041   Sanskrit texts
                  Including textual criticism
                  Class Sanskrit texts accompanied by translations
                  in notation 045 from this table; class Sanskrit texts
                  accompanied by commentaries in notation 047 from
                  this table
          045   Translations
                  Class here Sanskrit texts accompanied by translations
                  Add to 045 notation 1–9 from Table 6, e.g.,
                  translations into English 04521
                  Class texts accompanied by commentaries in notation
                  047 from this table
          046   Interpretation and criticism
                  *For textual criticism, see notation 041 from this
                  table; for commentaries, see notation 047 from this
                  table*
          047   Commentaries
                  Criticism and interpretation arranged in textual order
                  Including texts accompanied by commentaries
          048   Nonreligious subjects treated in sacred books and
                scriptures
                  Class a religious subject treated in sacred books and
                  scriptures with the subject, e.g., rites and ceremonies
                  294.538

.592 1   *Vedic literature

\>   294.592 12–294.592 15 The Vedas

      Class here Samhitas, Brahmanas, Aranyakas

      Class Upanishads in 294.59218; class Vedic religion in 294.509013; class
      comprehensive works on the Vedas in 294.5921

.592 12   *Rigveda

.592 13   *Samaveda

.592 14   *Yajurveda

.592 15   *Atharvaveda

.592 18   Upanishads

.592 2   *Ramayana

.592 3   *Mahabharata

                For Bhagavad Gita, see 294.5924

.592 4   *Bhagavad Gita

.592 5   Puranas

---

*Add as instructed under 294.592

.592 6	Dharmasastras

Including Code of Manu

.593	Oral traditions
.594	Laws and decisions
.595	Sources of sects and reform movements

Including Hindu tantras

.6 †Sikhism

.663	Founders of Sikhism

Number built according to instructions under 290

Class here role and function of the ten Sikh gurus

295 †Zoroastrianism (Mazdaism, Parseeism)

Class Mithraism in 299.15

See Manual at 200.92 and 201–209, 292–299; also at 201–209 and 292–299; also at 203.6, 263.9, 292–299 vs. 394.265–394.267; also at 207.5, 268 vs. 200.71, 230.071, 292–299; also at 322.1 vs. 201.72, 261.7, 292–299; also at 398.2 vs. 201.3, 230, 270, 292–299; also at 615.852 vs. 203.1, 234.131, 292–299; also at 616.86 vs. 158.1, 204.42, 248.8629, 292–299, 362.29

296 Judaism

See Manual at 200.92 and 201–209, 292–299; also at 201–209 and 292–299; also at 203.6, 263.9, 292–299 vs. 394.265–394.267; also at 322.1 vs. 201.72, 261.7, 292–299; also at 398.2 vs. 201.3, 230, 270, 292–299; also at 615.852 vs. 203.1, 234.131, 292–299; also at 616.86 vs. 158.1, 204.42, 248.8629, 292–299, 362.29

SUMMARY

296.01–.09	Standard subdivisions
.1	Sources
.3	Theology, ethics, views of social issues
.4	Traditions, rites, public services
.6	Leaders, organization, religious education, outreach activity
.7	Religious experience, life, practice
.8	Denominations and movements

[.06]	Organizations and management

Do not use; class in 296.6

.07	Education, research, related topics

†Add as instructed under 290

.071 Education

Class here Judaism as an academic subject

Class comprehensive works on Jewish religious education, religious education to inculcate religious faith and practice in 296.68

See Manual at 207.5, 268 vs. 200.71, 230.071, 292–299

.071 1 Higher education

Class here Jewish theological faculties, rabbinical seminaries, yeshivot, education of rabbis

.08 Groups of people

Class here Jewish attitudes toward social groups; discrimination, equality, inequality, prejudice

.09 History, geographic treatment, biography

Class here history of specific synagogues

See also 320.54095694 for Zionism; also 909.04924 for world history of Jews

---

\> 296.090 1–296.090 5 **Historical periods**

Add to each subdivision identified by * as instructed under —0901–0905 in Table 1, e.g., museums of ancient Judaism 296.0901074

Class comprehensive works in 296.09

.090 1 *To 499 A.D.

.090 13 *Earliest Judaism to 586 B.C.

.090 14 *Second Temple period, 586 B.C.–70 A.D.

.090 15 *Early rabbinic period, 70–499

.090 2–.090 5 6th-21st centuries

Add to base number 296.090 the numbers following —090 in notation 0902–0905 from Table 1, e.g., Judaism in the Middle Ages 296.0902

.092 Biography

Class here persons not associated with one activity or denomination

Class a person associated with one activity or denomination with the activity or denomination with which the person is associated, e.g., a theologian 296.3092, a Reform rabbi 296.8341092

See Manual at 296.092

*Add as instructed under 296.0901–296.0905

.1 Sources

Class Jewish theology based on these sources in 296.3

For Torah and sacred scripture (Tanakh, Old Testament), see 221

See Manual at 221

SUMMARY

296.12	**Talmudic literature**
.14	**Midrash**
.15	**Sources of specific sects and movements**
.16	**Cabalistic literature**
.18	**Halakhah (Legal literature)**
.19	**Aggadah (Nonlegal literature)**

(.11)   Tanakh

(Optional number; prefer 221)

Arranged as found in Jewish Bibles

See Manual at 221: Optional numbers for books of Bible

[.110 3]   Dictionaries, encyclopedias, concordances

Do not use for dictionaries and encyclopedias; class in 296.1113. Do not use for concordances; class in 296.1114–296.1115

(.111)   Special topics; generalities; geography, history, chronology, persons of Bible lands in times of the Tanakh

(Optional number; prefer 221)

(.111 04)   Special topics of Tanakh

(.111 046)   Apocalyptic passages

Class apocalyptic passages in a book or group of books with the book or group of books, plus notation 0046 from table under 221–229, e.g., apocalyptic passages in the prophets 296.1130046, in Book of Daniel 296.11650046

(.111 1–.111 8)   Generalities

Add to base number 296.111 the numbers following 221 in 221.1–221.8, e.g., criticism and interpretation 296.1116

(.111 9)   Geography, history, chronology, persons of Bible lands in times of the Tanakh

Add to base number 296.1119 the numbers following 221.9 in 221.91–221.95, e.g., archaeology 296.11193

(.112)   *‡Torah (Pentateuch)

(.112 1)   *‡Genesis

---

*Add as instructed under 221–229
‡(Optional number; prefer 222–224)

(.112 2)	*‡Exodus
	For Ten Commandments, see 296.1126
(.112 3)	*‡Leviticus
(.112 4)	*‡Numbers
(.112 5)	*‡Deuteronomy
	For Ten Commandments, see 296.1126
(.112 6)	*‡Ten Commandments (Decalogue)
(.113)	*‡Prophetic books (Nevi'im)
(.113 1)	*Former Prophets (Nevi'im rishonim)
	(Optional number; prefer 222)
	For individual books of Former Prophets, see 296.1132–296.1135
(.113 2)	*‡Joshua
(.113 3)	*‡Judges
(.113 4)	*‡Samuel
(.113 41)	*‡Samuel 1
(.113 42)	*‡Samuel 2
(.113 5)	*‡Kings
(.113 51)	*‡Kings 1
(.113 52)	*‡Kings 2
(.113 6)	*Later Prophets (Nevi'im aḥaronim)
	(Optional number; prefer 224)
	For Isaiah, see 296.1137; for Jeremiah, see 296.1138; for Ezekiel, see 296.1139; for Minor Prophets, see 296.114
(.113 7)	*‡Isaiah
(.113 8)	*‡Jeremiah
(.113 9)	*‡Ezekiel
(.114)	*‡Minor Prophets
	For Zephaniah, Haggai, Zechariah, Malachi, see 296.115
(.114 1)	*‡Hosea
(.114 2)	*‡Joel
(.114 3)	*‡Amos
(.114 4)	*‡Obadiah

*Add as instructed under 221–229
‡(Optional number; prefer 222–224)

(.114 5)	*‡Jonah
(.114 6)	*‡Micah
(.114 7)	*‡Nahum
(.114 8)	*‡Habakkuk
(.115)	*‡Zephaniah, Haggai, Zechariah, Malachi
(.115 1)	*‡Zephaniah
(.115 2)	*‡Haggai
(.115 3)	*‡Zechariah
(.115 4)	*‡Malachi
(.116)	*‡Writings (Ketuvim)
(.116 1)	*‡Psalms
(.116 2)	*‡Proverbs
(.116 3)	*‡Job
(.116 4)	*Megillot (Five scrolls)
	(Optional number; prefer 221.044)
(.116 41)	*‡Song of Solomon (Canticle of Canticles, Song of Songs)
(.116 42)	*‡Ruth
(.116 43)	*‡Lamentations
(.116 44)	*‡Ecclesiastes (Kohelet, Qohelet)
(.116 45)	*‡Esther
(.116 5)	*‡Daniel
(.116 6)	*‡Ezra
(.116 7)	*‡Nehemiah
(.116 8)	*‡Chronicles
(.116 81)	*‡Chronicles 1
(.116 82)	*‡Chronicles 2
(.118)	*Apocrypha
	(Optional number; prefer 229)

For pseudepigrapha, see 229.9

*Add as instructed under 221–229
‡(Optional number; prefer 222–224)

(.118 1)	*Esdras 1 and 2
	(Optional number; prefer 229.1)
	Variant names: Esdras 3 and 4
	See also 296.1166 for Ezra; also 296.1167 for Nehemiah
(.118 2)	*Tobit, Judith, Additions to Esther
	(Optional number; prefer 229.2)
(.118 22)	*Tobit
	(Optional number; prefer 229.22)
(.118 24)	*Judith
	(Optional number; prefer 229.24)
(.118 27)	*Additions to Esther
	(Optional number; prefer 229.27)
(.118 3)	*Wisdom of Solomon (Wisdom)
	(Optional number; prefer 229.3)
	Class here Apocryphal wisdom literature
	For Ecclesiasticus, see 296.1184
(.118 4)	*Ecclesiasticus (Sirach)
	(Optional number; prefer 229.4)
(.118 5)	*Baruch and Epistle of Jeremiah
	(Optional number; prefer 229.5)
(.118 6)	*Song of the Three Children, Susanna, Bel and the Dragon
	(Optional number; prefer 229.6)
(.118 7)	*Maccabees (Machabees)
	(Optional number; prefer 229.7)
(.118 73)	*Maccabees 1 and 2 (Machabees 1 and 2)
	(Optional number; prefer 229.73)
(.118 75)	*Maccabees 3 and 4 (Machabees 3 and 4)
	(Optional number; prefer 229.75)
(.118 8)	*Prayer of Manasseh
	(Optional number; prefer 229.6)

*Add as instructed under 221–229

>   296.12–296.14   Talmudic literature and Midrash

Add to each subdivision identified by ‡ as follows:

001–009	Standard subdivisions
04	Hebrew and Aramaic texts
	Including textual criticism
	Class texts accompanied by modern commentaries since 1500 in notation 07 from this table
05	Translations
	Add to 05 notation 1–9 from Table 6, e.g., literature in English 0521
	Class texts accompanied by modern commentaries since 1500 in notation 07 from this table
06	Interpretation and criticism (Exegesis)
0601	Philosophy and theory
	Class here hermeneutics
061–068	Subdivisions of interpretation and criticism (Exegesis)
	Add to 06 the numbers following 220.6 in 220.61–220.68, e.g., historical criticism 067
	For textual criticism, see notation 04 from this table; for modern commentaries since 1500, see notation 07 from this table
07	Modern commentaries since 1500
	Criticism and interpretation arranged in textual order
	Including texts accompanied by modern commentaries
	Commentaries written before 1500 are classed with the text without addition of 07
08	Nonreligious subjects treated in Talmudic literature and Midrash
	Add to 08 notation 001–999, e.g., natural sciences in Talmudic literature and Midrash 085
	Class a religious subject treated in Talmudic literature and Midrash with the subject, e.g., Jewish ethics 296.36

Class comprehensive works in 296.1

.12   ‡Talmudic literature

.120 092   Biography

           Number built according to instructions under 296.12–296.14

           Class here Soferim, Tannaim, Amoraim, Geonim

.123   ‡Mishnah

.123 1   ‡Order Zera'im

           Including tractates Berakhot, Bikkurim, Demai, Ḥallah, Kilayim, Ma'aser Sheni, Ma'aserot, Orlah, Pe'ah, Shevi'it, Terumot

.123 2   ‡Order Mo'ed

           Including tractates Beẓah, Eruvin, Ḥagigah, Megillah, Mo'ed Katan, Pesaḥim, Rosh Hashanah, Shabbat, Shekalim, Sukkah, Ta'anit, Yoma

‡Add as instructed under 296.12–296.14

.123 3	‡Order Nashim
	Including tractates Gittin, Ketubbot, Kiddushin, Nazir, Nedarim, Sotah, Yevamot
.123 4	‡Order Nezikin
	Including tractates Avodah Zarah, Bava Batra, Bava Kamma, Bava Meẓia, Eduyyot, Horayot, Makkot, Sanhedrin, Shevu'ot
.123 47	‡Tractate Avot (Pirke Avot)
.123 5	‡Order Kodashim
	Including tractates Arakhin, Bekhorot, Ḥullin, Keritot, Kinnim, Me'ilah, Menaḥot, Middot, Tamid, Temurah, Zevaḥim
.123 6	‡Order Tohorot
	Including tractates Kelim, Makhshirin, Mikva'ot, Nega'im, Niddah, Oholot (Ahilot), Parah, Tevul Yom, Tohorot, Ukẓin, Yadayim, Zavim
.123 7	Minor tractates
.124	‡Palestinian Talmud (Jerusalem Talmud, Talmud Yerushalmi)
.124 1–.124 7	Individual orders and tractates
	Add to base number 296.124 the numbers following 296.123 in 296.1231–296.1237, e.g., Order Zera'im in Palestinian Talmud 296.1241
.125	‡Babylonian Talmud
	Often called simply the Talmud
.125 1–.125 7	Individual orders and tractates
	Add to base number 296.125 the numbers following 296.123 in 296.1231–296.1237, e.g., tractate Shabbat in Babylonian Talmud 296.1252
.126	Tosefta and Baraita
.126 2	‡Tosefta
.126 21–.126 27	Individual orders and tractates
	Add to base number 296.1262 the numbers following 296.123 in 296.1231–296.1237, e.g., order Nezikin in Tosefta 296.12624
.126 3	‡Baraita
.127	Specific types of Talmudic literature
.127 4	‡Halakhah
.127 6	‡Aggadah
.14	‡Midrash
.141	‡Midrashic Halakhah

‡Add as instructed under 296.12–296.14

.142	‡Midrashic Aggadah
.15	Sources of specific sects and movements
.155	Writings of Qumran community

Class here comprehensive works on Dead Sea Scrolls

> *For Old Testament texts in Dead Sea Scrolls, see 221.44; for pseudepigrapha in Dead Sea Scrolls, see 229.91*
>
> *See also 296.815 for comprehensive works on Qumran community*

.16	Cabalistic literature

Class here interdisciplinary works on cabala

The texts of religious cabalistic works are classed here even if the editor introduces and annotates them from an occult or Christian point of view

Class Jewish mystical experience in 296.712; class Jewish mystical movements in 296.8

> *For cabalistic traditions in occultism, see 135.47*

.162	Zohar
.18	Halakhah (Legal literature)

Including early rabbinical legal writings, comprehensive works on rabbinical writings to 1400

Class here commandments (mitzvot) treated as laws, the 613 commandments, comprehensive works on Jewish law

Class commandments (mitzvot) treated as ethical values in 296.36; class Jewish law relating to secular matters in 340.58

> *For Torah, see 222.1; for Talmudic Halakhah, see 296.1274; for Midrashic Halakhah, see 296.141. For early rabbinical writings to 1400 on a specific subject, see the subject, e.g., creation 296.34; for laws on a specific religious topic, see the topic, e.g., laws concerning marriage rites 296.444*

.180 92	Biography

Class here Rishonim, Aharonim

.181	Legal writings of Maimonides

Class here comprehensive works on writings of Maimonides

> *For philosophical writings of Maimonides, see 181.06. For writings on a specific religious topic, see the topic, e.g., the Thirteen Articles of Faith 296.3*

.181 2	Mishneh Torah
.182	Work of Joseph Caro

Class here Shulḥan ʿarukh

‡Add as instructed under 296.12–296.14

.185	Responsa

Class responsa on a specific religious topic with the topic, e.g., responsa concerning marriage rites 296.444

.185 4	Responsa of reform movements

Add to base number 296.1854 the numbers following 296.834 in 296.8341–296.8344, e.g., Reform responsa 296.18541

.188	Nonreligious subjects treated in halakhah

.188 000 1–.188 000 9	Standard subdivisions

.188 001–.188 999	Specific nonreligious subjects treated in halakhah

Add to base number 296.188 notation 001–999, e.g., agriculture in halakhah 296.18863

.19	Aggadah (Nonlegal literature)

Stories, legends, parables, proverbs, anecdotes, ancient or modern, told for religious edification

Class here comprehensive works on Aggadah

Class Jewish folklore in 398.2089924

For Talmudic Aggadah, see 296.1276; for Midrashic Aggadah, see 296.142

See also 296.45371 for Passover Haggadah

.3	**Theology, ethics, views of social issues**

Standard subdivisions are added for theology, ethics, social issues together; for theology alone

Class here Biblical theology, the Thirteen Articles of Faith

See also 181.06 for Jewish philosophy

See Manual at 200 vs. 100

.31	God and spiritual beings

.311	God

.311 2	Attributes and names of God

.311 4	Relation to the world

For revelation, see 296.3115; for miracles, see 296.3116; for relation to and action in history, see 296.3117; for creation, see 296.34

.311 5	Revelation

.311 55	Prophecy

Class Biblical prophecy and prophecies in 221.15; class the prophetic books of the Bible in 224; class messianic prophecies in 296.336

.311 6	Miracles

.37	Judaism and secular disciplines

Class here attitudes of Judaism toward and influence on secular issues, religious views and teachings about secular disciplines, works treating relation between Jewish belief and a secular discipline

Class Jewish philosophy of a secular discipline and Jewish theories within a secular discipline with the discipline, e.g., Jewish philosophy 181.06

For Judaism and social issues, see 296.38

See also 296.12–296.14 for nonreligious subjects treated in Talmudic literature and Midrash; also 296.188 for nonreligious subjects treated in halakhah

.371	Judaism and philosophy, parapsychology and occultism, psychology
.375	Judaism and natural sciences, mathematics
.376	Judaism and technology

Including Judaism and medicine

.377	Judaism and the arts
.38	Judaism and social sciences

Attitudes of Judaism toward and influence on social issues

Including Judaism and ecology, Judaism and environment

Class here Judaism and socioeconomic problems, Jewish social theology

Class Jewish view of marriage and family in 296.74

.382	Judaism and politics

Attitude toward and influence on political activities and ideologies

Class here Judaism and civil rights

See Manual at 322.1 vs. 201.72, 261.7, 292–299

.382 7	International affairs, war and peace

Including attitude of Judaism toward civil and revolutionary wars, conscientious objectors, pacifism

.383	Judaism and economics

Class Judaism and ecology, Judaism and environment in 296.38

.39	Judaism and other systems of belief
.391	Judaism and irreligion

Class here Judaism and atheism

.396	Judaism and Christianity
.397	Judaism and Islam
.399	Judaism and other religions

Add to base number 296.399 the numbers following 29 in 294–299, e.g., relations with Buddhism 296.39943

.4   **Traditions, rites, public services**

Class individual observances not provided for here in 296.7

SUMMARY

.41   Sabbath

Class liturgy and prayers for Sabbath in 296.45

.412   Prohibited activity

> 296.43–296.44 Festivals, holy days, fasts; rites and customs for occasions that occur generally once in a lifetime

Class here personal ritual observances to be performed at specific times or in conjunction with specific rites

Class comprehensive works in 296.43

For specific rites of ancient Judaism to 70 A.D. not provided for elsewhere, see 296.49

.43   Festivals, holy days, fasts

For liturgy and prayers for festivals, holy days, fasts, see 296.453; for Sabbath, see 296.41

See Manual at 203.6, 263.9, 292–299 vs. 394.265–394.267

.431   High Holy Days

For Yom Kippur (Day of Atonement), see 296.432

.431 5   Rosh Hashanah (New Year)

.432   Yom Kippur (Day of Atonement)

.433   Sukkot (Feast of Tabernacles)

.433 9   Simḥat Torah

.435   Hanukkah (Feast of the Dedication)

.436   Purim (Feast of Lots)

.437   Pesach (Passover)

.438   Shavuot (Feast of Weeks, Pentecost)

.439   Other festivals, holy days, fasts

Including Lag b'Omer, Tishah b'Av

.439 1	Festivals, holy days, fasts associated with the land of Israel

Including Sabbatical Year (shemittah)

.44	**Rites and customs for occasions that occur generally once in a lifetime**

See also 296.7 for rites and customs which continue throughout life

For liturgy and prayers for occasions that occur generally once in a lifetime, see 296.454

.442	Special rites for male Jews
.442 2	Berit milah (Circumcision)
.442 3	Pidyon haben (Redemption of first-born male)
.442 4	Bar mitzvah
.443	Special rites for female Jews

Including naming ceremonies

For observance of laws of family purity, see 296.742

.443 4	Bat mitzvah
.444	Marriage and divorce rites and traditions

Standard subdivisions are added for marriage and divorce rites and traditions together, for marriage rites alone, for marriage traditions alone

Including issues concerning who may be married, descent of Jewish identity

For guides to marriage and family life, see 296.74

.444 3	Interreligious marriage
.444 4	Divorce rites and traditions

Standard subdivisions are added for either or both topics in heading

.445	Burial and mourning rites and traditions

Standard subdivisions are added for any or all topics in heading

Including memorial services

.446	Synagogue dedication
.45	Liturgy and prayers

Description, interpretation, conduct, texts of rites and public services; private and public prayers, blessings, benedictions

Including prayer at meals

Class here Ashkenazic liturgy; worship; liturgy and prayers for Sabbath; prayer books, e.g., siddurim

Class devotional reading for the individual in 296.72

.450 4	Liturgy of specific groups
	Including Ari liturgy
	Class Ashkenazic liturgy or liturgy of unspecified group in 296.45
[.450 401–.450 409]	Standard subdivisions
	Do not use; class in 296.4501–296.4509
.450 42	Sephardic liturgy
.450 44	Hasidic liturgy
.450 46	Reform liturgy
.450 47	Conservative liturgy
.450 48	Reconstructionist liturgy
.452	Piyyutim

> 296.453–296.454 Liturgy and prayers for festivals, holy days, fasts; for occasions that occur generally once in a lifetime

Add to each subdivision identified by * the numbers following 296.45 in 296.45042–296.45048, e.g., Passover Haggadah of the Sephardic rite 296.45371042

Class comprehensive works in 296.45

.453	*Liturgy and prayers for festivals, holy days, fasts
	Class here Mahzorim
.453 1–.453 6	Liturgy and prayers for High Holy Days, Sukkot, Hanukkah, Purim

Add to base number 296.453 the numbers following 296.43 in 296.431–296.436, e.g., liturgy and prayers for High Holy Days 296.4531; then add further as instructed under 296.453–296.454, e.g., Reform prayer books for High Holy Days 296.4531046

.453 7	*Liturgy and prayers for Pesach (Passover)
.453 71	*Passover Haggadah (Seder service)
.453 8–.453 9	Liturgy and prayers for Shavuot, other festivals, holy days, fasts

Add to base number 296.453 the numbers following 296.43 in 296.438–296.439, e.g., prayers for Shavuot 296.4538; then add further as instructed under 296.453–296.454, e.g., prayers for Shavuot of the Sephardic rite 296.4538042

.454	Liturgy and prayers for occasions that occur generally once in a lifetime

Add to base number 296.454 the numbers following 296.44 in 296.442–296.446, e.g., liturgy and prayers for weddings 296.4544; then add further as instructed under 296.453–296.454, e.g., Reform prayer books for weddings 296.4544046

*Add as instructed under 296.453–296.454

.46	Use of the arts and symbolism

> Including synagogue buildings

.461	Liturgical articles

> Including mezuzot, prayer shawls

.461 2	Phylacteries (Tefillin)
.461 5	Torah scrolls

> Class here scribes (soferim)

.462	Music

> Class here cantors

> Class works containing both text and music, interdisciplinary works on Jewish liturgical music in 782.36

.47	Sermons and preaching (Homiletics)

> Add to base number 296.47 the numbers following 296.4 in 296.41–296.44, e.g., High Holy Day sermons 296.4731

> Class sermons on a specific subject with the subject, e.g., sermons on social issues 296.38

.48	Pilgrimages and sacred places
[.480 93–.480 99]	Specific continents, countries, localities

> Do not use; class in 296.482–296.489

.481	Pilgrimages

> Class pilgrimages to specific sacred places in 296.482–296.489

.482	Jerusalem
.483–.489	Sacred places in specific continents, countries, localities

> Add to base number 296.48 notation 3–9 from Table 2, e.g., sacred places in Iraq 296.48567; however, for Jerusalem, see 296.482

> Class the Land of Israel as a theme in Jewish theology in 296.31173

.49	Traditions, rites, public services of ancient Judaism to 70 A.D.

> Not provided for elsewhere

.491	The Temple
.492	Sacrifices and offerings
.493	Ark of the Covenant
.495	Ancient priesthood
.6	**Leaders, organization, religious education, outreach activity**

.61   Leaders and their work

Role, function, duties

Class here ordination, work of rabbis; activities of leaders and other congregational workers designed to promote religious and social welfare of social groups in community, pastoral care; chaplaincy

For ancient priesthood, see 296.495

See also 296.4615 for scribes; also 296.462 for cantors

[.610 92]   Biography

Do not use for biography of religious leaders primarily associated with a specific religious activity; class in 296.1–296.7, e.g., a theologian 296.3092. Do not use for biography of religious leaders primarily associated with a specific denomination or movement; class in 296.8, e.g., a Reform rabbi 296.8341092. Do not use for biography of other religious leaders; class in 296.092

.65   Synagogues and congregations

Role and function

See also 296.46 for synagogue buildings

.650 9   History, geographic treatment, biography

Class history of specific synagogues in 296.09

.67   Organizations and organization

Theory and history of organizations other than synagogues and congregations

Including religious authority, excommunication, schism; sanhedrin

Class laws and decisions in 296.18. Class organizations sponsored by one denomination with the denomination in 296.8, e.g., Union of Orthodox Congregations of America 296.83206073

For synagogues and congregations, see 296.65

See also 369.3924 for Jewish service and fraternal associations, e.g., B'nai B'rith

.68   Religious education

Class Judaism as an academic subject in 296.071

For religious education at the level of higher education, see 296.0711

See Manual at 207.5, 268 vs. 200.71, 230.071, 292–299

.680 83   Young people

Do not use for religious training of children in the home; class in 296.74

Class here afternoon weekday schools, Hebrew schools, Jewish religious schools, Sunday schools; religious education in Jewish day schools

Class comprehensive works on Jewish day schools in 371.076

.69	Outreach activity for the benefit of converts and nonobservant Jews
.7	**Religious experience, life, practice**

> Standard subdivisions are added for religious experience, life, practice together; for religious life and practice together

> Practices which continue throughout life

> Including asceticism

> Class here guides to religious life, spirituality

> *For ethics, see 296.36; for traditions, rites, public services, see 296.4*

[.708 5]	Relatives

> Do not use; class in 296.74

.708 6	People by miscellaneous social attributes
[.708 655]	Married people

> Do not use; class in 296.74

.71	Religious experience
.712	Mysticism

> Class cabalistic literature in 296.16; class Jewish mystical movements in 296.8

.714	Conversion

> Class here conversion of non-Jews to Judaism

> Class outreach activity for the benefit of converts and nonobservant Jews in 296.69. Class conversion of Jews to another religion with the religion, e.g., conversion of Jews to Christianity 248.246

.715	Return of Jews from non-observance to religious observance
.72	Devotional reading for the individual

> Including meditation and meditations

> Class devotional literature in the form of Aggadah in 296.19

.73	Kosher observance (Kashrut observance)

> Observance of dietary laws

> Including ritual slaughter (shehitah)

.74	Marriage and family life

> Including child rearing, religious training of children in the home

> Class comprehensive works on Jewish religious training of children in 296.68083

> Class here social theology of marriage and family, comprehensive works on marriage

> *For ethics of marriage, see 296.363; for marriage and divorce rites and traditions, see 296.444*

.742   Observance of laws of family purity

                  For ritual bath (mikveh), see 296.75

.75   Ritual bath (Mikveh)

.76   People experiencing illness, trouble, bereavement

.8   **Denominations and movements**

                  Class specific aspects of denominations and movements in 296.1–296.7

.81   Denominations and movements of ancient origin

                  Including Hellenistic movement, Karaites, Zealots

.812   Pharisees

.813   Sadducees

.814   Essenes

                      For Qumran community, see 296.815

.815   Qumran community

                      See also 296.155 for writings of Qumran community

.817   Samaritans

.82   Medieval and early modern denominations and movements to ca. 1750

                  Including Sabbatianism

.83   Modern denominations and movements after ca. 1750

.832   Orthodox Judaism

.833   Mystical Judaism

.833 2   Hasidism

.833 22   Habad Lubavitch Hasidism

.834   Reform movements

                      Including Humanistic Judaism

.834 1   Reform Judaism

.834 2   Conservative Judaism

.834 4   Reconstructionist Judaism

.836   Black Hebrews

                      Including African Hebrew Israelite Nation of Jerusalem, Black Hebrew
                      Israelites

                      See also 296.0896073 for African-American Jews

297   Islam, Babism, Bahai Faith

Standard subdivisions are added for Islam, Babism, Bahai Faith together; for Islam alone

See Manual at 200.92 and 201–209, 292–299; also at 201–209 and 292–299; also at 203.6, 263.9, 292–299 vs. 394.265–394.267; also at 322.1 vs. 201.72, 261.7, 292–299; also at 398.2 vs. 201.3, 230, 270, 292–299; also at 615.852 vs. 203.1, 234.131, 292–299; also at 616.86 vs. 158.1, 204.42, 248.8629, 292–299, 362.29

SUMMARY

297.01–.09	Standard subdivisions
.1	Sources of Islam
.2	Islamic doctrinal theology ('Aqā'id and Kalām); Islam and secular disciplines; Islam and other systems of belief
.3	Islamic worship
.4	Sufism (Islamic mysticism)
.5	Islamic ethics and religious experience, life, practice
.6	Islamic leaders and organization
.7	Protection and propagation of Islam
.8	Islamic sects and reform movements
.9	Babism and Bahai Faith

[.06]   Organizations and management

Do not use; class in 297.6

.07   Education, research, related topics

.071   Education

Class here Islamic religion as an academic subject

Class comprehensive works on Islamic religious education, religious education to inculcate religious faith and practice in 297.77

See Manual at 207.5, 268 vs. 200.71, 230.071, 292–299

.09   History, geographic treatment, biography

Notation 09 from Table 1 as modified below

Class here religious aspects of Islamic fundamentalism

Class prophets prior to Muḥammad in 297.246; class political science aspects of Islam, of Islamic fundamentalism in 320

For religious aspects of Islamic fundamentalism in a specific sect or reform movement, see 297.8

See also 909.09767 for Islamic civilization

See Manual at 320.557 vs. 297.09, 297.272, 322.1

.090 2   610–1499

.090 21   610–1204

.090 211	Period of Revelation, 610–632

From first revelation to Muḥammad the Prophet until his death

Class biography of and comprehensive works on Muḥammad the Prophet in 297.63; class biography of and comprehensive works on his family and Companions in 297.64; class Hijrah (emigration from Mecca to Medina, 622) in relation to Muḥammad the Prophet and his family and Companions in 297.634; class Hijrah in general history in 953.802

.090 212	Period of Four Rightly-Guided Caliphs, 632–661

Class here 7th century, Rashidun Caliphate

Class religious biography and theological discussion of the first four caliphs in 297.648. Class interdisciplinary biographies of the first four caliphs with the subject in 950, e.g., Abu Bakr 953.02092

For 661–699, see 297.090213

.090 213	Period of Naissance, 661–718
.090 214	Period of Recording and Emergence of Islamic Schools of Thought, 718–912
.090 215	Period of Comprehensive Works, 912–1204
.090 22	1204–1499

Class here period of Explanations and Briefs, 1204–1495

.090 3–.090 5	16th-21st centuries

Add to base number 297.090 the numbers following —090 in notation 0903–0905 from Table 1, e.g., Islam in 20th century 297.0904

.092	Biography

Class interdisciplinary works on caliphs as civil and religious heads of state with the subject in 940–990, e.g., Abu Bakr 953.02092

For Muslims primarily associated with a specific religious activity, see 297.1–297.7; for founders of Sufi orders, see 297.48; for Muḥammad the Prophet, see 297.63; for Muḥammad's family and companions (including religious biography of the first four caliphs), see 297.64; for Muslims primarily associated with a specific sect or reform movement, see 297.8

See Manual at 297.092

> **297.1–297.8 Islam**

Class comprehensive works in 297

>   **297.1–297.3 Sources of Islam; Islamic doctrinal theology ('Aqā'id and Kalām); Islam and secular disciplines; Islam and other systems of belief; Islamic worship**

       Class comprehensive works in 297

.1   **Sources of Islam**

SUMMARY

297.12	**Koran and Hadith**
.14	**Religious and ceremonial laws and decisions**
.18	**Stories, legends, parables, proverbs, anecdotes told for religious edification**

.12   Koran and Hadith

       Class theology based on Koran and Hadith in 297.2

.122   Koran

.122 03   Topical dictionaries and encyclopedias

       Do not use for concordances or non-topical dictionaries; class in 297.1224–297.1225

.122 09   History, geographic treatment, biography

       Class here geography, history, chronology of the Middle East in Koran times in relation to Koran

       Class origin of Koran, commentary about historical occasions on which passages of Koran were revealed in 297.1221; class compilation and recording of Koran in 297.1224042; class comprehensive works on geography, history, chronology of the Middle East in Koran times in 939.4

.122 092   Biography

       For Muḥammad, see 297.63; for Muḥammad's family and companions, see 297.64; for prophets prior to Muḥammad, see 297.246

.122 1   Origin and authenticity

       Including inspiration, Koranic prophecy and prophecies

       Class compilation and recording of Koran in 297.1224042

.122 12   Revelation

       Class here occasions or circumstances of revelation (asbāb al-nuzūl)

       Class comprehensive works on doctrine of revelation in 297.2115

.122 2   Koran stories retold

       Including picture books

.122 3   Faḍā'il al-Qur'ān and prayers in Koran

.122 32   Faḍā'il al-Qur'ān (Virtues of Koran)

Class here excellent qualities of Koran

See also 297.5 for moral virtues as a topic in Koran

.122 34   Prayers in Koran

Verses used in prayer

Class how to pray as a topic in Koran, comprehensive works on Islamic prayers in 297.382

>   297.122 4–297.122 5 Texts

Class comprehensive works in 297.122

For texts of prayers in Koran, see 297.12234; for texts accompanied by commentaries, see 297.1227

.122 4   Arabic texts

Class Arabic texts accompanied by translations in 297.1225

.122 404   Special topics of Arabic texts

.122 404 2   Compilation and recording of Koran

Standard subdivisions are added for either or both topics in heading

Class here establishment of standard Uthmanic text

Class readings in 297.1224045

.122 404 5   Readings and recitation

Standard subdivisions are added for readings and recitation together, for readings alone

.122 404 52   Ten Readings (Al-qirā'āt al-'ashr)

The seven most authoritative readings plus three less authoritative readings

Including readings of Abū Ja'far al-Qāri', Yazīd ibn al-Qa'qā'; Ya'qūb al-Ḥaḍramī; Khalaf al-Qāri'

.122 404 522   Seven Readings (Al-qirā'āt al-sab')

Readings from authoritative readers with good chain of transmission

Including readings of Abū 'Amr ibn al-'Alā'; Kisā'ī, 'Alī ibn Ḥamzah; 'Āṣim ibn Abī al-Nujūd; Ibn 'Āmir, 'Abd Allāh; Ibn Kathīr, 'Abd Allāh; Kisā'ī, 'Alī ibn Ḥamzah; Qāri', Nāfi' ibn 'Abd al-Raḥmān

.122 404 59   Recitation

Class here art of melodic reading, science of tajwīd (proper pronunciation during recitation)

.122 42	Texts of parts of Koran

Class here selections

.122 421	Suras 1–4

Class here prologue and parts 1–6 together

For second portion of part 6, see 297.122422

.122 422	Suras 5–9

Class here parts 6–11 together

Class comprehensive works on part 6 in 297.122421

For second portion of part 11, see 297.122423

.122 423	Suras 10–16

Class here parts 11–14 together

Class comprehensive works on part 11 in 297.122422

.122 424	Suras 17–25

Class here parts 15–19 together

For second portion of part 19, see 297.122425

.122 425	Suras 26–36

Class here parts 19–23 together

Class comprehensive works on part 19 of Koran in 297.122424

For second portion of part 23, see 297.122426

.122 426	Suras 37–49

Class here parts 23–26 together

Class comprehensive works on part 23 of Koran in 297.122425

For second portion of part 26, see 297.122427

.122 427	Suras 50–114

Class here parts 26–30 together

Class comprehensive works on part 26 of Koran in 297.122426

.122 5	Translations

Class here Arabic texts accompanied by translations

Add to base number 297.1225 notation 1–9 from Table 6, e.g., the Koran in English 297.122521; then to the result add as follows:
001–009 Standard subdivisions
008–009 Groups of people; history, geographic treatment, biography
01–07 Parts of Koran
Add 0 and to the result add the numbers following 297.12242 in 297.122421–297.122427, e.g., English translation of sura 36 (Sūrat Yāsīn) 297.12252105

.122 6	Interpretation and exegesis

Including literary examination of the text in order to reach conclusions about its meaning

Class language and style of specific texts in 297.1224–297.1225; class art of recitation in 297.12240459

For commentaries, see 297.1227. For textual studies, see the topic in 297.1224, e.g., compilation and recording of Koran 297.1224042

See also 809.935297122 for Koran as literature

.122 601	Philosophy and theory

Class here hermeneutics, principles and methods of Koranic exegesis

.122 61	General introductions to the Koran

Class here sciences of the Koran

.122 612	Al-Nāsikh wa-al-mansūkh (Abrogation)

Class here comprehensive works on abrogation in Koran and Hadith

For abrogation in Hadith, see 297.125163

.122 67	Historical interpretation

Interpretation of texts in light of the cultural, historical, religious, social milieu in which written

Class history and chronology of the Middle East in Koran times in relation to the Koran, but not emphasizing interpretation and exegesis, in 297.12209

.122 68	Allegorical and numerical interpretations
.122 7	Commentaries

Interpretation and exegesis arranged in textual order

Class here texts accompanied by commentaries

.122 71	Specific kinds of commentaries

Class commentaries on parts of Koran in 297.12272; class commentaries by sect or reform movement in 297.12273–297.12276

[.122 710 1–.122 710 9]	Standard subdivisions

Do not use; class in 297.122701–297.122709

.122 711	Tafsīr al-ma'thūr (Commentary based on tradition)
.122 712	Tafsīr bi-al-ra'y (Commentary based on opinion, reasoning)

.122 712 2	Sufi commentary

> *For Sufi commentaries by sect or reform movement, see the sect or reform movement in 297.12273–297.12276, plus notation 122 from table under 297.12273–297.12276, e.g., Sufi commentaries of Sunnites 297.12273122*

.122 712 4	Jurisprudential commentary
.122 712 6	Philosophical commentary
.122 713	Tafsīr hadith (Modern commentary)
.122 713 4	Tafsīr al-mawḍūʿī (Topical commentary)
.122 72	Commentaries on parts of Koran

Add to base number 297.12272 the numbers following 297.12242 in 297.122421–297.122427, e.g., commentaries on sura 2 (Sūrat al-Baqarah) 297.122721

Class commentaries by sect or reform movement in 297.12273–297.12276

> 297.122 73–297.122 76 Commentaries by sect or reform movement

Except for modifications shown under specific entries, add to each subdivision identified by * as follows:
01–09   Standard subdivisions
1   Specific kinds of commentaries
[101–109]   Standard subdivisions
        Do not use; class in notation 01–09 from this table
11–13   Subdivisions for specific kinds of commentaries
        Add to 1 the numbers following 297.12271 in
        297.122711–297.122713, e.g., Sufi commentary 122, Sufi
        commentaries of Sunnites 297.12273122
2   Commentaries on parts of Koran
        Add to 2 the numbers following 297.12242 in
        297.122421–297.122427, e.g., commentaries on sura 2 (Sūrat
        al-Baqarah) 21, commentaries of Sunnites on sura 2 (Sūrat
        al-Baqarah) 297.1227321

Class comprehensive works on Sufi commentaries in 297.1227122; class comprehensive works on commentaries by sect or reform movement in 297.1227

.122 73	*Commentaries of Sunnites

Class here commentaries of Ṭabarī; Ibn Kathīr, Ismāʿīl ibn ʿUmar; Rāzī, Muḥammad ibn Abī Bakr; Baghawī, al-Ḥusayn ibn Masʿūd; Nasafī, ʿAbd Allāh ibn Aḥmad; Khāzin al-Baghdādī, ʿAlī ibn Muḥammad; Qurṭubī, Muḥammad ibn Aḥmad

Class commentaries of Motazilites in 297.12274

*Add as instructed under 297.12273–297.12276

.122 74	*Commentaries of Motazilites
	Class here commentaries of ʿAbd al-Jabbār ibn Aḥmad al-Asadābādī; Zamakhsharī, Maḥmūd ibn ʿUmar
.122 75	*Commentaries of Shiites
.122 753	*Commentaries of Twelvers (Ithna Asharites)
	Class here commentaries of Ṭūsī, Muḥammad ibn al-Ḥasan; Ṭabarsī, al-Faḍl ibn al-Ḥasan; Qummī, ʿAlī ibn Ibrāhīm
.122 754	*Commentaries of Seveners (Ismailites)
	Class here commentaries of Jaʿfar ibn Manṣūr al-Yaman
.122 755	*Commentaries of Zaydites
	Class here commentaries of Ibn Furāt al-Kūfī, Furāt; Ḥibarī, al-Ḥusayn ibn al-Ḥakam; Shawkānī, Muḥammad ibn ʿAlī
.122 77	*Commentaries of Ibadites
	Class here commentaries of Hawwārī, Hūd ibn Muḥakkam; Bayyūḍ, Ibrāhīm ibn ʿUmar; Aṭṭafayyish, Muḥammad ibn Yūsuf
.122 8	Nonreligious subjects treated in the Koran
	Class a religious subject treated in the Koran with the subject, e.g., Islamic ethics 297.5
.122 800 01–.122 800 09	Standard subdivisions
.122 800 1–.122 899 9	Specific nonreligious subjects treated in the Koran
	Add to base number 297.1228 notation 001–999, e.g., natural sciences in the Koran 297.12285
.125	Hadith (Traditions)
.125 012	Classification
	Do not use for musṭalaḥ al-Ḥadīth; class in 297.1252
.125 09	History, geographic treatment, biography
	Notation 09 from Table 1 as modified under 297.0902–297.0905
.125 1	General topics of Hadith
	Class texts of Hadith, works about specific Hadith and compilations of Hadith in 297.1254–297.1259
[.125 101–.125 109]	Standard subdivisions
	Do not use; class in 297.12501–297.12509
.125 12	Hadith stories retold
	Including picture books

*Add as instructed under 297.12273–297.12276

.125 16	Interpretation
	Class here riwayah (study of text of Hadith)
.125 160 1	Philosophy and theory
	Class here hermeneutics, principles and methods of interpretation of Hadith
.125 161	General introductions to Hadith
	Class here sciences of Hadith
	For dirāyah (science of authenticity of Hadith), see 297.1252
.125 162	Asbāb wurūd al-Ḥadīth (Causes and circumstances of Hadith)
.125 163	Al-Nāsikh wa-al-mansūkh (Abrogation of Hadith)
.125 18	Nonreligious subjects treated in Hadith
	Class a religious subject treated in Hadith with the subject, e.g., Islamic ethics 297.5
.125 180 001–.125 180 009	Standard subdivisions
.125 180 01–.125 189 99	Specific nonreligious subjects treated in Hadith
	Add to base number 297.12518 the notation 001–999, e.g., natural sciences in Hadith 297.125185
.125 2	Dirāyah (Science of authenticity of Hadith)
	Class here musṭalaḥ al-Ḥadīth (classification of Hadith)
	Unless other instructions are given, class a subject with aspects in two or more subdivisions of 297.1252 in the number coming last, e.g., Hadith that are ṣaḥiḥ (authentic) and mutawātir (have a large number of transmitters) 297.12523 (*not* 297.12521)
	Class texts of Hadith in 297.1254–297.1259. Class authenticity of specific Hadith with the Hadith in 297.1254–297.1259, plus notation 01 from table under 297.1254–297.1259, e.g., weak Hadith of Ibn Mājah, Muḥammad ibn Yazīd 297.1255201
.125 21	Al-ṣaḥiḥ (Authentic Hadith) and al-hasan (Good Hadith)
	Standard subdivisions are added for either or both topics in heading
	Including al-marfū' (narration attributed to the Prophet specifically), al-mawqūf (narration attributed to a Companion of the Prophet), al-maqtū' (narration attributed to the tabi'ī, the Successors of the Companions)
	Class here al-muttaṣil (Hadith with uninterrupted chain of transmission back to Prophet)

.125 22	Al-daʿīf (Weak Hadith)
	Including al-muʿallaq (discontinuity in the beginning of transmission chain), al-muḍal (two or more consecutive transmitters are dropped), al-munqatiʿ (chain of transmission is disconnected at any point), and al-shadh (reported by trustworthy transmitter but contradicts report of more trustworthy transmitter)
.125 222	Al-mursal (Hadith in which transmitter between Successor and Prophet is omitted from a given chain of transmission)
.125 225	Al-mawḍuʿ (Fabricated Hadith)
.125 23	Al-mutawātir (Hadith with large number of transmitters at all stages of transmission)
.125 24	Al-āḥād (Hadith with one or a few transmitters)
	Including al-mashhūr (Hadith with more than two transmitters), al-ʿazīz (Hadith with only two transmitters), al-gharīb (Hadith with only one transmitter)
.125 26	Al-jarḥ wa al-taʿdīl (Principles of disparagement and crediting of transmitters of Hadith)
.125 261	Ṭabaqāt al-ruwāh (Rankings of transmitters)
.125 262	Al-thiqāt (Trustworthy transmitters)
.125 263	Al-ḍuʿafāʿ (Untrustworthy transmitters)
.125 264	Asmāʾ al-ruwāh (Names of transmitters)
	Including al-muttafiq wa-al-muftariq (same name, different identity)
.125 264 2	Al-Muʿtalif wa-al-mukhtalif (Different names, written similarly but pronounced differently)

> **297.125 4–297.125 9 Texts of Hadith**

Class here texts of specific Hadith and compilations of Hadith, works about specific Hadith and compilations of Hadith

Add to each subdivision identified by * as follows:
  001–009 Standard subdivisions
  01–08 Generalities
    Add to 0 the numbers following 297.122 in 297.1221–297.1228, e.g., authenticity 01, interpretation 06

Class comprehensive works in 297.125

> **297.125 4–297.125 8 Texts of Hadith of Sunnites**

Class comprehensive works in 297.125

.125 4	*Jawāmiʻ (Comprehensive compilations), ṣiḥāḥ (Authentic compilations), mustadrākāt
	Subdivisions are added for jawāmiʻ, ṣiḥāḥ, mustadrākāt together, for jawāmiʻ alone, for ṣiḥāḥ alone
.125 41	*Al-Bukhārī, Muḥammad ibn Ismāʻīl
.125 42	*Muslim ibn al-Ḥajjāj al-Qushayrī
.125 43	*Al-Tirmidhī, Muḥammad ibn ʻĪsá
.125 45	Mustadrākāt (Compilations of Hadith meeting the conditions of other compilers but not found in their books)
.125 5	*Sunan (Compilations according to Islamic law hierarchy), muṣannafat, muwaṭṭaʻāt
	Subdivisions are added for sunan, muṣannafat, muwaṭṭaʻāt together, for sunan alone
.125 51	*Abū Dāʼūd Sulaymān ibn al-Ashʻath al-Sijistānī
.125 52	*Ibn Mājah, Muḥammad ibn Yazīd
.125 53	*Al-Nasāʼī, Aḥmad ibn Shuʻayb
.125 54	*Al-Dārimī, ʻAbd Allāh ibn ʻAbd al-Raḥmān
.125 56	*Muṣannafat (Compilations according to topics)
	Including muṣannaf of Ibn Abī Shaybah, ʻAbd Allāh ibn Muḥammad and muṣannaf of ʻAbd al-Razzāq ibn Hammām al-Ḥimyari
.125 58	*Muwaṭṭaʻāt (The well-trodden path of Hadith)
	Class here Muwaṭṭaʻ of Mālik ibn Anas
.125 6	Masānīd, aṭrāf, maʻājim, zawāʼid
.125 61	*Masānīd (Compilations arranged by first transmitter in the chain of transmission)
.125 612	*Ibn Ḥanbal, Aḥmad ibn Muḥammad
.125 613	*Al-Mawṣilī, Abū Yaʻlá Aḥmad ibn ʻAlī
.125 62	*Aṭrāf (Compilations of the beginnings, or the most well known words of a specific Hadith)
	Class here Mizzī, Yūsuf ibn al-Zakī ʻAbd al-Raḥmān
.125 63	*Maʻājim (Compilations arranged alphabetically according to names of the compilers' sheikhs)
	Class here al-Ṭabarānī, Sulaymān ibn Aḥmad
.125 64	*Zawāʼid (Compilations of Hadith found in one compilation but not another)
	Class here Haythamī, Nūr al-Dīn ʻAlī ibn Abī Bakr

*Add as instructed under 297.1254–297.1259

.125 7	*Mustakhrajat (Compilations containing Hadith of other compilers with different chains of transmission) and takhrījāt (Compilations that define the degree of verification of another compilation)
	Subdivisions are added for either or both topics in heading
	Class mustakhrajat and takhrījāt of a specific work with the work, e.g., takhrījāt of maʿājim of al-Ṭabarānī, Sulaymān ibn Aḥmad 297.12563
.125 8	*Al-Aḥādīth al-Qudsīyah (Sacred Hadith)
	Sayings of the Prophet Muḥammad divinely communicated to him
.125 9	Texts of Hadith of sects other than Sunnites
.125 92	Hadith of Shiites
.125 921	*Twelvers (Ithna Asharites)
.125 921 1	*Kulaynī, Muḥammad ibn Yaʿqūb
.125 921 2	*Ibn Bābawayh al-Qummī, Muḥammad ibn ʿAlī
.125 921 3	*Ṭūsī, Muḥammad ibn al-Ḥasan (Abū Jaʿfar)
.125 922	*Seveners (Ismailites)
.125 924	*Zaydites
.125 93	Hadith of other sects
.125 933	*Ibadites
.14	Religious and ceremonial laws and decisions
	Class here fiqh al-ʿibādāt (rituals law); fiqh in relation to religious and ceremonial laws and decisions, sharia in relation to religious and ceremonial laws and decisions
	Class Islamic law relating to secular matters, interdisciplinary works on Islamic law in 340.59. Class religious law on a specific topic with the topic, e.g., religious law concerning ḥajj 297.3524
.140 1	Philosophy and theory
	Notation 01 from Table 1 as modified below
.140 18	Schools of law
.140 181	Sunni schools
	Class here general or comparative works on several Sunni schools; or several authors belonging to different Sunni schools
	For works comparing Sunni law with other schools of Islamic law, see 297.140184
.140 181 1	Ḥanafī school
	Class here Ḥanafīyah (Hanafites)

*Add as instructed under 297.1254–297.1259

.140 181 2	Shāfiʿī school
	Class here Shāfiʿīyah (Shafiites)
.140 181 3	Mālikī school
	Class here Mālikīyah (Malikites)
.140 181 4	Ḥanbalī school
	Class here Ḥanbalīyah (Hanbalites)
.140 181 5	Ẓāhirī school
	Class here school of Zahirites
.140 182	Shiite schools

Including general or comparative works on several Shiite schools; or several authors belonging to different Shiite schools

For works comparing Shiite law with other schools of Islamic law, see 297.140184

.140 182 1	Jaʿfarī school
	Class here school of Twelvers (Ithna Asharites)
.140 182 2	Ismāʿīlī school
	Class here school of Seveners (Ismailites)
.140 182 4	Zaydī school
	Class here school of Zaydites
.140 183	Other schools
.140 183 3	ʿIbādī school
	Class here school of Ibadites
.140 184	Mixed schools and comparative treatment

Class here works comparing authors affiliated with different schools (e.g., Sunni and Shīʿī schools)

.18   Stories, legends, parables, proverbs, anecdotes told for religious edification

Class here comprehensive works on Islamic legends

Class Islamic folklore in 398.2088297

For Islamic legends on a specific topic, see the topic, e.g., Islamic legends about pre-Islamic prophets 297.246

.2   Islamic doctrinal theology ('Aqā'id and Kalām); Islam and secular disciplines; Islam and other systems of belief

> Standard subdivisions are added for Islamic doctrinal theology, Islam and secular disciplines, Islam and other systems of belief together; for Islamic doctrinal theology alone

> Class Islamic ethics in 297.5; class doctrines concerning Muḥammad the Prophet in 297.63

SUMMARY

.204   Doctrines of specific sects

> Add to base number 297.204 the numbers following 297.8 in 297.81–297.87, e.g., doctrines of Shiites 297.2042

> **297.21–297.24 Specific topics in Islamic doctrinal theology ('Aqā'id and Kalām)**

> Class comprehensive works in 297.2

> *For doctrines of specific sects, see 297.204; for apologetics and polemics, see 297.29; for shahāda (profession of faith), see 297.34*

.21   God and spiritual beings

.211   God

.211 2   Attributes and names of God

> Class vindication of God's justice and goodness in permitting existence of evil and suffering in 297.2118

> *For tawhid (unity of God), see 297.2113*

.211 3   Tawhid (Unity of God)

.211 4   Relation to the world

> Including relation to and action in history

> *For revelation, see 297.2115; for creation, see 297.242*

.211 5   Revelation

> Including prophecy

> Class Koranic prophecy in 297.1221; class prophets and prophethood in 297.246

.211 8	Theodicy	

Vindication of God's justice and goodness in permitting existence of evil and suffering

.215	Angels
.216	Devils
.217	Jinn
.22	Humankind

Including faith, repentance

For eschatology, see 297.23

.221	Creation

Class comprehensive works on creation in 297.242

.225	Nature

Including soul

Class free will and predestination in 297.227

.227	Free will and predestination

Class here freedom of choice between good and evil

.23	Eschatology

Including day of judgment, death, eternity, future life, heaven, hell, punishment, resurrection, rewards

Class doctrines of Hidden Imam, of Mahdi in 297.24

.24	Other doctrines

Including doctrines of Hidden Imam, of Mahdi

.242	Creation

Including origin of life

Class here Islamic cosmology

For creation of humankind, see 297.221

.246	Prophets prior to Muḥammad

Including Adam, Moses

Class here comprehensive works on prophets and prophethood in Islam

For Muḥammad the Prophet, see 297.63

.246 3	Abraham
.246 5	Jesus, son of Mary

.26   Islam and secular disciplines

Class here attitudes of Islam toward and influence on secular issues, Islamic views and teachings about secular disciplines

Class relation of a specific Islamic doctrine and a secular discipline with the doctrine in 297.2, e.g., relation of Islamic doctrine about creation and scientific theories about creation 297.242; class work influenced by Islam and Islamic theories within a secular discipline with the discipline, e.g., Islamic philosophy 181.07, architecture in the Islamic world 720.91767

For Islam and social sciences, see 297.27

See also 297.1228 for nonreligious subjects treated in Koran; also 297.12518 for nonreligious subjects treated in Hadith

See Manual at 297.26–297.27

.261   Islam and philosophy, parapsychology and occultism, psychology

.265   Islam and natural sciences, mathematics

.266   Islam and technology

.267   Islam and the arts

.27   Islam and social sciences

Attitudes of Islam toward and influence on social issues

Including environment, war and peace

Class here Islam and socioeconomic problems, Islamic social theology

Class Islamic view of marriage and family in 297.577

See Manual at 297.26–297.27

.272   Islam and politics

Including civil rights, international affairs, nationalism

Class political science view of religiously oriented political theories and ideologies in 320.55; class political science view of relation of state to religious organizations and groups in 322.1; class political science view of religious political parties in 324.2182

See Manual at 320.557 vs. 297.09, 297.272, 322.1

.273   Islam and economics

Including Islam and communism

See also 297.289 for Islam and atheism

.28   Islam and other systems of belief

Attitudes toward and relations with other systems of belief

Class apologetics and polemics in 297.29

.282   Islam and Judaism

Class Biblical figures as prophets prior to Muḥammad in 297.246

.283	Islam and Christianity

Class Biblical figures as prophets prior to Muḥammad in 297.246

.284	Islam and religions of Indic origin

Add to base number 297.284 the numbers following 294 in 294.3–294.6, e.g., Islam and Hinduism 297.2845

.286	Islam and other religions

Add to base number 297.286 the numbers following 29 in 292–299, e.g., Islam and Bahai Faith 297.286793

.289	Islam and irreligion

Class here Islam and atheism

.29	Apologetics and polemics
.292	Polemics against Judaism
.293	Polemics against Christianity
.294	Polemics against religions of Indic origin
.298	Polemics against scientists and materialists

.3	**Islamic worship**

Including use of arts and symbolism in worship

Class here comprehensive works on Islamic worship, on non-Sufi worship, on Islamic private worship, on non-Sufi private worship, public worship

Class Pillars of Islam (Pillars of the Faith) in 297.31. Class applications of the arts and symbolism in worship of specific sects with the sect in 297.301–297.307, e.g., use of arts and symbolism in Sunni worship 297.301; class applications of the arts and symbolism in specific aspects of worship with the aspect in 297.31–297.38, e.g., use of arts and symbolism in mosques 297.351

For Sufi worship, see 297.43

.300 1–.300 9	Standard subdivisions
.301–.307	Specific sects

Add to base number 297.30 the numbers following 297.8 in 297.81–297.87, e.g., Shiite rites 297.302

.31	Pillars of Islam (Pillars of the Faith)

Comprehensive works only

For shahāda (profession of faith), see 297.34; for ḥajj (pilgrimage to Mecca during second week of Dhū al-Ḥijjah), see 297.3524; for ṣawm Ramaḍān (annual fast of Ramadan), see 297.362; for ṣalāt (prayer five times daily), see 297.3822; for zakat, see 297.54

See also 297.72 for jihad

.34	Shahāda (Profession of faith)

.35   Sacred places and pilgrimages

Standard subdivisions are added for sacred places and pilgrimages together, for sacred places alone

Including non-Sufi pilgrimages, comprehensive works on Islamic pilgrimages

Class here rites and ceremonies associated with sacred places and pilgrimages

Class pilgrimages to specific places in 297.352–297.359

For Sufi pilgrimages, see 297.435

[.350 93–.350 99]   Specific continents, countries, localities

Do not use; class in 297.353–297.359

.351   Mosques

Class here interdisciplinary works

For organizational role and function of mosques, see 297.65; for architecture of mosques, see 726.2

[.351 093–.351 099]   Specific continents, countries, localities

Do not use; class in 297.352–297.359

.352   Mecca

Class here al-Masjid al-Ḥarām (the Holy Mosque), Kaʻbah

.352 4   Ḥajj

Annual pilgrimage to Mecca during second week of Dhū al-Ḥijjah

Class here manāsik (rituals of ḥajj)

Class comprehensive works on kinds of rituals not limited to the ḥajj with the kind, e.g., ritual slaughter of animals 297.576

.352 5   Umrah (Lesser pilgrimage to Mecca)

Pilgrimage to Mecca other than at time of annual ḥajj

.353–.359   Specific continents, countries, localities

Add to base number 297.35 notation 3–9 from Table 2, e.g., Medina 297.35538, Jerusalem 297.35569442; however, for Mecca, see 297.352

.36   Special days and seasons

Including Jumʻah (Friday prayer); ʻĀshūrāʼ (Tenth of Muḥarram); Mawlid al-Nabī (Prophet's birthday); ʻĪd al-Aḍḥā, ʻĪd al-Fiṭr

Class here rites and ceremonies associated with special days and seasons, Islamic religious calendar

See also 297.37 for sermons for special days and seasons

.362   Ṣawm Ramaḍān (Annual fast of Ramadan)

     Including Laylat al-Qadr

     Class comprehensive works on fasting in 297.53

.37   Sermons and preaching

     Class sermons on a specific subject with the subject, e.g., sermons on day of judgment 297.23

.38   Rites, ceremonies, prayer, meditation

     Conduct and texts

     Including ablutions

     Class ablutions associated with prayer and meditations in 297.382; class ablutions associated with burial and mourning in 297.385; class rites and ceremonies associated with sacred places and pilgrimages in 297.35; class rites and ceremonies associated with special days and seasons in 297.36

     See also 297.37 for sermons and preaching

.382   Prayer and meditation

     Standard subdivisions are added for prayer and meditation together, for prayer alone

     Including dhikr (remembrance), qiblah (direction of prayer)

     Class here practical works on prayer and meditation

     Class prayer and meditation associated with sacred places and pilgrimages in 297.35; class prayer and meditation associated with special days and seasons in 297.36. Class prayer and meditation associated with specific rites and ceremonies with the rites and ceremonies, e.g., funerals in 297.385; class prayers and meditations on a specific subject with the subject, e.g., unity of God 297.2113

.382 2   Ṣalāt (Prayer five times daily)

     For texts of prayers, see 297.3824

.382 4   Texts of prayers and meditations

     Class here prayer books

.385   Burial and mourning rites

.39   Popular practices

     Including controversial practices, e.g., divination and occultism

     Class occult practices not regarded as Islamic practices in 130; class Islamic views of occultism regarded as a secular topic in 297.261; class sociological studies of Islamic popular practices in 306.69739. Class popular practices associated with a topic provided elsewhere with the topic, e.g., popular practices associated with burial and mourning 297.385

.4   **Sufism (Islamic mysticism)**

.41   Sufi doctrinal theology; Sufism and secular disciplines; Sufism and
               non-Islamic systems of belief

               Standard subdivisions are added for Sufi doctrinal theology, Sufism and
               secular disciplines, Sufism and non-Islamic systems of belief together; for
               Sufi doctrinal theology alone

               Add to base number 297.41 the numbers following 297.2 in 297.21–297.29,
               e.g., Sufi concept of God 297.4111

               Class Sufi doctrines concerning Muḥammad the Prophet in 297.4; class Sufi
               ethics in 297.45

.43   Sufi worship

.430 01–.430 09   Standard subdivisions

.430 1–.430 7   Specific sects

               Add to base number 297.43 the numbers following 297.3 in
               297.301–297.307, e.g., Sunni Sufi orders 297.4301

.431–.438   Subdivisions of Sufi worship

               Add to base number 297.43 the numbers following 297.3 in
               297.31–297.38, e.g., Sufi pilgrimages 297.435, Sufi observance of ṣawm
               Ramaḍān 297.4362, Sufi prayer and meditation 297.4382

.44   Sufi religious life and practice

               Class here guides to Sufi religious life

               Class Sufi ethics in 297.45

               For Sufi worship, see 297.43

.446   Sufi individual observances

               Including Sufi ascetic practices, dietary laws and observance

               For Sufi fasting, see 297.45

.45   Sufi ethics

               Including Sufi almsgiving, fasting, ṣadaqah, zakat

               For Sufi observance of ṣawm Ramaḍān, see 297.4362

.48   Sufi orders

               Including Bektashi, Naqshabandiyah, Qādirīyah, Tijānīyah

               Class comprehensive works on Bektashi Sufi order and Alevis in 297.8252

               See also 297.835 for Kadarites (Islamic sect)

.482   Mevleviyeh

.5   Islamic ethics and religious experience, life, practice

Standard subdivisions are added for ethics and religious experience, life, practice together; for ethics alone

Including conscience; general works on duty, sin, vice, virtue

Class a specific duty, sin, vice, virtue in 297.56

For Pillars of Islam (Pillars of the Faith), see 297.31; for jihad, see 297.72

.53   Ṣawm (Fast)

Class here comprehensive works on fasting

For ṣawm Ramaḍān (Annual Fast of Ramadan), see 297.362

.54   Zakat

Class here almsgiving, ṣadaqah

.56   Specific vices, virtues, moral issues

Add to base number 297.56 the numbers following 17 in 172–179, e.g., Islamic sexual ethics 297.566; however, for almsgiving, see 297.54

Class comprehensive works on vices, on virtues in 297.5

.57   Religious experience, life, practice

Standard subdivisions are added for any or all topics in heading

Class here non-Sufi and comprehensive works on Islamic religious experience, life, practice; non-Sufi and comprehensive guides to religious life

Class Islamic ethics in 297.5

For worship, see 297.3; for mysticism and Sufi religious experience, see 297.4; for Sufi life and practice, see 297.44

[.570 85]   Relatives

Do not use; class in 297.577

.570 86   People by miscellaneous social attributes

[.570 865 5]   Married people

Do not use; class in 297.577

.574   Conversion

Class here conversion of non-Muslims to Islam

Class da'wah in 297.74. Class conversion of Muslims to another religion with the religion, e.g., conversion of Muslims to Christianity 248.246

.576   Individual observances

Including ascetic practices, dietary laws and observance, ritual slaughter of animals to conform with dietary laws

For pilgrimages, see 297.35; for fasting, see 297.53; for almsgiving, see 297.54

.577	Marriage and family life

Including child rearing, religious training of children in the home

Class comprehensive works on Islamic religious training of children in 297.77083

Class here comprehensive works on marriage, on family life

For ethics of marriage and family, see 297.563

.6	**Islamic leaders and organization**

.61	Leaders and their work

Role, function, duties

Class here ayatollahs, caliphate, caliphs, imamate, imams, ulama

For doctrine of Hidden Imam, see 297.24; for Muḥammad the Prophet, see 297.63; for Muḥammad's family and companions (including first four caliphs), see 297.64

[.610 92]	Biography

Do not use for biography of religious leaders primarily associated with a specific religious activity; class in 297.1–297.7, e.g., founders of Sufi orders 297.48. Do not use for biography of Muḥammad; class in 297.63. Do not use for biography of Muḥammad's family and companions (including first four caliphs); class in 297.64. Do not use for biography of Islamic leaders primarily associated with a specific sect or reform movement; class in 297.8. Do not use for biography of other religious leaders; class in 297.092

.63	Muḥammad the Prophet

Class here comprehensive works on Muḥammad and his family and companions

Class Hadith in 297.125

For Muḥammad's family and companions, see 297.64

.630 92	Biography

Do not use for Muḥammad the Prophet; class in 297.63

Class here scholars who specialize in the life and works of Muḥammad the Prophet

.632	Period prior to call to prophethood

Including birth, childhood

See also 297.36 for Mawlid al-Nabī (holiday of Prophet's birthday)

.633	Period at Mecca

Including Isrā' (Night Journey to Jerusalem) and Miʻrāj (Ascent to Heaven)

Class comprehensive works on prophetic career in 297.635

For period prior to call to prophethood, see 297.632

.634	Hijrah (Emigration from Mecca)
.635	Period at Medina

> *For emigration from Mecca to Medina, see 297.634*

.64	Muḥammad's family and companions

Standard subdivisions are added for family and companions together, for family alone

Including descendants of Muḥammad

.642	Wives
.644	Children
.648	Ṣaḥābah (Companions)

Including religious biography and theological discussion of the first four caliphs

Class interdisciplinary biographies of the first four caliphs with the subject in 950, e.g., Abu Bakr 953.02092

.65	Organizations and organization

Role and function

Including associations, congregations, mosques

Class Islamic organizations in relation to political affairs in 297.272; class a specific organization limited to a specific sect or reform movement in 297.8; class political science view of relation of state to religious organizations and groups in 322.1; class political science view of religious political parties in 324.2182; class interdisciplinary works on mosques in 297.351

.7	**Protection and propagation of Islam**
.72	Jihad
.74	Da'wah

Class here call to Islam, missionary work

.77	Islamic religious education

Class Islam as an academic subject in 297.071; class comprehensive works on madrasah education, treating both religious education and other subjects, in 371.077

> *For religious education at the level of higher education, see 297.0711*

> *See Manual at 207.5, 268 vs. 200.71, 230.071, 292–299*

.770 83	Young people

Do not use for religious training of children in the home; class in 297.577

Class here Islamic religious schools, religious education in Islamic schools that teach all subjects

Class comprehensive works on Islamic schools that teach all subjects in 371.077

.8   **Islamic sects and reform movements**

Class specific aspects of sects and reform movements in 297.1–297.7; class secular view of relation of state to religious organizations and groups in 322.1; class secular view of religious political parties in 324.2182

For Sufism, see 297.4

.804   Special topics of Islamic sects and reform movements

.804 2   Relations among sects and reform movements

Class here relations between Sunni and Shia Islam

.81   Sunnites

Class relations between Sunnites and Shiites in 297.8042; class Motazilites in 297.834

.814   Wahhābīyah

.82   Shiites

Class relations between Shiites and Sunnites in 297.8042

.821   Twelvers (Ithna Asharites)

.822   Seveners (Ismailites)

Including Mustalians, Nizaris

.824   Zaydites

.825   'Alawīs and Alevis

.825 1   'Alawīs (Alawites)

.825 2   Alevis

Class here Alevi-Bektashi sect, comprehensive works on Alevis and Bektashi Sufi order

For Bektashi Sufi order, see 297.48

.83   Other sects and reform movements

Including Kharijites

.833   Ibadites

.834   Motazilites

.835   Kadarites

See also 297.48 for Qādirīyah (Sufi order)

.837   Murjiites

.85   Druzes

.86   Ahmadiyya movement

.87   Black Muslim movement

Including American Muslim Mission, Nation of Islam, World Community of al-Islam in the West

.9	**Babism and Bahai Faith**
.92	Babism
.93	Bahai Faith
.931–.937	Specific aspects

> Add to base number 297.93 the numbers following 20 in 201–207, e.g., Bahai ethics 297.935

| .938 | Sources |
| .938 2 | Sacred books |

> *For works by the Bab, see 297.92*

.938 22	Works by Bahá'u'lláh
.938 24	Works by 'Abdu'l-Bahá
.938 6	Authoritative interpretation

Class here works by Shoghi Effendi

| .938 7 | Elucidation and legislation |

Class here works of the Universal House of Justice

(298)   (Permanently unassigned)

(Optional number used for Christianity if option A under 290 is chosen. Another option is described at 290)

299   Religions not provided for elsewhere

Including modern revivals of long dormant religions

Class syncretistic religious writings of individuals expressing personal views and not claiming to establish a new religion or to represent an old one in 200

> *See Manual at 200.92 and 201–209, 292–299; also at 201–209 and 292–299; also at 203.6, 263.9, 292–299 vs. 394.265–394.267; also at 207.5, 268 vs. 200.71, 230.071, 292–299; also at 322.1 vs. 201.72, 261.7, 292–299; also at 398.2 vs. 201.3, 230, 270, 292–299; also at 615.852 vs. 203.1, 234.131, 292–299; also at 616.86 vs. 158.1, 204.42, 248.8629, 292–299, 362.29*

(Options for giving local emphasis and shorter numbers for a specific religion are described at 290)

SUMMARY

299.1–.4	**Religions of Indo-European, Semitic, Non-Semitic Afro-Asiatic, North and West Asian, Dravidian origin**
.5	**Religions of East and Southeast Asian origin**
.6	**Religions originating among Black Africans and people of Black African descent**
.7	**Religions of North American native origin**
.8	**Religions of South American native origin**
.9	**Religions of other origin**

.1–.4   **Religions of Indo-European, Semitic, Non-Semitic Afro-Asiatic, North and West Asian, Dravidian origin**

Not otherwise provided for

Add to base number 299 the numbers following —9 in notation 91–94 from Table 5, e.g., Mithraism 299.15

Class modern revivals of long dormant religions in 299

.1   **Religions of Indo-European origin**

Number built according to instructions under 299.1–299.4

.16   Celtic religion

Number built according to instructions under 299.1–299.4

.161   Specific aspects of Celtic religion

Add to base number 299.161 the numbers following 20 in 201–209, e.g., Celtic mythology 299.16113

.3   **Religions of Non-Semitic Afro-Asiatic origin**

Number built according to instructions under 299.1–299.4

.31   †Ancient Egyptian religion

Number built according to instructions under 299.1–299.4

.5   **Religions of East and Southeast Asian origin**

See Manual at 200.9 vs. 294, 299.5

.51   Religions of Chinese origin

.511   Specific aspects of Chinese religions

Add to base number 299.511 the numbers following 20 in 201–209, e.g., Chinese gods and goddesses 299.511211

.512   †Confucianism

Class the Four books of Confucius, interdisciplinary works on Confucianism in 181.112

.514   †Taoism

.54   Religions of Tibetan origin

Class here Bon

.56   Religions of Japanese and Ryukyuan origin

.561   †Shinto

.57–.59   Other religions of East and Southeast Asian origin

Add to base number 299.5 the numbers following —95 in notation 957–959 from Table 5, e.g., Caodaism 299.592

---

†Add as instructed under 290

.6   **Religions originating among Black Africans and people of Black African descent**

> *For Black Muslims, see 297.87; for religions originating among peoples who speak, or whose ancestors spoke, Ethiopian languages, see 299.28; for religions originating among Cushitic and Omotic peoples, see 299.35; for religions originating among the Hausa, see 299.37; for religions originating among the Malagasy, see 299.923*

[.609 61–.609 69]   Religions in specific areas in Africa

>   Do not use; class in 299.691–299.699

.61   Specific aspects

> Add to base number 299.61 the numbers following 20 in 201–208, e.g., mythology and mythological foundations 299.6113
>
> Class specific aspects of specific religions and movements, of religions of specific groups and peoples in 299.67–299.68

.67   Specific religions and movements

> Class here doctrines; practices, rites, ceremonies; mythology and mythological foundations; and other specific aspects of specific religions and movements

.672   †Umbanda

.673   †Candomblé

.674   †Santeria

.675   †Vodou

>   Including zombiism
>
> *See also 133.4 for hoodoo*
>
> *See Manual at 130 vs. 200*

.676   †Ras Tafari movement

.68   Religions of specific groups and peoples

> Class here doctrines; practices, rites, ceremonies; mythology and mythological foundations; and other specific aspects of specific religions and movements
>
> Class specific religions and movements of specific groups and peoples in 299.67

.681   Religions of Khoikhoi and San

---

†Add as instructed under 290

.683–.685   Religions of peoples who speak, or whose ancestors spoke, Niger-Congo, Nilo-Saharan languages

> Add to base number 299.68 the numbers following —96 in notation 963–965 from Table 6, e.g., religion of the Yoruba 299.68333; then add further as follows:
> 001–009   Standard subdivisions
> 01–08   Specific aspects
> > Add to 0 the numbers following 20 in 201–208, e.g., mythology 013, Yoruba mythology 299.68333013

.686–.688   Religions of national groups in Africa

> Add to base number 299.68 the numbers following —6 in notation 66–68 from Table 2, e.g., religion of Ugandans 299.68761

> Class national groups that predominate in specific areas in Africa in 299.69

.689   Religions of other national groups of largely African descent

> Add to base number 299.689 notation 4–9 from Table 2, e.g., African religion of Haitians 299.6897294

> Class religions of such national groups in areas where they predominate in 299.609, e.g., African religion of Haitians in Haiti 299.6097294

.69   Religions of specific areas in Africa

> Add to base number 299.69 the numbers following —6 in notation 61–69 from Table 2, e.g., religions of West Africa 299.696

> Class specific aspects of religions of specific areas in 299.61; class specific religions and movements in specific areas in 299.67; class religions of specific groups and peoples in specific areas in 299.68

.7   **Religions of North American native origin**

[.709 71–.709 79]   Religions in specific areas in North America

> Do not use; class in 299.791–299.799

.71   Specific aspects

> Add to base number 299.71 the numbers following 20 in 201–208, e.g., mythology and mythological foundations 299.7113

> Class specific aspects of religions of specific groups and peoples in 299.78

.78   Religions of specific groups and peoples

> Add to base number 299.78 the numbers following —97 in notation 971–979 from Table 5, e.g., religion of Aztecs 299.78452; then add further as follows (*not* as instructed at —0):
> 001–009   Standard subdivisions
> 01–08   Specific aspects
> > Add to 0 the numbers following 20 in 201–208, e.g., mythology and mythological foundations 013, Aztec mythology 299.78452013

.79   Religions of specific areas in North America

> Add to base number 299.79 the numbers following —7 in notation 71–79 from Table 2, e.g., religions of Indians of Mexico 299.792

> Class religions of specific groups and peoples in specific areas in 299.78

.8   Religions of South American native origin

[.809 81–.809 89]   Religions of specific areas in South America

> Do not use; class in 299.891–299.899

.81   Specific aspects

> Add to base number 299.81 the numbers following 20 in 201–208, e.g., mythology and mythological foundations 299.8113

> Class specific aspects of religions of specific groups and peoples in 299.88

.88   Religions of specific groups and peoples

> Add to base number 299.88 the numbers following —98 in notation 982–989 from Table 5, e.g., religion of Incas 299.88323; then add further as follows (*not* as instructed at —0):
>   001–009   Standard subdivisions
>   01–08   Specific aspects
>   Add to 0 the numbers following 20 in 201–208, e.g., mythology and mythological foundations 013, Inca mythology 299.88323013

.89   Religions of specific areas in South America

> Add to base number 299.89 the numbers following —8 in notation 81–89 from Table 2, e.g., religions of Indians of the Amazon 299.8911

> Class religions of specific groups and peoples in specific areas in 299.88

.9   Religions of other origin

.92   Religions of other ethnic origin

> Add to base number 299.92 the numbers following —99 in notation 991–999 from Table 5, e.g., religion of Polynesians 299.924; then add further as follows (*not* as instructed at —0):
>   001–009   Standard subdivisions
>   01–08   Specific aspects
>   Add to 0 the numbers following 20 in 201–208, e.g., mythology and mythological foundations 013

.93	Religions of eclectic and syncretistic origin

Religions and applied religious philosophies of eclectic, syncretistic, universal nature

Including Eckankar, a Course in Miracles, Great White Brotherhood, New Thought, systems of Bhagwan Shree Rajneesh and Meher Baba, United Church of Religious Science, Urantia

Class here modern spiritual movements, New Age religions

Class syncretistic religious writings of individuals expressing personal views and not claiming to establish a new religion or to represent an old one in 200

See also 289.98 for Christian New Thought

See Manual at 299.93; also at 201–209 and 292–299

.932	Gnosticism

Including Manicheism

Class Christian gnosticism in 273.1; class Christian Manicheism in 273.2

.933	Subud
.934	Theosophy
.935	Anthroposophy
.936	Scientology

Including dianetics

.94	Modern paganism, neopaganism, wicca

Standard subdivisions are added for any or all topics in heading

Class here religions based on modern revivals of witchcraft

300

---

300 Social sciences

Class here behavioral sciences, social studies

Class a specific behavioral science with the science, e.g., psychology 150; class military, diplomatic, political, economic, social, welfare aspects of a war with the history of the war, e.g., Vietnamese War 959.7043

For language, see 400; for history, see 900

See Manual at 300 vs. 600; also at 300–330, 355–390 vs. 342–347, 352–354; also at 300, 320.6 vs. 352–354

SUMMARY

340	Law
.02–.09	Standard subdivisions
.1–.9	[Philosophy and theory of law, comparative law, law reform, legal systems, conflict of laws]
341	Law of nations
342	Constitutional and administrative law
343	Military, defense, public property, public finance, tax, commerce (trade), industrial law
344	Labor, social service, education, cultural law
345	Criminal law
346	Private law
347	Procedure and courts
348	Laws, regulations, cases
349	Law of specific jurisdictions, areas, socioeconomic regions, regional intergovernmental organizations
350	Public administration and military science
351	Public administration
352	General considerations of public administration
353	Specific fields of public administration
354	Public administration of economy and environment
355	Military science
356	Foot forces and warfare
357	Mounted forces and warfare
358	Air and other specialized forces and warfare; engineering and related services
359	Sea forces and warfare
360	Social problems and services; associations
361	Social problems and services
362	Social problems of and services to groups of people
363	Other social problems and services
364	Criminology
365	Penal and related institutions
366	Secret associations and societies
367	General clubs
368	Insurance
369	Associations
370	Education
.1–.9	Standard subdivisions, education for specific objectives, educational psychology
371	Schools and their activities; special education
372	Primary education (Elementary education)
373	Secondary education
374	Adult education
375	Curricula
378	Higher education (Tertiary education)
379	Public policy issues in education
380	Commerce, communications, transportation
.1–.9	Standard subdivisions
381	Commerce (Trade)
382	International commerce (Foreign trade)
383	Postal communication
384	Communications
385	Railroad transportation
386	Inland waterway and ferry transportation
387	Water, air, space transportation
388	Transportation
389	Metrology and standardization

390		**Customs, etiquette, folklore**
	.01–.09	Standard subdivisions of customs
	.1–.4	Customs of specific economic, social, occupational classes
391		**Costume and personal appearance**
392		**Customs of life cycle and domestic life**
393		**Death customs**
394		**General customs**
395		**Etiquette (Manners)**
398		**Folklore**
399		**Customs of war and diplomacy**

> **.1**   **Philosophy and theory**
>
> **.2**   **Miscellany**
>
> .21   Tabulated and related materials
>
>   Do not use for statistics; class in 310
>
> **.3–.9**   **Standard subdivisions**

301   Sociology and anthropology

Standard subdivisions are added for either or both topics in heading

Class here interdisciplinary works on society, humans

Class social problems and social welfare in 361–365

For specific topics in sociology and anthropology, see 302–307; for criminal anthropology, see 364.2; for customs, etiquette, folklore, see 390; for physical anthropology, see 599.9. For a specific aspect of society not provided for in 302–307, see the aspect, e.g., general history 900

See Manual at 301–307 vs. 361–365

[.019]   Psychological principles

             Do not use; class in 302

.7   **Nonliterate societies**

> ## 302–307   Specific topics in sociology and anthropology

Unless other instructions are given, observe the following table of preference, e.g., friendship among women 302.34082 (*not* 305.4):

Factors affecting social behavior	304
Social processes	303
Social interaction	302
Culture and institutions	306
Groups of people	305
Communities	307

Class comprehensive works in 301. Class effect of one factor on another with the factor affected, e.g., effect of climate on social change 303.4

See Manual at 301–307 vs. 361–365; also at 302–307 vs. 150, T1—019; also at 302–307 vs. 156; also at 302–307 vs. 320; also at 363 vs. 302–307, 333.7, 570–590, 600

302 Social interaction

Class here psychological principles of sociology, interpersonal relations, social psychology

Unless other instructions are given, class a subject with aspects in two or more subdivisions of 302 in the number coming last, e.g., social role in social interaction in complex groups 302.35 (*not* 302.15)

Class social psychology of a specific situation with the situation, e.g., social psychology of ethnic groups 305.8

> *See also 155.92 for effect of social environment upon individuals; also 158.2 for individual aspects of interpersonal relations*

SUMMARY

302.01–.09	**Standard subdivisions**
.1	**General topics of social interaction**
.2	**Communication**
.3	**Social interaction within groups**
.4	**Social interaction between groups**
.5	**Relation of individual to society**

.015 195   Statistical mathematics

Class here sociometry

> *See Manual at 519.5, T1—015195 vs. 001.422, T1—0727*

[.019]   Psychological principles

Do not use; class in 302

.072   Research

[.072 7]   Statistical methods

Do not use; class in 302.015195

.1   General topics of social interaction

.12   Social understanding

Including attribution, risk perception

> *For social learning, see 303.32; for perception of norms, see 303.37*

.13   Social choice

Including attraction, influence

.14   Social participation

Including communalism, competition, cooperation, encounter groups, sensitivity training, voluntarism

Class here social acceptance, social adjustment, social skills, success

> *See also 302.4 for intergroup aspects of participation*

.15 Social role (Role theory)

Including role conflict

Class social role of a specific group of people or institution with the group or institution in 305–306, e.g., social role of women 305.42

.17 Social dysfunction

Dysfunction affecting a substantial portion of society, e.g., mass hysteria, crazes

Including apathy, fear, panic

Class here social psychoanalysis

Class dysfunctional responses of individuals to society in 302.542

.2 **Communication**

Including failures and disruptions of communication

Class here interdisciplinary works on communication, content analysis, semiotics

For information theory, see 003.54; for censorship, see 303.376. For the semiotics of a specific subject, see the subject, plus notation 014 from Table 1, e.g., semiotics of biology 570.14

.22 Kinds of communication

> 302.222–302.224 Verbal and nonverbal communication

Class comprehensive works in 302.22; class comprehensive works on means of verbal and nonverbal communication in 302.23

.222 Nonverbal communication

Including drumbeats, smoke signals; body language, gestures; flower language

Class here means of nonverbal communication, interdisciplinary works on nonlinguistic communication (nonstructured communication)

Class sign languages for deaf people in 419

For iconography, see 704.9; for insignia, see 929.9

See also 302.226 for visual communication

.222 3 Symbols

Class here interdisciplinary works on symbols, on symbolism

For religious symbolism, see 203.7; for Christian religious symbols, see 246.55. For symbols in a specific subject other than religion, see the subject, plus notation 0148 from Table 1, e.g., symbols in electrical engineering 621.30148

.224 Verbal communication

> Class means of verbal communication in 302.23

> *For language, see 400*

.224 2 Oral communication

> Including listening

> *For conversation, see 302.346*

.224 4 Written communication

> Class here literacy, illiteracy

> > *See also 301.7 for nonliterate societies; also 302.226 for visual communication*

.226 Visual communication

> Including graphic design, typography

> Class means of visual communication in 302.23

> > *See also 302.222 for nonverbal communication; also 302.2244 for written communication*

.23 Media (Means of communication)

> Including signboards, signs

> Class here electronic media, mass media, sociology of journalism

> Class the effect of mass media on a specific subject other than social groups with the subject, e.g., effect on social change 303.4833, on a company's advertising policy 659.111; class interdisciplinary works on a specific medium with the medium, e.g., newspapers 070, television 384.55

> *For means of nonverbal communication, see 302.222*

.230 8 Groups of people

> Class here effect of mass media on specific groups, on social stratification

> Class portrayal of a specific group in mass media with the group in 305–306, e.g., minorities in mass media 305, scientists in mass media 306.45, gays in mass media 306.766

.231 Digital media

> Including Internet telephony

> Class here social media, user-generated content; digital audio, digital video; sociology of the Internet, sociology of the World Wide Web

> Class electronic publications in 302.232. Class digital media in a specific medium with the medium in 302.23, e.g., online newspapers 302.2322

> *For online social networks, see 302.30285*

.231 1   Electronic mail

Class here instant messaging; point-to-point communications

Class e-mail lists in 302.2312; class text messaging in 302.23445

.231 2   Discussion groups

Class here chat groups, electronic bulletin boards, e-mail lists, Internet forums, newsgroups; broadcast communications

Class electronic mail in 302.2311

.231 4   Blogs

.231 5   Wikis

.232   Print media

Class here electronic publications

.232 2   Newspapers

.232 4   Periodicals and journals

Standard subdivisions are added for either or both topics in heading

.234   Motion pictures, radio, television

Class here audiovisual media; podcasts, webcasts, streaming media

For a specific digital audiovisual medium provided for elsewhere, see the medium, e.g., blogs 302.2314

.234 3   Motion pictures

.234 4   Radio

.234 45   Radiotelephony

Including text messaging

Class here mobile telephone systems

.234 5   Television

Including videotelephony, videoconferencing, telepresence

Class here audiovisual media based on wireless communication; digital television, interactive television

.235   Telephony and telegraphy

Standard subdivisions are added for telephony and telegraphy together, for telephony alone

Class Internet telephony in 302.231; class mobile telephone systems in 302.23445

For radiotelephony, see 302.23445; for videotelephony, see 302.2345

.24   Content

Including gossip, rumor

See also 070.1 for journalistic aspect of content

.3   **Social interaction within groups**

Including teasing

Class here group decision-making processes, group dynamics, negotiation, social networks

.302 85   Computer applications

Class here online social networks

For computer science aspects of online social networks, see 006.754

.33   Social interaction in abstract and temporary groups

Including audiences, crowds, mobs

Class media audiences in 302.23

.34   Social interaction in primary groups

Groups small enough for all members to engage in face-to-face relationships at one time

Including committees, gangs

Class here friendship

Class family in 306.85

See also 362.74 for predelinquent gangs; also 364.1066 for gangs engaging in crime

.343   Bullying

Class bullying in a specific institution with the institution, e.g., bullying in school 371.58

.346   Conversation

Including conversational rhythm

.35   Social interaction in complex groups

Class here bureaucracies, hierarchically organized groups, organizational behavior, sociology of management

Class general works that emphasize how to manage in 658. Class works that emphasize how to manage in a specific field of activity with the field, plus notation 068 from Table 1, e.g., management of commercial banks 332.12068

.4   **Social interaction between groups**

Including ingroups and outgroups

Class social interaction between a specific group of people and other groups of people in 305

.5   **Relation of individual to society**

See also 155.92 for psychological effects of social environment upon the individual

.54   Response of individuals

> Including ambition

> Class here aggression, dysfunctional responses, individualism

> > *For conformity, see 303.32*

> > *See also 302.17 for mass manifestations of social dysfunction*

.542   Deviation

> Class here madness considered as a form of interaction of individuals with society

.544   Alienation

.545   Isolation

303   Social processes

> Unless other instructions are given, class a subject with aspects in two or more subdivisions of 303 in the number coming last, e.g., leadership in conflict resolution 303.69 (*not* 303.34)

> > *For social interaction, see 302; for factors affecting social behavior, see 304*

SUMMARY

303.3	**Coordination and control**
.4	**Social change**
.6	**Conflict and conflict resolution**

.3   Coordination and control

> Standard subdivisions are added for coordination and control together, for coordination alone

> Class here policy formulation, power

> Class coordination and control in and through specific institutions in 306

SUMMARY

303.32	Socialization
.33	Social control
.34	Leadership
.35	Utilitarian control
.36	Coercion
.37	Social norms
.38	Public opinion

.32   Socialization

> Including social learning

> Class here conformity

> Class interdisciplinary works on child development in 305.231

> > *For education, see 370*

.323   Socialization by family

.324   Socialization by school

.325   Socialization by religious organizations

.327   Socialization by peer group

> Class here peer pressure

.33   Social control

> *For socialization, see 303.32; for social control through specific means, see 303.34–303.38*

> 303.34–303.38 Social control through specific means

> Class socialization through specific means of control in 303.32; class comprehensive works in 303.33

.34   Leadership

.342   Persuasion

> By individuals

> Class here interdisciplinary works on persuasion

> *For a specific aspect of persuasion, see the aspect, e.g., individual psychology of persuasion 153.852, persuasion by media 302.23, persuasion by propaganda 303.375*

.35   Utilitarian control

> Use of rewards and incentives

.36   Coercion

> Including authority, punishment, restraint, threat

> *See also 364.6 for treatment and punishment of offenders*

.37   Social norms

> Including perception of norms

> *For public opinion, see 303.38*

.372   Belief systems and customs

> Standard subdivisions are added for either or both topics in heading

> Class here social ethics as a method of social control; justice, values

> Class rightness or wrongness of conduct as it affects individuals or society, interdisciplinary works on social ethics in 170

> *See also 361.61 for values in social policy toward welfare problems*

.375   Propaganda

.376   Censorship

> *See Manual at 363.31 vs. 303.376, 791.4*

.38   Public opinion

Class here attitudes, attitude formation and change

Class propaganda in 303.375. Class public opinion on a specific subject with the subject, e.g., public opinion on racial stereotypes 305.8, on the political process 324

See also 302.12 for social understanding

.380 81–.380 89   Groups of people by specific attributes; ethnic and national groups

Do not use for opinions held by groups of people with specific attributes; class in 303.386. Do not use for opinions held by ethnic and national groups; class in 303.387. Do not use for opinions held by occupational groups; class in 303.388

.385   Prejudice

Class here social stereotypes and stereotyping

Class prejudices regarding a specific group in 305

.385 081–.385 089   Groups of people by specific attributes; ethnic and national groups

Do not use for prejudices held by groups of people with specific attributes; class in 303.386. Do not use for prejudices held by ethnic and national groups; class in 303.387. Do not use for prejudices held by occupational groups; class in 303.388

.386   Opinions held by groups of people with specific attributes

Add to base number 303.386 the numbers following —08 in notation 081–088 from Table 1, e.g., opinions of young people 303.3863, opinions of Catholics 303.3868282

For opinions held by ethnic and national groups, see 303.387; for opinions held by occupational groups, see 303.388

.387   Opinions held by ethnic and national groups

Add to base number 303.387 notation 1–9 from Table 5, e.g., opinions of Canadians 303.38711

.388   Opinions held by occupational groups

Add to base number 303.388 notation 001–999, e.g., opinions of dentists 303.3886176

.4   Social change

Including evolutionary and revolutionary change

Class social change in a specific aspect of society with the aspect in 302–307, e.g., changes in religious institutions 306.6

[.401 12]   Forecasting and forecasts

Do not use; class in 303.49

.44 Growth and development

> Standard subdivisions are added for either or both topics in heading

> Class here progress, specialization

.45 Deterioration and decay

> Standard subdivisions are added for either or both topics in heading

.48 Causes of change

.482 Contact between cultures

> Class here acculturation, assimilation; social effects of international assistance, of commerce

> Class multicultural education in 370.117

.482 09 History and biography

> Do not use for geographic treatment; class in 303.4821–303.4829

.482 1–.482 9 Contact between specific areas

> Add to base number 303.482 notation 1–9 from Table 2, e.g., cultural exchanges with China 303.48251; then add 0* and again add notation 1–9 from Table 2, e.g., cultural exchange between China and Japan 303.48251052

> Give priority in notation to the nation most affected. If this cannot be determined, give priority to the one coming first in Table 2
> (Option: Give priority to the area requiring local emphasis, e.g., in United States class cultural exchange between United States and France in 303.48273044)

.483 Development of science and technology

> Class government policy on science in 338.926

> *See Manual at 303.483 vs. 306.45, 306.46*

.483 2 Transportation

.483 3 Communication

> Class here information technology

> Class government policy on information in 338.926

.483 4 Computers

> Class here automation, microelectronics, robots

*Add 00 for standard subdivisions; see instructions at beginning of Table 1

.484   Purposefully induced change

                  Including dissent, radicalism

                  Class here social innovation, social reform, social reform movements

                  Class political aspects of reform movements in 322.44; class role of reform movements in addressing social problems in 361–365. Class innovation and reform directed to a specific end with the end, e.g., reform of banking 332.1

.485   Disasters

                  Including earthquakes, pandemics, wars

.49   Social forecasts

                  Class here futurology, social forecasting

                  Class interdisciplinary works on forecasting in 003.2. Class forecasting in and forecasts of a specific subject with the subject, plus notation 0112 from Table 1, e.g., future of U.S. Democratic Party 324.27360112

.490 9   History and biography

                  Do not use for geographic treatment; class in 303.491–303.499

.491–.499   Forecasts for specific areas

                  Add to base number 303.49 notation 1–9 from Table 2, e.g., Eastern Europe in the year 2010 303.4947

.6   **Conflict and conflict resolution**

                  Class a specific form of conflict provided elsewhere in 302–306 with the form, e.g., bullying 302.343, racial conflict 305.8, spouse abuse 306.872; class a specific conflict considered an historical event with the event in 900, e.g., disturbances of May-June 1968 in France 944.0836

.61   Civil disobedience

                  Including hunger strikes, passive resistance, sit-ins

                  Class here nonviolence

.62   Civil disorder

                  For civil war and revolution, see 303.64

.623   Riots

.625   Terrorism

                  Class interdisciplinary works on terrorism in 363.325

.64   Civil war and revolution

                  Standard subdivisions are added for either or both topics in heading

                  Class terrorism in 303.625

.66 War and peace

Including pacifism, sociology of war

Class war as a cause of social change in 303.485; class prevention of war in 327.172; class causes of war in 355.027; class the art and science of warfare in 355–359. Class military, diplomatic, political, economic, social, welfare aspects of a specific war with the history of the war, e.g., of World War II 940.53

For civil war, see 303.64

.69 Conflict resolution

Including mediation

Class here conflict management

Class resolution of a specific kind of conflict with the kind of conflict, e.g., resolution of war 303.66

304 Factors affecting social behavior

Unless other instructions are given, class a subject with aspects in two or more subdivisions of 304 in the number coming last, e.g., interaction of environmental abuse and movement of people 304.8 (*not* 304.28)

.2 Human ecology

Class here ecological anthropology, human geography; interdisciplinary works on sustainability

For sustainable technology, see 628. For a specific social aspect of sustainability not provided for here, see the aspect in 300, without use of notation 0286 from Table 1, e.g., works on sustainability that emphasize conservation and protection of natural resources 333.72, economic aspects of sustainable development 338.927

See Manual at 578 vs. 304.2, 508, 910

.208 2 Women

Class here ecofeminism

.23 Geographic, space, time factors

Including territoriality

.237 Time factors

Class aspects of time in relation to a specific subject with the subject in 302–307, e.g., time and conversation 302.346, leisure activities 306.4812

See also 650.11 for time management

.25 Climatic and weather factors

.27 Biological factors

Other than human

For genetic factors, see 304.5

.28   Environmental abuse

Including greenhouse effect

Class here social consequences of pollution, of misuse of resources

Class interdisciplinary works on sustainability in 304.2; class interdisciplinary works on natural resources in 333.7; class interdisciplinary works on pollution in 363.73

See Manual at 333.72 vs. 304.28, 320.58, 363.7

.5   **Genetic factors**

Class here sociobiology (biosociology), study of genetic bases of human social behavior

Class a specific aspect of sociobiology with the aspect in 302–307, e.g., sociobiology of conflict 303.6

For sociobiology of plants and animals, see 577.8

See also 304.27 for biological factors

.6   **Population**

Class here demographic anthropology, demography; population composition, geography, size; comprehensive works on population

For movement of people, see 304.8

.61   Population characteristics

Including density

.62   Growth and decline

See also 304.63 for births; also 304.64 for deaths; also 304.8 for movement of people

.63   Births

Including birth intervals, family size

Class here comprehensive works on births and deaths

For deaths, see 304.64

See also 304.62 for growth and decline of population

.632   Fertility

.64   Deaths (Mortality)

.645   Life expectancy

.645 09   History and biography

Do not use for geographic treatment; class in 304.6451–304.6459

.645 1–.645 9   Geographic treatment

Add to base number 304.645 notation 1–9 from Table 2, e.g., life expectancy in Canada 304.64571

.66 Demographic effects of population control efforts

> Class population policy, comprehensive works on population control in 363.9

.663 Genocide

> Class here ethnic cleansing

.666 Family planning

> Class here birth control

>> *See also 363.96 for family planning programs; also 613.94 for birth control techniques*

.667 Abortion

.668 Infanticide

.8 **Movement of people**

> *For movement to, from, within communities, see 307.2*

.809 History, geographic treatment, biography

> Class here internal movement, emigration from specific areas

> *For emigration to specific areas, see 304.83–304.89*

.81 Causes

.82 International movement

> Class international emigration in 304.809; class international immigration in 304.83–304.89

> *See also 325 for political aspects of international movement*

.83–.89 Migration

> Add to base number 304.8 notation 3–9 from Table 2, e.g., migration to Australia 304.894; then add 0* and to the result add notation 1–9 from Table 2 for the place of origin, e.g., migration from United States to Australia 304.894073

---

*Add 00 for standard subdivisions; see instructions at beginning of Table 1

305 Groups of people

Class here minorities; culture and institutions of specific groups; subcultures of specific groups; consciousness-raising groups; problems, role, social status of specific groups; portrayal of a specific group in mass media; group identity, social identity; discrimination; social stratification, equality, inequality; interactions between a specific group and other groups

Unless other instructions are given, observe the following table of preference, e.g., African American male youths 305.235108996073 (*not* 305.3889607300835 or 305.896073008351):

People with disabilities and illnesses, gifted people	305.908
Age groups	305.2
People by gender or sex	305.3–305.4
People by social and economic levels	305.5
Religious groups	305.6
Ethnic and national groups	305.8
Language groups	305.7
People by occupation and miscellaneous social statuses (*except* 305.908)	305.9

Class effect of mass media on specific groups, on social stratification in 302.2308; class opinions of specific groups in 303.38; class interactions, problems, role, social status of specific groups, discrimination against and conflict involving specific groups in 305.2–305.9; class specific problems of, welfare services to groups of people in 362. Class role of a specific group in a specific institution with the institution, e.g., father-child relationship 306.8742, women in education 370.82; class people by sexual orientation with the sexual orientation in 306.76, e.g., middle-aged gay men 306.76620844; class people by kinship or marital status with the kinship or marital status in 306.8, e.g., African American mothers 306.874308996073; class a specific aspect of discrimination with the aspect, plus notation 08 from Table 1, e.g., sex discrimination against women in sports 796.082

See also 920.008 for general collections of biography of members of a specific group

See Manual at 306 vs. 305, 909, 930–990; also at 920.008 vs. 305–306, 362

SUMMARY

305.2	**Age groups**
.3	**People by gender or sex**
.4	**Women**
.5	**People by social and economic levels**
.6	**Religious groups**
.7	**Language groups**
.8	**Ethnic and national groups**
.9	**People by occupation and miscellaneous social statuses; people with disabilities and illnesses, gifted people**

[.08]   Specific groups of people

      Do not use; class in 305.2–305.9

[.085]   Relatives

      Do not use; class in 306.87

.2   **Age groups**

Class here comprehensive works on generation gap

For generation gap within families, see 306.874

SUMMARY

305.23	**Young people**
.24	**Adults**
.26	**People in late adulthood**

[.208 1–.208 4]   People by gender or sex; specific age groups

Do not use; class in 305.23–305.26

.23   **Young people**

Through age twenty

Class here interdisciplinary works on children

For a specific aspect of children, see the aspect, e.g., social welfare of children 362.7

.230 811   Boys

.230 82   Girls

[.230 83–.230 84]   Age groups

Do not use for young people in general; class in 305.23. Do not use for specific age groups; class in 305.232–305.235

.230 86   Children by miscellaneous social attributes

.230 869 23   Predelinquent children

Do not use for juvenile delinquents; class in 364.36

Class here runaway children

.231   **Child development**

Class here interdisciplinary works on child development

Class socialization in 303.32

For psychological development of children, see 155.4; for physical development of children, see 612.65

.232   **Infants**

Children from birth through age two

.233   **Children three to five**

Class here preschool children

.234   **Children six to eleven**

Class here preteens, school children

For school children over eleven, see 305.235

.235	Young people twelve to twenty

Variant names: adolescents, teenagers, young adults, youth

Class young people twenty-one and over in 305.242

[.235 081 1]	Men

Do not use; class in 305.2351

[.235 082]	Women

Do not use; class in 305.2352

[.235 083–.235 084]	Age groups

Do not use; class in 305.235

.235 1	Males
.235 2	Females
.235 5	Development

Class here interdisciplinary works on development of young people twelve to twenty

For psychological development, see 155.5; for physical development, see 612.661

.24	Adults

Class here adulthood

Class adult men in 305.31; class adult women in 305.4

For late adulthood, see 305.26

.242	People in early adulthood

Class here comprehensive works on young adults

For young adults under twenty-one, see 305.235

[.242 081 1]	Men

Do not use; class in 305.2421

[.242 082]	Women

Do not use; class in 305.2422

[.242 083–.242 084]	Age groups

Do not use; class in 305.242

.242 1	Young men
.242 2	Young women
.244	People in middle adulthood

Class here middle age

[.244 081 1]	Men

Do not use; class in 305.2441

[.244 082]	Women

Do not use; class in 305.2442

[.244 083–.244 084]	Age groups

Do not use; class in 305.244

.244 1   Middle-aged men

.244 2   Middle-aged women

.26   People in late adulthood

Class sociology of retirement in 306.38

See also 646.79 for guides to retirement

[.260 811]	Men

Do not use; class in 305.261

[.260 82]	Women

Do not use; class in 305.262

[.260 83–.260 84]	Age groups

Do not use; class in 305.26

.261   Older men

.262   Older women

.3   **People by gender or sex**

Standard subdivisions are added for either or both topics in heading

Class here interdisciplinary works on men and women, gender identity, gender role, sex role, the sexes

Class sex psychology, psychology of people by gender or sex, by sexual orientation in 155.3; class sexual division of labor in 306.3615; class the relations between the sexes and within the sexes in 306.7–306.8. Class the relation of a specific gender or sex to a specific subject with the subject, plus notation 081–082 from Table 1, e.g., women in U.S. history 973.082

For young and middle-aged men and women, see 305.24; for men and women in late adulthood, see 305.26; for women, see 305.4; for transgender and intersex people, see 306.768. For a specific aspect of gender identity, gender role, or sex role, see the aspect, e.g., psychology of gender identity 155.33

.31   Men

Class here interdisciplinary works on men, on males

For specific aspects of sociology of men, see 305.32–305.38. For a specific aspect of men not provided for in 305.3, see the aspect, e.g., men's clothing 391.1

[.310 8]	Groups of people

Do not use; class in 305.33–305.38

.310 9	History, geographic treatment, biography
.310 92	Biography

> *See also 920.71 for general biography of men*
>
> *See Manual at 920.008 vs. 305–306, 362*

.32–.38	Specific aspects of sociology of men

Add to base number 305.3 the numbers following 305.4 in 305.42–305.48, e.g., African American men 305.38896073; however, for engaged men, see 306.7340811; for men by sexual orientation, see 306.76; for gay men, see 306.7662; for single men, see 306.8152; for men by kinship characteristics, see 306.87; for married men, see 306.8722; for widowers, see 306.882; for separated and divorced men, see 306.892

Class comprehensive works in 305.31

.4   Women

Class here interdisciplinary works on women, on females

> *For a specific aspect of women not provided for here, see the aspect, e.g., women's suffrage 324.623*

[.408]	Groups of people

Do not use; class in 305.43–305.48

.409	History, geographic treatment, biography
.409 2	Biography

> *See also 920.72 for general biography of women*
>
> *See Manual at 920.008 vs. 305–306, 362*

.42	Social role and status of women

Standard subdivisions are added for either or both topics in heading

Class here discrimination against women, feminism, women's movements

> *For ecofeminism, see 304.2082*

Class social role and status of specific groups of women with the group in 305.43–305.48, e.g., role of housewives 305.4364 (*not* 305.4208864)

.43	Women by occupation

Add to base number 305.43 notation 001–999, e.g., women physicians 305.43610695

> *See also 331.4 for economic aspects of women by occupation*

.48   Specific groups of women

Class women by occupation in 305.43; class women with disabilities and illnesses, gifted women in 305.908

For engaged women, see 306.734082; for women by sexual orientation, see 306.76; for lesbians, see 306.7663; for single women, see 306.8153; for women by kinship characteristics, see 306.87; for married women, see 306.8723; for unmarried mothers, see 306.87432; for widows, see 306.883; for separated and divorced women, see 306.893

[.480 1–.480 9]   Standard subdivisions

Do not use; class in 305.401–305.409

.482   Women by social and economic levels

Class here women by level of cultural development

Add to base number 305.482 the numbers following —0862 in notation 08621–08625 from Table 1, e.g., working class women 305.4823

.484   Women by miscellaneous social statuses

Add to base number 305.484 the numbers following —0869 in notation 08691–08697 from Table 1, e.g., homeless women 305.48442; however, for women offenders, see 364.374; for women inmates of penal institutions, see 365.6082

.486–.488   Women by specific religious, language, ethnic, national groups

Add to base number 305.48 the numbers following 305 in 305.6–305.8, e.g., Muslim women 305.48697

.5   People by social and economic levels

Class here class struggle, people by level of cultural development, social classes

Unless other instructions are given, class a subject with aspects in two or more subdivisions of 305.5 in the number coming last, e.g., social mobility of people in working class 305.562 (*not* 305.513)

For theory of class struggle in Marxism, see 335.411

See Manual at 305.9 vs. 305.5

.51   General principles of social classes

.512   Principles of stratification

.512 2   Caste systems

.513   Social mobility

.52   Upper class

Class here aristocracy, elites

Class intellectual elites in 305.552

.522   Upper class by birth

Class here nobility, royalty

.523   Upper class by economic status

.523 2	Landowners with large estates and landed gentry
.523 4	Rich people

For landowners with large estates, see 305.5232

.524	Upper class by political status

Including cabinet ministers, commissars, judges, legislative representatives

.55	Middle class (Bourgeoisie)

Class here moderately well-to-do, white collar workers

Class working class in 305.562

.552	Intelligentsia

Class here intellectual elites

.553	Professional classes
.554	Managerial and entrepreneurial classes

Standard subdivisions are added for either or both topics in heading

.56	Lower, alienated, excluded classes

Class here people with cultural and social disadvantages, interdisciplinary works on nondominant groups

For a specific nondominant group, see the group, e.g., nondominant ethnic groups 305.8

.562	Working class

Variant names: laboring class, proletariat

Including migrant workers

Class here blue collar workers

Class agricultural laborers in 305.563; class slaves in 306.362

.563	Agricultural lower classes

Including agricultural laborers, migrant agricultural workers

For agricultural workers, see 305.963; for serfs, sharecroppers, see 306.365

.563 3	Peasants
.568	Alienated and excluded classes

For hoboes, tramps, vagrants, see 305.569

.568 8	Dalits

Variant names: scheduled castes, untouchables

.569	Poor people

Including hoboes, tramps, vagrants

.569 2	Homeless people

.6 **Religious groups**

Add to base number 305.6 the numbers following 2 in 230–299, e.g., Christians 305.67, Christians in Indonesia 305.67598, Christian Scientists 305.6895, Christian Scientists in France 305.689544, Orthodox Jews 305.696832

See Manual at 305.6 vs. 305.92, 306.6

.696 Jews as a religious group

Number built according to instructions under 305.6

Class comprehensive works on Jews in 305.8924

.7 **Language groups**

Add to base number 305.7 notation 1–9 from Table 6, e.g., English-speaking people 305.721; then add 0* and to the result add notation 1–9 from Table 2, e.g., English-speaking people of South Africa 305.721068

.8 **Ethnic and national groups**

Class here indigenous ethnic and national groups; ethnic and national groups associated with a specific language; ethnology, cultural ethnology, ethnography; race relations; racial groups, racism; treatment of biculturalism and multiculturalism in which difference in language is not a central element

Class physical ethnology in 599.97; class biculturalism and multiculturalism among residents in an area of divergent cultural traditions centered upon different languages in 306.446

See also 909.04 for the comprehensive history of specific ethnic and national groups; also 920.0092 for general collections of biography of members of a specific ethnic or national group

See Manual at 920.008 vs. 305–306, 362

.800 1–.800 9 Standard subdivisions

.805–.809 Ethnic and national groups with ethnic origins from more than one continent, of European descent

Add to base number 305.80 the numbers following —0 in notation 05–09 from Table 5, e.g., ethnic national groups of European descent 305.809

.81–.89 Specific ethnic and national groups

Add to base number 305.8 notation 1–9 from Table 5, e.g., comprehensive works on Jews 305.8924, Chinese 305.8951, Chinese Australians 305.8951094, Inuit 305.89712

For Jews as a religious group, see 305.696

*Add 00 for standard subdivisions; see instructions at beginning of Table 1

.9   People by occupation and miscellaneous social statuses; people with disabilities and illnesses, gifted people

> Standard subdivisions are added for all topics in heading together, for people by occupation alone
>
> Unless other instructions are given, class a subject with aspects in two or more subdivisions of 305.9 in the number coming last, e.g., unemployed librarians 305.9092 (*not* 305.90694)
>
> Class here occupational mobility
>
> Class men by occupation in 305.33; class women by occupation in 305.43; class comprehensive works on nonagricultural occupations in 306.368
>
> *See Manual at 305.9 vs. 305.5*

.900 1–.900 9   Standard subdivisions

.906   People by miscellaneous social statuses

> *For victims of crime, see 362.88*

.906 9   People with status defined by changes in residence; antisocial, asocial, unemployed people; victims of war; veterans

.906 91   People with status defined by changes in residence

> Class here aliens, expatriates, foreigners
>
> Class runaway children in 305.23086923; class migrant workers in 305.562; class tramps in 305.569; class people of a specific ethnic or national group in 305.8

.906 912   Immigrants

> Class displaced persons, refugees in 305.906914

.906 914   Displaced persons

> Class here exiles, refugees, stateless persons
>
> > *For a specific aspect of displaced persons or refugees, see the aspect, e.g., political aspects of refugees 325.21*

.906 918   Nomads

.906 92   Antisocial and asocial people

> *For offenders, see 364.3; for inmates of penal institutions, see 365.6*

.906 94   Unemployed people

.906 95   Victims of war

.906 97   Veterans of military service

.908   People with disabilities and illnesses, gifted people

> Add to base number 305.908 the numbers following —087 in notation 0871–0879 from Table 1, e.g., blind people 305.9081, deaf people 305.9082, gifted people 305.9089
>
> Class here people with physical disabilities

.909   Generalists

> Add to base number 305.909 the numbers following 0 in 001–099, e.g.,
> computer programmers 305.909051, librarians 305.9092

.91–.99   People by occupation other than generalists

> Add to base number 305.9 notation 100–999, e.g., religious occupations
> 305.92, postal workers 305.9383, farmers 305.963, office workers
> 305.96513

> *See Manual at 305.6 vs. 305.92, 306.6*

306   Culture and institutions

Culture: the aggregate of a society's beliefs, folkways, mores, science, technology, values, arts

Institutions: patterns of behavior in social relationships

Including the roles, functions, and patterns within which the groups and members of a society conduct their lives

Class here mass culture (popular culture), cultural and social anthropology

Unless other instructions are given, class a subject with aspects in two or more subdivisions of 306 in the number coming last, e.g., interaction of systems of labor and the family 306.85 (*not* 306.36)

Class cultural exchange in 303.482; class physical anthropology in 599.9; class history of a specific ethnic group in 900

> *For customs and folklore, see 390. For government policy on a specific aspect of culture, see the aspect, e.g., government policy on the arts 700*

> *See Manual at 306 vs. 305, 909, 930–990; also at 920.008 vs. 305–306, 362*

SUMMARY

306.1	**Subcultures**
.2	**Political institutions**
.3	**Economic institutions**
.4	**Specific aspects of culture**
.6	**Religious institutions**
.7	**Sexual relations**
.8	**Marriage, partnerships, unions; family**
.9	**Institutions pertaining to death**

[.08]   Groups of people

> Do not use for culture and institutions of a specific group not provided for here; class in 305

[.085]   Relatives

> Do not use; class in 306.87

.1   **Subcultures**

Including counterculture, drug culture

Class subcultures of specific groups in 305; class drug usage considered as a social problem in 362.29

>   **306.2–306.6 Cultural institutions**

Except for modifications shown under specific entries, add to each subdivision identified by * as follows:

01–07	Standard subdivisions
[08]	Groups of people
	Do not use; class in the specific subject, plus notation 08 from Table 1, e.g., women in education 370.82, women in sports 796.082
09	History, geographic treatment, biography

Class comprehensive works in 306

See Manual at T1—08 and 306.2–306.6

.2   ***Political institutions**

Institutions maintaining internal and external peace

Class here political sociology; comprehensive works on patronage, on client relationships

Class political science in 320; class law in 340; class public administration and military science in 350

For patronage and client relationships in a specific institution, see the institution, e.g., in systems of production 306.34, in art 306.47

See Manual at 320 vs. 306.2

>   306.23–306.25 Governmental institutions

Class comprehensive works in 306.2

.23   *Legislative institutions

.24   *Executive institutions

Class military institutions in 306.27; class police in 306.28

.25   *Judicial institutions

.26   *Political parties

.27   *Military institutions

Class here military sociology

See also 355 for military science

.28   *Police institutions

See also 363.2 for police services

*Add as instructed under 306.2–306.6

.3 ***Economic institutions**

> Social arrangements for production, distribution
>
> Class here economic anthropology; economic sociology; sociology of economic development, of consumption
>
> Class specific occupational groups in 305.909–305.99
>
> > *For economic institutions relating to housing, see 307.336*
> >
> > *See also 305.5 for social classes; also 330 for economics*

.32 ***Property systems**

> Including kinds of land tenure
>
> > *For agricultural land tenure systems, see 306.349*

.34 ***Systems of production and exchange**

> Standard subdivisions are added for either or both topics in heading
>
> Including cooperation, syndicalism
>
> Class here sociology of industrial conflict and relations
>
> > *See also 302.35 for organizational behavior; also 303.482 for commerce (trade) as agent of social change*

.342 ***Capitalism (Free enterprise)**

> > *See also 330.122 for economic aspects*

.345 ***Socialism**

> Class interdisciplinary works on socialism in 335
>
> > *See Manual at 335 vs. 306.345, 320.53*

.349 ***Agricultural systems**

> Including plantation as a system of production
>
> Class here agricultural sociology, land tenure systems
>
> > *For agricultural production systems not involving ownership of land, see 306.364*

.36 ***Systems of labor**

> Including free labor systems
>
> Class here industrial sociology, sociology of work
>
> Class sociology of industrial conflict and relations in 306.34; class economic aspects of work in 331

.361 ***General aspects of systems of labor**

> Including absenteeism, quality of work life, unemployment

---

*Add as instructed under 306.2–306.6

.361 3	Work ethic

See also 174 for philosophical aspects of ethics of work

.361 5	Sexual division of labor
.362	Slavery

Class here slaves, interdisciplinary works on slave trade

For a specific aspect of the slave trade, see the aspect, e.g., economic aspects of slave trade 381.44

.363	*Contract and indentured labor

Standard subdivisions are added for either or both topics in heading

.364	*Agricultural systems of labor

Class here systems of agricultural production not involving ownership of land, e.g., fishing, hunting, gathering systems

Class agricultural slavery in 306.362; class contract and indentured labor in agriculture in 306.363

For agricultural occupations in general, see 305.963; for agricultural shared return systems, see 306.365

.365	Agricultural shared return systems

Class here serfdom, serfs; sharecropping, sharecroppers

.368	*Nonagricultural occupations

Class here division of labor

Class social groups defined by occupation in 305.9

For sexual division of labor, see 306.3615

.38	Retirement

Class here retired people

See also 646.79 for guides to retirement

.4	**Specific aspects of culture**

Not provided for elsewhere

Including magic and witchcraft, symbols

.42	*Sociology of knowledge

Class here sociology of intellectual life, of information

Class specific instances of sociology of knowledge in 306.43–306.48

.43	*Education

Class here educational anthropology

See also 370.115 for education for social responsibility

---

*Add as instructed under 306.2–306.6

.432   School and society

Including interdisciplinary works on relations of teachers and society, on relations of colleges and universities with society

For community-school relations in education, see 371.19; for community-school relations in higher education, see 378.103

.44   Language

Including pragmatics

Class here anthropological linguistics, ethnolinguistics, sociolinguistics; endangered languages; responses to endangerment of languages, e.g., language documentation, language revitalization

Class interdisciplinary works on pragmatics in 401.45. Class effects of language endangerment on specific linguistic elements with the linguistic element, e.g., effects of language endangerment on morphology 415.9; class documentation of a specific language or language family with the language or language family, e.g., a grammar of Koroshi (a dialect of Baluchi) 491.598

See Manual at 401.43 vs. 306.44, 401.45, 401.9, 412, 415

.442   Anthropological linguistics, ethnolinguistics, sociolinguistics of a specific language

Add to base number 306.442 notation 2–9 from Table 6, e.g., sociolinguistics of French 306.44241; then add 0* and to the result add notation 1–9 from Table 2, e.g., sociolinguistics of French in Quebec 306.442410714
Subdivisions are added for any or all topics in heading

.446   Bilingualism and multilingualism

Standard subdivisions are added for either or both topics in heading

Class here biculturalism and multiculturalism among residents in an area of divergent cultural traditions centered upon different languages

Class treatment of biculturalism and multiculturalism in which difference in language is not a central element in 305.8; class treatment of bilingualism and multilingualism in context of language planning and policy formulation in 306.449

See also 404.2 for linguistic aspects of bilingualism

.449   Language planning and policy

Standard subdivisions are added for either or both topics in heading

Class here development of policies on language to solve communication problems of a community that uses more than one language

[.449 094–.449 099]   Specific continents, countries, localities in modern world

Do not use; class in 306.4494–306.4499

---

*Add 00 for standard subdivisions; see instructions at beginning of Table 1

.449 4–.449 9	Specific continents, countries, localities in modern world

Add to base number 306.449 notation 4–9 from Table 2, e.g., language policy of India 306.44954
> Subdivisions are added for language planning, language policy, or both

.45	*Science

Class here works contrasting scientific and humanistic cultures

See Manual at 303.483 vs. 306.45, 306.46

.46	*Technology

Class here material culture

See Manual at 303.483 vs. 306.45, 306.46

.461	*Medicine and health

Standard subdivisions are added for either or both topics in heading

Class here sociology of illness

Class social aspects of medical welfare problems and services in 362.1042

.461 3	*Personal health

Including body image, body shape, eating, physical fitness

.47	*Art

Including arts and crafts

.48	*Recreation and performing arts

Standard subdivisions are added for recreation and performing arts together, for recreation alone

For motion pictures, radio, television, see 302.234

.481	*General topics of recreation

Including play, pleasure, wit and humor

.481 2	*Leisure

Class here free time

.481 25	*Vacations (Holidays)
.481 9	*Travel and tourism

Standard subdivisions are added for either or both topics in heading

.482	*Gambling

Class here interdisciplinary works on gambling

For compulsive gambling, see 362.27; for gambling as a crime, see 364.172; for gambling as recreation, see 795

---

*Add as instructed under 306.2–306.6

.483	*Sports

Class gambling on athletic events in 306.482

.484	*Music, dance, theater

Class here performing arts

For motion pictures, radio, television, see 302.234

.484 2	Music
[.484 208]	Groups of people

Do not use; class in 780.8

.484 22–.484 29	Traditions of music

Add to base number 306.4842 the numbers following 781.6 in 781.62–781.69, e.g., jazz 306.48425; however, do not add notation 08 from Table 1 for groups of people; class in 781.62–781.69, plus notation 08 from Table 1, e.g., women and jazz 781.65082

.484 6	*Dance
.484 8	*Theater
.487	*Games and hobbies

Class gambling on games in 306.482; class sports in 306.483

.488	*Reading
.6	**Religious institutions**

Religious institutions considered from a secular, nonreligious viewpoint

Class here sociology of religion

See also 201.7 for social theology; also 261 for Christian social theology

See Manual at 305.6 vs. 305.92, 306.6

[.608]	Groups of people

Do not use; class in 200.8

.63–.69	Institutions of specific religions

Add to base number 306.6 the numbers following 2 in 230–290, e.g., comprehensive works on Christian institutions 306.63, Sunday school as a social institution 306.668, synagogue as a social institution 306.69665; however, do not add notation 08 from Table 1 for groups of people; class in 230–290, plus notation 08 from Table 1, e.g., women and Christianity 270.082

*Add as instructed under 306.2–306.6

.7   **Sexual relations**

Class here interdisciplinary works on relations between the sexes, sex, sexual love

For sexual ethics, see 176; for sex offenses, see 364.153; for customs pertaining to relations between the sexes, see 392.6; for sexual hygiene, see 613.95; for sexual techniques, see 613.96

.73   General institutions

Class here dating behavior

For marriage, see 306.81

See also 646.77 for practical guidance on dating behavior

.732   Celibacy

.733   Premarital sexual relations

Class premarital sexual relations as a crime in 364.153

.734   Courtship and engagement

Class here engaged people

See also 392.4 for customs of courtship

.736   Extramarital relations

Including lovers, mistresses, paramours

Class extramarital relations as a crime in 364.153

.74   Prostitution

Class here prostitutes

See also 331.76130674 for prostitution as an occupation; also 364.1534 for prostitution as a crime

.740 811   Men

Do not use for prostitution by males; class in 306.743

.740 82   Women

Do not use for prostitution by females; class in 306.742

.740 83   Young people

Do not use for prostitution by children; class in 306.745

.742   Prostitution by females

Class child prostitution in 306.745

.743   Prostitution by males

Class child prostitution in 306.745

.745   Prostitution by children

.76   Sexual orientation, transgender identity, intersexuality

Standard subdivisions are added for sexual orientation, transgender identity, intersexuality together; for sexual orientation and transgender identity together; for sexual orientation alone

Including asexuality, asexuals

Class here people by sexual orientation; interdisciplinary works on LGBT identity (Lesbian Gay Bisexual Transgender identity)

Class practices associated with specific orientations in 306.77

For medical aspects of LGBT identity, see 616.8583

.764   Heterosexuality

Class here heterosexuals

.765   Bisexuality

Class here bisexuals

.766   Homosexuality

Class here gay liberation movement, gays, homophobia

.766 2   Male homosexuality

Class here gay men

.766 3   Lesbianism

Class here lesbians

.768   Transgender identity and intersexuality

Standard subdivisions are added for transgender identity and intersexuality together, for transgender identity alone

Including female-to-male transgender people, male-to-female transgender people

Class here gender nonconformity, transsexuality; gender nonconforming people, transgender people, transsexuals

.768 5   Intersexuality

Class here intersex people

.77   Sexual and related practices

Standard subdivisions are added for sexual and related practices together, for sexual practices alone

Including sodomy

For sexual practices viewed as medical disorders, see 616.8583

See also 364.153 for sex crimes

.771   Pornography

Class pornography as a crime in 364.174

.772   Masturbation

.773	Group sex
.774	Oral sex
.775	Sadism

Class here sadomasochism

For masochism, see 306.776

.776	Masochism
.777	Fetishism
.778	Transvestism

Class here cross dressing

Class female impersonation, male impersonation in 792.028

.8   Marriage, partnerships, unions; family

See also 362.8286 for premarital and marriage counseling

.81   Marriage and marital status

Standard subdivisions are added for either or both topics in heading

Including remarriage

Class here people by marital status; interdisciplinary works on marriage, on marital status

Class patterns of mate selection in 306.82; class married people in 306.872; class alteration of marriage arrangements in 306.88

> *For types of marriage, see 306.84; for divorce, dissolution, annulment, separation, see 306.89. For other aspects of marriage and marital status, see the aspect, e.g., ethics of marriage, divorce, separation 173*

.810 89   Ethnic and national groups

Do not use for interethnic marriages, partnerships, unions; interracial marriages, partnerships, unions; marriages, partnerships, unions between citizens of different countries; class in 306.845

.815   Single marital status

Class here single people; people who have never been married; comprehensive works on single, divorced and widowed marital status

Class single parents in 306.856

For widowed people, see 306.88

[.815 081 1]   Men

Do not use; class in 306.8152

[.815 082]   Women

Do not use; class in 306.8153

.815 2	Single men

Class single fathers in 306.87422

.815 3	Single women

Class single mothers in 306.87432

.82	Patterns in mate selection

Including endogamy, exogamy

Class courtship in 306.734

> *See also 392.4 for the customs of mate selection; also 646.77 for practical guidance on choosing a mate and dating behavior*

.83	Types of kinship systems

Including matrilineal, patrilineal, totemic systems

.84	Specific types of marriages, partnerships, unions

Unless other instructions are given, observe the following table of preference, e.g., same-sex interreligious marriage 306.848 (*not* 306.843):

Same-sex marriages, partnerships, unions	306.848
Interethnic marriages, partnerships, unions	306.845
Interreligious marriages, partnerships, unions	306.843
Marriages, partnerships, unions by number of spouses	306.842
Temporary marriages, partnerships, unions	306.847
Partnerships and unions; common-law marriages	306.841

Class comprehensive works on marriage in 306.81

.841	Partnerships and unions; common-law marriages

Standard subdivisions are added for any or all topics in heading

Class here civil unions, domestic partnerships, registered partnerships; de facto relationships; unmarried couples living together (cohabitation); interdisciplinary works on partnerships and unions

> *For a specific kind of partnership or union, see the kind, e.g., interethnic partnerships or unions 306.845; for a specific aspect of partnerships and unions, see the aspect, e.g., ethics of partnerships and unions 173*

.842	Marriages, partnerships, unions by number of spouses

Limited to works that emphasize number of spouses

Class comprehensive works on marriage that do not emphasize number of spouses in 306.81

.842 2	Monogamous marriages, partnerships, unions
.842 3	Polygamous marriages, partnerships, unions

Including ménage à trois

Class here polyandry, polygyny; polygamists

.843   Interreligious marriages, partnerships, unions

> Marriages, partnerships, unions in which the partners belong to different religions or different branches of same religion

.845   Interethnic marriages, partnerships, unions

> Class here intercultural marriages, partnerships, unions; interracial marriages, partnerships, unions; marriages, partnerships, unions between citizens of different countries

.847   Temporary marriages, partnerships, unions

.848   Same-sex marriages, partnerships, unions

.85   Family

> Class here interdisciplinary works on family

> *For kinship systems, see 306.83; for intrafamily relationships, see 306.87; for stepfamilies, see 306.8747; for alteration of family arrangements, see 306.88. For a specific aspect of family, see the aspect, e.g., achieving harmonious family relations 646.78*

> *See also 155.924 for psychological influence of family on individual members*

.852   Rural family

> *See also 307.72 for rural sociology*

.854   Urban family

> *See also 307.76 for urban sociology*

.855   Nuclear family

> Class the single-parent family in 306.856

.856   Single-parent family

> Class here divorced families with single-parent custody, unmarried parents, unmarried parenthood

> *For single fatherhood, see 306.87422; for single motherhood, see 306.87432*

.857   Extended family

> Class kinship systems in extended family in 306.83

.858   Patriarchal family

.859   Matriarchal family

.87 Intrafamily relationships

Including abuse within family; birth order; childlessness; collateral relationships between aunts/uncles and nieces/nephews; collateral relationships between cousins; dysfunctional relationships; in-law relationships

Class incest in 306.877. Class abuse in a specific family relationship with the relationship, e.g., spouse abuse 306.872

For alteration of family arrangements, see 306.88

See also 362.82 for social services to families; also 646.78 for practical guides to harmonious family relationships

.872 Spousal relationship

Including dual-career families

Class here husband-wife relationship, married people

Class sexual practices in 306.77

For polygamists, see 306.8423

See also 613.96 for sexual techniques

.872 081 1 Men

Do not use for husbands; class in 306.8722

.872 082 Women

Do not use for wives; class in 306.8723

.872 2 Husbands

.872 3 Wives

.874 Parent-child relationship

Including adopted children, children of unmarried parents, only child

Class here generation gap within families

Class comprehensive works on generation gap in 305.2

See also 649.1 for child rearing (parenting)

.874 2 Father-child relationship

Including teenage fatherhood

Class here sociology of fatherhood

Class single teenage fatherhood in 306.87422

.874 22 Single fatherhood

Class here single fathers, unmarried fathers, unmarried fatherhood

.874 3	Mother-child relationship

Including surrogate motherhood, teenage motherhood

Class here sociology of motherhood

Class single teenage motherhood in 306.87432

.874 32	Single motherhood

Class here single mothers, unmarried mothers, unmarried motherhood

.874 5	Grandparent-child relationship
.874 7	Stepparent-stepchild relationship

Class here blended families; stepchildren, stepfamiles, stepparents

.875	Sibling relationships
.875 2	Brother-brother relationship
.875 3	Brother-sister relationship
.875 4	Sister-sister relationship
.877	Incest
.88	Alteration of family arrangements

Including desertion

Class here widowed people

For divorce, dissolution, annulment, separation, see 306.89

.880 811	Men

Do not use for widowers; class in 306.882

.880 82	Women

Do not use for widows; class in 306.883

.882	Widowers
.883	Widows
.89	Divorce, dissolution, annulment, separation

Standard subdivisions are added for any or all topics in heading

Including binuclear family, shared custody

Class here people from marriages, partnerships, unions that ended in divorce, dissolution, annulment; separated people

Class divorced families with single-parent custody in 306.856; class parent-child relationship in divorced families in 306.874

[.890 811]	Men

Do not use; class in 306.892

[.890 82]	Women

Do not use; class in 306.893

.892   Men from marriages, partnerships, unions that ended in divorce, dissolution, annulment; separated men

Standard subdivisions are added for any or all topics in heading

.893   Women from marriages, partnerships, unions that ended in divorce, dissolution, annulment; separated women

Standard subdivisions are added for any or all topics in heading

.9   Institutions pertaining to death

Class here interdisciplinary works on death

For a specific aspect of death, see the aspect, e.g., psychology of death 155.937, funeral rites and ceremonies 393.9

307   Communities

Unless other instructions are given, class a subject with aspects in two or more subdivisions of 307 in the number coming last, e.g., redevelopment of residential neighborhoods 307.34 (*not* 307.3362)

See Manual at 307

>   **307.1–307.3   Specific aspects of communities**

Add to each subdivision identified by * as follows:
1   Specific kinds of communities
        Add to 1 the numbers following 307.7 in 307.72–307.77, e.g., cities 16

Class comprehensive works in 307

.1   *Planning and development

.12   *Planning

See also 711 for the physical aspect of area planning

.14   *Development

Class here human settlement

Class resettlement in 307.2; class redevelopment in 307.34

.2   *Movement of people to, from, within communities

Including resettlement

Class comprehensive works on population in 304.6

.24   *Movement from rural to urban communities

Class here rural exodus

---

*Add as instructed under 307.1–307.3

.26	*Movement from urban to rural communities

Class here urban exodus

.3   *Structure

Class movement within communities in 307.2

.32	*Physical setting
.33	*Patterns of use
.332	*Industrial use
.333	*Commercial use

Class here business districts

.334	*Recreational use
.336	*Residential use

Including housing succession

Class here housing patterns, sociology of housing

See also 363.58 for housing programs

See Manual at 363.5 vs. 307.336, 307.34

.336 2	*Neighborhoods

Class ghettos in 307.3366

.336 4	*Slums
.336 6	*Ghettos
.34	*Redevelopment

Class community planning in 307.12

See Manual at 363.5 vs. 307.336, 307.34

.342	*City core

Class here inner cities

.344	*Slum clearance
.346	*Parks and recreational facilities

.7   Specific kinds of communities

Class a specific aspect of specific kinds of communities in 307.1–307.3

.72	Rural communities

Including plantations considered as communities

Class here rural sociology, rural villages

Class agricultural sociology, the plantation considered as a system of production in 306.349

*Add as instructed under 307.1–307.3

.74	Suburban communities
.740 9	History and biography

> Do not use for geographic treatment; class in 307.7609

.76	Urban communities

Class here urban policy (government policy on cities), urban sociology, interdisciplinary works on cities

For suburban communities, see 307.74. For a specific aspect of cities, see the aspect, e.g., public administration of cities 352.16

.760 9	History, geographic treatment, biography

Class here specific suburban communities, specific urban communities regardless of size or kind

---

> **307.762–307.764 Urban communities by size**

Class specific urban communities regardless of size in 307.7609; class comprehensive works in 307.76

.762	Small urban communities

Class here comprehensive works on villages

For rural villages, see 307.72

.763	Medium-sized urban communities
.764	Large urban communities

Class here metropolitan areas as communities

For medium-sized communities, see 307.763

> **307.766–307.768 Urban communities by kind**

Class specific urban communities regardless of kind in 307.7609; class comprehensive works in 307.76

.766	Mining and industrial towns

Class company towns in 307.767

.767	Company towns
.768	New towns
.77	Self-contained communities

Class here voluntary socialist and anarchist communities

.772	Tribal communities

Class tribal communities considered in context of culture and institutions of indigenous ethnic and national groups in 305.8

.774	Communes

Class kibbutzim in 307.776

.776   Kibbutzim and moshavim

> Standard subdivisions are added for either or both topics in heading

[308]   [Unassigned]

> Most recently used in Edition 16

[309]   [Unassigned]

> Most recently used in Edition 18

310   Collections of general statistics

> Class works on collecting statistical data in 001.433. Class statistics of a specific subject, other than general statistics of a place, with the subject, plus notation 021 from Table 1, e.g., statistics on deaths by crimes of violence 364.15021

> *See also 001.422 for analysis of statistical data; also 001.4226 for methods of presenting statistical data*

[.94–.99]   Specific continents, countries, localities in modern world

> Do not use; class in 314–319

[311]   [Unassigned]

> Most recently used in Edition 17

[312]   [Unassigned]

> Most recently used in Edition 19

[313]   [Unassigned]

> Most recently used in Edition 14

314–319 General statistics of specific continents, countries, localities in modern world

> Add to base number 31 notation 4–9 from Table 2, e.g., statistics of France 314.4

314   General statistics of Europe

> Number built according to instructions under 314–319

315   General statistics of Asia

> Number built according to instructions under 314–319

316   General statistics of Africa

> Number built according to instructions under 314–319

317   General statistics of North America

> Number built according to instructions under 314–319

318   General statistics of South America

> Number built according to instructions under 314–319

319   **General statistics of Australasia, Pacific Ocean islands, Atlantic Ocean islands, Arctic islands, Antarctica**

Number built according to instructions under 314–319

320   Political science (Politics and government)

Class sociology of political institutions and processes in 306.2

> *For law, see 340; for public administration and military science, see 350*
>
> *See Manual at 302–307 vs. 320; also at 320 vs. 306.2; also at 324 vs. 320; also at 909, 930–990 vs. 320*

SUMMARY

320.01–.09	Standard subdivisions
.1	The state
.3	Comparative government
.4	Structure and functions of government
.5	Political ideologies
.6	Policy making
.8	Local government
.9	Political situation and conditions
321	Systems of governments and states
.001–.009	Standard subdivisions
.01–.09	[Systems of relating parts of a state to the whole, kinds of states, change in system of government]
.1	Family-based government
.3	Feudalism
.5	Elitist systems
.6	Absolute monarchy
.8	Democratic government
.9	Authoritarian government
322	Relation of the state to organized groups and their members
.1	Religious organizations and groups
.2	Labor movements and groups
.3	Business and industry
.4	Political action groups
.5	Armed services
323	Civil and political rights
.01–.09	Standard subdivisions; citizen participation; resistance, repression, persecution
.1	Civil and political rights of nondominant groups
.3	Civil and political rights of other social groups
.4	Specific civil rights; limitation and suspension of civil rights
.5	Political rights
.6	Citizenship and related topics

324		The political process
	.09	History, geographic treatment, biography
	.1	International party organizations, auxiliaries, activities
	.2	Political parties
	.3	Auxiliary party organizations
	.4	Interest and pressure groups
	.5	Nominating candidates
	.6	Election systems and procedures; suffrage
	.7	Conduct of election campaigns
	.9	History and geographic treatment of elections
325		International migration and colonization
	.1	Immigration
	.2	Emigration
	.3	Colonization
	.4–.9	International migration to and colonization in specific continents, countries, localities in modern world
326		Slavery and emancipation
	.8	Emancipation
327		International relations
	.02–.09	Standard subdivisions
	.1	Foreign policy and specific topics in international relations
	.2	Diplomacy
	.3–.9	Foreign relations of specific continents, countries, localities
328		The legislative process
	.06	Organizations and management
	.1	Rules and procedures of legislative bodies
	.2	Initiative and referendum
	.3	Specific topics of legislative bodies
	.4–.9	The legislative process in specific continents, countries, localities in modern world

.01   Philosophy and theory

> Class general theory in 320.011

.011   General theory; systems

> Including theory of liberty

> Class here nature, legitimacy, role of government; political change, political justice

> Class systems in 320.0113; class biography of general theory in 320.092; class specific theories in the sense of ideologies in 320.5; class personal liberty in 323.44. Class theories on a specific aspect of political science with the aspect, e.g., social contract as a theory of origin of the state 320.11

.011 3   Systems

> The word "systems" here refers only to concepts derived from 003, e.g., systems theory, models

> Add to base number 320.0113 the numbers following 003 in 003.1–003.8, e.g., forecasting and forecasts 320.01132, computer modeling and simulation 320.01133; however, for forecasting and forecasts for a specific period or area, see 320.9

> Class systems of governments and states in 321

.014	Communication

Class here political persuasion and political propaganda

Class interdisciplinary works on persuasion in 303.342; class interdisciplinary works on propaganda in 303.375

.019	Psychological principles

Class political persuasion and propaganda in 320.014

.02–.08	Standard subdivisions

.09	History, geographic treatment, biography

Do not use for political situation and conditions, for forecasting and forecasts in a specific period or area; class in 320.9

.092	Biography

Do not use for biography of political thinkers identified with specific ideologies; class in 320.5

Class here political philosophers and political scientists

.1	**The state**

Class systems by which states are organized in 321

.101	Philosophy and theory

Do not use for theories of origin of the state; class in 320.11

.101 1	Systems

The word "systems" here refers only to concepts derived from 003, e.g., systems theory, models

Class systems of governments and states in 321

.11	Theories of origin

Class here social contract

.12	Territory

Including boundaries

Class here geopolitics

Class acquisition of territory in 325.32; class territory in law of nations in 341.42; class history of territorial changes in 911

For geopolitics in international relations, see 327.101

.15	Sovereignty

Class here national self-determination

Class states with restricted sovereignty in 321.08

.3	**Comparative government**

Class comparison of a specific aspect of government with the aspect, e.g., comparison of committee systems in different legislatures 328.365

.4	**Structure and functions of government**

Class here civics

Class analysis of systems by which government is structured in 321

For comparative government, see 320.3

See Manual at 320.9, 320.4 vs. 351; also at 909, 930–990 vs. 320.4, 321, 321.09

.404	Separation of powers

Class here interdisciplinary works on branches of government

Class systems of selecting chief executives in 324; class legislative control and oversight of executive branch in 328.3456

For legislative branch, see 328; for judicial branch, see 347; for executive branch, see 351

.404 09	History and biography

Do not use for geographic treatment; class in 320.41–320.49

.404 9	Vertical separation of powers

Class here relation of central governments with regional and local jurisdictions

For relation of local government to higher levels of government, see 320.8; for relation of federal to state, regional, provincial governments, see 321.023

.409	History and biography

Do not use for geographic treatment; class in 320.41–320.49

.41–.49	Geographic treatment

Class here systems of state and government in specific countries

Add to base number 320.4 notation 1–9 from Table 2, e.g., structure of government in Cuba 320.47291; then to the result add standard subdivisions as modified under 320.404, e.g., separation of powers in Cuba 320.4729104

.5	**Political ideologies**

Except as provided under 320.53209, use notation 09 from Table 1 for variants of basic ideologies formulated and practiced in specific nations, e.g., Titoism 320.532309497, apartheid 320.5690968

Class ideologies with respect to a specific aspect of political science with the aspect, e.g., ideologies with respect to revolution 321.094

See Manual at 324 vs. 320.5, 320.9, 909, 930–990

.508	Groups of people

Do not use for ideologies based on groups of people; class in 320.56

.51	Liberalism

.512   Classical liberalism

Ideologies and theories stressing rationalism, individualism, limited government

Class here fiscal conservatism, libertarianism

Class social conservatism, ideologies that combine classical liberalism with social conservatism in 320.52

.513   Modern liberalism

Ideologies and theories stressing responsibility of the state for welfare of its citizens

Class ideologies that combine modern liberalism with social conservatism in 320.52

.52   Conservatism

Ideologies and theories stressing limits of human reason and virtue, value of tradition, caution in effecting social change

Class here social conservatism, ideologies that combine social conservatism with classical or modern liberalism

Class comprehensive works on classical liberalism in 320.512; class comprehensive works on modern liberalism in 320.513

See also 320.512 for fiscal conservatism

.53   Collectivism and fascism

Standard subdivisions are added for collectivism and fascism together, for collectivism alone

Class here new left, radicalism, totalitarianism, comprehensive works on authoritarianism

For religiously oriented authoritarianism, see 320.55

See Manual at 335 vs. 306.345, 320.53

>   320.531–320.532   Specific collectivist ideologies

Class comprehensive works in 320.53

.531   Socialism

Nonauthoritarian systems

Class authoritarian systems of socialism in 320.532; class interdisciplinary works on socialism in 335

.531 2   Non-Marxian and quasi-Marxian socialism

Including Christian socialism, Fabian socialism

.531 5   Marxian socialism (Democratic socialism, Social democracy)

Class comprehensive political works on Marxian systems of collectivism in 320.532

.532   Communism

              Class here authoritarian systems of socialism, comprehensive political
              works on Marxian systems of collectivism

              Class interdisciplinary works on Marxism in 335.4

              For nonauthoritarian Marxian socialism, see 320.5315

.532 093–.532 099   Specific continents, countries, localities

              Class communism as formulated and practiced in former
              Soviet Union in 320.5322; class systems of communism as
              formulated and practiced in specific nations outside of former
              Soviet Union in 320.5323093–320.5323099, e.g., Maoism
              320.53230951

.532 2   Marxism-Leninism

              Class here communism as formulated and practiced in former Soviet
              Union

              For variant forms of Marxism-Leninism, see 320.5323

.532 3   Variant forms of communism

              Systems of communism, of Marxism-Leninism, other than ones
              accepted in former Soviet Union

              Including Trotskyism

.533   Fascism

              Class here falangism, national socialism, neo-Nazism

              Class interdisciplinary works on fascism in 335.6

              See also 320.569924 for anti-Semitism

.54   Nationalism, regionalism, internationalism

              Standard subdivisions are added for nationalism, regionalism,
              internationalism together; for nationalism and regionalism together; for
              nationalism alone; for regionalism alone

              Class here regional nationalism, ethnic nationalism, pan-nationalism

.540 899 6   Africans and people of African descent

              Do not use for Black nationalism; class in 320.546

.540 9   History, geographic treatment, biography

.540 91   Areas, regions, places in general

Add to base number 320.54091 the numbers following
—1 in notation 11–19 from Table 2, e.g., Arab nationalism
320.5409174927; then add further as follows:
    01–07   Standard subdivisions [*formerly* 320.5401–320.5407]
    08   Groups of people [*formerly* 320.5408]
    08996   Africans and people of African descent
                     Do not use for Black nationalism; class in
                     320.546
    09   History, geographic treatment, biography
    092   Biography [*formerly* 320.54092]

.540 92   Biography

Do not use for biography of nationalism and regionalism
with respect to groups of people by areas, regions, places in
general; class in 320.54091, plus notation 092 from add table
under 320.54091. Do not use for biography of nationalism
and regionalism with respect to groups of people by specific
continents, countries, localities; class in 320.54093–320.54099,
plus notation 092 from add table under 320.54093–320.54099

.540 93–.540 99   Specific continents, countries, localities

Add to base number 320.5409 notation 3–9 from Table 2, e.g.,
Swedish nationalism 320.5409485; then add further as follows:
    01–07   Standard subdivisions [*formerly* 320.5401–320.5407]
    08   Groups of people [*formerly* 320.5408]
    08996   Africans and people of African descent
                     Do not use for Black nationalism; class in
                     320.546
    09   History, geographic treatment, biography
    092   Biography [*formerly* 320.54092]

.540 956 94   Palestine; Israel

Number built according to instructions under
320.54093–320.54099

Class here Zionism

.540 96   Africa

Number built according to instructions under
320.54093–320.54099

Class here Pan-Africanism

.546   Black nationalism

See also 320.54096 for Pan-Africanism

.548   Internationalism

Ideology based on political activity that focuses on the universal human
condition rather than the narrow interests of a particular nation

.55	Religiously oriented ideologies

Including theocracy

Class Black Muslim movement in 297.87; class Zionism in 320.54095694

For Christian socialism, see 320.5312

.557	Islamic ideologies

Class here Islamic fundamentalism, Islamism

See Manual at 320.557 vs. 297.09, 297.272, 322.1

.56	Ideologies based on groups of people

Unless other instructions are given, class a subject with aspects in two or more subdivisions of 320.56 in the number coming last, e.g., multicultural feminism 320.5622 (*not* 320.561)

.561	Multiculturalism

Ideologies based on preserving the various cultural identities within a society

.562	Ideologies by gender or sex

.562 2	Feminism

Ideologies based on equality of the sexes

.566	Ideologies by miscellaneous social statuses

.566 2	Populism

Ideologies based on defending the interests of the common people

.569	Ideologies by ethnic and national groups

Class here racism (ideologies based on assumptions of racial superiority)

Class Nazism in 320.533

For multiculturalism, see 320.561

.569 001–.569 009	Standard subdivisions

.569 05–.569 09	People of mixed ancestry with ethnic origins from more than one continent; Europeans and people of European descent

Add to base number 320.569 notation 05–09 from Table 5, e.g., white supremacy as a political ideology 320.56909

.569 1–.569 9	Specific ethnic and national groups

Add to base number 320.569 notation 1–9 from Table 5, e.g., anti-Semitism as a political ideology 320.569924

.57	Anarchism

Class interdisciplinary works on anarchism in 335.83

.58   Environmentalist political ideologies

Class here ecologism, environmentalism, green politics

See Manual at 333.72 vs. 304.28, 320.58, 363.7

.6   Policy making

Class here decision making, planning, formulation of programs and proposals, policy studies, public policy

Class a specific aspect of policy making with the aspect, e.g., policy making on religion 322.1, legislative lobbying 328.38

For policy making in a specific subject, see the subject, e.g., policy making for economic development 338.9

See Manual at 300, 320.6 vs. 352–354: Public policy

.8   Local government

Including boundaries and forms of local government

Class here relation of local government to higher levels of government

Class boundaries and forms of specific kinds of local governments in 320.83–320.85; class comprehensive works on relation of parts of a state to the whole in 321.01

For local administration, see 352.14

.83   Intermediate levels

Government levels between national, state, or large provincial government and local municipalities

Class here arrondissements, counties, districts, Landkreise, provinces as intermediate level units

For provinces as state-level units, see 321.023

See Manual at 352.13 vs. 352.15

.84   Rural government

.85   City government

Including incorporation

Class here urban government

See also 321.06 for city-states

.854   Forms of city government

Including city manager, commission, mayor-council government

.859   Annexation

.9   Political situation and conditions

Class general political history in 900

See Manual at 320.9, 320.4 vs. 351; also at 324 vs. 320.5, 320.9, 909, 930–990; also at 909, 930–990 vs. 320

.900 1–.900 8   Standard subdivisions

[.900 9]   History, geographic treatment, biography

> Do not use for history; class in 320.901–320.905. Do not use for geographic treatment and biography; class in 320.91–320.99

.901–.905   History

> Add to base number 320.9 notation 01–05 from Table 2, e.g., political conditions in 19th century 320.9034

.91–.99   Geographic treatment and biography

> Add to base number 320.9 notation 1–9 from Table 2, e.g., political conditions in Egypt 320.962

321   Systems of governments and states

Class here kinds of states

Class selecting chief executives in 324; class comprehensive works on heads of state and administration in 352.23. Class a kind of head of state or administration characteristic of a specific system of government with the system, e.g., prime ministers responsible to legislatures 321.8043, constitutional monarchs 321.87

See Manual at 909, 930–990 vs. 320.4, 321, 321.09

SUMMARY

321.001–.009	Standard subdivisions
.01–.09	[Systems of relating parts of a state to the whole, kinds of states, change in system of government]
.1	Family-based government
.3	Feudalism
.5	Elitist systems
.6	Absolute monarchy
.8	Democratic government
.9	Authoritarian government

.001–.009   Standard subdivisions

.01   *Systems of relating parts of a state to the whole

> Class here unitary states (states in which full control is vested in central governments)
>
> Class systems of relating parts of a state to the whole in specific kinds of states in 321.02–321.08

> 321.02–321.08 Kinds of states

> Class kinds of states in specific jurisdictions in 320.43–320.49; class comprehensive works in 321

> *For comprehensive works on unitary states, see 321.01; for kinds of states defined by source or exercise of governmental authority, see 321.3–321.9*

---

*Do not use notation 093–099 from Table 1 for systems of governments and states in a specific jurisdiction; class in 320.43–320.49

.02   *Federations

                    Class here confederations

                    For proposed regional and world federations, see 321.04

.023   *Relation of federal to state, regional, provincial governments

                    Standard subdivisions are added for any or all topics in heading

                    Class here states and provinces in federal systems

.03   Empires

                    Systems in which a group of states are governed by a single sovereign power

                    See also 325.32 for imperialism

.04   Proposed regional and world unions

                    Unitary or federal

                    Class here supranational states

.040 94   Europe

                        Class European Union in 341.2422

.05   *Nation-states

                    States considered as political embodiments of ethnic groups

                    Class a national state or nation in the sense of a sovereign state in 320.1

.06   *Small states

                    Including city-states, ministates

                    See also 320.85 for cities as local governments; also 327.101 for international role of small states

.07   Ideal states (Utopias)

                    Including anarchy as an ideal system

                    Class proposed regional and world unions in 321.04

.08   *States with restricted sovereignty and non-self-governing territories

                    Including colonies, mandates, protectorates

.09   Change in system of government

                    Including coups d'état

                    See Manual at 909, 930–990 vs. 320.4, 321, 321.09

.094   Revolution

                    Class interdisciplinary works on revolution in 303.64

---

*Do not use notation 093–099 from Table 1 for systems of governments and states in a specific jurisdiction; class in 320.43–320.49

.1   Family-based government

Ancient and modern

Class here government in nonliterate societies, tribal government

---

>   **321.3–321.9 Systems of government defined by source or exercise of authority**

Class here kinds of states defined by source or exercise of governmental authority

Class comprehensive works in 321

.3   *Feudalism

.5   *Elitist systems

Including aristocracy, oligarchy, plutocracy, theocracy

.6   *Absolute monarchy

Including divine right of kings

Class here autocracy

.8   *Democratic government

.804   Systems defined by method of selecting chief executives

.804 2   *Presidential government

Government by a chief executive selected independently of a legislature

.804 3   *Cabinet government

Government by a cabinet of ministers (including a chief executive) responsible to a legislature

.86   *Republics

Class republics defined by method of selecting chief executives in 321.804

.87   *Limited monarchy (Constitutional monarchy)

Class cabinet government in limited monarchies in 321.8043

.9   *Authoritarian government

Class here despotism, dictatorship, totalitarian government

For elitist systems, see 321.5; for absolute monarchy, see 321.6

---

*Do not use notation 093–099 from Table 1 for systems of governments and states in a specific jurisdiction; class in 320.43–320.49

.92   *Communist government

Class here proletarian dictatorship

Class communism as a political ideology in 320.532; class interdisciplinary works on communism in 335.4

.94   *Fascist government

Including corporate state

Class here Nazi system

Class fascism as a political ideology in 320.533; class interdisciplinary works on fascism in 335.6

322   Relation of the state to organized groups and their members

Relation of the state to groups other than regular political parties

For groups organized for a specific purpose not provided for here, see the purpose, e.g., groups organized to promote political rights 323.5

.1   Religious organizations and groups

Class here church and state, religion and state; government policy on religion

Class freedom of religion in 323.442

See Manual at 320.557 vs. 297.09, 297.272, 322.1; also at 322.1 vs. 201.72, 261.7, 292–299

.2   Labor movements and groups

Including general strikes

For general strikes directed primarily toward employers or focused upon limited economic objectives, see 331.8925

See also 323.3223 for relation of the state to the working class

.3   Business and industry

.4   Political action groups

Class here protest groups; nonelectoral tactics used by political action groups, e.g., civil disobedience; specific kinds of conflicts between political action groups and constituted authorities, e.g., riots

Class political action committees (United States fund-raising groups) in 324.4; class interdisciplinary works on conflicts and their resolution in 303.6

---

*Do not use notation 093–099 from Table 1 for systems of governments and states in a specific jurisdiction; class in 320.43–320.49

.42   Revolutionary and subversive groups

> Standard subdivisions are added for either or both topics in heading

> Class here revolutionary and subversive activities and branches of political parties

> Class comprehensive works on parties and international party organizations engaged in both nonviolent political activity and revolutionary activity in 324.2

.420 93–.420 99   Specific continents, countries, localities

>> Class here specific revolutionary and subversive groups irrespective of political persuasion or stated goals, e.g., Ku Klux Klan 322.420973

>> Class impact of specific revolutionary and subversive groups on general history in 930–990

.43   Pressure groups

> Groups striving for immediate and relatively limited goals

> Class a pressure group working for a specific goal with the goal, e.g., a group working for better law enforcement 363.23

.44   Reform movements

> Groups seeking to change a substantial social function

> Class interdisciplinary works on social reform in 303.484. Class a movement seeking to reform a specific social function with the function, e.g., women's suffrage movement 324.623, welfare reform 361.68

.5   **Armed services**

323   Civil and political rights

> Standard subdivisions are added for civil and political rights together, for civil rights alone

> Class here civil liberties, human rights, individual freedom, rights of humanity; relations of the state to its residents

> Class welfare aspects of human rights in 361.614

> *For relation of the state to organized groups other than political parties and related organizations, see 322; for relation of the state to political parties and related organizations, see 324; for human rights law, see 341.48; for civil rights law, see 342.085*

SUMMARY

323.01–.09	**Standard subdivisions; citizen participation; resistance, repression, persecution**
.1	**Civil and political rights of nondominant groups**
.3	**Civil and political rights of other social groups**
.4	**Specific civil rights; limitation and suspension of civil rights**
.5	**Political rights**
.6	**Citizenship and related topics**

.01   Philosophy and theory

>   Class here natural rights

.04   Citizen participation; resistance, repression, persecution

.042   Citizen participation

>   Class here participation of citizens in governmental processes, participatory democracy
>
>   Class citizen participation in a specific issue with the issue, e.g., participation in public school evaluation 379.158

.044   Resistance, repression, persecution

>   Class limitation and suspension of civil rights in 323.49

.08   Groups of people

>   Class here groups of people enforcing civil and political rights, groups of people participating in the abuse of civil and political rights, groups of people working for civil and political rights in general
>
>   Do not use for civil and political rights of nondominant groups; class in 323.1. Do not use for civil and political rights of other social groups; class in 323.3

.1   Civil and political rights of nondominant groups

>   Standard subdivisions are added for either civil or political rights or both
>
>   Class specific civil rights of nondominant groups in 323.4; class specific political rights of nondominant groups in 323.5; class interdisciplinary works on nondominant groups in 305.56
>
>   *For civil and political rights of specific nondominant groups other than members of ethnic and national groups, see 323.3*

[.109 3–.109 9]   Specific continents, countries, localities

>   Do not use; class in 323.13–323.19

.11   Ethnic and national groups

>   Standard subdivisions are added for either civil or political rights or both
>
>   Class interdisciplinary works on ethnic and national groups in 305.8

[.110 93–.110 99]   Specific continents, countries, localities

>   Do not use; class in 323.13–323.19

.111–.119   Specific ethnic and national groups

>   Add to base number 323.11 notation 1–9 from Table 5, e.g., civil rights of Jews 323.11924, of African Americans 323.1196073
>   Subdivisions are added for either civil or political rights or both
>   (Option: Class civil and political rights of North American native peoples in 970.5; prefer 323.1197
>   (Option: Class civil and political rights of South American native peoples in 980.5; prefer 323.1198)
>
>   Class members of specific ethnic and national groups who are also members of other social groups in 323.3

.13–.19   Nondominant groups, ethnic and national groups in specific continents, countries, localities

> Add to base number 323.1 notation 3–9 from Table 2, e.g., civil rights of national minorities in China 323.151
> > Subdivisions are added for either civil or political rights or both
>
> Class specific ethnic and national groups in specific continents, countries, localities in 323.111–323.119; class other specific nondominant groups in specific continents, countries, localities in 323.3

.3   Civil and political rights of other social groups

> Groups other than ethnic and national groups
>
> Unless other instructions are given, observe the following table of preference, e.g., young women 323.34 (*not* 323.352):
>
> | | |
> |---|---|
> | Occupational and religious groups | 323.38 |
> | People with disabilities and illnesses, gifted people | 323.37 |
> | Groups identified by miscellaneous social attributes | 323.32 |
> | People by gender or sex | 323.33–323.34 |
> | Age groups | 323.35 |
> | Relatives | 323.36 |
>
> Class a specific civil right of social groups in 323.4; class a specific political right of social groups in 323.5

[.301–.309]   Standard subdivisions

> Do not use; class in 323.01–323.09

.32   Groups identified by miscellaneous social attributes

> Add to base number 323.32 the numbers following —086 in notation 0862–0869 from Table 1, e.g., intellectuals 323.32222, working class 323.3223
> > Subdivisions are added for either civil or political rights or both

.33   People by gender or sex

> Standard subdivisions are added for either civil or political rights or both
>
> *For transgender and intersex people, see 323.327; for women, see 323.34*

.331   Men

> Standard subdivisions are added for either civil or political rights or both
>
> Class here males

.34   Women

> Standard subdivisions are added for either civil or political rights or both
>
> Class here females

.35   Age groups

> Standard subdivisions are added for either civil or political rights or both

.352   Young people

> Standard subdivisions are added for either civil or political rights or both
>
> Class here children

.353   Young and middle-aged adults

> Standard subdivisions are added for either civil or political rights or both
>
> Class comprehensive works on adults in 323

.354   People in late adulthood

> Standard subdivisions are added for either civil or political rights or both

.36   Relatives

> Add to base number 323.36 the numbers following —085 in —0851–0855, e.g., progeny 323.364
> Subdivisions are added for either civil or political rights or both

.37   People with disabilities and illnesses, gifted people

> Add to base number 323.37 the numbers following —087 in —0871–0879, e.g., people with mobility impairments 323.373
> Subdivisions are added for either civil or political rights or both

.38   Occupational and religious groups

> Add to base number 323.38 the notation 001–999, e.g., nondominant religious groups 323.382
> Subdivisions are added for either civil or political rights or both

.4   **Specific civil rights; limitation and suspension of civil rights**

[.401–.409]   Standard subdivisions

> Do not use; class in 323.01–323.09

.42   Equal protection of law

.43   Personal security

> Including right to bear arms, right to life
>
> Class right to privacy in 323.448; class legal aspects of right to life in 342.085

.44   Freedom of action (Liberty)

> Class here freedom of expression, intellectual freedom
>
> *For rights of assembly and association, see 323.47; for right of petition, see 323.48*

.442   Freedom of conscience and religion

.443   Freedom of speech

.445   Freedom of publication

> Class here freedom of information, freedom of the press

.448   Right to privacy

.448 2	Freedom from government surveillance
	Surveillance by interception of mail, electronic monitoring, other means
	Class governmental databases in 323.4483
.448 3	Freedom from misuse of information in databases and government records
.46	Property rights
	Including freedom of contract
	Class interdisciplinary works on economic rights in 330
.47	Rights of assembly and association
.48	Right of petition
	Class here comprehensive works on rights of petition and assembly
	For right of assembly, see 323.47
.49	Limitation and suspension of civil rights
	Including harassment through abuse of power, e.g., detention of dissidents for alleged mental health problems
	Class limitation and suspension of specific rights in 323.42–323.48
[.490 8]	Groups of people
	Do not use for limitation and suspension of rights of nondominant groups; class in 323.1. Do not use for limitation and suspension of rights of other social groups; class in 323.3
.5	**Political rights**
	Including right to hold office, right to representation
	Class right of assembly in 323.47; class right of petition in 323.48; class exercise of political rights in 324
	For citizenship and related rights, see 323.6; for voting rights, see 324.62
[.508]	Groups of people
	Do not use for political rights of nondominant groups; class in 323.1. Do not use for political rights of other social groups; class in 323.3
.6	**Citizenship and related topics**
	Standard subdivisions are added for citizenship and related topics together, for citizenship alone
.62	Acquisition of citizenship
	Including acquisition of citizenship by marriage
.623	Naturalization
.63	Relation of the state to aliens and people with citizenship problems
	Including dual nationality, stateless persons

.631 Aliens

Including asylum

Class naturalization of aliens in 323.623

.64 Expatriation and repatriation

Class comprehensive works on refugees in 325.21

.65 Duties and obligations of citizens

Standard subdivisions are added for either or both topics in heading

Including loyalty, loyalty oaths

.67 Passports and visas

324 The political process

Class here elections

See Manual at 324 vs. 320; also at 324 vs. 320.5, 320.9, 909, 930–990; also at 909, 930–990 vs. 320

SUMMARY

324.09	**History, geographic treatment, biography**
.1	**International party organizations, auxiliaries, activities**
.2	**Political parties**
.3	**Auxiliary party organizations**
.4	**Interest and pressure groups**
.5	**Nominating candidates**
.6	**Election systems and procedures; suffrage**
.7	**Conduct of election campaigns**
.9	**History and geographic treatment of elections**

[.023] Politics as a profession, occupation, hobby

Do not use; class in 324.22

.09 History, geographic treatment, biography

Do not use for history and geographic treatment of elections; class in 324.9

.1 International party organizations, auxiliaries, activities

Not directly controlled by specific national parties

Class revolutionary and subversive activities and branches of party organizations in 322.42

> 324.13–324.17 International organizations, auxiliaries, activities of parties identified primarily by position on right-to-left spectrum

Class organizations, auxiliaries, activities of parties not primarily identified by position on right-to-left spectrum in 324.18; class comprehensive works in 324.1

.13 International organizations of rightist parties

Including international anticommunist leagues and their activities, monarchist parties

.14 International organizations of conservative parties

.15 International organizations of centrist parties

.16 International organizations of liberal parties

For international organizations of social democratic parties, see 324.172

.17 International organizations of leftist and labor-oriented parties

Including First International

.172 International organizations of social democratic parties

.174 International organizations of nonauthoritarian socialist parties

Including Second and Socialist Internationals

For international organizations of social democratic parties, see 324.172

.175 International organizations of communist parties

Including Third (Communist) and Fourth (Trotskyist) Internationals, Cominform

.18 International organizations of other parties

Not primarily identified by position on right-to-left spectrum

Including libertarian parties

Add to base number 324.18 the numbers following 08 in notation 082–087 from table under 324.24–324.29, e.g., international organizations of religious parties 324.182

.2 Political parties

For revolutionary and subversive activities and branches of parties, see 322.42; for international party organizations and activities, see 324.1; for auxiliary organizations, see 324.3

SUMMARY

324.201–.209		Standard subdivisions and relation of political parties to state and government
	.21	Kinds of parties
	.22	Leadership
	.23	Programs and ideologies
	.24–.29	Parties in specific countries and localities in modern world

[.202 3] Party politics as a profession, occupation, hobby

Do not use; class in 324.22

.204 Relation of political parties to state and government

Including political patronage

.209   History, geographic treatment, biography

.209 4–.209 9   Specific continents, countries, localities in modern world

> Do not use for parties in specific countries and localities; class in 324.24–324.29

> *See Manual at 324.2094–324.2099 and 324.24–324.29*

.21   Kinds of parties

> Class here party finance, membership, organization; political machines

.210 94–.210 99   Specific continents, countries, localities in modern world

> Do not use for kinds of parties in specific countries and localities; class in 324.24–324.29. Do not use for party finance, membership, organizations of parties in specific countries and localities; class in 324.24–324.29, plus notation 011 from table under 324.24–324.29

.212–.218   Specific kinds of parties

> Add to base number 324.21 the numbers following 0 in notation 02–08 from table under 324.24–324.29, e.g., centrist parties 324.215

> *For leadership of specific kinds of parties, see 324.22; for programs and ideologies of specific kinds of parties, see 324.23; for specific parties and kinds of parties in a specific country or part of a country in modern world, see 324.24–324.29; for campaign finance of specific kinds of parties, see 324.78*

.218 2   Religious parties

> Number built according to instructions under 324.212–324.218

> Class here comprehensive works on Christian democratic parties

> *For nominally religious parties identified primarily by position on right-to-left spectrum or other ideology, see the position or ideology, e.g., conservative, secular Christian democratic parties 324.214*

.22   Leadership

> Including selection of leaders

> Class here politics as a profession, occupation, hobby; politicians as a type of person

> *For nominating candidates, see 324.5*

.220 94–.220 99   Specific continents, countries, localities in modern world

> Do not use for party leadership in specific countries and localities; class in 324.24–324.29, plus notation 012 from table under 324.24–324.29

.23 Programs and ideologies

Standard subdivisions are added for either or both topics in heading

Class here platforms, campaign literature

For campaign literature on a specific subject, see the subject, e.g., campaign literature on United States participation in Vietnamese War 959.7043373

.230 94–.230 99 Geographic areas in modern world other than specific countries and states

Do not use for party programs and ideologies in specific countries and localities; class in 324.24–324.29, plus notation 013 from table under 324.24–324.29

.232–.238 Programs and ideologies of specific kinds of parties

Add to base number 324.23 the numbers following 0 in notation 02–08 from table under 324.24–324.29, e.g., programs of centrist parties 324.235

For programs and ideologies of specific parties and kinds of parties in a specific country or part of a country in modern world, see 324.24–324.29

.24–.29   Parties in specific countries and localities in modern world

The following add table is limited to countries and localities other than the United Kingdom, Germany, Austria, Italy, Switzerland, Canada, United States, Australia; special developments for those countries follow the add table

Except where specifically instructed to the contrary below, for a country or for localities within a country add to base number 324.2 notation 4–9 from Table 2 for the specific country, e.g., parties of France 324.244; then add to the number according to the table below, e.g., parties in Paris 324.24400944361, French Communist Party 324.244075, French Communist Party in Paris 324.2440750944361:

001–009	Standard subdivisions
01	General topics
	Class general topics of specific parties in notation 02–08 from this table
011	Organization, membership, finance
	Class here political machines
	Class leadership in notation 012 from this table; class comprehensive works on party organization, membership, finance in 324.21
012	Leadership
	Including selection of leaders
	Class nominating candidates in notation 015 from this table; class comprehensive works on party leadership in 324.22
013	Programs and ideologies
	Standard subdivisions are added for either or both topics in heading
	Class here platforms, campaign literature
	Class comprehensive works on party programs and ideologies in 324.23
	For campaign literature on a specific subject, see the subject, e.g., campaign literature on United States participation in Vietnamese War 959.7043373
014	Auxiliary party organizations
	Class comprehensive works on auxiliary party organizations in 324.3
015	Nominating party candidates
	Class here nomination campaigns; results of campaigns, e.g., delegate counts
	Class comprehensive works on nominating candidates in 324.5; class comprehensive works on nomination and election campaigns in 324.9
0152	Nominating by caucuses and co-optation
0154	Nominating by primaries
0156	Nominating by conventions
	For selecting delegates to nominating conventions by caucuses and co-optation, see notation 0152 from this table; for selecting delegates to nominating conventions by primaries, see notation 0154 from this table
02	Parties existing only prior to 1945
	Class comprehensive works on parties existing only prior to 1945 in 324.212

.24–.29 Parties in specific countries and localities in modern world

>03–08 Parties founded or in existence after 1945

Class here parties existing prior to 1945 and ceasing existence after 1945

Class comprehensive works on specific kinds of parties founded or in existence after 1945 in 324.21; class comprehensive works on parties founded or in existence after 1945 in specific countries in base number for the country in 324.24–324.29

>03–07 Parties founded or in existence after 1945 identified primarily by position on right-to-left spectrum

Class parties that are identified by position on right-to-left spectrum and another ideology in notation 08 from this table; class comprehensive works in base number for the country in 324.24–324.29 without adding from this table

03 Rightist parties

Including monarchist parties

038 Neofascist and neo-Nazi parties

Standard subdivisions are added for either or both topics in heading

See also 02 for fascist and Nazi parties founded before 1945

04 Conservative parties

05 Centrist parties

06 Liberal parties

07 Leftist and worker parties

072 Social democratic parties

074 Socialist parties

For social democratic parties, see notation 072 from this table

075 Communist parties

08 Parties founded or in existence after 1945 not identified primarily by position on right-to-left spectrum

Including libertarian, farmers' parties

082 Religious parties

Class nominally religious parties identified primarily by position on right-to-left spectrum or other ideology with the position or ideology, e.g., centrist, secular Christian democratic parties 05

083 Nationalist parties

084 Regionalist parties

Class here separatist, sovereigntist parties

087 Environmentalist parties (Green parties)

(Option: Arrange specific parties of a specific country alphabetically, e.g., Labour Party of United Kingdom 324.241)

Class comprehensive works on parties in 324.2; class comprehensive works on specific kinds of parties in 324.21

See Manual at 324.2094–324.2099 and 324.24–324.29

Special developments follow for selected specific countries whose party systems deviate from the above pattern

SUMMARY

.241   Parties of United Kingdom

.241 001–.241 009   Standard subdivisions

.241 01   General topics of parties of United Kingdom

Add to base number 324.24101 the numbers following 01 in notation 011–015 from table under 324.24–324.29, e.g., campaign literature of parties of United Kingdom 324.241013

Class general topics of specific parties of United Kingdom in 324.24102–324.24109

.241 02   Parties existing only prior to 1945

Class here parties of Great Britain before union with Ireland, of England and Wales before union with Scotland

———————————

>   324.241 04–324.241 09 Parties founded or in existence after 1945

Class here parties existing prior to 1945 and ceasing existence after 1945

Class comprehensive works in 324.241

.241 04   Conservative Party

.241 06   Liberal Party and its successors

Standard subdivisions are added for any or all liberal parties

Class here Liberal Democrats

.241 07   Labour Party

.241 09   Other parties

Add to base number 324.24109 the numbers following 0 in notation 03–08 from table under 324.24–324.29, e.g., Communist Party 324.2410975

.243   Parties of Germany

.243 001–.243 009   Standard subdivisions

.243 01	General topics

> Add to base number 324.24301 the numbers following 01 in notation 011–015 from table under 324.24–324.29, e.g., campaign literature of parties of Germany 324.243013

> Class general topics of specific parties of Germany in 324.24302–324.24308

.243 02	Parties existing only prior to 1945
.243 023	Rightist parties

> Including monarchist parties

> Class here rightist nationalist parties

.243 023 8	National Socialist German Labor Party (Nazi Party)
.243 024	Conservative parties
.243 025	Centrist parties

> Class here German Center Party

.243 026	Liberal parties
.243 027	Leftist and worker parties

> 324.243 03–324.243 08 Parties founded or in existence after 1945

Class here parties existing prior to 1945 and ceasing existence after 1945

Class comprehensive works in 324.243

> 324.243 03–324.243 07 Parties founded or in existence after 1945 identified primarily by position on right-to-left spectrum

Class parties that are identified by position on right-to-left spectrum and another ideology in 324.24308; class comprehensive works in 324.243

.243 03	Rightist parties

> Including monarchist parties

> Class here rightist nationalist parties, German People's Union, National Democratic Party of Germany; Republican Party of Germany

.243 038	Neofascist and neo-Nazi parties

> Standard subdivisions are added for either or both topics in heading

> *See also 324.2430238 for National Socialist German Labor Party (Nazi Party)*

.243 04	Conservative parties

> Class here conservative religious parties, Christian Democratic Union of Germany (CDU), Christian Social Union (CSU)

.243 05	Centrist parties
.243 06	Liberal parties

Class here Free Democratic Party

.243 07	Leftist and worker parties
.243 072	Social democratic parties

Class here Social Democratic Party of Germany (SPD)

.243 074	Socialist parties

Class here Party of Democratic Socialism, The Left

For social democratic parties, see 324.243072

.243 075	Communist parties

Class here German Communist Party, Communist Party of Germany, Socialist Unity Party of Germany (SED)

.243 08	Parties founded or in existence after 1945 not identified primarily by position on right-to-left spectrum

Including libertarian, farmers' parties

.243 082	Religious parties

Class conservative religious parties, Christian Democratic Union of Germany, Christian Social Union in 324.24304

.243 083	Nationalist parties

Class rightist nationalist parties, National Democratic Party of Germany in 324.24303

.243 084	Regionalist parties

Class here separatist, sovereigntist parties

.243 087	Environmentalist parties (Green parties)

Class here Greens

.243 6	Parties of Austria
.243 600 1–.243 600 9	Standard subdivisions
.243 601	General topics

Add to base number 324.243601 the numbers following 01 in notation 011–015 from table under 324.24–324.29, e.g., campaign literature of parties in Austria 324.2436013

Class general topics of specific parties of Austria in 324.243602–324.243608

.243 602	Parties existing only prior to 1945
.243 602 3	Rightist parties

Class here rightist Pan-German national parties, Pan-German People's Party (GDVP), Rural Federation (LB)

.243 602 38	National socialist parties

Class here German National Socialist Labor Party (DNSAP), National Socialist German Labor Party (NSDAP), National Socialist Labor Party (NSAP)

.243 602 4	Conservative parties

Class here Christian Social Party (CSP), Homeland Bloc

.243 602 43	Fatherland Front
.243 602 6	Liberal parties
.243 602 7	Leftist and worker parties

Class here Social Democratic Worker Party (SDAP)

> 324.243 603–324.243 608 Parties founded or in existence after 1945

Class here parties existing prior to 1945 and ceasing existence after 1945

Class comprehensive works in 324.2436

> 324.243 603–324.243 607 Parties founded or in existence after 1945 identified primarily by position on right-to-left spectrum

Class parties that are identified by position on right-to-left spectrum and another ideology in 324.243608; class comprehensive works in 324.2436

.243 603	Rightist parties

Class here rightist populist parties, Freedom Party of Austria (FPÖ), Alliance for the Future of Austria (BZÖ);rightist Pan-German nationalist parties, Federation of Independents (VdU)

.243 603 8	Neofascist and neo-Nazi parties

Standard subdivisions are added for either or both topics in heading

Class here National Democratic Party (NDP)

See also 324.24360238 for national socialist parties

.243 604	Conservative parties

Class here Austrian People's Party (ÖVP)

.243 606	Liberal parties

Class here Liberal Forum (LiF)

.243 607	Leftist and worker parties
.243 607 2	Social democratic parties

Class here Social Democratic Party of Austria (SPÖ)

.243 607 5	Communist parties

Class here Communist Party of Austria (KPÖ)

.243 608	Parties founded or in existence after 1945 not identified primarily by position on right-to-left spectrum
.243 608 3	Nationalist parties
.243 608 7	Environmental parties (Green parties)

Class here Greens (Austrian Green Party)

.245	Parties of Italy
.245 001–.245 009	Standard subdivisions
.245 01	General topics

Add to base number 324.24501 the numbers following 01 in notation 011–015 from table under 324.24–324.29, e.g., campaign literature of parties in Italy 324.245013

Class general topics of specific parties of Italy in 324.24502–324.24508

.245 02	Parties existing only prior to 1945

> 324.245 023–324.245 027 Parties existing only prior to 1945 identified primarily by position on right-to-left spectrum

Class parties that are identified by position on right-to-left spectrum and another ideology in 324.245028; class comprehensive works in 324.24502

.245 023	Rightist parties
.245 023 8	Fascist parties

Including Fascist Republican Party

Class here National Fascist Party

.245 024	Conservative parties
.245 025	Centrist parties
.245 026	Liberal parties

Including Action Party (1853–1867)

See also 324.24506 for Action Party (1942–1947)

.245 027	Leftist parties

Including Party of Italian Workers, Socialist Party of Italian Workers (1893–1895), Socialist Party of Italian Workers (1925–1927), United Socialist Party (1922–1930)

See also 324.2450722 for Socialist Party of Italian Workers (1947–1951), United Socialist Party (1969–1971)

.245 028	Parties existing only prior to 1945 not identified primarily by position on right-to-left spectrum

.245 028 2	Religious parties

Class here Italian Popular Party (1919–1926)

Class comprehensive works on Italian Popular Party (1919–1926) and Christian Democracy in 324.2450822

See also 324.245082 for Italian Popular Party (1994–2002)

> 324.245 03–324.245 08 Parties founded or in existence after 1945

Class comprehensive works in 324.245

> 324.245 03–324.245 07 Parties founded or in existence after 1945 identified primarily by position on right-to-left spectrum

Class parties that are identified by position on right-to-left spectrum and another ideology in 324.24508; class comprehensive works in 324.245

.245 03	Rightist parties

Including monarchist parties

.245 038	Neofascist parties

Including Italian Social Movement, Italian Social Movement-Right National

Class National Alliance in 324.24504

.245 04	Conservative parties

Including Forward Italy, Italian Liberal Party (1943–1994), Italian Liberal Party (2004–), National Alliance

.245 05	Centrist parties

Including Democracy is Freedom-Daisy (Daisy), Italian Republican Party

Class Democratic Party in 324.24506

.245 06	Liberal parties

Including Action Party (1942–1947), Democratic Party, Radical Party, Transnational Radical Party

See also 324.245026 for Action Party (1853–1867); also 324.24504 for Italian Liberal Party (1943–1994), Italian Liberal Party (2004–)

.245 07	Leftist and worker parties

Including Democratic Party of the Left, Democrats of the Left

Class Democratic Party in 324.24506

.245 072   Social democratic parties

                                  Including Italian Democratic Socialist Party (2004–)

See also 324.2450722 for Italian Democratic Socialist Party (1954–1995)

.245 072 2   Italian Democratic Socialist Party (1952–1995)

Class here Socialist Party of Italian Workers (1947–1951), United Socialist Party (1969–1971)

See also 324.245027 for Socialist Party of Italian Workers (1893–1895), Socialist Party of Italian Workers (1925–1927), United Socialist Party (1922–1930); also 324.245072 for Italian Democratic Socialist Party (2004–)

.245 074   Socialist parties

Including Socialist Party of Proletarian Unity (1947–1951)

For social democratic parties, see 324.245072

See also 324.2450742 for Socialist Party of Proletarian Unity (1943–1947)

.245 074 2   Italian Socialist Party

Class here Socialist Party of Proletarian Unity (1943–1947)

See also 324.245074 for Socialist Party of Proletarian Unity (1947–1951)

.245 075   Communist parties

Including Communist Refoundation Party, Party of Italian Communists

Class Democratic Party of the Left, Democrats of the Left in 324.24507

.245 075 2   Italian Communist Party

.245 08   Parties founded or in existence after 1945 not identified primarily by position on right-to-left spectrum

.245 082   Religious parties

Including Christian Democratic Center, Italian Popular Party (1994–2002), Union of Christian and Center Democrats, United Christian Democrats

See also 324.2450282 for Italian Popular Party (1919–1926)

.245 082 2   Christian Democracy

                                  Class here comprehensive works on Italian Popular Party
                                  (1919–1926) and Christian Democracy together; on Italian
                                  Popular Party (1919–1926), Christian Democracy, Italian
                                  Popular Party (1994–2002) together

                                  Class Italian Popular Party (1994–2002) in 324.245082

                                  *For Italian Popular Party (1919–1926), see
                                  324.2450282*

.245 083   Nationalist parties

.245 084   Regionalist parties

                                  Including Northern League, South Tyrolean People's Party,
                                  Valdotanian Union

                                  Class here separatist, sovereigntist parties

.245 087   Environmentalist parties (Green parties)

                                  Class here Federation of the Greens

.245 1–.245 9   Parties of regions and provinces of Italy

                                  Add to base number 324.245 the numbers following —45 in notation
                                  451–459 from Table 2 for region or province, e.g., parties in Veneto
                                  region 324.2453; then add 0* and to the result add the numbers
                                  following 324.2450 in 324.24501–324.24508, e.g., Venetian League
                                  324.2453084

.249 4   Parties of Switzerland

.249 400 1–.249 400 9   Standard subdivisions

.249 401   General topics

                                  Add to base number 324.249401 the numbers following 01
                                  in notation 011–015 from table under 324.24–324.29, e.g.,
                                  campaign literature of parties in Switzerland 324.2494013

                                  Class general topics of specific parties of Switzerland in
                                  324.249402–324.249408

.249 402   Parties existing only prior to 1945

>   324.249 403–324.249 408 Parties founded or in existence after 1945

           Class here parties existing prior to 1945 and ceasing existence after 1945

           Class comprehensive works in 324.2494

>   324.249 403–324.249 407 Parties founded or in existence after 1945 identified
           primarily by position on right-to-left spectrum

           Class parties that are identified by position on right-to-left spectrum and another
           ideology in 324.249408; class comprehensive works in 324.2494

*Add 00 for standard subdivisions; see instructions at beginning of Table 1

.249 403	Rightist parties
	Class here rightist national parties, Freedom Party of Switzerland (FPS), National Action for People and Homeland (NA), Swiss Democrats (SD), Swiss Peoples Party (SVP)
.249 404	Conservative parties
	Class here conservative religious parties, Christian Democratic People's Party of Switzerland (CVP)
.249 405	Centrist parties
.249 406	Liberal parties
	Class here FDP.The Liberals, Radical Democratic Party (FDP, Free Democratic Party, Freethinking Democratic Party, Liberal Democratic Party, Radical Free Democratic Party), Swiss Liberal Party (LPS)
.249 407	Leftist and worker parties
	Class here leftist religious parties, Christian Social Party (CSP)
.249 407 2	Social democratic parties
	Class here Social Democratic Party of Switzerland (SPS)
.249 407 4	Socialist parties
	Class here Swiss Labour Party (PdA)
	For social democratic parties, see 324.2494072
.249 407 5	Communist parties
	Class here Revolutionary Marxist League (RML), Socialist Worker Party (SAP)
.249 408	Parties founded or in existence after 1945 not identified primarily by position on right-to-left spectrum
	Including libertarian parties, farmers' parties
	Class here National Alliance of Independents (LdU)
.249 408 2	Religious parties
	Class here Protestant People's Party of Switzerland (EVP), Confederal Democratic Union (EDU)
.249 408 3	Nationalist parties
.249 408 4	Regionalist parties
	Class here separatist, sovereigntist parties; Ticino League
.249 408 7	Environmental parties (Green parties)
	Class here Green Party of Switzerland (GPS), Green Alliance (GB)
.271	Parties of Canada
.271 001–.271 009	Standard subdivisions

.271 01   General topics of parties of Canada

> Add to base number 324.27101 the numbers following 01 in notation 011–015 from table under 324.24–324.29, e.g., campaign literature of parties of Canada 324.271013

> Class general topics of specific parties of Canada in 324.27102–324.27109

.271 02   Parties existing only prior to 1945

\>   324.271 04–324.271 09   Parties founded or in existence after 1945

Class here parties existing prior to 1945 and ceasing existence after 1945

Class comprehensive works in 324.271

.271 04   Conservative Party of Canada (2003–) and its predecessors

> Including Reform Party of Canada, Canadian Reform Conservative Alliance

> Class here Conservative Party of Canada (1938–1942) and the party under former names, e.g., Liberal-Conservative Party; Progressive Conservative Party

.271 05   Social Credit Party of Canada

.271 06   Liberal Party of Canada

.271 07   New Democratic Party of Canada

.271 09   Other parties

> Add to base number 324.27109 the numbers following 0 in notation 03–08 from table under 324.24–324.29, e.g., nationalist parties 324.2710983

.271 098 4   Regionalist parties

> Number built according to instructions under 324.27109

> Class here separatist, sovereigntist parties; Bloc québécois

> *See also 324.27140984 for Parti québécois*

.271 1–.271 9   Parties of provinces and territories of Canada

> Add to base number 324.271 the numbers following —71 in notation 711–719 from Table 2 for province or territory, e.g., parties in the Yukon Territory 324.27191; then add 0* and to the result add the numbers following 324.2710 in 324.27101–324.27109, e.g., Yukon Party 324.2719104

---

*Add 00 for standard subdivisions; see instructions at beginning of Table 1

.271 409 84	Regionalist parties of Quebec

Number built according to instructions under 324.2711–324.2719

Class here separatist, sovereigntist parties; Parti québécois

See also 324.2710984 for Bloc québécois

.273	Parties of United States

For parties in specific states and District of Columbia, see 324.274–324.279

.273 01–.273 09	Standard subdivisions
.273 1	General topics of parties of United States

Add to base number 324.2731 the numbers following 01 in notation 011–015 from table under 324.24–324.29, e.g., campaign literature of parties of United States 324.27313

Class general topics of specific parties of United States in 324.2732–324.2738

.273 2	Parties existing only prior to 1945

Including American ("Know-Nothing") Party, Free Soil Party

.273 22	Federalist Party

Variant name: Federal Party

.273 23	Whig Party

Including National Republican Party

.273 26	Jeffersonian Republican Party

Variant name: Anti-federalist Party

.273 27	Populist and progressive parties

Including Progressive ("Bull Moose") Party

See also 324.2737 for Progressive Party (1948)

>	324.273 3–324.273 8 Parties founded or in existence after 1945

Class here parties existing prior to 1945 and ceasing existence after 1945

Class comprehensive works in 324.273

.273 3	Nationalist parties of the right

Including American Independent Party; sectionalist parties, e.g., States' Rights Party (Dixiecrats)

.273 38	National Socialist White People's Party

Former name: American Nazi Party

.273 4	Republican Party

.273 6	Democratic Party
	Including Democratic-Republican Party
.273 7	Leftist and worker parties
	Including Progressive Party (1948), Socialist Labor Party, Socialist Party, Socialist Workers Party
	See also 324.27327 for Progressive ("Bull Moose") Party
.273 75	Communist Party
.273 8	Other parties founded or in existence after 1945
	Including environmentalist, libertarian, prohibitionist, religious, separatist parties
	See also 324.2733 for sectionalist parties
.274–.279	Parties of states of United States and District of Columbia
	Add to base number 324.27 the numbers following —7 in notation 74–79 from Table 2 for state or District of Columbia, e.g., parties in New York State 324.2747; then add 0*, and to the result add the numbers following 324.273 in 324.2731–324.2738, e.g., Republican Party in New York State 324.274704
	Class comprehensive works in 324.273
	For parties in Hawaii, see 324.2969
	A development for New York follows
.274 7	Parties in New York
.274 700 1–.274 700 9	Standard subdivisions
.274 701–.274 702	General topics and parties existing only prior to 1945
	Add to base number 324.27470 the numbers following 324.273 in 324.2731–324.2732, e.g., Whig Party 324.2747023
.274 703	Nationalist parties of the right
.274 704	Republican Party
.274 706	Democratic Party
.274 707	Leftist and worker parties
.274 707 5	Communist Party
.274 708	Other parties founded or in existence after 1945
	Including Conservative Party, Liberal Party
.294	Parties of Australia
.294 001–.294 009	Standard subdivisions

---

*Add 00 for standard subdivisions; see instructions at beginning of Table 1

.294 01 General topics of parties of Australia

Add to base number 324.29401 the numbers following 01 in notation 011–015 from table under 324.24–324.29, e.g., campaign literature of parties of Australia 324.294013

Class general topics of specific parties of Australia in 324.29402–324.29409

.294 02 Parties existing only prior to 1945

\> 324.294 04–324.294 09 Parties founded or in existence after 1945

Class here parties existing prior to 1945 and ceasing existence after 1945

Class comprehensive works in 324.294

.294 04 The Nationals

Former names: Australian Country Party, National Country Party, National Party of Australia

.294 05 Liberal Party of Australia

.294 06 Democratic Labor Party

.294 07 Australian Labor Party

.294 09 Other parties

Add to base number 324.29409 the numbers following 0 in notation 03–08 from table under 324.24–324.29, e.g., Australian Democrats 324.294095

.294 1–.294 8 Parties in states and territories of Australia

Add to base number 324.294 the numbers following —94 in notation 941–948 from Table 2 for state or territory, e.g., parties in New South Wales 324.2944; then add 0* and to the result add the numbers following 324.2940 in 324.29401–324.29409, e.g., Australian Labor Party in New South Wales 324.294407

.296 9 Parties in Hawaii

.296 900 1–.296 900 9 Standard subdivisions

.296 901–.296 908 Parties in Hawaii

Add to base number 324.29690 the numbers following 324.273 in 324.2731–324.2738, e.g., Democratic Party in Hawaii 324.296906

.3 Auxiliary party organizations

Organizations attached to political parties, e.g., political clubs, women's organizations, youth groups

Class revolutionary and subversive branches of political parties in 322.42

For auxiliary organizations of international party organizations, see 324.1

---

*Add 00 for standard subdivisions; see instructions at beginning of Table 1

.309 4–.309 9   Geographic areas in modern world other than specific countries and states

> Do not use for auxiliary party organizations in a specific country or state; class in 324.24–324.29, plus notation 014 from table under 324.24–324.29

.4   Interest and pressure groups

Class here influence and activities of groups in extragovernmental processes; political action committees (PACs, United States fund-raising groups); comprehensive works on lobbying

Class comprehensive works on interest groups, political action groups in 322.4; class comprehensive works on pressure groups in 322.43

> *For legislative lobbying, see 328.38. For lobbying for a specific goal, see the goal, e.g., lobbying for penal reform 364.6*

.5   Nominating candidates

Class here campaigns for nomination; results of campaigns, e.g., delegate counts

Class comprehensive works on nomination and election campaigns in 324.9

.509 4–.509 9   Geographic areas in modern world other than specific countries and states

> Do not use for nominating party candidates in a specific country or state; class in 324.24–324.29, plus notation 015 from table under 324.24–324.29

.52   Nominating by caucuses and co-optation

.520 94–.520 99   Geographic areas in modern world other than specific countries and states

> Do not use for nominating party candidates by caucuses and co-optation in a specific country or state; class in 324.24–324.29, plus notation 0152 from table under 324.24–324.29

.54   Nominating by primaries

.540 94–.540 99   Geographic areas in modern world other than specific countries and states

> Do not use for nominating party candidates by primaries in a specific country or state; class in 324.24–324.29, plus notation 0154 from table under 324.24–324.29

.56   Nominating by conventions

> *For selecting delegates to nominating conventions by caucuses and co-optation, see 324.52; for selecting delegates to nominating conventions by primaries, see 324.54*
>
> *See also 324.21 for convention finance*

.560 94–.560 99 Geographic areas in modern world other than specific countries and states

> Do not use for nominating party candidates by conventions in a specific country or state; class in 324.24–324.29, plus notation 0156 from table under 324.24–324.29

.6 Election systems and procedures; suffrage

Standard subdivisions are added for election systems and procedures, suffrage together; for election systems alone; for election procedures alone

Class here comprehensive works on systems and procedures for nominations and elections

Class conduct of election campaigns in 324.7

> *For nominating candidates, see 324.5; for manuals outlining election procedures that discuss laws or administrative regulations, see 342.07*

.62 Suffrage

Class here qualifications for voting, voting rights

Class comprehensive works on political rights in 323.5

[.620 82] Women's suffrage

Do not use; class in 324.623

.623 Women's suffrage

.63 Electoral systems

Including direct and indirect elections, electoral colleges

> *For electoral basis of representation in legislative bodies, see 328.3347*

.64 Registration of voters

.65 Voting procedures

Including absentee voting, ballots and ballot systems, counting and certification of votes, election monitoring, election officials, procedures for contested elections, voting machines

.66 Election fraud

Class irregularities in campaign finance in 324.78; class election fraud as a crime in 364.1324

.68 Recall

Removal of an official from office by popular vote

.7 Conduct of election campaigns

Variant name: practical politics

Class here public relations for conduct of political election campaigns

> *See also 324.5 for conduct of campaigns for nomination*

.72	Strategy

Including citizen participation

For use and effect of media, see 324.73

.73	Use and effect of media

Class here advertising for political election campaigns

.78	Campaign finance

Class party finance in 324.21

.9	**History and geographic treatment of elections**

Class here election returns and results, studies of voting behavior; comprehensive works on campaigns

Class platforms, campaign literature in 324.23

For campaigns for nomination, see 324.5; for conduct of election campaigns, see 324.7

.900 1–.900 8	Standard subdivisions

[.900 9]	History, geographic treatment, biography

Do not use for comprehensive works on history; class in 324.9. Do not use for geographic treatment; class in 324.91–324.99

[.900 901–.900 905]	Historical periods

Do not use; class in 324.901–324.905

[.900 92]	Biography

Do not use; class in 324.092

.901–.905	Historical periods

Add to base number 324.90 the numbers following —090 in notation 0901–0905 from Table 1, e.g., election campaigns in 19th century 324.9034

.91–.99	Geographic treatment

Add to base number 324.9 the numbers following 9 in 930–990, e.g., political campaigns in the United Kingdom 324.941, election campaign of 1997 in the United Kingdom 324.9410859; however, for historical periods of United States elections, see 324.97301–324.97309

.973 01–.973 09	Historical periods of United States

Add to base number 324.9730 the numbers following 973 in 973.1–973.9, e.g., election of 1992 in United States 324.9730928

325   International migration and colonization

Standard subdivisions are added for international migration and colonization together, for international migration alone

Including population transfers

Class interdisciplinary works on international movement of people in 304.82. Class movement of people associated with a specific event in world history with the event in 909, e.g., Jewish Diaspora 909.04924; class movement of people associated with a specific event in the history of a country or region with the event in 930–990, e.g., emigration of Jews as a consequence of the Holocaust 940.5318142

[.094–.099]   Specific continents, countries, localities in modern world

> Do not use; class in 325.4–325.9

.1   Immigration

For illegal immigration, see 364.137

[.109 4–.109 9]   Specific continents, countries, localities in modern world

> Do not use; class in 325.4–325.9

.2   Emigration

[.209 3–.209 9]   Specific continents, countries, localities

> Do not use; class in 325.23–325.29

.21   Refugees

Class here displaced persons, exiles, political refugees

Class interdisciplinary works on displaced persons, refugees in 305.906914

.210 93–.210 99   Specific continents, countries, localities

> Refugees from one country in another country are classed in country of origin, e.g., Polish political refugees in Canada 325.21094380971

.23–.29   Emigration from specific continents, countries, localities

Add to base number 325.2 notation 3–9 from Table 2, e.g., emigration from Japan 325.252, emigration from Japan to United States 325.2520973

.3   Colonization

Class here exercise of political dominion over distant territories, decolonization

.309 3   Ancient world

> Do not use for colonization by specific countries in ancient world; class in 325.33

.309 4–.309 9   Specific continents, countries, localities in modern world

> Do not use for colonization by specific countries in modern world; class in 325.34–325.39. Do not use for colonization in specific places in modern world; class in 325.4–325.9

.32   Imperialism

The policy, practice, or advocacy of acquiring political dominion over territories outside the natural boundaries of a country

Class comprehensive works on foreign policy in 327.1

.33–.39   Colonization by specific countries

Add to base number 325.3 notation 3–9 from Table 2, e.g., colonization by United Kingdom 325.341, colonization by United Kingdom in West Africa 325.3410966

Class imperialism of specific countries in 325.32093–325.32099

.4–.9   International migration to and colonization in specific continents, countries, localities in modern world

Add to base number 325 notation 4–9 from Table 2, e.g., migration to Israel 325.5694
Subdivisions are added for either or both topics in heading

Class emigration from specific continents, countries, localities in modern world to specific continents, countries, localities in 325.24–325.29; class colonization by specific countries in modern world in specific continents, countries, localities in 325.34–325.39; class comprehensive works on colonization by and in specific continents, countries, localities in modern world in 325.3094–325.3099

326   Slavery and emancipation

Standard subdivisions are added for slavery and emancipation together, for slavery alone

Class interdisciplinary works on slavery in 306.362

.8   Emancipation

Class here abolitionism, antislavery movements

327   International relations

Class military science in 355; class interdisciplinary works on relations among countries in 303.482

For international relations with respect to a specific subject, see the subject, e.g., commerce between United Kingdom and communist bloc 382.094101717

See Manual at 341 vs. 327

SUMMARY

327.02–.09	**Standard subdivisions**	
.1	**Foreign policy and specific topics in international relations**	
.2	**Diplomacy**	
.3–.9	**Foreign relations of specific continents, countries, localities**	

[.01]   Philosophy and theory

Do not use; class in 327.101

.06   Organizations

For intergovernmental organizations, see 341.2

[.068]   Management

                Do not use; class in 353.13

.09   History, geographic treatment, biography

                Class here diplomatic history, international relations of or in areas, regions, places in general, not limited by continent, country, locality, e.g., foreign relations of former Communist bloc 327.091717

.092   Biography

                Do not use for diplomats; class in 327.2092

[.093–.099]   Foreign relations of specific continents, countries, localities

                Do not use; class in 327.3–327.9

.1   Foreign policy and specific topics in international relations

                Standard subdivisions are added for foreign policy

                Class here imperialism in international relations, international politics, power politics

                Class comprehensive works on imperialism, imperialism as national policy in 325.32

                For diplomacy, see 327.2

.101   Philosophy and theory of international relations, of foreign policy

                Including role and position of small states, economic bases of international relations

                Class here geopolitics in international relations, nature of power in international relations

                Class comprehensive works on geopolitics in 320.12

.102–.108   Standard subdivisions of foreign policy

.109   History, geographic treatment, biography of foreign policy

.109 2   Biography

                Do not use for diplomats; class in 327.2092

[.109 3–.109 9] Foreign relations of specific continents, countries, localities

                Do not use; class in 327.3–327.9

.11   Specific means of attaining foreign policy goals

                Including government information services

                For espionage and subversion, see 327.12; for propaganda and war of nerves, see 327.14

.111   Economic activities

                Including foreign aid

                Class boycotts and sanctions in 327.117

.112   Balance of power

.114	Spheres of influence
.116	Alliances

Class here collective security

.117	Use of force and threats of force

Including boycotts, sanctions, terrorism

Class war of nerves in 327.14; class war in 355.02

.12	Espionage and subversion

Standard subdivisions are added for either or both topics in heading

Class here interdisciplinary works on espionage, subversion, intelligence gathering

For military espionage, see 355.3432; for military subversion, see 355.3437

.120 93–.120 99	Specific continents, countries, localities

Do not use for espionage and subversion by specific nations; class in 327.123–327.129

.123–.129	Espionage and subversion by specific nations

Add to base number 327.12 notation 3–9 from Table 2, e.g., espionage by France 327.1244; then for espionage and subversion by that country in another area add 0* and to the result add notation 1–9 from Table 2, e.g., espionage by France in developing countries 327.124401724
Subdivisions are added for either or both topics in heading

.14	Propaganda and war of nerves

Including disinformation activities

Class comprehensive works on political propaganda in 320.014; class comprehensive works on use of force and threats of force in 327.117; class interdisciplinary works on propaganda in 303.375

.16	International conflict

Class war in 355.02; class conflict involving specific means of attaining foreign policy goals in 327.117

See also 327.17 for peaceful resolution of international conflict

.17	International cooperation

Class here internationalism, conflict resolution

Class international governmental organizations in 341.2; class interdisciplinary works on conflict resolution in 303.69

For law of international cooperation, see 341.7

.172	Promotion of peace and international order
.174	Disarmament and arms control

*Add 00 for standard subdivisions; see instructions at beginning of Table 1

.174 3   Conventional weapons limitation

.174 5   Chemical and biological disarmament

> Standard subdivisions are added for either or both topics in heading

> Class here disarmament of weapons of mass destruction, of specific chemical and biological weapons

> *For nuclear disarmament, see 327.1747*

.174 7   Nuclear disarmament

> Class here strategic arms limitation, limitation of specific nuclear weapons

.2   Diplomacy

Including protocol

Use 327.2 for methods and style of diplomacy; 327 for substance and content of diplomatic relations

> *For law of diplomacy, see 341.33*

.209 2   Biography

> Do not use for biography of diplomats of specific nations; class in 327.3–327.9

.3–.9   Foreign relations of specific continents, countries, localities

Class here foreign policy

Add to base number 327 notation 3–9 from Table 2, e.g., foreign relations of Brazil 327.81, of eastern European countries 327.47, in Middle East 327.56; then, for relations between that nation or region and another nation or region, add 0* and to the result add notation 1–9 from Table 2, e.g., relations between Brazil and France 327.81044, between Brazil and Arab world 327.810174927

Give priority in notation to the nation or region emphasized. If emphasis is equal, give priority to the nation or region coming first in Table 2
(Option: Give priority in notation to the nation or region requiring local emphasis, e.g., libraries in the United States class foreign relations between the United States and France in 327.73044)

Class specific topics in international relations of specific nations or regions in 327.11–327.17

> *See Manual at T1—092: Comprehensive biography: Public figures; also at 920.009, 920.03–920.09 vs. 909.09, 909.1–909.8, 930–990*

328   The legislative process

Class here legislative branch, legislative bodies

> *See Manual at 909, 930–990 vs. 320*

---

*Add 00 for standard subdivisions; see instructions at beginning of Table 1

SUMMARY

.060 1   International organizations

Class here interparliamentary unions

.068   Management

Do not use for management of members' offices; class in 328.331068. Do not use for public administration of legislative branch of specific jurisdiction; class in 328.4–328.9, plus notation 0068 from table under 328.4–328.9

Class here public administration of legislative branch

[.094–.099]   The legislative process in specific continents, countries, localities in modern world

Do not use; class in 328.4–328.9

.1   **Rules and procedures of legislative bodies**

Including rules and procedures for reporting legislative sessions, e.g., television coverage

Class comprehensive rules of order in 060.42

For rules of committees of legislative bodies, see 328.3653

.109 4–.109 9   Specific continents and localities in modern world

Do not use for rules and procedures of specific legislative bodies in modern world; class in 328.4–328.9, plus notation 05 from table under 328.4–328.9

.2   **Initiative and referendum**

.209 4–.209 9   Specific continents and localities in modern world

Do not use for treatment in specific jurisdictions in modern world; class in 328.24–328.29

.22   Initiative

.220 94–.220 99   Specific continents and localities in modern world

Do not use for initiative in specific jurisdictions in modern world; class in 328.24–328.29

.23   Referendum

.230 94–.230 99   Specific continents and localities in modern world

Do not use for referendum in specific jurisdictions in modern world; class in 328.24–328.29

.24–.29   Initiative and referendum in specific jurisdictions in modern world

> Add to base number 328.2 notation 4–9 from Table 2, e.g., initiative in California 328.2794
> Subdivisions are added for either or both topics in heading

.3   Specific topics of legislative bodies

> Class specific topics of legislative bodies of specific jurisdictions in modern world in 328.4–328.9, plus notation 07 from table under 328.4–328.9

For rules and procedures of legislative bodies, see 328.1

SUMMARY

328.304	Legislative reform
.31	Upper houses
.32	Lower houses
.33	Members and membership
.34	Powers, privileges, restrictions
.35	Sessions
.36	Internal organization and discipline
.37	Enactment of legislation
.38	Lobbying
.39	Forms of legislative bodies

[.301–.303]   Standard subdivisions

> Do not use; class in 328.01–328.03

.304   Legislative reform

> *For reform of basis of representation, see 328.334; for reform of internal organization, see 328.36*

[.305–.309]   Standard subdivisions

> Do not use; class in 328.05–328.09

.31   Upper houses

> Class comprehensive works on upper and lower houses in 328.39. Class a specific aspect of upper houses with the aspect, e.g., treaty making power of upper houses 328.346

.32   Lower houses

> Class a specific aspect of lower houses with the aspect, e.g., basis of representation of lower houses 328.334

.33   Members and membership

> Including qualifications, term of office, term limitation

> Class comprehensive biography of members in 328.092; class biography of members of specific legislative bodies in modern world in 328.4–328.9, plus notation 092 from table under 328.4–328.9

> *For personal privileges, see 328.347; for officers and leaders, see 328.362; for discipline of members, see 328.366*

.331   Work and activity of individual members

> Class here constituency services, work of members' offices

.334	Basis of representation
.334 5	Election districts
	Class here apportionment and reapportionment, redistricting
	For districts used in proportional representation, see 328.3347
.334 55	Gerrymandering
.334 7	Proportional representation
.34	Powers, privileges, restrictions
	Class here legislative duties
	Class enactment of legislation in 328.37
.341	General powers
	For treaty and war powers, see 328.346
.341 2	Financial power
	Power over appropriation, borrowing and lending, currency, taxation
.341 3	General economic and public welfare powers
.345	Extralegislative powers
	Including control and oversight of judicial branch
	Class here hearings
	For hearings on a specific subject, see the subject, e.g., hearings on laws 348.01
.345 2	Investigative power
	Including ombudsman role
	Class interdisciplinary works on ombudsmen in 352.88
.345 3	Judicial power
	Including power to impeach
.345 4	Electoral power
.345 5	Power over appointments
.345 6	Control and oversight of executive branch
	Class here general relations with executive branch
	Class cabinet system of executives in 321.8043; class control of foreign relations in 328.346
	For ombudsman role, see 328.3452
.346	Treaty and war powers
	Class here control of international relations
.347	Personal privileges of legislators
	For legislative immunity, see 328.348

.375	Passage of legislation

Including votes and voting procedures

.377	Enactment of resolutions
.378	Enactment of special types of legislation

Including private bills, procedures for legislative enactment of budgets

For enactment of resolutions, see 328.377; for enactment of budgets, see 352.48

.38	Lobbying
.39	Forms of legislative bodies

Unicameral, bicameral

Do not use for description of various legislatures that happen to be of one form or another

For upper houses, see 328.31; for lower houses, see 328.32

.4–.9   **The legislative process in specific continents, countries, localities in modern world**

> Add to base number 328 notation 4–9 from Table 2, e.g., the legislative process in the Canadian Parliament or in the provincial legislatures of Canada 328.71, in eastern Europe 328.47; then add further as follows:

001–008	Standard subdivisions
[009]	History and biography
	Do not use; class in notation 09 from this table
01	Journals and calendars
02	Debates
	Including collections of speeches by individual members
03	Abstracts
04	Other documents
	Class here series of miscellaneous parliamentary papers and documents
05	Rules and procedures
	Including legislative manuals
	Class committee rules in notation 07653 from this table
07	Specific topics of legislative bodies
	For rules and procedures, see notation 05 from this table
[0701–0703]	Standard subdivisions
	Do not use; class in notation 001–003 from this table
0704	Legislative reform
[0705–0708]	Standard subdivisions
	Do not use; class in notation 005–008 from this table
[0709]	History and biography
	Do not use; class in notation 09 from this table
071–079	Other topics of legislative bodies
	Add to 07 the numbers following 328.3 in 328.31–328.39, e.g., specific committees 07658
09	History and biography
092	Biography
	See Manual at T1—092: Comprehensive biography: Public figures; also at 920.009, 920.03–920.09 vs. 909.09, 909.1–909.8, 930–990

> *For initiative and referendum in specific jurisdictions in modern world, see 328.24–328.29*

[329]   [Unassigned]

> Most recently used in Edition 18

330   Economics

Including interdisciplinary works on economic rights

Class here comprehensive works on economics and management

Unless other instructions are given, observe the following table of preference, e.g., finance as an economic factor in international economics 332.042 (*not* 337):

Cooperatives	334
Public finance	336
Economics of labor, finance, land, energy	331–333
Production, Commerce (381–382), Communications	
(383–384), Transportation (385–388)	338
Macroeconomics and related topics	339
International economics	337
Socialism and related systems	335

Class economic rights in the sense of welfare rights in 361.614

For management, see 658. For a specific kind or aspect of economic rights, see the kind or aspect, e.g., political aspects of property rights 323.46

See Manual at 330 vs. 650, 658

SUMMARY

330.01–.09	**Standard subdivisions**
.1	**Systems, schools, theories**
.9	**Economic situation and conditions**
331	**Labor economics**
.01–.09	**Standard subdivisions and industrial relations by industry and occupation**
.1	**Labor force and market**
.2	**Conditions of employment**
.3	**Workers by age group**
.4	**Women workers**
.5	**Workers by personal attributes other than age**
.6	**Workers by ethnic and national origin**
.7	**Labor by industry and occupation**
.8	**Labor unions, labor-management bargaining and disputes**
332	**Financial economics**
.01–.09	**Standard subdivisions, personal finance, special topics of financial economics**
.1	**Banks**
.2	**Specialized banking institutions**
.3	**Credit and loan institutions**
.4	**Money**
.5	**Barter, commercial paper, social credit money**
.6	**Investment**
.7	**Credit**
.8	**Interest**
.9	**Counterfeiting, forgery, alteration**

333		**Economics of land and energy**
	.001–.009	Standard subdivisions
	.01–.08	[Theories and land surveys]
	.1	Public ownership of land
	.2	Ownership of land by nongovernmental groups
	.3	Private ownership of land
	.4	Absentee ownership
	.5	Renting and leasing land
	.7	Land, recreational and wilderness areas, energy
	.8	Subsurface resources
	.9	Other natural resources
334		**Cooperatives**
	.1	Housing cooperatives
	.2	Banking and credit cooperatives
	.5	Consumer cooperatives
	.6	Producers' cooperatives
	.7	Benefit societies
335		**Socialism and related systems**
	.001–.009	Standard subdivisions
	.02	Utopian systems and schools
	.1	Systems of English origin
	.2	Systems of French origin
	.3	Systems of American origin
	.4	Marxian systems
	.5	Democratic socialism
	.6	Fascism
	.7	Christian socialism
	.8	Other systems
336		**Public finance**
	.001–.008	Standard subdivisions
	.01–.09	[Public finance by governmental level; revenue; history, geographic treatment, biography; associations of sovereign states]
	.1	Nontax revenues
	.2	Taxes
	.3	Public debt and expenditures
	.4–.9	Public finance of specific continents, countries, localities in modern world
337		**International economics**
	.1	Multilateral economic cooperation
	.3–.9	Foreign economic policies and relations of specific jurisdictions and groups of jurisdictions
338		**Production**
	.001–.008	Standard subdivisions
	.01–.09	[General topics]
	.1	Agriculture
	.2	Extraction of minerals
	.3	Other extractive industries
	.4	Secondary industries and services
	.5	General production economics
	.6	Organization of production
	.7	Business enterprises
	.8	Combinations
	.9	Economic development and growth
339		**Macroeconomics and related topics**
	.2	Distribution of income and wealth
	.3	Product and income accounts
	.4	Factors affecting income and wealth
	.5	Macroeconomic policy

.01	Philosophy and theory

> Do not use for theories; class in 330.1

.015 1	Mathematical principles

> *See also 330.1543 for mathematical economics as a school of economics*

.015 195	Statistical mathematics

> Class here econometrics

> *See Manual at 519.5, T1—015195 vs. 001.422, T1—0727*

.02–.08	Standard subdivisions
.09	History, geographic treatment, biography of economics as a discipline

> Do not use for economic situation and conditions; class in 330.9

.1	**Systems, schools, theories**

> *For economic rent, see 333.012; for law of supply and demand, see 338.521*

.12	Systems
.122	Free enterprise economy

> Including open economy (the economy of an area in which trade with other areas is unrestricted)

> Class here capitalism

> Class laissez-faire economic theory in 330.153

> *See also 382.7 for trade barriers and restrictions*

.124	Planned economies

> Class here command economies

> Class schools of thought featuring planned economies in 335

> *See also 338.9 for economic planning*

.126	Mixed economies

> Including interventionism, social market economy, welfare state systems

> *See also 330.1556 for welfare economics as a school of economic thought*

.15	Schools of economic thought

> *For socialist and related schools, see 335*

.151	Pre-classical schools

> *For physiocracy, see 330.152*

.151 2	Ancient and medieval theories
.151 3	Mercantilism

.152	Physiocracy
	Class here school of Quesnay
.153	Classical economics
	Class here schools of Smith, Ricardo, Malthus, Mill, Say; laissez-faire economic theory

See also 330.157 for neoclassical school

.154	Historical and mathematical schools
.154 2	Historical school
	Class here the schools of Roscher, Knies, Hildebrand, Schmoller, Bücher, Knapp
.154 3	Mathematical school
	Class here schools of Cournot, Dupuit, Pareto
	Class mathematical economics in 330.0151

See also 330.157 for marginal utility school

.155	Miscellaneous schools
	Only those named below
	Including school of Henry George (single-tax school)
.155 2	Institutional economics
	Class economics of institutions in 330
.155 3	Chicago school of economics (Monetarism)
	Class monetary theory in 332.401
.155 4	Supply-side economics
.155 6	Welfare economics school
.156	Keynesian economics
	Class here post-Keynesian economics
.157	Marginal utility school
	Variant names: Austrian school, neoclassical school
	Class here schools of Jevons, Menger, Walras, Wieser, Böhm-Bawerk, Von Mises; utility theory

See also 330.1543 for schools of Cournot, Dupuit, Pareto

(.159)	Socialist and related schools
	(Optional number; prefer 335)
	Add to base number 330.159 the numbers following 335 in 335.1–335.8, e.g., Marxian systems 330.1594
.16	Theories of wealth
	Class macroeconomic aspects of wealth in 339

.17   Theories of property

.9   Economic situation and conditions

> Standard subdivisions are added for either or both topics in heading
>
> Class here economic geography, economic history; works describing situation and conditions at both macroeconomic and microeconomic levels
>
> Class policies to promote economic growth and development in 338.9; class macroeconomic policies in 339.5

.900 1–.900 8   Standard subdivisions

[.900 9]   History, geographic treatment, biography

> Do not use for comprehensive works on history, on geographic treatment; class in 330.9

[.900 901–.900 905]   Historical periods

> Do not use; class in 330.901–330.905

[.900 91]   Areas, regions, places in general

> Do not use; class in 330.91

[.900 92]   Biography

> Do not use; class in 330.092

[.900 93–.900 99]   Specific continents, countries, localities

> Do not use; class in 330.93–330.99

.901–.905   Historical periods

> Add to base number 330.90 the numbers following —090 in notation 0901–0905 from Table 1, e.g., economic situation in 1960–1969 330.9046

.91   Areas, regions, places in general

> Add to base number 330.91 the numbers following —1 in notation 11–19 from Table 2, e.g., economic situation and conditions in developing countries 330.91724; then add 0* and to the result add the numbers following 909 in 909.1–909.8, e.g., economic situation and conditions in developing countries in 1980–1989 330.917240828
>> Use 0 plus notation 0112 from Table 1 for forecasting and forecasts, e.g., forecasting and forecasts of economic situation and conditions in developing countries 330.9172400112. Do not use historical periods for forecasting and forecasts
>
> (Option: Class in 910.13301)

---

*Add 00 for standard subdivisions; see instructions at beginning of Table 1

.93–.99   Specific continents, countries, localities

> Add to base number 330.9 the numbers following 9 in 930–990, e.g., economic situation and conditions in France 330.944, economic situation and conditions in France under Louis XIV 330.944033; however, for historical periods of economic situation and conditions in United States, see 330.97301–330.97309
>> Use 0 or 00 plus notation 0112 from Table 1 for forecasting and forecasts, e.g., forecasting and forecasts of economic situation and conditions in France 330.94400112. Do not use historical periods for forecasting and forecasts

> (Option: Class in 910.13303–910.13309)

.973 01–.973 09   Historical periods of United States

> Add to base number 330.9730 the numbers following 973 in 973.1–973.9, e.g., economic situation in the United States during Reconstruction period 330.97308

> ## 331–333 Economics of labor, finance, land, energy

Class comprehensive works on economics of labor, finance, land, energy in 330; class comprehensive works on labor, capital, land considered as factors of production in 338.01

331 Labor economics

Class here industrial relations, interdisciplinary works on labor

Unless other instructions are given, observe the following table of preference, e.g., compensation of women in banking 331.42813321 (*not* 331.2813321 or 331.7613321):

Choice of vocation	331.702
Labor force by personal attributes	331.3–331.6
Labor force and market	331.1
Conditions of employment	331.2
Labor unions, labor-management bargaining and disputes	331.8
Labor by industry and occupation (*except* 331.702)	331.7

Class economic conditions of working class in 330.9; class relations between management and labor unions in 331.8; class full employment policy in 339.5

For a specific noneconomic aspect of labor, see the aspect, e.g., relation of labor movements to the state 322.2, managerial aspects of labor 658.3

See also 305.562 for sociology of working class; also 306.36 for sociology of labor

SUMMARY

.01   Philosophy and theory

> Notation 01 from Table 1 as modified below

> Do not use for value of labor; class in 331.013

.011   Rights and position of labor

> Do not use for systems analysis applied to labor economics; class in 331.01. Do not use for systems of labor; class in 331.117

> Standard subdivisions are added for either or both topics in heading

> Class here employment rights

> *For open shop, right to work, see 331.8892*

.011 2   Industrial democracy

> Class producer cooperatives in 334.6; class guild socialism in 335.15; class syndicalism in 335.82; class worker control of industry in 338.6; class employee representation in management discussed from the managerial viewpoint in 658.3152

> *For role of labor unions in industrial democracy, see 331.88*

.012   Satisfactions and dissatisfactions of labor

> Do not use for classification of occupations; class in 331.70012

> Standard subdivisions are added for either or both topics in heading

.013   Freedom, dignity, value of labor

.04   Industrial relations by industry and occupation

> Standard subdivisions are added for either or both topics in heading

.041   Industrial relations in industries and occupations other than extractive, manufacturing, construction

> Standard subdivisions are added for industries, occupations, or both

> Class here industrial relations in service industries and occupations

.041 000 1–.041 000 9   Standard subdivisions

.041 001–.041 999   Subdivisions for industrial relations in industries and occupations other than extractive, manufacturing, construction

> Add to base number 331.041 notation 001–999, e.g., industrial relations in clerical occupations 331.04165137
> Subdivisions are added for industries, occupations, or both

.042–.049   Industrial relations in extractive, manufacturing, construction industries and occupations

> Add to base number 331.04 the numbers following 6 in 620–690, e.g., industrial relations in chemical industries 331.046
> Subdivisions are added for industries, occupations, or both

.08   Groups of people

> Do not use for discrimination; class in 331.133

> Class here labor force by personal attributes, comprehensive works on minorities in the labor force

[.081]   People by gender or sex

> Do not use; class in 331.56

[.082]   Women

> Do not use; class in 331.4

[.083–.084]   Age groups

> Do not use; class in 331.3

[.086]   People by miscellaneous social attributes

> Do not use; class in 331.5

[.087]   People with disabilities and illnesses, gifted people

> Do not use; class in 331.5

[.088]   Occupational and religious groups

> Do not use for religious groups; class in 331.58. Do not use for occupational groups; class in 331.7

[.089]   Ethnic and national groups

> Do not use; class in 331.6

.1   **Labor force and market**

> Class here comprehensive works on employment and unemployment

> Class employment in 331.125; class unemployment in 331.137

SUMMARY

331.11	**Labor force**
.12	**Labor market**
.13	**Discrimination in employment, labor shortages, unemployment**

.11	Labor force

Class here human resources, labor supply, size of labor force, work force

Class labor force in relation to demand for labor in 331.12

See also 331.8732 for union membership

.114	Qualifications
.114 2	Qualifications by level of skills

Including semiskilled, unskilled employees

.114 22	Skilled workers
.114 4	Qualifications by level of education
.114 43	High school graduates
.114 45	College graduates

Regardless of degree obtained

.117	Systems of labor

See also 306.36 for social aspects of systems of labor

.117 2	Free labor
.117 3	Compulsory labor
.117 32	State labor (Drafted workers)
.117 34	Slave labor
.118	Labor productivity

Class industrial productivity in 338.06

.119	Labor force by industry and occupation

Standard subdivisions are added for either or both topics in heading

Class qualifications of labor force by industry and occupation in 331.114; class systems of labor by industry and occupation in 331.117; class labor productivity by industry and occupation in 331.118; class comprehensive works on labor by industry and occupation in 331.7

.119 04	Special topics of labor force by industry and occupation
.119 042	Labor force in general categories of occupations

Including blue collar, civilian, governmental (public service), service, white collar occupations

.119 1	Labor force in industries and occupations other than extractive, manufacturing, construction

Standard subdivisions are added for industries, occupations, or both

Class here labor force in service industries and occupations

.119 100 01–.119 100 09	Standard subdivisions

.119 100 1–.119 199 9   Subdivisions for labor force in industries and occupations other
                             than extractive, manufacturing, construction

                                  Add to base number 331.1191 notation 001–999, e.g.,
                                  labor force in stenography 331.11916513741; however,
                                  for labor force in general categories of occupations, e.g.,
                                  governmental (public service) occupations, see 331.119042
                                       Subdivisions are added for industries, occupations, or
                                       both

.119 2–.119 9   Labor force in extractive, manufacturing, construction industries and
                             occupations

                                  Add to base number 331.119 the numbers following 6 in 620–690,
                                  e.g., labor force in automotive manufacturing 331.119292
                                       Subdivisions are added for industries, occupations, or both

.12   Labor market

                 Class here supply of labor in relation to demand

                 Class job creation in 331.120424

                     For discrimination in employment, labor shortages, unemployment,
                     underemployment, see 331.13

                                 SUMMARY

         331.120 4   **Special topics of labor market**
            .123   **Demand for labor**
            .124   **Job vacancies (Job openings)**
            .125   **Labor actively employed**
            .126   **Labor turnover**
            .127   **Labor mobility**
            .128   **Placement**
            .129   **Labor market by industry and occupation**

.120 4   Special topics of labor market

.120 42   Government policy on labor market

                             For policy with respect to a specific aspect of labor force and
                             market, see the aspect, e.g., assistance in finding jobs 331.128

                             See also 362.85 for social programs for working class; also
                             370 for education

.120 424   Full employment policies

                         Class here job creation

                         Class policies designed to secure full employment through
                         fiscal and monetary policy in 339.5

                             See Manual at 331.120424 vs. 331.1377

.123   Demand for labor

                 Class here labor requirements

                     For job vacancies, see 331.124; for shortages, see 331.136; for
                     surpluses, see 331.137

.123 1   Demand for labor in industries and occupations other than extractive, manufacturing, construction

                          Standard subdivisions are added for industries, occupations, or both

                          Class here demand for labor in service industries and occupations

.123 100 01–.123 100 09   Standard subdivisions

.123 100 1–.123 199 9   Subdivisions for demand for labor in industries and occupations other than extractive, manufacturing, construction

                          Add to base number 331.1231 notation 001–999, e.g., demand for teachers 331.12313711
                              Subdivisions are added for industries, occupations, or both

.123 2–.123 9   Demand for labor in extractive, manufacturing, construction industries and occupations

                          Add to base number 331.123 the numbers following 6 in 620–690, e.g., demand for carpenters 331.12394
                              Subdivisions are added for industries, occupations, or both

.124   Job vacancies (Job openings)

.124 1   Job vacancies in industries and occupations other than extractive, manufacturing, construction

                          Standard subdivisions are added for industries, occupations, or both

                          Class here job vacancies in service industries and occupations

.124 100 01–.124 100 09   Standard subdivisions

.124 100 1–.124 199 9   Subdivisions for job vacancies in industries and occupations other than extractive, manufacturing, construction

                          Add to base number 331.1241 notation 001–999, e.g., opportunities in librarianship 331.124102
                              Subdivisions are added for industries, occupations, or both

.124 2–.124 9   Job vacancies in extractive, manufacturing, construction industries and occupations

                          Add to base number 331.124 the numbers following 6 in 620–690, e.g., openings in paper manufacture 331.12476
                              Subdivisions are added for industries, occupations, or both

.125   Labor actively employed

                          Class here employment, utilization of human resources, comprehensive works on employment and compensation

                          Class comprehensive works on employment and unemployment in 331.1

                          For compensation, see 331.21

                          See also 331.126 for turnover; also 331.137 for unemployment

.125 1   Labor actively employed in industries and occupations other than
                 extractive, manufacturing, construction

                     Standard subdivisions are added for industries, occupations, or both

                     Class here labor actively employed in service industries and
                     occupations

.125 100 01–.125 100 09   Standard subdivisions

.125 100 1–.125 199 9   Subdivisions for labor actively employed in industries and
                                  occupations other than extractive, manufacturing, construction

                                      Add to base number 331.1251 notation 001–999, e.g., labor
                                      actively employed in education 331.125137
                                          Subdivisions are added for industries, occupations, or
                                          both

.125 2–.125 9   Labor actively employed in extractive, manufacturing, construction
                 industries and occupations

                     Add to base number 331.125 the numbers following 6 in 620–690,
                     e.g., labor actively employed in the plumbing industry 331.125961
                         Subdivisions are added for industries, occupations, or both

.126   Labor turnover

.126 1   Labor turnover in industries and occupations other than extractive,
                 manufacturing, construction

                     Standard subdivisions are added for industries, occupations, or both

                     Class here turnover in service industries and occupations

.126 100 01–.126 100 09   Standard subdivisions

.126 100 1–.126 199 9   Subdivisions for turnover in industries and occupations other
                                  than extractive, manufacturing, construction

                                      Add to base number 331.1261 notation 001–999, e.g.,
                                      turnover of nurses 331.126161073
                                          Subdivisions are added for industries, occupations, or
                                          both

.126 2–.126 9   Labor turnover in extractive, manufacturing, construction industries and
                 occupations

                     Add to base number 331.126 the numbers following 6 in 620–690,
                     e.g., turnover of miners 331.12622
                         Subdivisions are added for industries, occupations, or both

.127   Labor mobility

.127 09   History and biography

                     Do not use for geographic treatment; class in 331.1279

.127 2   Occupational mobility

.127 9   Geographic mobility

.127 91   International mobility

                     Including brain drain

| .127 93–.127 99 | Geographic mobility within specific countries and smaller areas |

Add to base number 331.1279 notation 3–9 from Table 2, e.g., mobility of labor within Canada 331.127971

Class mobility between countries and continents in 331.12791

| .128 | Placement |

Class here employment agencies, job banks, labor exchanges, sources of job information

Class job vacancies in 331.124

See also 362.0425 for employment services viewed as a solution to social welfare problems; also 650.14 for success in, techniques of job hunting

| .129 | Labor market by industry and occupation |

Standard subdivisions are added for either or both topics in heading

For specific aspects of labor market by industry and occupation, see 331.123–331.128

| .129 04 | Special topics of labor market by industry and occupation |

| .129 042 | Labor market by general categories of occupations |

Including blue collar, civilian, governmental (public service), service, white collar occupations

| .129 1 | Labor market by industries and occupations other than extractive, manufacturing, construction |

Standard subdivisions are added for industries, occupations, or both

Class here labor market in service industries and occupations

| .129 100 01–.129 100 09 | Standard subdivisions |

| .129 100 1–.129 199 9 | Subdivisions for labor market by industries and occupations other than extractive, manufacturing, construction |

Add to base number 331.1291 notation 001–999, e.g., labor market in stenography 331.12916513741; however, for labor market in general categories of occupations, e.g., governmental (public service) occupations, see 331.129042
    Subdivisions are added for industries, occupations, or both

| .129 2–.129 9 | Labor market by extractive, manufacturing, construction industries and occupations |

Add to base number 331.129 the numbers following 6 in 620–690, e.g., labor market in automotive manufacturing 331.129292
    Subdivisions are added for industries, occupations, or both

| .13 | Discrimination in employment, labor shortages, unemployment |

Including underemployment

Class here maladjustments in labor market, programs to prevent or provide relief from maladjustments

.133	**Discrimination in employment**	

Class here affirmative action in employment, equal employment opportunity programs, programs for workplace diversity; hostile work environments

Class discrimination against workers with specific personal attributes in 331.3–331.6; class personnel aspects of discrimination in government employment in 352.608; class comprehensive works on work environment in 331.256; class comprehensive works about personnel policies on discrimination in 658.3008

> *For discrimination in relation to a specific aspect of industrial relations, see the aspect, e.g., discrimination as a factor affecting compensation 331.2153, discrimination by unions 331.8732*

.136   **Labor shortages**

.137   **Unemployment**

Class here labor surpluses, unemployed people

.137 04   Kinds of unemployment

.137 041   Structural unemployment

> *For technological unemployment, see 331.137042*

.137 042   Technological unemployment

.137 044   Seasonal unemployment

.137 045   Frictional unemployment

.137 047   Cyclical unemployment

[.137 09]   History, geographic treatment, biography

Do not use; class in 331.1379

.137 2   Causes of unemployment

> *For macroeconomic causes, see 339. For a cause of unemployment that defines a specific kind of unemployment, see the kind in 331.13704, e.g., structural unemployment 331.137041*

.137 3   Effects of unemployment

.137 7   Prevention and relief of unemployment

Standard subdivisions are added for either or both topics in heading

> *For a specific measure of prevention or relief, see the measure, e.g., work sharing 331.2572, economic stabilization 339.5, welfare 362.85*

> *See Manual at 331.120424 vs. 331.1377*

.137 8   Unemployment among general groups of labor, unemployment by industry and occupation

Class specific elements regardless of group, industry, occupation in 331.1372–331.1377

.137 804	General groups of unemployed people

> Groups defined by level of education, skill, experience
>
> Class unemployed people having specific personal attributes in 331.3–331.6

.137 81	Unemployment in industries and occupations other than extractive, manufacturing, construction

> Standard subdivisions are added for industries, occupations, or both
>
> Class here unemployment in service industries and occupations

.137 810 001–.137 810 009	Standard subdivisions
.137 810 01–.137 819 99	Subdivisions for unemployment in industries and occupations other than extractive, manufacturing, construction

> Add to base number 331.13781 notation 001–999, e.g., unemployment in clerical occupations 331.1378165137
>> Subdivisions are added for industries, occupations, or both

.137 82–.137 89	Unemployment in extractive, manufacturing, construction industries and occupations

> Add to base number 331.1378 the numbers following 6 in 620–690, e.g., unemployment in the automotive industry 331.1378292
>> Subdivisions are added for industries, occupations, or both

.137 9	History, geographic treatment, biography

> Class history of specific elements of unemployment in 331.1372–331.1377; class history of unemployment among general groups of labor and by industry and occupation in 331.1378

.137 900 1–.137 900 8	Standard subdivisions
[.137 900 9]	History

> Do not use; class in 331.1379

.137 901–.137 905	Historical periods

> Add to base number 331.13790 the numbers following —090 in notation 0901–0905 from Table 1, e.g., unemployment in 20th century 331.137904

.137 91–.137 99	Geographic treatment and biography

> Add to base number 331.1379 notation 1–9 from Table 2, e.g., unemployment in the United States 331.137973
>
> Class geographic treatment of specific elements of unemployment in 331.1372–331.1377; class geographic treatment and biography of unemployment among general groups of labor and by industry and occupation in 331.1378

.2   **Conditions of employment**

Class here comprehensive works on collective bargaining to determine conditions of employment and the resulting conditions of employment

Class conditions of employment discussed from the managerial viewpoint in 658.312

For collective bargaining to determine conditions of employment, see 331.89

SUMMARY

.204   Conditions of employment by industry and occupation

Standard subdivisions are added for either or both topics in heading

.204 1   Conditions of employment in industries and occupations other than extractive, manufacturing, construction

Standard subdivisions are added for industries, occupations, or both

Class here conditions of employment in service industries and occupations

.204 100 01–.204 100 09   Standard subdivisions

.204 100 1–.204 199 9   Subdivisions for conditions of employment in industries and occupations other than extractive, manufacturing, construction

Add to base number 331.2041 notation 001–999, e.g., conditions of employment in clerical occupations 331.204165137
Subdivisions are added for industries, occupations, or both

.204 2–.204 9   Conditions of employment in extractive, manufacturing, construction industries and occupations

Add to base number 331.204 the numbers following 6 in 620–690, e.g., conditions of employment in chemical industries 331.2046
Subdivisions are added for industries, occupations, or both

.21   Compensation

Class here wages, wage policy

Class incomes policy (wage-price policy) in 339.5

For compensation differentials, see 331.22; for employee benefits (fringe benefits), see 331.255; for compensation by industry and occupation, see 331.28

.210 1	Philosophy and theory

Including bargain theory, marginal productivity theory, national income theory, subsistence theory ("iron law"), wages fund theory

[.210 9]	History, geographic treatment, biography

Do not use; class in 331.29

.215	Factors affecting compensation

Including methods of determination, e.g., intraindustry and interindustry comparison; criteria used in determination, e.g., cost of living as a compensation determinant

For minimum-wage policies, see 331.23

See also 332.415 for wage-price controls to combat inflation; also 339.5 for wage control as a factor in economic stabilization

.215 08	Groups of people

Do not use for discrimination in compensation; class in 331.2153

.215 3	Discrimination and anti-discrimination policies

Standard subdivisions are added for either or both topics in heading

Class here equal pay for equal work, pay equity

Class discrimination because of a specific personal characteristic in 331.3–331.6

.216	Methods of compensation

Class here wage payment systems

Class employee benefits (fringe benefits) in 331.255

.216 2	Time payments

Including hourly, weekly, monthly, annual periods; overtime pay

Class guaranteed-wage plans in 331.23

.216 4	Incentive compensation

Including bonuses, merit pay, performance awards; piecework, combined timework and piecework

Class tips in 331.2166

.216 47	Profit sharing

Class here gain sharing

.216 49	Employee stock ownership plans

Class here employee stock options, employee stock purchase plans

Class stock options as a form of speculation in 332.632283; class comprehensive works on employee ownership in 338.69

.216 6   Other methods of compensation

                Including longevity pay, locality pay (weighting), professional and subcontracting fees, severance pay, tips

                Class paid leave in 331.2576

.22   Compensation differentials

                Including differences among, firms, industries, occupations, regions

                Class differentials as a factor affecting compensation in 331.215

.220 9   History, geographic treatment, biography

                Class geographic treatment of compensation not emphasizing differentials in 331.29

.23   Guaranteed-wage plans

                Class here minimum wage

                Class guaranteed minimum income in 362.582

.236   Guaranteed annual wage

.25   Other conditions of employment

SUMMARY

331.252	**Pensions**	
.255	**Employee benefits (Fringe benefits)**	
.256	**Work environment**	
.257	**Hours**	
.259	**Training, worker security, regulation of worker conduct**	

.252   Pensions

                Including retirement age

                Class here retirement benefits, superannuation, interdisciplinary works on pensions

                Class pensions for government (public service) employees in 331.25291351

                For pensions provided by unions, see 331.8735; for retirement planning, see 332.024014; for public administration of pensions for government workers, see 353.549; for pensions (annuities) provided through insurance, see 368.37; for government pension plans for the population at large, see 368.43; for comprehensive works on administration of pensions, see 658.3253

.252 2   Pension reform

                Class here preservation, transfer of vested rights in pensions

.252 4   Pension funds

                Class investment by pension funds in 332.67254

.252 9   Pensions by industry and occupation

                Standard subdivisions are added for either or both topics in heading

.252 91   Pensions in industries and occupations other than extractive, manufacturing, construction

> Standard subdivisions are added for industries, occupations, or both

> Class here pensions in service industries and occupations

.252 910 001–.252 910 009   Standard subdivisions

.252 910 01–.252 919 99   Subdivisions for pensions in industries and occupations other than extractive, manufacturing, construction

> Add to base number 331.25291 notation 001–999, e.g., military pensions 331.25291355
> > Subdivisions are added for industries, occupations, or both

.252 92–.252 99   Pensions in extractive, manufacturing, construction industries and occupations

> Add to base number 331.2529 the numbers following 6 in 620–690, e.g., pensions in construction trades 331.252924
> > Subdivisions are added for industries, occupations, or both

.255   Employee benefits (Fringe benefits)

> Class here employee assistance programs, insurance, interdisciplinary works on employee benefits

> *For stock ownership and purchase plans, see 331.21649; for pensions, see 331.252; for benefits provided by unions, see 331.8735; for benefits for veterans of military service and their survivors, see 362.86; for benefits provided through insurance, see 368.3; for benefits provided through government-sponsored social insurance, see 368.4; for comprehensive works on administration of employee benefits, see 658.325*

.255 2   Unemployment compensation

> Class interdisciplinary works on unemployment insurance in 368.44

.255 4   Health services

> Class interdisciplinary works on health insurance in 368.382

.256   Work environment

> Class here physical working conditions, quality of work life, working facilities, workplace relationships; work stress

> *For hostile work environment caused by hostile and discriminatory behavior, see 331.133*

.256 7   Home labor

> Producing goods at home for an outside employer

> Class here cottage industries, comprehensive works on work at home

> *For telecommuting, see 331.2568*

.256 8   Telecommuting

.257   Hours

Including reduced workweek

Class here workweek

.257 2   Alternative work schedules; workday

Including overtime, work sharing

.257 22   Compressed workweek

Including four-day forty-hour week

.257 23   Workday

Class a specific alternative workday schedule with the alternative work schedule elsewhere in 331.2572, e.g., part-time schedule 331.25727

For rest periods, see 331.2576

.257 24   Flexible hours

See also 331.2567 for home labor; also 331.2568 for telecommuting; also 331.25722 for compressed workweek

.257 25   Shift work

See also 331.2574 for night work

.257 27   Part-time work

.257 277   Job sharing

See also 331.2572 for work sharing

.257 29   Temporary employment

Class here temporary employees

Class services to provide temporary help in 331.128

.257 4   Night, holy day, Sunday, holiday work

See also 331.2572 for shift work

.257 6   Leave and rest periods (breaks)

Standard subdivisions are added for leave and rest periods together, for leave alone

Including sabbatical leave

Class here annual leave, holidays, paid vacations

.257 62   Sick leave

Class here interdisciplinary works on employer-sponsored and government-sponsored paid sick leave

For government-sponsored paid sick leave, see 368.452

.257 63	Parental leave

Class here leave for pregnancy, birth, longer-term care of children; adoption leave, parental leave taken by legal guardians; interdisciplinary works on government-sponsored and employer-sponsored paid parental leave

For government-sponsored paid parental leave, see 368.454

.257 630 851	Fathers

Class here paternity leave, parental leave taken by fathers

.257 630 852	Mothers

Class here maternity leave, parental leave taken by mothers

.257 630 86	People by miscellaneous social attributes
.257 630 866 4	Gays

Class here parental leave taken by same-sex partners

.257 64	Educational leave
.259	**Training, worker security, regulation of worker conduct**
.259 2	Training

Not related to a specific industry

Class here interdisciplinary works on on-the-job vocational training, on vocational training provided by industry

Class interdisciplinary works on vocational education conducted by an educational institution in 370.113

For managerial aspects of training by the employer, see 658.3124. For on-the-job training in a specific occupation, see the occupation, plus notation 07155 from Table 1, e.g., on-the-job apprenticeship of plumbers 696.107155

.259 22	Apprenticeship

For apprentices as a special class of workers, see 331.55; for work experience as part of education, see 371.227

.259 24	Retraining
.259 6	Worker security

Including dismissal of employees; employment security, job tenure; right to organize, rights of transfer and promotion, seniority

.259 8	Regulation of worker conduct

Class here discipline

.259 88	Absenteeism

.28   Compensation by industry and occupation

> Standard subdivisions are added for either or both topics in heading

> Class specific elements of compensation by industry and occupation in 331.21–331.23

.281   Compensation in industries and occupations other than extractive, manufacturing, construction

> Standard subdivisions are added for industries, occupations, or both

> Class here compensation in service industries and occupations

.281 000 1–.281 000 9   Standard subdivisions

.281 001–.281 999   Subdivisions for compensation in industries and occupations other than extractive, manufacturing, construction

> Add to base number 331.281 notation 001–999, e.g., compensation of legislators 331.28132833
> > Subdivisions are added for industries, occupations, or both

.282–.289   Compensation in extractive, manufacturing, construction industries and occupations

> Add to base number 331.28 the numbers following 6 in 620–690, e.g., compensation in the mining industry 331.2822, average factory compensation 331.287
> > Subdivisions are added for industries, occupations, or both

.29   History, geographic treatment, biography of compensation

> Class history of factors affecting compensation and history of methods of compensation in 331.215–331.216; class history of compensation differentials and history of guaranteed-wage plans in 331.22–331.23; class history of compensation by industries and occupations in 331.28; class wage-price policies in relation to stabilizing the economy in 339.5

.290 01–.290 08   Standard subdivisions

[.290 09]   History

> Do not use; class in 331.29

.290 1–.290 5   Historical periods

> Add to base number 331.290 the numbers following —090 in notation 0901–0905 from Table 1, e.g., compensation in 20th century 331.2904

.291–.299   Geographic treatment and biography

> Add to base number 331.29 notation 1–9 from Table 2, e.g., compensation in Australia 331.2994

> Class geographic treatment and biography of specific elements of compensation in 331.215–331.23; class geographic treatment and biography of compensation by industries and occupations in 331.28

> ### 331.3–331.6 Labor force by personal attributes

Class here labor force and market, conditions of employment, industries and occupations, labor unions, labor-management bargaining with respect to special groups of workers

Unless other instructions are given, class a subject with aspects in two or more subdivisions of 331.3–331.6 in the number coming first, e.g., young North American native women 331.34408997 (*not* 331.408997 or 331.6397)

Class choice of vocation for people with specific personal attributes in 331.702; class comprehensive works on groups of people in 331.08. Class employment services as a form of social service to a specific group of people with the group in 362.6–362.8, e.g., sheltered employment for people in late adulthood 362.64

.3　　Workers by age group

.31　　Children

Through age thirteen

See also 364.15554 for criminal aspects of child labor

.318　　Children through age thirteen by industry and occupation

Standard subdivisions are added for either or both topics in heading

.34　　Young workers

Through age thirty-five

For children through age thirteen, see 331.31; for young workers by industry and occupation, see 331.38

.341–.342　　Specific aspects of employment of young workers

Add to base number 331.34 the numbers following 331 in 331.1–331.2, e.g., training of young workers 331.342592

Class specific aspects of employment of specific kinds of young workers in 331.344–331.346

.344–.346　　Employment of specific kinds of young workers

Add to base number 331.34 the numbers following 331 in 331.4–331.6, e.g., African American youth 331.346396073; however, for apprentices, see 331.55

.347　　Workers aged 14 through 20

Class employment of specific groups of workers aged 14 through 20 in 331.344–331.346

For specific aspects of employment of workers aged 14 through 20, see 331.341–331.342

.38   **Young workers by industry and occupation**

         Standard subdivisions are added for either or both topics in heading

         Through age thirty-five

         Class employment of specific kinds of young workers by industry and occupation in 331.344–331.346

> *For children through age thirteen by industries and occupations, see 331.318; for specific aspects of employment of young workers by industry and occupation, see 331.341–331.342*

.381   **Young workers in industries and occupations other than extractive, manufacturing, construction**

         Standard subdivisions are added for industries, occupations, or both

         Class here young workers in service industries and occupations

.381 000 1–.381 000 9   Standard subdivisions

.381 001–.381 999   Subdivisions for young workers in industries and occupations other than extractive, manufacturing, construction

         Add to base number 331.381 notation 001–999, e.g., young workers in clerical occupations 331.38165137
         Subdivisions are added for industries, occupations, or both

.382–.389   **Young workers in extractive, manufacturing, construction industries and occupations**

         Add to base number 331.38 the numbers following 6 in 620–690, e.g., young textile workers 331.3877
         Subdivisions are added for industries, occupations, or both

.39   **Other age groups**

.394   **Middle-aged workers**

.398   **Older workers**

.398 1–.398 2   Specific aspects on employment of older workers

         Add to base number 331.398 the numbers following 331 in 331.1–331.2, e.g., discrimination against older workers 331.398133

.398 8   Older workers by industry and occupation

         Standard subdivisions are added for either or both topics in heading

.398 81   Older workers in industries and occupations other than extractive, manufacturing, construction

         Standard subdivisions are added for industries, occupations, or both

         Class here older workers in service industries and occupations

.398 810 001–.398 810 009   Standard subdivisions

.398 810 01–.398 819 99   Subdivisions for older workers in industries and occupations other than extractive, manufacturing, construction

> Add to base number 331.39881 notation 001–999, e.g., older workers in clerical occupations 331.3988165137
>> Subdivisions are added for industries, occupations, or both

.398 82–.398 89   Older workers in extractive, manufacturing, construction industries and occupations

> Add to base number 331.3988 the numbers following 6 in 620–690, e.g., older agricultural workers in 331.39883
>> Subdivisions are added for industries, occupations, or both

.4   Women workers

Unless other instructions are given, observe the following table of preference, e.g., women clothing workers in labor unions 331.478187 (*not* 331.4887):

Working mothers	331.44
Married women	331.43
Labor unions and labor-management bargaining and disputes	331.47
Specific aspects of employment of women	331.41–331.42
Women workers by industry and occupation	331.48

See also 305.43 for sociology of women's occupations

.41–.42   Specific aspects of employment of women

> Add to base number 331.4 the numbers following 331 in 331.1–331.2, e.g., discrimination against women 331.4133

.43   Married women

.44   Working mothers

> Including pregnant workers

> Class maternity leave, parental leave taken by mothers in 331.257630852

.47   Labor unions and labor-management bargaining and disputes

> Add to base number 331.47 the numbers following 331.8 in 331.87–331.89, e.g., women in labor unions 331.478

.48   Women workers by industry and occupation

> Standard subdivisions are added for either or both topics in heading

.481   Women workers in industries and occupations other than extractive, manufacturing, construction

> Standard subdivisions are added for industries, occupations, or both

> Class here women in service industries and occupations

.481 000 1–.481 000 9   Standard subdivisions

.481 001–.481 999   Subdivisions for women workers in industries and occupations other than extractive, manufacturing, construction

> Add to base number 331.481 notation 001–999, e.g., women in advertising 331.4816591
> > Subdivisions are added for industries, occupations, or both

.482–.489   Women workers in extractive, manufacturing, construction industries and occupations

> Add to base number 331.48 the numbers following 6 in 620–690, e.g., women clothing workers 331.4887
> > Subdivisions are added for industries, occupations, or both

.5   Workers by personal attributes other than age

> Including transgender and intersex people, retired people

> *For immigrants and aliens, see 331.62; for native-born workers by ethnic group, see 331.63*

.51   Prisoners and ex-convicts

> Standard subdivisions are added for either or both topics in heading

> Including political and war prisoners

.52   Veterans

> *See also 331.25291355 for pensions received because of military service; also 331.761355 for military labor*

.53   Gays

> Class here gay men

> Class parental leave taken by same-sex partners in 331.2576308664

.54   Workers in special economic situations

> Class here economically disadvantaged workers not provided for elsewhere

> Class unemployed workers in 331.137

.542   Contract workers

.544   Migrant and casual workers

> Standard subdivisions are added for migrant and casual workers together, for migrant workers alone

> Class here migrant agricultural laborers

> *See also 331.62 for immigrant and alien workers*

.55   Apprentices

> Class training of apprentices in 331.25922

.56   Workers by gender or sex

> Class transgender and intersex people in 331.5

> *For women, see 331.4*

.561   Men

> Class paternity leave, parental leave taken by fathers in 331.257630851

.58   Workers by religious group

> Add to base number 331.58 the numbers following 2 in 230–299, e.g., Catholics 331.5882, Muslims 331.5897

.59   Workers with disabilities and illnesses

> Class here workers with physical disabilities

> Add to base number 331.59 the numbers following —087 in notation 0871–0877 from Table 1, e.g., workers with impaired vision 331.591

.6   **Workers by ethnic and national origin**

.62   Immigrants and aliens

> Standard subdivisions are added for either or both topics in heading

> *See also 331.544 for migrant workers*

.620 9   History, geographic treatment, biography

> Class here immigrant and alien workers in specific areas, e.g., immigrant workers in Canada 331.620971

> > *For immigrant and alien workers from specific jurisdictions, see 331.621–331.629*

> 331.621–331.629   Immigrants and aliens by place of origin

> Class comprehensive works in 331.62

> *See also 331.6209 for immigrant and alien workers in specific areas*

.621   Immigrants and aliens from areas, regions, places in general

> Add to base number 331.621 the numbers following —1 in notation 11–19 from Table 2, e.g., immigrant workers from developing regions 331.621724; then add 0* and to the result add notation 1–9 from Table 2, e.g., immigrant workers from developing regions in California 331.6217240794
> Subdivisions are added for either or both topics in heading

.623–.629   Immigrants and aliens from specific continents, countries, localities

> Add to base number 331.62 notation 3–9 from Table 2 for place of origin, e.g., immigrant workers from China 331.6251; then, for area located, add 0* and to the result add notation 1–9 from Table 2, e.g., immigrant workers from China in California 331.62510794
> Subdivisions are added for either or both topics in heading

.63   Native-born workers by ethnic group

.630 01–.630 07   Standard subdivisions

.630 08   Groups of people

*Add 00 for standard subdivisions; see instructions at beginning of Table 1

[.630 089]	Ethnic and national groups
	Do not use for comprehensive works on native-born ethnic groups; class in 331.63. Do not use for native-born workers of mixed ancestry with ethnic origins from more than one continent, native-born European workers and native-born workers of European descent; class in 331.6305–331.6309. Do not use for native-born workers of other ethnic groups; class in 331.631–331.639
.630 09	History, geographic treatment, biography
.630 5–.630 9	Native-born workers of mixed ancestry with ethnic origins from more than one continent, native-born European workers and native-born workers of European descent
	Add to base number 331.63 notation 05–09 from Table 5, e.g., native-born workers of European descent 331.6309, native-born workers of European descent in Australia 331.6309094
.631–.639	Native-born workers of other ethnic groups
	Add to base number 331.63 notation 1–9 from Table 5, e.g., African Americans 331.6396073, African American workers in Alabama 331.63960730761, Aboriginal Australians 331.639915, Aboriginal Australian workers in Queensland 331.6399150943

.7 **Labor by industry and occupation**

Standard subdivisions are added for either or both topics in heading

Class comprehensive works on industrial occupations in 331.794

For professional relationships in a specific industry or occupation, see the industry or occupation, plus notation 023 from Table 1, e.g., professional relationships in accounting 657.023

.700 1–.700 9	Standard subdivisions
.702	Choice of vocation
	Class here choice of vocation for people with specific personal attributes, e.g., veterans; interdisciplinary works describing vocations and occupational specialties; interdisciplinary works on career opportunities and vocational counseling
	Class studies of vocational interest in 158.6; class job hunting in 650.14
	For vocational counseling in schools, see 371.425. For descriptions of, career opportunities in, choice of vocation with regard to specific vocations and occupational specialties, see the vocation or specialty, plus notation 023 from Table 1, e.g., career opportunities in accounting 657.023
.702 3	Choice of vocation for people at specific educational levels
[.702 301–.702 309]	Standard subdivisions
	Do not use; class in 331.70201–331.70209
.702 33	Choice of vocation for high school graduates

.702 35   Choice of vocation for college graduates

                            Regardless of degree obtained

.71   Professional occupations

                For specific professional occupations, see 331.761

.76   Specific industries and occupations

                Class specific groups of occupations in 331.79

[.760 1–.760 9]   Standard subdivisions

                    Do not use; class in 331.7001–331.7009

.761   Industries and occupations other than extractive, manufacturing, construction

                Standard subdivisions are added for industries, occupations, or both

                Class comprehensive works on service industries and occupations in 331.793

.761 000 1–.761 000 9   Standard subdivisions

.761 001–.761 999   Subdivisions for industries and occupations other than extractive, manufacturing, construction

                        Add to base number 331.761 notation 001–999, e.g., managerial occupations 331.761658; however, for governmental (public service) occupations, see 331.795
                            Subdivisions are added for industries, occupations, or both

.762–.769   Extractive, manufacturing, construction industries and occupations

                Add to base number 331.76 the numbers following 6 in 620–690, e.g., food processing 331.7664
                    Subdivisions are added for industries, occupations, or both

                Class comprehensive works on industrial occupations in 331.794

.79   General occupation groups and government occupations

                Occupational groups not defined by industry or discipline

                Unless other instructions are given, class a subject with aspects in two or more subdivisions of 331.79 in the number coming last, e.g., white collar governmental (public service) occupations 331.795 (*not* 331.792)

                For professional occupations, see 331.71

[.790 1–.790 9]   Standard subdivisions

                    Do not use; class in 331.7001–331.7009

.792   White collar occupations

.793   Service occupations

                Class here labor in service industries

.794 Industrial occupations

Including the work of artisans and supervisors; skilled, semiskilled work

For unskilled work, see 331.798

.795 Governmental occupations (Public service occupations)

Including elected civil servants

.798 Unskilled work

.8 Labor unions, labor-management bargaining and disputes

Class here interdisciplinary works on labor movements

Class comprehensive works on labor relations (all relations between management and individual employees or employee groups) in 331; class comprehensive works on industrial democracy in 331.0112

For a specific aspect of labor movements, see the aspect, e.g., political activities of labor movements 322.2

SUMMARY

331.87	**Labor union organization**
.88	**Labor unions (Trade unions)**
.89	**Labor-management bargaining and disputes**

.87 Labor union organization

Class comprehensive works on labor unions in 331.88

.871 Constitutions, bylaws, rules

.872 Levels of organization

Including locals, national unions, union federations

Class international unions in 331.88091; class descriptions of individual unions and federations, comprehensive works on unions in specific areas in 331.8809

.873 Specific aspects of union organization

Including discipline of members

[.873 01–.873 09] Standard subdivisions

Do not use; class in 331.8701–331.8709

.873 2 Membership

Class here membership policies

Class discrimination by unions against workers with specific personal attributes with the attribute in 331.3–331.6, e.g., discrimination against women 331.47732

.873 3	Officers
	Including shop stewards
	Class here union leaders
	Class biography of union leaders in 331.88092
.873 5	Benefits, funds, property
.874	Union elections and conventions

Standard subdivisions are added for union elections and conventions together, for union elections alone

.88   **Labor unions (Trade unions)**

Class here unions organized along religious lines, e.g., Christian trade unions

Class right of workers to organize in 331.2596

For labor union organization, see 331.87; for managerial viewpoint on labor unions, see 658.3153

See also 322.2 for political activities of labor unions

.880 1   Philosophy and theory

Including countermonopoly theory; theories of unions as instruments of class struggle, as instruments of industrial democracy, as instruments for worker control of industry

See also 331.0112 for industrial democracy; also 338.69 for worker control of industry

.880 9   History, geographic treatment, biography

.880 91   Areas, regions, places in general

Class here international unions

Class international unions with members from only two countries in 331.88094–331.88099, using the comprehensive notation from Table 2 for the two countries, e.g., unions with United States and Canadian workers 331.880973

.881   Labor unions by industry and occupation

Standard subdivisions are added for either or both topics in heading

.881 1   Labor unions in industries and occupations other than extractive, manufacturing, construction

Standard subdivisions are added for industries, occupations, or both

Class here labor unions in service industries and occupations

.881 100 01–.881 100 09   Standard subdivisions

.881 100 1–.881 199 9	Subdivisions for labor unions (trade unions) in industries and occupations other than extractive, manufacturing, construction

> Add to base number 331.8811 notation 001–999, e.g., teachers' unions 331.88113711
>> Subdivisions are added for industries, occupations, or both

.881 2–.881 9	Labor unions in extractive, manufacturing, construction industries and occupations

> Add to base number 331.881 the numbers following 6 in 620–690, e.g., garment workers' unions 331.88187
> Subdivisions are added for industries, occupations, or both

.883   Kinds of unions

> Class blue-collar unions in 331.88; class specific kinds of unions by industry and occupation in 331.881
>
> *For revolutionary unions, see 331.886*

.883 2   Craft unions

> Class semi-industrial unions in 331.8833

.883 3   Industrial unions

> Class here semi-industrial unions

.883 4   Company unions

.883 6   White collar unions

.886   Revolutionary unions

> Class Industrial Workers of the World (IWW) in 331.8860973

.889   Union security issues

.889 2   Open and closed shop

> Standard subdivisions are added for either or both topics in heading
>
> Class here right to work, agency shop, union shop; general arrangements for union security
>
> Class specific issues of union security in 331.8896; class comprehensive works on rights of labor in 331.011

.889 6   Other union security issues

> Including control of hiring, layoffs, apprenticeships; preferential hiring, sole bargaining rights; dues checkoff, featherbedding
>
> Class general arrangements for union security in 331.8892

[.889 601–.889 609]   Standard subdivisions

> Do not use; class in 331.88901–331.88909

.889 66   Grievance procedures

.89   Labor-management bargaining and disputes

Standard subdivisions are added for either or both topics in heading

Variant name for labor-management bargaining: collective bargaining

Class conditions of work determined by collective bargaining in 331.2; class grievance procedures to resolve disputes in 331.88966; class works treating collective bargaining from the managerial viewpoint in 658.3154

SUMMARY

331.890 4	**Labor-management bargaining and disputes by industry and occupation**
.891	**Contracts and related topics**
.892	**Strikes**
.893	**Other labor measures**
.894	**Management measures**
.898	**Government measures**

.890 4   Labor-management bargaining and disputes by industry and occupation

Standard subdivisions are added for any or all topics in heading

.890 41   Labor-management bargaining and disputes in industries and occupations other than extractive, manufacturing, construction

Standard subdivisions are added for any or all topics in heading

Class here labor-management bargaining and disputes in service industries and occupations

.890 410 001–.890 410 009   Standard subdivisions

.890 410 01–.890 419 99   Subdivisions for labor-management bargaining and disputes in industries and occupations other than extractive, manufacturing, construction

Add to base number 331.89041 notation 001–999, e.g., labor-management bargaining in hospitals 331.8904136211
Subdivisions are added for any or all topics in heading

.890 42–.890 49   Labor-management bargaining and disputes in extractive, manufacturing, construction industries and occupations

Add to base number 331.8904 the numbers following 6 in 620–690, e.g., labor-management bargaining and disputes in the garment industry 331.890487
Subdivisions are added for any or all topics in heading

.891   Contracts and related topics

Standard subdivisions are added for contracts and related topics, for contracts alone

.891 2   Organizing and contract negotiation

Including negotiation during life of contract, recognition of unions

Class conciliation measures in 331.8914

.891 4	Conciliation measures
.891 42	Mediation
.891 43	Arbitration
.892	Strikes

> *For management measures with respect to strikes, see 331.894; for government measures with respect to strikes, see 331.898*
>
> *See also 331.8914 for conciliation measures*

.892 01	Philosophy and theory

> Including right to strike, general theories about effects of strikes
>
> Class effects of strikes on a specific thing with the thing, e.g., effect of strikes on profitability of mining industries 338.23

[.892 09]	History, geographic treatment, biography

> Do not use; class in 331.8929

.892 5	General strikes

> Class interdisciplinary works on general strikes in 322.2

.892 7	Picketing
.892 8	Strikes by industry and occupation

> Standard subdivisions are added for either or both topics in heading

.892 81	Strikes in industries and occupations other than extractive, manufacturing, construction

> Standard subdivisions are added for industries, occupations, or both
>
> Class here strikes in service industries and occupations

.892 810 001–.892 810 009	Standard subdivisions
.892 810 01–.892 819 99	Subdivisions for strikes in industries and occupations other than extractive, manufacturing, construction

> Add to base number 331.89281 notation 001–999, e.g., teachers' strikes 331.892813711
> Subdivisions are added for industries, occupations, or both

.892 82–.892 89	Strikes in extractive, manufacturing, construction industries and occupations

> Add to base number 331.8928 the numbers following 6 in 620–690, e.g., strikes of rubber workers 331.8928782
> Subdivisions are added for industries, occupations, or both

.892 9	History, geographic treatment, biography
.892 900 1–.892 900 8	Standard subdivisions

[.892 900 9]	History

Do not use; class in 331.8929

.892 901–.892 905	Historical periods

Add to base number 331.89290 the numbers following —090 in notation 0901–0905 from Table 1, e.g., strikes in 20th century 331.892904

Class general strikes in specific periods in 331.8925; class strikes by industry and occupations in specific periods in 331.8928

.892 91–.892 99	Geographic treatment and biography

Add to base number 331.8929 notation 1–9 from Table 2, e.g., strikes in Great Britain 331.892941

Class general strikes in specific places in 331.8925; class strikes by industry and occupations in specific places in 331.8928

.893	Other labor measures

Including boycotts, injunctions, sabotage

Class here comprehensive works on labor violence

For violence in strikes, see 331.892

.894	Management measures

Including blacklisting, injunctions, labor espionage, lockouts, strikebreaking, yellow-dog contracts

Class comprehensive works on strikes in 331.892

.898	Government measures

For conciliation measures, see 331.8914

See also 331.8892 for right to work

.898 4	Use of troops

332 Financial economics

For public finance, see 336

See Manual at 332, 336 vs. 339; also at 332 vs. 338, 658.15

SUMMARY

332.01–.09	**Standard subdivisions, personal finance, special topics of financial economics**
.1	**Banks**
.2	**Specialized banking institutions**
.3	**Credit and loan institutions**
.4	**Money**
.5	**Barter, commercial paper, social credit money**
.6	**Investment**
.7	**Credit**
.8	**Interest**
.9	**Counterfeiting, forgery, alteration**

.02   Miscellany and personal finance

Notation 02 from Table 1 as modified below

.024   Personal finance

Do not use for works on financial economics for people in specific occupations; class in 332.02

Including prevention of identity theft

Class here management of household finances

> *For a specific aspect of personal finance not provided for here, see the aspect, e.g., investing in stocks 332.6322, consumer information 381.33*

.024 001–.024 009   Standard subdivisions

.024 01   Increasing income, net worth, financial security

Standard subdivisions are added for any or all topics in heading

Class here financial independence

.024 014   Retirement planning

.024 014 5   Retirement investment plans

Class here individual retirement accounts (IRAs), 401(k) plans, Keogh plans, other investment plans regardless of name; annuities

.024 016   Estate planning

.024 02   Personal debt management

.04   Special topics of financial economics

.041   Capital

> *For international aspects of capital, see 332.042*

.041 2   Working capital

Including cash, inventories

.041 4   Fixed capital

> *For land, see 333*

.041 5   Capital formation and saving

Standard subdivisions are added for either or both topics in heading

Class here capital markets, interdisciplinary works on raising money for investment in capital assets

> *For capital formation discussed in relation to production in specific kinds of industries, see 338.1–338.4; for financing of firms, see 338.6041; for savings and investment as a factor affecting national income, see 339.43*

[.041 506 8]   Management

Do not use; class in 658.1522

.041 52   Self-financing

                 Class here retained profits

                 Class managerial aspects of self-financing in 658.15226

.041 54   Venture capital

.042   International finance

                 Class international monetary system in 332.45; class comprehensive
                 works on international economics in 337

                 *For international banking, see 332.15; for international investment,
                 see 332.673*

.042 4   Capital movements

                 Class here currency movements

                 *For exchange of currencies, see 332.45; for international
                 exchange of securities, see 332.65; for balance of payments, see
                 382.17*

.042 46   Emigrant remittances

                 *For a specific aspect of emigrant remittances, see the aspect,
                 e.g., impact of emigrant remittances on economic development
                 in Latin America 338.98*

.06   Organizations

                 Do not use for financial institutions and their management; class in 332.1

.1   **Banks**

                 Including bank failures

                 Class here banking; comprehensive works on money and banking, on financial
                 institutions and their functions

                 Class government guaranty of deposits in 368.854

                 *For specialized banking institutions, see 332.2; for credit and loan
                 institutions, see 332.3; for money, see 332.4; for credit, see 332.7; for credit
                 unions, see 334.22. For a specific nonbanking activity of a bank, see the
                 activity, e.g., banks selling real estate 333.33*

SUMMARY

332.11	**Central banks**
.12	**Commercial banks**
.15	**International banks**
.16	**Banks with multiple outlets**
.17	**Banking services**

.11   Central banks

                 Specific central banks are classed here, e.g., United States Board of
                 Governors of the Federal Reserve System 332.110973

.112   Relation to monetary policy

       Including issuance of bank notes

       Class role of central bank in carrying out macroeconomic policy in 339.53; class comprehensive works on bank notes in 332.4044

       For interest rates, reserve requirements, see 332.113; for open-market operations, see 332.114

.113   Relation to commercial banks

       Including clearance, interest rates (discount rates), loans, reserve requirements

.114   Open-market operations

       Including purchase of government securities

.12   Commercial banks

       Class here clearing banks, clearing houses

       Class relation to central banks in 332.113; class commercial banks with multiple outlets in 332.16

       For international operations of commercial banks, see 332.15; for other banking services of commercial banks, see 332.17

.122   Incorporated banks

       Class here chartered banks

.122 3   National banks

       See also 332.11 for central banks

.122 4   State and provincial banks

       Class state and provincial chartered private banks in 332.123

.123   Private banks

.15   International banks

       Class here international operations of commercial and other banks, role of banks in international borrowing and debt

       Class comprehensive works on international borrowing and debt in 336.3435

.152   International banks for monetary stabilization and balance of payments

       Standard subdivisions are added for either or both topics in heading

       Class here International Monetary Fund

       Class comprehensive works on balance of payments in 382.17

.153	**International banks for development of resources and production**
	Standard subdivisions are added for either or both topics in heading
	Including International Development Association, International Finance Corporation
	Class here comprehensive works on development banks
	Class banks for development of resources and production in a specific region in 332.15309
	For development banks serving one country, see 332.28
.153 094	Europe
	For European Investment Bank, see 332.1534
.153 097	North America
	For Inter-American Development Bank, see 332.1538
.153 2	International Bank for Reconstruction and Development (World Bank)
.153 4	European Investment Bank
.153 8	Inter-American Development Bank
.154	**International banks for promotion and facilitation of trade**
	Standard subdivisions are added for either or both topics in heading
.155	**International banks for international settlements**
	Class here Bank for International Settlements
.16	**Banks with multiple outlets**
	Class here branch banks, chain banks, interstate banking; bank holding companies, mergers, syndicates
.17	**Banking services**
	For international operations, see 332.15; for services of specialized banking institutions, see 332.2
	See also 332.7 for credit functions not limited to a specific type of financial institution
.175	**General banking services**
.175 2	Deposits
	Including time deposits, e.g., certificates of deposit, savings accounts; savings departments
.175 22	Checking accounts
	Including NOW (negotiable order of withdrawal) accounts
	Class here demand deposits
.175 3	Loans

.175 4		Investments

> *See also 332.66 for investment banks*

.178		Special banking services

> Including clearing services, debit and smart cards, electronic funds transfers, safe-deposit services, trust services

.178 8		Credit cards

> Class comprehensive works on credit cards in 332.765

.2		**Specialized banking institutions**

> *For international banks, see 332.15; for agricultural institutions, see 332.31; for investment banks, see 332.66; for banking cooperatives, see 334.2*

.21		Savings banks

> Including government savings banks
>
> Class here mutual savings banks
>
> Class comprehensive works on thrift institutions in 332.32
>
> *For postal savings banks, see 332.22*

.22		Postal savings banks
.26		Trust companies
.28		Development banks serving one country

> Variant name: industrial development banks
>
> Class banks for development of agriculture in 332.31; class comprehensive works on development banks in 332.153

.3		**Credit and loan institutions**

> Standard subdivisions are added for either or both topics in heading
>
> Including credit and loan functions of enterprises whose primary function is not credit and loan, e.g., credit function of retail stores, travel agencies
>
> Class credit and loan functions of insurance companies in 332.38

.31		Agricultural institutions

> Including land banks

.32		Savings and loan associations

> Variant names: building and loan associations, building societies, home loan associations, mortgage institutions
>
> Class here comprehensive works on thrift institutions
>
> *For savings banks, see 332.21; for credit unions, see 334.22*

.34		Pawnshops

> Class here pawnbrokers, pawnbroking

.35   Consumer and sales finance institutions

Standard subdivisions are added for either or both topics in heading

.37   Labor and employee banks

Standard subdivisions are added for either or both topics in heading

For credit unions, see 334.22

See also 332.35 for banks specializing in consumer loans

.38   Credit and loan functions of insurance companies

Standard subdivisions are added for either or both topics in heading

Class interdisciplinary works on insurance companies in 368.0065

.4   **Money**

Class here mediums of exchange

Class monetary policy in 332.46; class comprehensive works on money and banking in 332.1

For barter, commercial paper, social credit money, see 332.5

SUMMARY

332.401–.408	**Standard subdivisions and forms and units of money**
.41	**Value of money**
.42	**Monetary standards**
.45	**Foreign exchange**
.46	**Monetary policy**
.49	**History, geographic treatment, biography of money and monetary policy**

.401   Philosophy and theory

Including circulation and velocity theory, equation of exchange theory, income and cash balance theories, quantity theory, supply and demand theory

.404   Forms and units of money

.404 2   Gold and silver coins

Class here interdisciplinary works on coins

For token coins, coins of nonprecious metals, see 332.4043. For a specific aspect of coins not provided for here, see the aspect, e.g., coins as an investment 332.63, artistic aspect of coins 737.4

.404 3   Token coins

Coins with an intrinsic value less than their nominal value

Class here coins of nonprecious metals

.404 4   Paper money

Class here bank notes

[.409]	History, geographic treatment, biography

Do not use; class in 332.49

.41 Value of money

Class here inflation, stagflation, deflation; purchasing power

Class the personal financial problem of coping with changing value of money in 332.024; class comprehensive works on purchasing power in 339.42

See also 331.1372 for effects of inflation on unemployment

.414 Factors affecting fluctuations in value

Including variations in money supply

For stabilization measures, see 332.415

.414 2 Devaluation

.415 Stabilization measures

Including wage-price policy to combat inflation

Class monetary policy in 332.46; class fiscal policy in 336.3; class comprehensive works on economic stabilization policies, on wage-price policy in 339.5

.42 Monetary standards

Class here credit, fiat, paper money; bank notes; legal tender; paper standard

For paper money as a form of currency, see 332.4044

.422 Monometallic standards

.422 2 Gold standard

.422 3 Silver standard

Class silver question in 332.4230973

.423 Bimetallism

Class here bimetallism based on gold and silver

.45 Foreign exchange

Class here forward exchange (foreign exchange futures), international monetary systems, special drawing rights

Class Eurocurrency and Eurodollar market in 332.456094; class Euro in 332.494; class comprehensive works on international finance in 332.042; class comprehensive works on financial futures in 332.632; class comprehensive works on speculation in 332.645; class comprehensive works on balance of payments in 382.17

See also 332.152 for International Monetary Fund

.452 Foreign exchange with a gold standard

.456 Exchange rates

Class here currency convertibility

.456 01–.456 08	Standard subdivisions

Class standard subdivisions of specific currencies and groups of currencies in 332.45609

.456 09	History, geographic treatment, biography

.456 091	Exchange rates of specific currencies and groups of currencies in areas, regions, places in general

Add to base number 332.456091 the numbers following —1 in notation 11–19 from Table 2, e.g., exchange rates of currencies of developing countries 332.456091724; then add 0* and to the result add notation 1–9 from Table 2, e.g., exchange rate between currencies of developing countries and Europe 332.45609172404
Do not follow add instructions under —091 in Table 1

Give priority in notation to the currency of a jurisdiction or group of jurisdictions coming first in Table 2
(Option: Give priority in notation to the currency of the jurisdiction requiring local emphasis, e.g., libraries in Europe class exchange rate between currencies of Europe and developing countries in 332.45609401724)

.456 093–.456 099	Exchange rates of specific currencies and groups of currencies in specific continents, countries, localities

Add to base number 332.45609 notation 3–9 from Table 2, e.g., exchange rates of currency of United Kingdom 332.4560941; then add 0* and to the result add notation 1–9 from Table 2, e.g., exchange rate between currencies of United Kingdom and United States 332.4560941073
Do not use add table under —093–099 in Table 1

Give priority in notation to the currency of a jurisdiction or group of jurisdictions coming first in Table 2
(Option: Give priority in notation to the currency of the jurisdiction requiring local emphasis, e.g., libraries in United States class exchange rate between currencies of United States and United Kingdom in 332.4560973041)

.456 2	Floating exchange rates (Fluctuating exchange rates)

Class managed floating rates in 332.4564

.456 4	Fixed and flexible exchange rates

For determination by international agreement, see 332.4566

.456 6	Determination by international agreement

Class here international monetary policy, international monetary reform

Class International Monetary Fund in 332.152; class comprehensive works on monetary policy in 332.46

*Add 00 for standard subdivisions; see instructions at beginning of Table 1

.46 Monetary policy

Including minting policies and practices

Class here currency question, managed currency

For relation of central banks to monetary policy, see 332.112; for international monetary policy, see 332.4566; for use of monetary policy for economic stabilization, see 339.53

[.460 9] History, geographic treatment, biography

Do not use; class in 332.49

.49 History, geographic treatment, biography of money and monetary policy

Standard subdivisions are added for money, monetary policy, or both

.490 01–.490 08 Standard subdivisions

[.490 09] History

Do not use; class in 332.49

.490 1–.490 5 Historical periods

Add to base number 332.490 the numbers following —090 in notation 0901–0905 from Table 1, e.g., money and monetary policy in 20th century 332.4904
Subdivisions are added for money, monetary policy, or both

.491–.499 Geographic treatment and biography

Add to base number 332.49 notation 1–9 from Table 2, e.g., money and monetary policy in India 332.4954
Subdivisions are added for money, monetary policy, or both

.5 Barter, commercial paper, social credit money

.54 Barter

.55 Commercial paper as medium of exchange

Class comprehensive works on commercial paper in 332.77

.56 Social credit money

.6 Investment

Class here investments, domestic investment, individual investment, private investment; investment prospectuses, portfolio analysis and management

Class investment guides in 332.678; class description and analysis of business enterprises issuing securities in 338.7

SUMMARY

[.601 12]   Forecasting

Do not use; class in 332.678

.604   Special topics of investment

.604 2   Investment for specific purposes

Including socially responsible investment

Class retirement investment plans in 332.0240145

[.604 201–.604 209]   Standard subdivisions

Do not use; class in 332.601–332.609

.604 22   Tax shelters

.62   Securities brokers

Including discount brokers

Class here investment brokers, investment counselors

Class real estate brokerage in 333.33

.63   Specific forms of investment

Including art, coins, stamps

Class here speculation in specific forms of investment

Class speculation in multiple forms of investment, comprehensive works on speculation in 332.645; class investment in specific kinds of enterprises regardless of form in 332.6722

[.630 1–.630 9]   Standard subdivisions

Do not use; class in 332.601–332.609

.632   Securities, real estate, commodities

                Standard subdivisions are added for securities, real estate, commodities together; for securities alone

                Class here valuation (value); speculation in securities; comprehensive works on financial futures

                Class evaluation techniques in 332.632042; class buying and selling procedures for securities and commodities in 332.64; class buying and selling procedures for real estate in 333.33; class comprehensive works on speculation, on futures in 332.645

                For forward exchange (foreign exchange futures), see 332.45

.632 04   Special topics of securities, real estate, commodities

.632 042   Evaluation techniques for securities, real estate, commodities

                Including analyzing corporate balance sheets, reading financial pages and ticker tapes

                Class the valuation given to securities, real estate and commodities in 332.632

.632 044   General types of securities

                Including fixed rate, variable rate securities; gilt-edged securities

                Class stocks in 332.6322; class bonds in 332.6323

                See Manual at 332.632044 vs. 332.6323

.632 2   Stocks (Shares)

                Including rights and warrants

                Class here common stock

                See Manual at 332.6322 vs. 332.6323

.632 21   Valuation

                Including dividends paid, price-earnings ratio

                For prices, see 332.63222

.632 22   Prices

.632 220 21   Tabulated and related materials

                Do not use for statistics; class in 332.63222

.632 25   Preferred stock

                Class valuation in 332.63221; class prices in 332.63222; class speculation in 332.63228

.632 28   Stock speculation

                Including buying on margin, day trading, stock index futures

                Class comprehensive works on speculation in 332.645

.632 283	Options

        Class here puts and calls

        See also 331.21649 for employee stock options

.632 3	Bonds

        Including mortgage bonds and certificates

        Class here interest rate futures and options

        See Manual at 332.632044 vs. 332.6323; also at 332.6322 vs. 332.6323

.632 32	Government securities

        Class here government or treasury bonds, bills, certificates, notes

        For municipal bonds, see 332.63233

.632 33	Municipal bonds
.632 34	Corporate bonds
.632 4	Real estate

        Class real estate finance in 332.72; class comprehensive works on fixed capital in 332.0414; class comprehensive works on real estate business in 333.33

.632 42	Land
.632 43	Buildings and other fixtures

        Standard subdivisions are added for buildings and other fixtures, for buildings alone

        See also 647.92–647.94 for management of multiple dwellings

.632 44	Mortgages

        See also 332.6323 for mortgage bonds

.632 47	Real estate investment trusts

        Including real estate syndication

.632 7	Investment company securities

        Including closed-end mutual funds, money market funds

        Class here mutual funds, open-end mutual funds, investment companies, investment trusts, unit trusts

        For real estate investment trusts, see 332.63247

.632 8	Commodities

        Class here commodity futures and options, speculation in commodities

.64   Exchange of securities and commodities; speculation

Class here security and commodity exchanges

See also 332.632 for advice on investing in specific forms of securities and commodities; also 332.678 for general investment guides

.642   Exchange of securities

Including initial public offerings, tender offers

Class here securities exchanges, stock exchanges, stock market

Class brokerage firms in 332.62; class speculation in securities in 332.632

For over-the-counter markets, see 332.643; for international exchange of securities, see 332.65

[.642 094–.642 099]   Specific continents, countries, localities in modern world

Do not use; class in 332.6424–332.6429

.642 4–.642 9   Exchange of securities in specific continents, countries, localities in modern world

Add to base number 332.642 notation 4–9 from Table 2, e.g., exchange of securities in the Netherlands 332.642492
    When adding from Table 2 for a specific exchange, use the number for the primary area served by the exchange, e.g., New York Stock Exchange 332.64273, Pacific Stock Exchange 332.64279

.643   Over-the-counter markets

.644   Exchange of commodities

Class here commodity exchanges, commodity futures and options markets

Class speculation in 332.645

.644 1   Products of agriculture

Add to base number 332.6441 the numbers following 63 in 633–638, e.g., soybeans 332.6441334

.644 2   Products of mineral industries

Add to base number 332.6442 the numbers following 553 in 553.2–553.9, e.g., copper 332.644243

.645   Speculation

Including arbitrage, buying on margin

Class here speculation in multiple forms of investment

Class speculation in specific forms of investment in 332.63; class guides to speculation in 332.678

See also 332.45 for speculation in foreign exchange

.645 2   Futures

.645 24	Hedging

.645 3	Options

Class here puts and calls

.645 7	Derivatives

.65	International exchange of securities

Class comprehensive works on international investment in 332.673

.66	Investment banks

Class here investment banking, issuing houses

For international investment banks, see 332.15

See also 332.1754 for investment services of commercial banks

.67	Investments in specific industries, in specific kinds of enterprise, by specific kinds of investors; international investment; investment guides

Class investment in a specific form of securities with the form in 332.63, e.g., investment in railroad stocks 332.6322 (*not* 332.6722); class a specific aspect of investment with the aspect in 332.64–332.66, e.g., speculation by pension funds 332.645 (*not* 332.67254)

SUMMARY

332.672	**Investment in specific industries, in specific kinds of enterprises, by specific kinds of investors**
.673	**International investment**
.678	**Investment guides**

[.670 1–.670 9]	Standard subdivisions

Do not use; class in 332.601–332.609

.672	Investment in specific industries, in specific kinds of enterprises, by specific kinds of investors

Class foreign investment in specific industries, in specific kinds of enterprises, by specific kinds of investors in 332.673

[.672 01–.672 09]	Standard subdivisions

Do not use; class in 332.601–332.609

.672 2	Investment in specific industries and kinds of enterprises

Including insurance companies, railroads

Class here domestic investment in specific industries and specific kinds of enterprises

Class investment in specific industries and kinds of enterprises by specific kinds of investors in 332.6725

See Manual at 332 vs. 338, 658.15

[.672 201–.672 209]	Standard subdivisions

Do not use; class in 332.67201–332.67209

.672 22	Small business
.672 5	Investment by specific kinds of investors

Other than investment by private investors in general or by individual investors

Class here domestic investment by specific kind of investors

[.672 501–.672 509]	Standard subdivisions

Do not use; class in 332.67201–332.67209

.672 52	Investment by governments and their agencies

Standard subdivisions are added for either or both topics in heading

.672 53	Investment by institutional investors

Class here domestic investment by specific kinds of institutions other than pension funds

Class investments by banks in 332.1754

For investment by pension funds, see 332.67254

.672 532	Insurance companies
.672 54	Investment by pension funds
.673	International investment

Class here foreign investment

Class international investment banking in 332.15; class specific forms of foreign investment in 332.63; class history and description of multinational business ventures and subsidiaries in 338.88; class initiation of international business enterprises (including subsidiaries) in 658.1149

For international exchange of securities, see 332.65

.673 09	History, geographic treatment, biography

Class here the advantages and disadvantages of establishing businesses in specific areas, investment in specific areas not originating in other specific areas

Class the advantages and disadvantages of establishing businesses in specific areas resulting from government policy in 332.6732

See also 338.09 for works describing where in fact industry is located

See Manual at 338.091–338.099 vs. 332.67309, 338.6042

.673 093–.673 099	Specific continents, countries, localities

For investment originating in specific continents and countries, see 332.6733–332.6739

.673 1	International investment by specific kinds of investors
	Other than investment by private investors in general
	Including individual investors
[.673 101–.673 109]	Standard subdivisions
	Do not use; class in 332.67301–332.67309
.673 12	International investment by governments
.673 14	International investment by institutional investors
.673 2	Government policy
	Including international control
.673 209 3–.673 209 9	Specific continents, countries, localities

Class incentives and obstacles in country of investment in 332.67322; class incentives and obstacles in country of investor in 332.67324

.673 22	Incentives and obstacles in country of investment

Class here incentives and obstacles in specific continent and region of investment

Add to base number 332.67322 notation 3–9 from Table 2, e.g., incentives and obstacles in Brazil 332.6732281
Subdivisions are added for either or both topics in heading

.673 24	Incentives and obstacles in country of investor

Class here incentives and obstacles in specific continent and region of investor

Add to base number 332.67324 notation 3–9 from Table 2, e.g., incentives and obstacles to overseas investment by British citizens 332.6732441
Subdivisions are added for either or both topics in heading

.673 3–.673 9	Investment originating in specific continents and countries

Add to base number 332.673 notation 3–9 from Table 2 for origin of investment, e.g., British foreign investments 332.67341; then add 0* and to the result add notation 1–9 from Table 2, e.g., British foreign investments in Brazil 332.67341081

Class policies of specific governments in 332.6732

---

*Add 00 for standard subdivisions; see instructions at beginning of Table 1

.678   Investment guides

> Including forecasting, formula plans, speculation

> Class here guides to domestic investment in general, guides to investment by private investors in general, by individual investors in general

> Class guides to specific forms of investment in 332.63; class guides to investment in specific industry, by kind of enterprise, by kind of investor (other than private investors in general and individual investors) in 332.672; class guides to foreign investment in 332.673

.7   **Credit**

> Class here loans

> Class credit functions of banks in 332.1; class credit functions of specialized banking institutions in 332.2; class credit functions of credit and loan institutions in 332.3

> *For interest, see 332.8*

.71   Agricultural credit

.72   Real estate finance and mortgages

> Standard subdivisions are added for either or both topics in heading

> Class here discrimination in mortgage loans; mortgage delinquencies and defaults

> Class finance on farm real estate in 332.71

> > *See also 332.32 for mortgage institutions; also 332.6323 for mortgage bonds and certificates; also 332.63244 for mortgages as an investment*

.722   Home finance (Residential finance)

.74   Other forms of credit

> Class credit instruments facilitating a specific form of credit in 332.76

.742   Commercial, mercantile, industrial credit

> Including export credit, small business loans

.743   Personal loans

> Including consumer credit

.75   Insolvency and credit restrictions

> Standard subdivisions are added for insolvency and credit restrictions together, for insolvency alone

> Class here bankruptcy

.76   Credit instruments

Including checks, debit cards, money orders, smart cards

Class certificates of deposit in 332.1752

For commercial paper, see 332.77. For credit instruments issued by a specific type of financial institution, see the type in 332.1, e.g., commercial banks 332.178

.765   Credit cards

Class here comprehensive works on credit cards

.77   Commercial paper

Including acceptances, drafts, letters of credit, promissory notes

Class here comprehensive works on commercial paper

For commercial paper as medium of exchange, see 332.55

.8   **Interest**

See also 332.6323 for interest rate futures

.83   Usury

.84   Discount

Including rediscount

.9   **Counterfeiting, forgery, alteration**

Class comprehensive works on counterfeiting in 364.1334; class comprehensive works on forgery in 364.1635

See also 737.4 for counterfeit coins; also 769.55 for counterfeit paper money; also 769.562 for counterfeit stamps

333   Economics of land and energy

Land: all natural and man-made resources over which possession of the earth gives control

Standard subdivisions are added for land and energy together, for land alone

Class here land as a factor of production

See Manual at 333.73–333.78 vs. 333, 333.1–333.5

SUMMARY

333.001–.009	**Standard subdivisions**
.01–.08	**[Theories and land surveys]**
.1	**Public ownership of land**
.2	**Ownership of land by nongovernmental groups**
.3	**Private ownership of land**
.4	**Absentee ownership**
.5	**Renting and leasing land**
.7	**Land, recreational and wilderness areas, energy**
.8	**Subsurface resources**
.9	**Other natural resources**

.001	Philosophy and theory

Do not use for theories; class in 333.01

.001 2	Classification

For land classification, see 333.73012

.002–.009	Standard subdivisions
.01	Theories
.012	Rent theories

Including Ricardo's theory of earning power of land in terms of its marginal productivity

Class here economic rent

Class comprehensive works on rent in 333.5

.08	Land surveys

Class here work of chartered surveyors (United Kingdom)

For land surveying techniques, see 526.9. For a specific kind of land survey, see the kind, e.g., public land surveys 333.18, land use surveys 333.7313

See also 631.47 for surveys that focus on agricultural use of soils

---

> **333.1–333.5 Ownership of land**

Ownership: right to possession and use; right to transfer of possession and use

Land: all natural and man-made resources over which possession of the earth gives control

Class here the kind of control that stems from ownership; ownership of natural resources

Class comprehensive economic works on ownership of land in 333.3; class interdisciplinary works on economic and legal aspects of ownership and transfer of land in 346.043

See also 333.7–333.9 for usage of natural resources, for control of such usage not stemming from ownership

See Manual at 333.73–333.78 vs. 333, 333.1–333.5

.1	**Public ownership of land**

Class public control of privately owned lands in 333.717; class comprehensive works on land policy in 333.73

See also 333.2 for ownership and control of land by peoples subordinate to another jurisdiction; also 343.02 for law of public property

.11	Acquisition and disposal of specific kinds of lands

Including forests, roads, recreational lands

[.110 1–.110 9]   Standard subdivisions

> Do not use; class in 333.1

.13   Acquisition

> Including eminent domain, expropriation, purchase
>
> Class here evaluation of lands for government acquisition
>
> Class acquisition of specific kinds of land in 333.11
>
> *For nationalization, see 333.14*

.14   Nationalization

.16   Disposal

> Including grants, leases, sale
>
> Class disposal of specific kinds of land in 333.11

.18   Public land surveys

> Class surveys of public land use in 333.7313; class interdisciplinary works on land surveys in 333.08
>
> *See also 526.9 for surveying techniques*

.2   Ownership of land by nongovernmental groups

> Including common lands; enclosure of common lands; open-field system; ownership and control of land by peoples subordinate to another jurisdiction, e.g., lands of American native peoples in United States
>
> *For corporate ownership, see 333.324*

.3   Private ownership of land

> Including subdivision of private land
>
> Class here comprehensive works on land ownership (land tenure)
>
> *For public ownership, see 333.1; for ownership by nongovernmental groups, see 333.2; for absentee ownership, see 333.4*

SUMMARY

333.31	**Land reform**
.32	**Types of tenure**
.33	**Transfer of possession and of right to use**

.31   Land reform

> Class here land redistribution, settlement and resettlement of people on the land
>
> *See also 333.2 for enclosure of common lands*

[.310 94–.310 99]   Specific continents, countries, localities in modern world

> Do not use; class in 333.314–333.319

.314–.319	Land reform in specific continents, countries, localities in modern world

Add to base number 333.31 notation 4–9 from Table 2, e.g., land reform in Latin America 333.318

.32	Types of tenure

.322	Feudal tenure

.323	Individual tenure

For corporate ownership, see 333.324

.323 2	Ownership in fee simple

.323 4	Qualified ownership

Including easements, entails, life estates, time-sharing

.324	Corporate ownership

.33	Transfer of possession and of right to use

Standard subdivisions are added for either or both topics in heading

Including consolidation of holdings

Class here comprehensive works on real estate business

Class land reform in 333.31

For government acquisition and disposal, see 333.1; for renting and leasing, see 333.5; for real estate development, see 333.7315

See also 332.6324 for real estate investment; also 332.72 for real estate finance

.332	Value and price of land

Standard subdivisions are added for value and price together, for value alone

Class here valuation (appraisal)

Class valuation for government acquisition and disposal in 333.11–333.16; class value and price of specific kinds of land in 333.335–333.339; class valuation for tax purposes in 352.44

.332 2	Real estate market

Class here economic and social factors affecting exchange of real estate

Class price in 333.3323

.332 3	Price

.332 302 1	Tabulated and related materials

Do not use for statistics; class in 333.3323

.333   Sale and gift

> Standard subdivisions are added for sale and gift together, for sale alone
>
> Class sale and gift of specific kinds of land in 333.335–333.339

>   333.335–333.339 Transfer of possession and use of specific kinds of land

Except for modifications shown under specific entries, add to each subdivision identified by * as follows:

    2   Value and price

>   Standard subdivisions are added for value and price together, for value alone
>
>   Class here valuation (appraisal)

   22   Real estate market

>   Class here economic and social factors affecting exchange of real estate
>
>   Class price in notation 23 from this table

   23   Price

    3   Sale and gift

>   Standard subdivisions are added for sale and gift together, for sale alone

    5   Renting and leasing

>   Standard subdivisions are added for renting and leasing together, for renting alone
>
>   Add to 5 the numbers following 333.5 in 333.53–333.56, e.g., share renting 563

Class comprehensive works in 333.33

.335   *Rural lands

> Class here agricultural lands

.335 7   *Forest lands

.336   *Industrial lands

> Including transportation space, e.g., right of way
>
> Class works that emphasize buildings in 333.338

.337   *Urban lands

> Residential and commercial lands
>
> Class works that emphasize buildings in 333.338
>
> *For industrial lands, see 333.336*

.338   *Buildings and other fixtures

> Including apartment houses, condominiums, mobile homes
>
> Class here residential buildings
>
> *See also 643.12 for the homemakers approach to buying and selling housing*

---

*Add as instructed under 333.335–333.339

.338 7   *Commercial and industrial buildings

         Subdivisions are added for either or both topics in heading

.339   Other natural resources

        Appraisal, gift, leasing, renting, sale, market

        Including rights to use of minerals, water, air space

.4   **Absentee ownership**

.5   **Renting and leasing land**

      Class renting and leasing specific kinds of land in 333.335–333.339

       For renting and leasing public land, see 333.16; for renting and leasing land owned by nongovernmental groups other than private corporations and partnerships, see 333.2; for absentee ownership, see 333.4

.53   Tenancy

       Including tenancy for years (for a specified time period), tenancy from year to year, tenancy at will

       For landlord-tenant relations, see 333.54

.54   Landlord-tenant relations

.56   Types of renting

.562   Cash renting

.563   Share renting

       Class here percentage renting

       For sharecropping, see 333.335563

---

*Add as instructed under 333.335–333.339

> **333.7–333.9 Natural resources and energy**

Aspects other than ownership

Class here raw materials

Except for modifications shown under specific entries, add to each subdivision identified by * as follows:

01–09 Standard subdivisions

1 General topics

Class comprehensive works on specific topics in 333.71

[101–109] Standard subdivisions

Do not use; class in notation 01–09 from this table

11 Reserves

Variant names: stock, supply

Including shortages

12 Requirements

Variant names: need, demand

13 Consumption (Utilization)

Class consumption control in notation 17 from this table

Do not add for specific uses (e.g., water for irrigation); class with the subject in 333.7–333.9 without adding from this table

Class interdisciplinary works on consumption in 339.47

137 Abuse and wastage

Standard subdivisions are added for either or both topics in heading

Class here description of abused resources, consequences of abuse and wastage

Class reclamation, rehabilitation, restoration of abused resources in notation 153 from this table; class prevention of abuse and wastage in notation 16 from this table; class pollution in 363.73

14 Environmental impact studies

Class studies emphasizing abuse and wastage in notation 137 from this table. Class impact on a specific environment or resource with the impact, e.g., economic impact on Rome of a major new waste treatment facility 330.945632, impact of the same treatment plant on the waters of the Tiber River 333.916214094562; class projected impacts with the program or development that is being studied, e.g., projected impact of proposed standards for water pollution 363.739462

>15–17 Management and control

Class here citizen participation, planning, policy

Class comprehensive works in 333.7–333.9 without adding from this table

15 Development

152 Improvement

153 Reclamation, rehabilitation, restoration

Standard subdivisions are added for any or all topics in heading

Class reclamation that is not restoration to a previous state in notation 152 from this table

158 Subsidies

> **333.7–333.9 Natural resources and energy**

    16   Conservation and protection

                 Standard subdivisions are added for either or both topics in heading

                 Class control of usage in notation 17 from this table; class comprehensive works on conservation and protection in 333.72

    17   Control of usage

                 Including allocation, price control, rationing, ways and means of efficient use

                 Do not add for specific uses (e.g., water for irrigation); class with the subject in 333.7–333.9 without adding from this table

Class ownership of land and other natural resources in 333.1–333.5; class economic geology in 553; class comprehensive works on natural resources and energy in 333.7

See Manual at 333.7–333.9 vs. 363.1, 363.73, 577; also at 333.7–333.9 vs. 363.6; also at 333.7–333.9 vs. 508, 913–919, 930–990

.7   **Land, recreational and wilderness areas, energy**

Class here comprehensive works on environmental economics; interdisciplinary works on the environment, on natural resources

Class environmentalism in 333.72; class interdisciplinary works on sustainability in 304.2

For ownership aspects of natural resources, see 333.1–333.5; for subsurface resources, see 333.8; for natural resources other than land, recreational and wilderness areas, energy, subsurface resources, see 333.9; for development policy in environmental economics, see 338.927. For noneconomic aspects of the environment, of natural resources, see the aspect, e.g., environmental protection 363.7, conservation technology 639.9

See Manual at 363 vs. 302–307, 333.7, 570–590, 600

SUMMARY

333.71	**General topics of land, recreational and wilderness areas, energy**
.72	**Conservation and protection**
.73	**Land**
.74	**Grasslands**
.75	**Forest lands**
.76	**Rural lands**
.77	**Urban lands**
.78	**Recreational and wilderness areas**
.79	**Energy**

.71   General topics of land, recreational and wilderness areas, energy

Add to base number 333.71 the numbers following 1 in notation 11–17 from table under 333.7–333.9, e.g., development 333.715; however, for conservation and protection, see 333.72

.72   Conservation and protection

               Standard subdivisions are added for either or both topics in heading

               Class here comprehensive works on conservation and protection of natural
               resources; interdisciplinary works on environmentalism

                   *For conservation and protection with respect to energy or a specific type
                   of natural resource, see the resource in 333.73–333.95, plus notation
                   16 from table under 333.7–333.9, e.g., conservation of wilderness areas
                   333.78216; for a specific social aspect of environmentalism not provided
                   for here, see the aspect in 300, e.g., environmentalist political ideologies
                   320.58*

                   See Manual at 333.72 vs. 304.28, 320.58, 363.7

.73   Land

               Aspects other than ownership

               Including kinds of land by physical condition, e.g., mountainous land, sand
               dunes

               Class here government policy on land; river basins

               Class ownership aspects of land in 333.1–333.5; class arid and semiarid
               lands in 333.736

                   *For kinds of land by use, see 333.74–333.78; for shorelands and related
                   areas, see 333.917; for wetlands and submerged lands, see 333.918*

                   See Manual at 333.73–333.78 vs. 333, 333.1–333.5

.731   General topics of land

               Add to base number 333.731 the numbers following 1 in notation 11–17
               from table under 333.7–333.9, e.g., real estate development 333.7315,
               comprehensive works on soil and water conservation 333.7316

               Class soil and water conservation in rural lands in 333.7616; class real
               estate development in urban lands in 333.7715; class zoning of urban
               lands in 333.7717; class water conservation in 333.9116; class pollution
               control in 363.73966; class comprehensive works on real estate business
               in 333.33

                   *For a specific type of natural areas established for conservation, see
                   the type, e.g., wilderness areas 333.782*

.736   *Arid lands

               Class here semiarid lands, desertification

               _____

>   333.74–333.78 Kinds of land by use

               Class comprehensive works in 333.73

                   See Manual at 333.73–333.78 vs. 333, 333.1–333.5

*Add as instructed under 333.7–333.9

.74   *Grasslands

    Class here grazing lands, pasture lands

.75   *Forest lands

    Class here national forests; jungles, rain forests, woodlands; old-growth forests

    Class parks, recreational, wilderness areas in 333.78

    See also 333.95397 for wood as a fuel

.751 1   Reserves

    Number built according to instructions under 333.7–333.9

    Class here forest reserves, timber reserves

    Class supply of cut timber, comprehensive works on timber in 338.17498

.751 2   Requirements

    Number built according to instructions under 333.7–333.9

    Class here requirements for timber discussed in terms of effect on forest land and supply of uncut timber

    Class requirements for timber discussed in terms of how much timber will need to be cut to meet demand in 338.17498

.751 3   Consumption (Utilization)

    Number built according to instructions under 333.7–333.9

    Class here consumption of forest products in terms of effect on future forest resources

    Class utilization of forests to provide products for sale in 338.17498

.751 5   Development

    Number built according to instructions under 333.7–333.9

    Class here measures to promote growth of forests as long-term resources

    Class development of ways to exploit forest products in 338.17498

.76   *Rural lands

    Class here agricultural lands

    Class rural lands of a specific physical condition not devoted to a specific use in 333.73; class rural recreational lands in 333.78

    For grasslands, see 333.74; for forest lands, see 333.75

.765   *Mined lands

    Class here surface-mined lands

*Add as instructed under 333.7–333.9

.77   *Urban lands

   Including commercial, industrial, residential lands; streets

   Class urban mined lands in 333.765; class urban recreational lands in 333.78

.78   *Recreational and wilderness areas

   Subdivisions are added for recreational and wilderness areas together, for recreational areas alone

   Class wildlife in 333.954; class wildlife refuges in 333.95416

   See also 363.68 for park and recreation services

.782   *Wilderness areas

   For specific kinds of wilderness areas, see 333.784

.783   *Parks

.784   Specific kinds of recreational and wilderness areas

   Including forests, mountains

[.784 01–.784 09]   Standard subdivisions

   Do not use; class in 333.7801–333.7809

\>   333.784 4–333.784 5   Recreational use of water

   Class here recreational use of land adjoining water, e.g., beaches, shores

   Class comprehensive works on recreational use of water in 333.7844; class comprehensive works on uses of water and land adjoining it in 333.91

.784 4   *Recreational use of lakes

   Class here comprehensive works on recreational use of water

   For recreational use of rivers and streams, see 333.7845; for recreational use of reservoirs, see 333.7846

.784 5   *Recreational use of rivers and streams

   Standard subdivisions are added for either or both topics in heading

.784 6   *Recreational use of reservoirs

   Class comprehensive works on lakes and reservoirs in 333.7844

*Add as instructed under 333.7–333.9

.79   ‡Energy

Class here power resources, production of energy, interdisciplinary works on energy

Class electric power in 333.7932; class extraction of energy resources and comprehensive works on the economics of mineral fuels in 338.2; class comprehensive works on production economics of processing and manufacturing fuels in 338.476626; class interdisciplinary works on mineral fuels in 553

> *For a specific form of energy not provided for here, see the form, e.g., wind energy 333.92; for a specific energy resource not provided for here, see the resource, e.g., fossil fuels 333.82; for a noneconomic aspect of energy, see the aspect, e.g., technology of photovoltaic power generation 621.31244*

SUMMARY

333.791 37	**Abuse and wastage**
.792	**Primary forms of energy**
.793	**Secondary forms of energy**
.794	**Renewable energy resources**
.796	**Energy for specific uses**

.791 37   Abuse and wastage

Number built according to instructions under 333.7–333.9

Class utilization of waste heat in 333.793

.792   †Primary forms of energy

Resources used directly to perform work, to produce other forms of energy

.792 3   †Solar energy

Including electricity derived from solar energy, e.g., with photovoltaic cells

Class distribution of electricity derived from solar energy in 333.7932

.792 33   Financial aspects

Including prices

.792 4   †Nuclear energy

Class here electricity derived from nuclear energy

Class distribution of electricity derived from nuclear energy in 333.7932; class nuclear fuels in 333.85

.792 43   Financial aspects

Including prices

---

†Add as instructed under 333.7–333.9, except use 15 for both development and generation of energy
‡Add as instructed under 333.7–333.9, except class utilization of waste heat in 333.793

.793   †Secondary forms of energy

Energy produced through use of other resources

Including cogeneration of electric power and heat, district heating, waste heat

Class economics of synthetic fuel production in 338.4766266

For secondary forms of energy derived from a specific resource, see the resource, e.g., electricity derived from nuclear energy 333.7924

.793 2   †Electrical energy

Including distribution of electrical energy regardless of resource from which the electricity was derived, rural electrification

Class here electricity derived from fossil fuels, electrical utilities, comprehensive works on electrical energy

For electricity derived from a specific resource other than fossil fuels, see the resource, e.g., electricity derived from water 333.914

.793 23   Financial aspects

.793 231   Prices

.793 8   †Energy from waste materials

Class distribution of electricity derived from waste materials in 333.7932; class production economics of making fuel from waste materials in 338.4766287; class chemical technology of energy from waste materials in 662.87

For energy from biological wastes, see 333.9539

.794   †Renewable energy resources

Class here alternative energy resources

Class distribution of electricity derived from renewable energy resources in 333.7932

For a specific renewable or alternative energy resource, see the resource, e.g., solar energy 333.7923

.796   Energy for specific uses

Including energy for military use

Unless other instructions are given, class a subject with aspects in two or more subdivisions of 333.796 in the number coming last, e.g., energy use in school buildings 333.7964 (*not* 333.7962)

Class a specific kind of energy for specific uses with the kind of energy, e.g., energy from petroleum for transportation use 333.8232 (*not* 333.7968)

[.796 01–.796 09]   Standard subdivisions

Do not use; class in 333.7901–333.7909

---

†Add as instructed under 333.7–333.9, except use 15 for both development and generation of energy

.796 2	*Energy for use in buildings

Including use in construction

See also 624 for technical aspects of energy use in construction

.796 3	*Energy for residential use
.796 4	*Energy for social service institutions

Including churches, hospitals, prisons, schools

.796 5	*Energy for industrial use

Class here manufacturing use

Class energy use in construction of buildings in 333.7962

For food processing use, see 333.7966

.796 6	*Energy for use in agriculture and food processing
.796 8	*Energy for use in transportation and commerce

Subdivisions are added for transportation and commerce together, for transportation alone

.796 89	*Energy for commercial use

.8 Subsurface resources

Class here strategic materials

Class mined lands, including surface-mined lands, in 333.765; class extraction of subsurface resources and comprehensive works on the economics of subsurface resources in 338.2; class interdisciplinary works on subsurface resources in 553

For ownership aspects of subsurface resources, see 333.1–333.5; for groundwater, see 333.9104

.81	General topics of subsurface resources

Add to base number 333.81 the numbers following 1 in notation 11–17 from table under 333.7–333.9, e.g., reserves in storage of subsurface resources 333.811; however, for development, see 338.2

.82	Fossil fuels

Class here nonrenewable fuels

Class electricity derived from fossil fuels in 333.7932

For nuclear fuels, see 333.85493

.821	General topics of fossil fuels

Add to base number 333.821 the numbers following 1 in notation 11–17 from table under 333.7–333.9, e.g., reserves in storage of fossil fuels 333.8211; however, for development, see 338.272; for reserves in nature, see 553.2

.822	Coal

*Add as instructed under 333.7–333.9

.822 1   General topics of coal

> Add to base number 333.8221 the numbers following 1 in notation 11–17 from table under 333.7–333.9, e.g., reserves in storage of coal 333.82211; however, for development, see 338.2724; for reserves in nature, see 553.24

.823   Oil and natural gas

.823 1   General topics of oil and natural gas

> Add to base number 333.8231 the numbers following 1 in notation 11–17 from table under 333.7–333.9, e.g., reserves in storage of oil and natural gas 333.82311; however, for development, see 338.2728; for reserves in nature, see 553.28

.823 2   Oil

> Petroleum limited to oil

> Class petroleum covering oil and natural gas in 333.823

.823 21   General topics of oil

> Add to base number 333.82321 the numbers following 1 in notation 11–17 from table under 333.7–333.9, e.g., reserves in storage of oil 333.823211; however, for development, see 338.27282; for reserves in nature, see 553.282

.823 3   Natural gas

> *See also 363.63 for gas distribution services of public utilities*

.823 31   General topics of natural gas

> Add to base number 333.82331 the numbers following 1 in notation 11–17 from table under 333.7–333.9, e.g., reserves in storage of natural gas 333.823311; however, for development, see 338.27285; for reserves in nature, see 553.285

.85   Minerals

> Class comprehensive works on the economics of minerals in 338.2; class interdisciplinary works on nonmetallic minerals in 553; class interdisciplinary works on metals in 669

.851   General topics of minerals

> Add to base number 333.851 the numbers following 1 in notation 11–17 from table under 333.7–333.9, e.g., reserves in storage of minerals 333.8511; however, for development, see 338.2; for reserves in nature, see 553

.852–.859   Specific minerals

> Add to base number 333.85 the numbers following 553 in 553.2–553.9, e.g., tin 333.85453, uranium 333.854932; however, for fossil fuels, see 333.82; for groundwater, see 333.9104

> Class nuclear energy in 333.7924

.88 *Geothermal energy

Class here electricity derived from geothermal energy, thermal waters

Class distribution of electricity derived from geothermal energy in 333.7932

.9 **Other natural resources**

For ownership aspects of other natural resources, see 333.1–333.5

SUMMARY

333.91	**Water and lands adjoining bodies of water**
.92	**Air**
.94	**Space**
.95	**Biological resources**

.91 Water and lands adjoining bodies of water

Standard subdivisions are added for water and lands adjoining bodies of water together, for water alone

Class here aquatic resources, comprehensive works on the economics of aquatic resources

Class interdisciplinary works on water in 553.7

For a specific aquatic resource, see the resource, e.g., minerals 333.85, fishes 333.956; for a specific aspect of water not provided for here, see the aspect, e.g., recreational use of water and lands adjoining bodies of water 333.7844–333.7845, regulation and control of distribution of water to consumers 363.61

See Manual at 363.61

.910 01–.910 09 Standard subdivisions

.910 4 †Groundwater (Subsurface water)

For subsurface thermal waters, see 333.88

.911 General topics of water

Class water for specific uses in 333.912–333.915; class comprehensive works on soil and water conservation in 333.7316. Class general topics of a specific kind of water with the kind, e.g., general topics of rivers and streams 333.9162

[.911 01–.911 09] Standard subdivisions

Do not use; class in 333.91001–333.91009

.911 1–.911 7 Subdivisions for topics of water

Add to base number 333.911 the numbers following 1 in notation 11–17 from table under 333.7–333.9, e.g., reserves in storage, as in reservoirs and storage tanks 333.9111; however, for water pollution, see 363.7394; for reserves in nature, see 553.7

---

*Add as instructed under 333.7–333.9
†Add as instructed under 333.7–333.9, except use 11 only for reserves in storage; class reserves in nature in 553.7

> 333.912–333.915 Water for specific uses

Class comprehensive works in 333.91

For recreational use, see 333.7844

.912 †Water for domestic and industrial uses

.912 2 †Water for domestic use

Including drinking and washing

.912 3 †Water for industrial use

Class water for generation of energy in 333.914; class water for transportation in 333.915

.913 †Water for irrigation

.914 *Water for generation of energy

Including thermal ocean power conversion

Class here hydroelectricity

.914 11 Reserves

Number built according to instructions under 333.7–333.9

Class here energy-producing potential of water

.914 15 Development

Number built according to instructions under 333.7–333.9

Class here development and generation of energy

.915 †Water for transportation

> 333.916–333.918 Specific bodies of water, shorelands, wetlands and related areas

Class specific uses of water, shorelands, wetlands, and related areas in 333.912–333.915; class comprehensive works in 333.91

.916 Specific bodies of water

Class specific uses of specific bodies of water in 333.912–333.915; class lands adjoining specific bodies of water in 333.917; class wetlands and submerged lands related to specific bodies of water in 333.918

.916 2 †Rivers and streams

Subdivisions are added for either or both topics in heading

Class river basins in 333.73

---

*Add as instructed under 333.7–333.9

†Add as instructed under 333.7–333.9, except use 11 only for reserves in storage; class reserves in nature in 553.7

.916 3 †Lakes and ponds

Subdivisions are added for either or both topics in heading

For saltwater lakes, see 333.9164

.916 4 ‡Oceans and seas

Including bays, estuaries, gulfs, salt lakes

Subdivisions are added for either or both topics in heading

.917 *Lands adjoining bodies of water

Including beaches, floodplains, tidelands (lands that are overflowed by the tide but exposed by low water)

Class here coasts, seashores, shorelands

Class river basins in 333.73; class comprehensive works on tidelands in 333.918

For wetlands and submerged lands, see 333.918

.918 *Wetlands and submerged lands

Including continental shelves, tidelands (lands underlying the ocean beyond the low tidemark but within a nation's territorial waters), comprehensive works on tidelands

Subdivisions are added for wetlands and submerged lands together, for wetlands alone

Class recreational use in 333.784

For tidelands (lands that are overflowed by the tide but exposed by low water), see 333.917

See also 333.916 for works focusing on bodies of water rather than the land they submerge

.92 *Air

Class here wind energy, use of wind for generation of electricity

Class distribution of wind-generated electricity in 333.7932

.94 Space

Class industrialization of space in 338.0919

.95 *Biological resources

Class here biodiversity, biosphere

Unless other instructions are given, class a subject with aspects in two or more subdivisions of 333.95 in the number coming last, e.g., game birds 333.95829 (*not* 333.9549)

---

*Add as instructed under 333.7–333.9

†Add as instructed under 333.7–333.9, except use 11 only for reserves in storage; class reserves in nature in 553.7

‡Add as instructed under 333.7–333.9, except class reserves in 551.46

SUMMARY

.952   Specific kinds of biological resources

> Not limited by kind of organisms

> *For genetic and germ plasm resources, see 333.9534; for biomass energy, see 333.9539*

[.952 01–.952 09]   Standard subdivisions

> Do not use; class in 333.9501–333.9509

.952 2   *Rare and endangered species

> Class here extinction, threatened species, vanishing species

> Subdivisions are added for either or both topics in heading

.952 3   *Nonnative species

> Class here alien, exotic, introduced, invasive, naturalized species

.952 8   *Aquatic biological resources

> Class here freshwater biological resources

> *For marine biological resources, see 333.956*

.952 88   *Wetland biological resources

.953   *Plants and microorganisms

> Subdivisions are added for plants and microorganisms together, for plants alone

> *For forests, comprehensive works on timber resources, see 333.75*

> *See also 333.82 for peat*

.953 2   *Rare and endangered plants

> Class here threatened, vanishing plants

> Subdivisions are added for either or both topics in heading

---

*Add as instructed under 333.7–333.9

.953 3	*Nonnative and native plants

Standard subdivisions are added for nonnative and native plants together, for nonnative plants alone

Class here alien, exotic, introduced, invasive, naturalized plants

Class rare and endangered nonnative and native plants in 333.9532

.953 4	*Germ plasm resources

Class here plant varieties; interdisciplinary works on genetic resources, on germ plasm

> *For animal genetic resources, germ plasm, see 333.954; for germ plasm, plant varieties in agriculture, see 631.523*

.953 8	*Seaweeds

Class here algae, kelp

.953 9	†Plants as sources of energy

Class here interdisciplinary works on biomass energy

> *For animal biomass as an energy resource, see 333.954; for production economics of making biomass fuel, see 338.4766288; for biomass fuel engineering, see 662.88*

.953 97	*Fuelwood
.954	*Animals

Including biomass energy, genetic resources, germ plasm

Class here wildlife; comprehensive works on mammals, on vertebrates

> *For invertebrates, see 333.955; for fishes, see 333.956; for reptiles and amphibians, see 333.957; for birds, see 333.958; for specific kinds of mammals, see 333.959*

.954 11	Reserves

Number built according to instructions under 333.7–333.9

Class here supply of uncaught animals in nature, statistics of catches used in estimating population of animals in nature

Class catches from fishing, whaling, hunting, trapping industries in 338.372

.954 15	Development

Number built according to instructions under 333.7–333.9

Class here measures to increase supply of animals in nature

.954 2	*Rare and endangered animals

Class here threatened, vanishing animals

Subdivisions are added for either or both topics in heading

---

*Add as instructed under 333.7–333.9
†Add as instructed under 333.7–333.9, except use 15 for both development and generation of energy

.954 3	*Nonnative animals

Class here alien, exotic, introduced, invasive, naturalized animals

.954 8	*Aquatic animals

For marine animals, see 333.956

.954 88	*Wetland animals
.954 9	*Game animals

Class economics of hunting in 338.3729

For big game animals, see 333.9596

> 333.955–333.959 Specific taxonomic groups of animals

Class comprehensive works in 333.954

See Manual at 333.955–333.959 vs. 639.97

.955	*Invertebrates

Class here marine invertebrates, shellfish

> 333.955 3–333.955 5 Marine invertebrates

Class comprehensive works in 333.955

.955 3	*Coral reefs

> 333.955 4–333.955 5 Shellfish

Class comprehensive works in 333.955

.955 4	*Mollusks

Class here Bivalvia

Class comprehensive works on shellfish in 333.955

.955 41–.955 48	Specific kinds of mollusks

Add to base number 333.9554 the numbers following 639.4 in 639.41–639.48, e.g., scallops 333.95546; then add further as instructed under 333.7–333.9 (*not* as instructed under 592–599), e.g., supply of scallops 333.9554611

.955 5	*Crustaceans

Class here Decapoda

.955 54–.955 58	Specific kinds of crustaceans

Add to base number 333.9555 the numbers following 595.38 in 595.384–595.388, e.g., lobsters 333.95554; then add further as instructed under 333.7–333.9 (*not* as instructed under 592–599), e.g., consumption of lobsters 333.9555413

*Add as instructed under 333.7–333.9

.955 7	*Insects
.956	*Fishes

Class here marine biological resources, comprehensive works on finfish and shellfish

For shellfish, see 333.955. For a specific kind of marine biological resource not provided for below, see the kind, e.g., marine algae 333.9538, marine mammals 333.9595

.956 2–.956 7	Specific kinds of fishes

Add to base number 333.956 the numbers following 597 in 597.2–597.7, e.g., salmon 333.95656; then add further as instructed under 333.7–333.9 (*not* as instructed under 592–599), e.g., restoration of salmon fisheries 333.95656153

.956 8	*Rare and endangered fishes

Subdivisions are added for either or both topics in heading

Class specific kinds of rare and endangered fishes in 333.9562–333.9567

.956 9	*Game fishes

Class specific kinds of game fishes in 333.9562–333.9567; class game fishes (salmonids) in 333.95655; class economics of fishing in 338.3727

.957	*Reptiles and amphibians

Subdivisions are added for reptiles and amphibians together, for reptiles alone

.957 2	*Rare and endangered reptiles and amphibians

Subdivisions are added for all topics in heading together, for rare reptiles alone, for endangered reptiles alone

.957 8–.957 9	Amphibians, specific reptiles

Add to base number 333.957 the numbers following 597 in 597.8–597.9, e.g., sea turtles 333.957928; then add further as instructed under 333.7–333.9 (*not* as instructed under 592–599), e.g., protection of sea turtles 333.95792816; however, for comprehensive works on reptiles, on reptiles and amphibians, see 333.957

.958	*Birds
.958 2	Specific nontaxonomic kinds of birds
[.958 201–.958 209]	Standard subdivisions

Do not use; class in 333.9501–333.9509

.958 22	*Rare and endangered birds

Class here threatened, vanishing birds

Subdivisions are added for either or both topics in heading

*Add as instructed under 333.7–333.9

.958 28	*Aquatic birds

Class here water birds

Class waterfowl in 333.95841

.958 287	*Sea birds
.958 29	*Game birds

Class lowland game birds in 333.95841; class upland game birds in 333.9586

.958 3–.958 9	Specific kinds of birds

Add to base number 333.958 the numbers following 598 in 598.3–598.9, e.g., wild turkeys 333.958645; then add further as instructed under 333.7–333.9 (*not* as instructed under 592–599), e.g., demand for wild turkeys 333.95864513

.959	Specific kinds of mammals

Class comprehensive works in 333.954

[.959 01–.959 09]	Standard subdivisions

Do not use; class in 333.95401–333.95409

.959 2–.959 8	Subdivisions for specific kinds of mammals

Add to base number 333.959 the numbers following 599 in 599.2–599.8, e.g., marine mammals, whales 333.9595, big game animals, ungulates 333.9596, carnivores, fur-bearing animals 333.9597; then add further as instructed under 333.7–333.9 (*not* as instructed under 592–599), e.g., supply of big game 333.959611

334 Cooperatives

.1 Housing cooperatives

Class here building cooperatives

Class cooperative building associations that are also cooperative savings and loan associations in 334.2

.2 Banking and credit cooperatives

Standard subdivisions are added for either or both topics in heading

.22 Credit unions

Class comprehensive works on thrift institutions in 332.32

.5 Consumer cooperatives

Class consumer housing cooperatives in 334.1; class comprehensive works on cooperative marketing in 334.6

[.506 88]	Management of distribution (Marketing)

Do not use; class in 658.87

*Add as instructed under 333.7–333.9

.6 **Producers' cooperatives**

Class here marketing, production cooperatives

For consumer cooperatives, see 334.5

.68 Producers' cooperatives by industry

.681 Producers' cooperatives in industries other than extractive, manufacturing, construction

Class here service industries

.681 000 1–.681 000 9 Standard subdivisions

.681 001–.681 999 Subdivisions for producer's cooperatives in industries other than extractive, manufacturing, construction

Add to base number 334.681 notation 001–999 (but not 381–382), e.g., cooperative legal services 334.68134; however, for banking and credit cooperatives, see 334.2

.682–.688 Producers' cooperatives in extractive, manufacturing, construction industries

Class here cooperative marketing by producers in extractive, manufacturing, construction industries

Add to base number 334.68 the numbers following 6 in 620–680, e.g., agricultural cooperatives 334.683; however, for kibbutzim and moshavim, see 307.776; for Communist collective farms, see 338.763

For building cooperatives, see 334.1

.7 **Benefit societies**

Class here benevolent, friendly, fraternal benefit, mutual aid, provident societies

Class a specific function of a benefit society with the function, e.g., insurance 368.3

335 Socialism and related systems

Standard subdivisions are added for socialism and related systems together, for socialism alone

Class here schools of thought featuring planned economies, state socialism, interdisciplinary works on socialism and related systems

Class socialism (communism) in 335.43; class comparisons of Communism (Marxism-Leninism) with other systems in 335.437; class socialism (democratic socialism) in 335.5

For socialism as a political ideology, see 320.53; for socialist and communist political parties, see 324.217. For a specific topic of economics treated from a socialist or communist point of view, see the topic in economics, e.g., interest 332.8

See Manual at 335 vs. 306.345, 320.53

(Option: Class in 330.159)

SUMMARY

.001–.009   Standard subdivisions

.02   Utopian systems and schools

> Standard subdivisions are added for either or both topics in heading

> *For specific utopian systems, see 335.1–335.3*

> *See also 301 for ideal societies; also 321.07 for ideal states*

>   **335.1–335.3 Non-Marxian and quasi-Marxian socialism**

> Class comprehensive works in 335

> *For national socialism, see 335.6; for Christian socialism, see 335.7*

> *See also 307.77 for voluntary socialist communities*

.1   **Systems of English origin**

.12   Utopian socialism

> Including Owenism

.14   Fabian socialism

.15   Guild socialism

.2   **Systems of French origin**

> Including Babouvism, Icarianism

.22   Saint-Simonism

.23   Fourierism (Phalansterianism)

.3   **Systems of American origin**

.4   **Marxian systems**

> Class here Marxism

> *For democratic Marxian systems, see 335.5*

.401   Philosophy

> Do not use for philosophic foundations; class in 335.411. Do not use for comprehensive works on theory of Marxian systems; class in 335.4

[.409 034]	19th century, 1800–1899
	Do not use; class in 335.42
.409 04	20th century, 1900–1999
.409 041	1917–1919
	Do not use for 1900–1917; class in 335.423
.41	Philosophic foundations, economic concepts, aims
	Including social ownership of means of production
.411	Philosophic foundations
	Including theory of class struggle
	For the philosophic foundations of Marxian economics, see 335.412
.411 2	Dialectical materialism
	Class comprehensive works on dialectical materialism in 146.32
.411 9	Historical materialism
.412	Economic concepts
	Including labor theory of value
.42	Marxian systems, 1848–1917
.422	Early Communism, 1848–1875
	Period of Communist manifesto
.423	Scientific socialism, 1875–1917
	Class scientific socialism of Lenin (Marxism-Leninism) in 335.43
	For democratic socialism, see 335.5
.43	Communism (Marxism-Leninism)
	Class here former Soviet communism, democratic centralism
	For communism as a political ideology, see 320.532
.430 9	History, geographic treatment, biography
	Do not use for national variants as schools of thought; class in 335.434
.433	Trotskyist doctrines
.434	National variants as schools of thought
	Use 335.4309 for communism in specific nations viewed as actual economic systems rather than schools of thought, e.g., Cuban communism as an existing system 335.43097291 (*not* 335.4347)
	Soviet communism as a school of thought is classed in 335.43, as the economic system of the former Soviet Union in 335.430947
[.434 094–.434 099]	Specific continents, countries, localities in modern world
	Do not use; class in 335.434

.434 4   Communism of Yugoslavia (1918–1991)

                 Class here Titoism

.434 5   Chinese communism

                 Class here Maoism

                 Class comprehensive works on Asian national variants of communism in 335.4346

.434 6   Asian national variants

                 Including North Korean, Vietnamese communism

                 For Chinese communism, see 335.4345

.434 7   Cuban communism (Castroism)

                 Including ideas of Che Guevara

.437   Comparative studies

                 Comparison of communism with capitalism, cooperation, democratic socialism, other forms of collectivism

.5   **Democratic socialism**

         Marxian and non-Marxian socialism

             For Fabian socialism, see 335.14; for Christian socialism, see 335.7

             See also 307.77 for voluntary socialist communities

.6   **Fascism**

         Class here falangism, national socialism, Neo-Nazism

             For fascism as a political ideology, see 320.533

.7   **Christian socialism**

             For Christian socialism as a political ideology, see 320.5312

.8   **Other systems**

.82   Syndicalism

         Class here anarcho-syndicalism

.83   Anarchism

             For anarchism as a political ideology, see 320.57; for anarcho-syndicalism, see 335.82

             See also 307.77 for voluntary anarchist communities

336   Public finance

Class here intergovernmental fiscal relations, comprehensive works on public finance and financial administration of governments

For public financial administration and budgets, see 352.4

See Manual at 332, 336 vs. 339

SUMMARY

336.001–.008	**Standard subdivisions**
.01–.09	**[Public finance by governmental level; revenue; history, geographic treatment, biography; associations of sovereign states]**
.1	**Nontax revenues**
.2	**Taxes**
.3	**Public debt and expenditures**
.4–.9	**Public finance of specific continents, countries, localities in modern world**

.001–.005   Standard subdivisions

.006   Organizations

.006 01   International organizations

> Class associations of sovereign states in 336.0916

[.006 8]   Management

> Do not use; class in 352.4

.007–.008   Standard subdivisions

[.009]   History, geographic treatment, biography

> Do not use for treatment by governmental level; class in 336.01. Do not use for history and biography for treatment by areas, regions, places in general, for ancient world; class in 336.09

[.009 4–.009 9]   Specific continents, countries, localities in modern world

> Do not use; class in 336.4–336.9

.01   Public finance by governmental level

> Class here public finance in three or more jurisdictions at a specific level

> Class public finance at a specific level in one or two specific jurisdictions in ancient world in 336.093; class public finance at a specific level in one or two specific jurisdictions in modern world in 336.4–336.9

.012   Public finance at national level

[.012 091]   Areas, regions, places in general

> Do not use; class in 336.0121

[.012 093–.012 099]   Specific continents, countries

> Do not use for specific continents; class in 336.0123–336.0129. Do not use for specific countries in ancient world; class in 336.093. Do not use for specific countries in modern world; class in 336.4–336.9

.012 1   Public finance at national level in areas, regions, places in general

> Add to base number 336.0121 the numbers following —1 in notation 11–19 from Table 2, e.g., national public finance in developing countries 336.0121724

.012 3–.012 9	Public finance at national level in specific continents

Add to base number 336.012 notation 3–9 from Table 2, e.g., national public finance in Europe 336.0124

Class public finance at national level in specific nations in ancient world in 336.093; class public finance at national level in specific nations in modern world in 336.4–336.9

.013	Public finance at state and provincial level
[.013 091]	Areas, regions, places in general

Do not use; class in 336.0131

[.013 093–.013 099]	Specific continents, countries, localities

Do not use for specific continents, countries; class in 336.0133–336.0139. Do not use for specific states and provinces in ancient world; class in 336.093. Do not use for specific states and provinces in modern world; class in 336.4–336.9

.013 1	Public finance at state and provincial level in areas, regions, places in general

Add to base number 336.0131 the numbers following —1 in notation 11–19 from Table 2, e.g., state and provincial public finance in developing countries 336.0131724

.013 3–.013 9	Public finance at state and provincial level in specific continents, countries

Add to base number 336.013 notation 3–9 from Table 2, e.g., provincial public finance in Canada 336.01371

Class public finance at state and provincial level in specific states and provinces in ancient world in 336.093; class public finance at state and provincial level in specific states and provinces in modern world in 336.4–336.9

.014	Public finance at local level
[.014 091]	Areas, regions, places in general

Do not use; class in 336.0141

[.014 093–.014 099]	Specific continents, countries, localities

Do not use for specific continents, countries, states and provinces; class in 336.0143–336.0149. Do not use for specific localities in ancient world; class in 336.093. Do not use for specific localities in modern world; class in 336.4–336.9

.014 1	Public finance at local level in areas, regions, places in general

Add to base number 336.0141 the numbers following —1 in notation 11–19 from Table 2, e.g., local public finance in developing countries 336.0141724

.014 3–.014 9   Public finance at local level in specific continents, countries, states and provinces

> Add to base number 336.014 notation 3–9 from Table 2, e.g., local public finance in Pennsylvania 336.014748

> Class public finance at local level in specific localities in ancient world in 336.093; class public finance at local level in specific localities in modern world in 336.4–336.9

.02   Revenue

> *For specific forms of revenue, see 336.1–336.2*

[.020 91]   Areas, regions, places in general

> Do not use; class in 336.021

[.020 93–.020 99]   Specific continents, countries, localities

> Do not use; class in 336.023–336.029

.021   Revenue in areas, regions, places in general

> Add to base number 336.021 the numbers following —1 in notation 11–19 from Table 2, e.g., revenue in developing countries 336.021724

.023–.029   Revenue in specific continents, countries, localities

> Add to base number 336.02 notation 3–9 from Table 2, e.g., revenue in France 336.0244

.09   History; areas, regions, places in general; associations of sovereign states; biography; ancient world

.090 1–.090 5   Historical periods

> Add to base number 336.090 the numbers following —090 in notation 0901–0905 from Table 1, e.g., public finance in the 19th century 336.09034

.091   Areas, regions, places in general; associations of sovereign states

.091 6   Associations of sovereign states

.091 62   League of Nations

.091 63   United Nations

.091 68   Regional associations

> Including League of Arab States

> Class regional associations limited to specific continents in 336.4–336.9

.091 7   Socioeconomic regions

> Add to base number 336.0917 the numbers following —17 in notation 171–177 from Table 2, e.g., public finance in developing countries 336.091724; however, for public finance in socioeconomic regions by governmental level, see 336.01

> Class regional associations of sovereign states in 336.09168

.092   Biography

> Add to base number 336.092 the numbers following —092 in notation
> 0922–0929 from Table 1, e.g., collected biography 336.0922

.093   Ancient world

> Add to base number 336.093 the numbers following —3 in notation
> 31–39 from Table 2, e.g., public finance in Roman Empire 336.0937;
> however, for public finance in ancient world by governmental level, see
> 336.01

> **336.1–336.2 Specific forms of revenue**

Class comprehensive works in 336.02

.1   **Nontax revenues**

For public borrowing, see 336.34

> 336.12–336.15 Commercial revenues

Class revenue from franchises in 336.16; class comprehensive works in 336.1

For revenues from public industries and services, see 336.19

.12   Commercial revenues from public lands

Including revenue from rent, mineral rights

.15   Commercial revenues from deposits, investments, loans

.16   Administrative revenues

Including revenue from franchises, fines, gifts, profits on coinage, user and
license fees

.17   Revenues from lotteries

.18   Intergovernmental and intragovernmental revenues

Standard subdivisions are added for intergovernmental and
intragovernmental revenues together, for intergovernmental revenues alone

.182   Revenues from reparations and interest on war loans

.185   Revenues from one government unit to another

Including grants from higher units, payment in lieu of taxes, technical
assistance funds

.188   Revenues from international grants

.19   Revenue from public industries and services

Standard subdivisions are added for either or both topics in heading

.2   Taxes

Class here taxation, internal (inland) revenue, interdisciplinary works on taxes

For tax law, see 343.04; for tax administration, see 352.44

See Manual at 343.04–343.06 vs. 336.2, 352.44

SUMMARY

336.200 1–.200 9	Standard subdivisions
.201–.207	General topics of taxes
.22	Real property taxes
.23	Personal property taxes
.24	Income taxes
.25	Poll taxes
.26	Customs (Tariff)
.27	Other taxes
.29	Principles of taxation

.200 1–.200 8   Standard subdivisions

.200 9   History, geographic treatment, biography

Do not use for general works on taxes by governmental level; class in 336.201

>   **336.201–336.207 General topics of taxes**

Unless other instructions are given, class a subject with aspects in two or more subdivisions of 336.201–336.207 in the number coming last, e.g., local business taxes 336.207 (*not* 336.2014)

Class comprehensive works in 336.2

.201   Taxes by governmental level

Class here taxes in three or more jurisdictions at the same level

Class taxes in one or two specific jurisdictions at a specific level in 336.20093–336.20099

.201 2   National taxes

[.201 209 1]   Areas, regions, places in general

Do not use; class in 336.20121

[.201 209 3–.201 209 9]   Specific continents, countries

Do not use for specific countries; class in 336.20093–336.20099. Do not use for specific continents; class in 336.20123–336.20129

.201 21   National taxes in areas, regions, places in general

Add to base number 336.20121 the numbers following —1 in notation 11–19 from Table 2, e.g., national taxes in developing countries 336.20121724

.201 23–.201 29   National taxes in specific continents

         Add to base number 336.2012 notation 3–9 from Table 2, e.g., national taxes in Europe 336.20124

         Class national taxes in specific nations in 336.20093–336.20099

.201 3   State and provincial taxes

[.201 309 1]   Areas, regions, places in general

         Do not use; class in 336.20131

[.201 309 3–.201 309 9]   Specific continents, countries

         Do not use for specific states or provinces; class in 336.20093–336.20099. Do not use for specific continents, countries; class in 336.20133–336.20139

.201 31   State and provincial taxes in areas, regions, places in general

         Add to base number 336.20131 the numbers following —1 in notation 11–19 from Table 2, e.g., provincial taxes in developing countries 336.20131724

.201 33–.201 39   State and provincial taxes in specific continents, countries

         Add to base number 336.2013 notation 3–9 from Table 2, e.g., provincial taxes in Canada 336.201371

         Class state and provincial taxes in specific states or provinces in 336.20093–336.20099

.201 4   Local taxes

[.201 409 1]   Areas, regions, places in general

         Do not use; class in 336.20141

[.201 409 3–.201 409 9]   Specific continents, countries, localities

         Do not use for local taxes in specific local jurisdictions; class in 336.20093–336.20099. Do not use for local taxes in specific continents, countries, states or provinces; class in 336.20143–336.20149

.201 41   Local taxes in areas, regions, places in general

         Add to base number 336.20141 the numbers following —1 in notation 11–19 from Table 2, e.g., local taxes in developing countries 336.20141724

.201 43–.201 49   Local taxes in specific continents, countries, states and provinces

         Add to base number 336.2014 notation 3–9 from Table 2, e.g., local taxes in Pennsylvania 336.2014748

         Class local taxes in specific local jurisdictions in 336.20093–336.20099

.205   Tax reform

     Class here proposals and innovations

     Class reform of taxes at a specific governmental level in 336.201

.206   **Provisions that allow tax avoidance**

> Including tax credits, deductions, incentives, rebates

> Class here loopholes, tax expenditure (reductions in government revenue through preferential tax treatment)

.207   **Business taxes**

> Including taxes on manufacturing, small business, international business

.22   **Real property taxes**

> Variant name: rates (United Kingdom)

> Class here comprehensive works on property taxes

> Class comprehensive works on taxes on personal wealth in 336.24

> *For personal property taxes, see 336.23*

.222   **Rates and assessment**

> Class rates and assessment of specific kinds of real property in 336.225

.225   **Specific kinds of real property**

> Including commercial, farm, residential property; land value taxation

[.225 01–.225 09]   Standard subdivisions

> Do not use; class in 336.2201–336.2209

.23   **Personal property taxes**

> On tangible and intangible property

> Including mobile homes

> Class comprehensive works on property taxes in 336.22

.24   **Income taxes**

> Class here comprehensive works on taxes on personal wealth

> *For property taxes, see 336.22; for estate, inheritance, gift taxes, see 336.276*

.241   **General topics of income taxes**

> Class general topics applied to personal income tax in 336.242; class general topics applied to corporate income tax in 336.243

[.241 01–.241 09]   Standard subdivisions

> Do not use; class in 336.2401–336.2409

.241 5   Reform

> Class reform of taxes on business income in 336.2417

.241 6   Provisions that allow tax avoidance

> Class provisions allowing avoidance of taxes on business income in 336.2417

.241 7   Taxes on business income

.242	Personal income taxes (Individual income taxes)

See also 362.582 for negative income tax

.242 1	General topics of personal income taxes

Class general topics applied to taxes on specific kinds of personal income in 336.2422–336.2428

[.242 101–.242 109]	Standard subdivisions

Do not use; class in 336.24201–336.24209

.242 15	Reform
.242 16	Provisions that allow tax avoidance
.242 2	Income from wages

Including withholding tax

.242 3	Self-employment income

Including income from individual proprietorships, from partnerships

Class here small business income

For small corporation income, see 336.243

.242 4	Capital gains

Including capital loss deduction

Class here comprehensive works on taxation of individual and corporate capital gains and losses

For taxation of corporate capital gains, see 336.243

.242 6	Interest income

Class here comprehensive works on taxation of individual and corporate interest income

For taxation of corporate interest income, see 336.243

.242 8	Retirement income
.243	Corporate income taxes

Including capital gains taxes, interest income

Class comprehensive works on business taxes in 336.207; class comprehensive works on business income tax in 336.2417

.243 1	General topics of corporate income taxes

Class general topics applied to profits taxes in 336.2432

[.243 101–.243 109]	Standard subdivisions

Do not use; class in 336.24301–336.24309

.243 15	Reform
.243 16	Provisions that allow tax avoidance

Including oil depletion allowance

.243 2   Excess and undistributed profits taxes

> Standard subdivisions are added for excess and undistributed profits taxes together, for excess profits tax alone

.249   Social security taxes

> Class actuarial and administrative aspects of finance for social security in 368.401; class actuarial and administrative aspects of rates and rate making for social security in 368.4011

.25   Poll taxes

.26   Customs (Tariff)

> Class interdisciplinary works on customs (tariff) in 382.7

.263   Export and transit taxes

> Standard subdivisions are added for export and transit taxes together, for export taxes alone

.264   Import taxes

> *For import tax schedules, see 336.265; for import taxes on specific products, see 336.266*

.265   Import tax schedules

> *For import tax schedules on specific products, see 336.266*

.266   Import taxes and tax schedules on specific products

[.266 000 1–.266 000 9]   Standard subdivisions

> Do not use for import taxes; class in 336.26401–336.26409. Do not use for import tax schedules; class in 336.26501–336.26509

.266 001–.266 999   Subdivisions of import taxes and tax schedules on specific products

> Add to base number 336.266 notation 001–999, e.g., import taxes on paintings 336.26675
> Subdivisions are added for either or both topics in heading

.27   Other taxes

.271   Excise, sales, value-added, related taxes

> Including luxury, use taxes

.271 3   Sales tax

.271 4   Value-added tax

.271 6   Severance tax

.272   Stamp tax and revenue stamps

> Standard subdivisions are added for either or both topics in heading

.276   Estate, inheritance, gift taxes

> Standard subdivisions are added for any or all topics in heading
>
> Class here death duties, death tax
>
> Class estate planning in 332.024016; class comprehensive works on taxes on personal wealth in 336.24

.278   Taxes on products, services, industries

> Standard subdivisions are added for any or all topics in heading
>
> Class a specific kind of tax on a product, service, industry with the kind of tax, e.g., import taxes on coal 336.26655324, severance taxes on coal 336.2716

.278 000 1–.278 000 9   Standard subdivisions

.278 001–.278 999   Taxes on specific products, services, industries

> Add to base number 336.278 notation 001–999, e.g., coal industry taxes 336.2783382724
> Subdivisions are added for any or all topics in heading

.29   Principles of taxation

> Class principles of specific kinds of taxes in 336.22–336.27

.291   General principles of taxation

> Including adequacy (yield), certainty, diversity, economy and convenience of collection, justice

.293   Kinds of rate

> Including progressive, proportional, regressive rates

.294   Incidence

> The final burden of tax payment and the people on whom it falls
>
> Including direct, indirect, double taxation

.3   **Public debt and expenditures**

> Class here fiscal policy, comprehensive works on monetary and fiscal policy
>
> *For monetary policy, see 332.46; for use of fiscal and monetary policy in economic stabilization, see 339.5*

SUMMARY

336.31	**Government securities**
.34	**Public debt**
.36	**Debt management**
.39	**Public expenditures**

.31   Government securities

> Including short-term securities, Eurobonds
>
> Class comprehensive works on government securities in 332.63232

.34 Public debt

Class here public borrowing

For public securities, see 336.31; for debt management, see 336.36

.340 9 History, geographic treatment, biography

Do not use for general works on domestic public debt by governmental level; class in 336.343

.343 Public debt by governmental level

Class here public debt in three or more jurisdictions at a specific level

Class public debt in one or two jurisdictions at the same level in 336.34093–336.34099; class international public debt regardless of jurisdiction or level in 336.3435; class flotation of loans regardless of level in 336.344; class debt limits regardless of level in 336.346

.343 1 Local level

[.343 109 1] Areas, regions, places in general

Do not use; class in 336.34311

[.343 109 3–.343 109 9] Specific continents, countries, localities

Do not use for specific continents, countries, states and provinces; class in 336.3409. Do not use for specific localities; class in 336.34313–336.34319

.343 11 Local public debt in areas, regions, places in general

Add to base number 336.34311 the numbers following —1 in notation 11–19 from Table 2, e.g., local public debt in developing countries 336.34311724

.343 13–.343 19 Local public debt in specific continents, countries, states and provinces

Add to base number 336.3431 notation 3–9 from Table 2, e.g., local public debt in Pennsylvania 336.3431748

Class local public debt in specific localities in 336.34093–336.34099

.343 2 State and provincial level

[.343 209 1] Areas, regions, places in general

Do not use; class in 336.34321

[.343 209 3–.343 209 9] Specific continents, countries, localities

Do not use for specific states and provinces; class in 336.34093–336.34099. Do not use for specific continents, countries; class in 336.34323–336.34329

.343 21 State and provincial public debt in areas, regions, places in general

Add to base number 336.34321 the numbers following —1 in notation 11–19 from Table 2, e.g., state and provincial public debt in developing countries 336.34321724

.343 23–.343 29	State and provincial public debt in specific continents, countries

Add to base number 336.3432 notation 3–9 from Table 2, e.g., provincial public debt in Canada 336.343271

Class state and provincial public debt in specific states and provinces in 336.34093–336.34099

.343 3	National level

For borrowing by one nation from another nation, see 336.3435

[.343 309 1]	Areas, regions, places in general

Do not use; class in 336.34331

[.343 309 3–.343 309 9]	Specific continents, countries, localities

Do not use for specific countries; class in 336.34093–336.34099. Do not use for specific continents; class in 336.34333–336.34339

.343 31	National public debt in areas, regions, places in general

Add to base number 336.34331 the numbers following —1 in notation 11–19 from Table 2, e.g., national public debt in developing countries 336.34331724

.343 33–.343 39	National public debt in specific continents

Add to base number 336.3433 notation 3–9 from Table 2, e.g., national public debt in Europe 336.34334

Class national public debt in specific countries in 336.34093–336.34099

.343 5	International public debt

Borrowing by one nation from another, public debts owed by one nation to another

Class here comprehensive works on international borrowing and debts

For role of banks in international borrowing and debts, see 332.15

.344	Flotation of government securities

Including forced loans

Class government securities in 336.31

.346	Debt limits
.36	Debt management

Class debt limits in 336.346

See also 339.523 for deficit financing in macroeconomic policy

.363	Repayment and redemption

Standard subdivisions are added for either or both topics in heading

Including sinking funds

.368   Repudiation

      Class here public insolvency

.39   Public expenditures

      Class tax expenditure in 336.206

      For expenditure in macroeconomic policy, see 339.522. For expenditures by a specific agency or on a specific activity, see the agency or activity in 352–354, plus notation 249 from table under 352–354, e.g., expenditures on transportation 354.76249

.4–.9   Public finance of specific continents, countries, localities in modern world

      Add to base number 336 notation 4–9 from Table 2, e.g., public finance of Australia 336.94; however, for general works on public finance by governmental level, see 336.01

337   International economics

      Class here international economic planning; comprehensive works on international economic relations, on international economic cooperation

      For a specific aspect of international economics not provided for here, see the aspect, e.g., multinational business enterprises 338.88, international commerce 382

[.093–.099]   Specific continents, countries, localities

      Do not use; class in 337.3–337.9

.1   Multilateral economic cooperation

      Class here economic integration, multilateral agreements and multistate organizations for economic cooperation

      Class bilateral economic cooperation in 337.3–337.9; class interdisciplinary works on intergovernmental organizations in 341.2

      For trade agreements, see 382.9

      See Manual at 337.3–337.9 vs. 337.1

.109   History and biography

      Do not use for geographic treatment; class in 337.11–337.19

.11   Multilateral economic cooperation in areas, regions, places in general

      Add to base number 337.11 the numbers following —1 in notation 17–18 from Table 2, e.g., multilateral economic cooperation in developing regions 337.11724

.14   European multilateral cooperation

.142   European Union

      Class here European Common Market, European Community, European Economic Community

.143   European Free Trade Association (EFTA)

.147   Council for Mutual Economic Assistance (COMECON)

.15–.19   Multilateral cooperation in continents other than Europe

> Add to base number 337.1 notation 5–9 from Table 2, e.g., Andean Group 337.18

.3–.9   Foreign economic policies and relations of specific jurisdictions and groups of jurisdictions

> Class here bilateral economic cooperation
>
> Add to base number 337 notation 3–9 from Table 2, e.g., economic policy of United Kingdom 337.41; then, for foreign economic relations between two jurisdictions or groups of jurisdictions, add 0* and to the result add notation 1–9 from Table 2, e.g., economic relations between United Kingdom and France 337.41044
>
> Give priority in notation to the jurisdiction or group of jurisdictions emphasized. If the emphasis is equal, give priority to the one coming first in Table 2
> (Option: Give priority in notation to the jurisdiction or group of jurisdictions requiring local emphasis, e.g., libraries in the United States class foreign economic relations between the United States and France in 337.73044)
>
> Class multilateral economic cooperation in 337.1
>
> *See Manual at 337.3–337.9 vs. 337.1*

338   Production

> Class here interdisciplinary works on industry, on production
>
> *For specific factors of production, see 331–333; for production economics of financial industries, see 332; for production economics of real estate business, see 333.33; for production economics of energy production, see 333.79; for economics of cooperative production, see 334; for production economics of insurance industry, see 368; for commerce, communications, transportation, see 380. For a specific noneconomic aspect of industry and production, see the aspect, e.g., law of industry 343.07, production technology 620–690*
>
> *See Manual at T1—025 vs. T1—029; also at 332 vs. 338, 658.15; also at 363.5, 363.6, 363.8 vs. 338*

SUMMARY

338.001–.008	**Standard subdivisions**
.01–.09	**[General topics]**
.1	**Agriculture**
.2	**Extraction of minerals**
.3	**Other extractive industries**
.4	**Secondary industries and services**
.5	**General production economics**
.6	**Organization of production**
.7	**Business enterprises**
.8	**Combinations**
.9	**Economic development and growth**

---

*Add 00 for standard subdivisions; see instructions at beginning of Table 1

.001   Philosophy and theory

> *For a specific theory, see the theory, e.g., law of diminishing marginal utility 338.5212*

.001 12   Forecasting

> Do not use for forecasting of products and services; class in 338.020112. Do not use for general production forecasting; class in 338.544

.002–.008   Standard subdivisions

[.009]   History, geographic treatment, biography

> Do not use; class in 338.09

.01   Factors of production

> Class here comprehensive and theoretical works on factors of production

> Class factors of production as part of industrial conditions and situation in 338.09; class factors of production as costs of production in 338.512

> *For labor, see 331; for capital, see 332; for land, see 333*

.02   Products and services

> Standard subdivisions are added for products and services together, for products alone

> Class general production economics in 338.5; class consumption in 339.47; class shipments and sales in 381

> *For specific products, see 338.1–338.4; for services alone, see 338.47*

> *See Manual at T1—025 vs. T1—029*

.020 12   Classification

> Class here standard industrial classifications

> Add to base number 338.02012 notation 4–9 from Table 2, e.g., standard industrial classifications of Canada 338.0201271

.04   Entrepreneurship

.06   Production efficiency

> Including cost-output ratio

> Class here industrial productivity

> Class conservation of energy in 333.7916

> *For labor productivity, see 331.118*

.064   Effect of technological innovations

Class here effect of automation, comprehensive works on effect of technological innovations on the economy

For effect of technological innovations on a specific aspect of the economy, see the aspect, e.g., effect on working conditions 331.25, effect on banking 332.1

See also 303.483 for effect of technological innovation on society

.09   History, geographic treatment, biography

Class here history, geographic treatment, biography of general principles and theories; existing and potential resources for production, industrial conditions and situation, industrial surveys, location of industry

Class a specific resource with the resource, e.g., water for power 333.914

.090 01–.090 08   Standard subdivisions

.090 09   Archaeology

Do not use for history, geographic treatment, biography together; class in 338.09. Do not use for historical periods; class in 338.0901–338.0905. Do not use for geographic treatment and biography; class in 338.091–338.099

Class interdisciplinary works on industrial archaeology in 609.009

.090 1–.090 5   Historical periods

Add to base number 338.090 the numbers following —090 in notation 0901–0905 from Table 1, e.g., industrial surveys in 20th century 338.0904

.091–.099   Geographic treatment and biography

Add to base number 338.09 notation 1–9 from Table 2, e.g., industrial surveys of Canada 338.0971

See also 338.6042 for rationale for and process of locating business enterprises

See Manual at 338.091–338.099 vs. 332.67309, 338.6042

.092   Biography

Number built according to instructions under 338.091–338.099

See Manual at 338.092

> ### 338.1–338.4 Specific kinds of industries

Class here finance, general production economics of specific kinds of industries

Class results of market surveys; supply and demand in relation to trade, to marketing opportunities in 381; class comprehensive works in 338; class interdisciplinary works on capital formation in 332.0415

> *For financial industries, see 332; for credit for specific kinds of industries, see 332.7; for real estate business, see 333.33; for energy production, see 333.79; for cooperatives in specific kinds of industries, see 334; for organization of production in specific kinds of industries, see 338.6; for business enterprises other than cooperatives in specific kinds of industries, see 338.7; for commerce, communications, transportation, see 380. For biographies of entrepreneurs in a specific kind of industry, see the kind of industry in 338.6–338.8, e.g., biographies of small-business owners 338.642092, biographies of entrepreneurs in textile manufacturing 338.76770092; for biographies of people known for their contributions in a specific type of technology, see the type of technology in 600, e.g., biographies of mining engineers 622.092*

> ### 338.1–338.3 Primary industries (Extractive industries)

Class comprehensive works in 338

.1 **Agriculture**

Class agricultural cooperatives in 334.683; class government farm policies in 338.18

See Manual at 338.1 vs. 631.558

.13 Financial aspects

Class here capital formation and other investment in agriculture, costs, prices received by farmers, farm income

Add to base number 338.13 the numbers following 63 in 633–638, e.g., prices of rice 338.13318

Class government policies that affect financial aspects in 338.18; class food prices in 338.19

> *For agricultural credit, see 332.71*

> *See also 338.16 for production efficiency*

> *See Manual at 332 vs. 338, 658.15*

.14 Factors affecting production

Including drought, plant and animal diseases, shortages of materials and equipment used in farming

> *For financial factors, see 338.13; for production efficiency, see 338.16; for surpluses and shortages of farm products, see 338.17; for government policies, see 338.18*

.16   Production efficiency

              Including cost-output ratio, size of farm, use of labor

              Class here agricultural productivity; science, technological innovation in
              agriculture

              Class energy conservation in agriculture in 333.7966; class comprehensive
              works on factors affecting production in 338.14

              For labor productivity, see 331.118

.161   Mechanization

              Class here automation

              Class mechanization of harvesting methods in 338.163

.162   Agricultural methods

              Including crop rotation; use of fertilizers, of insecticides

              For harvesting methods, see 338.163

.163   Harvesting methods

.17   Products

              Including seed industry as a whole

              Class here surpluses and shortages of farm products, forecasts and
              projections of supply and demand

              Class specific elements of production applied to specific products and
              groups of products in 338.13–338.16; class government farm policies
              applied to specific products and groups of products in 338.18; class
              supply, surpluses, shortages of food in 338.19; class specific producers in
              338.763. Class a specific kind of seed with the kind, e.g., corn (maize) seed
              338.17315

              See also 338.47637 for dairy and related products

.173–.176 Products of culture of plants, of domestic mammals, of domestic
              birds

              Add to base number 338.17 the numbers following 63 in 633–636,
              e.g., rice or seed rice 338.17318, forestry 338.1749, forest products
              338.17498; however, for supply of timber in nature, see 333.7511; for
              demand for timber, see 333.7512

.174 98   Forest products

                  Number built according to instructions under 338.173–338.176

                  Class here supply of cut timber, comprehensive works on timber

                  For uncut timber, timber reserves, see 333.7511

.178   Products of insect culture

              Add to base number 338.178 the numbers following 638 in 638.1–638.5,
              e.g., honey 338.17816

.18   Government farm policies

Class here acreage allotments, agricultural credit, drought relief, price supports, subsidies

Class government policies with respect to food supply in 338.19

[.180 93–.180 99]   Specific continents, countries, localities

Do not use; class in 338.183–338.189

.181   International policies

Policies and programs of international bodies

.183–.189   Specific continents, countries, localities

Add to base number 338.18 notation 3–9 from Table 2, e.g., government farm policies of India 338.1854; however, for international policies, see 338.181

.19   Food supply

Class here economic causes and effects of, economic remedies for maladjustments in food supply; measures for attaining and maintaining adequate amounts of food; food requirements (demand); reserves (stocks, supply) of food; prices of food to the consumer; comprehensive works on the economics of production, storage, distribution of food

Class interdisciplinary works on food supply in 363.8

For production of food, see 338.13–338.18; for supply of specific food commodities, see 338.17; for food processing, see 338.47664; for distribution of food, see 381.41

See Manual at 363.5, 363.6, 363.8 vs. 338

[.190 91]   Areas, regions, places in general

Do not use; class in 338.191

[.190 93–.190 99]   Specific continents, countries, localities

Do not use; class in 338.193–338.199

.191   Food supply in areas, regions, places in general

Add to base number 338.191 the numbers following —1 in notation 11–19 from Table 2, e.g., food supply in developing countries 338.191724

.193–.199   Food supply in specific continents, countries, localities

Add to base number 338.19 notation 3–9 from Table 2, e.g., food supply in Africa 338.196

.2   Extraction of minerals

Class here extraction of energy resources, comprehensive works on economics of extraction and processing of minerals and energy resources

Class conservation of mineral and energy resources in 333.7–333.9; class mined lands in 333.765

For processing of minerals and raw materials of energy, see 338.47

.23   Financial aspects

Class here capital formation and other investment in industries engaged in extraction of minerals; costs, income, prices

Add to base number 338.23 the numbers following 553 in 553.2–553.9, e.g., prices of tin 338.23453

Class production efficiency in 338.26

For industrial credit, see 332.742

See Manual at 332 vs. 338, 658.15

.26   Production efficiency

Including automation, cost-output ratio, effect of technological innovation, factors of production

Class here industrial productivity

Class energy conservation in mineral extraction industries in 333.7965

For labor productivity, see 331.118

.27   Products

Add to base number 338.27 the numbers following 553 in 553.2–553.9, e.g., coal 338.2724

Class supply in storage, shortages, surpluses, demand, and projections of these in 333.8; class specific elements of production applied to specific products in 338.23–338.26; class specific producers doing extraction only in 338.7622; class specific producers doing both extraction and processing in 338.766; class supply in nature in 553.2–553.9

.3   **Other extractive industries**

Including financial aspects, production efficiency

Class energy conservation in extractive industries in 333.7965

For industrial credit, see 332.742

See Manual at 332 vs. 338, 658.15

.37   Products

Class specific producers in 338.763

.371   Products of culture of invertebrates and cold-blooded vertebrates; aquaculture

Add to base number 338.371 the numbers following 639 in 639.3–639.8, e.g., culture of oysters 338.37141, aquaculture 338.3718; however, for insect culture, see 338.178

Class comprehensive works on fishing and the culture of fishes and other water animals in 338.3727

.372   Products of fishing, whaling, hunting, trapping

Class here catches from fishing, whaling, hunting, trapping industries

Add to base number 338.372 the numbers following 59 in 592–599, e.g., fishing for mollusks, comprehensive works on shellfishing 338.3724; fishing for crustaceans 338.3753; finfishing, comprehensive works on fishing 338.3727; then add further as follows:

01–08   Standard subdivisions
09   History, geographic treatment, biography
          Use number for the area in which industry is based, not the place where fishes or other animals are caught, e.g., fishing fleet based at Los Angeles 338.37270979494, not 338.372709722 or 338.3727091641

Class supply of uncaught animals in nature in 333.95411; class measures to increase supply of animals in nature in 333.95415; class culture of invertebrates and cold-blooded vertebrates in 338.371. Class supply of a specific non-taxonomic kind of uncaught animals in nature, statistics of catches of a specific non-taxonomic kind of animal used in estimating its population in nature, with the kind of animal in 333.9542–333.9549, plus notation 11 from table under 333.7–333.9, e.g., supply of uncaught aquatic animals 333.9594811, statistics of game animal catches used in estimating population of game animals 333.954911; class supply of a specific taxonomic kind of uncaught animals in nature, statistics of catches of a specific taxonomic kind of animal used in estimating its population in nature, with the kind of animal in 333.955–333.959, plus notation 11 from table under 333.7–333.9, e.g., supply of uncaught deer 333.9596511, statistics of game bird catches used in estimating population of game birds 333.9582911; class measures to increase supply of a specific non-taxonomic kind of animals in nature with the kind in 333.9542–333.9549, plus notation 15 from table under 333.7–333.9, e.g., development of game animals in nature 333.954915; class measures to increase supply of a specific taxonomic kind of animals in nature with the kind in 333.955–333.959, plus notation 15 from table under 333.7–333.9, e.g., development of fishes in nature 333.95615

.4   **Secondary industries and services**

Standard subdivisions are added for secondary industries and services together, for secondary industries alone

Class here products of secondary industries

Class government policies in 338.48; class comprehensive works on products in 338.02; class comprehensive works on service industries, on services in 338.47

See Manual at T1—025 vs. T1—029

.43   Financial aspects

Class here capital formation and other investments, costs, income, prices

Class production efficiency in 338.45

For industrial credit, see 332.742

See Manual at 332 vs. 338, 658.15

.430 001–.430 009   Standard subdivisions

.430 01–.439 99   Specific industries and services

> Add to base number 338.43 notation 001–999, e.g., automobile prices 338.43629222; however, for financial aspects of financial industries, see 332; for financial aspects of real estate, see 333.33; for financial aspects of energy production, see 333.79; for financial aspects of cooperative production, see 334; for financial aspects of insurance industry, see 368.01; for financial aspects of commerce, communications, transportation, see 380
> Subdivisions are added for either or both topics in heading

.45   Production efficiency

> Including cost-output ratio, factors of production (land, labor, capital), production capacity

> Class here industrial productivity

> Class energy conservation in secondary industries in 333.796516

> *For labor productivity, see 331.118*

.454   Automation

> *For automation in specific industries, see 338.456*

.456   Production efficiency in specific industries and groups of industries

> Class here automation in specific industries

[.456 01–.456 09]   Standard subdivisions

> Do not use; class in 338.4501–338.4509

.456 1   Production efficiency in industries other than extractive, manufacturing, construction

> Class here service industries

.456 100 01–.456 100 09   Standard subdivisions

.456 100 1–.456 199 9   Subdivisions for production efficiency in industries other than extractive, manufacturing, construction

> Add to base number 338.4561 notation 001–999, e.g., production efficiency in hospital services 338.456136211; however, for production efficiency in financial industries, see 332; for production efficiency in real estate business, see 333.33; for production efficiency in cooperative enterprises, see 334; for production efficiency in the insurance industry, see 368; for production efficiency in commerce, communications, transportation, see 380

.456 2–.456 9   Production efficiency in manufacturing and construction industries

> Add to base number 338.456 the numbers following 6 in 620–690, e.g., power equipment in textile manufacture 338.456770285; however, for production efficiency in energy production, see 333.79; for production efficiency in cooperative enterprises, see 334

.46   Professional services

> Class specific elements of production applied to professional services in 338.43–338.45; class specific professional services in 338.47

.47   Services and specific products

Class here quantities produced, shortages, surpluses, stockpiles, forecasts and projections of supply and demand; comprehensive works on service industries, on economics of services

Class specific elements of production applied to services and specific products in 338.43–338.45; class specific producers in 338.76; class comprehensive works on products of secondary industries in 338.4

For comprehensive works on professional services, see 338.46

.470 001–.470 009   Standard subdivisions of services

.470 01–.479 99   Subdivisions for products and services

Add to base number 338.47 notation 001–999, e.g., pharmaceutical industry 338.476151, tourist industry 338.4791; however, for production economics of financial industries, see 332; for production economics of real estate business, see 333.33; for production economics of energy production, see 333.79; for production economics of cooperative enterprises, see 334; for production economics of commerce, communications, transportation, see 380
Subdivisions are added for either or both topics in heading

.476 626   Fuel industry

Number built according to instructions under 338.47001–338.47999

Class here comprehensive works on processing and manufacturing fuels

For processing or manufacturing a specific fuel, see the fuel, e.g., biomass fuel 338.4766288, gasoline 338.4766553827

.48   Government policies

Class government policies with respect to a specific aspect of secondary industries and services in 338.43–338.47

.5   General production economics

Including risk

Class here microeconomics (economics of the firm)

Class production economics of specific kinds of industries in 338.1–338.4

For organization of production, see 338.6

[.501 12]   Forecasting

Do not use; class in 338.544

.51   Costs

.512   Factors of production as costs of production

Including law of diminishing marginal returns, of factor proportions

Class comprehensive works on factors of production in 338.01

.514	Elements in cost calculation
.514 2	Kinds of cost
	Including average, fixed, marginal, variable costs
.514 4	Size of enterprise
	Including economies and diseconomies of scale
.516	Profits
	Including relation of marginal cost to marginal revenue
.52	Prices

> Class here price determination, effects of changes, comprehensive works on prices

> Class effect of money on prices in 332.41; class effect of costs on prices in 338.516

> *For a specific aspect of prices not provided for here, see the aspect, e.g., effects of prices on the whole economy 339.42*

.520 1	Philosophy and theory

> Do not use for theories; class in 338.521

.520 2	Miscellany
.520 21	Tabulated and related materials

> Do not use for statistics; class in 338.528

.521	Price theories

> Class here law of supply and demand, theories of value

> *For Marxian labor theory of value, see 335.412*

> *See also 333.7 for supply and demand for natural resources and energy; also 338.1–338.4 for supply and demand for specific products*

.521 2	Theory of demand
	Including law of diminishing marginal utility, price-demand relationship
.521 3	Theory of supply
	Including price-supply relationship

> **338.522–338.526 Price determination**

Class comprehensive works in 338.52

.522	Price determination in free markets
	Including interproduct competition, e.g., butter versus margarine
.523	Price determination by monopolies, oligopolies
	Including price fixing, price leadership

| .526 | Price determination by government regulation (Price control) |
| .528 | Price levels |

       Class here indexes, statistics

       See also 339.42 for cost of living

| .528 021 | Tabulated and related materials |

       Do not use for statistics; class in 338.528

| .54 | Economic fluctuations |

       Including seasonal variations, secular trends

| [.540 112] | Forecasting |

       Do not use; class in 338.544

| .542 | Business cycles |

       Including prosperity, recession, depression, recovery; panics

       Class remedial and preventive measures in 338.543. Class comprehensive economic works on a specific period of prosperity or depression with the economic conditions of the specific time or place in 330.9, e.g., worldwide depression in 1930s 330.9043, economic prosperity in Germany, 1949–1962 330.9430875

| .543 | Remedial and preventive action |

       Standard subdivisions are added for either or both topics in heading

       Class comprehensive works on economic stabilization in 339.5

| .544 | General production forecasting and forecasts |

       See also 658.40355 for forecasting as a technique of managerial decision-making

| .544 2 | Methods of forecasting |

       Class comprehensive works on economic forecasting in 330.0112

| .544 3 | Forecasts |

       Class forecasts of economic situation in 330.900112

| **.6** | **Organization of production** |

       Class here organization of production in specific kinds of industries

       For business enterprises and their structure, see 338.7

       See Manual at 338.092

| .604 | Special topics of organization of production |
| .604 1 | Finance |

       Class finance of specific kinds of industries in 338.1–338.4; class interdisciplinary works on capital formation in 332.0415

.604 2	Location

Class here proximity to sources of power, raw materials, labor supply, transportation, markets

See Manual at 338.091–338.099 vs. 332.67309, 338.6042

.604 6	Specialization and comparative advantage

Standard subdivisions are added for either or both topics in heading

Class works on specialization and comparative advantage that emphasize international commerce in 382.1042

.604 8	Competition and restraint

Standard subdivisions are added for either or both topics in heading

Class monopoly and monopolies in 338.82

.61	Private enterprise

Class specific systems of private enterprise in 338.63; class specific sizes of private enterprise in 338.64

.62	Public enterprise
.63	Systems of production

For factory system, see 338.65

.632	Guild system
.634	Domestic system

Class here cottage industry

.64	Size of enterprises

Including downsizing

Class relation of size of enterprise to cost of production in 338.5144; class specific types of enterprises of specific sizes in 338.7–338.8

.642	Small business

Including custom production

Class here small industry

Class cottage industry in 338.634

.642 089	Ethnic and national groups

Class minority enterprises in 338.6422

.642 2	Minority enterprises

Class handicraft industries operated by minorities in 338.6425

.642 5	Handicraft industries
.644	Big business

Class here large industry

Class monopoly and monopolies in 338.82

.65   Factory system

.69   Worker control of industry

Class here employee ownership, worker self-management

Class role of unions in achieving worker control of industry in 331.8801; class guild socialism in 335.15; class syndicalism in 335.82; class employee participation in management in 658.3152

For employee stock ownership plans, see 331.21649

.7   Business enterprises

Not limited to private or capitalist enterprises

Class here structure of business enterprises; interdisciplinary works on business enterprises, on organizations for production

For cooperatives, see 334; for combinations, see 338.8

See Manual at T1—025 vs. T1—029; also at 338.092

.71   Initiation and dissolution of business enterprises

>   338.72–338.74 Specific kinds of business enterprises

Class specific kinds of business enterprises in specific industries and groups of industries in 338.76; class comprehensive works in 338.7

.72   Individual proprietorships

.73   Partnerships

.74   Corporations

Open and closed

See Manual at T1—025 vs. T1—029

.749   Government corporations

Class here interdisciplinary works on government corporations

For a specific aspect of government corporations, see the aspect, e.g., law 346.067, public administration of government corporations 352.266

[.749 068]   Management

Do not use; class in 352.266

.76   Business enterprises by industry

Class here specific individual business enterprises, biographies of entrepreneurs in specific fields

For biographies of people known for their contribution to technology, see the kind of contribution in 600, plus notation 092 from Table 1, e.g., biographies of mining engineers 622.092

See Manual at T1—025 vs. T1—029

.761   Business enterprises in industries other than extractive,
                manufacturing, construction

    Class here service industries

.761 000 1–.761 000 9   Standard subdivisions

.761 001–.761 999   Subdivisions for business enterprises in industries other than
                extractive, manufacturing, construction

    Add to base number 338.761 notation 001–999, e.g., law
firms 338.76134; however, for financial institutions, see
332.1–332.6; for real estate business enterprises, see 333.33;
for cooperative enterprises, see 334; for insurance companies,
see 368.0065; for enterprises engaged in commerce,
communications, transportation, see 380

.762–.769   Business enterprises in extractive, manufacturing, construction
                industries

    Add to base number 338.76 the numbers following 6 in 620–690, e.g.,
agriculture 338.763; however, for enterprises engaged in production of
energy, see 333.79; for cooperative enterprises, see 334.682–334.688

.8   **Combinations**

    Organization and structure for massive production and control of production

    Class here antitrust policies, economic concentration

    To be classed here, works about specific individual enterprises must stress that
they are combinations; otherwise, the works are classed in 338.76

    See Manual at 338.092

SUMMARY

338.804	**Special topics of combinations**	
.82	**Restrictive practices**	
.83	**Mergers**	
.85	**Trusts**	
.86	**Holding companies**	
.87	**Informal arrangements**	
.88	**Multinational business enterprises**	

.804   Special topics of combinations

.804 2   Kinds of combinations

    Including horizontal, vertical, conglomerate

.82   Restrictive practices

    Class here monopoly and monopolies, oligopoly and oligopolies

    Class price determination in 338.523; class restrictive practices of
multinational business enterprises in 338.884

.826   Restrictive practices in specific industries, groups of industries,
                fields of enterprise

[.826 01–.826 09]   Standard subdivisions

Do not use; class in 338.8201–338.8209

.826 1   Restrictive practices in industries and fields of enterprise other than extractive, manufacturing, construction

Class here service industries

.826 100 01–.826 100 09   Standard subdivisions

.826 100 1–.826 199 9   Subdivisions for restrictive practices in industries and fields of enterprise other than extractive, manufacturing, construction

Add to base number 338.8261 notation 001–999, e.g., restrictive practices in publishing 338.82610705; however, for restrictive practices by combinations in the financial industries, see 332.1–332.6; for restrictive practices by combinations in real estate business, see 333.33; for restrictive practices by combinations in cooperative enterprise, see 334; for restrictive practices by combinations in the insurance industry, see 368; for restrictive practices by combinations in commerce, communications, transportation, see 380

.826 2–.826 9   Restrictive practices in extractive, manufacturing, construction industries and fields of enterprise

Add to base number 338.826 the numbers following 6 in 620–690, e.g., restrictive practices by combinations engaged in computer engineering 338.8262139; however, for restrictive practices by combinations engaged in energy production, see 333.79; for restrictive practices by cooperatives, see 334

>   338.83–338.87 Specific forms of combinations and their practices

Class international combinations regardless of form in 338.88; class comprehensive works in 338.8

.83   Mergers

Class here acquisitions, amalgamations

.836   Mergers in specific industries, groups of industries, fields of enterprise

[.836 01–.836 09]   Standard subdivisions

Do not use; class in 338.8301–338.8309

.836 1   Mergers in industries and fields of enterprise other than extractive, manufacturing, construction

Class here service industries

.836 100 01–.836 100 09   Standard subdivisions

.836 100 1–.836 199 9   Subdivisions for mergers in industries and fields of enterprise other than extractive, manufacturing, construction

> Add to base number 338.8361 notation 001–999, e.g., mergers of publishers 338.83610705; however, for mergers of financial institutions, see 332.1–332.6; for mergers of real estate business enterprises, see 333.33; for mergers of cooperatives, see 334; for mergers of enterprises in the insurance industry, see 368.0065; for mergers of enterprises engaged in commerce, communications, transportation, see 380

.836 2–.836 9   Mergers in extractive, manufacturing, construction industries and fields of enterprise

> Add to base number 338.836 the numbers following 6 in 620–690, e.g., mergers of automotive companies 338.836292; however, for mergers of enterprises engaged in energy production, see 333.79; for mergers of cooperatives, see 334

.85   Trusts

.86   Holding companies

.87   Informal arrangements

> Including cartels, interlocking directorates, pools

.88   Multinational business enterprises

> Class here foreign-owned and mostly foreign-owned enterprises, enterprises with mostly international operations

SUMMARY

338.880 9	**History and biography**
.881	**Growth, expansion, power**
.883	**Role in international economic development**
.884	**Restrictive practices and their control**
.887	**Multinational business enterprises in specific industries, groups of industries, fields**
.888	**Multinational business enterprises by location of operations**
.889	**Multinational business enterprises by location of owners**

.880 9   History and biography

> Do not use for geographic treatment; class in 338.888–338.889

.881   Growth, expansion, power

> Standard subdivisions are added for any or all topics in heading

> Class growth, expansion, power of multinational enterprises engaged in specific fields in 338.887

> *See also 322.3 for political influence of multinational enterprises*

.881 09   History and biography

> Do not use for geographic treatment; class in 338.888–338.889

.883	Role in international economic development

Class role in international economic development of multinational enterprises engaged in specific fields in 338.887

.883 09	History and biography

Do not use for geographic treatment; class in 338.888–338.889

.884	Restrictive practices and their control

Standard subdivisions are added for either or both topics in heading

Class here international monopoly, oligopoly

Class restrictive practices of multinational enterprises engaged in specific fields in 338.887

.884 09	History and biography

Do not use for geographic treatment; class in 338.888–338.889

.887	Multinational business enterprises in specific industries, groups of industries, fields

[.887 01–.887 08]	Standard subdivisions

Do not use; class in 338.8801–338.8808

[.887 09]	History

Do not use for history; class in 338.8809. Do not use for geographic treatment; class in 338.888–338.889

[.887 092]	Biography

Do not use; class in 338.88092

.887 1	Multinational business enterprises in industries and fields of enterprise other than extractive, manufacturing, construction

Class here service industries

.887 100 01–.887 100 09	Standard subdivisions

.887 100 1–.887 199 9	Subdivisions for multinational business enterprises in industries and fields of enterprise other than extractive, manufacturing, construction

Add to base number 338.8871 notation 001–999, e.g., multinational enterprises engaged in advertising 338.88716591; however, for multinational enterprises in financial industries, see 332.1–332.6; for multinational enterprises in real estate business, see 333.33; for multinational cooperatives, see 334; for multinational enterprises in the insurance industry, see 368.0065; for multinational enterprises in commerce, communications, transportation, see 380

.887 2–.887 9	Multinational business enterprises in extractive, manufacturing, construction industries and fields of enterprise

Add to base number 338.887 the numbers following 6 in 620–690, e.g., multinational enterprises engaged in mining petroleum and natural gas 338.88722338; however, for multinational enterprises engaged in energy production, see 333.79; for multinational cooperatives, see 334

.888   **Multinational business enterprises by location of operations**

Class multinational enterprises in specific industries and groups of industries in 338.887; class multinational enterprises by location of owners in 338.889

[.888 01–.888 08]   Standard subdivisions

Do not use; class in 338.8801–338.8808

[.888 09]   History

Do not use; class in 338.8809

[.888 091]   Areas, regions, places in general

Do not use; class in 338.8881

[.888 092]   Biography

Do not use; class in 338.88092

[.888 093–.888 099]   Specific continents, countries, localities

Do not use; class in 338.8883–338.8889

.888 1   Multinational business enterprises in areas, regions, places in general

Add to base number 338.8881 the numbers following —1 in notation 11–19 from Table 2, e.g., multinational enterprises in developing countries 338.8881724

.888 3–.888 9   Multinational enterprises in specific continents, countries, localities

Add to base number 338.888 notation 3–9 from Table 2, e.g., multinational enterprises in Europe 338.8884

.889   **Multinational business enterprises by location of owners**

Class multinational enterprises in specific industries or groups of industries in 338.887; class multinational enterprises in a specific area without regard to location of owners in 338.888

[.889 01–.889 08]   Standard subdivisions

Do not use; class in 338.8801–338.8808

[.889 09]   History

Do not use; class in 338.8809

[.889 091]   Areas, regions, places in general

Do not use; class in 338.8891

[.889 092]   Biography

>Do not use; class in 338.88092

[.889 093–.889 099]   Specific continents, countries, localities

>Do not use; class in 338.8893–338.8899

.889 1   Multinational business enterprises by owners residing in areas, regions, places in general

>Add to base number 338.8891 the numbers following —1 in notation 11–19 from Table 2, e.g., multinational enterprises owned by citizens of developing countries 338.8891724; then, for area in which enterprise is located, add 0* and to the result add notation 1–9 from Table 2, e.g., multinational enterprises owned by citizens of developing countries and located in Africa 338.889172406

.889 3–.889 9   Multinational business enterprises by owners residing in specific continents, countries, localities

>Add to base number 338.889 notation 3–9 from Table 2, e.g., multinational enterprises owned by United States nationals 338.88973; then, for area in which enterprise is located, add 0* and to the result add notation 1–9 from Table 2, e.g., multinational enterprises owned by United States nationals in Canada 338.88973071

.9   Economic development and growth

>Standard subdivisions are added for either or both topics in heading

>Including autarky and interdependence

>Class here economic planning, government policies and programs

>>*For economic development and growth with respect to specific kinds of industries, see 338.1–338.4. For economic development and growth with respect to a specific subject not provided for here, see the subject, e.g., international development banks 332.153*

>>*See also 330.124 for planned economies*

.900 1–.900 8   Standard subdivisions

.900 9   History, geographic treatment, biography

[.900 93–.900 99]   Specific continents, countries, localities

>Do not use; class in 338.93–338.99

.91   International development and growth

>Standard subdivisions are added for either or both topics in heading

>Class here assistance by international organizations, foreign aid, technical assistance

>Class foreign economic policies and relations of specific jurisdictions and groups of jurisdictions in 337.3–337.9

---

*Add 00 for standard subdivisions; see instructions at beginning of Table 1

.910 91   Areas, regions, places in general

> Do not use for assistance given by specific groups of jurisdictions in areas, regions, places in general to other jurisdictions; class in 338.911

> Class here assistance given to specific groups of jurisdictions in areas, regions, places in general

.910 93–.910 99   Specific continents, countries, localities

> Do not use for assistance given by specific jurisdictions and groups of jurisdictions to other jurisdictions; class in 338.913–338.919

> Class here assistance given to specific jurisdictions and groups of jurisdictions

.911   International assistance by specific groups of jurisdictions in areas, regions, places in general

> Add to base number 338.911 the numbers following —1 in notation 11–19 from Table 2, e.g., assistance by countries where Arabs predominate 338.91174927; then, for assistance by a specific group of jurisdictions to another group of jurisdictions or to a specific jurisdiction, add 0* and to the result add notation 1–9 from Table 2, e.g., assistance by Arab countries to Africa 338.9117492706

.913–.919   International assistance by specific jurisdictions and groups of jurisdictions in specific continents, countries, localities

> Add to base number 338.91 notation 3–9 from Table 2, e.g., assistance by United Kingdom 338.9141; then, for assistance by a specific jurisdiction or group of jurisdictions to another jurisdiction or group of jurisdictions, add 0* and again add notation 1–9 from Table 2, e.g., assistance by United Kingdom to Nigeria 338.91410669

.92   Specific policies

[.920 1–.920 8]   Standard subdivisions

> Do not use; class in 338.9001–338.9008

[.920 9]   History, geographic treatment, biography

> Do not use; class in 338.9009

[.920 93–.920 99]   Specific continents, countries, localities

> Do not use; class in 338.93–338.99

.922   †Subsidies and grants

> Standard subdivisions are added for either or both topics in heading

> Including government loans

---

*Add 00 for standard subdivisions; see instructions at beginning of Table 1
†Do not use notation 093–099 from Table 1 for specific policies in specific areas; class in 338.93–338.99

.924	†Nationalization

Class here expropriation

.925	†Privatization

Class here denationalization

.926	†Information policy

Class here science policy, technology transfer

See Manual at 338.926 vs. 352.745, 500

.927	†Appropriate technology

Class here alternative technology, environmental economics, sustainable development

Class comprehensive works on environmental economics in 333.7; class interdisciplinary works on sustainability in 304.2

.93–.99	Economic development and growth in specific continents, countries, localities

Add to base number 338.9 notation 3–9 from Table 2, e.g., economic policies of United Kingdom 338.941; then add 0* and to the result add the numbers following 338.92 in 338.922–338.927, e.g., subsidies in United Kingdom 338.94102
Subdivisions are added for either or both topics in heading

339   Macroeconomics and related topics

Standard subdivisions are added for macroeconomics and related topics together, for macroeconomics alone

For economic fluctuations, see 338.54

See Manual at 332, 336 vs. 339

SUMMARY

339.2	Distribution of income and wealth
.3	Product and income accounts
.4	Factors affecting income and wealth
.5	Macroeconomic policy

.2	Distribution of income and wealth

Standard subdivisions are added for either or both topics in heading

Class product and income accounts in 339.3; class factors affecting income and wealth in 339.4; class income redistribution in 339.52; class transfer payments in 339.522

---

*Add 00 for standard subdivisions; see instructions at beginning of Table 1
†Do not use notation 093–099 from Table 1 for specific policies in specific areas; class in 338.93–338.99

.21   Distribution of income and wealth among factors of production

      Factors of production: land, labor, capital, entrepreneurship, corporate profits

      Standard subdivisions are added for either or both topics in heading

.22   Distribution of aggregate personal income and wealth

      Standard subdivisions are added for either or both topics in heading

      Class here consumer income, household income

      Class income in relation to consumption, household budget, in 339.41; class poverty in 339.46

.23   Input-output analysis (Interindustry analysis)

      Including data on specific industries

.26   Flow-of-funds accounts

.3   **Product and income accounts**

      For distribution of income and wealth, see 339.2; for factors affecting income and wealth, see 339.4

[.309 3–.309 9] Specific continents, countries, localities

      Do not use for specific countries and localities; class in 339.33–339.39

.31   Product accounts

      Class here gross domestic product (GDP), gross national product (GNP)

      For net national product (NNP), see 339.32

[.310 93–.310 99] Specific continents, countries, localities

      Do not use for specific countries and localities; class in 339.33–339.39

.32   Income accounts

      Class here net national product (NNP), national income (NI), personal income (PI), disposable personal income (DPI)

      For distribution of aggregate personal income, see 339.22

[.320 93–.320 99] Specific continents, countries, localities

      Do not use for specific countries and localities; class in 339.33–339.39

.33–.39   Product and income accounts of specific continents, countries, localities

      Class here product accounts of specific continents, income accounts of specific continents

      Add to base number 339.3 notation 3–9 from Table 2, e.g., gross national product of United States 339.373
        Subdivisions are added for product accounts, income accounts, or both

.4   **Factors affecting income and wealth**

Standard subdivisions are added for either or both topics in heading

For economic stabilization, see 339.5

.41   Income in relation to consumption

Including acceleration principle, consumer responses to decreases and increases in income, household budgets as a measure of relation of income to consumption

Class purchasing power, effect of prices on consumption in 339.42; class multiplier, relation of consumption and savings, in 339.43

See also 658.834 for consumer research in marketing management

.42   Cost of living

Including effect of rising costs of specific commodities on consumers

Class here purchasing power, effect of prices on consumers

Class price statistics and indexes in 338.528

For purchasing power of money, see 332.41

.43   Savings and investment

Standard subdivisions are added for either or both topics in heading

Including multiplier, relation of consumption and savings

Class here capital formation

Class interdisciplinary works on capital formation and saving in 332.0415

.46   Poverty

Class here economic causes of poverty

Class comprehensive works on poverty in 362.5

.47   Consumption (Spending)

Class here standard of living, interdisciplinary works on consumption

Class consumption in relation to income in 339.41; class consumption in relation to cost of living in 339.42; class consumption in relation to savings and investment in 339.43; class consumption in relation to poverty in 339.46; class government spending in 339.522; class consumption as a measure of marketing opportunities or volume and value of trade in 381

For sociology of consumption, see 306.3; for consumption as utilization of natural resources and energy, see 333.713; for consumption of specific products and services, of specific groups of products and services, see 339.48

See also 658.834 for consumer research in marketing management

.48   Consumption of specific products and services, of specific groups of products and services

[.480 001–.480 009]   Standard subdivisions

                Do not use; class in 339.4701–339.4709

.480 01–.489 99   Subdivisions for consumption of specific products and services, of specific groups of products and services

                Add to base number 339.48 notation 001–999, e.g., consumption of agricultural products 339.4863; however, for consumption in the sense of utilization of specific natural resources, see 333.7–333.9

.49   Conservation of economic resources

                Economic resources: the sum total of economic resources of a nation or other area, e.g., natural resources, human resources, resources that result from human activities

                For conservation of natural resources, see 333.72

[.490 91]   Areas, regions, places in general

                Do not use; class in 339.491

[.490 93–.490 99]   Specific continents, countries, localities

                Do not use; class in 339.493–339.499

.491   Conservation of economic resources in areas, regions, places in general

                Add to base number 339.491 the numbers following —1 in notation 11–19 from Table 2, e.g., conservation of economic resources of developing countries 339.491724

.493–.499   Conservation of economic resources in specific continents, countries, localities

                Add to base number 339.49 notation 3–9 from Table 2, e.g., conservation of economic resources of India 339.4954

.5   **Macroeconomic policy**

                Class here incomes policy (wage-price policy), economic stabilization and growth, equilibrium, full employment policy

                Class wage-price policies of specific jurisdictions in 331.29

                For wage policy, see 331.21; for measures to combat inflation, see 332.415; for price policy, see 338.52; for measures to control economic fluctuations, see 338.543; for measures to promote growth and development, see 338.9

.52   Use of fiscal policy

                Class here income redistribution

.522   Government spending

                Including transfer payments

.523   Budget surpluses and deficits

.525   Taxes

.53   Use of monetary policy

> Including discount rates, reserve requirements, open-market operations, regulation of bank credit

> Class comprehensive works on relation of central banks to monetary policy in 332.112; class comprehensive works on monetary policy in 332.46

340   Law

Class here jurisprudence

Instructions for building classification numbers for works on law of a jurisdiction or area are found at 342–349

> *See Manual at 340 vs. 808.06634; also at 340, 342–347 vs. 340.56; also at 340, 342–347 vs. 340.57; also at 342–349*

SUMMARY

340.02–.09	**Standard subdivisions**
.1	**Philosophy and theory of law**
.2	**Comparative law**
.3	**Law reform**
.5	**Legal systems**
.9	**Conflict of laws**
341	**Law of nations**
.01–.09	**Standard subdivisions; treaties, codes, cases; relation of law of nations and domestic law**
.1	**Sources of law of nations**
.2	**The world community**
.3	**Relations between states**
.4	**Jurisdiction over physical space; human rights**
.5	**Disputes and conflicts between states**
.6	**Law of war**
.7	**International cooperation**
342	**Constitutional and administrative law**
.001–.009	**Standard subdivisions; laws, regulations, cases, procedure, courts**
.02	**Basic instruments of government**
.03	**Revision and amendment of basic instruments of government**
.04	**Structure, powers, functions of government**
.05	**Legislative branch of government**
.06	**Executive branch of government**
.07	**Election law**
.08	**Jurisdiction over persons**
.09	**Local government**
.1	**Socioeconomic regions**
.2	**Regional intergovernmental organizations**
.3–.9	**Specific jurisdictions and areas**

343	Military, defense, public property, public finance, tax, commerce (trade), industrial law
.001–.009	Standard subdivisions; laws, regulations, cases, procedure, courts
.01	Military and defense law, veterans' law
.02	Law of public property
.03	Law of public finance
.04	Tax law
.05	Kinds of taxes by base
.06	Kinds of taxes by incidence
.07	Regulation of economic activity
.08	Regulation of commerce (trade)
.09	Control of public utilities
.1	Socioeconomic regions
.2	Regional intergovernmental organizations
.3–.9	Specific jurisdictions and areas

344	Labor, social service, education, cultural law
.001–.009	Standard subdivisions; laws, regulations, cases, procedure, courts
.01	Labor
.02	Government-sponsored insurance
.03	Social service
.04	Miscellaneous social problems and services
.05	Police services, other aspects of public safety, matters concerning public morals and customs
.06	Public works
.07	Education
.08	Educational and cultural exchanges
.09	Culture and religion
.1	Socioeconomic regions
.2	Regional intergovernmental organizations
.3–.9	Specific jurisdictions and areas

345	Criminal law
.001–.009	Standard subdivisions; laws, regulations, cases, procedure, courts
.01	Criminal courts
.02	Criminal offenses
.03	Offenders
.04	Liability, responsibility, guilt
.05	Criminal procedure
.06	Evidence
.07	Trials
.08	Juvenile procedure and courts
.1	Socioeconomic regions
.2	Regional intergovernmental organizations
.3–.9	Specific jurisdictions and areas

346	**Private law**	
.001–.009	Standard subdivisions; laws, regulations, cases, procedure, courts; equity	
.01	Persons and domestic relations	
.02	Juristic acts, contracts, agency	
.03	Torts (Delicts)	
.04	Property	
.05	Inheritance, succession, fiduciary trusts, trustees	
.06	Organizations (Associations)	
.07	Commercial law	
.08	Banks and insurance	
.09	Investment and negotiable instruments	
.1	Socioeconomic regions	
.2	Regional intergovernmental organizations	
.3–.9	Specific jurisdictions and areas	
347	**Procedure and courts**	
.001–.009	Standard subdivisions; laws, regulations, cases, procedure, courts	
.01	Courts	
.02	Courts with general original jurisdiction	
.03	Appellate courts	
.04	Courts with specialized jurisdiction	
.05	Procedure	
.06	Evidence	
.07	Trials	
.08	Appellate procedure	
.09	Dispute resolution	
.1	Socioeconomic regions	
.2	Regional intergovernmental organizations	
.3–.9	Specific jurisdictions and areas	
348	**Laws, regulations, cases**	
.001–.009	Standard subdivisions and codification	
.01	Preliminary materials	
.02	Laws and regulations	
.04	Cases	
.05	Advisory opinions of attorneys-general (ministers of justice)	
.1	Socioeconomic regions	
.2	Regional intergovernmental organizations	
.3–.9	Specific jurisdictions and areas	
349	**Law of specific jurisdictions, areas, socioeconomic regions, regional intergovernmental organizations**	
.1	Law of specific socioeconomic regions	
.2	Law of regional intergovernmental organizations	
.4–.9	Law of specific jurisdictions and areas of modern world	

[.01]   Philosophy and theory

> Do not use; class in 340.1

> 340.02–340.09 Standard subdivisions

Class comprehensive works in 340

See Manual at 340.02–340.09 vs. 349

.02   Miscellany

.023	Law as a profession, occupation, hobby

Class here legal personnel, nature of duties, characteristics of profession

Class professional ethics of legal personnel in 174.3. Class works that emphasize procedures of work performed by legal personnel with the subject without adding notation 023 from Table 1, e.g., works that emphasize procedures of conducting a lawsuit 347.0504

.03–.07	Standard subdivisions
.08	Groups of people
.089	Ethnic and national groups

Do not use for nondominant legal systems associated with specific ethnic groups; class in 340.52

.09	History, geographic treatment, biography of law

Do not use for comprehensive works on law of specific jurisdictions and areas in modern world; class in 349

[.091 7]	Socioeconomic regions

Do not use; class in 349.1

.092	Biography

Do not use for theorists; class in 340.1092

[.093]	Ancient world

Do not use; class in 340.53

.1	**Philosophy and theory of law**

Class here methodology, schools of thought

For theory of specific legal systems, see 340.5

.11	Special topics of philosophy and theory of law

Including origin, sources, nature, limits of law; rule of law; legal reasoning; equal protection of the law

Class interdisciplinary works on equal protection of the law in 323.42

.112	Law and ethics

Class here civil rights, law and morality, legal positivism, natural law

Class social justice in 340.115

.114	Justice

For distributive justice, social justice, see 340.115

.115	Law and society

Including distributive justice, social justice

Class here sociological jurisprudence

.12–.19 Specific aspects of philosophy and theory

> Add to base number 340.1 the numbers following —01 in notation 012–019 from Table 1, e.g., classification of law 340.12

.2 **Comparative law**

> Limited to methodological works

> Class comparison of specific branches of law in 342–347

> (If option A under 342–349 is chosen, class comparative law in 349

> (If option B under 342–349 is chosen, class comparative law in 342)

.3 **Law reform**

.5 **Legal systems**

> History and theory

> Class here customary law

> Class customary law as a source for another system of law with the other system, e.g., customary law as a source for civil law systems 340.56, 'ādāt law as a source for Islamic law 340.59135; class conflict of laws on a specific subject in specific systems of law with the subject in 340.9, e.g., conflict of divorce laws in ancient Roman law 340.91660937, conflict of divorce laws in civil law 340.9166; class a specific subject in specific systems of law with the subject in 341–347, e.g., juristic persons in Islamic law 346.167013, in ancient Roman law 346.37013, in Byzantine law 346.495013, in civil law 346.013; class religious and ceremonial laws of a specific religious body with the body, e.g., Christian canon law 262.9

.508 9 Ethnic and national groups

> Do not use for nondominant legal systems associated with specific ethnic groups; class in 340.52

.52 Nondominant legal systems associated with specific ethnic groups

> Limited to legal systems that are currently nondominant, even though they may have been dominant in the past

> Class here ethnological jurisprudence; customary law associated with specific ethnic groups; law of indigenous peoples; law of minority ethnic groups

> Class nondominant legal systems associated with specific ethnic groups in medieval Europe as a whole in 340.55. Class law that is nondominant only because it is law of a subordinate level of government, e.g., provincial law in a country with a federal government, in 342–349; class a nondominant legal system that is primarily religious with the religious law, e.g., Jewish law 340.58

> *See Manual at 340.52*

[.520 93] Ancient world

> Do not use; class in 340.53

[.520 94–.520 99]   Specific continents, countries, localities in modern world

Do not use; class in 340.524–340.529

.524–.529   Specific continents, countries, localities in modern world

Add to base number 340.52 notation 4–9 from Table 2, e.g., customary law of indigenous peoples of Africa 340.526; however, for nondominant legal systems associated with specific ethnic groups in medieval Europe as a whole, see 340.55; for nondominant legal systems associated with specific ethnic groups in a specific jurisdiction of medieval Europe, see 349.41–349.49

.53   Ancient law

Add to base number 340.53 the numbers following —3 in notation 31–39 from Table 2, e.g., law of ancient Greece 340.538; however, for Roman law, see 340.54

Class ancient Oriental law in 340.5

(If option B under 342–349 is chosen, class here branches of the law in jurisdictions of the ancient world by adding to the number for the jurisdiction facet indicator 0*, notation for the branch of law, and notation for the subordinate subject in branch of law, e.g., criminal law of ancient Greece 340.53805, law of criminal trials of ancient Greece 340.538057)

.54   Roman law

Including Byzantine law

Class comprehensive works on Roman-derived law in specific jurisdictions and areas in modern world in 349

For medieval Roman law, see 340.55

(If option B under 342–349 is chosen, class here branches of the law in Roman Empire by adding to base number 340.54 facet indicator 0*, notation for the branch of law, and notation for the subordinate subject in branch of law, e.g., criminal law of Roman Empire 340.5405, law of criminal trials of Roman Empire 340.54057)

>   340.55–340.59 Medieval, modern, religious systems of law

Class comprehensive works in 340.5; class nondominant legal systems associated with specific ethnic groups in 340.52; class comprehensive works on law of specific jurisdictions and areas in modern world in 349

---

*Add 00 for standard subdivisions; see instructions at beginning of Table 1

.55 Medieval European law

> Limited to comprehensive works on Europe as a whole, but without regard to whether the legal systems are dominant or nondominant

> Including feudal law, medieval Roman law

> Class medieval civil law in 340.56; class medieval common law in 340.57

> *For comprehensive works on medieval European law operative in a specific jurisdiction, see the jurisdiction in 349.41–349.49, plus notation from Table 1 for the historical period, e.g., comprehensive works on law operative in medieval England 349.420902, comprehensive works on law operative in England during the Anglo-Saxon period 349.4209021*

[.550 94] Europe

> Do not use; class in 340.55

[.550 941–.550 949] Specific countries, localities in medieval Europe

> Do not use; class in 349.41–349.49

.56 Civil law systems

> Systems of law derived from Roman law

> Including Roman-Dutch law

> *See Manual at 340, 342–347 vs. 340.56*

.57 Common law systems

> *See Manual at 340, 342–347 vs. 340.57*

.58 Jewish law

> *For religious and ceremonial law of Judaism, see 296.18*

.59 Islamic law

> Class here fiqh, sharia, comprehensive works on furū' al-fiqh and uṣūl al-fiqh

> Class conflict of laws, private international law from the viewpoint of Islamic law in 340.9091767; class law of nations, public international law from the viewpoint of Islamic law in 341.091767. Class conflict of laws from the viewpoint of Islamic law with respect to a branch other than private law with the branch, e.g., conflict of laws from the viewpoint of Islamic law with respect to criminal law 345.167

> *For religious and ceremonial law of Islam, fiqh and sharia in relation to religious and ceremonial laws and decisions, see 297.14. For a specific branch or topic of Islamic law, see the branch or topic, e.g., private law 346.167, marriage law 346.167016*

.590 1 Philosophy and theory

> Notation 01 from Table 1 as modified below

> Do not use for schools of law; class in 340.59018. Do not use for methodology; class in 340.591

.590 18   Schools of Islamic law

> Add to base number 340.59018 the numbers following 297.14018 in notation 297.140181–297.140184, e.g., Islamic law according to Ḥanafī school 340.5901811

.590 9   History, geographic treatment, biography

> Do not use for comprehensive collections of Islamic laws, regulations, cases, fatwas, and their guides operative in a specific jurisdiction; class in 348, plus notation from Table 2 for the jurisdiction, e.g., comprehensive collections of laws, cases, fatwas operative in Indonesia 348.598, comprehensive collections of fatwas operative in Indonesia 348.59806. Do not use for comprehensive treatises on Islamic law operative in a specific jurisdiction; class in 349, plus notation from Table 2 for the jurisdiction, e.g., comprehensive treatise on Islamic law operative in Saudi Arabia 349.538

.591   †Uṣūl al-fiqh (Fundamentals of Islamic law)

> Including works on derivation of furūʿ al-fiqh (branches of Islamic law) from uṣūl al-fiqh

> Class comprehensive works on furūʿ al-fiqh and uṣūl al-fiqh in 340.59

.591 1   †Maqāṣid al-sharīʿah (Object and objective of law)

.591 2   †Ḥukm (Legal qualification)

> Including works on legal qualification for facts and acts such as wājib (obligation), ibāḥah (permission), fasād and buṭlān (validity and invalidity), ʿillah (cause), sabab (occasions)

.591 3   †Sources of fiqh

> Including istiṣḥāb (presumption of continuity)

.591 31   †Koran

.591 32   †Hadith (Traditions)

.591 33   †Ijmāʿ (Consensus)

.591 34   †Qiyās (analogical deduction) and istiḥsān (scholarly discretion in breach of strict analogy)

> Standard subdivisions are added for qiyās and istiḥsān together, for qiyās alone

.591 35   †ʿUrf, ʿādāt (Custom)

> Standard subdivisions are added for either or both topics in heading

.591 36   †Istiṣlāḥ, maṣāliḥ al-mursalah (Public interest)

> Standard subdivisions are added for either or both topics in heading

---

†Use notation 01 from Table 1 as modified at 340.5901

.591 38   †Ijtihād (sound judgment), ijtihād al-ra'y (individual reasoning), taqlīd (legal conformism; relying upon opinion of another)

Ijtihād and ijtihād al-ra'y: rational deduction and derivation of law from scriptural sources for lack of a definitive revelation

Standard subdivisions are added for ijtihād, ijtihād al-ra'y, taqlīd together, for ijtihād and ijtihād al-ra'y together; for ijtihād alone

.592   †Islamic substantive law

Limited to comprehensive collections of and treatises on law not associated with a specific jurisdiction

Class here comprehensive laws, regulations, cases of regions where Islam predominates; comprehensive treatises on furū' al-fiqh (branches of Islamic law)

Class comprehensive works on furū' al-fiqh and uṣūl al-fiqh in 340.59. Class comprehensive collections of Islamic laws, regulations, cases, fatwas, and their guides operative in a specific jurisdiction with the jurisdiction in 348, e.g., comprehensive collections of Islamic laws, cases, fatwas operative in Iran 348.55; class comprehensive treatises on Islamic law operative in a specific jurisdiction with the jurisdiction in 349, e.g., comprehensive treatises on Islamic law operative in Pakistan 349.5491

For a specific branch or topic of Islamic substantive law, see the branch or topic, e.g., private law 346.167, marriage law 346.167016

.592 2   †Fatwas (Legal opinions)

Not limited to a specific branch or topic, not associated with a specific jurisdiction

.592 22   †The fatwa

Limited to general discussions of the fatwa not associated with a specific jurisdiction

.592 24   †Collected fatwas

Limited to general collections of fatwas not associated with a specific jurisdiction

Class fatwas on a specific topic with the topic, e.g., fatwas on marriage 346.167016; class fatwas limited to a specific jurisdiction with the jurisdiction in 348.3–348.9, plus notation 06 from add table under 348.3–348.9, e.g., fatwas from Indonesia 348.59806

.592 5   †General concepts

Including ignorance of the law, necessity, nīyah (intention)

†Use notation 01 from Table 1 as modified at 340.5901

.9 **Conflict of laws**

Body of rules governing choice of jurisdiction in cases in private law that fall under laws of two or more such jurisdictions

Class here private international law

Add to base number 340.9 the numbers following 346.0 in 346.01–346.09, e.g., conflict of divorce laws 340.9166

> *For comparative law, see 340.2; for domestic conflict of laws, see 342.042. For a specific aspect of conflict of laws and of private international law not provided for here, see the aspect in 342–345, e.g., citizenship 342.083, air transportation 343.097*
>
> *See also 341 for international law*
>
> *See Manual at 340.9*

341 Law of nations

Class here international law, public international law

Class comprehensive works on public law in 342

> *See also 340.9 for private international law*
>
> *See Manual at 341 vs. 327*

(Option: Class law of nations of a specific subject with the subject, plus notation 026 from Table 1, e.g., international disarmament law 327.174026, not 341.733)

SUMMARY

341.01–.09	**Standard subdivisions; treaties, codes, cases; relation of law of nations and domestic law**
.1	**Sources of law of nations**
.2	**The world community**
.3	**Relations between states**
.4	**Jurisdiction over physical space; human rights**
.5	**Disputes and conflicts between states**
.6	**Law of war**
.7	**International cooperation**

.02 Miscellany; treaties, codes, cases

Notation 02 from Table 1 as modified below

.026 Treaties, codes, cases

Texts of treaties, codes, cases; guides, e.g., checklists, citators, digests, indexes

Class here conventions, protocols

Class treaties as a source of law of nations in 341.1; class comprehensive works on treaties in 341.37. Class treaties on a specific subject in law of nations with the subject in 341.2–341.7, plus notation 026 from table under 341.2–341.7, e.g., collections of disarmament treaties 341.733026; class text of treaties on a specific subject in domestic law with the subject in 342–347, plus notation 0261 from table under 342–347, e.g., text of commercial treaties 346.070261

>   341.026 1–341.026 6 Texts of treaties

          Class comprehensive works in 341.026

>   341.026 1–341.026 3 Series of treaties compiled by intergovernmental organizations

          Class specific kinds of treaties regardless of the organization compiling them in 341.0265–341.0266; class comprehensive works in 341.026

.026 1   League of Nations series of treaties

            Class a League of Nations series relating to a specific area in 341.0264

.026 2   United Nations series of treaties

            Class a United Nations series relating to a specific area in 341.0264

.026 3   Series of treaties compiled by regional organizations

            Add to base number 341.0263 the numbers following 341.24 in 341.242–341.249, e.g., a series compiled by Organization of American States 341.02635

.026 4   Collections of treaties by area

            Add to base number 341.0264 notation 1–9 from Table 2, e.g., treaties on Philippines 341.0264599

            Class collections of treaties relating to a specific area compiled by regional organizations in 341.0263; class collections of specific kinds of treaties by area in 341.0265–341.0266

>   341.026 5–341.026 6 Kinds of treaties

          Collections and individual treaties

          Class comprehensive works in 341.026

.026 5   Multilateral treaties

            Class an agreement between an intergovernmental organization and a specific country in 341.026

.026 6   Bilateral treaties

            Add to base number 341.0266 notation 3–9 from Table 2, e.g., treaties of the United Kingdom 341.026641; then add 0* and again add notation 3–9 from Table 2, e.g., treaties between United Kingdom and France 341.026641044

            Give priority in notation to the country coming first in Table 2 (Option: Give priority in notation to the country requiring local emphasis, e.g., libraries in United States class treaties between United Kingdom and the United States in 341.026673041)

---

*Add 00 for standard subdivisions; see instructions at beginning of Table 1

.026 7	Codes

Class codes of a specific subject in law of nations with the subject in 341.2–341.7, plus notation 0267 from table under 341.2–341.7, e.g., disarmament codes 341.7330267; class codes of a specific subject in domestic law with the subject in 342–347, plus notation 02632 from table under 342–347, e.g., commercial codes 346.0702632

.026 8	Cases

Decisions and reports

Class here general collections of cases on international matters tried in any court system

Add to base number 341.0268 notation 3–9 from Table 2, e.g., cases brought by United Kingdom 341.026841; then, for cases brought by that nation against another nation, add 0* and again add notation 3–9 from Table 2, e.g., cases brought by United Kingdom against United States 341.026841073
> (Option: Give priority in notation to the nation requiring local emphasis, e.g., libraries in United States class all cases involving United States and United Kingdom in 341.026873041)

Class cases about a specific subject in law of nations with the subject in 341.2–341.7, plus notation 0268 from table under 341.2–341.7, e.g., disarmament cases 341.7330268; class cases about a specific subject in domestic law with the subject in 342–347, plus notation 0264 from table under 342–347, e.g., commercial cases 346.070264

.04	Relation of law of nations and domestic law

Class here works on whether domestic law or law of nations prevails in a certain situation

Class the law of a nation or lesser jurisdiction that carries out the provisions of an international agreement in 342–347

.09	History, geographic treatment, biography

Notation 09 from Table 1 as modified below

.091 767	Regions where Islam predominates

Class here law of nations from the viewpoint of Islamic law

(.091 767 1–.091 767 3)	Schools of Islamic law

(Optional numbers; prefer 341.091767)

Add to base number 341.091767 the numbers following 297.14018 in notation 297.140181–297.140183, e.g., law of nations as viewed by Ḥanafī school 341.09176711

(.091 767 4)	Mixed schools of Islamic law and comparative treatment

Class here works comparing authors affiliated with different schools (e.g., Sunni and Shīʿī schools)

(Optional number; prefer 341.091767)

---

*Add 00 for standard subdivisions; see instructions at beginning of Table 1

[.091 767 8]   Regions where specific Islamic sects and reform movements predominate

> Do not use; class in 341.091767

.092   Biography

> Do not use for critical works on individual publicists; class in 341.1

.1   Sources of law of nations

Treaties, judicial decisions, custom, general principles of law, works of publicists (theorists)

Class here critical works on individual publicists (theorists)

Class texts of treaties and reports of judicial decisions in 341.026; class comprehensive works on treaties in 341.37. Class writings of publicists on a specific subject with the subject in 341–347, e.g., international rivers 341.442, international commerce 343.087

>   **341.2–341.7 Specific topics**

Add to each subdivision identified by † as follows:

01   Philosophy and theory
           Notation 01 from Table 1 as modified below
011   Special topics of philosophy and theory of law
           Including origin, sources, nature, limits of law; rule of law; legal reasoning; equal protection of the law; law and ethics; justice; law and society
02   Miscellany
           Notation 02 from Table 1 as modified below
023   Law as a profession, occupation, hobby
           Class here legal personnel, nature of duties, characteristics of profession
           Class professional ethics of legal personnel in 174.3; class comprehensive works on legal personnel in 340.023. Class works that emphasize procedures of work performed by legal personnel with the subject without adding notation 023 from Table 1, e.g., works that emphasize procedures of adjudicating matters of public international law 341.55
026   Treaties, codes, cases
           Texts of treaties, codes, cases; guides, e.g., checklists, citators, digests, indexes
           Do not use for discussions, commentaries, or popular works; class with the subject in 341.2–341.7 without adding from this table
           Class here conventions, protocols
           Class texts of treaties on a specific subject in domestic law with the subject in 342–347, plus notation 0261 from add table under 342–347, e.g., text of commercial treaties 346.070261
0261–0266   Text of treaties
           Add to 026 the numbers following 341.026 in 341.0261–341.0266, e.g., multilateral treaties 0265
0267   Codes
           Class codes of a specific subject in domestic law with the subject in 342–347, plus notation 02632 from table under 342–347, e.g., commercial codes 346.0702632
0268   Cases
           Decisions and reports
           Class here general collections of cases on international matters tried in any court system
           Add to 0268 notation 3–9 from Table 2, e.g., cases brought by United Kingdom 026841; then, for cases brought by that nation against another nation, add 0* and again add notation 3–9 from Table 2, e.g., cases brought by United Kingdom against United States 026841073
              (Option: Give priority in notation to the nation requiring local emphasis, e.g., libraries in United States class all cases involving United States and United Kingdom in 026873041)
           Class cases about a specific subject in domestic law with the subject in 342–347, plus notation 0264 from table under 342–347, e.g., commercial cases 346.070264

---

*Add 00 for standard subdivisions; see instructions at beginning of Table 1

> **341.2–341.7 Specific topics**

03–08	Standard subdivisions	
09	History, geographic treatment, biography	
	Notation 09 from Table 1 as modified below	
	See Manual at 342–349	
091767		Regions where Islam predominates

                  Class here law of nations from the viewpoint of Islamic law

(0917671–0917673)   Schools of Islamic law

                  (Optional numbers; prefer 091767)
                  Add to 091767 the numbers following 297.14018 in notation 297.140181–297.140183, e.g., law of nations as viewed by Ḥanafī school 09176711

(0917674)   Mixed schools of Islamic law and comparative treatment

                  Class here works comparing authors affiliated with different schools (e.g., Sunni and Shīʿī schools)
                  (Optional number; prefer 091767)

[0917678]   Regions where specific Islamic sects and reform movements predominate

                  Do not use; class in 091767

Class comprehensive works in 341

.2   The world community

Class here international legal personality

.21   World government

Proposals and schemes

> 341.22–341.24 Intergovernmental organizations

Class here legal responsibilities of officials; privileges and immunities; interdisciplinary works on intergovernmental organizations

Class comprehensive works on intergovernmental organizations in 341.2; class interdisciplinary works on international organizations in 060. Class comprehensive works on the laws of a specific intergovernmental organization with the organization in 349, e.g., laws of European Union 349.24

For administration of intergovernmental organizations, see 352.11. For a specialized intergovernmental organization, see the subject with which it deals, plus notation 0601 from Table 1, e.g., Interpol 363.20601; for legal aspects of a specialized intergovernmental organization, see the subject with which it deals in 341–347, e.g., Interpol 345.052; for treaties, codes, cases on a specific subject in domestic law of a non-specialized intergovernmental organization, see the specific subject in 342–347, e.g., economic law of European Union 343.2407; for a nonlegal aspect of an intergovernmental organization, see the aspect, e.g., economic aspects of European Union 337.142

*Add 00 for standard subdivisions; see instructions at beginning of Table 1

.22	**League of Nations**
[.220 68]	Management
	Do not use; class in 352.112
.221–.229	**Functions, activities, organization, general relations with specific nations**
	Add to base number 341.22 the numbers following 341.23 in 341.231–341.239, e.g., Covenant of the League 341.222
.23	**United Nations**
.230 1	Philosophy and theory
	Notation 01 from Table 1 as modified below
	Do not use for value; class in 341.23013
.230 13	Value
	Evaluation of and opinions about the effectiveness and worth of the United Nations
[.230 68]	Management
	Do not use; class in 352.113
.231	†Functions and activities
	Class functions and activities of specific branches of the United Nations in 341.232. Class a specific function or activity with the function or activity in 341–347, e.g., role in the peaceful settlement of disputes 341.523, role of UNICEF in child welfare 344.0327
.232	†Organization
	Including charter
	Class here rules of procedure
	For legal responsibility of officials, see 341.233; for Secretariat, see 352.113
.232 2	†General Assembly
.232 3	†Security Council
.232 5	†Economic and Social Council
.233	†Admission and membership
	For organization, see 341.232

†Add as instructed under 341.2–341.7

.234–.239   General relations with specific nations

> Add to base number 341.23 notation 4–9 from Table 2, e.g., relations with United States 341.2373

> Class relations dealing with a specific subject with the subject in 341–347, e.g., United Nations peacekeeping operations in Serbia 341.584094971, United Nations human rights activities in the United States 342.73085

.24   Regional organizations

> *For comprehensive works on the laws of regional intergovernemental organizations, see 349.2*

.242   European regional organizations

.242 1   †Council of Europe

> Class laws promulgated by Council of Europe with the subject in 341–347, e.g., protection of rights of individuals 342.24085

.242 2   †European Union

> Class here European Common Market, European Community, European Economic Community

> Class political integration of European Union member states in 320.94; class economic integration of European Union member states in 337.142. Class laws promulgated by European Union with the subject in 341–347, e.g., copyright laws 346.240482

.242 202 65   Multilateral treaties

> Number built according to instructions under 341.2–341.7

> Class here texts of founding treaties, e.g., Treaty Establishing the European Community, Maastricht Treaty on European Union; texts of treaties amending founding treaties, e.g., Treaty of Nice; Treaty Establishing a Constitution for Europe (2004)

> Class texts of accession treaties in 341.242230265

[.242 206 8]   Management

> Do not use; class in 352.114

.242 209   History, geographic treatment, biography

> Notation 09 from Table 1 as modified below

.242 209 4–.242 209 9   Specific continents, countries, localities; extraterrestrial worlds

> Class here general relations with specific nations

> Class relations dealing with a specific subject with the subject in 341–347, e.g., admission to European Union 341.24223, relations concerning antitrust law and competition law 343.240721, effect of European Union law on national law of Germany 349.43

†Add as instructed under 341.2–341.7

.242 22	†Organization

        Class here rules of procedure

        Class legislative process in European Union in 328.4

        For legal responsibility of officials, see 341.24223

.242 222	†Council of the European Union
.242 224	†European Parliament
.242 226	†European Commission
.242 228	†Courts of the European Union

        For European Court of Human Rights, see 342.240850269

.242 228 2	†Court of First Instance of the European Communities
.242 228 4	†Court of Justice of the European Communities
.242 23	†Admission and membership

        Subdivisions are added for either or both topics in heading

        For organization, see 341.24222

.242 230 265	Multilateral treaties

        Number built according to instructions under 341.2–341.7

        Class here texts of accession treaties

.242 24	†Relationship between European Union law and national law of European Union countries

        Class here effect of European Union law on national law of European Union countries, harmonization of national law of European Union countries

        For relationship of European Union law on a specific branch or subject of law with national law of a specific member state, see the branch or subject of national law in 342–347, e.g., Italian labor law regulated by European Union law 344.4501; for comprehensive works on relationship of European Union law on a specific branch or subject and national law of member countries, see the branch or subject in 342–347 plus the notation for European regional intergovernmental organizations, e.g., effect of European Union law on labor law of member states 344.2401; for comprehensive works on relationship of European Union law and national law of a specific member state, see the national law in 349, e.g., effect of European Union law on national law of Italy 349.45

.242 7	†Council for Mutual Economic Assistance
.243	Atlantic regional organizations

†Add as instructed under 341.2–341.7

.245　　　　Western Hemisphere regional organizations

　　　　　　　Including Organization of American States

.246　　　　Pacific regional organizations

.247　　　　Asian regional organizations

.247 3　　　　Far East regional organizations

　　　　　　　Including ASEAN (Association of East Asian Nations)

.247 7　　　　Western Asia regional organizations

　　　　　　　Including League of Arab States

　　　　　　　Class here Middle East organizations

.249　　　　African regional organizations

　　　　　　　For League of Arab States, see 341.2477

.26　　　†States

　　　　　　Including recognition of states and governments; mergers, self-determination, liability, sovereignty, succession of states; liability of states to aliens

　　　　　　Class liability of states with respect to a specific subject in law of nations with the subject in 341.2–341.7, e.g., liability for damages caused by testing nuclear weapons 341.734; class liability of states with respect to a specific subject in other branches of law with the subject in 342–347, e.g., liability for breach of contract 346.022

　　　　　　　For semisovereign states, see 341.27; for relations between states, see 341.3; for jurisdiction over physical space, see 341.4

.27　　　†Semisovereign states

　　　　　　Including mandates, protectorates, trusteeships

.28　　　†Non-self-governing territories

　　　　　　Class here colonies

.29　　　†Areas having special status in international law

　　　　　　Including partitioned areas, e.g., Antarctica, Cyprus

.3　　†Relations between states

　　　　　　For jurisdictional relations, see 341.4; for disputes and conflicts, see 341.5; for international cooperation, see 341.7

†Add as instructed under 341.2–341.7

.302 6	Treaties, codes, cases

Number built according to instructions under 341.2–341.7

Class here texts of treaties limited to general relations between states

Class works about treaties in 341.37. Class text of treaties on a specific subject in law of nations with the subject in 341.2–341.7, plus notation 026 from table under 341.2–341.7, e.g., text of disarmament treaties 341.733026, text of a disarmament treaty between Russia and the United States 341.733026647073; class text of treaties on a specific subject in domestic law with the subject in 342–347, plus notation 0261 from table under 342–347, e.g., text of copyright treaties 346.04820261

.33	†Diplomatic law

Including legal aspects of functions, immunities, privileges, status of diplomatic personnel and agencies; delegations to international organizations and their staffs

Class officials and employees of intergovernmental organizations in 341.22–341.24; class interdisciplinary works on diplomacy in 327.2

For consular law, see 341.35

.35	†Consular law
.37	Treaties

Including negotiation and ratification, validity and binding force, termination, interpretation

Class treaties on a specific subject in law of nations with the subject in 341.2–341.7, e.g., disarmament treaties 341.733; class treaties on a specific subject in domestic law with the subject in 342–347, e.g., copyright treaties 346.0482

For general collections of texts of treaties, see 341.026; for treaties as sources of law of nations, see 341.1

.4	**†Jurisdiction over physical space; human rights**

Class here conservation and development of extraterritorial natural resources; extraterritoriality; jurisdiction over physical space; servitudes and easements; right of innocent passage

Subdivisions are added for jurisdiction over physical space and human rights together, for jurisdiction over physical space alone

See also 346.044 for conservation and development of territorial natural resources

---

>	341.42–341.47 Jurisdiction over physical space

Class comprehensive works in 341.4

---

†Add as instructed under 341.2–341.7

.42	†Territory

Including acquisition, boundaries, border disputes

Class mergers of states in 341.26; class boundary rivers in 341.442

.44	†Bodies of water

For high seas, see 341.45

.442	†Rivers

National, semi-national, boundary, internationalized rivers

Including combined river, lake, canal systems, e.g., Saint Lawrence Seaway

Class canalized rivers in 341.446

.444	†Lakes and inland seas

Subdivisions are added for either or both topics in heading

Class combined river, lake, canal systems in 341.442

.446	†Canals and straits

Class combined river, lake, canal systems in 341.442

.448	†Territorial waters

Including bays, continental shelves

Class access to the sea, comprehensive works on ocean and sea waters in 341.45

.45	†High seas

Class here comprehensive works on international law of ocean and sea waters

Class ocean transportation in 343.0962; class oceanographic research in 344.0955

For territorial waters, see 341.448

See Manual at 341.45 vs. 343.0962

.455	†Seabed (Ocean bottom)
.46	†Airspace

Class air transportation in 343.097; class meteorological research in 344.0955

.47	†Extraterrestrial space

Including the moon, planets

Class space transportation in 343.0979; class space research in 344.0952

†Add as instructed under 341.2–341.7

.48   Human rights

Class jurisdiction over persons in 342.08; class civil rights in 342.085; class personal property in 346.047; class interdisciplinary works on human rights in 323

See Manual at 342.085 vs. 341.48

.480 2   Miscellany

Notation 02 from Table 1 as modified below

.480 26   Treaties, codes, cases

Add to base number 341.48026 the numbers following 341.026 in 341.0261–341.0268, e.g., text of multilateral treaties 341.480265

[.480 8]   Groups of people

Do not use; class in 341.485

.483   Specific human rights

Class specific rights of specific social groups in 341.485

[.483 01–.483 09]   Standard subdivisions

Do not use; class in 341.4801–341.4809

.483 2–.483 8   Subdivisions for specific human rights

Add to base number 341.483 the numbers following 342.085 in 342.0852–342.0858, e.g., freedom of religion 341.4832

.485   Rights of specific social groups

Class rights of religious groups in 341.4832

[.485 01–.485 09]   Standard subdivisions

Do not use; class in 341.4801–341.4809

.485 2–.485 8   Subdivisions for rights of specific social groups

Add to base number 341.485 the numbers following 342.087 in 342.0872–342.0878, e.g., rights of women 341.4858; however, for rights of stateless persons and refugees, see 341.486

.486   †Rights of stateless persons and refugees

Class jurisdiction over stateless persons and refugees in 342.083

.5   †Disputes and conflicts between states

Class disputes on a specific subject with the subject in 341–347, e.g., jurisdictional disputes 341.4

For law of war, see 341.6

†Add as instructed under 341.2–341.7

†Add as instructed under 341.2–341.7

.66	Termination of war

Including indemnification, reparations, restitution; laws of occupation

Class here military government of occupied countries

For war claims by private individuals of one country against another country, see 340.9

.660 2	Miscellany

Notation 02 from Table 1 as modified below

.660 26	Treaties and cases

Class here text of treaties limited to termination of war

Add to base number 341.66026 the numbers following 341.026 in 341.0261–341.0268, e.g., text of multilateral treaties 341.660265

Class texts of treaties that are signed at termination of a war but cover topics other than termination of the war in 341.026

.67	†Humanitarian law

Including status of enemy aliens and their property, nationals of neutral nations, combatants, noncombatants, war victims

For treatment of prisoners, see 341.65

.68	†Law of nations and civil war

Including responsibility of the state for acts of unsuccessful insurgent governments

.69	†War crimes
.690 268	Cases

Number built according to instructions under 341.2–341.7

Class here trials of war criminals, e.g., Tokyo war crime trials

.7	**†International cooperation**
.72	†Mutual security

Including international security forces

Class here legal aspects of international mutual security pacts, e.g., NATO (North Atlantic Treaty Organization)

Class military and defense law in 343.01; class civil defense in 344.0535; class interdisciplinary works on international mutual security pacts in 355.031

.722	†Peaceful occupation (Friendly occupation)

---

†Add as instructed under 341.2–341.7

.73 †Peace and disarmament

> Class here peace conferences, general efforts to gain acceptance of renunciation of war as an instrument of national policy

> Subdivisions are added for peace and disarmament together, for peace alone

> Class peaceful settlement of disputes in 341.52

.733 †Disarmament

> Including suspension of weapons testing

> Class the abolition and control of specific kinds of weapons in 341.734–341.738

.734 †Control of nuclear weapons

.735 †Control of chemical and biological weapons

> Class here control of weapons of mass destruction

> *For control of nuclear weapons, see 341.734*

.738 †Control of strategic weapons during time of peace

> Class control of nuclear strategic weapons in 341.734; class control of chemical and biological strategic weapons in 341.735

†Add as instructed under 341.2–341.7

> ## 342–349 Branches of law; laws, regulations, cases; law of specific jurisdictions, areas, socioeconomic regions

Classification numbers for law of specific jurisdictions and areas are built from five elements, which can be arranged in different ways to produce standard or optional numbers, according to instructions following this table:

(1)   34, the base number, indicating law

(2)   A digit indicating specific branch of law, original materials, or comprehensive works as follows:

     2   Constitutional and administrative law

     3   Military, defense, public property, public finance, tax, trade (commerce), industrial law

     4   Labor, social service, education, cultural law

     5   Criminal law

     6   Private law

     7   Procedure and courts

     8   Laws, regulations, cases not limited to a specific branch

     9   Comprehensive works

(3)   The facet indicator 0*

(4)   One or more digits indicating a subject subordinate to specific branch of law or type of original material

     Example: 1 Courts (from 345.01 under 345 Criminal law)

(5)   Notation from Table 2 indicating the jurisdiction or area

     Example: —94 Australia

To show comprehensive works on a specific jurisdiction or area in modern world, arrange the elements as follows, using law of Australia as an example:

Base number: 34

Digit indicating comprehensive works: 9

Jurisdiction or area: Australia, —94

The complete number is 349.94

To show a specific branch, a specific subject, or a kind of original material, arrange the elements as follows, using criminal courts of Australia as an example:

Base number: 34

Branch of law: Criminal law, 5

Jurisdiction or area: Australia, —94

Facet indicator: 0*

Subordinate subject in branch of law: Courts, 1

The complete number is 345.9401

Class comprehensive works in 340; class comprehensive works on law of specific ancient jurisdictions, areas, socioeconomic regions in 340.53; class comprehensive works on law of specific jurisdictions, areas, socioeconomic regions in 349

See Manual at 342–349

(Option: To give preferred treatment to the law of a specific jurisdiction, to jurisdictions in general, to branch of law and its subordinate subjects, or to subject, use one of the following options or the option at 342–347:

---

*Add 00 for standard subdivisions; see instructions at beginning of Table 1

> **342–349 Branches of law; laws, regulations, cases; law of specific jurisdictions, areas, socioeconomic regions**

(Option A: To give local emphasis and a shorter notation to law of a specific jurisdiction or area, e.g., Australia, arrange the elements as follows, using criminal courts of Australia as an example:
    Base number: 34
    Branch of law: Criminal law, 5
    Facet indicator: 0*
    Subordinate subject in the branch of law: Courts, 1
    The complete number is 345.01

(For law of a jurisdiction subordinate to the emphasized jurisdiction or area, insert between the branch of law and facet indicator the notation indicating the subordinate jurisdiction

(To show subordinate jurisdictions of an area with regular notation from Table 2, derive the notation by dropping from the area number for subordinate jurisdiction all digits that apply to preferred jurisdiction. For example, drop area number for Australia —94 from area number for Tasmania —946 to obtain notation 6, which is used for Tasmania. Thus, the number for criminal procedure of Tasmania is 345.605

(To show subordinate jurisdictions of an area with irregular notation from Table 2, i.e., with numbers for subdivisions that are coordinate with the number for the entire area, derive notation by dropping the digits from area number that all subdivisions have in common. For example, Sudan's area number is —624, while the numbers for its regions and provinces are —625–628. Drop —62 from full area number for Darfur region —627 to obtain the notation 7, which is used for Darfur region. Thus, the number for criminal procedure of the Darfur region is 345.705

(Class comprehensive works on law of the preferred jurisdiction or area in 342; class comparative law and law of other jurisdictions and areas in 349

(Option B: To give preferred treatment to jurisdictions in general, arrange the elements as follows, using criminal courts of Australia as an example:
    Base number: 34
    Jurisdiction or area: Australia, —94
    Facet indicator: 0*
    Branch of law: Criminal law, 5
    Subordinate subject in branch of law: Courts, 1
    The complete number is 349.4051. Other examples: criminal courts of Tasmania 349.46051, texts of welfare laws of Hobart 349.4610430263

(Class law of jurisdictions in the ancient world in 340.53–340.54; class comparative law in 342; class law of socioeconomic regions in 343.1; class law of regional intergovernmental organizations in 343.2

(Option C: To give preferred treatment to branch of law and its subordinate subjects, arrange the elements as follows, using criminal courts of Australia as an example:
    Base number: 34
    Branch of law: Criminal law, 5
    Subordinate subject in branch of law: Courts, 1

*Add 00 for standard subdivisions; see instructions at beginning of Table 1

> **342–349 Branches of law; laws, regulations, cases; law of specific jurisdictions, areas, socioeconomic regions**

Facet indicator: 0*
Jurisdiction or area: Australia, —94
The complete number is 345.1094)

*Add 00 for standard subdivisions; see instructions at beginning of Table 1

> ## 342–347 Branches of law

Class here comprehensive works on specific subjects of law

Except for modifications shown under specific entries, add to each subdivision identified by * as follows:

01	Philosophy and theory
	Notation 01 from Table 1 as modified below
011	Special topics of philosophy and theory of law
	Including origin, sources, nature, limits of law; rule of law; legal reasoning; equal protection of the law; law and ethics; justice; law and society
02	Miscellany
	Notation 02 from Table 1 as modified below
023	Law as a profession, occupation, hobby
	Class here legal personnel, nature of duties, characteristics of profession
	Class professional ethics of legal personnel in 174.3; class comprehensive works on legal personnel in 340.023. Class works that emphasize procedures of work performed by legal personnel with the subject without adding notation 023 from Table 1, e.g., works that emphasize procedures of conducting a lawsuit 347.0504
026	Laws, regulations, cases, procedure, courts
	Standard subdivisions may be added to 026 and its subdivisions
	(Option: Class laws, regulations, cases on specific subjects in law in 348)
0261	Treaties
	Including negotiation and ratification, validity and binding force, termination, interpretation
	Class here bilateral and multilateral treaties
	Do not use for commentaries and criticism; class with the subject in 342–347 without adding from this table
	Add to 0261 notation 3–9 from Table 2, e.g., bilateral treaties with Great Britain 026141
0262	Preliminary materials
	Including bills, hearings, reports, executive messages, statements of witnesses, legislative histories, slip laws
	Do not use for commentaries and critical works; class with the subject in 342–347 without adding from this table
	See Manual at 300–330, 355–390 vs. 342–347, 352–354
0263	Laws and regulations
	Do not use for commentaries and criticism; class with the subject in 342–347 without adding from this table
02632	Individual and collected laws
	Including codes
02636	Administrative regulations
	Collections and individual regulations
02638	Guides to laws and regulations
	Digests, citators, checklists, tables, indexes
0264	Cases
	Do not use for casebooks, for popular works; class with the subject in 342–347 without adding from this table
02642	Reports

>   **342–347 Branches of law**

02643	Court decisions
	Class here official court decisions
	Do not use for treatises on court decisions and popular treatment of cases; class with the subject in 342–347 without adding from this table
02646	Decisions (Rulings) of regulatory agencies
02648	Guides to cases
	Including digests, citators, checklists, tables, indexes, loose-leaf services
	Class here guides to laws, regulations, cases
	For guides to laws and regulations, see notation 02638 from this table
0265	Advisory opinions of attorneys-general (ministers of justice)
0269	Courts and procedure
	Including administrative courts, regulatory agencies; practice, rules, form books, legal costs and fees
	(Option: Class courts and procedure in specific fields in 347)
03–05	Standard subdivisions
06	Organizations and management
	Notation 06 from Table 1 as modified below
	Class regulation of associations engaged in a specific type of enterprise with the enterprise in 343.076–343.078, e.g., regulation of law partnerships 343.07834; class organization of associations engaged in specific types of enterprises with the kind of association in 346.06, e.g., laws for forming a law partnership 346.0682
0601	International organizations
	Law limited to a specific regional intergovernmental organization is classed under the area of the organization before indicating the subject of a branch of law, e.g., economic law of European Union 343.2407. Further instructions are given under 342–349
07–08	Standard subdivisions
09	History, geographic treatment, biography
[0917]	Socioeconomic regions
	Law limited to a specific socioeconomic region is classed under the region before indicating the subject of a branch of law, e.g., railroad law in developing countries 343.124095 (*not* 343.095091724)
093–099	Specific localities
	Limited to application of law of a specific jurisdiction to a limited area within that jurisdiction
	Law limited to a specific jurisdiction or area is classed under the jurisdiction before indicating the subject of a branch of law, e.g., railroad law of Germany 343.43095 (*not* 343.0950943). Once the jurisdiction has been specified, notation 093–099 may be added for application of law of that jurisdiction to a limited area within the jurisdiction, e.g., application of German railroad law in Bavaria 343.4309509433
	See Manual at 342–349

Class general laws, regulations, cases in 348; class comprehensive works in 340

> ## 342–347 Branches of law

For a specific subject in law of nations, see the subject in 341, e.g., disarmament law 341.73

See Manual at 340, 342–347 vs. 340.56; also at 340, 342–347 vs. 340.57

(Option: Class the law of a specific subject with the subject, plus notation 026 from Table 1, e.g., law of education 370.26, not 344.07)

342 Constitutional and administrative law

Standard subdivisions are added for constitutional and administrative law together, for constitutional law alone

Class here comprehensive works on public law

For law of nations, see 341. For constitutional law on a specific subject not provided for here, see the subject in 343–347, e.g., criminal law 345

(If option A under 342–349 is chosen, class here comprehensive works on the law of preferred jurisdiction, e.g., [assuming Australia to be preferred jurisdiction] comprehensive works on law of Australia 342, on law of Tasmania 342.6. Class specific branches of the law of preferred jurisdiction in 342–348

(If option B under 342–349 is chosen, class here comparative law and law without jurisdiction by adding to base number 342 the numbers following 34 in 342–348, but omitting the first 0 after decimal point, e.g., comparative criminal procedure 342.55 [*not* 342.505])

SUMMARY

342.001–.009	Standard subdivisions; laws, regulations, cases, procedure, courts
.02	Basic instruments of government
.03	Revision and amendment of basic instruments of government
.04	Structure, powers, functions of government
.05	Legislative branch of government
.06	Executive branch of government
.07	Election law
.08	Jurisdiction over persons
.09	Local government
.1	Socioeconomic regions
.2	Regional intergovernmental organizations
.3–.9	Specific jurisdictions and areas

.001–.008   Standard subdivisions

Notation from Table 1 as modified in notation 01–08 from table under 342–347, e.g., cases 342.00264

.009   History, geographic treatment, biography

[.009 17]   Socioeconomic regions

Do not use; class in 342.1

[.009 3–.009 9]   Specific continents, countries, localities

Do not use; class in 342.3–342.9

.02	*Basic instruments of government

Class here constitutions, municipal charters

For revision and amendment, see 342.03. For constitutional provisions dealing with a specific subject, see the subject in 342–347, e.g., individual rights 342.085

[.020 9]	History, geographic treatment, biography

Do not use; class in 342.029

.023	Texts of constitutions

Including texts of proposed constitutions

.024	Sources

Class commentary on source documents without text in 342.0292

.024 2	Convention proceedings

Including debates, journals, minutes

.024 3	Other convention documents

Including enabling acts, memoranda, proposals, rules

.029	Constitutional history

For sources, see 342.024

.029 2	History of conventions

Class proceedings and documents of conventions in 342.024; class constitutional conventions dealing with revision and amendment of constitutions in 342.03

.03	Revision and amendment of basic instruments of government

Class here constitutional reform

Class proposals for and formation of new constitutions in 342.02

For amendments dealing with a specific subject, see the subject in 342–347, e.g., an amendment establishing an income tax 343.052

[.030 9]	History, geographic treatment, biography

Do not use; class in 342.039

.032	*Amendment procedure
.035	Proposed and pending amendments

Class here collected texts of constitutional amendments

Class texts of proposed constitutions in 342.023

.039	History of amendments

Including defeated amendments not limited to a specific subject

*Add as instructed under 342–347

.04   *Structure, powers, functions of government

> Class government corporations in 346.067

.041   *Powers and functions of government

> *For jurisdiction over persons, see 342.08*

.041 2   *Conduct of relations with foreign governments

> Including military assistance and missions; power to regulate foreign diplomatic and consular personnel, to wage war; comprehensive works on power to acquire territory from or cede it to other jurisdictions

> Class military and defense law in 343.012–343.019

> *For municipal annexation, see 342.0413*

> *See also 342.0418 for police powers; also 342.062 for war and emergency powers of executives*

.041 3   *Jurisdiction over territory, dependencies, colonies

> Including municipal annexation

> Class comprehensive works on the power to acquire territory from or cede it to other jurisdictions in 342.0412

.041 8   *Police powers

> Powers to exercise control in interests of general security, health, safety, morals, welfare

> Class individual rights in 342.085. Class the exercise of a specific police power with the power in 342–347, e.g., exclusion of undesirable aliens 342.082, regulation of public health 344.04

> *See also 342.062 for war and emergency powers of executives*

.042   *Levels of government

> Including federal structure; relations between levels, relations among subordinate units of same level; domestic conflict of laws; home rule; interstate compacts

> Class levels of government with respect to a specific subject with the subject in 342–347, e.g., interstate compacts on seaports and their facilities 343.0967

> *See also 342.09 for local governments*

.044   *Branches of government

> Including distribution and separation of powers, relations between branches

> Class relations of a specific branch of government with government institutions at a different level in 342.042

> *For legislative branch, see 342.05; for executive branch, see 342.06; for judicial branch, see 347*

*Add as instructed under 342–347

.05　　　*Legislative branch of government

　　　　　Class here lobbying

　　　　　Class relations of legislative branch with government institutions at a different level in 342.042

.052　　*Duties, functions, powers

.053　　*Basis of representation

　　　　　Including apportionment, districting

.055　　*Membership

　　　　　Including qualifications, terms of office

.057　　*Organization and procedure

　　　　　For preliminary materials, see 348.01

.06　　　*Executive branch of government

　　　　　Class here administrative law

　　　　　Class relations of executive branch with governmental institutions at a different level in 342.042. Class standards set by an agency in connection with a specific subject with the subject outside of law, e.g., standards for safety in health care facilities 363.1562

　　　　　For administrative law on a specific subject, see the subject in 342–347, e.g., air traffic control 343.0976

.062　　*Chief and deputy chief executives

　　　　　Including impeachment; war and emergency powers

　　　　　Subdivisions are added for either or both topics in heading

.062 8　　*Martial law

.064　　*Executive departments (Ministries) and agencies

　　　　　Class departments and agencies dealing with a specific subject with the subject in 342–347, e.g., revenue agencies 343.036

.066　　*Administrative procedure

　　　　　Class maintenance of privacy in 342.0858

　　　　　See also 344.0531 for information control laws

.066 2　　*Public records

　　　　　Class here privacy of government records, right to information, sunshine laws

*Add as instructed under 342–347

.066 4   *Administrative courts and regulatory agencies

Including hearing examiners, provisional courts

Class executive function of administering and enforcing the law in 351–354. Class administrative courts, regulatory agencies dealing with a specific subject with the subject in 342–347, plus notation 0269 from table under 342–347, e.g., agencies regulating civil aeronautics 343.0970269

.066 7   *Ombudsmen

.068   *Officials and employees

Including impeachment

Class here civil service

Class labor-management bargaining in government service in 344.018904135

For chief and deputy chief executives, see 342.062; for official and employees involved with administrative procedure, see 342.066

.068 4   *Employee rights and discipline

Including conflict of interest, loyalty oaths, political activity of employees, security measures

.068 6   *Conditions of employment

Including compensation, fringe benefits, leave, retirement benefits, tenure, training

.07   *Election law

Class here manuals of election procedures that discuss laws or administrative regulations

Class manuals of election procedures limited to political aspects in 324.6; class apportionment, districting in 342.053

For electing legislators, see 342.055; for electing executives, see 342.068

.072   *Voting rights and qualifications for voting

Subdivisions are added for either or both topics in heading

.075   *Voting procedures

Including absentee voting, voter registration

.078   *Campaign practices

Including finance

.08   *Jurisdiction over persons

Including census law

*Add as instructed under 342–347

.082   *Entrance to and exit from national domain

Including immigration, passports, visas, emigration

Class entry and exit of diplomatic and consular personnel in 342.0412

.083   *Citizenship and nationality

Including right of asylum, status of aliens, jurisdiction over stateless persons and refugees

Subdivisions are added for either or both topics in heading

Class liability of states to aliens in 341.26; class status of enemy aliens in 341.67; class status of diplomatic and consular personnel in 342.0412

.084   *Abortion

Class here comprehensive works

For rights of fetuses, see 342.085; for rights of women, see 342.0878; for medical aspects, see 344.04192; for abortion for population control, see 344.048; for abortion control, see 344.0546; for criminal abortion, see 345.0285

.085   *Rights and activities of individuals

Including individual rights of military personnel, rights of fetuses

Class here civil rights; comprehensive works on individual rights

Class constitutional rights of aliens in 342.083; class constitutional rights of specific social groups in 342.087; class comprehensive works on abortion in 342.084; class interdisciplinary works on civil rights, on individual rights in 323

For a specific right not provided for here, see the right, e.g., right to vote 342.072, right to education 344.079

See Manual at 342.085 vs. 341.48

.085 2   *Religious groups and religious activities

Class here affirmative action, discrimination; legal status

Subdivisions are added for either or both topics in heading

.085 21   Specific religious activities

Add to base number 342.08521 the numbers following 20 in 201–207, e.g., religious healing 342.0852131; then add further as instructed under 342–347, e.g., cases involving religious healing 342.08521310264

Class specific religious activities in relation to specific religious groups in 342.08522–342.08529

*Add as instructed under 342–347

.085 22	*People associated with free thought, humanism, secularism, agnosticism, skepticism, atheism

Not associated with religious groups provided in 342.08523–342.08529

Including people associated with secular humanism

.085 222	*People associated with atheism
.085 23–.085 29	Specific religious groups

Class here specific religious activities associated with specific religious groups

Add to base number 342.0852 the numbers following 2 in 230–299, e.g., Christians 342.08527, Catholics 342.085282, Christian sacred places 342.085263042, Buddhists 342.0852943, Buddhist sacred places 342.0852943435, Muslims 342.085297, Islamic sacred places 342.08529735; then add further as instructed under 342–347, e.g., cases involving Buddhists 342.08529430264, cases involving Buddhist sacred places 342.08529434350264

Class people associated with free thought, humanism, secularism, agnosticism, skepticism, atheism, not associated with religious groups provided here in 342.08522

.085 3	*Freedom of information and opinion

Including freedom of speech, freedom of the press

Subdivisions are added for either or both topics in heading

Class fairness doctrine in 343.09945; class censorship and information control laws in 344.0531; class relation of freedom of the press to the judicial process in 347.05

For freedom of political opinion, see 342.0854; for academic freedom, see 344.078

See also 342.0662 for access to public records; also 344.0547 for obscenity and pornography laws

.085 4	*Political activity

Including civil disobedience and dissent, rights of assembly and petition

Class election law in 342.07

For political activity of government employees, see 342.0684

.085 8	*Maintenance of privacy

Class privacy of government records in 342.0662

*Add as instructed under 342–347

.087	*Groups of people

Including slaves

Class here affirmative action, discrimination; legal status

For aliens, displaced persons, refugees, see 342.083; for religious groups, see 342.0852

See also 342.085 for rights and activities of individuals

[.087 08]	Groups of people

Do not use; class in 342.087

.087 2	*Indigenous and aboriginal peoples

Subdivisions are added for either or both topics in heading

Class women in 342.0878

.087 3	*Ethnic and national groups

Class indigenous and aboriginal peoples of specific ethnic and national groups in 342.0872; class women of specific ethnic and national groups in 342.0878

.087 7	*Age groups

Class women regardless of age group in 342.0878

.087 72	*Young people

Class here children

.087 74	*People in late adulthood
.087 8	*Women

Including abortion rights

Class comprehensive works on abortion in 342.084

.088	*Government liability

Including liability for abuse of power, corruption, denial of civil rights

Class liability in a specific field with the field in 342–347, e.g., liability of military units 343.013, liability of schools, of school officials, of school districts 344.075

.09	*Local government

Including municipal corporations, municipal government

Class home rule in 342.042; class specific local governments in 342.3–342.9. Class a specific aspect of local government with the aspect in 342–347, e.g., local real estate taxation 343.054

*Add as instructed under 342–347

.1 Socioeconomic regions

Add to base number 342.1 the numbers following —17 in notation 171–177 from Table 2, e.g., constitutional and administrative law of developing countries 342.124, constitutional and administrative law of Islamic countries, Islamic constitutional and administrative law 342.167; then to the result add as follows:

001–009 Standard subdivisions

Notation from Table 1 as modified under 342–347

02–09 Topics of constitutional and administrative law

Add the numbers following 342 in 342.02–342.09, e.g., citizenship law of developing countries 342.124083, citizenship law of Islamic countries 342.167083, administrative regulations concerning citizenship in developing countries 342.12408302636, administrative regulations concerning citizenship in Islamic countries 342.16708302636

Class socioeconomic regions of a specific regional intergovernmental organization in 342.2; class socioeconomic regions of a specific jurisdiction or area in 342.3–342.9

.167 Regions where Islam predominates

Number built according to instructions under 342.1

Class here Islamic public law

(.167 1–.167 3) Schools of Islamic law

(Optional numbers; prefer 342.167)

Add to base number 342.167 the numbers following 297.14018 in notation 297.140181–297.140183, e.g., Islamic public law according to Ḥanafī school 342.16711; then to the result add as instructed under 342.1, e.g., Islamic law concerning citizenship according to Ḥanafī school 342.16711083

(.167 4) Mixed schools of Islamic law and comparative treatment

Class here works comparing authors affiliated with different schools (e.g., Sunni and Shīʿī schools)

(Optional number; prefer 342.167)

[.167 8] Regions where specific Islamic sects and reform movements predominate

Do not use; class in 342.167

.2   **Regional intergovernmental organizations**

> Class here relationship between the organization's law and national law of member countries
>
> Add to base number 342.2 notation 3–9 from Table 2, e.g., harmonization of national constitutional and administrative law of European Union countries 342.24; then to the result add as follows:
>
> > 001–009   Standard subdivisions
> > > Notation from Table 1 as modified in notation 01–09 from table under 342–347
> >
> > 02–09   Topics of constitutional and administrative law
> > > Add the numbers following 342 in 342.02–342.09, e.g., harmonization of national citizenship law of European Union countries 342.24083, harmonization of administrative regulations of citizenship law of European Union countries 342.2408302636
>
> Class relationship of organization's law and national law of a specific member country with the national law in 342.3–342.9, e.g., effect of European Union laws on national constitutional and administrative law of Germany 342.43
>
> *See Manual at 342–349*

.24   Regional intergovernmental organizations of Europe

> Number built according to instructions under 342.2

.240 2   Basic instruments of government

> Class founding treaties, basic legal instruments of European Union in 341.2422
>
> Class here effect of European Union law on and harmonization of national constitutions of European Union countries
>
> Number built according to instructions under 342.2

.240 8   Jurisdiction over persons

> Number built according to instructions under 342.2
>
> Class here European Union law itself, effect of European Union law on and harmonization of national laws of European Union countries

.240 85   Rights and activities of individuals

> Number built according to instructions under 342.2

.240 850 261   Treaties

> Number built according to instructions under 342.2
>
> Class here Charter of Fundamental Rights of the European Union, European Convention on Human Rights

.240 850 269   Courts and procedure

> Number built according to instructions under 342.2
>
> Class here European Court of Human Rights

.3–.9 Specific jurisdictions and areas

Add to base number 342 notation 3–9 from Table 2, e.g., constitutional and administrative law of Australia 342.94, of New South Wales 342.944, of African states 342.6; then to the result add as follows:

001–009   Standard subdivisions
> Notation from Table 1 as modified in notation 01–09 from table under 342–347

02–09   Topics of constitutional and administrative law
> Add the numbers following 342 in 342.02–342.09, e.g., election law of Australia 342.9407, of New South Wales 342.94407, of African states 342.607, administrative regulations for elections in Australia 342.940702636

For regional intergovernmental organizations, relationship between the organization's laws and national laws of all member states, see 342.2

See Manual at 342–349

343 Military, defense, public property, public finance, tax, commerce (trade), industrial law

(If option B under 342–349 is chosen, class here law of socioeconomic regions and of regional intergovernmental organizations; however, for law of jurisdictions in the ancient world, see 340.53)

SUMMARY

343.001–.009	Standard subdivisions; laws, regulations, cases, procedure, courts
.01	Military and defense law, veterans' law
.02	Law of public property
.03	Law of public finance
.04	Tax law
.05	Kinds of taxes by base
.06	Kinds of taxes by incidence
.07	Regulation of economic activity
.08	Regulation of commerce (trade)
.09	Control of public utilities
.1	Socioeconomic regions
.2	Regional intergovernmental organizations
.3–.9	Specific jurisdictions and areas

.001–.008   Standard subdivisions

> Notation from Table 1 as modified in notation 01–08 from table under 342–347, e.g., cases 343.00264

.009   History, geographic treatment, biography

> Notation 09 from Table 1 as modified below

[.009 17]   Socioeconomic regions

> Do not use; class in 343.1

[.009 3–.009 9]   Specific continents, countries, localities

> Do not use; class in 343.3–343.9

.01   *Military and defense law, veterans' law

     Class here national security, war and emergency legislation

     Subdivisions are added for two or more topics in heading, for military law alone, for defense law alone

     For war claims, see 341.66; for martial law, see 342.0628

.011   *Veterans' law

     Class here veterans' welfare law

     Class veterans' insurance claims in 346.086364

.011 2   *Veterans' pensions

     Including benefits to survivors of veterans

.011 3   *Education and training for veterans

     Subdivisions are added for either or both topics in heading

.011 4   *Employment for veterans

.011 5   *Health care and rehabilitation for veterans

     Subdivisions are added for either or both topics in heading

     Class disability compensation in 343.0116

.011 6   *Disability compensation for veterans

>   343.012–343.019 Military and defense law

     Class comprehensive works in 343.01. Class a specific aspect of military or defense law not provided for here with the aspect in 342–347, e.g., regulation of industry 343.07

.012   *Manpower procurement

     Including voluntary enlistment

     Class reserve officers' training corps and military academies in 344.0769

     For manpower procurement of a specific service other than the army in general, see the service in 343.015–343.019, e.g., manpower procurement of mercenary troops 343.015354, naval manpower procurement 343.01922

.012 2   *Draft and selective service

     Including draft resistance

     Subdivisions are added for either or both topics in heading

     Class individual rights of military personnel in 342.085; class treatment of conscientious objectors in 343.0126

.012 6   *Conscientious objectors

*Add as instructed under 342–347

.013   *Military life, customs, resources

Including rank, pay, promotion, demotion, leave, allowances, living conditions

Class individual rights of military personnel in 342.085

For civilian employees of military services, see 342.068; for manpower procurement, see 343.012; for discipline and conduct, see 343.014. For military life, customs, resources of a specific service other than the army in general, see the service in 343.015–343.019, e.g., military resources of mercenary troops 343.015354, naval military resources 343.0192

.014   *Discipline and conduct

Including desertion

Subdivisions are added for either or both topics in heading

For discipline and conduct of a specific service other than the army in general, see the service in 343.015–343.019, e.g., discipline and conduct of mercenary troops 343.015354, naval discipline and conduct 343.01913

[.014 026 9]   Courts and procedure

Do not use; class in 343.0143

.014 3   *Military courts and procedure

Including procedural rights of military personnel in military courts

Subdivisions are added for either or both topics in heading

Class international war crime trials in 341.69; class procedural rights in nonmilitary courts in 347.05

See also 342.085 for general rights of military personnel

.014 6   *Military penology

For military prisons, see 344.03548

.015–.019   Specific aspects of military and defense law

Add to base number 343.01 the numbers following 35 in 355–359, e.g., organization 343.0153, training 343.0155, military installations and bases 343.0157, naval law 343.019; then add further as instructed under 342–347, e.g., cases involving naval law 343.0190264; however, for military assistance to foreign nations, see 342.0412; for manpower procurement, see 343.012; for military life, customs, resources, see 343.013; for discipline and conduct, see 343.014

.02   *Law of public property

.023   *Personal property

.025   *Real property

*Add as instructed under 342–347

.025 2   *Acquisition

                Including nationalization of alien property, condemnation, eminent
                domain (expropriation); comprehensive works on nationalization

                For acquisition of territory from other jurisdictions, see 342.0412

.025 3   *Disposal

                See also 342.0412 for cession of territory to other jurisdictions

.025 6   *Control and use

                Including construction and maintenance of government buildings

                Subdivisions are added for either or both topics in heading

                Class regulation of construction of government buildings in
                343.07869051; class comprehensive works on control and use of
                public and private real property, control of natural resources in
                346.044

.03   *Law of public finance

                Class here international financial law

                For banks, see 346.082; for government securities, see 346.0922

.032   *Monetary law

                Including coinage

                Class here currency

                Class comprehensive works on commemorative medals in 344.091; class
                comprehensive works on central banks in 346.0821

.032 1–.032 6   Specific aspects of monetary law

                Add to base number 343.032 the numbers following 332.4 in
                332.41–332.46, e.g., foreign exchange 343.0325, monetary policy
                343.0326; then add further as instructed under 342–347, e.g., cases
                involving foreign exchange 343.03250264

.034   *Budgeting and expenditure

                Including fiscal policy, accounting and auditing, economic stabilization,
                grants-in-aid, intergovernmental financial relations, revenue sharing

                Subdivisions are added for either or both topics in heading

                Class revenue law, revenue sharing as revenue in 343.036; class
                budgets and their preparation in 352.48. Class bills for authorization of
                expenditure for a specific purpose with the purpose in 342–347, e.g.,
                price supports 343.0742

                *See also 343.083 for regulation of prices; also 346.063 for public
                accounting*

.036   *Revenue law

                For public borrowing and debt, see 343.037; for tax law, see 343.04

*Add as instructed under 342–347

.037　　　　　*Public borrowing and debt

Including government bankruptcy and insolvency

.04　　　　　*Tax law

Class here internal revenue law; tax auditing, avoidance, planning

Class fiscal policy in 343.034; class tax planning applied to a specific kind of tax in 343.05–343.06; class tax evasion in 345.0233; class interdisciplinary works on taxes in 336.2

For specific kinds of taxes, see 343.05–343.06

See Manual at 343.04–343.06 vs. 336.2, 352.44

.042　　　　　*Tax assessment and collection

Including tax accounting, tax appeals

Class assessment and collection of taxes at specific levels in 343.043; class assessment and collection of specific kinds of taxes in 343.05–343.06

.043　　　　　Taxes by level

National, state and provincial, local

Class here only comprehensive works and comparisons, e.g., national taxes in North America 343.7043, state taxes in the United States 343.73043, local taxes of the jurisdictions of Pennsylvania 343.748043

Class a specific kind of tax regardless of level with the kind in 343.05–343.06, e.g., income tax law of Michigan 343.774052

Taxes of a specific jurisdiction are classed in 343.3–343.9, plus notation 04 from 343.04, e.g., United States taxes 343.7304

>　　　　　343.05–343.06　Specific kinds of taxes

Class comprehensive works in 343.04

See Manual at 343.04–343.06 vs. 336.2, 352.44

.05　　　　　Kinds of taxes by base

SUMMARY

343.052	Income tax
.053	Estate, inheritance, gift taxes
.054	Property taxes
.055	Excise and turnover taxes
.056	Customs taxes (Tariff)
.057	Stamp taxes

.052　　　　　*Income tax

Class internal revenue law in 343.04

.052 04　　　　　Special topics of income tax

*Add as instructed under 342–347

.052 042	*Assessment of income taxes
.052 044	*Preparation of returns
.052 3	*Provisions that allow tax avoidance
.052 304	*Tax incentives
.052 32	*Charitable deductions
.052 33	*Individual retirement accounts

Including Keogh plans

| .052 34 | *Depreciation and depletion allowances |

Subdivisions are added for either or both topics in heading

| .052 36 | *Business losses |

Including bad debts

.052 37	*Tax credits
.052 38	*Tax shelters
.052 4	Taxes on specific types of income

Including proceeds from insurance, retirement income

Class reductions in taxes on specific types of income in 343.0523

| .052 42 | *Wages |

Including payroll taxes, social security taxes

.052 424	*Withholding tax
.052 44	*Profits
.052 45	*Capital gains
.052 46	*Investment income

Including income from bonds, deposits, stocks

> *For taxes on capital gains, see 343.05245; for taxes on real estate transactions, see 343.0546*

| .052 48 | *Foreign income |

Class taxes on specific types of foreign income in 343.05242–343.05246

*Add as instructed under 342–347

.052 6	Income taxes by incidence

Including taxes on citizens resident in foreign countries, on self-employed persons

Class here double taxation

Add to base number 343.0526 the numbers following 343.06 in 343.062–343.068, e.g., corporation income taxes 343.05267; then add further as instructed under 342–347, e.g., cases involving corporation income taxes 343.052670264; however, for reduction in taxation regardless of incidence, see 343.0523; for taxes on specific types of income regardless of incidence, see 343.0524

.053	*Estate, inheritance, gift taxes

Standard subdivisions are added for estate, inheritance, gift taxes together; for estate taxes alone; for inheritance taxes alone

Class here death duties, death tax, estate planning

Subdivisions are added for estate, inheritance, gift taxes together; for estate taxes alone; for inheritance taxes alone

For taxes on fiduciary trusts, see 343.05264

.053 5	*Gift taxes
.054	*Property taxes

Real and personal property

.054 2	*Assessment
.054 3	*Exemptions
.054 6	*Taxes on real estate transactions

Including real estate sales tax

Class a specific aspect of real estate tax not provided for here with the aspect in 342–347, e.g., tax assessment 343.0542

.055	*Excise and turnover taxes

Including luxury, severance, transfer, use, value-added taxes; user fees

For taxes on real estate transactions, see 343.0546

.055 2	*Sales taxes

Class sales taxes on specific commodities and services in 343.0558

.055 3	*Excise taxes

Class excise taxes on specific commodities and services in 343.0558

.055 8	Taxes on specific commodities and services

Class comprehensive works on sales taxes in 343.0552; class comprehensive works on excise taxes in 343.0553

*Add as instructed under 342–347

[.055 801–.055 809]   Standard subdivisions

Do not use; class in 343.05501–343.05509

.055 81–.055 85   Subdivisions for taxes on specific commodities and services

Add to base number 343.0558 the numbers following 381.4 in 381.41–381.45, e.g., taxes on products of secondary industries 343.05585, on cigarettes 343.0558567973; then add further as instructed under 342–347, e.g., cases involving taxes on cigarettes 343.0558679730264

.056   *Customs taxes (Tariff)

Including custom taxes (tariff) on specific commodities

.057   *Stamp taxes

.06   Kinds of taxes by incidence

Class taxes on specific bases regardless of incidence in 343.05

.062   *Taxes on individuals

Class here poll tax

.064   *Taxes on fiduciary trusts

Including pension trusts

.066   *Taxes on organizations

Class here tax-exempt organizations

For taxes on corporations, see 343.067

.066 2   *Partnerships

.066 8   *Charitable foundations and trusts

Subdivisions are added for either or both topics in heading

.067   *Taxes on corporations

.068   *Taxes on business enterprises

Including small business taxes

Class taxes on individuals engaged in business in 343.062; class taxes on specific types of business organizations in 343.066

*Add as instructed under 342–347

.07   *Regulation of economic activity

Including daylight saving time, nationalization of industry, rationing

Class here international economic law, international economic organizations; comprehensive works on regulation of small business, licensing, industry and commerce

Class regulation of the practice of specific occupations in 344.01; class public health in 344.04; class safety measures in 344.047; class regulation of organizations in 346.06

For regulation of commerce, see 343.08

See also 346 for impact of economic activity upon private persons and corporate bodies

SUMMARY

343.071	**Consumer protection**
.072	**Unfair practices**
.074	**Economic assistance**
.075	**Production controls**
.076	**Agricultural industries**
.077	**Mineral industries**
.078	**Secondary industries and services**

.071   *Consumer protection

Class a specific aspect of consumer protection with the aspect in 342–347, e.g., protection against misleading advertising 343.082

>   343.072–343.075 Specific aspects of regulation

Class regulation of specific industries and services regardless of aspect in 343.076–343.078; class regulation of public utilities regardless of aspect in 343.09; class comprehensive works in 343.07. Class a specific aspect of industrial regulation not provided for here with the aspect in 342–347, e.g., wages 344.0121

.072   *Unfair practices

Including monopoly, industrial espionage

.072 1   *Antitrust law

Class here competition law

For restraint of trade, see 343.0723; for price fixing and discrimination, see 343.0725

.072 3   *Restraint of trade

.072 5   *Price fixing and discrimination

Subdivisions are added for either or both topics in heading

---

*Add as instructed under 342–347

.074   *Economic assistance

Class here technology transfer

Class assistance to specific industries and services in 343.076–343.078

\>   343.074 2–343.074 6   Domestic economic assistance

Class comprehensive works in 343.074

.074 2   Specific kinds of assistance

Including loans, mortgage insurance, price supports, subsidies

.074 5   *Rural development

Class specific kinds of assistance to rural areas in 343.0742; class assistance to agriculture in 343.076

.074 6   *Regional development

Class specific kinds of assistance in 343.0742; class development of rural regions in 343.0745

.074 8   *Foreign economic assistance (Foreign aid)

.075   *Production controls

Including standardization, weights and measures, packaging (containers)

See also 344.042 for product control

\>   343.076–343.078   Regulation of specific industries and services

Class here regulating the production of and commerce in specific goods and services

Class comprehensive works in 343.07

For commerce in specific goods and services, see 343.085; for public utilities, see 343.09; for regulation of labor of specific occupations, see 344.0176

See also 346.07 for commercial law

.076   *Agricultural industries

Including agricultural assistance

Class here comprehensive works on primary industries

For mineral industries, see 343.077

See also 343.078637 for regulation of dairy and related products industries; also 344.049 for veterinary public health

---

*Add as instructed under 342–347

.076 1	Specific production controls

Including acreage allotments, price supports, production quotas

Class controls of specific commodities in 343.0763–343.0769

.076 3–.076 6   Specific commodities of culture of plants, of domestic mammals, of domestic birds

Add to base number 343.076 the numbers following 63 in 633–636, e.g., forest products 343.076498; then add further as instructed under 342–347, e.g., cases involving forest products 343.0764980264

.076 8–.076 9   Specific commodities of insect culture, of culture of invertebrates and cold-blooded vertebrates, of aquaculture

Add to base number 343.076 the numbers following 63 in 638–639, e.g., products of fishing 343.07692, products of whaling 343.076928, products of sealing 343.076929, products of fishery of invertebrates 343.07694; then add further as instructed under 342–347, e.g., cases involving products of fishing 343.076920264

.077   *Mineral industries

See also 346.043 for mineral rights; also 346.04685 for conservation of minerals

.077 2   *Oil, oil shales, tar sands, natural gas

.077 5   *Mining of coal and nonfuel minerals

.077 52   *Coal

.077 55   *Nonfuel minerals

.078   Secondary industries and services

See Manual at 343.078 vs. 343.08

.078 000 1–.078 000 9   Standard subdivisions

Notation from Table 1 as modified in notation 01–09 from table under 342–347, e.g., cases 343.078000264

.078 001–.078 999   Specific secondary industries and services

Add to base number 343.078 notation 001–999, e.g., regulation of tourist industry 343.07891, regulation of shipbuilding industry 343.07862382; then add further as instructed under 342–347, e.g., cases involving shipbuilding industry 343.078623820264; however, for regulation of advertising industry, see 343.082; for regulation of marketing, see 343.08; for regulation of closely regulated industries, such as transportation and communication, see 343.09; for regulation of health services, see 344.0321

*Add as instructed under 342–347

.08   *Regulation of commerce (trade)

Including guarantees, warranties

Class here commodity exchanges, marketing, domestic trade, exchange transactions

Unless other instructions are given, observe the following table of preference, e.g., retail trade of agricultural commodities 343.0851 (*not* 343.0811):

International commerce (Foreign trade)	343.087
Specific commodities	343.085
Retail and wholesale trade, interstate commerce	343.081
Prices	343.083
Advertising and labeling	343.082

Class regulation of real estate business in 346.0437; class law of sale in 346.072; class regulation of banks in 346.082; class regulation of insurance companies and agencies in 346.086; class regulation of organizations engaged in marketing securities in 346.0926; class comprehensive works on regulation of industry and trade in 343.07

See Manual at 343.078 vs. 343.08

.081   Retail and wholesale trade, interstate commerce

[.081 01–.081 09]   Standard subdivisions

Do not use; class in 343.0801–343.0809

.081 1   *Retail trade

Including auctions

Class here wholesale trade through specific marketing channels, marketing channels

.081 14   Retail channels by merchandising pattern

[.081 140 1–.081 140 9]   Standard subdivisions

Do not use; class in 343.081101–343.081109

.081 142   *Electronic commerce; mail-order, telephone-order, television shopping

Class here online shopping, teleshopping

Subdivisions are added for electronic commerce, mail-order, telephone-order, television shopping together; for electronic commerce alone

Class online auctions in 343.0811

[.081 142 028 5]   Computer applications

Do not use; class in 343.081142

---

*Add as instructed under 342–347

.081 142 8	*Mail-order, telephone-order, television shopping
	Class here catalog shopping
	Subdivisions are added for any or all topics in heading
.081 2	*Wholesale trade

For wholesale trade through specific marketing channels, see 343.0811

.081 5	*Interstate commerce

Class interstate retail commerce in 343.0811; class interstate wholesale commerce in 343.0812

.082	*Advertising and labeling

Class restrictions on posting advertisements in 346.045

.083	*Prices

Class price supports in 343.0742; class price supports for a specific industry or service in 343.076–343.078

.085	Specific commodities

Class international commerce of a specific commodity in 343.0871–343.0875

[.085 01–.085 09]	Standard subdivisions

Do not use; class in 343.0801–343.0809

.085 1–.085 5	Subdivisions for specific commodities

Class here domestic trade of specific commodities

Add to base number 343.085 the numbers following 381.4 in 381.41–381.45, e.g., agricultural commodities 343.0851, rice 343.0851318; then add further as instructed under 342–347, e.g., cases involving rice 343.08513180264

.087	*International commerce (Foreign trade)

Class here combined treatment of trade, tariffs, and general shipping

For tariffs, see 343.056; for shipping, see 343.096

.087 1–.087 5	Specific commodities

Add to base number 343.087 the numbers following 381.4 in 381.41–381.45, e.g., agricultural commodities 343.0871, rice 343.0871318; then add further as instructed under 342–347, e.g., cases involving rice 343.08713180264

.087 7	*Imports

Class imports of specific commodities in 343.0871–343.0875

.087 8	*Exports

Class exports of specific commodities in 343.0871–343.0875

*Add as instructed under 342–347

.09   *Control of public utilities

SUMMARY

343.091	**General considerations of control of public utilities**
.092	**Water and power supply**
.093	**Transportation**
.094	**Road transportation**
.095	**Railroad transportation**
.096	**Water transportation**
.097	**Air transportation and space transportation**
.098	**Local transportation**
.099	**Communications**

.091   *General considerations of control of public utilities

Including rates, operations, facilities, services

Class general considerations applied to specific utilities in 343.092–343.099

.092   *Water and power supply

Subdivisions are added for water and power supply together, for power supply alone

.092 4   *Water

.092 5   *Nuclear energy

.092 6   *Oil and gas

Class extraction in 343.0772; class processing in 343.0786655–343.0786657

.092 7   *Coal

Class extraction in 343.07752; class processing in 343.07866262

.092 8   *Solar energy

.092 9   *Electric power

Including cogeneration of heat and electricity

Class a specific source of electric power with the source in 342–347, e.g., nuclear power 343.0925

.093   *Transportation

Class here comprehensive works on ground transportation, on the law of carriers

Class transportation insurance in 346.0862

For specific kinds of transportation and ground transportation, see 343.094–343.098

.093 2   *Freight services

Including transportation of specific goods

*Add as instructed under 342–347

.093 22	*Hazardous materials
.093 3	*Passenger services

Class here mass transportation

.093 8	*Transportation safety

Class private law of transportation accidents in 346.0322

.093 9	*Pipeline transportation
.093 95	*Oil (Petroleum)
.093 96	*Natural gas
.093 97	*Coal

Class here coal slurry

> 343.094–343.098 Specific kinds of transportation and ground transportation

Class comprehensive works in 343.093

For pipeline transportation, see 343.0939

.094	*Road transportation

Class here highway transportation

Class comprehensive works on ground transportation in 343.093

For street traffic, see 343.0982

.094 2	*Roads

Class here highways

.094 4	*Vehicles

Including licensing, registration

Class vehicle operation in 343.0946; class commercial vehicular services in 343.0948; class vehicle product liability in 346.038; class property laws relating to vehicles in 346.047

See also 346.043 for mobile homes

.094 6	*Vehicle operation and traffic control

Including drivers' licenses, speed limits, traffic signals

Subdivisions are added for either or both topics in heading

Class police traffic services in 344.052332; class traffic offenses in 345.0247

.094 8	*Commercial services

Class commercial vehicles in 343.0944; class operation of commercial vehicles in 343.0946

---

*Add as instructed under 342–347

.094 82	*Bus
.094 83	*Truck
.095	*Railroad transportation
.095 2	*Stationary facilities

Including signals, terminals, tracks, yards

| .095 5 | *Rolling stock |

Including cars, locomotives

| .095 8 | *Services |

Passenger, freight

| .096 | *Water transportation |

Including prize law

Class here maritime, admiralty law

Class a specific subject of maritime or admiralty law not provided for here with the subject in 342–347, e.g., maritime contracts 346.022

>   343.096 2–343.096 4 Specific kinds of water transportation

Class facilities, operations, services of specific kinds of transportation in 343.0965–343.0968; class comprehensive works in 343.096

| .096 2 | *Ocean transportation |

Class interoceanic waterways in 343.0964

See Manual at 341.45 vs. 343.0962

| .096 4 | *Inland waterway transportation |

Including interoceanic canals

>   343.096 5–343.096 8 Facilities, operations, services

Class comprehensive works in 343.096

| .096 5 | *Ships |

Including pilot's license

| .096 6 | *Navigation |

Class here rule of the road at sea

| .096 7 | *Ports |

Including piloting, tug services

*Add as instructed under 342–347

.096 8   *Services

                  Including freight, passenger services; salvage operations

                  Class services of ports in 343.0967

.097   *Air transportation and space transportation

                  Subdivisions are added for air and space transportation together, for air
                  transportation alone

>   343.097 5–343.097 8 Air transportation

                  Class comprehensive works in 343.097

.097 5   *Aircraft

                  Including pilot's license

.097 6   *Air navigation and traffic control

                  Subdivisions are added for either or both topics in heading

.097 7   *Airports

                  Class here landing fields

                  For traffic control, see 343.0976

.097 8   *Air transportation services

                  Including freight, passenger services

                  Class services of airports and landing fields in 343.0977

.097 9   *Space transportation

.098   *Local transportation

                  Class police traffic services in 344.052332; class traffic offenses in
                  345.0247

                  *For local water transportation, see 343.096; for local air
                  transportation, see 343.097*

.098 1   *Pedestrian traffic

.098 2   *Vehicular traffic

                  Including parking facilities

                  Class traffic control in 343.0946

.098 3   *Rail transit systems

                  Surface, subsurface, elevated

*Add as instructed under 342–347

.099	*Communications

Class here mass media law

Class censorship in 344.0531; class criminal libel in 345.0256; class libel as a tort in 346.034

.099 2	*Postal service

Class postal offenses in 345.0236

.099 23	*Postal rates

.099 25	*Postal organization

Including routes

.099 4	*Telecommunication

Including telegraph

.099 43	*Telephone

Class radiotelephony in 343.09945

.099 44	*Computer communications

Class comprehensive works on computer law in 343.0999

.099 45	*Radio

Including radiotelephony, comprehensive works on fairness doctrine

Class here wireless communication

For fairness doctrine related to television, see 343.09946

.099 46	*Television

Including cable television

.099 8	*Press law

Class here publishing law

Class freedom of the press in 342.0853

.099 9	*Information storage and retrieval

Class here comprehensive works on computer law

For a specific aspect of computer law, see the aspect in 342–347, e.g., invasion of privacy 342.0858

*Add as instructed under 342–347

.1 **Socioeconomic regions**

Add to base number 343.1 the numbers following —17 in notation 171–177 from Table 2, e.g., miscellaneous public law of developing countries 343.124, miscellaneous public law of Islamic countries, miscellaneous Islamic public law 343.167; then to the result add as follows:

001–009   Standard subdivisions

Notation from Table 1 as modified under 342–347

01–09   Topics of military, defense, public property, public finance, tax, commerce (trade), industrial law

Add the numbers following 343 in 343.01–343.09, e.g., tax law of developing countries 343.12404, tax law of Islamic countries 343.16704, administrative regulations on taxes of developing countries 343.1240402636, administrative regulations on taxes of Islamic countries 343.1670402636

Class socioeconomic regions of a specific regional intergovernmental organization in 343.2; class socioeconomic regions of a specific jurisdiction or area in 343.3–343.9

(If option B under 342–349 is chosen, class here law of socioeconomic regions by adding to base number 343.1 the numbers following —17 in notation 171–177 from Table 2, e.g., law of developing countries 343.124, then adding facet indicator 0*, notation for the branch of law, and notation for the subordinate subject in branch of law, e.g., private law of developing countries 343.12406, banking law of developing countries 343.1240682)

.167   Regions where Islam predominates

Number built according to instructions under 343.1

(.167 1–.167 3)   Schools of Islamic law

(Optional numbers; prefer 343.167)

Add to base number 343.167 the numbers following 297.14018 in notation 297.140181–297.140183, e.g., Islamic miscellaneous public law according to Ḥanbalī school 343.16714; then to the result add as instructed under 343.1, e.g., Islamic tax law according to Ḥanbalī school 343.1671404

(.167 4)   Mixed schools of Islamic law and comparative treatment

Class here works comparing authors affiliated with different schools (e.g., Sunni and Shīʿī schools)

(Optional number; prefer 343.167)

[.167 8]   Regions where specific Islamic sects and reform movements predominate

Do not use; class in 343.167

*Add 00 for standard subdivisions; see instructions at beginning of Table 1

.2   Regional intergovernmental organizations

Class here relationship between the organization's law and national law of member countries

Add to base number 343.2 notation 3–9 from Table 2, e.g., miscellaneous public law of European Union 343.24; then to the result add as follows:

001–009	Standard subdivisions
	Notation from Table 1 as modified in notation 01–09 from table under 342–347
01–09	Topics of military, defense, public property, public finance, tax, commerce (trade), industrial law
	Add the numbers following 343 in 343.01–343.09, e.g., economic law of European Union 343.2407, administrative regulations of economic law of European Union 343.240702636

Class relationship of organization's law and national law of a specific member country with the national law in 343.3–343.9, e.g., effect of European Union laws on national economic law of Germany 343.43

See Manual at 342–349

(If option B under 342–349 is chosen, class here law of regional intergovernmental organizations by adding to base number 343.2 notation 4–9 from Table 2, e.g., law of the European Union 343.24, then adding facet indicator 0*, notation for the branch of law, and notation for the subordinate subject in branch of law, e.g., private law of the European Union 343.2406, banking law of the European Union 343.240682)

.240 7   Regulation of economic activity

Number built according to instructions under 343.2

Class here comprehensive works on Four Freedoms of European Union

For a specific aspect of the Four Freedoms, see the aspect, e.g., prohibition of customs duties on goods moving from one country to another within European Union 343.24056

.3–.9   Specific jurisdictions and areas

Add to base number 343 notation 3–9 from Table 2, e.g., miscellaneous public law of Australia 343.94, of New South Wales 343.944, of African states 343.6; then to the result add as follows:

001–009	Standard subdivisions
01–09	Topics of military, defense, public property, public finance, tax, commerce (trade), industrial law
	Add the numbers following 343 in 343.01–343.09, e.g., tax law of Australia 343.9404, of New South Wales 343.94404, of African states 343.604, administrative regulations on taxes of Australia 343.940402636

For regional intergovernmental organizations, relationship between the organization's laws and national laws of all member states, see 343.2

See Manual at 342–349

.730 43

---

*Add 00 for standard subdivisions; see instructions at beginning of Table 1

344 Labor, social service, education, cultural law

SUMMARY

.001–.008   Standard subdivisions

> Notation from Table 1 as modified in notation 01–08 from table under 342–347, e.g., cases 344.00264

.009   History, geographic treatment, biography

[.009 17]   Socioeconomic regions

> Do not use; class in 344.1

[.009 3–.009 9]   Specific continents, countries, localities

> Do not use; class in 344.3–344.9

.01   *Labor

> Class here social law, social legislation

> *For social insurance, see 344.02; for public welfare, see 344.0316*

.010 1   Philosophy and theory

> Including job and labor rights

.011–.018   Specific aspects of labor

> Add to base number 344.01 the numbers following 331 in 331.1–331.8, e.g., child labor law 344.0131; then add further as instructed under 342–347, e.g., cases involving child labor law 344.01310264; however, for government officials and employees, see 342.068; for military personnel, see 343.013–343.019; for medical personnel, see 344.041; for certification and licensing of teachers, see 344.078

*Add as instructed under 342–347

.02   *Government-sponsored insurance

Class here social insurance

Class comprehensive works on insurance in 346.086

> *For a type of government-sponsored insurance not provided for here, see the type in 346.0861–346.0868, e.g., crop insurance 346.086121, bank deposit insurance 346.086854*
>
> *See also 344.03 for social service law; also 343.05242 for social security taxes*
>
> *See Manual at 363 vs. 344.02–344.05, 353–354*

.021   *Workers' compensation insurance (Workmen's compensation insurance)

Class disability compensation for veterans in 343.0116

.021 7   Occupations and industries

Class disabilities and injuries in specific occupations and industries in 344.0218

.021 8   Disabilities and injuries

.022   *Health and accident insurance

Subdivisions are added for health and accident insurance together, for health insurance alone

Class health benefits for veterans in 343.0115

> *For workers' compensation insurance, see 344.021*

[.022 084 6]   Insurance for people in late adulthood

Do not use; class in 344.0226

.022 4   *Maternity insurance

.022 6   *Accident and health insurance for people in late adulthood

.023   *Old age and survivors' insurance

Class accident and health insurance for people in late adulthood in 344.0226

.024   *Unemployment insurance

.028   *Insurance against crimes of violence

.03   *Social service

> *For social insurance, see 344.02; for miscellaneous social problems and services, see 344.04; for police services, other aspects of public safety, matters concerning public morals and customs, see 344.05; for public works, see 344.06; for insurance, see 346.086*
>
> *See Manual at 363 vs. 344.02–344.05, 353–354*

---

*Add as instructed under 342–347

.031 Specific topics of social service in general

Class specific topics of a specific social problem or service in 344.032–344.035

[.031 001–.031 009] Standard subdivisions

Do not use; class in 344.0301–344.0309

.031 02–.031 06 Subdivisions for specific kinds of assistance in social service in general

Add to base number 344.031 the numbers following 361 in 361.02–361.06, e.g., laws governing counseling 344.03106; then add further as instructed under 342–347, e.g., cases involving counseling 344.031060264

.031 1–.031 8 Social problems and social action

Add to base number 344.031 the numbers following 361 in 361.1–361.8, e.g., laws governing charitable trusts 344.0317632; then add further as instructed under 342–347, e.g., cases involving charitable trusts 344.03176320264

.032 Social welfare problems and services

.032 01 Philosophy and theory

Notation 01 from Table 1 as modified in notation 01 from table under 342–347, e.g., sources of law 344.032011

.032 02 Miscellany

Notation 02 from Table 1 as modified in notation 02 from table under 342–347, e.g., cases 344.0320264

.032 03 Dictionaries, encyclopedias, concordances

.032 04 Special topics of social problems of and services to groups of people

Add to base number 344.03204 the numbers following 362.04, e.g., social action law 344.0320425; then add further as instructed under 342–347, e.g., cases involving social action law 344.03204250264

.032 05–.032 07 Standard subdivisions

Notation from Table 1 as modified in notation 05–07 from table under 342–347

[.032 08] Groups of people

Do not use; class in 344.0321–344.0328

.032 09 History, geographic treatment, biography

Notation 09 from Table 1 as modified in notation 09 from table under 342–347

.032 1–.032 8   Specific social welfare problems and services

Add to base number 344.032 the numbers following 362 in 362.1–362.8, e.g., child welfare law 344.0327; then add further as instructed under 342–347, e.g., cases involving child welfare 344.03270264; however, for veterans' welfare, see 343.011; for comprehensive works on public health, see 344.04; for medical personnel and their activities, see 344.041; for mental and emotional illnesses and disturbances, see 344.044; for adoption, see 346.0178

.033   *Food supply

.035   *Penal institutions

.035 3–.035 7   Specific aspects of penal institutions

Add to base number 344.035 the numbers following 365 in 365.3–365.7, e.g., law governing convict labor 344.03565; then add further as instructed under 342–347, e.g., cases involving convict labor 344.035650264

.04   Miscellaneous social problems and services

Only those named below

Class here comprehensive works on public health

For an aspect of public health not provided for here, see the aspect, e.g., emergency medical services 344.03218

See Manual at 363 vs. 344.02–344.05, 353–354

SUMMARY

344.041	**Medical personnel and their activities**
.042	**Product control**
.043	**Control of disease**
.044	**Mental health services and services to substance abusers**
.045	**Disposal of dead**
.046	**Environmental protection**
.047	**Safety**
.048	**Population control**
.049	**Veterinary public health**

.041   *Medical personnel and their activities

Subdivisions are added for either or both topics in heading

Class military medicine in 343.013; class medical institutions and their services in 344.03211–344.03216

For control of disease, see 344.043

.041 1   *Medical malpractice

Class medical malpractice by a specific kind of medical personnel in 344.0412–344.0416; class medical malpractice related to a specific medical problem in 344.0419

See also 344.03211 for malpractice by hospitals and other medical institutions

*Add as instructed under 342–347

> 　　　　　344.041 2–344.041 6 Specific medical personnel and their activities

　　　　　Class a specific type of medical personnel involved with specific problems in 344.0419; class comprehensive works in 344.041

.041 2　　　　　　　*Physicians and their activities

　　　　　　　　Including informed consent

　　　　　　　　Subdivisions are added for either or both topics in heading

.041 21　　　　　　　　*Malpractice

　　　　　　　　Works specifically emphasizing physicians

.041 3　　　　　　　*Dentists and dentistry

　　　　　　　　Including dental assistants, dental technicians

　　　　　　　　Subdivisions are added for either or both topics in heading

.041 4　　　　　　　*Nurses and nursing

　　　　　　　　Subdivisions are added for either or both topics in heading

.041 5　　　　　　　*Midwives and midwifery

　　　　　　　　Subdivisions are added for either or both topics in heading

.041 6　　　　　　　*Pharmacists and pharmacy

　　　　　　　　Subdivisions are added for either or both topics in heading

.041 9　　　　　　　Problems in medical practice

.041 92　　　　　　　　*Abortion

　　　　　　　　Class comprehensive works in 342.084

.041 94　　　　　　　　*Oversight of the human body and its parts

　　　　　　　　Including blood transfusion, organ donation, transplants

　　　　　　　　Class rights regarding frozen embryos in 346.0171

.041 96　　　　　　　　*Human experimentation

　　　　　　　　Including medical genetics

.041 97　　　　　　　　*Terminal care

　　　　　　　　Class here euthanasia, right to die

.042　　　　　　*Product control

　　　　　　Including recall of unsafe products

　　　　　　For motor vehicle recall, see 343.0944

.042 3　　　　　　*Food, drugs, cosmetics, clothing, toys

*Add as instructed under 342–347

.042 32   *Food

                         Including food additives

.042 33   *Drugs

.042 35   *Clothing and toys

.042 4   *Chemicals

                         Class food additives, drugs, cosmetics in 344.0423

.043   *Control of disease

                         Including control of carriers, quarantine, immunization measures

                         Class control of carriers, quarantine, immunization measures of a specific disease in 344.0436–344.0438

.043 6–.043 8   Control of specific diseases

                         Add to base number 344.043 the numbers following 61 in 616–618, e.g., control of AIDS 344.04369792; then add further as instructed under 342–347, e.g., cases involving control of AIDS 344.043697920264; however, for control of mental diseases, see 344.044

.044   *Mental health services and services to substance abusers

                         Subdivisions are added for mental health services and services to substance abusers together, for mental health services alone

                         Class capacity and status of persons with mental illness and disabilities in 346.0130874

.044 6   *Services to substance abusers

                         Class here addiction

.044 61   *Alcoholics

                         Class control of trade in alcoholic beverages in 344.0541

.044 63–.044 69   Other kinds of substance abusers

                         Add to base number 344.0446 the numbers following 362.29 in 362.293–362.299 for the substance only, e.g., heroin abusers 344.04463; then add further as instructed under 342–347, e.g., cases involving heroin abusers 344.044630264

                         Class control of drug traffic in 344.0545

.045   *Disposal of dead

*Add as instructed under 342–347

.046	*Environmental protection

Class here liability for environmental damages, comprehensive works on environmental law

Class conservation of natural resources in 346.044

For an aspect of environmental law not provided for here, see the aspect, e.g., government control and regulation of natural resources 346.044

.046 2	*Wastes

Including recycling

Class here waste disposal, management

.046 22	Kinds of waste

Including sewage; animal, chemical, solid wastes

Class disposal of specific kinds of wastes into specific environments in 344.04626

.046 26	Disposal into specific environments

Including dumping into oceans

.046 3	*Pollution and noise
.046 32	*Pollution

Class waste disposal in 344.0462

For pollutants, see 344.04633; for pollution of specific environments, see 344.04634

.046 33	*Pollutants
.046 332	*Oil
.046 334	*Pesticides
.046 335	*Asbestos
.046 336	*Acid rain
.046 34	Pollution of specific environments

Including soil pollution

Class pollution of specific environments by specific pollutants in 344.04633

.046 342	*Air pollution
.046 343	*Water pollution
.046 38	*Noise

*Add as instructed under 342–347

.046 4	*Sanitation in places of public assembly
	Including hotels
	For industrial sanitation, see 344.0465
.046 5	*Industrial sanitation and safety
.047	*Safety

For transportation safety, see 343.0938; for product safety, see 344.042; for industrial safety, see 344.0465; for other aspects of public safety, see 344.053

| .047 2 | *Safety in use of hazardous materials and devices |

Class safety in use of hazardous materials in industry in 344.0465

| .047 6 | *Safety in recreation |
| .048 | *Population control |

Class here birth control

| .049 | *Veterinary public health |

Including animal welfare, humane law

| .05 | Police services, other aspects of public safety, matters concerning public morals and customs |

See Manual at 363 vs. 344.02–344.05, 353–354

| .052–.053 | Police services, other aspects of public safety |

Add to base number 344.05 the numbers following 363 in 363.2–363.3, e.g., disasters 344.0534, civil defense 344.0535, fire protection 344.0537; then add further as instructed under 342–347, e.g., cases involving fire protection 344.05370264; however, for criminal investigation and law enforcement, see 345.052

Class comprehensive works on public safety in 344.047

.054	Matters concerning public morals and customs
.054 1	*Alcoholic beverages
.054 2	*Gambling
.054 4	*Prostitution
.054 5	*Drug traffic
.054 6	*Abortion
.054 7	*Obscenity and pornography
.06	Public works

Public programs not provided for elsewhere

*Add as instructed under 342–347

.060 001–.060 009	Standard subdivisions

Notation from Table 1 as modified in notation 01–09 from table under 342–347, e.g., cases 344.06000264

.060 01–.069 99	Specific kinds of public works

Add to base number 344.06 notation 001–999, e.g., public housing 344.063635; then add further as instructed under 342–347, e.g., cases involving public housing 344.0636350264

.07	*Education

Class here schools

Unless other instructions are given, class a subject with aspects in two or more subdivisions of 344.07 in the number coming last, e.g., finance of primary public schools by local governments 344.07682 (*not* 344.074, 344.073, or 344.071)

For educational exchanges, see 344.08

> 344.071–344.074 Kinds of education

Class comprehensive works in 344.07

.071	*Public education
.072	*Private education
.073	Education by level of government

National, state, local

.074	Education by level of education

Primary, secondary, higher, adult

.075	*Liability of schools, of school officials, of school districts
.076	*Finance

Public and private education

Class financial aid to students in 344.0795

.076 2	*Financial resources

Including investments, natural resources, tax receipts

For aid to education, see 344.0763

.076 3	*Aid to education by higher levels of government
.076 5	*Expenditure
.076 7	Kinds of schools

Including trade, vocational schools

.076 8	Levels of education and schools

*Add as instructed under 342–347

.076 82	*Preschool and primary education
	Subdivisions are added for preschool and primary education together, for primary education alone
.076 83	*Secondary education
.076 84	*Higher education
.076 85	*Adult education
.076 9	Educational programs
	Including medical and public health education; schools devoted to specific educational programs, e.g., military, merchant marine academies

.077   *Curricula and educational materials

.078   *Teachers and teaching

Including academic freedom

Subdivisions are added for either or both topics in heading

Class employment rights in 344.0101

.079   *Students

Including authority of the law over students, compulsory education, right to education

.079 1	*Education of specific groups of students
	Class here special education
	Class finance in 344.0769
.079 11–.079 15	Specific groups of students
	Add to base number 344.0791 the numbers following 371.9 in 371.91–371.95, e.g., education of students with visual impairments 344.079111; then add further as instructed under 342–347, e.g., cases involving education of students with visual impairments 344.0791110264
.079 2	*Attendance
	Including school year and day, truancy
.079 3	*Discipline and student rights
	See also 342.085 for general rights of students
.079 4	*Student services
	Including counseling
.079 42	*School lunch programs
.079 5	*Financial aid to students
	Including loans, scholarships

*Add as instructed under 342–347

.079 6	*Religion and the student
	Including prayer in public schools
.079 8	*Segregation and discrimination
.08	*Educational and cultural exchanges
.09	*Culture and religion

Including information exchange, flag code, language code (the official language or languages of a specific jurisdiction)

Subdivisions are added for culture and religion together, for culture alone

For education, see 344.07; for educational and cultural exchanges, see 344.08

.091	*Historic commemoration and patriotic events

Subdivisions are added for either or both topics in heading

Class commemorative medals and coins that are legal tender in 343.032

.092	*Libraries and archives

Subdivisions are added for either or both topics in heading

.093	*Museums and galleries

Subdivisions are added for either or both topics in heading

.094	*Historic preservation

Including archaeology, antiquities

Class here historical buildings, monuments

Class historic commemoration and patriotic events in 344.091

.095	*Science and technology

Subdivisions are added for either or both topics in heading

.095 2	*Astronomy and space research

Subdivisions are added for either or both topics in heading

.095 3	*Physics and applied physics

Subdivisions are added for either or both topics in heading

.095 4	*Chemistry and chemical technology

Subdivisions are added for either or both topics in heading

.095 5	*Geology

Including weather control, meteorology, oceanography

.095 7	*Agriculture and biology

Subdivisions are added for either or both topics in heading

*Add as instructed under 342–347

.096   *Religion

.097   *Arts and humanities

> *For museums and galleries, see 344.093*

.099   *Amusements

> Including sports law; comprehensive works on gambling
>
> Class here recreation law
>
> Class arts and humanities in 344.097
>
> *For gambling as a social problem, see 344.0542*

.1   Socioeconomic regions

> Add to base number 344.1 the numbers following —17 in notation 171–177
> from Table 2, e.g., social law of developing countries 344.124, social law of
> Islamic countries, Islamic social law 344.167; then to the result add as follows:
>
> 001–009   Standard subdivisions
>   Notation from Table 1 as modified under 342–347
> 01–09   Topics of labor, social service, education, cultural law
>   Add the numbers following 344 in 344.01–344.09, e.g., labor
>   law of developing countries 344.12401, labor law of Islamic
>   countries 344.17601, administrative regulations on labor
>   in developing countries 344.1240102636, administrative
>   regulations on labor in Islamic countries 344.1670102636

> Class socioeconomic regions of a specific regional intergovernmental
> organization in 344.2; class socioeconomic regions of a specific jurisdiction or
> area in 344.3–344.9

.167   Regions where Islam predominates

> Number built according to instructions under 344.1

(.167 1–.167 3)   Schools of Islamic law

> (Optional numbers; prefer 344.167)
>
> Add to base number 344.167 the numbers following 297.14018 in
> notation 297.140181–297.140183, e.g., Islamic social law according
> to Shāfiʿī school 344.16712; then to the result add as instructed under
> 344.1, e.g., Islamic social service law according to Shāfiʿī school
> 344.1671203

(.167 4)   Mixed schools of Islamic law and comparative treatment

> Class here works comparing authors affiliated with different schools
> (e.g., Sunni and Shīʿī schools)
>
> (Optional number; prefer 344.167)

[.167 8]   Regions where specific Islamic sects and reform movements predominate

> Do not use; class in 344.167

---

*Add as instructed under 342–347

.2 **Regional intergovernmental organizations**

Class here relationship between the organization's law and national law of member countries

Add to base number 344.2 notation 3–9 from Table 2, e.g., social law of European Union 344.24; then to the result add as follows:
001–009 Standard subdivisions
Notation from Table 1 as modified in notation 01–09 from table under 342–347
01–09 Topics of labor, social service, education, cultural law
Add the numbers following 344 in 344.01–344.09, e.g., labor law of European Union 344.2401, administrative regulations of labor law of European Union 344.240102636

Class relationship of organization's law and national law of a specific member country with the national law in 344.3–344.9, e.g., effect of European Union laws on national social law of France 344.44

See Manual at 342–349

.3–.9 **Specific jurisdictions and areas**

Add to base number 344 notation 3–9 from Table 2, e.g., social law of Australia 344.94, of New South Wales 344.944, of African states 344.6; then to the result add as follows:
001–009 Standard subdivisions
Notation from Table 1 as modified in notation 01–09 from table under 342–347
01–09 Topics of labor, social service, education, cultural law
Add the numbers following 344 in 344.01–344.09, e.g., labor law of Australia 344.9401, of New South Wales 344.94401, of African states 344.601, administrative regulations on labor in Australia 344.940102636

For regional intergovernmental organizations, relationship between the organization's laws and national laws of all member states, see 344.2

See Manual at 342–349

345 Criminal law

Class here international criminal law

Class comprehensive works on civil and criminal procedure and courts in 347; class interdisciplinary works on criminal justice in 364. Class civil actions linked to crimes with the subject in 342–344 or 346–347, e.g., employers' civil tort liability 346.031

SUMMARY

345.001–.009	Standard subdivisions; laws, regulations, cases, procedure, courts
.01	Criminal courts
.02	Criminal offenses
.03	Offenders
.04	Liability, responsibility, guilt
.05	Criminal procedure
.06	Evidence
.07	Trials
.08	Juvenile procedure and courts
.1	Socioeconomic regions
.2	Regional intergovernmental organizations
.3–.9	Specific jurisdictions and areas

.001–.008   Standard subdivisions

> Notation from Table 1 as modified in notation 01–08 from table under 342–347, e.g., cases 345.00264

.009   History, geographic treatment, biography

[.009 17]   Socioeconomic regions

> Do not use; class in 345.1

[.009 3–.009 9]   Specific continents, countries, localities

> Do not use; class in 345.3–345.9

.01   *Criminal courts

> Courts specializing in criminal cases, general and other specialized courts considered with respect to their functions in criminal cases

> Class appellate courts hearing both civil and criminal cases in 347.03

> *For juvenile courts, see 345.081*

.012   General considerations, administration and personnel, legal aid

.012 2   *General considerations of criminal courts

> Including criminal jurisdiction, judicial cooperation in criminal cases, judicial discretion, judicial error, judicial review, letters rogatory

.012 3   *Judicial administration of criminal courts

> *For judges, see 345.0124; for court officials other than judges, see 345.0126*

.012 4   *Criminal court judges

> Class judges associated with a specific criminal court with the court, e.g., judges of a juvenile court 345.081

.012 6   Other criminal court officials

> Including coroners

*Add as instructed under 342–347

.012 62	*Public prosecutors
	Class here district attorneys
.012 63	*Public defenders
.012 7	*Legal aid in criminal cases
	Class legal aid as a welfare service, interdisciplinary works on legal aid in 362.58

.014 Criminal courts with specific kinds of jurisdiction

Add to each subdivision identified by † as follows:

01–09		Standard subdivisions
		Notation from Table 1 as modified under 342–347, e.g., cases 0264
2		General considerations
		Including functions, jurisdiction, organization, powers
3		Judicial administration
34		Judges
36		Other criminal court officials
		Including coroners
362		Public prosecutors
		Class here district attorneys
363		Public defenders
5		Procedure
		For evidence, see 345.06; for trials, see 345.07; for juvenile procedure, see 345.08
504		Special topics of criminal procedure
		Add to 504 the numbers following 345.0504 in 345.05042–345.05044, e.g., prosecution 5042
52–56		Criminal investigation and law enforcement, rights of suspects
		Add to 5 the numbers following 345.05 in 345.052–345.056, e.g., rights of suspects 56

.014 2	†Courts with original jurisdiction
	Class here courts of first instance, local courts, trial courts
.014 4	†Appellate courts
	Class here comprehensive works on appellate procedure in criminal cases
	For appellate courts with specialized jurisdiction, see 345.0148
.014 42	†Intermediate appellate courts
	Class here courts of second instance, courts of first appeal
.014 44	†Courts of last resort (Supreme courts)
	Class here courts of third instance, courts of second appeal, courts of final appeal

*Add as instructed under 342–347
†Add as instructed under 345.014

.014 8   †Courts with specialized jurisdiction

Class courts dealing with a specific subject with the subject in 342–347, plus notation 0269 from table under 342–347 if needed, e.g., military courts 343.0143

>   345.02–345.04   General considerations

Class comprehensive works in 345

.02   *Criminal offenses

Class here contraventions, crimes, crimes without victims

See Manual at 345.02 vs. 346.03

.023–.028   Specific crimes and classes of crime

Class here specific trials of specific crimes and classes of crime, e.g., trials of offenses against the person 345.025, a specific trial for murder 345.02523

Add to base number 345.02 the numbers following 364.1 in 364.13–364.18, e.g., terrorism 345.02317, genocide 345.0251, hijacking 345.02552, piracy 345.0264, drug traffic 345.0277, white collar crime 345.0268; then add further as instructed under 342–347, e.g., court decisions on white collar crime 345.026802643

Class defenses for a specific crime in 345.04

.03   *Offenders

Including juvenile delinquents

Class here criminals

.04   *Liability, responsibility, guilt

Including criminal capacity; criminal intent; double jeopardy; defenses, e.g., duress; defenses for a specific crime, e.g., self-defense

Subdivisions are added for any or all topics in heading

See also 345.05044 for defense

*Add as instructed under 342–347
†Add as instructed under 345.014

.05	*Criminal procedure

Including legal costs and fees

Class here administration of criminal justice, court rules, participants in criminal proceedings

Class procedure in specific courts devoted exclusively to criminal cases in 345.01; class procedure in specific courts hearing both civil and criminal cases in 347.02–347.04. Class participants in criminal proceedings provided for elsewhere with the subject, e.g., criminal court judges 345.0124, witnesses 345.066

For evidence, see 345.06; for trials and trial procedures, see 345.07; for juvenile procedure, see 345.08

.050 4	Special topics of criminal procedure
.050 42	*Prosecution

Including prosecutorial discretion

Class district attorneys, public prosecutors in 345.01262

.050 44	*Defense

Class public defenders in 345.01263; class defenses in 345.04; class right to counsel in 345.056

.050 46	*Victims of crime

Class a specific role of victims in criminal procedure with the role, e.g., witness 345.066; class a specific use of victim impact statements with the use, e.g., use of victim impact statements at sentencing 345.0772. Class social services for victims of crime in 362.88

.052	*Criminal investigation and law enforcement

Including extradition, judicial assistance

Class here Interpol, manuals on what police may legally do in course of carrying out their duties

Class rights of suspects in 345.056; class admissibility of evidence in 345.062

.052 2	*Search and seizure

Subdivisions are added for either or both topics in heading

.052 7	*Arrest

Including preventive detention

See also 346.0334 for false arrest

---

*Add as instructed under 342–347

.056		*Rights of suspects

Including habeas corpus, jury trial, protection from self-incrimination, right to counsel

Class legal aid in 345.0127

.06		*Evidence

Including confessions

.062–.067		Specific aspects of evidence

Add to base number 345.06 the numbers following 347.06 in 347.062–347.067, e.g., admissibility of evidence 345.062; then add further as instructed under 342–347, e.g., cases involving admissibility of evidence 345.0620264

.07		*Trials

Class trials of specific offenses in 345.02; class hearings and trials in juvenile cases in 345.087; class comprehensive works on criminal procedure in 345.05; class comprehensive works on appellate procedure in criminal cases in 345.0144

.072		*Pretrial procedure

Including arraignment, discovery, grand jury proceedings, indictment, plea bargaining, pleading, preliminary hearings, pretrial release, summons

.075		*Trial procedure (Courtroom procedure)

Including juries and jury selection, examination of witnesses, instructions to juries, verdicts

For final disposition of cases, see 345.077

.077		*Final disposition of cases

Including pardon, parole, probation, rehabilitation

.077 2		*Sentencing

For penalties, see 345.0773

.077 3		*Penalties

Including death penalty

.08		*Juvenile procedure and courts

Subdivisions are added for procedure and courts together, for procedure alone

Class juvenile offenders in 345.03; class liability, responsibility, guilt of juveniles in 345.04

.081		*Juvenile courts
.087		*Hearings, trials, disposition of cases

*Add as instructed under 342–347

.1 **Socioeconomic regions**

> Add to base number 345.1 the numbers following —17 in notation 171–177
> from Table 2, e.g., criminal law of developing countries 345.124, criminal law
> of Islamic countries, Islamic criminal law 345.167; then to the result add as
> follows:
>
> > 001–009 Standard subdivisions
> > > Notation from Table 1 as modified under 342–347
> > 01–08 Topics of criminal law
> > > Add the numbers following 345 in 345.01–345.08, e.g., the
> > > law of evidence in developing countries 345.12406, the law
> > > of evidence in Islamic countries, Islamic law of evidence
> > > 345.16706, decisions on evidence in developing countries
> > > 345.1240602643, decisions on evidence in Islamic countries
> > > 345.1670602643
>
> Class socioeconomic regions of a specific regional intergovernmental
> organization in 345.2; class socioeconomic regions of a specific jurisdiction or
> area in 345.3–345.9

.167 **Regions where Islam predominates**

> Number built according to instructions under 345.1

> Class here Islamic criminal law

(.167 1–.167 3) Schools of Islamic law

> (Optional numbers; prefer 345.167)

> Add to base number 345.167 the numbers following 297.14018
> in notation 297.140181–297.140183, e.g., Islamic criminal law
> according to Ḥanafī school 345.16711; then to the result add as
> instructed under 345.1, e.g., Islamic criminal law concerning theft
> according to Ḥanafī school 345.167110262

(.167 4) Mixed schools of Islamic law and comparative treatment

> Class here works comparing authors affiliated with different schools
> (e.g., Sunni and Shīʿī schools)

> (Optional number; prefer 345.167)

[.167 8] Regions where specific Islamic sects and reform movements predominate

> Do not use; class in 345.167

.2   Regional intergovernmental organizations

Class here relationship between the organization's law and national law of member countries

Add to base number 345.2 notation 3–9 from Table 2, e.g., criminal law of European Union 345.24; then to the result add as follows:

001–009   Standard subdivisions
> Notation from Table 1 as modified in notation 01–09 from table under 342–347

01–08   Topics of criminal law
> Add the numbers following 345 in 345.01–345.08, e.g., law of evidence of European Union 345.2406, administrative regulations of law of evidence of European Union 345.240602636

Class relationship of organization's law and national law of a specific member country with the national law in 345.3–345.9, e.g., effect of European Union laws on national criminal law of Spain 345.46

See Manual at 342–349

.3–.9   Specific jurisdictions and areas

Add to base number 345 notation 3–9 from Table 2, e.g., criminal law of Australia 345.94, of New South Wales 345.944, of African states 345.6; then to the result add as follows:

001–009   Standard subdivisions
> Notation from Table 1 as modified in notation 01–09 from table under 342–347

01–08   Topics of criminal law
> Add the numbers following 345 in 345.01–345.08, e.g., the law of evidence in Australia 345.9406, in New South Wales 345.94406, in African states 345.606, decisions on evidence in Australia 345.940602643

For regional intergovernmental organizations, relationship between the organization's laws and national laws of all member states, see 345.2

See Manual at 342–349

Special developments for Scotland and England follow

.411   Criminal law of Scotland

.411 001–.411 009   Standard subdivisions

.411 01   *Criminal courts

Including Crown Counsel, Lord Advocate, Solicitor-General; procurators fiscal

Class here appellate courts devoted exclusively to criminal cases

Class appellate courts hearing both civil and criminal cases in 347.41103

For Children's Hearings (juvenile courts), see 345.41108

.411 012   *District Court

---

*Add as instructed under 342–347

.411 014	*Sheriff Court
.411 016	*High Court of Justiciary
.411 016 2	*Court of First Instance
.411 016 3	*Court of Appeal
.411 02–.411 07	General considerations and procedure

Add to base number 345.4110 the numbers following 345.0 in 345.02–345.07, e.g., general criminal procedure 345.41105

.411 08	*Juvenile procedure

Including Children's Hearings (juvenile courts)

Class juvenile offenders in 345.41103; class liability, responsibility, guilt of juveniles in 345.41104

.42	Criminal law of England
.420 01–.420 09	Standard subdivisions
.420 1	*Criminal courts

Including Attorney-General, Director of Public Prosecutions

Class here appellate courts devoted exclusively to criminal cases

Class appellate courts hearing both civil and criminal cases in 347.4203

For juvenile courts, see 345.42081

.420 12	*Magistrates Court

For civil jurisdiction of Magistrates Court, see 347.42023

.420 14	*Crown Court
.420 16	*Divisional Court of Queen's Bench Division of High Court of Justice
.420 18	*Criminal Division of Court of Appeal
.420 2–.420 8	General considerations, procedure, juvenile courts and procedure

Add to base number 345.420 the numbers following 345.0 in 345.02–345.08, e.g., juvenile courts 345.42081

346 Private law

See also 340.9 for private international law

*Add as instructed under 342–347

SUMMARY

346.001–.009	Standard subdivisions; laws, regulations, cases, procedure, courts; equity
.01	Persons and domestic relations
.02	Juristic acts, contracts, agency
.03	Torts (Delicts)
.04	Property
.05	Inheritance, succession, fiduciary trusts, trustees
.06	Organizations (Associations)
.07	Commercial law
.08	Banks and insurance
.09	Investment and negotiable instruments
.1	Socioeconomic regions
.2	Regional intergovernmental organizations
.3–.9	Specific jurisdictions and areas

.001   Philosophy and theory

> Notation 01 from Table 1 as modified in notation 01 from table under 342–347, e.g., sources of law 346.0011

.002   Miscellany

> Notation 02 from Table 1 as modified below and under 342–347, e.g., cases 346.00264

.002 3   Private law as a profession, occupation, hobby

> Class here nature of duties, characteristics of profession of civil-law notaries, of other notaries required to have legal education

> Class lay notaries in 347.016. Class works that emphasize procedures of work performed by notaries with the subject without adding notation 023 from Table 1, e.g., private international law 340.9, transfer of real property 346.0436

.003   Dictionaries, encyclopedias, concordances

.004   *Equity

.005–.008   Standard subdivisions

.009   History, geographic treatment, biography

[.009 17]   Socioeconomic regions

> Do not use; class in 346.1

[.009 3–.009 9]   Specific continents, countries, localities

> Do not use; class in 346.3–346.9

.01   *Persons and domestic relations

.012   *Persons

> Including names of persons

> *For capacity and status of persons, see 346.013*

> *See also 346.048 for business names*

*Add as instructed under 342–347

.013   *Capacity and status of persons

> Capacity: the attribute of persons (personal or corporate) which enables them to perform civil or juristic acts

> Subdivisions are added for either or both topics in heading

> Class individual rights in 342.085

.013 08   Groups of people

.013 083   Young people

> Class here minors; age of majority

> *For age of majority in jurisdictions where the age is older than twenty, see the age, e.g., jurisdictions where the age of majority is twenty-one 346.0130842*

.013 086 5   People by marital status

[.013 086 53]   Separated and divorced people

> Do not use for divorced people; class in 346.0166. Do not use for separated people; class in 346.01668

[.013 086 55]   Married people

> Do not use; class in 346.0163

[.013 086 56]   People in partnerships and unions

> Do not use; class in 346.0163

[.013 086 59]   Polygamists

> Do not use; class in 346.0163

.013 086 91   People with status defined by changes in residence

> Class liability of states to aliens in 341.26

.013 086 927   Offenders

> Class the rehabilitation of a criminal's personal rights lost by judicial sentence in 345.077

> *For criminal capacity, see 345.04*

.015   *Domestic relations (Family law)

> Class here comprehensive works on domestic relations and inheritance and succession

> *For marriage, partnerships, unions, see 346.016; for parent and child, see 346.017; for inheritance and succession, see 346.052*

*Add as instructed under 342–347

.016   *Marriage, partnerships, unions

Subdivisions are added for marriage, partnerships, unions together; for marriage alone

Unless other instructions are given, observe the following table of preference, e.g., same-sex divorce 346.0166 (*not* 346.0168):

Divorce, dissolution, annulment, separation	346.0166
Spouses	346.0163
Actions before marriage, partnerships, unions; requirements for validity	346.0162
Same-sex marriages, partnerships, unions	346.0168
Interethnic marriages, partnerships, unions	346.016764
Interreligious marriages, partnerships, unions	346.016762
Marriages, partnerships, unions by number of spouses	346.01672
Temporary marriages, partnerships, unions	346.01677
Partnerships and unions; common-law marriages	346.01671

Class comprehensive works about a specific kind of marriage, partnership, union with the kind in 346.0167–346.0168, e.g., same-sex marriage and divorce 346.0168

.016 089   Ethnic and national groups

Do not use for interethnic marriages, partnerships, unions; interracial marriages, partnerships, unions; marriages, partnerships, unions between citizens of different countries; class in 346.016764

.016 2   *Actions before marriage, partnerships, unions; requirements for validity

Including courtship, engagement; arranged marriage, dowry, marriage contracts; minimum age, consent, lack of impediments

For prenuptial and related contracts concerning dissolution of marriage, partnerships, unions; prenuptial and related contracts concerning death of a spouse or member of a partnership or union, see 346.01662

See also 345.0254 for forced marriage in criminal law

.016 3   *Spouses

Rights and duties, capacity and status

Class here husband and wife, married people, people with the same rights and duties as spouses

*Add as instructed under 342–347

.016 6   *Divorce, dissolution, annulment, separation

> Subdivisions are added for divorce, dissolution, annulment, separation together; for divorce alone; for dissolution alone

> Class comprehensive works about a specific kind of marriage, partnership, union that includes divorce with the kind in 346.0167–346.0168, e.g., interethnic marriages, partnerships, unions and divorce or dissolution of interethnic marriages, partnerships, unions 346.016764

\>   346.016 62–346.016 64   Specific aspects of divorce, dissolution, annulment, separation

Class comprehensive works in 346.0166

For specific aspects of annulment, see 346.01665; for specific aspects of separation, see 346.01668

.016 62   *Prenuptial contracts (Antenuptial contracts)

> Class here contracts concerning dissolution of partnerships and unions, contracts concerning death of a spouse or member of a partnership or union

> Class contracts made before marriage that apply to ongoing marriages, partnerships, unions; comprehensive works on contracts that cover both ongoing relationships and dissolution of relationships in 346.0162

> *For support aspects of the contract, see 346.01663; for marital property aspects of the contract, see 346.01664*

.016 63   *Support

> Class here alimony

> *For separate maintenance, see 346.01668; for child support, see 346.0172*

.016 64   *Marital property in divorce, dissolution, annulment, separation

> Including community and separate property in divorce, dissolution, annulment, separation

.016 65   *Annulment

.016 68   *Separation

> Including separate maintenance

.016 7   Specific types of marriages, partnerships, unions

> *For same-sex marriages, partnerships, unions, see 346.0168*

---

*Add as instructed under 342–347

.016 71   *Partnerships and unions; common-law marriages

Subdivisions are added for any or all topics in heading

Class here civil unions, domestic partnerships, registered partnerships; de facto relationships; unmarried couples living together (cohabitation); comprehensive works on partnerships and unions

For a specific kind of partnership or union, see the kind, e.g., interethnic partnerships and unions 346.016764

.016 72   Marriages, partnerships, unions by number of spouses

Limited to works that emphasize number of spouses

Class comprehensive works on marriage that do not emphasize number of spouses in 346.016

See also 345.0283 for bigamy

.016 722   *Monogamous marriages, partnerships, unions

.016 723   *Polygamous marriages, partnerships, unions

Class here polyandry, polygyny

.016 76   *Interreligious marriages, partnerships, unions; interethnic marriages, partnerships, unions

.016 762   *Interreligious marriages, partnerships, unions

Marriages, partnerships, unions in which the partners belong to different religions or different branches of same religion

.016 764   *Interethnic marriages, partnerships, unions

Class here intercultural marriages, partnerships, unions; interracial marriages, partnerships, unions; marriages, partnerships, unions between citizens of different countries

.016 77   *Temporary marriages, partnerships, unions

.016 8   *Same-sex marriages, partnerships, unions

.017   *Parent and child

Including surrogate motherhood

Class here parental rights and duties regardless of marital status of parents

.017 1   *Unborn children

For a specific aspect of unborn children, see the aspect, e.g., rights of fetuses 342.085

.017 2   *Child support

.017 3   *Custody of children

Class here joint custody, visitation rights

*Add as instructed under 342–347

.017 5	*Paternity
.017 8	*Adoption
.018	*Guardian and ward
.02	*Juristic acts, contracts, agency

Subdivisions are added for juristic acts, contracts, and agency together; for juristic acts alone

Class juristic acts dealing with a specific legal aspect not provided for here with the aspect in 342–347, e.g., personal property 346.047

.021	General considerations of juristic acts

Including cause, form, object, declaration of will

.022	*Contracts

Including breach of contract, parties to contract, rescission, subcontracting

Class here comprehensive works on liability

Class sale in 346.072; class loan in 346.073. Class contractual aspects of specific subjects in law with the subject in 342–347, e.g., partnership contracts 346.0682; class nonlegal aspects of contracts concerning a specific nonlegal subject with the subject, e.g., materials management aspects of roofing contracts 695.0687

For government liability, see 342.088; for liability of schools, of school officials, of school districts, see 344.075; for criminal liability, see 345.04; for specific kinds of contracts, see 346.023–346.025; for extracontractual liability, see 346.03

.023	*Public contracts (Government contracts)

Including defense, research and development contracts

Class governmental contracts themselves in 352.53

.024	*Contracts of service

Including master-servant relationships, mechanics' liens

Class labor contracts in 344.01891; class public contracts of service in 346.023; class contracts of service involving bailments in 346.025; class agency in 346.029

See also 346.074 for liens in secured transactions

.025	*Contracts involving bailments

Including bills of lading, pawnbroking

Class public contracts involving bailments in 346.023

.029	*Agency and quasi contract

Including power of attorney, unjust enrichment

Subdivisions are added for either or both topics in heading

*Add as instructed under 342–347

.03   *Torts (Delicts)

     Class here liability for the torts of others, e.g., employees

     Class remedies in 347.077

     See Manual at 345.02 vs. 346.03

.031   Liability of specific classes of persons

     Including liability of employers, directors of corporations, hospitals

     Class liability of specific classes of persons in specific situations in 346.032–346.038

     For personal liability of government officials, see 342.068

.032   *Negligence

     Including contributory negligence

     Class environmental liability and negligence in 344.046; class malpractice in 346.033

.032 2   *Accidents

     Class accidents resulting in personal injury and wrongful death in 346.0323

.032 3   *Personal injury and wrongful death

.033   *Torts against the person

     Including assault and battery, invasion of privacy, malpractice (professional liability)

     For accidents, see 346.0322; for injury through negligence, see 346.0323; for libel and slander, see 346.034. For malpractice pertaining to a specific profession, see the profession in 342–347, e.g., malpractice of lay notaries 347.016, malpractice of lawyers 347.05041

.033 4   *Malicious prosecution

     Class here false arrest and imprisonment

.034   *Libel and slander (Defamation)

     Class libel and slander as crimes in 345.0256

.036   *Torts involving property

     Including nuisance, trespass, trover and conversion, wrongful entry

     Class wrongful entry as invasion of privacy in 346.033

.038   *Product liability

     Class here strict liability

.04   *Property

     For property of enemy aliens, see 341.67; for public property, see 343.02

*Add as instructed under 342–347

SUMMARY

.040 869 1   Property of people with status defined by changes in residence

Class here alien property

For nationalization of alien property, see 343.0252

.042   Kinds of interest in property

Including joint tenancy, future interests; comprehensive works on marital, community, separate property

For marital, community, separate property in divorce, annulment, separation, see 346.01664

.043   *Real property

Land, permanent fixtures, natural resources

Including mobile homes

Class here interdisciplinary works on economic and legal aspects of ownership and transfer of land

For economic aspects of ownership and transfer of land, see 333.1–333.5; for government control and regulation of real property, see 346.044

See also 343.0944 for motorized homes

.043 2   *Ownership (Land tenure)

Including incidents of ownership, e.g., riparian rights, water rights; recovery, squatter's right; types of estate, e.g., fee simple

For joint tenancy, see 346.042

.043 3   *Horizontal property and cooperative ownership

Variant name for horizontal property: condominium

Including time-sharing

.043 4   *Tenancy

Including eviction

Class here landlord and tenant

Class ejectment in 346.0432

*Add as instructed under 342–347

.043 44	*Rent
	Including rent control
.043 46	*Leases
.043 462	*Commercial leases
.043 48	*Farm tenancy
	Class rent in 346.04344; class leases in 346.04346
.043 5	*Easements and servitudes
	Including right of way
.043 6	*Transfer
	Including consolidation of land holdings, restrictions on alienation
	Class inheritance and succession in 346.052
	For conveyancing, see 346.0438
.043 62	*Acquisition and purchase
.043 63	*Sale
	Class real estate business in 346.0437
.043 64	*Mortgages
	Class here foreclosure
.043 7	*Real estate business
	Including valuation of real property
	Class regulation of a specific general administrative function of real estate business with the function in 342–347, e.g., wages 344.0128133333, organization 346.065
.043 71	*Malpractice
	Class malpractice pertaining to closing and settlements in 346.04373; class malpractice pertaining to subdivision in 346.04377
.043 73	*Closing and settlements
	Including escrows
.043 77	*Subdivision
.043 8	*Conveyancing
	Including deeds, registration and description of land, title examinations, titles

*Add as instructed under 342–347

.044   *Government control and regulation of real property

> Class here conservation of natural resources; land reform; comprehensive works on government control and regulation of public and private real property

> Subdivisions are added for either or both topics in heading

> Class government as landlord or tenant in 346.0434; class comprehensive works on environmental law in 344.046

>> *For control and use of public real property, see 343.0256; for rent control, see 346.04344; for regional and local community planning, see 346.045; for control of specific kinds of land and natural resources, see 346.046*

>> *See also 341.4 for conservation of extraterritorial natural resources*

.045   *Regional and local community planning

> Variant name for local community planning: city planning

> Including building codes that relate to regional or local community planning or land use; land use; restrictions on posting advertisements; zoning

> Class regulations governing construction of buildings in 343.07869

.046   Government control and regulation of specific kinds of land and natural resources

> Class here protection of specific resources

> Add to base number 346.046 the numbers following 333 in 333.7–333.9, e.g., control of power and power resources 346.04679, control of recreational lands 346.04678; then add further as instructed under 342–347, e.g., cases involving control of recreational lands 346.046780264

> Class comprehensive works in 346.044

.047   *Personal property

> Movable property

> Including leasing of personal property, e.g., a truck

> Class mobile homes in 346.043

>> *For intangible property, see 346.048; for sale, see 346.072*

.048   *Intangible property

> Including public lending rights

> Class here intellectual property, industrial property (intangible property of an industrial nature, e.g., business names, franchises)

>> *For negotiable instruments, see 346.096*

.048 2   *Copyright

---

*Add as instructed under 342–347

.048 4	*Design protection
.048 6	*Patents
.048 8	*Trademarks
.05	*Inheritance, succession, fiduciary trusts, trustees
.052	*Inheritance and succession

Class here estate planning, probate practice

Subdivisions are added for either or both topics in heading

Class comprehensive works on domestic relations and inheritance and succession in 346.015

For estate planning to avoid taxes, see 343.053; for wills, see 346.054; for administration of estates, see 346.056

.054	*Wills
.056	*Administration of estates

Including execution of wills

For unclaimed estates, see 346.057

.057	*Unclaimed estates
.059	*Fiduciary trusts
.06	*Organizations (Associations)

Class here organization of associations engaged in specific types of enterprises, e.g., an organization of railroad companies

Class organization of labor unions in 344.0187. Class operation of organizations engaged in a specific type of enterprise with the type of enterprise, e.g., operation of railroad companies 343.095

.063	*Accounting

Class accounting for specific kinds of organizations in 346.064–346.068

See also 343.034 for government accounting

.063 1	*Malpractice
.064	*Nonprofit organizations

Including trade associations, unincorporated societies

.064 2	*Charitable trusts and foundations

Subdivisions are added for either or both topics in heading

*Add as instructed under 342–347

.065   *Business enterprises

Including combinations, record requirements, sale, valuation

Class record requirements for a specific kind of organization with the kind in 342–347, e.g., record requirements for a government corporation 346.067; class record requirements for a specific subject with the subject in 342–347, e.g., workers' compensation insurance records 344.021

For corporations, see 346.066; for unincorporated business enterprises, see 346.068

.065 2   *Small business

Class small corporations in 346.066

.066   *Corporations (Companies)

Class comprehensive works on corporate and commercial law in 346.07

For government corporations, see 346.067

See also 342.09 for municipal corporations

.066 2   *Organization

Including investment banking, liquidation

.066 22   *Incorporation

.066 26   *Reorganization

Including acquisitions and mergers

.066 4   *Management

Including records

.066 42   *Officers

.066 45   *Meetings

Class shareholders' meetings in 346.0666

.066 48   *Accounting

.066 6   *Securities and security holders

Including shareholders' voting and meetings

Standard subdivisions are added for either or both topics in heading

Class tender offers for corporate stock in 346.0662; class securities marketing in 346.092

---

*Add as instructed under 342–347

.066 8   Kinds of corporations (Kinds of companies)

                         Including close corporations; cooperatives; credit unions; holding, limited, public limited companies

                         Class specific aspects of corporate law applied to specific kinds of corporations in 346.0662–346.0666

                         For nonprofit corporations, see 346.064; for government corporations, see 346.067

.067   *Government corporations

                         Including quangos

                         Class municipal corporations in 342.09

.068   *Unincorporated business enterprises

                         Including land trusts, sole traders

.068 2   *Partnerships

                             Class here joint ventures

.07   *Commercial law

                         Class here commercial contracts, conduct of business; laws of a specific jurisdiction governing business investment by foreign nationals, e.g., laws of China governing the conduct of business in China by foreign nationals 346.5107; comprehensive works on business law

                         For a specific subject of commercial law, of business law not provided for here, see the subject in 342–347, e.g., tax law 343.04, insurance law 346.086

.072   *Sale

                         Class sale of real property in 346.04363; class sale of business enterprises in 346.065; class conditional and secured sales transactions in 346.074

.073   *Loan

                         Including agricultural and consumer credit, interest, truth in lending, usury

                         Class here credit

                         Class secured loan transactions in 346.074

.074   *Secured transactions

                         Including chattel mortgages; conditional, installment sales; guaranty, liens, suretyship

                         Class comprehensive works on mortgages in 346.04364

                         See also 346.024 for mechanics' liens

---

*Add as instructed under 342–347

.077   *Debtor and creditor

Including collection of debts

For bankruptcy, see 346.078

.078   *Bankruptcy

Including receivership

Class here insolvency

.08   *Banks and insurance

.082   *Banks

Class here banking

Class investment banking in 346.0662. Class regulation of a specific general administrative function with the function in 342–347, e.g., wages 344.012813321, corporate organization 346.0662

For loan, see 346.073

.082 1–.082 3   Specific topics of banks

Add to base number 346.082 the numbers following 332 in 332.1–332.3, e.g., international banks 346.08215, specialized banking institutions 346.0822, credit and loan institutions 346.0823, commercial banks 346.08212; then add further as instructed under 342–347, e.g., cases involving commercial banks 346.082120264

.086   Insurance

Class regulation of a specific general administrative function with the function in 342–347, e.g., wages 344.01281368, corporate organization 346.0662

.086 000 1–.086 000 9   Standard subdivisions

Notation from Table 1 as modified in notation 01–09 from table under 342–347, e.g., cases 346.086000264

.086 01   General principles

Add to base number 346.08601 the numbers following 368.01 in 368.011–368.019, e.g., underwriting 346.086012; then add further as instructed under 342–347, e.g., cases involving underwriting 346.0860120264

.086 02   *Malpractice

.086 06–.086 09   Risks and sales groupings

Add to base number 346.0860 the numbers following 368.0 in 368.06–368.09, e.g., automobile insurance 346.086092; then add further as instructed under 342–347, e.g., cases involving automobile insurance 346.0860920264

*Add as instructed under 342–347

.086 1–.086 8   Specific topics of insurance

Add to base number 346.086 the numbers following 368 in 368.1–368.8, e.g., fire insurance 346.08611; then add further as instructed under 342–347, e.g., cases involving fire insurance 346.086110264; however, for government-sponsored insurance, social insurance, see 344.02

.09   *Investment and negotiable instruments

.092   *Investment

Class here investments

.092 2   Specific types of investments

Including bonds, government securities, mutual funds, stocks; commodities, real estate

Class here securities

Class initial promotion of securities in 346.0662; class what a corporation must do to make certain a security is valid in 346.0666; class organizations marketing specific types of securities in 346.0926

See also 346.074 for secured transactions

[.092 201–.092 209]   Standard subdivisions

Do not use; class in 346.09201–346.09209

.092 6   *Marketing agents and arrangements

Including securities brokers; exchange of securities, stock exchanges

Class investment banking in 346.0662. Class regulation of a specific general administrative function of organizations engaged in marketing securities with the function in 342–347, e.g., wages 344.01281332642, organization 346.065

For commodity exchanges, see 343.08

.096   *Negotiable instruments

Including bills of exchange, checks (cheques), promissory notes, trade acceptances, warehouse receipts

For securities, see 346.092

*Add as instructed under 342–347

.1   **Socioeconomic regions**

Add to base number 346.1 the numbers following —17 in notation 171–177 from Table 2, e.g., private law of developing countries 346.124, private law of Islamic countries, Islamic private law 346.167; then to the result add as follows:

     001–009   Standard subdivisions

                Notation from Table 1 as modified under 342–347

     01–09   Topics of private law

                Add the numbers following 346 in 346.01–346.09, e.g., property law of developing countries 346.12404, property law of Islamic countries, Islamic property law 346.16704, cases involving property law in developing countries 346.124040264, cases involving property law in Islamic countries, cases involving Islamic property law 346.167040264

Class socioeconomic regions of a specific regional intergovernmental organization in 346.2; class socioeconomic regions of a specific jurisdiction or area in 346.3–346.9

.167   **Regions where Islam predominates**

Number built according to instructions under 346.1

Class here Islamic private law

(.167 1–.167 3)   Schools of Islamic law

(Optional numbers; prefer 346.167)

Add to base number 346.167 the numbers following 297.14018 in notation 297.140181–297.140183, e.g., Islamic private law according to Mālikī school 346.16713; then to the result add as instructed under 346.1, e.g., Islamic property law according to Mālikī school 346.1671304

(.167 4)   Mixed schools of Islamic law and comparative treatment

Class here works comparing authors affiliated with different schools (e.g., Sunni and Shīʿī schools)

(Optional number; prefer 346.167)

[.167 8]   Regions where specific Islamic sects and reform movements predominate

Do not use; class in 346.167

.2 **Regional intergovernmental organizations**

Class here relationship between the organization's law and national law of member countries

Add to base number 346.2 notation 3–9 from Table 2, e.g., private law of European Union 346.24; then to the result add as follows:

001–009   Standard subdivisions
           Notation from Table 1 as modified in notation 01–09 from table under 342–347

01–09   Topics of private law
           Add the numbers following 346 in 346.01–346.09, e.g., property law of European Union 346.2404, administrative regulations of property law of European Union 346.240402636

See Manual at 342–349

Class relationship of organization's law and national law of a specific member country with the national law in 346.3–346.9, e.g., effect of European Union laws on national private law of Italy 346.45

.3–.9 **Specific jurisdictions and areas**

Add to base number 346 notation 3–9 from Table 2, e.g., private law of Australia 346.94, of New South Wales 346.944, of African states 346.6; then to the result add as follows:

001–009   Standard subdivisions
           Notation from Table 1 as modified in notation 01–09 from table under 342–347

01–09   Topics of private law
           Add the numbers following 346 in 346.01–346.09, e.g., family law of Australia 346.94015, of New South Wales 346.944014, of African states 346.6015, cases involving family law of Australia 346.940150264

For regional intergovernmental organizations, relationship between the organization's laws and national laws of all member states, see 346.2

See Manual at 342–349

.510 7

.940 13

347   Procedure and courts

Class here civil procedure and courts; comprehensive works on civil and criminal procedure and courts, judicial branch of government, administration of justice, legal services

For administrative procedure, see 342.066; for criminal procedure and courts, see 345

See Manual at 347

(Option: Class here courts and procedure in a specific field of law; prefer specific field in 342–347, plus notation 0269 from table under 342–347)

SUMMARY

.001–.005   Standard subdivisions

> Notation from Table 1 as modified in notation 01–05 from table under 342–347, e.g., cases 347.00264

.006   Organizations

[.006 8]   Management

> Do not use; class in 347.013

.007–.008   Standard subdivisions

.009   History, geographic treatment, biography

[.009 17]   Socioeconomic regions

> Do not use; class in 347.1

[.009 3–.009 9]   Specific continents, countries, localities

> Do not use; class in 347.3–347.9

.01   *Courts

> Class provisional courts in 342.0664

> *For juvenile courts, see 345.081; for courts with specific kinds of jurisdiction, see 347.02–347.04*

.012   *General considerations of courts

> Including judicial cooperation, letters rogatory; judicial discretion, judicial error, judicial review, jurisdiction of courts

> Class criminal contempt of court in 345.0234; class general considerations of specific aspects of courts in 347.013–347.017

> *See Manual at 347*

*Add as instructed under 342–347

.013　　　　　　*Judicial administration (Court management)

Including court calendars, records

For judges, see 347.014; for court officials other than judges, see 347.016

.014　　　　　　*Judges

Class judges associated with a specific court with the court, e.g., judges of a juvenile court 345.081, judges of the High Court of Justice in England 347.4202534

.016　　　　　　Other officials

Including clerks, coroners, court reporters, justices of the peace, marshals, lay notaries, sheriffs

Class nature of duties, characteristics of profession of civil-law notaries, of other notaries required to have legal education in 346.0023. Class the work of court officials with respect to a specific subject with the subject, e.g., justices of the peace and domestic relations 346.015

.017　　　　　　*Legal aid

Class legal aid in criminal cases in 345.0127; class legal aid as a welfare service, interdisciplinary works on legal aid in 362.58

\>　　　　347.02–347.04　Courts with specific kinds of jurisdiction

Add to each subdivision identified by † as follows:
01–09　　Standard subdivisions
　　　　　　　Notation from Table 1 as modified under 342–347, e.g., cases 0264
2　　　　General considerations
　　　　　　　Including functions, jurisdiction, organization, powers
3　　　　Judicial administration
34　　　　　Judges
36　　　　　Other officials
5　　　　Procedure
　　　　　　　For evidence, see 347.06; for trials, see 347.07; for appellate procedure, see 347.08
504　　　　　Practice
　　　　　　　Form, manner, order of instituting and conducting a suit, court case, or other judicial proceeding through its successive stages to its end in accordance with rules and principles laid down by law or by regulations and precedents of the courts
5041　　　　　　Malpractice
51–57　　Specific topics of procedure
　　　　　　　Add to 5 the numbers following 347.05 in 347.051–347.057, e.g., formbooks 55
　　　　　　　Class practice in notation 504 from this table

Class comprehensive works in 347.01

---

*Add as instructed under 342–347

\>   **347.02–347.03 Courts with general jurisdiction**

Class procedure in specific levels of courts in 347.05–347.08; class comprehensive works in 347.01

.02   †Courts with general original jurisdiction

Class here comprehensive works on courts of first instance, local courts, trial courts, on courts that have names such as Circuit, District, County, Municipal, Superior Court

.03   †Appellate courts

For appellate courts devoted exclusively to criminal cases, see 345.0144; for appellate courts with specialized jurisdiction, see 347.04

.033   †Intermediate appellate courts

Class here courts of second instance, courts of first appeal

.035   †Courts of last resort (Supreme courts)

Class here courts of third instance, courts of second appeal, courts of final appeal

.04   †Courts with specialized jurisdiction

Including admiralty courts, small-claims courts

Class courts dealing with a specific subject with the subject in 342–347, plus notation 0269 from table under 342–347, e.g., tax courts 343.040269

.05   *Procedure

Class here procedure in specific levels of courts, relation of a fair trial to freedom of the press, comprehensive works on procedure

Class procedure in a specific court with the court in 347.02–347.04, plus notation 5 from table under 347.02–347.04, e.g., practice in supreme courts 347.035504; class procedure with respect to a specific subject with the subject in 342–347, plus notation 0269 from table under 342–347, e.g., court procedure in tax matters 343.040269

For evidence, see 347.06; for trials, see 347.07; for appellate procedure, see 347.08

.050 4   *Practice

Form, manner, order of instituting and conducting a suit, court case, or other judicial proceeding through its successive stages to its end in accordance with rules and principles laid down by law or by regulations and precedents of the courts

See also 340.023 for practice of law as a profession

.050 41   *Malpractice

---

*Add as instructed under 342–347
†Add as instructed under 347.02–347.04

.051   *Court rules

> Class rules about legal costs and fees in 347.057; class rules of specific courts, of courts having specific kinds of jurisdiction in 347.02–347.04

.052   Motions, limitation of actions, parties to trial, jury trial

> Class here advocacy

.053   Kinds of actions

> Including class actions, lawsuits

.055   Forms and form books

> Standard subdivisions are added for either or both topics in heading

.057   Legal costs and fees

> Standard subdivisions are added for either or both topics in heading

> Rules and guidelines

> Class ethical aspects of legal costs and fees in 174.3; class financial management of law firms in 340.0681; class economics of salaries of legal personnel in 331.28134; class economics of law firms in 338.7–338.8; class interdisciplinary works on legal costs and fees in 338.4334

.057 2   Fees for legal professional services

> Class here lawyers' fees, contingent or conditional fees

.06   *Evidence

.062   *Admissibility

.064   Kinds of evidence

> *For witnesses, see 347.066*

.066   *Witnesses

> Class examination of witnesses in 347.075

> *For expert testimony, see 347.067*

.067   *Expert testimony

> Class forensic science in 363.25; class medical jurisprudence, forensic medicine, forensic psychiatry in 614.1

.07   *Trials

> Class a trial dealing with a specific subject with the subject in 342–347, e.g., a product liability trial 346.038; class procedures of trials dealing with a specific subject with the subject in 342–347, plus notation 0269 from table under 342–347, e.g., procedures of product liability trials 346.0380269

.072   *Pretrial procedure

> Including discovery, pleading, service of process, summons

---

*Add as instructed under 342–347

.075   *Trial procedure (Courtroom procedure)

Including examination of witnesses, summations, verdicts

.075 2   *Juries

Class here jury selection

Class instructions to juries in 347.0758

.075 8   *Instructions to juries

.077   *Judgments

Including attachment and garnishment, legal costs and fees awarded as part of judgments, executions of judgment, remedies

.08   *Appellate procedure

Class here comprehensive works on appellate procedure in civil and criminal cases

For procedure in specific appellate courts hearing both civil and criminal cases, specific appellate courts devoted exclusively to civil cases, see 347.03–347.04; for procedure in appellate courts devoted exclusively to criminal cases, see 345.0144

.09   *Dispute resolution

Class here arbitration, conciliation, mediation

.1   **Socioeconomic regions**

Add to base number 347.1 the numbers following —17 in notation 171–177 from Table 2, e.g., civil procedure and courts of developing countries 347.124, civil procedure and courts of Islamic countries, civil procedure and courts in Islamic law 347.167; then to the result add as follows:

001–009   Standard subdivisions

              Notation from Table 1 as modified under 342–347

01–09   Topics of procedure and courts

              Add the numbers following 347 in 347.01–347.09, e.g., the law of evidence in developing countries 347.12406, law of evidence in Islamic countries, Islamic law of evidence 347.16706, court decisions on evidence in developing countries 347.1240602643, court decisions on evidence in Islamic countries 347.1670602643

Class socioeconomic regions of a specific regional intergovernmental organization in 347.2; class socioeconomic regions of a specific jurisdiction or area in 347.3–347.9

.167   Regions where Islam predominates

Number built according to instructions under 347.1

---

*Add as instructed under 342–347

(.167 1–.167 3)   Schools of Islamic law

(Optional numbers; prefer 347.167)

Add to base number 347.167 the numbers following 297.14018 in notation 297.140181–297.140183, e.g., civil procedure and courts according to Ja'farī school 347.16721; then to the result add as instructed under 347.1, e.g., law of evidence according to Ja'farī school 347.1672106

(.167 4)   Mixed schools of Islamic law and comparative treatment

Class here works comparing authors affiliated with different schools (e.g., Sunni and Shī'ī schools)

(Optional number; prefer 347.167)

[.167 8]   Regions where specific Islamic sects and reform movements predominate

Do not use; class in 347.167

.2   Regional intergovernmental organizations

Class here effect of organization's law on and harmonization of national laws of member countries

Add to base number 347.2 notation 3–9 from Table 2, e.g., harmonization of national laws on procedure and courts of European Union countries 347.24; then to the result add as follows:
001–009   Standard subdivisions
    Notation from Table 1 as modified in notation 01–09 from table under 342–347
01–09   Topics of procedure and courts
    Add the numbers following 347 in 347.01–347.09, e.g., harmonization of national law of evidence of European Union 347.2406, harmonization of individual and collected laws of evidence of European Union countries 347.240602632
    Class effect of organization's laws on national laws of a specific member country with the national laws, e.g., effect of European Union laws on national laws on procedures and courts of France 347.44

Class relationship of organization's law and national law of a specific member country with the national law in 347.3–347.9, e.g., effect of European Union laws on national German laws on procedure and courts 347.43

See Manual at 342–349

.24   Regional intergovernmental organizations of Europe

Number built according to instructions under 347.2

Class here effect of European Union law on and harmonization of national laws on procedure and courts of European Union countries

Class effect of European Union law on national laws of a specific member country with the national law, e.g., effect of European Union laws on national French laws on procedures and courts 347.44

.240 1   Courts

Number built according to instructions under 347.2

Class here effect of European Union law on courts of European Union countries, harmonization of aspects of courts of European Union countries

Class courts of a regional intergovernmental organization of Europe with the law of the organization, e.g., Court of Justice of European Free Trade Association States (EFTA Court) 341.242, Courts of European Union 341.242228

.3–.9   Specific jurisdictions and areas

Add to base number 347 notation 3–9 from Table 2, e.g., civil procedure and courts of Australia 347.94, of New South Wales 347.944, of African states 347.6; then to the result add as follows:

 001–009 Standard subdivisions
       Notation from Table 1 as modified in notation 01–09 from
       table under 342–347
 01–09 Topics of procedure and courts
       Add the numbers following 347 in 347.01–347.09, e.g., the
       law of evidence in Australia 347.9406, in New South Wales
       347.94406, in African states 347.606; Australian court decisions
       on evidence in 347.940602643

For regional intergovernmental organizations, relationship between the organization's laws and national laws of all member states, see 347.2

See Manual at 342–349

Special developments for Scotland, England, the United States follow

.411   Civil procedure and courts of Scotland

.411 001–.411 009   Standard subdivisions

.411 01   *Courts

For courts with specific kinds of jurisdiction, see 347.41102–347.41104

.411 012–.411 017   Specific aspects of courts

Add to base number 347.41101 the numbers following 347.01 in 347.012–347.017, e.g., general considerations 347.411012

>   347.411 02–347.411 04 Courts with specific kinds of jurisdiction

Add to each subdivision identified by † as instructed under 347.02–347.04, e.g., jurisdiction of the Sheriff Court 347.4110212

Class comprehensive works in 347.41101

*Add as instructed under 342–347

>   347.411 02–347.411 03   Courts with general jurisdiction

Class procedure in specific levels of courts in 347.41105–347.41108; class comprehensive works in 347.41101

.411 02   †Courts with original jurisdiction

.411 021   †Sheriff Court

For criminal jurisdiction of Sheriff Court, see 345.411014; for appellate jurisdiction of Sheriff-Principal, see 347.411032

.411 023   †Court of Session

For Outer House, see 347.411024; for Inner House, see 347.411035

.411 024   †Outer House of Court of Session

.411 03   †Courts with appellate jurisdiction

Class here comprehensive works on appellate courts

For appellate courts devoted exclusively to criminal cases, see 345.41101; for appellate courts with specialized jurisdiction, see 347.41104

.411 032   †Sheriff-Principal

.411 035   †Inner House of Court of Session

.411 039   †House of Lords (Court of last resort)

.411 04   †Courts with specialized jurisdiction

Including Court of the Lord Lyon, Licensing Appeals Courts, Licensing Courts

Class courts dealing with a single specific subject with the subject in 342–347, plus notation 0269 from table under 342–347, e.g., Court of Exchequer 343.411040269

.411 05–.411 09   Procedure and arbitration

Add to base number 347.4110 the numbers following 347.0 in 347.05–347.09, e.g., evidence 347.41106

.42   **Civil procedure and courts of England**

.420 01–.420 09   Standard subdivisions

.420 1   *Courts

For courts with specific kinds of jurisdiction, see 347.4202–347.4204

---

*Add as instructed under 342–347
†Add as instructed under 347.02–347.04

.420 12–.420 17   Specific aspects of courts

> Add to base number 347.4201 the numbers following 347.01 in
> 347.012–347.017, e.g., general considerations 347.42012

> 347.420 2–347.420 4 Courts with specific kinds of jurisdiction

Add to each subdivision identified by † as instructed under 347.02–347.04, e.g.,
jurisdiction of County Court 347.420212

Class comprehensive works in 347.4201

> 347.420 2–347.420 3 Courts with general jurisdiction

Class procedure in specific levels of courts in 347.4205–347.4208; class
comprehensive works in 347.4201

.420 2   †Courts with original jurisdiction

.420 21   †County Court

.420 23   †Domestic Court of Magistrates Court

Class comprehensive works on Magistrates Court in 345.42012

.420 25   †High Court of Justice

*For Family Division, see 346.420150269; for Chancery
Division, see 347.42026; for Queen's Bench Division, see
347.42027*

.420 26   †Chancery Division of the High Court of Justice

.420 27   †Queen's Bench Division of High Court of Justice

*For Divisional Court of Queen's Bench Division, see
345.42016*

.420 29   †Supreme Court of Judicature

*For Crown Court, see 345.42014; for High Court of Justice,
see 347.42025; for Court of Appeal, see 347.42032*

.420 3   †Courts with appellate jurisdiction

Class here comprehensive works on appellate courts

*For appellate courts devoted exclusively to criminal cases, see
345.4201; for appellate courts with specialized jurisdiction, see
347.4204*

.420 32   †Court of Appeal

*For Criminal Division, see 345.42018; for Civil Division, see
347.42035*

.420 35   †Civil Division of Court of Appeal

---

†Add as instructed under 347.02–347.04

.420 39	†House of Lords (Court of last resort)
	Criminal and civil jurisdiction
.420 4	†Courts with specialized jurisdiction

Including Judicial Committee of the Privy Council

Class courts dealing with a specific subject with the subject in 342–347, plus notation 0269 from table under 342–347, e.g., Lands Tribunal 346.420430269

.420 5–.420 9	Procedure and arbitration

Add to base number 347.420 the numbers following 347.0 in 347.05–347.09, e.g., evidence 347.4206

.73	Civil procedure and courts of the United States

Federal procedure and courts; national and regional treatment of state and local procedure and courts

For civil procedure and courts of specific states and localities, see 347.74–347.79

.730 01–.730 09	Standard subdivisions
.731	*Courts

For specific court systems, see 347.732–347.734

.731 2–.731 7	Specific aspects of courts

Add to base number 347.731 the numbers following 347.01 in 347.012–347.017, e.g., judges 347.7314

>	347.732–347.734 Specific court systems

Class comprehensive works in 347.731

.732	Federal courts

Add to base number 347.7320 as instructed under 347.02–347.04, e.g., periodicals about federal courts 347.732005, federal judges 347.732034

>	347.732 2–347.732 8 Federal courts with specific kinds of jurisdiction

Class here procedure in specific courts

Add to each subdivision identified by † as instructed under 347.02–347.04, e.g., Supreme Court rules 347.732651

Class comprehensive works in 347.732

*Add as instructed under 342–347
†Add as instructed under 347.02–347.04

> 347.732 2–347.732 6 Federal courts with general jurisdiction

Class procedure in specific levels of courts in 347.735–347.738; class comprehensive works in 347.732

.732 2 †District courts

Courts of original jurisdiction

.732 4 †Courts of appeal

For Supreme Court, see 347.7326

.732 6 †Supreme Court

.732 8 †Courts of specialized jurisdiction

Including United States Court of Customs and Patent Appeals

Class courts dealing with a specific subject with the subject in United States law, plus notation 0269 from table under 342–347, e.g., tax courts 343.73040269

.733 *State courts

Class courts of specific states in 347.74–347.79

.733 2–.733 8 Specific aspects of state courts

Add to base number 347.733 the numbers following 347.732 in 347.7322–347.7328, e.g., state supreme courts 347.7336

.734 *Local courts

Class courts of specific localities in 347.74–347.79

.735–.738 Procedure

Class here procedure in specific levels of federal courts

Add to base number 347.73 the numbers following 347.0 in 347.05–347.08, e.g., rules of evidence 347.736

Class procedure in specific courts in 347.732–347.734

.739 *Arbitration, mediation, conciliation

Subdivisions are added for any or all topics in heading

*Add as instructed under 342–347
†Add as instructed under 347.02–347.04

.74–.79   Civil procedure and courts of specific states and localities of the United States

Add to base number 347 notation 74–79 from Table 2, e.g., civil procedure and courts of Pennsylvania 347.748, of Philadelphia 347.74811; then to the result add as follows:
001–009   Standard subdivisions
Notation from Table 1 as modified in notation 01–09 from table under 342–347
01–09   Topics of procedure and courts
Add the numbers following 347 in 347.01–347.09, e.g., the Supreme Court of Pennsylvania 347.748035, courts of Philadelphia 347.7481101

Class regional treatment of state and local procedure and courts in 347.73; class civil procedure and courts of Hawaii in 347.969

348   Laws, regulations, cases

Original materials and their guides listed here are comprehensive in nature, covering the whole of the law of a specific jurisdiction or a major portion thereof

Class treatises on the whole law of a specific jurisdiction in 349. Class original materials and their guides limited to a specific branch or subject with the branch or subject in 342–347, plus notation 026 from table under 342–347, e.g., a digest of tax laws 343.0402638
(Option: Class here laws, regulations, cases covering specific subjects in law; prefer specific subject in 342–347, plus notation 026 from table under 342–347)

SUMMARY

348.001–.009	Standard subdivisions and codification
.01	Preliminary materials
.02	Laws and regulations
.04	Cases
.05	Advisory opinions of attorneys-general (ministers of justice)
.1	Socioeconomic regions
.2	Regional intergovernmental organizations
.3–.9	Specific jurisdictions and areas

.001–.003   Standard subdivisions

.004   Codification

Class proposed codes in 348.023

.005   Serial publications

.006   Organizations and management

Notation 06 from Table 1 as modified below

.006 01   International organizations

Laws, regulations, cases limited to a specific regional intergovernmental organization are classed under the area of the organization before indicating the subject of a branch of law, e.g., regulations of European Union 348.24025. Further instructions are given under 342–349

.007–.008   Standard subdivisions

.009   History, geographic treatment, biography

[.009 17]   Socioeconomic regions

                                  Do not use; class in 348.1

[.009 3–.009 9]   Specific continents, countries, localities

                         Do not use; class in 348.3–348.9

.01   *Preliminary materials

             Including bills; legislative hearings, histories; slip laws; statistical reports of
             bills passed or vetoed, reports on the status of bills

.02   *Laws and regulations

             Standard subdivisions are added for laws and regulations together, for laws
             alone

             Class here statutes

             Including laws arranged in alphabetical order

             (If option under 348 is chosen, class here individual laws)

>   348.022–348.024 Laws

             Class guides to laws in 348.026–348.028; class comprehensive works in 348.02

.022   *Laws arranged in chronological order

                 Including session laws

.023   *Codes

                 Compilations of laws in classified order

                 Including compiled and consolidated statutes

.024   *Selected laws

.025   *Regulations

                 Class guides to regulationss in 348.026–348.028

>   348.026–348.028 Guides to laws and regulations

             Class comprehensive works and guides in 348.026. Class guides to a specific
             collection of laws with the collection, e.g., a citator to the U.S. Code 348.7323

---

*Do not use notation 0601 from Table 1 for a specific regional intergovernmental organization;
class in 348.2. Do not use notation 0917 from Table 1 for socioeconomic regions; class in 348.1.
Do not use notation 093–099 from Table 1 for specific continents, countries, localities; class in
348.3–348.9

.026   *Digests of laws and regulations

        Standard subdivisions are added for either or both topics in heading

        Including summaries of changes

        Class here comprehensive guides to laws and regulations

        For citators to laws and regulations, see 348.027; for checklists, tables, indexes of laws and regulations, see 348.028

.027   *Citators to laws and regulations

        Standard subdivisions are added for either or both topics in heading

.028   *Checklists, tables, indexes of laws and regulations

        Standard subdivisions are added for any or all topics in heading

        Class union lists of legal material in 016.34

.04   *Cases

        Do not use for casebooks; class with the subject in 342–347 without further subdivision

        Class cases in a specific subject in law with the subject in 343–347, plus notation 0264 from table under 342–347, e.g., cases involving tax law 344.040264

>   348.041–348.043 Reports

        Reports of cases contain a relatively full treatment of each case as well as the ultimate decision

        Class comprehensive works in 348.04

.041   *National reports

.042   *Regional reports

.043   *State and provincial reports

        Standard subdivisions are added for either or both topics in heading

.044   *Court decisions

        Texts of decisions with or without accompanying information

.045   *Decisions (Rulings) of regulatory agencies

---

*Do not use notation 0601 from Table 1 for a specific regional intergovernmental organization; class in 348.2. Do not use notation 0917 from Table 1 for socioeconomic regions; class in 348.1. Do not use notation 093–099 from Table 1 for specific continents, countries, localities; class in 348.3–348.9

>   348.046–348.048 Guides to cases

       Class here combined guides to laws, regulations, cases

       Class comprehensive works and guides in 348.046. Class guides to a specific set of court reports with the reports, e.g., a citator to U.S. Supreme Court reports 348.73413

       For guides to laws and regulations, see 348.026–348.028

.046   *Digests of cases

       Class here comprehensive guides to cases

       For citators to cases, see 348.047; for checklists, tables, indexes of cases, see 348.048

.047   *Citators to cases

.048   *Checklists, tables, indexes of cases

       Standard subdivisions are added for any or all topics in heading

.05   *Advisory opinions of attorneys-general (ministers of justice)

.06   *Other advisory opinions

       Class collected fatwas not associated with a specific jurisdiction in 340.59224. Class collected fatwas associated with a specific jurisdiction with the jurisdiction in 348.3–348.9, plus notation 06 from add table under 348.3–348.9, e.g., fatwas from Indonesia 348.59806

.1   **Socioeconomic regions**

       Add to base number 348.1 the numbers following —17 in notation 171–177 from Table 2, e.g., laws, regulations, cases of developing countries 348.124; however, for laws, regulations, cases of regions where Islam predominates, see 340.592; then to the result add as follows:

       001–009   Standard subdivisions
                Notation from Table 1 as modified under 348.001–348.009
       01–06   Topics of laws, regulations, cases
                Add the numbers following 348 in 348.01–348.06, e.g., selected laws of developing countries 348.124024

       Class socioeconomic regions of a specific regional intergovernmental organization in 348.2; class socioeconomic regions of a specific jurisdiction or area, Islamic law of a specific jurisdiction in 348.3–348.9

---

*Do not use notation 0601 from Table 1 for a specific regional intergovernmental organization; class in 348.2. Do not use notation 0917 from Table 1 for socioeconomic regions; class in 348.1. Do not use notation 093–099 from Table 1 for specific continents, countries, localities; class in 348.3–348.9

.2   **Regional intergovernmental organizations**

> Add to base number 348.2 notation 3–9 from Table 2, e.g., laws, regulations, cases of European Union 348.24; then to the result add as follows:
>
>   001–009   Standard subdivisions
> > Notation from Table 1 as modified under 348.001–348.009
>
>   01–06   Topics of laws, regulations, cases
> > Add the numbers following 348 in 348.01–348.06, e.g., selected laws of European Union 348.24024
>
> *See Manual at 342–349*

.3–.9   **Specific jurisdictions and areas**

> Class here general collections of repealed laws
>
> Add to base number 348 notation 3–9 from Table 2, e.g., laws, regulations, cases of Australia 348.94, of New South Wales 348.944, of African states 348.6; then to the result add as follows:
>
>   001–009   Standard subdivisions
> > Notation from Table 1 as modified under 348.001–348.009
>
>   01–06   Topics of laws, regulations, cases
> > Add the numbers following 348 in 348.01–348.06, e.g., selected laws of Australia 348.94024, of New South Wales 348.944024, of African states 348.6024
>
> Class the legislative procedure involved in enacting or repealing a law in 328.37. Class repealed laws on a specific subject with the subject in 342–347, e.g., repeal of a prohibition on the sale and consumption of alcohol 344.0541
>
> *For regional intergovernmental organizations, relationship between the organization's laws and national laws of all member states, see 348.2*
>
> *See Manual at 342–349*
>
> **A special development for the United States follows**

.73   Federal laws, regulations, cases of the United States

> Including national and regional treatment of state and local laws, regulations, cases
>
> *For laws, regulations, cases of specific states and localities, see 348.74–348.79*

.730 4   Codification

> Class proposed codes in 348.7323

.731   Preliminary materials

> Including bills; legislative hearings, histories; slip laws

.732   Federal laws and regulations

> Standard subdivisions are added for federal laws and regulations together, for federal laws alone
>
> Class here federal statutes
>
> (If option under 348 is chosen, class here individual laws)

>   348.732 2–348.732 4 Federal laws

              Class guides to federal laws in 348.7326–348.7328; class comprehensive works in 348.732

.732 2   Federal laws in chronological order

.732 3   United States Code

.732 4   Selected Federal laws

.732 5   Federal regulations

              Class guides to federal regulations in 348.7326–348.7328

>   348.732 6–348.732 8 Guides to federal laws and regulations

              Class comprehensive works and guides in 348.7326

.732 6   Digests of federal laws and regulations

              Standard subdivisions are added for either or both topics in heading

              Including summaries of changes

              Class here comprehensive guides to federal laws and regulations

                For citators to federal laws and regulations, see 348.7327; for checklists, tables, indexes of federal laws and regulations, see 348.7328

.732 7   Citators to federal laws and regulations

              Standard subdivisions are added for either or both topics in heading

.732 8   Checklists, tables, indexes of federal laws and regulations

              Standard subdivisions are added for any or all topics in heading

.734   Federal cases

              Do not use for casebooks; class with the subject in 342–347 without further subdivision

>   348.734 1–348.734 2 Reports of federal cases

              Class comprehensive works and reports in 348.734

.734 1   Federal court reports

.734 13   Supreme Court

.734 15   Lower Federal courts

.734 2   National reporter system

.734 22   Atlantic federal reporter system

.734 23   Northeastern federal reporter system

.734 24   Northwestern federal reporter system

.734 25	Southeastern federal reporter system
.734 26	Southwestern federal reporter system
.734 27	Southern federal reporter system
.734 28	Pacific federal reporter system
.734 4	Court decisions
.734 5	Decisions of regulatory agencies (Rulings of regulatory agencies)

>   348.734 6–348.734 8   Guides to federal cases

Class here combined guides to federal laws, regulations, cases

Class comprehensive works and guides to federal cases in 348.7346

For guides to federal laws and regulations, see 348.7326–348.7328

.734 6   Digests of federal cases

Class here comprehensive guides to federal cases

For citators to federal cases, see 348.7347; for checklists, tables, indexes of federal cases, see 348.7348

.734 7   Citators to federal cases

.734 8   Checklists, tables, indexes of federal cases

Standard subdivisions are added for any or all topics in heading

.735   **Advisory opinions of Attorney-General**

.74–.79   **Laws, regulations, cases of specific states and localities of the United States**

Add to base number 348 notation 74–79 from Table 2, e.g., laws, regulations, cases of Pennsylvania 348.748, of Philadelphia 348.74811; then to the result add the numbers following 348 in 348.001–348.05, e.g., Pennsylvania statutes 348.748022, Philadelphia code of ordinances 348.74811023

Class national and regional treatment of state and local laws, regulations, cases in 348.73; class laws, regulations, cases of Hawaii in 348.969

349 Law of specific jurisdictions, areas, socioeconomic regions, regional intergovernmental organizations

For law of specific ancient jurisdictions, areas, socioeconomic regions, see 340.53; for specific branches of law of a specific jurisdiction, area, socioeconomic region, regional intergovernmental organization, see 342–347; for original materials on law of a specific jurisdiction, area, socioeconomic region, regional intergovernmental organization, see 348

See Manual at 340.02–340.09 vs. 349; also at 342–349

(If option A under 342–349 is chosen, class here comparative law and law of jurisdictions other than the preferred jurisdiction by adding to base number 349 the numbers following 34 in 342–348, e.g., comparative criminal procedure 349.505, criminal procedure of New Zealand 349.59305. Assuming Australia to be the preferred jurisdiction, criminal procedure of Australia 345.05. Class comprehensive works on law of jurisdictions other than the preferred jurisdiction in 349.9)

.1 Law of specific socioeconomic regions

Add to base number 349.1 the numbers following —17 in notation 171–177 from Table 2, e.g., works on ordinances from developing countries 349.124; however, for Islamic law, see 340.59

Class socioeconomic regions of a specific regional intergovernmental organization in 349.2; class law of specific socioeconomic regions of a specific jurisdiction or area in 349.4–349.9

.2 Law of regional intergovernmental organizations

Add to base number 349.2 notation 3–9 from Table 2, e.g., works on the ordinances of European Union 349.24

Class comprehensive works on regional intergovernmental organizations themselves in 341.2

.24 Regional intergovernmental organizations of Europe

Number built according to instructions under 349.2

Class comprehensive works on effect of European Union laws on national laws of member states in 341.24224. Class effect of European Union laws on national laws of a specific member state with the laws of the member state, e.g., effect on laws of Italy 349.45

.4–.9 Law of specific jurisdictions and areas in modern world

Add to base number 349 notation 4–9 from Table 2, e.g., works on law of England 349.42, works on law of medieval England 349.420902; however, for law of nondominant legal systems associated with specific ethnic groups in specific jurisdictions and areas in modern world, see 340.524–340.529; for comprehensive works on law of medieval Europe as a whole, see 340.55

For regional intergovernmental organizations, see 349.2

.9   **Law of other parts of world**

Number built according to instructions under 349.4–349.9

(If option A under 342–349 is chosen, class here law of specific jurisdictions, areas, socioeconomic regions, regional intergovernmental organizations

(For law of specific ancient jurisdictions, areas, socioeconomic regions, see 340.53)

(.91)   Law of specific socioeconomic regions

(Optional number; prefer 349.1)

(If option A under 342–349 is chosen, add to base number 349.91 the numbers following —17 in notation 171–177 from Table 2, e.g., works on ordinances from developing countries 349.9124; however, for Islamic law, see 340.59

(Class socioeconomic regions of a specific regional intergovernmental organization in 349.92; class law of specific socioeconomic regions of a specific jurisdiction or area in 349.94–349.99)

(.92)   Law of regional intergovernmental organizations

(Optional number; prefer 349.2)

(If option A under 342–349 is chosen, add to base number 349.92 notation 3–9 from Table 2, e.g., works on the ordinances of European Union 349.924)

.93–.99   Law of Australasia, Pacific Ocean islands, Atlantic Ocean islands, Arctic islands, Antarctica

Number built according to instructions under 349.4–349.9

(If option A under 342–349 is chosen, class here law of specific jurisdictions and areas of modern world other than the preferred jurisdiction, adding to base number 349.9 notation 4–9 from Table 2, e.g., works on the ordinances of the City of Los Angeles 349.979494. Assuming Australia to be the preferred jurisdiction, works on the ordinances of Australia 342

(For law of regional intergovernmental organizations, see 349.92)

350   Public administration and military science

SUMMARY

359	Sea forces and warfare
.001–.009	Standard subdivisions
.03–.07	[Situation and policy, naval research and development]
.1–.2	Naval life and resources
.3	Organization and personnel of naval forces
.4–.7	Naval operations, training, administration, installations
.8	Naval equipment and supplies (Naval matériel)
.9	Specialized combat forces; engineering and related services

351   Public administration

Class here executive branch of government, programs administered by executive branch, civil service in the sense of all units of public administration outside armed services

Class relation of executive branch to other branches, works that deal comprehensively with more than one branch of government in 320.404; class civil service in the sense of merit system in 352.63; class interdisciplinary works on management in 658. Class management of government-owned enterprises operating a service with the service, plus notation 068 from Table 1, e.g., management of public hospitals 362.11068, of nationalized railroads 385.068

For administration of legislative branch, see 328.068; for administration of judicial branch, see 347.013; for specific topics of public administration, see 352–354

See Manual at T1—068 vs. 353–354; also at 320.9, 320.4 vs. 351; also at 351 vs. 352.29

SUMMARY

351.01–.09	Standard subdivisions
.1	Administration in areas, regions, places in general
.3–.9	Administration in specific continents, countries, localities

.025   Directories of persons and organizations

Class directories of elected public officials in 324.025

.05   Serial publications

Class here official gazettes, serial administrative reports of governmental organizations

.06   Nongovernmental organizations

Do not use for governmental organizations; class in 351. Do not use for serial administrative reports of governmental organizations; class in 351.05

See Manual at T1—0601–T1—0609

[.068]   Management

Do not use; class in 351

.07   Education, research, related topics

.076   Review and exercise

Class here interdisciplinary works on civil service examinations

*For civil service examinations in a specific subject, see the subject,
plus notation 076 from Table 1, e.g., examinations in accounting
657.076*

(Option: Class here civil service examinations in specific subjects; prefer
the subject in 001–999, plus notation 076 from Table 1. If option is
chosen, add to base number 351.076 notation 001–999, e.g., civil service
examinations in accounting 351.076657)

.08   Groups of people

Do not use for programs directed to groups of people; class in 353.53

.09   History and biography

[.091]   Areas, regions, places in general

Do not use; class in 351.1

[.093–.099]   Specific continents, countries, localities

Do not use; class in 351.3–351.9

.1   Administration in areas, regions, places in general

Not limited by continent, country, locality

Add to base number 351.1 the numbers following —1 in notation 11–19 from
Table 2, e.g., administration in developing regions 351.1724; however, for
urban administration, see 352.16; for rural administration, see 352.17

.3–.9   **Administration in specific continents, countries, localities**

Class here administration of specific jurisdictions, practical works on administration of specific subordinate jurisdictions, e.g., specific provinces

Add to base number 351 notation 3–9 from Table 2, e.g., public administration in Germany 351.43

Class theoretical works on specific kinds of subordinate jurisdictions in 352.13–352.19

See Manual at 351.3–351.9 vs. 352.13–352.19

(Option A: Class here treatment of specific topics of public administration in specific continents, countries, localities; prefer 352–354, plus notation 09 from table under 352–354. If option is chosen, add to each geographic subdivision as follows:

001–007	Standard subdivisions Notation from Table 1 as modified under 351, e.g., serial administrative reports 005
008	Groups of people Class programs directed to groups of people in notation 0353 from this table
009	History, geographic treatment, biography Use for geographic treatment only when area of interest is narrower than area of jurisdiction, e.g., United States federal administration in Gulf Coast states 351.7300976
02–04	Specific topics of public administration Add to 0 the numbers following 35 in 352–354, e.g., social welfare administration 035, programs directed to groups of people 0353

(Option B: Class here treatment of specific topics of public administration in specific continents, countries, localities not requiring local emphasis; prefer 352–354, plus notation 09 from table under 352–354. If option B is chosen, add to each geographic subdivision as instructed under option A)

> ## 352–354 Specific topics of public administration

Class here public administration of specific departments and agencies

Except for modifications shown under specific entries, add to each subdivision identified by * as follows:

01–07   Standard subdivisions
        Notation from Table 1 as modified under 01–07, e.g., serial administrative reports 05

08   Groups of people
        Class here programs directed to groups of people; equal opportunity programs

09   History, geographic treatment, biography

093–099   Specific continents, countries, localities
        (Option A: Class treatment of specific topics of public administration by specific continents, countries, localities in 351.3–351.9
        (Option B: In order to provide local emphasis and shorter notation, class specific topics of public administration treated in jurisdictions requiring local emphasis in 352–354 without adding notation 09 from this table, and class specific topics of public administration in specific continents, countries, localities not requiring local emphasis in 351.3–351.9)

2   General considerations of public administration

21   Jurisdictional levels

2101–2109   Standard subdivisions
        Add to 210 the numbers following 352.10 in 352.101–352.109, e.g., nongovernmental organizations 2106

211–219   Specific jurisdictional levels
        Add to 21 the numbers following 352.1 in 352.11–352.19, e.g., international administration 211
        Class administration at national level, combined treatment of national and other levels (*except* works that emphasize differences between administration at different levels) in base number without use of notation 21 from this table

22–26   Specific topics in management
        Add to 2 the numbers following 352 in 352.2–352.6, e.g., governing boards and commissions 225, contracts and procurement 253; however; for planning and policy making of a specific subject, see the subject outside of public administration, e.g., government policy on arts 700

27–28   Public administration of supporting and controlling functions of government
        Do not use when redundant
        Add to 2 the numbers following 352 in 352.7–352.8, e.g., promoting and disseminating knowledge 274, regulation 28

Unless other instructions are given, class a subject with aspects in two or more subdivisions of 352–354 in the number coming last, e.g., chief executive of a department of agriculture 354.52293 (*not* 352.293)

Class misconduct in office regardless of topic in 353.46; class comprehensive works in 351

See Manual at 352–354; also at 300–330, 355–390 vs. 342–347, 352–354; also at 300, 320.6 vs. 352–354

352   General considerations of public administration

Class here general considerations of public administration applying to two or more branches of government, e.g., financial administration of the legislative and judicial branches 352.4

Class general considerations of public administration applied to a specific field with the field in public administration, plus notation 2 from table under 352–354, e.g., local safety administration 353.9214

See Manual at 352–354

SUMMARY

352.1	Jurisdictional levels of administration	
.2	Organization of administration	
.3	Executive management	
.4	Financial administration and budgets	
.5	Property administration and related topics	
.6	Personnel management (Human resource management)	
.7	Public administration of general forms of assistance	
.8	Public administration of general forms of control	

[.01–.09]   Standard subdivisions

Do not use; class in 351.01–351.09

.1   Jurisdictional levels of administration

Class programs directed to specific groups of people at specific levels of administration in 353.5321. Class a specific topic in administrative management, support, control at a specific jurisdictional level of administration with the topic in 352.2–352.8, plus notation 21 from table under 352–354, e.g., financial administration and budgets of international agencies 352.4211, regulation by local government 352.8214

Use 351 for combined treatment of national and other levels of administration except for works that emphasize differences between administration at different levels

For administration at national level, see 351

SUMMARY

352.101–.109	Standard subdivisions	
.11	International administration	
.13	State and provincial administration	
.14	Local administration	
.15	Intermediate units of local administration	
.16	Urban administration	
.17	Rural administration	
.19	Administration of special service districts	

.105   Serial publications

Class here official gazettes, serial administrative reports of governmental organizations

.106	Nongovernmental organizations

Do not use for governmental organizations; class in 352.1. Do not use for serial administrative reports of governmental organizations; class in 352.105

[.106 8]	Management

Do not use; class in 352.1

.108	Groups of people

Do not use for programs at specific levels of administration directed toward groups of people; class in 353.5321

.11	International administration

Class here administration of intergovernmental organizations

Class interdisciplinary works on intergovernmental organizations in 341.2

.110 5	Serial publications

Class here official gazettes, serial administrative reports of government organizations

.110 6	Nongovernmental organizations

Do not use for governmental organizations; class in 352.11. Do not use for serial administrative reports of governmental organizations; class in 352.1105

[.110 68]	Management

Do not use; class in 352.11

.110 8	Groups of people

Do not use for international programs directed to groups of people; class in 353.53211

.110 9	History, geographic treatment, biography
[.110 94–.110 99]	Specific continents, countries, localities in modern world

Do not use; class in 352.114–352.119

.112	League of Nations
.113	United Nations

Class here secretariat

Class interdisciplinary works on United Nations in 341.23

.114–.119	International administration in specific continents and parts of continents

Class here administration of international organizations serving continents and parts of continents

Add to base number 352.11 notation 4–9 from Table 2, e.g., international administration in southeast Asia 352.1159, Organization of American States 352.117

>

352.13–352.19 Administration of subordinate jurisdictions

Except for modifications shown under specific entries, add to each subdivision identified by † as follows:

01–07   Standard subdivisions
> Notation from Table 1 as modified under 01–07, e.g., serial administrative reports 05

08   Groups of people
> Do not use for programs directed to groups of people; class in 353.53213

09   History, geographic treatment, biography

093–099   Specific continents, countries, localities
> Limited to comprehensive, theoretical, comparative treatment, e.g. administration of Länder in Germany 352.130943
>
> Class administration of or in a specific subordinate jurisdiction with the jurisdiction in 351.3–351.9 (*not* notation 093–099 from this table), e.g., administration of Bavaria 351.433
>
> *See Manual at 351.3–351.9 vs. 352.13–352.19*

3   Administrative cooperation among subordinate jurisdictions
> Class here administrative relations among subordinate jurisdictions that do not involve support and control by a higher jurisdiction, e.g., relations among coordinate city and county governments
>
> Class comprehensive works on administrative cooperation among subordinate jurisdictions in 352.143
>
> *See also 353.33 for support and control of subordinate jurisdictions by higher jurisdictions*

301–308   Standard subdivisions
> Notation from Table 1 as modified under 01–08, e.g., serial administrative reports 305

309   History, geographic treatment, biography

Class comprehensive works on administration of subordinate jurisdictions in 352.14. Class administration of or in a specific subordinate jurisdiction with the jurisdiction in 351.3–351.9, e.g., administration of Bavaria 351.433

See Manual at 351.3–351.9 vs. 352.13–352.19

.13   †State and provincial administration

States and provinces: regularly constituted territorial subdivisions of large countries, with responsibilities cutting across several fields of administration, and usually encompassing many local units

Subdivisions are added for either or both topics in heading

See Manual at 352.13 vs. 352.15

†Add as instructed under 352.13–352.19

.14   †Local administration

Limited to comprehensive and comparative treatment, e.g., local administration in Germany 352.140943

Class here comprehensive works on administration of subordinate jurisdictions

Class local government, combined treatment of local government and local administration in 320.8; class regional divisions of administrative agencies in 352.288. Class administration in or of a specific subordinate jurisdiction with the jurisdiction in 351.3–351.9, e.g., administration of Nuremberg 351.43324

> *For state and provincial administration, see 352.13; for administration of specific kinds of local jurisdictions, see 352.15–352.19; for support and control of subordinate jurisdictions by higher jurisdictions, see 353.33*

See Manual at 351.3–351.9 vs. 352.13–352.19

.143

>   352.15–352.19   Administration of specific kinds of local jurisdictions

Class comprehensive works in 352.14

.15   †Intermediate units of local administration

Intermediate units: regularly constituted relatively local territorial subdivisions, with responsibilities cutting across several fields of administration, and usually containing few component units

Class here arrondissements, counties, shires, territorial departments; provinces of small countries

See Manual at 352.13 vs. 352.15

.16   †Urban administration

Class here city administration

See also 354.2793 for public administration of urban development

.167   †Administration of metropolitan regions

.169   †Suburban administration

.17   †Rural administration

See also 354.2794 for public administration of rural development

†Add as instructed under 352.13–352.19

.19   †Administration of special service districts

Local districts or authorities established to provide one or a few services

Class regional divisions of state and national agencies in 352.288. Class administration of specific kinds of special service districts with the service they administer, e.g., metropolitan districts to coordinate administration of health services 353.6219, local rail transit authorities that operate trains 388.42065

.193   Administrative cooperation among jurisdictions served by special service districts

Number built according to instructions under 352.13–352.19

Class here control of special service districts by higher jurisdictions and by other local authorities

---

>   **352.2–352.6   Specific topics of management in public administration**

Except for modifications shown under specific entries, add to each subdivision identified by ‡ as follows:
   01–09   Standard subdivisions
            Add to 0 the numbers following 0 in notation 01–09 from table
            under 352–354, e.g., programs directed to groups of people 08
   2   General considerations of public administration
   21   Jurisdictional levels
   2101–2109   Standard subdivisions
            Add to 210 the numbers following 352.10 in
            352.101–352.109, e.g., nongovernmental organizations
            2106
   211–219   Specific jurisdictional levels
            Add to 21 the numbers following 352.1 in 352.11–352.19,
            e.g., international administration 211
            Class administration at national level, combined treatment
            of national and other levels (*except* works that emphasize
            differences between administration at different levels) in base
            number without use of notation 21 from this table
   22–26   Specific topics in management
            Add to 2 the numbers following 352 in 352.2–352.6, e.g.,
            governing boards and commissions 225, planning and policy
            making 234, contracts and procurement 253

Class comprehensive works on administrative aspects in 351; class interdisciplinary works on management, on specific topics of management in 658

.2   ‡**Organization of administration**

Class comprehensive works on executive management in public administration in 352.3; class interdisciplinary works on organization in management in 658.1

---

†Add as instructed under 352.13–352.19
‡Add as instructed under 352.2–352.6

SUMMARY

.23   ‡Chief executives

Class here presidents, prime ministers, monarchs; comprehensive works on heads of state

Class governing boards and commissions in 352.25

For heads of departments and agencies, see 352.293. For a specific aspect of heads of state, see the aspect, e.g., presidential government 321.8042

.230 92   Biography

Do not use for collected biographies of chief executives; class in 930–990, plus notation 0099 from table under 930–990, e.g., collected biography of kings and queens of Great Britain 941.0099. Do not use for individual biographies of chief executive; class in 930–990, plus notation 01–09 for the period of the person's administration from table under 930–990, plus notation 092 from Table 1, e.g., biography of Queen Elizabeth of England 942.055092

Class here biography of chief executives as administrators

See Manual at T1—092: Comprehensive biography: Public figures; also at 920.009, 920.03–920.09 vs. 909.09, 909.1–909.8, 930–990

.233   ‡Heads of state lacking administrative powers

Presidents in countries where prime ministers are head of administration; constitutional monarchs and their representatives, e.g., governors-general in Commonwealth of Nations countries

.233 092   Biography

Do not use for collected biographies of heads of states lacking administrative powers; class in 930–990, plus notation 0099 from table under 930–990, e.g., collected biography of constitutional monarchs of Great Britain 941.0099. Do not use for individual biographies of heads of states lacking administrative powers; class in 930–990, plus notation 01–09 for the period of the person's administration from table under 930–990, plus notation 092 from Table 1, e.g., biography of Queen Elizabeth of Great Britain 941.085092

See Manual at T1—092: Comprehensive biography: Public figures; also at 920.009, 920.03–920.09 vs. 909.09, 909.1–909.8, 930–990

‡Add as instructed under 352.2–352.6

.235   ‡Powers and privileges of chief executives

Class abuse of power in 353.46

.236   ‡Leadership role of chief executives

.237   ‡Office of chief executive

.237 229 3   Heads and deputy heads of office of chief executive

Number built according to instructions under 352.2–352.6

Class here chief of staff to chief executive

.238   ‡Executive messages, speeches, writings

Collections, history, description, criticism

> *For messages, speeches, writings on a specific subject, see the subject, e.g., budget messages of specific jurisdictions 352.493–352.499, messages on German budget 352.4943013, executive messages on economics 330, executive messages on economy of Germany 330.943*

.238 4   ‡Addresses to legislatures

.238 6   ‡Inaugural addresses

.239   ‡Deputy chief executives

.239 092   Biography

Do not use for collected biographies of deputy chief executives; class in 930–990, plus notation 0099 from table under 930–990, e.g., collected biography of deputy prime ministers of Australia 994.0099. Do not use for individual biographies of deputy chief executives; class in 930–990, plus notation 01–09 for the period of the person's administration from table under 930–990, plus notation 092 from Table 1, e.g., biography of Deputy Prime Minister Tim Fischer of Australia 994.066092

Class here biographies of deputy chief executives as administrators

> *See Manual at T1—092: Comprehensive biography: Public figures; also at 920.009, 920.03–920.09 vs. 909.09, 909.1–909.8, 930–990*

.24   ‡Cabinets and cabinet-level committees

Class here councils of ministers, executive councils

Subdivisions are added for either or both topics in heading

> *For a cabinet-level committee charged with a specific activity, see the activity, plus notation 224 from table under 352–354, e.g., cabinet councils on the economy 354.224*

.243   ‡Cabinet secretariats

‡Add as instructed under 352.2–352.6

.243 229 3	Heads and deputy heads of cabinet secretariats
	Number built according to instructions under 352.2–352.6
	Class here cabinet secretaries, ministers with a portfolio of cabinet affairs
.246	‡Domestic councils
.25	‡Governing boards and commissions

Multimember bodies (other than cabinets and cabinet-level committees) selecting executives and or participating in executive decisions

Subdivisions are added for either or both topics in heading

Class a specific board or commission with the topic it administers, plus notation 09 (*not* 225) from table under 352–354, e.g., United States National Labor Relations Board 354.970973 (*not* 354.972250973)

> *For regulatory boards and commissions, see 352.8*

> *See also 352.743 for advisory bodies*

| .26 | ‡Special kinds of agencies |

> *For a special kind of agency not provided for here, see the kind, e.g., cabinets 352.24*

| .264 | ‡Independent agencies |

Agencies that are not parts of larger (cabinet-level) departments

Avoid using notation 2264 from table under 352–354 for specific independent agencies, e.g., independent regulatory agencies 352.8 (*not* 352.82264)

Class autonomous authorities of local scope in 352.19

| .266 | ‡Government corporations (Public enterprises) |

Class interdisciplinary works on government corporations in 338.749

| .28 | ‡Internal organization |

Class here levels of management

> *For supervision, see 352.66*

| .283 | ‡Distribution and delegation of authority |

Including centralization, decentralization

Class here line and staff organization

Subdivisions are added for either or both topics in heading

> *For regional divisions of administrative departments, see 352.288*

| .284 | ‡Middle management |
| .285 | ‡Top management |

‡Add as instructed under 352.2–352.6

.288   ‡Regional divisions of administrative agencies

Class here field offices, regional offices

.29   ‡Organization and structure of departments and agencies

Limited to generalities of organization and structure

Subdivisions are added for either or both topics in heading

Class description and purposes of departments and agencies in general in 351. Class organization and structure of a specific kind of department or agency with the kind, plus notation 22 (*not* 229) from table under 352–354, e.g., structure of governing boards 352.2522, structure of governing boards in Germany 352.25220943

See Manual at 351 vs. 352.29; also at 352–354

.293   ‡Heads and deputy heads of departments and agencies

Class here cabinet officers, ministers of state, secretaries of state

Class cabinet secretaries, ministers with a portfolio of cabinet affairs in 352.2432293; class secretaries of state of specific states of United States in 352.3870974–352.3870979; class secretaries of state for foreign affairs in 353.132293; class prime ministers, comprehensive works on chief executives in 352.23

See also 352.39 for executive development

See Manual at 352–354

.3   ‡Executive management

Class here interdisciplinary works on public administrators

Class interdisciplinary works on executive management in 658.4

For internal organization, see 352.28. For a specific aspect of public administrators, see the aspect, e.g., biography 351.092, law 342.068

.33   ‡Decision making

Class specific means of obtaining guidance for decision making in 352.37

.34   ‡Planning and policy making

Subdivisions are added for either or both topics in heading

Class specific means of obtaining guidance for planning and policy making in 352.37

See Manual at 300, 320.6 vs. 352–354

‡Add as instructed under 352.2–352.6

.35   ‡Internal control

Including internal inspection, agency ombudsmen

Class here accountability in public administration, administrative responsibility, oversight

Class legislative oversight in 328.3456; class administration of control of society by government in 352.8

For oversight by outside agencies, see 352.88

.357   ‡Quality control

Class quality control by managerial accounting in 352.43

.36   ‡Objectives of administration

Class here management by objective (MBO)

Class means of obtaining objectives in 352.37

.365   ‡Project management

.367   ‡Managing change

Class here modernization

.37   ‡Means of obtaining objectives

Class here specific means of obtaining guidance for policy and decision making

Class comprehensive works on decision making in 352.33; class comprehensive works on policy in 352.34; class management by objectives in 352.36

For use of information, see 352.38; for fact-finding and advisory bodies, see 352.743

.373   ‡Use of consultants

.375   ‡Promotion of efficiency

.379   ‡Intelligence and security

Including computer and office security, security classification

Class military security classification in 355.3433

See also 353.1 for administration of external and national security

.38   ‡Information management

Class fact-finding and advisory bodies in 352.743

.384   ‡Communication in management

‡Add as instructed under 352.2–352.6

.387   ‡Records management

Class here maintaining official records

Class archival treatment of public records in 025.1714; class secretaries of state in specific states of United States in 352.3870974–352.3870979; class programs supporting archives in 352.744

See Manual at 352–354

.39   ‡Managing executive personnel

Class here executive development, leadership, management environment

For leadership role of chief executive, see 352.236; for specific aspects of managing of executive personnel, see 352.6

.4   ‡Financial administration and budgets

Class here management of public finance; treasury departments and ministries; works covering both government financial administration and administration of financial institutions, money, credit

Subdivisions are added for financial administration and budgets together, for financial administration alone

Class interdisciplinary works on public finance in 336; class interdisciplinary works on financial management in 658.15

For administration of financial institutions, money, credit, see 354.8

See also 332.46 for monetary policy; also 336.3 for fiscal policy

.43   ‡Financial control

Class here managerial accounting (financial and nonfinancial); agencies that perform management, performance, program auditing, e.g., general accounting offices

Class ordinary accounting of government agencies in 657.835

.439   ‡Management, performance, program audits

Internal or external audits or comparable reviews to evaluate efficiency, conformance to policies and standards, and effectiveness of expenditures of funds or other administrative activities

Class here reports of general accounting offices

Subdivisions are added for any or all topics in heading

Class financial auditing of government agencies in 657.835045

.44   ‡Revenue administration

Class here tax administration, tax collection

See also 353.43 for tax litigation

See Manual at 343.04–343.06 vs. 336.2, 352.44

.448   ‡Customs administration

‡Add as instructed under 352.2–352.6

.45   ‡Debt management

.46   ‡Public expenditures

> *For payroll administration, see 352.47; for contracts, see 352.53; for financial assistance, see 352.73*

.47   ‡Payroll administration

> *See also 352.67 for wage and salary scales of government workers; also 354.98 for wages and salaries of labor and professions*

.48   ‡Budgeting

Including adoption of budgets, budget messages; specific kinds of budgets, e.g., capital, estimated, legislative budgets

Class here comprehensive works on budgets

> *For procedures for legislative enactment of budgets, see 328.378; for budgets of specific international organizations and specific jurisdictions, see 352.49*

.49   Budgets for specific international organizations and specific jurisdictions

Class comprehensive works on budgets in 352.48

[.490 1–.490 9]   Standard subdivisions

Do not use; class in 352.4801–352.4809

.491   Budgets for specific international organizations

Add to base number 352.491 the numbers following 352.11 in 352.112–352.119, e.g., budgets for United Nations 352.4913; then add further as instructed under 352.493–352.499, e.g., proposed budgets for United Nations 352.491301

---

‡Add as instructed under 352.2–352.6

.493–.499   Budgets for specific jurisdictions

Add to base number 352.49 notation 3–9 from Table 2, e.g., a budget of Germany 352.4943; then add further as follows:

001–007	Standard subdivisions
	Notation from Table 1 as modified under 351, e.g., official serial reports on budgets 005
008–009	Standard subdivisions
>01–03	Comprehensive budgets in specific stages of adoption
	Class here operating budgets
	Class partial budgets in specific stages of adoption in notation 04–08 from this table; class comprehensive works in 352.493–352.499 without adding from this table
01	Proposed budgets
	Class here estimated budgets, executive budgets, budget requests from recipient agencies
	For budgets in legislative process, see notation 02 from this table
013	Executive budget messages and supporting documents
02	Budgets in legislative process
	Class here legislative budgets, legislative authorizations
023	Legislative hearings and reports on budgets
	Hearings that concentrate on the objectives that a budget is to achieve are usually classed with the subject outside public administration, e.g., a hearing on the prospect that a budget will help achieve economic stabilization and growth 339.522
	See Manual at 300–330, 355–390 vs. 342–347, 352–354
03	Adopted budgets
>04–08	Partial budgets
	Class comprehensive works in 352.493–352.499 without adding from this table. Class budgets for a specific jurisdiction limited to a specific subject with the subject, plus notation 249 from table under 352–354, e.g., agricultural budgets in specific jurisdictions 354.5249, agricultural budgets for Germany 354.524943
	For operating budgets, see notation 01–03 from this table
04	Revenue budgets
05	Capital budgets
08	Supplemental budgets

Class works on budgeting, on budgets in general in 352.48

.5   ‡**Property administration and related topics**

Class here general services agencies

Subdivisions are added for property administration and related topics together, for property administration alone

Class records management in 352.387

---

‡Add as instructed under 352.2–352.6

.53 ‡Contracts and procurement

Class here procurement of property, comprehensive works on public contracts

Subdivisions are added for either or both topics in heading

For procurement of equipment and supplies, see 352.553; for procurement of buildings and their utilities, see 352.563; for procurement of public lands, see 352.573. For public contracts not related to property, see the subject, plus notation 253 from table under 352–354, e.g., personnel contracts 352.65253

.538 ‡Contracting for services

Class here contracting out

Class use of consultants in 352.373

.54 ‡Maintenance, utilization, disposal of property

Including inventory

For maintenance, utilization, disposal of equipment and supplies, see 352.554; for maintenance, utilization, disposal of buildings and their utilities, see 352.564; for maintenance, utilization, disposal of public lands, see 352.574

.55 *Equipment and supplies

Subdivisions are added for either or both topics in heading

Class interdisciplinary works on supply management in 658.7

.553 *Contracts and procurement

Subdivisions are added for either or both topics in heading

.554 *Maintenance, utilization, disposal

.56 *Buildings and their utilities

Class here plant management

Subdivisions are added for buildings and their utilities, for buildings alone

Class interdisciplinary works on plant management in 658.2

For public land management, see 352.57

.563 *Contracts and procurement

Subdivisions are added for either or both topics in heading

.564 *Maintenance, utilization, disposal

.57 *Public lands

Class comprehensive works on land resources in 354.34

*Add as instructed under 352–354
‡Add as instructed under 352.2–352.6

.573	*Contracts and procurement

Subdivisions are added for either or both topics in heading

.574	*Maintenance, utilization, disposal

.6	**‡Personnel management (Human resource management)**

Use subdivisions of 352.6 for specific aspects of management of executive personnel

Class contracting out in 352.538; class interdisciplinary works on personnel management in 658.3

For general management of executive personnel, see 352.39

.602 5	Directories of people and organizations in personnel management

Class directories of public officials and employees in 351.025

.608	Groups of people

Class here equal employment opportunity programs for government employees

Class comprehensive works on equal employment opportunity programs in 354.908

.63	‡Civil service system

Government service in which appointments are determined by merit and examination rather than by political patronage

Including management of office workers

Class here government service, merit system, interdisciplinary works on government workers

Class civil service in the sense of all units of public administration other than armed services in 351; class civil service examinations in 351.076

For a specific aspect of government service and government workers, see the aspect, e.g., labor economics 331.795, wage and salary scales 352.67

.64	‡Job description

Including job analysis and classification

.65	‡Recruiting and selection

.650 8	Groups of people

Class here preferential hiring

.66	‡Utilization and training

Including discipline, evaluation, motivation, placement, supervision; absenteeism, turnover

Subdivisions are added for utilization and training, for utilization alone

---

*Add as instructed under 352–354
‡Add as instructed under 352.2–352.6

.669   ‡Training

.67   ‡Conditions of employment

Including fringe benefits, e.g., counseling, health services; hours of work, work environment

Class here compensation

Class payroll administration in 352.47; class public administration of pensions for government workers in 353.549; class comprehensive works on conditions of employment for all workers in 354.98

For training, see 352.669

.68   ‡Employer-employee relationships

Including labor unions and collective bargaining, other employee organizations, employee participation in management, grievances

Class comprehensive works on grievances against government in 352.885; class comprehensive works on labor unions and collective bargaining for all workers in 354.97

.69   ‡Separation from service

Including dismissal, layoffs, reduction in force, retirement

Class public administration of pensions for government workers in 353.549

>   **352.7–352.8 Public administration of supporting and controlling functions of government**

Class comprehensive works in 351. Class public administration of support and control of a specific topic of management with the topic, plus notation 27–28 from table under 352–354, e.g., support for commerce and trade 354.7327, advisory bodies in commerce and trade 354.732743

.7   ***Public administration of general forms of assistance**

Class here the promotional and supporting role of administration when considered apart from its restraining and limiting role; administration of research and development in noneconomic fields

Class comprehensive works on public administration of research and development in 354.27

See also 352.8 for the restraining and limiting role of administration

*Add as instructed under 352–354
‡Add as instructed under 352.2–352.6

SUMMARY

352.73	**Financial assistance**
.74	**Promoting and disseminating knowledge**
.75	**Census and surveys**
.76	**Promoting museums and exhibitions**
.77	**Public works**
.78	**Sponsorship of volunteers and public service activities**
.79	**Assistance to urban, suburban, rural areas**

.73   *Financial assistance

Financial assistance to subordinate jurisdictions or to private parties

Class here grants, grants-in-aid, revenue sharing

Class comprehensive works on support and control of subordinate jurisdictions in 353.33

For price supports, see 352.85

.734   Financial support for specific kinds of subordinate jurisdictions

Add to base number 352.734 the numbers following 352.1 in 352.13–352.19, e.g., grants to states and provinces 352.7343, grants to local governments from either national governments or states and provinces 352.7344

.736   *Loans and loan guarantees

Subdivisions are added for either or both topics in heading

.74   *Promoting and disseminating knowledge

Class here promoting research

Subdivisions are added for either or both topics in heading

Class governmental publishers in 070.595

For census and surveys, see 352.75; for promoting museums and exhibitions, see 352.76; for public administration of agencies supporting and controlling education, see 353.8

.743   *Fact-finding and advisory bodies

Bodies advising the government or the public

Temporary and permanent

Class here counseling bodies, royal commissions

Subdivisions are added for either or both topics in heading

See also 352.25 for governing boards and commissions

*Add as instructed under 352–354

.744   *Promoting libraries and historical research

          Class here programs supporting archives

          Subdivisions are added for either or both topics in heading

          Class library administration in 025.1; class archives administration in 025.1714; class records management in 352.387

          For public administration of agencies supporting public libraries, see 353.73

.745   *Promoting general fields of knowledge

          Including natural sciences, social and behavioral sciences, technology; specific field of knowledge not provided for elsewhere, e.g., physics, space

          Class here promoting experimental research

          Class promoting museums and exhibitions in 352.76. Class promoting a specific field of knowledge provided for elsewhere with the field in public administration, plus notation 274 (*not* 2745) from table under 352–354 if not redundant, e.g., promoting environmental knowledge by an environmental protection agency 354.328274, but promoting public libraries 353.73 (*not* 353.73274)

          For promoting arts and humanities, see 353.77

          See also 338.926–338.927 for science policy, policies to promote economic development through use of science and technology; also 355.07 for military research and development

          See Manual at 338.926 vs. 352.745, 500

.746   *Consumer information programs

          Class here consumer protection

          Class interdisciplinary works on consumer information in 381.33; class interdisciplinary works on consumer protection in 381.34

          For a specific aspect of consumer protection, see the aspect, e.g., price and cost controls 352.85

.748   *Publicity activities

          Publicity for government's own activities

          Class here public relations

          Class interdisciplinary works on public relations in 659.2

.749   *Protecting intellectual property

          Regardless of subject or field

          Including copyright, patents, trademarks

*Add as instructed under 352–354

.75   *Census and surveys

           Class here public administration of descriptive research

           Subdivisions are added for either or both topics in heading

.76   *Promoting museums and exhibitions

           Class here government participation in fairs and expositions

           Subdivisions are added for either or both topics in heading

           Class comprehensive works on public administration of culture and related activities in 353.7

           See also 069 for government policy on museums

.77   *Public works

           For a specific program of public works, see the program, e.g., transportation public works 354.76277

.78   *Sponsorship of volunteers and public service activities

           Subdivisions are added for either or both topics in heading

.79   *Assistance to urban, suburban, rural areas

           Class specific forms of assistance to urban and rural areas in 352.73–352.78; class comprehensive works on public administration of urban and rural development in 354.279

           See also 352.7091724 for assistance to underdeveloped areas

.793   *Urban and suburban areas

           Including community planning

           Subdivisions are added for either or both topics in heading

           Class community planning for rural areas in 352.794; class community action programs in 353.52793; class comprehensive works on public administration of community development in 354.2793

           See also 353.5333 for programs directed to residents of disadvantaged urban areas

.794   *Rural areas

           See also 353.5334 for programs directed to residents of rural areas

.8   *Public administration of general forms of control

           Class here the restraining and limiting role of administration when considered apart from its promotional and supporting role; regulation, regulatory agencies, quasi-judicial agencies

           Class internal control of administrative activities in 352.35; class watchdog agencies in 352.88

           See also 352.7 for promotional and supporting role of administration

*Add as instructed under 352–354

.83   *Setting standards

     Class here inspection, establishing weights and measures

     Class inspection as a form of internal control in 352.35

.84   *Licensing, accreditation, certification, chartering, registration; incorporation

     Class here interdisciplinary works on licensing, accreditation, certification, chartering, registration

     Subdivisions are added for any or all topics in heading

     Class interdisciplinary works on incorporation in 346.06622

        For licensing, accreditation, certification, chartering by nongovernmental organizations, see 060

.85   *Price and cost controls

     Class here price supports

     Subdivisions are added for either or both topics in heading

.86   *Rationing

     Class here allocation

.88   *Use of watchdog and oversight agencies

     Including ethics agencies

     Class here promotion of procedural rights, agencies providing checks and balances to administrative operations, interdisciplinary works on ombudsmen

     Subdivisions are added for either or both topics in heading

     Class oversight in executive management, ombudsmen within agencies in 352.35; class quasi-judicial agencies in 352.8; class misconduct in office in 353.46

        For ombudsman role in legislative bodies, see 328.3452

        See also 342.06 for administrative law

.885   *Processing claims against government

     Class here government liability, grievances against government

        For government-employee grievances, see 352.68; for international claims, see 353.44

353   Specific fields of public administration

     For public administration of economy and environment, see 354

     See Manual at T1—068 vs. 353–354; also at 352–354; also at 363 vs. 344.02–344.05, 353–354

*Add as instructed under 352–354

SUMMARY

[.01–.09]   Standard subdivisions

> Do not use; class in 351.01–351.09

.1   *Public administration of external and national security affairs

> Subdivisions are added for external and national security affairs together, for national security affairs alone

> Class interdisciplinary works on national security in 355.03

> *For military and defense administration, see 355.6*

> *See also 352.379 for intelligence and security in executive management*

.122 4   Cabinet-level national security councils

> Number built according to instructions under 352–354

.13   *Foreign and diplomatic relations

> Class here departments and ministries of foreign affairs

> Subdivisions are added for either or both topics in heading

> Class interdisciplinary works on foreign relations in 327

.132 63   Foreign service

> Number built according to instructions under 352–354

> Class here consular and diplomatic services

.132 73   Financial assistance

> Number built according to instructions under 352–354

> Class here foreign aid

> Class use of foreign aid to attain foreign policy objectives in 327.111; class interdisciplinary works on foreign aid in 338.91

.132 74   Promotion and dissemination of knowledge

> Number built according to instructions under 352–354

> Class here government information services

> Class interdisciplinary works on government information services in 327.11

*Add as instructed under 352–354

.15   *Administration of non-self-governing territories

Class here administration of colonies, of semisovereign states

Class military government of occupied territories in 355.49

.150 93–.150 99   Specific continents, countries, localities

Do not use for administration of specific non-self-governing territories; class in 351.3–351.9, e.g., British colonial administration in Kenya 351.67620904

Limited to administration of more than one jurisdiction, e.g., British colonial administration 353.150941, British colonial administration in Africa 353.150941096

.159   Administration of territories under international control

.17   *Intelligence and counterintelligence

Limited to administration of operations primarily focused on foreign threats

Class here espionage, subversion

Subdivisions are added for either or both topics in heading

Class activities of domestic police services relating to intelligence and subversion in 363.23; class interdisciplinary works on espionage, subversion, intelligence in 327.12

(.2)   **Military and defense administration**

(Optional number; prefer 355.6)

Class here army administration

For specific topics in military and defense administration, see 355.6

(.25)   Naval administration

(Optional number; prefer 359.6)

For specific topics in naval administration, see 359.6

(.27)   Air forces administration

(Optional number; prefer 358.416)

For specific topics in air forces administration, see 358.416

(.29)   Administration of other military forces

(Optional number; prefer numbers for specific forces in 356–359)

For specific topics in administration of other specific forces, see the specific force, plus notation 6 from table under 356–359, e.g., executive management of marine forces 359.966

---

*Add as instructed under 352–354

> **353.3–353.9 Public administration in domestic fields not related to economy and environment**

Many works classed here will concern activities of national or state and provincial governments to regulate, control, or support services provided by local government agencies. These activities are in contrast to those of local governments which provide the actual services. Works on managing local agencies that directly serve the ultimate recipients are usually classed with the service outside public administration, e.g., management of city police departments 363.2068 (*not* 353.36216), of parole boards 364.62068 (*not* 353.39), of local school systems 371.2 (*not* 353.8214)

Class comprehensive works in 351

See Manual at T1—068 vs. 353–354

.3   *Public administration of services related to domestic order

Class here home departments and ministries, European style interior ministries

For public administration of justice, see 353.4

See also 354.30973 for United States Department of the Interior

.33   *Support and control of subordinate jurisdictions by higher jurisdictions

Subdivisions are added for either or both topics in heading

Class comprehensive works on administration of subordinate jurisdictions in 352.14

For financial support of subordinate jurisdictions, see 352.73

.332 13–.332 19   Administration by subordinate jurisdictions

Numbers built according to instructions under 352–354

Class support and control of specific kinds of subordinate jurisdictions in 353.333–353.339

.333–.339   Support and control of specific kinds of subordinate jurisdictions

Unless it is redundant, add to base number 353.33 the numbers following 352.1 in 352.13–352.19, e.g., support and control of counties 353.335, but comprehensive works on support and control of local administration by states and provinces or by unitary national administration 353.33 (*not* 353.334); however, for control of special service districts, see 352.193; for support of urban, suburban, rural areas, see 352.79

.36   *Police services

Including control of crowds, explosives, guns; crime prevention

Class operational management of police services in 363.2068; class operational management of bureaus of investigation in 363.25068

For regulating personal conduct, see 353.37

*Add as instructed under 352–354

.37 *Regulating personal conduct

Including public administration of censorship; control of alcohol, drugs, gambling, pornography, prostitution, sexual mores and morals

Class personal liberty in 323.44; class police control of personal conduct in 363.23; class censorship in 363.31

.39 *Corrections

Including parole and probation services

Class here prisons

Class interdisciplinary works on administration of correctional activities in 364.6068; class interdisciplinary works on parole administration in 364.62068; class interdisciplinary works on probation administration in 364.63068; class interdisciplinary works on prison administration in 365.068

.4 *Public administration of justice

Class here public administration of criminal justice, departments of justice

For judicial administration, see 347.013; for police services, see 353.36; for correctional activities, see 353.39

.43 *Criminal matters

Including antitrust and tax litigation

Class here criminal prosecution

Class marshals service in 347.016; class criminal litigation to promote civil rights in 353.48; class administration of police services in 363.25068; class interdisciplinary works on criminal procedure in 345.05

.44 *Civil matters

Including international-claims litigation

Class administrative processing of claims against government in 352.885; class civil litigation to promote citizenship and rights in 353.48; class interdisciplinary works on civil procedure in 347.05

.46 *Misconduct in office

Regardless of topic or field

Class here abuse of power, civil rights violations, conflict of interest, corruption, whistle blowing

Class problems resolvable by routine administrative procedures in 352.88; class interdisciplinary works on misconduct in office in 364.132

*Add as instructed under 352–354

.463   *Public investigations and inquiries

Other than normal administrative and legislative oversight

Subdivisions are added for either or both topics in heading

Class legislative oversight hearings on administrative matters with the subject in public administration, e.g., on public administration of social welfare 353.5

> See also 328.3452 for legislative investigative power; also 352.88 for normal administrative oversight and watchdog agencies

.465   Misconduct in specific areas of public administration

Add to base number 353.465 the numbers following 35 in 352–354, e.g., misconduct in treasury departments 353.46524

.48   *Exercise of citizenship and rights

Including litigation

Class here promotion of civil rights

Class election procedures in 324.6

> For administration of public defenders, see 345.01263; for promotion of procedural rights, see 352.88

.484   *Immigration and naturalization services

Subdivisions are added for either or both topics in heading

Class comprehensive works on activities relating to population and settlement in 353.59

.5   ***Public administration of social welfare**

Class here human services, social security in the sense of social welfare

Class social security in the sense of retirement income in 353.54

> For public administration of health services, see 353.6

> See Manual at 361–365 vs. 353.5

SUMMARY

353.508	**Groups of people**
.53	**Programs directed to groups of people**
.54	**Income maintenance**
.55	**Housing**
.56	**Nutrition and food**
.59	**Activities relating to population and settlement**

.508   Groups of people

Do not use for programs directed to groups of people; class in 353.53

---

*Add as instructed under 352–354

.53   ***Programs directed to groups of people**

Class here equal opportunity programs; programs for minorities, for socially disadvantaged groups; comprehensive works on programs in public administration directed to groups of people

Class programs directed to victims of crime and political oppression regardless of other group characteristic in 353.5337–353.5338; class programs directed to ethnic minorities in 353.5339. Class a program directing a specific kind of service to groups of people with the kind of service, plus notation 08 from Table 1, e.g., personnel programs directed to minorities 352.608, administrative support for children's recreation 353.78083

For programs directed to labor and professional groups, see 354.9

.533   **Specific miscellaneous groups**

Only those named below

[.533 01–.533 09]   Standard subdivisions

Do not use; class in 353.5301–353.5309

.533 1   ***Families**

Class here unmarried mothers

See also 353.536 for children

.533 2   ***Poor people**

Class poor residents of disadvantaged urban and suburban areas in 353.5333; class poor residents of disadvantaged rural and sparsely populated areas in 353.5334

.533 3   ***Residents of disadvantaged urban and suburban areas**

Class here residents of inner cities, of slums

Subdivisions are added for either or both topics in heading

Class comprehensive works on assistance to urban and suburban areas in 352.793

See also 354.2793 for urban and suburban development

.533 4   ***Residents of rural and sparsely populated areas**

Subdivisions are added for either or both topics in heading

Class comprehensive works on assistance to rural areas in 352.794

See also 354.2794 for rural development

.533 7   ***Victims of crime**

Regardless of other group characteristics or kind of crime

Class people who are victims of both crime and political oppression in 353.5338

*Add as instructed under 352–354

.533 8   *Victims of oppression

   Regardless of other group characteristics or of reason for oppression

   Class here refugees, victims of religious persecution

.533 9   *Ethnic and national groups in general

   Class here programs directed to ethnic minorities

   For specific ethnic and national groups, see 353.534

.534   Specific ethnic and national groups

[.534 001–.534 009]   Standard subdivisions

   Do not use; class in 353.533901–353.533909

.534 05–.534 09   Specific ethnic and national groups with ethnic origins from more than one continent, of European descent

   Add to base number 353.534 notation 05–09 from Table 5, e.g., programs directed to ethnic groups of European descent 353.53409

.534 1–.534 9   Specific ethnic groups with other origins

   Add to base number 353.534 notation 1–9 from Table 5, e.g., programs for Spanish Americans 353.53468

.535   *Women

.536   *Young people to age twenty

   Class here children

.536 5   Young people twelve to twenty

   Variant names: adolescents, teenagers, young adults, youth

.537   *People in late adulthood

.538   *Veterans

.539   *People with disabilities and illnesses

   Programs not predominantly health related, e.g., access for people with disabilities

   Subdivisions are added for either or both topics in heading

   Class health programs for people with disabilities and illnesses in 353.6

*Add as instructed under 352–354

.54   *Income maintenance

> Including guaranteed minimum income, unemployment insurance
>
> Class here pensions, social security in the sense of retirement income, comprehensive works on public administration of government sponsored insurance
>
> Class social security in the sense of social welfare in 353.5; class comprehensive works on insurance in 354.85
>
> *For government-sponsored health insurance, see 353.69*

.548   Public administration of pensions limited to specific occupations and groups of occupations

> Add to base number 353.548 the numbers following 354.9 in 354.93–354.95, e.g., public administration of railroad pensions 353.5485385
>
> *For pensions of government workers, see 353.549*
>
> *See also 331.252 for pension benefits*

.549   *Public administration of pensions for government workers

> *See also 352.69 for retirement of government workers*

.55   *Housing

> Including public housing, assistance to home owners

.56   *Nutrition and food

> *For food purity, designation of nutritional content, see 353.997*

.59   *Activities relating to population and settlement

> Including birth and death certificates, birth control, population movement
>
> *For immigration and naturalization services, see 353.484*

.6   *Public administration of health services

> Including disposal of the dead
>
> Class here rehabilitation services, services for physical illness
>
> Class comprehensive works on public administration of social welfare in 353.5

.627 4   Promoting and disseminating knowledge

> Number built according to instructions under 352–354
>
> Class here health promotion, physical fitness programs

.628   General forms of control

> Number built according to instructions under 352–354
>
> Class here disease control, medical screening

---

*Add as instructed under 352–354

.63	Specific kinds of physical diseases

Including cancer, communicable diseases

.64	*Mental health services

Including services for substance abuse

For services for people with mental retardation, see 353.65

.65	*Services for people with mental retardation
.66	*Services for people with physical disabilities
.68	*Health care facilities
.69	*Health insurance

Including workers' compensation insurance

Class here hospital insurance; specific health insurance programs, e.g., United States Medicaid and Medicare 353.690973

.7	***Public administration of culture and related activities**

Including programs to support and control religion, language programs

Subdivisions are added for culture and related activities together, for culture alone

Class public administration of communications in 354.75

For promoting museums and exhibitions, see 352.76; for public administration of education, see 353.8

See also 306 for government policy on culture; also 322.1 for government policy on religion; also 353.48 for promotion of religious freedom

.73	*Public libraries

Public administration of agencies supporting and controlling public libraries and library systems

Class administration of public libraries and library systems in 025.1974; class public administration of support for libraries in general in 352.744

[.732 25]	Governing boards and commissions

Do not use; class in 021.82

.77	*Arts and humanities

Including crafts, performing arts, celebrations, historical preservation

For recreation, see 353.78

See also 001.3 for government policy on humanities; also 306.449 for government policy on language; also 700 for government policy on arts

*Add as instructed under 352–354

.78   *Recreation

Including parks, recreational use of environment, sports hunting and fishing

Class here sports

Class comprehensive works on hunting in 354.349; class comprehensive works on fishing in 354.57

For crafts and performing arts, see 353.77

.8   ***Public administration of agencies supporting and controlling education**

Class here agencies supporting and controlling primary education, supporting and controlling secondary education

Class school administration and management in 371.2; class public policy issues in education in 379; class comprehensive works on promotion and dissemination of knowledge in 352.74

See Manual at 371 vs. 353.8, 371.2, 379

.822 5   Governing boards and commissions

Number built according to instructions under 352–354

For local school boards, see 379.1531

.824   Financial administration of public education

Number built according to instructions under 352–354

Class here financial administration of agencies supporting and controlling public education

Class financial management of schools and school systems in 371.206

.84   *Adult education

.88   *Higher education

.89   *Special education

.9   ***Public administration of safety, sanitation, waste control**

Subdivisions are added for public administration of safety, sanitation, waste control together, for public administration of safety alone

.93   *Sanitation and waste control

Including cleanup of pollution, recycling

Subdivisions are added for either or both topics in heading

Class operational management of waste control and disposal services in 363.728068; class comprehensive works on public administration of pollution in 354.335

For sanitation in public facilities, see 353.94; for hazardous wastes, see 353.994

*Add as instructed under 352–354

.94   *Sanitation in public facilities

> Including sanitation in common carriers, eating and drinking places, health facilities, streets, workplaces
>
> Class operational management of sanitary services in 363.72068

\>   **353.95–353.99   Public administration of safety**

> Class here accidents, public administration of safety in economy and environment
>
> Class comprehensive works in 353.9
>
> *For police services, see 353.36; for contagious diseases, see 353.63*

.95   *Preparation for disasters

> Class here civil defense, emergency planning
>
> Class management of disaster relief in 363.348068

.96   *Industrial and occupational safety

> Standard subdivisions are added for either or both topics in heading
>
> Class here workplace safety
>
> Class workplace sanitation in 353.93

.966   Safety in specific extractive, manufacturing, construction occupations

> Add to base number 353.966 the numbers following 6 in 620–690, e.g., mine safety 353.96622

.97   *Safety in miscellaneous areas

> Including domestic, outdoor, sports safety
>
> Class here safety in public facilities
>
> *For workplace safety, see 353.96; for transportation safety, see 353.98*

.979   *Fire safety

> Class management of fire departments in 363.37068

.98   *Transportation safety

> Including space transportation safety
>
> Class here ground-transportation safety
>
> Class comprehensive works on transportation in 354.76

.987   *Water-transportation safety

> Class here water safety
>
> *For water-sports safety, see 353.97*

*Add as instructed under 352–354

.988   *Air-transportation safety

.99   *Hazardous products and materials

            Including medical instruments and supplies

            Class here hazardous machinery

            Subdivisions are added for hazardous products and materials together, for hazardous products alone

.993   *Hazardous materials

            Class hazardous wastes in 353.994

            For radioactive materials, see 353.999

.994   *Hazardous wastes

            For radioactive wastes, see 353.999

.997   *Food safety

            Class here food purity, designation of nutritional content

            Class comprehensive works on nutrition and food services in 353.56

.998   *Drugs and medicines

            Class here drug safety

            Subdivisions are added for either or both topics in heading

.999   *Radioactive products

            Including radioactive wastes

            Class here radiation safety, radioactive materials

354 *Public administration of economy and environment

Subdivisions are added for public administration of economy and environment together, for public administration of economy alone

Class public administration of safety in economy and environment in 353.95–353.99

See Manual at T1—068 vs. 353–354; also at 352–354; also at 363 vs. 344.02–344.05, 353–354

SUMMARY

354.08	Groups of people
.2	General considerations of public administration
.3	Public administration of environment and natural resources
.4	Public administration of energy and energy-related industries
.5	Public administration of agriculture
.6	Public administration of construction, manufacturing, service industries
.7	Public administration of commerce, communications, transportation
.8	Public administration of financial institutions, money, credit
.9	Public administration of labor and professions

*Add as instructed under 352–354

.08   Groups of people

Class here equal economic opportunity programs

.27   General forms of assistance

Number built according to instructions under 352–354

Class here comprehensive works on public administration of development, on public administration of research and development

Class urban and community development in 354.2793; class rural development in 354.2794; class comprehensive works on public administration of research and development in noneconomic fields in 352.7; class interdisciplinary works on research and development in 338.9. Class public administration of research and development of a specific economic activity with the activity in 354, plus notation 27 from table under 352–354, e.g., development of agriculture 354.527

.274   Promotion and dissemination of knowledge

Number built according to instructions under 352–354

Class protection of intellectual property in 352.749

.279   Assistance to urban, suburban, rural areas; to small business

Number built according to instructions under 352–354

.279 9   *Assistance to small business

For a specific form of assistance to small business, see the form, e.g., assistance in securing government contracts 352.5327, small business loans 354.2736

>
354.3–354.8 Public administration of specific fields of economic and environmental activity

Class here public administration of industries associated with specific fields of economic and environmental activity

Class public administration of labor and professions in specific fields of economic and environmental activity in 354.9; class comprehensive works in 354

.3   *Public administration of environment and natural resources

Class here departments of natural resources, public administration of primary industries

Subdivisions are added for either or both topics in heading

For public administration of recreational use of environment, see 353.78; for public administration of sanitation and waste control, see 353.93; for public administration of energy and energy-related resources, see 354.4; for public administration of agriculture, see 354.5

*Add as instructed under 352–354

SUMMARY

.327   General forms of assistance

> Number built according to instructions under 352–354

> Class here natural resources development

> Class interdisciplinary works on natural resources development in 333.715

.328   General forms of control

> Number built according to instructions under 352–354

> Class here environmental protection

> Class interdisciplinary works on environmental protection in 363.7

> *For special forms of environmental protection and control, see 354.33*

.33   Special forms of environmental protection and control

> Not provided for in subdivisions of 354.328

> Class comprehensive works on public administration of environmental protection and control in 354.328. Class public administration of a special form of protection and control relating to a specific environment with the form of protection and control in 354.34–354.37, plus notation 3 from table under 354.34–354.37, e.g., water conservation 354.3634

.333   *Resource use planning

> Class here zoning

> Class urban zoning in 354.353; class interdisciplinary works on zoning in 333.7317

.334   *Conservation

> Class interdisciplinary works on conservation in 333.72

.335   *Prevention and control of pollution

> Class here comprehensive works on public administration of pollution

> Class public administration of cleanup of pollution in 353.93; class interdisciplinary works on pollution in 363.73

.338   *Noise control

> Regardless of environment

---

*Add as instructed under 352–354

.339   *Pest control

Regardless of environment

>   354.34–354.37   Specific environments

Except for modifications shown under specific entries, add to each subdivision identified by † as follows:

01–09   Standard subdivisions

Add as instructed under 352–354, e.g., equal opportunity programs 08

2   General considerations of administration

Add as instructed under 352–354, e.g., state and provincial administration of the topic 213

3   Special forms of protection and control

Add to 3 the numbers following 354.33 in 354.333–354.335, e.g., conservation 34

Class noise control in specific environments in 354.338; class pest control in specific environments in 354.339; class mineral resources derived from a specific environment in 354.39; class comprehensive works on administration of environment in 354.3

.34   †Land and biological resources

Including wetlands

Class here real estate, real property

Subdivisions are added for land and biological resources together, for land alone

Class parks in 353.78

For public lands, see 352.57; for urban land, see 354.35

.349   †Biological resources

Including hunting

Class here animal resources

For sports hunting, see 353.78; for forestry, see 354.55; for aquatic biological resources, fishing and fisheries, see 354.57

.35   *Urban land

.353   *Land use planning

Class here city planning, urban zoning

Class comprehensive works on public administration of zoning in 354.333; class interdisciplinary works on city planning in 307.1216; class interdisciplinary works on urban zoning in 333.7717

*Add as instructed under 352–354
†Add as instructed under 354.34–354.37

.36 †Water

Including groundwater, estuaries

For aquatic biological resources, fishing and fisheries, see 354.57

.362 7 General forms of assistance

Number built according to instructions under 354.34–354.37

Class here development of water resources, of electricity from water resources; flood control

Class distribution of electricity derived from water power in 354.49

.366 †Water supply

For irrigation projects, see 354.367

.367 †Irrigation projects

.369 †Oceans

.37 †Air and atmospheric phenomena

Class here weather bureaus

.39 *Mineral resources

Class here geological surveys, mining bureaus, subsurface resources

For mineral energy resources, see 354.4

.393 *Conservation of mineral resources

.4 *Public administration of energy and energy-related industries

Class here departments of energy; public administration of energy resources, public administration of mineral energy resources

Subdivisions are added for either or both topics in heading

For development of water power, see 354.3627

.428 General forms of control

Number built according to instructions under 352–354

Class here control of public utilities supplying energy

Class energy conservation in 354.43; class comprehensive works on control of public utilities in 354.728. Class control of a specific energy utility with the form of energy, plus notation 28 from table under 352–354, e.g., a gas utility 354.4628

.43 *Energy conservation

Class energy conservation for a specific form of energy with the form, plus notation 3 from table under 354.44–354.49, e.g., petroleum conservation 354.453

---

*Add as instructed under 352–354
†Add as instructed under 354.34–354.37

\>   354.44–354.49 **Specific energy resources and electricity**

Except for modifications shown under specific entries, add to each subdivision identified by ‡ as follows:
01–09   Standard subdivisions
      Add as instructed under 352–354, e.g., equal opportunity programs 08
2   General considerations of administration
      Add as instructed under 352–354, e.g., international administration of the topic 211
3   Conservation
301–309   Standard subdivisions
      Add as instructed under 352–354, e.g., equal opportunity programs 308
32   General considerations of administration
      Add as instructed under 352–354, e.g., international administration of the topic 3211

Class comprehensive works in 354.4

\>   354.44–354.48 **Specific energy resources**

Class distribution of electricity derived from specific energy resources in 354.49; class comprehensive works on energy resources in 354.4

.44   ‡Fossil fuels

Including coal

For oil and gas, see 354.45

.45   ‡Oil

Class here comprehensive works on petroleum

For gas, see 354.46

.46   ‡Gas

Natural and manufactured

.47   ‡Nuclear fuels

Class radiation safety, radioactive wastes in 353.999

.472 7   General forms of assistance

Number built according to instructions under 354.44–354.49

Class here development of electricity from nuclear fuels

Class distribution of electricity derived from nuclear fuels in 354.49

.48   ‡Other energy resources

Including geothermal and solar energy

.49   ‡Electricity

‡Add as instructed under 354.44–354.49

.492 7   General forms of assistance

> Number built according to instructions under 354.44–354.49

> Class here comprehensive works on development of electricity

> Class development of electricity from a specific resource with the resource, plus notation 27 from table under 354.44–354.49, e.g., from water power 354.3627, from nuclear fuels 354.4727

.492 8   General forms of control

> Number built according to instructions under 354.44–354.49

> Class here control of electric utilities, of distribution of electricity regardless of resource from which it is derived

> Class development of electricity in 354.4927

.5   ***Public administration of agriculture**

> Class nutrition and food programs in 353.56; class rural development in 354.2794; class soil conservation in 354.3434; class irrigation projects in 354.367; class agricultural price supports in 354.5285; class agricultural credit in 354.86

> *For hunting, see 354.349*

> *See also 354.66 for public administration of dairy and related products industries*

.54   *Plant crops

> *For forestry, see 354.55*

.55   *Forestry

.56   *Animal husbandry

.57   *Fishing and fisheries

> Class here aquatic biological resources, marine biological resources

> Subdivisions are added for either or both topics in heading

> Class comprehensive works on resources derived from water in 354.36

> *For sports fishing, see 353.78*

.59   *Commodity programs

> Including marketing services

> Class here farm produce

> Class programs that combine inspection and marketing in 354.59283

> *For agricultural price supports, see 354.5285*

> *See also 354.88 for commodity exchanges*

---

*Add as instructed under 352–354

.6   ***Public administration of construction, manufacturing, service industries**

    Class here administration of secondary industries

.64   *Construction

    Class public works in 352.77

.66   *Manufacturing

.68   *Service industries

> *For commerce, communications, transportation, see 354.7; for financial services, see 354.8*

.7   ***Public administration of commerce, communications, transportation**

SUMMARY

354.728	**General forms of control**
.73	**Commerce**
.74	**Foreign commerce**
.75	**Communications**
.76	**Transportation**
.77	**Road transportation**
.78	**Water transportation**
.79	**Air and space transportation**

.728   General forms of control

    Number built according to instructions under 352–354

    Class here comprehensive works on control of public utilities

> *For control of a specific public utility, see the utility, plus notation 28 from table under 352–354, e.g., control of electric utilities 354.4928*

.73   *Commerce

    Including tourist trade regardless of origin

    Class here domestic commerce

> *For consumer protection, see 352.746; for foreign commerce, see 354.74*

> *See also 354.76280973 for United States Interstate Commerce Commission*

.74   *Foreign commerce

    Class foreign tourism in 354.73

---

*Add as instructed under 352–354

.75   *Communications

Class here telecommunications

Class management, business organizations, and description of facilities, activities, services of a publicly owned communications system with the system in 384, e.g., business organization of a publicly owned telephone system 384.6065

See Manual at T1—068 vs. 353–354; also at 380: Add table: 09 vs. 065

.759   *Postal service

Class operational management of postal service in 383.068; class postal organization in 383.4

.76   *Transportation

Class here ground transportation

Class transportation safety in 353.98

For road transportation, see 354.77; for water transportation, see 354.78; for air and space transportation, see 354.79

.763   *Passenger services

Class passenger service in a specific form of transportation with the form in 354.765–354.79, e.g., rail passenger service 354.7673

.764   *Freight services

Including pipeline transportation

Class freight service in a specific form of transportation with the form in 354.765–354.79, e.g., rail freight service 354.7674

.765   *Automotive transportation

Including parking facilities

For road transportation, see 354.77

.765 284   Licensing, accreditation, certification, chartering, registration; incorporation

Number built according to instructions under 352–354

Class here licensing to drive, registration of passenger automobiles for general use

For licensing to drive and registration of passenger automobiles for hire, see 354.7653284

.765 3   *Passenger service

*Add as instructed under 352–354

.765 328 4	Licensing, accreditation, certification, chartering, registration; incorporation

Number built according to instructions under 352–354

Class here licensing to drive, registration of passenger vehicles for hire

For licensing to drive, registration of passenger automobiles for general use, see 354.765284

.765 4	*Freight service
.767	*Railroad transportation

Class urban rail transportation in 354.769

.767 3	*Passenger service
.767 4	*Freight service
.769	*Urban mass transportation

Class here local bus transportation, local rail transportation, comprehensive works on local transportation

For a specific form of local transportation not provided for here, see the form, e.g., taxi service 354.7653, helicopter service 354.79

.769 3	*Passenger service
.769 4	*Freight service
.77	*Road transportation
.772 8	General forms of control

Number built according to instructions under 352–354

Class here traffic control, traffic engineering

.773	*Passenger service
.774	*Freight service
.78	*Water transportation

Class here inland water transportation, ocean transportation

.783	*Passenger service
.784	*Freight service
.79	*Air and space transportation

Subdivisions are added for air and space transportation together, for air transportation alone

.793	*Passenger service
.794	*Freight service

*Add as instructed under 352–354

.8 ***Public administration of financial institutions, money, credit**

> Subdivisions are added for financial institutions, money, credit together; for financial institutions alone

> Class works covering public administration of both financial system and government finances in 352.4

> *See also 332.46 for monetary policy*

.84 ***Money**

> Class credit institutions in 354.86

.85 ***Insurance**

> *For government-sponsored insurance, see 353.54; for government-sponsored health insurance, see 353.69*

.86 ***Credit institutions**

> Class here banks, savings and loan institutions

> Class government loans and loan guarantees in 352.736

.88 ***Securities and investments**

.9 ***Public administration of labor and professions**

> Class here departments of labor

> Subdivisions are added for labor and professions together, for labor alone

> Class occupational safety in 353.96

.908 Groups of people

> Class here affirmative action programs, equal employment opportunity programs

> Class affirmative action programs for a government's own employees in 352.608

.927 General forms of assistance

> Number built according to instructions under 352–354

> Class here job creation

.93 Labor in specific groups of occupations

> Including blue collar, industrial, professional occupations

> Class labor in specific extractive, manufacturing, construction occupations in 354.94; class labor in specific occupations other than extraction, manufacturing, construction in 354.95

> *For government workers, see 352.63*

.94 Labor in specific extractive, manufacturing, construction occupations

> Add to base number 354.94 the numbers following 6 in 620–690, e.g., miners 354.9422

*Add as instructed under 352–354

.95   **Labor in other specific occupations**

> Add to base number 354.95 notation 001–999, e.g., railroad workers 354.95385

> **354.96–354.98 Specific programs for labor and professions**

Not provided for in subdivisions of 354.927 derived from 352.7

Except for modifications shown under specific entries, add to each subdivision identified by † as follows:
01–09   Standard subdivisions
        Add as instructed under 352–354, e.g., programs directed to groups of people 08
2   General considerations of administration
        Add as instructed under 352–354, e.g., state and provincial administration of the topic 213
3   Specific groups of occupations
        Class specific extractive, manufacturing, construction occupations in notation 4 from this table; class other specific occupations in notation 5 from this table
        For government workers, see 352.63
4   Specific extractive, manufacturing, construction occupations
        Add to 4 the numbers following 6 in 620–690, e.g., miners 422
5   Other specific occupations
        Add to 5 notation 001–999, e.g., railroad workers 5385

Class comprehensive works in 354.9

.96   †**Employment and related services**

> Subdivisions are added for employment and related services together, for employment services alone

.968   †**Promoting training**

> Class here promoting apprenticeship

> *See also 352.669 for training of government's own workers*

.97   †**Labor unions and collective bargaining**

> Class here employer-employee relationships

> Subdivisions are added for either or both topics in heading

.98   †**Conditions of employment**

> Class here compensation

> Class pensions, unemployment insurance in 353.54; class workers' compensation insurance in 353.69

†Add as instructed under 354.96–354.98

355 Military science

Class here armed forces and services, ground forces and services

Class sociology of military institutions in 306.27

> *For specific kinds of military forces and warfare, see 356–359*

> *See also 322.5 for relation of the state to military organizations; also 327.174 for disarmament; also 343.01 for military and defense law*

> *See Manual at 355–359 vs. 623; also at 930–990 vs. 355.009, 355–359*

SUMMARY

355.001–.009	**Standard subdivisions**
.02–.07	**Basic considerations of military science**
.1	**Military life and customs**
.2	**Military resources**
.3	**Organization and personnel of military forces**
.4	**Military operations**
.5	**Military training**
.6	**Military administration**
.7	**Military installations**
.8	**Military equipment and supplies (Matériel)**

.001   Philosophy and theory

.002   Miscellany

[.002 8]   Auxiliary techniques and procedures; apparatus, equipment, materials

Do not use; class in 355.8

.003–.005   Standard subdivisions

.006   Organizations

[.006 8]   Management

Do not use; class in 355.6

.007   Education and related topics

.007 1   Education

Do not use for reserve training; class in 355.2232

.007 11   Higher education

Class here military colleges and universities

> *For mid-career training of officers at academically accredited armed forces schools, see 355.55*

> *See Manual at 378.4–378.9 vs. 355.00711*

.007 113–.007 119   Specific continents, countries, localities

Official service academies are classed in notation at the country level only, e.g., Royal Military Academy (Sandhurst, England) 355.0071141

[.007 155]		On-the-job training

> Do not use; class in 355.5

[.007 2]	Research

> Do not use; class in 355.07

.008	Groups of people
.009	History, geographic treatment, biography

> Class historical and geographic treatment of military situation and policy in 355.033
>
> *See Manual at 930–990 vs. 355.009, 355–359*

.009 3–.009 9	Specific continents, countries, localities

> Class organization of specific national armies in 355.3093–355.3099
>
> *For military history of a specific war, see the war in 930–990, e.g., military history of Vietnamese War 959.70434*

> 355.02–355.07 **Basic considerations of military science**

> Class comprehensive works in 355

.02	War and warfare

> Class here conventional warfare, total war; comprehensive works on military strategy
>
> Class defense in 355.03
>
> *For strategy in military operations, see 355.4*
>
> *See also 341.6 for law of war*

.020 11	Systems

> Do not use for models; class in 355.48

.021	General topics of war and warfare
[.021 01–.021 09]	Standard subdivisions

> Do not use; class in 355.0201–355.0209

.021 3	Militarism

> Class here antimilitarism, interdisciplinary works on military-industrial complex
>
> Class relation of military organizations to the state in 322.5; class promotion of peace in 327.172
>
> *For economic aspects of military-industrial complex, see 338.47355*

.021 5	Limited war

.021 7   Nuclear warfare

        Including issues of deterrence

        Class here comprehensive works on nuclear forces

        Class comprehensive works on warfare with weapons of mass destruction in 358.3

         For a specific nuclear force and its warfare, see the force, e.g., nuclear missile forces and warfare 358.17

         See also 327.1747 for nuclear disarmament

.021 8   Insurgent, resistance, revolutionary warfare

        Standard subdivisions are added for any or all topics in heading

        Class here civil war, guerrilla warfare

        Class guerrilla tactics in 355.425

.027   Causes of war

        For causes of specific wars, see 930–990

.027 2   Political and diplomatic causes

.027 3   Economic causes

.027 4   Social causes

        See also 303.66 for sociology of war

.027 5   Psychological causes

.028   Aftermath of war

        Including military occupation

        Class here dislocation, reconstruction

        Class government of occupied territories in 355.49

        For aftermath of specific wars, see 930–990

.03   Military situation and policy

        Class here defense

        Class defense operations in 355.4

[.030 9]   History and geographic treatment

        Do not use; class in 355.033

[.030 92]   Biography

        Do not use; class in 355.0092

.031   Military relations

        Class here military alliances, mutual security pacts

        For military assistance, see 355.032

.031 09 History, geographic treatment, biography

> Class here military relations between two regions or countries, e.g., military relations of China 355.0310951, then for relations between that nation and another nation or region add as instructed under —093–099 in Table 1, e.g., military relations between China and Myanmar 355.031095109591

.032 Military assistance

> Class here military attachés, military missions

.032 093–.032 099 Specific continents, countries, localities

> Do not use for military assistance to specific continents, countries, localities; class in 355.0323–355.0329

.032 3–.032 9 Military assistance to specific continents, countries, localities

> Add to base number 355.032 notation 3–9 from Table 2, e.g., military assistance to Vietnam 355.032597

.033 General history and description

> Class general history and description of military relations in 355.031

.033 000 1–.033 000 8 Standard subdivisions

[.033 000 9] History, geographic treatment, biography

> Do not use for biography; class in 355.0092. Do not use for history without subdivision; class in 355.033. Do not use for historical periods; class in 355.033001–355.033005. Do not use for areas, regions, places in general; class in 355.03301. Do not use for specific continents, countries, localities; class in 355.03303–355.03309

.033 001–.033 005 Historical periods

> Add to base number 355.03300 the numbers following —090 in notation 0901–0905 from Table 1, e.g., military situation and policy in 1930s 355.0330043

.033 01 Areas, regions, places in general

> Add to base number 355.03301 the numbers following —1 in notation 11–19 from Table 2, e.g., military situation and policy in developing countries 355.03301724

.033 03–.033 09 Specific continents, countries, localities

> Add to base number 355.0330 notation 3–9 from Table 2, e.g., military situation of Brazil 355.033081

.033 2 Military capability

> Class here combat readiness

> Class combat readiness of specific units in 355.3

[.033 209 1–.033 209 9] Geographic treatment and biography

> Do not use; class in 355.03321–355.03329

.033 21–.033 29   Geographic treatment and biography of military capability

> Add to base number 355.0332 notation 1–9 from Table 2, e.g., military capability of Sweden 355.0332485

.033 5   Military policy

[.033 509 1–.033 509 9]   Geographic treatment and biography

> Do not use; class in 355.03351–355.03359

.033 51–.033 59   Geographic treatment and biography of military policy

> Add to base number 355.0335 notation 1–9 from Table 2, e.g., military policy of Italy 355.033545

.07   Military research and development

> Limited to military aspects

> Class here relation of military science to science and technology; comprehensive works on military aspects of research and development of equipment, supplies, weapons

> Class interdisciplinary works on military research and development in 338.4735507

> *For procurement and contracting aspects of research and development of equipment and supplies, see 355.6212; for military aspects of research and development (other than procurement and contracting) of specific kinds of equipment and supplies, see 355.8*

.1   Military life and customs

> Class here conditions of military employment

> *For social and welfare services provided to soldiers and dependents, see 355.34*

SUMMARY

355.11	**Service periods, promotion and demotion, termination**
.12	**Living conditions**
.13	**Conduct and rewards**
.14	**Uniforms**
.15	**Colors and standards**
.16	**Celebrations, commemorations, memorials**
.17	**Ceremonies**

.11   Service periods, promotion and demotion, termination

.111   Length of service

.112   Promotion and demotion

.113   Inactive periods

> Including furloughs, leaves, missing in action, reserve status, status during captivity or internment

> Class reserve training in 355.2232

.114	Termination of service

Including resignation, retirement; reinstatement

.12	Living conditions

Class here living conditions of dependents, comprehensive works on military housing

For quarters for personnel at military installations, see 355.71

.123	Morale and motivation
.129	Living conditions in specific situations

Class morale in specific situations in 355.123

For life in military prisons and prison camps (other than prisoner-of-war camps), see 365.48

.129 2	Living conditions in regular quarters

Including quarters during basic training

.129 3	Living conditions during maneuvers, aboard ship, in transit
.129 4	Living conditions in combat zones
.129 6	Living conditions in prisoner-of-war camps
.13	Conduct and rewards

Class here discipline, soldierly qualities

See also 343.014 for law of discipline and conduct

.133	Regulation of conduct

Class rewards in 355.134

.133 2	Enforcement and punishment

Class offenses in 355.1334

.133 23	Enforcement

Including criminal investigation, military police

Class interdisciplinary works on police in 363.2

.133 25	Punishment

Class military prisons in 365.48

.133 4	Offenses against military discipline

Including desertion, mutiny

Class interdisciplinary works on mutinies in 364.131

See also 364.138 for war crimes

.133 6	Etiquette

Class dress regulations, etiquette of uniforms in 355.14

.134   Rewards

         Including special privileges

         Class here awards, citations

.134 092   Biography

            Class a military awardee who is associated with another subject with the subject, e.g., biography of an awardee who is also a movie star 791.43028092

.134 2   Honorary insignia

         Including badges, decorations, medals

         Class here comprehensive works on insignia

         Class comprehensive works on insignia and uniforms in 355.14

         For insignia of rank, see 355.14

.134 9   Gifts and gun salutes

.14   Uniforms

         Including accessories, insignia of rank and service

         Class here etiquette of uniforms, comprehensive works on insignia and uniforms

         Class issue and use of uniforms in 355.81

         For honorary insignia, comprehensive works on insignia, see 355.1342

.140 9   History, geographic treatment, biography

         See Manual at 355.1409

.15   Colors and standards

         Standard subdivisions are added for either or both topics in heading

         Class here flag presentations

.16   Celebrations, commemorations, memorials

         Standard subdivisions are added for any or all topics in heading

.17   Ceremonies

         Class ceremonies for a specific occasion with the occasion, e.g., gun salutes 355.1349, military celebrations 355.16

.2   **Military resources**

.21   Preparation, evaluation, preservation

         Class preparation, evaluation, preservation of specific resources in 355.22–355.27

\>   355.22–355.27   Specific resources

         Class comprehensive works in 355.2

.22	**Human resources**

For civilian personnel, see 355.23

[.220 68]	Management

Do not use for management of human resources other than recruiting; class in 355.61. Do not use for recruiting; class in 355.223

.223	**Recruiting and reserve training**

Standard subdivisions are added for recruiting and reserve training together, for recruiting alone

Class here enlistment

.223 2	Reserve training
.223 207 11	Higher education

Class here reserve training in academic settings, e.g., United States Reserve Officers' Training Corps 355.2232071173

.223 4	Qualifications for service
.223 6	Specific methods and procedures of recruiting

Including registration, commissioning

[.223 601–.223 609]	Standard subdivisions

Do not use; class in 355.22301–355.22309

.223 62	Voluntary enlistment

Class here all-volunteer army

.223 63	Draft (Conscription)

For universal military service, see 355.225

.224	**Conscientious objectors**

Class here draft resistance

Class ethics of conscientious objection in 172.1; class techniques for evading draft in 355.22363

.225	**Universal military training**

Class here universal military service

.23	**Civilian workers**
[.230 68]	Management

Do not use; class in 355.619

.24	**Raw materials**

Class here strategic materials, comprehensive works on nonhuman resources

For industrial resources, see 355.26; for transportation and communication facilities, see 355.27

.242   Metals

.243   Nonmetallic minerals

.245   Agricultural products

.26   Industrial resources

> Military appraisal and utilization

> Class here manufacturing war matériel

.27   Transportation and communications facilities

.28   Mobilization

> Including commandeering, requisition

> Class mobilization of specific resources in 355.22–355.27

.29   Demobilization

> Class demobilization of specific resources in 355.22–355.27

.3   **Organization and personnel of military forces**

> Standard subdivisions are added for organization and personnel together, for organization alone

> Class here organization of national armies, combat readiness of specific units

> Class comprehensive works on combat readiness in 355.0332

SUMMARY

355.31	**Kinds of military units**
.33	**Personnel and their hierarchy**
.34	**Noncombat services**
.35	**Combat units according to field of service**
.37	**Reserves**

.31   Kinds of military units

> Including armies, regiments, squads; districts

> Class here combat units

> Class organization of national armies in 355.3

>> *For a specific kind of unit limited to a specific service, see the service, e.g., reserve units 355.37, armored units 358.183*

.33   Personnel and their hierarchy

> Including labor relations and military employee organizations

> Class biography of soldiers in 355.0092; class promotion and demotion in 355.112

.330 4   Line and staff organization

.330 41	Line organization

Including evaluation, leadership, supervision

Class here command and control systems, command functions

For motivation, see 355.123

.330 42	Staff organization

Class here general staffs, joint chiefs of staff

For line functions of chiefs of staff, see 355.33041

.331	General and flag officers

Officers above rank of colonel (naval rank of captain)

.332	Commissioned and warrant officers

Standard subdivisions are added for commissioned and warrant officers together, for commissioned officers alone

Class officers' manuals in 355

For general and flag officers, see 355.331

.338	Enlisted personnel

Including noncommissioned officers

Class noncommissioned officers' manuals in 355

See also 331.8811355 for military unions

.34	Noncombat services

Including propaganda, social services for dependents, interdisciplinary works on civic action of armed forces

Class here operations of noncombat services, social services for soldiers; interdisciplinary works on private military companies

For a specific noncombat service not provided for here, see the service, e.g., housing 355.12, personnel management 355.61; for a specific civic action of armed forces, see the action, e.g., civil works program of U.S. Army Corps of Engineers 363.0973; for a specific service of a private military company, see the service, e.g., service as a combat unit 355.354, logistics 355.411, non-military security services 363.2898

.341	Supply issuing and related services

Including canteens, mess services, post exchanges

Class officers' and noncommissioned officers' clubs in 355.346; class comprehensive works on supply services in 355.621

.342	Public relations
.343	Unconventional warfare services

.343 2	Intelligence
	Including cryptanalysis, mapping, weather forecasting; torture in intelligence gathering
	Class here military espionage
	Class counterintelligence in 355.3433; class interdisciplinary works on espionage in 327.12; class interdisciplinary works on torture in 364.675
.343 3	Counterintelligence
	Including security classification
.343 4	Psychological warfare
.343 7	Subversion and sabotage
	Class interdisciplinary works on subversion in 327.12
.345	Health services
	Including ambulance, sanitation, veterinary services
	Class here medical services
	Class technology of medical services in 610; class technology of health services in 613.6; class sanitation engineering in 623.75; class veterinary sciences in 636.089
.346	Recreational services
	Including library services, officers' and noncommissioned officers' (NCO) clubs
	Class library and informational sciences in 020; class recreational arts in 790
.347	Religious services
	Standard subdivisions are added for specific religions, e.g., history of Jewish services 355.34709
	Class care of military personnel by religious leaders in general in 206.1; class Christian pastoral care of military personnel in 259.088355
.348	Women's units
	Class women in armed forces in 355.0082; class women as a military resource in 355.22082. Class a specific service performed by women with the service, plus notation 082 from Table 1, e.g., women in intelligence services 355.3432082, women in combat 355.4082
.35	Combat units according to field of service
	Class comprehensive works on combat units in 355.31
.351	Units serving wholly within national or local frontiers
	Class here frontier troops, active units called home guards
	Class reserve units called home guards in 355.37

.352	Expeditionary forces

Class here expeditionary forces of colonies, forces of mother countries dedicated to service in colonies

.354	Mercenary troops

Class here soldiers of fortune

.356	Allied and coalition forces

Standard subdivisions are added for either or both topics in heading

Class here multinational forces

Class joint operations of allied and coalition forces in 355.46

> For multinational forces commanded by international bodies, see 355.357

.357	International forces

Troops serving under command of international bodies

Including peacekeeping forces

Class interdisciplinary works on peaceful resolution of conflict in 327.17

> See also 341.58 for legal aspects of international forces

.359	Foreign legions

Units of national armies consisting primarily of foreign recruits

Class here auxiliaries (troops of foreign countries serving with a state's armies)

.37	Reserves

Class here home guards, home reserves, militia, national guards; military departments devoted to reserve or national guard affairs

Class training of reserves in 355.2232; class active units called home guards in 355.351. Class reserve units of a specific kind of military force with the force, e.g., army engineer reserves 358.223

.4	**Military operations**

Including mine clearing operations, peacekeeping operations, security measures

Class here attack and defense operations, combat; strategy in military operations

Class interdisciplinary works on security measures provided by private military companies in 363.2898

> For mine clearing operations by civilians, see 363.34988; for engineering of mine clearing, see 623.26

[.409 1]	Areas, regions, places in general

Do not use; class in 355.471

[.409 3–.409 9]	Specific continents, countries, localities

Do not use; class in 355.473–355.479

.41	Support operations

Including camouflage, deception, handling prisoners of war

Class support operations in a specific situation with the situation, e.g., logistics of siege warfare 355.44

.411	Logistics

Including troop movements

For troop support, see 355.415

.412	Encampment
.413	Reconnaissance

Class here patrolling

.415	Troop support

Operations for providing immediate necessities for maintenance of troops

Class comprehensive works on operations for provisioning troops in 355.411

For a specific aspect of troop support, see the aspect, e.g., medical service 355.345

.42	Tactics

For nuclear tactics, see 355.43; for tactics of siege warfare, see 355.44; for tactics of defense of home territory, see 355.45

.422	Specific tactics

Including antiaircraft defenses, attacks and counterattacks, debarkation and landing, prevention of friendly fire casualties, retreats, skirmishing; mobile (blitz), commando (hit-and-run), infiltration tactics

Class specific tactics in specific conditions in 355.423–355.426

[.422 01–.422 09]	Standard subdivisions

Do not use; class in 355.4201–355.4209

>   355.423–355.426 Tactics in specific conditions

Class comprehensive works in 355.42

.423	Tactics in various kinds of terrain, climate, weather; night tactics
.424	Use of animals
.425	Guerrilla tactics

Class here tribal fighting

Class guerrilla warfare in 355.0218

.426	Tactics in cities

Class here house-to-house fighting, street fighting, urban warfare

Class siege warfare in 355.44

.43　　　　Nuclear operations

　　　　　　Class nuclear warfare in 355.0217

.44　　　　Siege and trench warfare, blockades

　　　　　　Class urban warfare in 355.426; class naval blockades in 359.44

.45　　　　Defense of home territory

　　　　　　Class defensive forts and installations in 355.7

.46　　　　Combined operations

　　　　　　Joint operations of two or more kinds of military forces

　　　　　　Including operations of forces of more than one nation

　　　　　　Class here amphibious operations

　　　　　　Class amphibious operations in which marines are main land component in 359.9646

.47　　　　Military geography

[.470 91–.470 99]　　　Geographic treatment and biography

　　　　　　　　　Do not use; class in 355.471–355.479

.471–.479　　Geographic treatment and biography of military geography

　　　　　　Class here geographic treatment of military operations

　　　　　　Add to base number 355.47 notation 1–9 from Table 2, e.g., military geography of Russia 355.4747

.48　　　　Technical analyses of military events

　　　　　　Including real and imaginary wars, campaigns, battles

　　　　　　Class here war games

　　　　　　See also 793.92 for recreational war games

.49　　　　Occupation of conquered territory

　　　　　　Including military government

　　　　　　Class occupation as an aftermath of war in 355.028

.5　　　Military training

　　　　　　Training of individuals and units

　　　　　　For reserve training, see 355.2232; for universal military training, see 355.225. For military training in a specific subject, see the subject, plus notation 0715 from Table 1, e.g., military training in computer engineering 621.390715

.507 1　　　Education in military training

　　　　　　　　Class military training in a specific country with the country in 355.5093–355.5099, e.g., military training in Switzerland 355.509494 (*not* 355.50710494)

.52　　　　Maneuvers

.54	Basic training

Including drill, survival training, tactical exercises

.544	Encampment and field training

Including setting up and dismantling camps, constructing temporary fortifications, running obstacle courses

.547	Small arms and bayonet practice

Class here manual of arms

If emphasis is on use by infantry, class in 356.115

.548	Self-defense

Unarmed combat and combat with knife

If emphasis is on use by infantry, class in 356.115

.55	Training of officers

Class here mid-career training at academically accredited armed forces schools

Class training through war games in 355.48; class comprehensive works on university-level service academies in 355.00711

.56	Technical training

.6	**Military administration**

Class here defense administration, departments of defense

Class administration of a function not provided for here with the function, plus notation 068 from Table 1, e.g., administration of installations 355.7068

For organization of military forces, see 355.3

(Option: Class comprehensive works in 353.2. If option is chosen, change heading to "Specific topics in military administration," and do not add standard subdivisions)

[.606 8]	Management

Do not use; class in 355.6

.609 1	Areas, regions, places in general

Class here international military and defense administration

Class administration of international peacekeeping troops in 355.357068

(If option under 355.6 is chosen, class international military and defense administration in 353.2211)

.61	Personnel management (Human resource management)

For service periods, promotion and demotion, termination, see 355.11; for motivation, see 355.123; for personnel and their hierarchy, see 355.33; for wage and salary administration, see 355.64

.614		Job description for military personnel

Including job analysis and classification

.619   Civilian workers

Add to base number 355.619 the numbers following 352.6 in 352.63–352.69, e.g., recruiting civilian personnel 355.6195

Class civilian workers as a military resource in 355.23

.62   Supply and financial administration and related topics

.621   Supply administration and related topics

Class here administration of specific kinds of equipment and supplies

For product development, see 355.07; for supply issuing and related services, see 355.341; for supply depots and installations, see 355.75

.621 2   Contracts and procurement

Standard subdivisions are added for either or both topics in heading

Class here comprehensive works on military contracts

For contracts for a specific nonsupply item, see the item, plus notation 068 from Table 1, e.g., contracts for real property 355.70681

.621 3   Internal control and disposal of supplies

Including warehouse management

.621 32   Inventory control

.621 37   Surplus supplies and their disposal

Standard subdivisions are added for either or both topics in heading

.622   Financial administration

Add to base number 355.622 the numbers following 352.4 in 352.43–352.49, e.g., defense budget 355.6229, defense budget of United States 355.622973

For payroll administration, see 355.64

.64   Salary administration

Class here wage and payroll administration

.68   Executive management

Add to base number 355.68 the numbers following 352.3 in 352.33–352.38, e.g., inspection 355.685; however, for intelligence, see 355.3432; for counterintelligence, see 355.3433

Class command and control systems in 355.33041

For managing executive personnel, see 355.33

.69   Military mail; graves registration and burial services

.693   Military mail

.699   Graves registration and burial services

.7   **Military installations**

Including security measures

Class interdisciplinary works on security measures provided by private military companies in 363.2898

.709 3–.709 9   Specific continents, countries, localities

Class here specific forts or systems of fortifications, installations having two or more functions

Use notation for area of installation, not country maintaining it, e.g., United States bases in Panama Canal Area 355.70972875

.71   Quarters for personnel

Housing at military installations

Including barracks, prisoner-of-war camps

Class comprehensive works on military housing in 355.12

.72   Medical installations

Class medical supply depots in 355.75; class veterans' hospitals in 362.11; class comprehensive works on medical services in 355.345

.73   Artillery installations

Class army artillery installations in 358.127

.74   Engineering installations

Class army engineering installations in 358.227

.75   Supply depots and installations

Class comprehensive works on supply services in 355.621

.79   Land

.8   **Military equipment and supplies (Matériel)**

Limited to equipment and supplies common to two or more land forces, or to at least two of the three major defense forces, e.g., missiles and tanks, supplies of land and sea forces

Including auxiliary techniques and procedures

Class here ordnance; apparatus, equipment, materials; military aspects of research and development (other than procurement and contracting) of specific kinds of equipment and supplies

Class mobilization of military industrial resources in 355.28; class comprehensive works on military aspects of research and development of equipment and supplies, of weapons in 355.07. Class interdisciplinary works on research and development of a specific kind of supplies and equipment with the kind in 338.47, e.g., small arms 338.4762344

For administration of specific kinds of equipment and supplies, see 355.621

[.806 8]	Management
	Do not use; class in 355.621
[.807 2]	Research
	Do not use; class in 355.07
.81	Clothing, food, camp equipment, office supplies
.82	Weapons

Class a kind of weapon limited to a specific land force in 356–357

Class here nonlethal weapons

For combat vehicles, see 355.83

See also 327.174 for problems of arms limitation and of verifying arms-control treaty provisions for specific kinds of weapons

See Manual at 355–359 vs. 623

.821	Artillery

Class army artillery in 358.1282

For specific pieces of artillery, see 355.822; for artillery projectiles, see 355.82513

.822	Specific pieces of artillery

Class specific pieces of army artillery in 358.1282

.823–.826	Other specific kinds of weapons

Add to base number 355.82 the numbers following 623.4 in 623.43–623.46, e.g., nuclear weapons 355.825119, artillery projectiles 355.82513; however, for comprehensive works on missiles, see 358.17182; for comprehensive works on chemical, biological, radiological weapons, on weapons of mass destruction, see 358.3; for ordnance of a force or service dedicated to a specific kind of weapon, see the force or service in 356–359, plus notation 82 or 83 from table at 356–359, e.g., tank ammunition 358.1882

.825 1	Charge-containing devices

Number built according to instructions under 355.823–355.826

Class here interdisciplinary works on bombs

For military engineering of bombs, see 623.451

.83	Transportation equipment and supplies

Including fuel; aircraft used outside air forces, ships used outside naval forces, support vehicles, trains

Class here combat vehicles

Class comprehensive works on aircraft in 358.4183; class comprehensive works on ships in 359.83

.85 Communication equipment

Class army communication equipment in 358.248

.88 Medical supplies

Class ambulances in 355.83

> ## 356–359 Specific kinds of military forces and warfare

Class here history of specific military forces not limited to any one war, services and units dedicated to specific forces, countermeasures against specific forces

All notes under 355 are applicable here

Except for modifications shown under specific entries, add to each subdivision identified by * as follows:

01–09	Standard subdivisions
	Notation from Table 1 as modified under 355.001–355.009, e.g., management 6 (*not* 068), management of artillery forces 358.126 (*not* 358.12068); however, class research, statistical methods in notation 072 from this table
1	Military life and customs
14	Uniforms
3	Organization and personnel
	Class here units
	For personnel management, see notation 6 from this table
309	History, geographic treatment, biography
	Class here units of specific countries regardless of size of unit
4	Operations
	Class here tactics
5	Training
6	Administration
	Including administration of equipment and supplies, executive management, financial administration, personnel management
	For administration of a specific topic not provided for here, see the topic, plus notation 068 from Table 1, e.g., administration of installations 7068
	(Option: Class comprehensive works on administration in 353.29. If option is chosen, change heading to "Specific topics in administration," and do not add standard subdivisions)
7	Installations
8	Equipment and supplies (Matériel)
	Class here ordnance
[8068]	Management
	Do not use; class in notation 6 from this table
82	Weapons
	Class here nonlethal weapons
	For combat vehicles, see 83 from this table
83	Combat vehicles

Class comprehensive works in 355. Class a specific countermeasure with the force wielding it, e.g., coast artillery 358.16 (*not* 359)

See Manual at 355–359 vs. 623; also at 930–990 vs. 355.009, 355–359

> ### 356–357 Land forces and warfare

Class comprehensive works in 355

> *For artillery, missile, armored forces, see 358.1; for chemical, biological, radiological warfare, see 358.3*

356 Foot forces and warfare

Standard subdivisions are added for either or both topics in heading

.1 Infantry

.11 General topics of infantry

Class general topics of irregular troops in 356.15; class general topics of troops having special combat functions in 356.16

[.110 1–.110 9] Standard subdivisions

Do not use; class in 356.101–356.109

.111–.118 Specific topics of infantry

Add to base number 356.11 notation 1–8 from table under 356–359, e.g., infantry training 356.115

.15 *Irregular troops

Including guerrillas, partisans

.16 Troops having special combat functions

Including motorized infantry

.162 Troops specializing in specific weapons

Including bazookamen, grenadiers, machine gunners, sharpshooters (snipers)

.164 *Mountain and ski troops

Subdivisions are added for either or both topics in heading

.166 *Paratroops

.167 *Commandos and rangers

Subdivisions are added for either or both topics in heading

357 Mounted forces and warfare

Standard subdivisions are added for either or both topics in heading

.04 General topics of mounted forces and warfare

[.040 1–.040 9] Standard subdivisions

Do not use; class in 357.01–357.09

.041 Military life and customs

---

*Add as instructed under 356–359

.041 4	Uniforms
.043	Organization and personnel

> Class here comprehensive works on units that served as horse cavalry and mechanized or armored cavalry, e.g., U.S. Third Cavalry Division 357.0430973
>
> Class a specific period of service of a unit which changed kinds of mounts with the kind of mount, e.g., U.S. Third Cavalry Division as a horse unit 357.1830973

.044–.048	Operations, training, administration, installations, equipment and supplies

> Add to base number 357.04 notation 4–8 from table under 356–359, e.g., training mounted forces 357.045

.1 Horse cavalry

> Class here dragoons, lancers
>
> *For remount services, see 357.2*
>
> *See also 358.12 for horse artillery*

.18	General topics of horse cavalry
[.180 1–.180 9]	Standard subdivisions

> Do not use; class in 357.101–357.109

.181–.188	Special topics of horse cavalry

> Add to base number 357.18 notation 1–8 from table under 356–359, e.g., uniforms of horse cavalry 357.1814

.2 Remount services

.5 Mechanized cavalry

> *For armored cavalry, see 358.18*

.52	*Bicycle troops
.53	*Motorcycle troops
.54	Large motor-vehicle cavalry

> Including jeep and truck cavalry

358 Air and other specialized forces and warfare; engineering and related services

*Add as instructed under 356–359

SUMMARY

358.1	**Missile forces; army artillery and armored forces**
.2	**Army engineering and related services**
.3	**Chemical, biological, radiological warfare**
.4	**Air forces and warfare**
.8	**Space forces**

.1   **Missile forces; army artillery and armored forces**

.12   *Army artillery forces

Including antitank artillery forces

Class here field artillery forces

> *For antiaircraft artillery forces, see 358.13; for coast artillery forces, see 358.16*

.13   *Antiaircraft artillery forces

.16   *Coast artillery forces

.17   Guided missile forces

Class here strategic missile forces, nuclear missile forces

Class strategic land missile forces in 358.1754

> *For air guided missile forces, see 358.42; for naval guided missile forces, see 359.9817*

.171   General topics of guided missile forces

Class general topics of specific missile forces in 358.174–358.176

[.171 01–.171 09]   Standard subdivisions

Do not use; class in 358.1701–358.1709

.171 1–.171 8   Specific topics of guided missile forces

Add to base number 358.171 notation 1–8 from table under 356–359, e.g., training of missile forces 358.1715

.171 82   Weapons other than combat vehicles

Number built according to instructions under 358.1711–358.1718

Class here comprehensive works on missiles

> *For military engineering of missiles, see 623.451*

.174   *Antimissile defense forces

Class here Strategic Defense Initiative (SDI, star wars), surface-to-air missile forces

Class a specific defense other than surface-to-air missiles with the defense, e.g., beam weapon forces 358.39, air-to-air missile forces 358.43

*Add as instructed under 356–359

.175	Specific surface-to-surface missile forces

[.175 01–.175 09]   Standard subdivisions

Do not use; class in 358.1701–358.1709

| .175 2 | *Short-range missile forces |

Class here tactical missile forces

| .175 3 | *Intermediate-range missile forces |

| .175 4 | *Long-range missile forces |

Class here strategic land missile forces

| .176 | *Surface-to-underwater missile forces |

| .18 | *Armored forces |

Class here tank forces, armored cavalry

| **.2** | **Army engineering and related services** |

| .22 | *Engineering services |

Including property maintenance

Class here construction engineer services

Class communications services in 358.24; class transportation services in 358.25; class civil activities of army engineering services in 363

| .23 | *Demolition services |

Including bomb disposal units

| .24 | *Communications forces (Signal forces) |

Including military cryptography services

| .25 | *Transportation services |

| **.3** | **Chemical, biological, radiological warfare** |

Regardless of service or force to which assigned

Class here warfare with weapons of mass destruction; interdisciplinary works on chemical, biological, radiological warfare; interdisciplinary works on weapons of mass destruction

For nuclear warfare, see 355.0217. For a specific aspect of weapons of mass destruction, see the aspect, e.g., disarmament of weapons of mass destruction 327.1745

| .34 | *Chemical warfare |

| .38 | *Biological warfare |

| .39 | *Radiation and beam warfare |

Class here passive defense against nuclear radiation

---

*Add as instructed under 356–359

.4   **Air forces and warfare**

> Standard subdivisions are added for either or both topics in heading

> *For naval air forces, see 359.94*

.400 1–.400 9   Standard subdivisions

> Notation from Table 1 as modified under 355.001–355.009, e.g., air forces administration 358.416 (*not* 358.40068)

.403   Situation and policy

> Standard subdivisions are added for either or both topics in heading

> Class air defense operations in 358.414

.407   Air force research and development

> Limited to air force aspects

> Class here relation of air force and warfare to science and technology, comprehensive works on air force aspects of research and development of equipment and supplies

> Class interdisciplinary works on air force research and development in 338.47358407

> *For procurement and contracting aspects of research and development of air force supplies and equipment, see 358.416212; for air force aspects of research and development (other than procurement and contracting) of specific kinds of equipment and supplies, see 358.418*

.41   General topics of air forces and warfare

> Class general topics of specific forces in 358.42–358.47

[.410 1–.410 9]   Standard subdivisions

> Do not use; class in 358.4001–358.4009

.411–.418   Specific topics of air forces and warfare

> Add to base number 358.41 the numbers following 355 in 355.1–355.8, e.g., uniforms 358.4114, comprehensive works on military aircraft 358.4183; however, for aircraft of specific forces, see 358.42–358.47

>   358.42–358.47 Specific forces

> Class chemical, biological, radiological warfare in 358.3; class comprehensive works in 358.4

.42   *Bombing forces

Including air-to-underwater guided missile forces

Class here strategic missions of air forces; air-to-surface guided missile forces; comprehensive works on air guided missile forces, on air nuclear forces

For air-to-air guided missile forces, air-to-air nuclear forces, see 358.43

.43   *Pursuit and fighter forces

Standard subdivisions are added for either or both topics in heading

Including air-to-air guided missile forces, air-to-air nuclear forces, air artillery

Class here tactical missions of air forces

.44   *Transportation services

.45   *Reconnaissance forces and operations

Including antisubmarine reconnaissance

.46   *Communications services

Class here signal services

.47   *Engineering services

.8   *Space forces

See also 358.17 for missile forces when either launch or target is from or to the earth or its atmosphere

359   Sea forces and warfare

Standard subdivisions are added for either or both topics in heading

Class here naval forces and warfare

SUMMARY

359.001–.009	**Standard subdivisions**
.03–.07	**[Situation and policy, naval research and development]**
.1–.2	**Naval life and resources**
.3	**Organization and personnel of naval forces**
.4–.7	**Naval operations, training, administration, installations**
.8	**Naval equipment and supplies (Naval matériel)**
.9	**Specialized combat forces; engineering and related services**

.001–.009   Standard subdivisions

Notation from Table 1 as modified under 355.001–355.006, e.g., naval administration 359.6 (*not* 359.0068)

*Add as instructed under 356–359

.03 Situation and policy

> Standard subdivisions are added for either or both topics in heading
>
> Class here naval defense
>
> Class naval defense operations in 359.4

.07 Naval research and development

> Limited to naval aspects
>
> Class here relation of naval science to science and technology; comprehensive works on naval aspects of research and development of equipment, supplies, weapons
>
> Class interdisciplinary works on naval research and development in 338.4735907
>
> > *For procurement and contracting aspects of research and development of naval equipment and supplies, see 359.6212; for naval aspects of research and development (other than procurement and contracting) of specific kinds of equipment and supplies, see 359.81–359.88*

.1–.2 **Naval life and resources**

> Add to base number 359 the numbers following 355 in 355.1–355.2, e.g., uniforms 359.14

.3 **Organization and personnel of naval forces**

.31 Naval units

> Including fleets, squadrons, flotillas, divisions
>
> Class noncombat services in 359.34; class reserves in 359.37
>
> > *For ships as naval units, see 359.32*

.32 Ships as naval units

> Class here crews of ships
>
> Class comprehensive works on ships in the navy in 359.83
>
> > *See Manual at 359.32 vs. 359.83*

.322 Sailing ships as naval units

> Class here sailing ships of war

.325–.326 Specific kinds of powered ships as naval units

> Add to base number 359.32 the numbers following 623.82 in 623.825–623.826, e.g., cruisers 359.3253; however, for submarines, see 359.933; for aircraft carriers, see 359.9435; for military supply and transport ships, see 359.9853

.33–.37 Personnel, noncombat services, fields of combat service, reserves

> Add to base number 359.3 the numbers following 355.3 in 355.33–355.37, e.g., noncombat services 359.34

.4–.7   Naval operations, training, administration, installations

Add to base number 359 the numbers following 355 in 355.4–355.7, e.g., naval blockades 359.44

.8   Naval equipment and supplies (Naval matériel)

Including auxiliary techniques and procedures

Class here weapons (ordnance); apparatus, equipment, materials; naval aspects of research and development (other than procurement and contracting) of specific kinds of supplies and equipment

Class mobilization of naval industrial resources in 359.28. Class interdisciplinary works on research and development of a specific kind of naval supplies and equipment with the kind in 338.47, e.g., warships 338.47623825

[.806 8]   Management

Do not use; class in 359.621

[.807 2]   Research

Do not use; class in 359.07

.81–.88   Specific kinds of naval equipment and supplies

Add to base number 359.8 the numbers following 355.8 in 355.81–355.88, e.g., clothing 359.81; however, for ordnance on specific kinds of ships, see 359.83; for artillery, see 359.981282; for guided missiles, see 359.981782

.83   Transportation equipment and supplies

Number built according to instructions under 359.8

Including fuel, support vehicles

Class here comprehensive works on ships in armed forces

> *For ships as naval units, see 359.32. For ships used outside the naval forces, see the force using them, e.g., coast guard ships 359.9783*
>
> *See Manual at 359.32 vs. 359.83*

.832   Sailing ships as equipment

Class here sailing ships of war

.835–.836   Specific kinds of power-driven warships as equipment

Add to base number 359.83 the numbers following 623.82 in 623.825–623.826, e.g., cruisers 359.8353; however, for submarines, see 359.9383; for aircraft carriers, see 359.94835; for military supply and transport ships, see 359.98583

.9   Specialized combat forces; engineering and related services

Class chemical, biological, radiological warfare in 358.3

.93   *Submarine forces

*Add as instructed under 356–359

.933	Organization and personnel
	Number built according to instructions under 356–359
	Class here units, submarines as units
	See Manual at 359.32 vs. 359.83
.938	Equipment and supplies (Matériel)
	Number built according to instructions under 356–359
.938 3	Ships as equipment
	Number built according to instructions under 356–359
	Class here submarines as equipment
	See Manual at 359.32 vs. 359.83
.938 32	Conventionally powered submarines
.938 34	Nuclear powered submarines
.94	*Naval air forces
.943	Organization and personnel
	Number built according to instructions under 356–359
	Class here units
.943 4	Aircraft units
	Including flights, groups, squadrons, wings
.943 5	Aircraft carriers as units
	See Manual at 359.32 vs. 359.83
.948	Equipment and supplies (Matériel)
	Number built according to instructions under 356–359
.948 3	Combat vehicles
	Number built according to instructions under 356–359
	Class combat vehicles as units in 359.943
.948 34	Aircraft
.948 35	Aircraft carriers as equipment
	See Manual at 359.32 vs. 359.83
.96	Marine forces
	Add to base number 359.96 the numbers following 355 in 355.1–355.8, e.g., training 359.965

*Add as instructed under 356–359

.97   *Coast guard

As a military service

Class coast guard as a police service, interdisciplinary works on coast guard in 363.286

.98   Artillery and guided missile forces; engineering and related services

.981   Artillery and guided missile forces

.981 2   *Artillery services

Class artillery units aboard specific kinds of ships in 359.32; class artillery ordnance aboard specific kinds of ships in 359.83

.981 7   *Guided missile forces

Class guided missile units aboard specific kinds of ships in 359.32; class guided missile ordnance aboard specific kinds of ships in 359.83

.982   *Engineering services

.983   *Communications services (Signal services)

.984   Special warfare services

Including frogmen, underwater demolition units, underwater reconnaissance operations; sea, air, land teams

.985   *Transportation services

Class here military sealift commands

.985 3   Organization and personnel

Number built according to instructions under 356–359

Including troopships as units

Class here units, military supply ships as units

See Manual at 359.32 vs. 359.83

.985 8   Supplies and equipment (Matériel)

Number built according to instructions under 356–359

.985 83   Military supply ships as equipment

Number built according to instructions under 356–359

Including troopships

See Manual at 359.32 vs. 359.83

360   Social problems and services; associations

*Add as instructed under 356–359

SUMMARY

367		General clubs
	.9	History, geographic treatment, biography

368		Insurance
	.001–.009	Standard subdivisions and insurance companies
	.01–.09	[General principles, specific forms of risk, sales groupings]
	.1	Insurance against damage to and loss of property
	.2	Insurance against damage to and loss of property in transit
	.3	Old-age insurance and insurance against death, illness, injury
	.4	Government-sponsored insurance
	.5	Liability insurance
	.6	Glass insurance
	.7	Insurance against industrial casualties (accidents)
	.8	Other casualty insurance
	.9	Insurance by specific continents, countries, localities in modern world

369		Associations
	.01–.09	Standard subdivisions
	.1	Hereditary, military, patriotic societies of United States
	.2	Hereditary, military, patriotic societies
	.3	Ethnic clubs
	.4	Young people's societies
	.5	Service clubs

361   Social problems and services

Class here social welfare; work and policy of government agencies that enforce the law in matters of social problems and services; interdisciplinary works on socioeconomic planning and development, on programs and services covering several branches of social sciences, on social problems and services

Class law of social services, including draft laws, enforcement of the law by courts, in 344.02–344.05; class the internal administration of governmental agencies dealing with social services, including their administrative annual reports, in 353.5; class insurance in 368; class personal health and safety in 613; class description of present or past social conditions in 930–990

> *For social problems treated purely as social phenomena, see 301–307; for community planning and development, see 307.1; for economic planning and development, see 338.9; for social services in armed forces, see 355–359; for specific problems and services, see 362–365; for school social services, see 371.7; for social services in specific wars, see 900. For a specific topic treated as a social problem but not provided for here, see the topic, e.g., premarital sexual relations 306.733*

> *See Manual at 361–365; also at 301–307 vs. 361–365; also at 361–365 vs. 353.5; also at 361 vs. 362–363*

SUMMARY

361.001–.008	Standard subdivisions
.02–.06	Specific kinds of assistance
.1	Social problems
.2	Social action
.3	Social work
.4	Group work
.6	Governmental action
.7	Private action
.8	Community action
.9	History, geographic treatment, biography

.001–.007	Standard subdivisions

.008   Groups of people

> Do not use for social problems of and services to groups of people; class in 362

[.009]   History, geographic treatment, biography

> Do not use; class in 361.9

>   361.02–361.06   Specific kinds of assistance

> Class here general discussions covering various problems and client groups, and both governmental and private assistance

> Class comprehensive works in 361. Class assistance with respect to a specific problem with the problem, e.g., free assistance to people in late adulthood 362.6

> *For governmental assistance, see 361.6; for private assistance, see 361.7*

.02   Free assistance

> Class specific kinds of free assistance in 361.05–361.06

.04   Paid assistance

> Assistance for which the recipient pays all or part of cost

> Class specific kinds of paid assistance in 361.05–361.06

.05   Material assistance

> Including direct provision of food, clothing, shelter (temporary housing); financial aid; institutional care; recreational activities and facilities; relief

.06   Counseling, guidance, related services

> Standard subdivisions are added for counseling, guidance, related services together; for counseling alone; for guidance alone

> Services directed toward enabling individuals and groups to assist themselves

> Including citizens advice bureaus; telephone counseling, e.g., hot lines

> Class social work in 361.3

.1   **Social problems**

> History, description, appraisal of areas and kinds of social breakdown, of problems endemic to human society

> Including risk assessment

> *For specific problems, see 362–363*

.2   **Social action**

> Class change as a social phenomenon in 303.4

> *For a specific aspect of social action not provided for here, see the aspect in 361.3–361.8, e.g., social work 361.3*

.23   Dissent and protest

> Standard subdivisions are added for either or both topics in heading

.24   Reform movements

.25   Action within established social framework

> Class here planning, policy, programs, proposals; citizen participation; comprehensive works on governmental and private action
>
> *For international action, see 361.26; for social work, see 361.3; for governmental action, see 361.6; for private action, see 361.7; for combined governmental and private community action, see 361.8*

.26   International action

> Class governmental international action in 361.6; class private international action in 361.77

.3   Social work

.32   Practice of social work

> Class here casework
>
> *For counseling, see 361.06; for group work, see 361.4*

.322   Interviewing

.37   Volunteer social work

> *For a specific aspect of volunteer social work, see the aspect, e.g., interviewing 361.322*

.4   Group work

> Class counseling in group work in 361.06

.43   Self-help groups

> Class here mutual aid, support groups

.6   Governmental action

> Class here intergovernmental assistance and planning, governmental international action, interdisciplinary works on government-sponsored socioeconomic planning and development
>
> Class combined governmental and private action in 361.25; class governmental social work in 361.3; class combined governmental and private community action in 361.8
>
> *For management of governmental agencies regulating social welfare services, see 353.5*

.61   Social policy

> Class welfare reform in 361.68

.612   Goals, values, priorities

.613   Relation of politics and social action

> Class effect of social action on political structures and values in 320

.614	Relation of welfare and human rights

Including use of compulsory remedial action

Class interdisciplinary works on human rights in 323

.615	Relation of government and private sectors

Class welfare state in 361.65

.65	Welfare state

Class economics of welfare state in 330.126

.68	Welfare reform
.7	**Private action**

Class combined governmental and private action in 361.25; class private social work in 361.3; class relation of government and private sectors in 361.615; class combined governmental and private community action in 361.8

.706	Organizations and management

Do not use for a specific kind of organization; class in 361.75–361.77 with the kind, e.g., nonprofit organizations 361.763

.706 81	Organization and financial management

Class here fund raising

Class charity, thrift shops in 381.19

.708	Groups of people

Do not use for private action to a group of people; class in 362

.74	Individual philanthropy

Class an organization that controls the use of the money donated by a philanthropist with the organization, e.g., Rockefeller Foundation 361.7632

.75	Religious organizations
.76	Private organizations

Class religious organizations in 361.75; class private international organizations in 361.77

.763	Nonprofit organizations

Including CARE

.763 2	Charitable foundations and trusts
.763 4	National Red Cross and Red Crescent societies

Standard subdivisions are added for either or both topics in heading

Class here affiliated national societies, e.g., Red Crystal

Class comprehensive works on International Committee of the Red Cross, International Federation of Red Cross and Red Crescent Societies in 361.772

| .765 | Business organizations |
| | Class ways that management can deal with charitable donations in 658.153; class programs of employers for employees in 658.38 |

.766   Labor unions

.77   Private international organizations

See also 361.76 for local organizations providing services worldwide

.772   International Committee of the Red Cross; International Federation of Red Cross and Red Crescent Societies

Standard subdivisions are added for either or both topics in heading

For Red Cross, Red Crescent, affiliated societies of a specific nation, see 361.7634

.8   **Community action**

Including community chests, united charities

Class community development in 307.14; class governmental community action in 361.6; class private community action in 361.7

.9   **History, geographic treatment, biography**

Class history, geographic treatment, biography of specific kinds of social action in 361.2–361.8

.901–.905   Historical periods

Add to base number 361.90 the numbers following —090 in notation 0901–0905 from Table 1, e.g., welfare work in 20th century 361.904

.91–.99   Geographic treatment, biography

Add to base number 361.9 notation 1–9 from Table 2, e.g., welfare work in Arizona 361.9791

> **362–363 Specific social problems and services**

Except for modifications shown under specific entries, add to each subdivision identified by * as follows:

01	Philosophy and theory
02	Miscellany
[0218]	Standards
	Do not use; class in notation 62 from this table
[0289]	Safety measures
	Do not use; class in 363.1
03–05	Standard subdivisions
06	Organizations and management
0681	Organization and financial management
	Including managerial cost control
	Class social measures to hold down costs in notation 5 from this table
07	Education, research, related topics
08	Groups of people
	Do not use for discrimination as social cause; class in notation 1 from this table. Do not use for actions against discrimination; class in notation 5 from this table
	See also notation 3 from this table for people close to those with a problem
09	History, geographic treatment, biography

>1–4   Characteristics of problem

Class comprehensive works in 362–363 without adding from this table

1   Social causes

Including discrimination

Class here sources

2   Incidence, extent, severity

Standard subdivisions are added for any or all topics in heading

Including risk assessment

3   Effects on people close to those with a problem

Including effects on co-workers, on neighbors

Class here families

Class aftereffects on people close to those with a problem in notation 4 from this table; class family problems in 362.82

4   Aftereffects of people with a problem

Either effects on the individual with the problem that occur after the problem has ceased, or effects on other people that occur after the problem has ceased or the other people are no longer close to the individual with the problem

Class here adult children of people with a problem

Class a specific aftereffect with the aftereffect, e.g., social aspects of alcoholism in victims of child abuse 362.292, medical aspects of depression in adult victims of child abuse 616.8527

5   Social action

Class here social action to relieve discrimination, social measures to hold down costs

Add to 5 the numbers following 361 in 361.2–361.8, e.g., international action 526, social work 53, rationing 56

Class governmental administration of rationing programs in 352.86; class comprehensive works on social action in 361.2

For specific forms of action, see notation 6–8 from this table

362–363 Specific social problems and services

> 6–8 Specific forms of action
Class comprehensive works in notation 5 from this table
Works containing topics from any two of these subdivisions are
classed in notation 5 from this table

6 Control
Elimination and reduction of hazards, of sources and causes of
difficulty
Class measures to protect against and to limit effects of problems in
notation 7 from this table

62 Standards

63 Monitoring, surveillance, reporting
Standard subdivisions are added for any or all topics in heading

64 Inspection and testing
Standard subdivisions are added for either or both topics in
heading

65 Investigation of specific incidents
Class criminal investigation of specific incidents in 364.1

66 Certification

7 Measures to prevent, protect against, limit effects of problems
Class here preparedness
Class measures that both control and prevent problems in notation
6 from this table
For safety measures, see 363.1

72 Protective measures
Including design of environments, warning and guidance
systems

8 Remedial measures, services, forms of assistance
Measures applicable primarily to individuals, even if in large
groups
Class here material assistance
Class remedial measures directed toward altering a social function,
e.g., cost control, in 5; class social work in notation 53 from this
table; class comprehensive works on material assistance in 361.05

809 History, geographic treatment, biography
Class here the area receiving assistance, e.g., relief to Italy
provided by the United States 809450973
Class the area providing assistance in notation 8 from this
table without adding from Table 1, e.g., relief provided by the
United States to many countries 8, not 80973

81 Rescue operations

82 Financial assistance
Class social insurance in 368.4

83 Provision of food, shelter (temporary housing), household
assistance, clothing, other related necessities; recreation
Class long-term housing in 363.59

84 Employment services
Including vocational rehabilitation

85 Residential care
Care within institutions existing for the purpose

> **362–363 Specific social problems and services**

86   Counseling and guidance
>> Standard subdivisions are added for either or both topics in heading
>> Including legal aid
>> Class comprehensive works on counseling and guidance in 361.06

Class discrimination in 305; class comprehensive works in 361

For criminology, see 364

See Manual at 361 vs. 362–363; also at 362–363 vs. 364.1

362   Social problems of and services to groups of people

Class here social security

Unless other instructions are given, observe the following table of preference, e.g., mentally ill veterans 362.208697 (*not* 362.860874):

People with physical illnesses	362.1
People with mental illness and disabilities	362.2
People with mental retardation	362.3
People with physical disabilities	362.4
Displaced persons	362.87
Victims of crimes and war	362.88
Veterans of military service	362.86
People in late adulthood	362.6
Young people	362.7
Working class	362.85
Women	362.83
Transgender and intersex people	362.897
People by sexual orientation	362.896
People with status defined by changes in residence	362.8991
Retired people	362.8996
Poor people	362.5
Unemployed people	362.8994
People by miscellaneous social attributes (without subdivisions)	362.899
People by social and economic levels	362.892
Miscellaneous groups of people (without subdivisions)	362.89
Families	362.82
Ethnic and national groups	362.84
Other groups of people (without subdivisions)	362.8
History, geographic treatment, biography	362.9

Use notation 08 from Table 1 to indicate the specific group of people to whom the service is rendered, e.g., young adults addicted to narcotics 362.293084, poor veterans of military service 362.86086942. Do not use notation 08 from Table 1 to indicate services rendered by groups of people, e.g., services rendered by young adults to people addicted to narcotics 362.293, not 362.2930842

> *For social problems of and services to military personnel, see 355.34; for social problems of and services to prisoners, see 365.66; for social security as a form of social insurance, see 368.4; for social problems of and services to students, see 371.7*

> *See also 920.008 for general collections of biography of members of a specific group that share a social problem*

> *See Manual at 920.008 vs. 305–306, 362*

SUMMARY

.04   Special topics of social problems of and services to groups of people

.042   Social problems

.042 2   Incidence, extent, severity

Including social effects

.042 3   Social causes

.042 4   Prevention

.042 5   Social action

Including remedial measures

Class prevention in 362.0424

[.08]   Groups of people

Do not use; class in 362.1–362.8

[.09]   History, geographic treatment, biography

Do not use; class in 362.9

>   **362.1–362.4 People with illnesses and disabilities**

Class incidence of and public measures to prevent physical diseases in 614.4–614.5; class comprehensive works in 362.1

See Manual at 362.1–362.4 vs. 610; also at 362.1–362.4 and 614.4–614.5

.1   **People with physical illnesses**

Class here interdisciplinary works on illness and disability, on medical care and treatment, on medical missions, on public health

For religious aspects of medical missions, see 266; for sociology of medicine, of health, of illness, see 306.461; for mental illness, see 362.2; for mental retardation, see 362.3; for problems of and services to people with a specific physical disability regardless of cause, see 362.4; for technology of medicine, see 610

SUMMARY

.102 3   Services to people with physical illnesses as a profession, occupation, hobby

Class here interdisciplinary works on health occupations peripheral to the medical and paramedical professions

Class works covering both the medical and peripheral occupations in 610

For a specific peripheral profession, see the profession, e.g., medical social workers 362.10425, hospital secretaries 651.3741

.104   Special topics of people with physical illnesses

.104 2   Social aspects

Class preventive measures in 614.44–614.48

.104 22   Social effects

Class incidence in 614.42

.104 25   Forms of assistance

Including medical social work

Class here comprehensive works on health assistance and health and accident insurance

For health and accident insurance, see 368.382; for government sponsored health and accident insurance, see 368.42

.104 252   Financial assistance

.104 256   Counseling and guidance

Standard subdivisions are added for either or both topics in heading

.104 257   Rural health services

.104 258   Managed care plans

.104 258 4   Health maintenance organizations (HMOs)

.106 8   Management

Class here peer reviews

Class the result of a peer review with the result, e.g., the result of the evaluation of New York City hospitals 362.11097471

.108	Groups of people

> Do not use for services rendered by groups of people; class in 362.1

> Class physical illness among groups of people in 616.008

.108 3	Young people

> Do not use for infants and children up to puberty; class in 362.19892

.108 4	People in specific stages of adulthood
[.108 46]	People in late adulthood

> Do not use; class in 362.19897

.109	History, geographic treatment, biography
[.109 173 4]	Rural regions

> Do not use; class in 362.104257

\>   362.11–362.19 Medical services

Free and paid

Class medical treatment in 616; class comprehensive works in 362.1

\>   362.11–362.16 Services of specific kinds of institutions

Class services of health maintenance organizations in 362.1042584; class specific kinds of services provided by a specific institution in 362.17; class services by a specific institution to patients with specific conditions in 362.19; class comprehensive works in 362.1

.11	Hospitals and related institutions

Standard subdivisions are added for hospitals and related institutions together, for hospitals alone

> *For clinics and related institutions, see 362.12; for extended medical care facilities, see 362.16*

.12	Clinics and related institutions

Standard subdivisions are added for clinics and related institutions together, for clinics alone

Including dispensaries, health centers, outpatient departments of general hospitals

Class here ambulatory care, community health services

.14	Professional home care

Including visiting nurses' services, services of health visitors

> *See also 649.8 for home care by family members*

.16   **Extended medical care facilities**

Including convalescent homes, sanatoriums for people suffering from chronic diseases

Class here extended medical care facilities for people in late adulthood, institutions providing complete medical care, nursing homes providing complete medical care

Class comprehensive works on life care communities in 362.61

[.160 846]   People in late adulthood

Do not use; class in 362.16

.17   **Specific services**

Class here social provision of specific kinds of medical services, interdisciplinary works covering both social provision and technology of specific kinds of medical services

Unless other instructions are given, class a subject with aspects in two or more subdivisions of 362.17 in the number coming last, e.g., diagnostic services by doctors 362.177 (*not* 362.172)

Class forms of assistance in 362.10425; class specific kinds of services to patients with specific conditions in 362.19; class group practice in 610.65

For emergency services, see 362.18; for technology of medical services, see 610; for preventive services, see 614.44

.172   **Services of physicians**

Including referral and consulting services

.173   **Services of nurses**

Class visiting nurses' services in 362.14

.173 068   Management of services of nurses

Class here nonmedical aspects of ward management

.174   **Intensive care**

.175   **Terminal care**

.175 6   Hospices

.176   **Nutritional services**

Class here feeding of sick, comprehensive works on the provision of special diets for various classes of people with illnesses

Class nutritional programs for the population at large in 363.8

For nutritional services applied to nutrition disorders, see 362.19639

.177   **Diagnostic and screening services**

Including radiology services

.178   **Therapeutic services**

.178 2   Pharmaceutical services

                     Class nutritional services in 362.176

.178 3   Organ and tissue banks

                     Standard subdivisions are added for either or both topics in heading

                     Including eye banks

                     For blood and blood plasma banks, see 362.1784

.178 4   Blood and blood plasma banks

                     Standard subdivisions are added for either or both topics in heading

.178 6   Rehabilitation services

.18   Emergency services

                     Including trauma centers

.188   Ambulance services

.19   Services to patients with specific conditions

                     Class here living with a physical disease

                     Class incidence of and public measures to prevent specific diseases in 614.5

                     See also 362.10425 for indigent patients; also 362.175 for terminal patients

[.190 1–.190 9]   Standard subdivisions

                     Do not use; class in 362.101–362.109

.196–.198   Specific conditions

                     Except for modifications shown under specific entries, add to base number 362.19 the numbers following 61 in 616–618 for the condition only, e.g., services to patients with diabetes 362.196462, dental care 362.1976, maternity services 362.1982; then add further as follows (*not* as instructed under 616.1–616.9, 617, or 618.1–618.8):
                     001–009   Standard subdivisions
                                    Notation from Table 1 as modified under 616.1–616.9, e.g., biography of an individual with diabetes 362.1964620092, periodicals on dental care 362.1976005
                     02–08   Specific services
                                    Add to 0 the numbers following 362.17 in 362.172–362.178, e.g., intensive care 04

                     For services to people with mental illness, see 362.2

[.198 18]   Birth control services

                     Do not use; class in 363.96

.198 88		Abortion services

Number built according to instructions under 362.196–362.198

Class here interdisciplinary works on abortion

> *For a specific aspect of abortion, see the aspect, e.g., abortion as a crime 364.185, medical aspects of abortion 618.88*

.198 92   Pediatric care

Number built according to instructions under 362.196–362.198

.198 920 001–.198 920 009   Standard subdivisions

Notation from Table 1 as modified under 001–009, e.g., periodicals on pediatric care 362.198920005

.198 920 02–.198 920 08   Specific services

Add to base number 362.1989200 the numbers following 362.17 in 362.172–362.178, e.g., pediatric intensive care 362.19892004

.2   †People with mental illness and disabilities

Standard subdivisions are added for either or both topics in heading

Class here mental disabilities that consist of mental retardation combined with mental illness

Class life with a psychiatric disorder in 616.890092

> *For mental retardation, see 362.3*

SUMMARY

362.204	**Special topics of people with mental illness and disabilities**
.21	**Mental health facilities**
.22	**Community mental health services**
.23	**Extended care facilities**
.24	**Professional home care**
.25	**Neuroses**
.26	**Psychoses**
.27	**Disorders of personality, intellect, impulse control**
.28	**Suicide**
.29	**Substance abuse**

.204   Special topics of people with mental illness and disabilities

.204 2   Social aspects

.204 22   Incidence, extent, severity

Including social effects

.204 25   Prevention and forms of assistance

Class here psychiatric social work

---

†Do not use notation 08 from Table 1 to indicate services rendered by groups of people; class in base number

.204 251		Emergency and rescue operations

           Standard subdivisions are added for either or both topics in heading

           Class here hot lines

.204 252   Financial assistance

.204 256   Counseling and guidance

           Standard subdivisions are added for either or both topics in heading

---

\>   **362.21–362.24 Medical services**

           Class care for specific problems in 362.25–362.29; class medical treatment in 616.8; class comprehensive works in 362.2

.21   **Mental health facilities**

           Class here psychiatric hospitals

           For psychiatric clinics, see 362.22; for nursing homes and sanatoriums, see 362.23

.22   **Community mental health services**

           Class here psychiatric clinics

.223   **Group homes**

.23   **Extended care facilities**

           Class here nursing homes, sanatoriums

.24   **Professional home care**

\>   **362.25–362.29 Specific problems**

           Class comprehensive works in 362.2

.25   †**Neuroses**

           Including anorexia nervosa, depression

.26   †**Psychoses**

           Including schizophrenia

.27   †**Disorders of personality, intellect, impulse control**

           Including food addiction, kleptomania; interdisciplinary works on compulsive gambling

           Class interdisciplinary works on gambling in 306.482

           For suicide, see 362.28; for substance abuse, see 362.29; for compulsive gambling in medicine, see 616.85841

†Do not use notation 08 from Table 1 to indicate services rendered by groups of people; class in base number

.28   *†Suicide

      Class here suicidal behavior

.288 1   Rescue operations

      Number built according to instructions under 362–363

      Class here emergency services, hot lines

.29   †Substance abuse

      Class here drug abuse; interdisciplinary works on substance abuse, addiction, habituation, intoxication

      Class works on drug abuse limited to narcotic abuse in 362.293

      For subculture of substance abusers, see 306.1; for drug traffic, see 364.13365; for illegal sale, possession, use of drugs, see 364.177; for drug use as a custom, see 394.1; for medical aspects of substance abuse, see 616.86

      See also 362.27 for food addiction

      See Manual at 616.86 vs. 158.1, 204.42, 248.8629, 292–299, 362.29

.291   Aspects of substance abuse

      Class aspects of a specific substance in 362.292–362.299

[.291 01–.291 09]   Standard subdivisions

      Do not use; class in 362.2901–362.2909

.291 1–.291 8   Specific aspects of substance abuse

      Add to base number 362.291 notation 1–8 from table under 362–363, e.g., prevention of substance abuse 362.2917; however, for control of drug traffic, see 364.13365

      Notation 1–8 from table under 362–363 is added for both specific aspects of two or more of the substances provided for in 362.292–362.298 and for a combination of substances provided for in 362.292–362.298 and in 362.299, e.g., counseling for alcohol and cocaine abuse, for narcotics and stimulant abuse 362.29186

.292   *†Alcohol

      Class here interdisciplinary works on alcoholism

      For a specific aspect of alcoholism, see the aspect, e.g., medical aspects 616.861

[.292 6]   Control of sale of alcoholic beverages

      Do not use; class in 364.1332

.292 8   Remedial measures, services, forms of assistance

      Number built according to instructions under 362–363

*Add as instructed under 362–363
†Do not use notation 08 from Table 1 to indicate services rendered by groups of people; class in base number

.292 86	Counseling and guidance

Number built according to instructions under 362–363

Class here services of Alcoholics Anonymous

.293	*†Narcotics

Opium and its derivatives and synthetic equivalents

Class here specific narcotics, e.g., heroin, morphine

.294	*†Hallucinogens and psychedelics

Class here specific hallucinogens and psychedelics, e.g., LSD, mescaline, PCP

Subdivisions are added for either or both topics in heading

Class cannabis in 362.295

.295	*†Cannabis

Class here specific kinds of cannabis, e.g., hashish, marijuana

.296	*†Tobacco
.298	*†Cocaine

Class here specific forms of cocaine, e.g., crack

.299	†Other substances

Including analgesics, depressants, sedatives

Class here designer drugs (synthetic drugs of abuse), prescription drugs

Class alcohol in 362.292; class cocaine in 362.298

For designer hallucinogens, see 362.294

.299 3	*†Inhalants

Class here gases and solvents used as inhalants; individual gases or solvents, e.g., amyl nitrate, glue

.299 5	*†Stimulants

Class here specific kinds of stimulants, e.g., amphetamine, ephedrine, methamphetamine

Class cocaine in 362.298

.3   *†People with mental retardation

Class comprehensive works on problems of and services to people with developmental disabilities (those who have neurological diseases combined with mental retardation and whose problems exhibit themselves before age 18) in 362.1968; class comprehensive works on treatment of mental retardation and mental illness in 362.2

---

*Add as instructed under 362–363

†Do not use notation 08 from Table 1 to indicate services rendered by groups of people; class in base number

.4   †People with physical disabilities

Regardless of cause

Class here comprehensive works on people with disabilities, people with physical and mental disabilities

Class comprehensive medical works in 617

For people with mental disabilities, see 362.3

.404   Special topics of people with physical disabilities, people with physical and mental disabilities

Add to base number 362.404 notation 1–8 from table under 362–363, e.g., social work with people with physical disabilities 362.40453 Subdivisions are added for either or both topics in heading

.404 8   People with disabilities — material assistance

.404 84   Employment services

Number built according to instructions under 362–363

.404 848   Sheltered employment

.41   *†People with blindness and visual impairments

Class here people who are blind-deaf

Subdivisions are added for either or both topics in heading

For people who are deaf, see 362.42

.42   *†People with hearing impairments

Class here people who are deaf

Class comprehensive works on people with linguistic and communication disabilities in 362.196855; class people who are blind-deaf in 362.41

See also 371.912 for teaching people who are deaf

.43   *†People with mobility impairments

Subdivisions are added for services to people with specific mobility impairments, e.g., residential care for paraplegics 362.4385

.5   *†Poor people

Class economic causes and effects of poverty in 339.46

.508   Groups of people

Do not use for services rendered by groups of people; class in 362.5

[.508 3]   Young people

Do not use for poor young people through age seventeen; class in 362.77569

*Add as instructed under 362–363
†Do not use notation 08 from Table 1 to indicate services rendered by groups of people; class in base number

[.508 35]	Young people eighteen to twenty
	Do not use; class in 362.77569
.508 6	People by miscellaneous social attributes
[.508 694 1]	Unemployed people
	Do not use; class in 362.594
[.508 694 2]	Homeless people
	Do not use; class in 362.592
.57	Measures to prevent, protect against, limit effects of poverty

Number built according to instructions under 362–363

Class economic measures to prevent poverty in 339

.58	Remedial measures, services, forms of assistance

Number built according to instructions under 362–363

Class birth control as a remedy for poverty in 363.96; class assistance to poor people under social security in 368.4

For food stamp programs, see 363.882

.582	Financial assistance

Number built according to instructions under 362–363

Including guaranteed minimum income, negative income tax

Class here supplementary social security for low income people

Class aid to families with dependent children (AFDC) in 362.713

.583	Provision of shelter (temporary housing), clothing, other related necessities; recreation

Number built according to instructions under 362–363

Do not use for food programs; class in 363.8

Class long-term housing in 363.5

.586	Counseling and guidance

Number built according to instructions under 362–363

Including interdisciplinary works on legal aid

For law of legal aid, see 347.017

.59	Homeless and unemployed people
.592	*†Homeless people
.594	*†Unemployed people

*Add as instructed under 362–363
†Do not use notation 08 from Table 1 to indicate services rendered by groups of people; class in base number

.6   **People in late adulthood**

Class here social gerontology

[.608]   Groups of people

Do not use; class in 362.69

>   362.61–362.66 Remedial measures, services, forms of assistance

Class comprehensive works in 362.63

For specific problems, see 362.68; for services to groups of people in late adulthood, see 362.69

.61   Residential care

Class here assisted living; facilities providing minimal medical care, e.g., medication maintenance; services of life care communities (continuing care retirement communities), old age homes, rest homes

Class institutions providing complete medical care in 362.16; class housing in 363.5946

.63   Remedial measures, services, forms of assistance

Measures applicable primarily to individuals, even if in large groups

Class here material assistance

Including provision of financial aid, food, shelter (temporary housing), household assistance, clothing, recreation

Class remedial measures directed toward altering a social function, e.g., cost control, in 362.675; class social work in 362.6753

For residential care, see 362.61; for employment services, see 362.64; for counseling and guidance, see 362.66; for specific problems, see 362.68; for services to groups of people, see 362.69

.64   Employment services

Including vocational rehabilitation

.66   Counseling and guidance

Standard subdivisions are added for either or both topics in heading

.67   Characteristics of problems, social action

Add to base number 362.67 notation 1–7 from table under 362–363, e.g., effects on families 362.673

For remedial measures, services, forms of assistance, see 362.63; for specific problems, see 362.68; for problems of groups of people in late adulthood, see 362.69

.68   Specific problems

For problems of groups of people, see 362.69

.682   †Elder abuse

> Class parent abuse in 362.8292; class elder abuse as a crime in 364.1555.
> Class elder abuse in a specific situation with the situation, e.g., elder
> abuse in nursing homes 362.16

.69   Groups of people

.691–.698   Miscellaneous specific groups of people

> Add to base number 362.69 the numbers following —08 in notation
> 081–088 from Table 1, e.g., women in late adulthood 362.692; then add
> further as follows:
> 001–007   Standard subdivisions
> 008   Groups of people
>   Do not use for services rendered by groups of people;
>   class in base number
> 009   History, geographic treatment, biography
> 01–08   Characteristics of problems, social action
>   Add to 0 notation 1–8 from table under 362–363, e.g.,
>   effects on families of women in late adulthood 362.6923

.699   People in late adulthood by ethnic or national group

> Class treatment with respect to miscellaneous specific groups of people
> in late adulthood of a specific ethnic and national group with the kind
> of people in 362.691–362.698, e.g., Chinese women in late adulthood
> 362.692

.699 001–.699 007   Standard subdivisions

.699 008   Groups of people

> Do not use for services rendered by groups of people; class in
> 362.699

.699 009   History, geographic treatment, biography

.699 05–.699 09   †People in late adulthood of mixed ancestry with ethnic origins from
more than one continent, Europeans in late adulthood and people in
late adulthood of European descent

> Add to base number 362.6990 the numbers following —0 in
> notation 05–09 from Table 5, e.g., people in late adulthood of
> European descent 362.69909, people in late adulthood of European
> descent in Australia 362.69909094

.699 1–.699 9   †People in late adulthood by specific ethnic or national groups

> Add to base number 362.699 notation 1–9 from Table 5, e.g.,
> people in late adulthood of Italian descent 362.69951, people in late
> adulthood of Italian descent in United States 362.69951073

.7   Young people

Through age twenty

Class here children

---

†Do not use notation 08 from Table 1 to indicate services rendered by groups of people; class in base
number

SUMMARY

362.708	**Groups of people**
.71	**Remedial measures, services, forms of assistance**
.72	**Characteristics of problems, social action**
.73	**Institutional and related services**
.74	**Troubled young people**
.76	**Abused and neglected young people**
.77	**Specific groups of young people**
.78	**Transgender and intersex young people, young people by sexual orientation, young people in intrafamily relationships**

.708   Groups of people

Do not use for services rendered by groups of people; class in 362.7

.708 3   Young people twelve to twenty

Do not use for children; class in 362.7

Class here young men and women twelve to twenty

Class remedial measures, services, forms of assistance in 362.71; class characteristics of problems, social action in 362.72; class specific groups of young people twelve to twenty, other than young men and women, in 362.77; class young people twenty-one and over, comprehensive works on young men and women in 362

[.708 35]   Young people twelve to twenty

Do not use; class in 362.7083

.708 5   Relatives

Do not use for young people as parents; class in 362.7874

[.708 6]   Young people by miscellaneous social attributes

Do not use; class in 362.77

[.708 66]   Young people by sexual orientation

Do not use; class in 362.786

[.708 67]   Transgender and intersex young people

Do not use; class in 362.785

[.708 9]   Ethnic and national groups

Do not use; class in 362.778

>   362.71–362.73 Specific kinds of services to young people

Class services to maladjusted young people in 362.74; class services to abused and neglected children in 362.76; class comprehensive works in 362.7

.71	Remedial measures, services, forms of assistance

Measures applicable primarily to individuals, even if in large groups

Including recreational services

Class here material assistance

Class remedial measures directed toward altering a social function, e.g., cost control, in 362.725; class social work in 362.7253

> *For institutional and related services, see 362.73; for services to groups of young people, see 362.77*

.712	Day care services
.713	Aid to families with dependent children (AFDC)
.716	Counseling and guidance

Standard subdivisions are added for either or both topics in heading

Including legal aid

.72	Characteristics of problems, social action

Add to base number 362.72 notation 1–7 from table under 362–363, e.g., effects on families 362.723

> *For remedial measures, services, forms of assistance, see 362.71; for problems of groups of young people, see 362.77*

.723	Effects on people close to those with a problem

Number built according to instructions under 362.72

Class here a family problem when focused on the child

Class a family problem when focused on the parent with the problem in 362.82, e.g., families with missing children 362.8297

.73	Institutional and related services

Class here abandoned children, orphans

.732	Institutional care

Including children's homes, orphanages; houseparents

.733	Foster home care

Class here comprehensive works on foster home care and adoption

> *For adoption, see 362.734*

.734	Adoption

Including confidentiality of adoption records

Class comprehensive works on the activities of adopted people seeking their natural parents in 362.8298

>   **362.74–362.78 Groups of young people**

Unless other instructions are given, observe the following table of preference, e.g., poor gay abused young people 362.76 (*not* 362.77569 or 362.7866):

Troubled young people	362.74
Abused and neglected young people	362.76
Young people by intrafamily relationships	362.787
Young people by sexual orientation	362.786
Transgender and intersex young people	362.785
Transgender and intersex young people, young people by sexual orientation, young people by intrafamily relationships (without subdivision)	362.78
Young people by social and economic levels	362.775
Young people by religious groups	362.776
Young people by ethnic and national group	362.778
Young people by language groups	362.77
Unemployed young people	362.7794
Young people with status defined by changes in residence	362.7791
Young people with status defined by changes in residence, unemployed young people (without subdivision)	362.779
Specific groups of young people (without subdivision)	362.77

Class comprehensive works in 362.7

>   **362.74–362.76 Specific kinds of young people**

Class comprehensive works in 362.7

For abandoned children, orphans, see 362.73

.74   ***†Troubled young people**

Including predelinquents, runaways

Class here halfway houses for young people who have not committed any crimes

Class young people with mental illness in 362.2083; class families with missing children in 362.8297; class halfway houses for the transition from reform school to society in 365.42

For juvenile delinquents, see 364.36

.76   ***†Abused and neglected young people**

Subdivisions are added for either or both topics in heading

Class child abuse as a crime in 364.15554

---

*Add as instructed under 362–363

†Do not use notation 08 from Table 1 to indicate services rendered by groups of people; class in base number

.77 Specific groups of young people

Class here young people by miscellaneous social attributes

For transgender and intersex young people, see 362.785; for young people by sexual orientation, see 362.786; for young people in intrafamily relationships, see 362.787

[.770 1–.770 9] Standard subdivisions

Do not use; class in 362.701–362.709

.775–.777 Young people by social and economic levels, religious groups, language groups

Add to base number 362.77 the numbers following 305 in 305.5–305.7, e.g., poor young people 362.77569; then add further as follows:
001–007 Standard subdivisions
008 Groups of people
Do not use for services rendered by groups of people; class in base number
009 History, geographic treatment, biography
01–08 Characteristics of problems, social action
Add to 0 notation 1–8 from table under 362–363, e.g., effects on families of poor young people 362.7756903

For abandoned children, orphans, see 362.73; for abused children, see 372.76

.775 69 †Poor young people

Number built according to instructions under 362.775–362.777

Class aid to families with dependent children in 362.713

.778 †Young people by ethnic or national group]

.778 001–.778 007 Standard subdivisions

.778 008 Groups of people

Do not use for services rendered by groups of people; class in 362.778

.778 009 History, geographic treatment, biography

.778 05–.778 09 †Young people of mixed ancestry with ethnic origins from more than one continent, European young people and young people of European descent

Add to base number 362.7780 the numbers following —0 in notation 05–09 from Table 5, e.g., young people of European descent 362.77809, young people of European descent in Australia 362.77809094

.778 1–.778 9 †Specific ethnic and national groups

Add to base number 362.778 notation 1–9 from Table 5, e.g., young people of Italian descent 362.77851, young people of Italian descent in United States 362.77851073

†Do not use notation 08 from Table 1 to indicate services rendered by groups of people; class in base number

.779   Young people with status defined by changes in residence,
                       unemployed youth

.779 1   Young people with status defined by changes in residence

                            Class here aliens, expatriates, foreigners

.779 100 1–.779 100 7   Standard subdivisions

.779 100 8   Groups of people

                                    Do not use for services rendered by groups of people; class
                                    in 362.7791

.779 100 9   History, geographic treatment, biography

.779 101–.779 108   Characteristics of problems, social action

                                    Add to base number 362.77910 notation 1–8 from table under
                                    362–363, e.g., effects on families of young aliens 362.779103

.779 12   *†Immigrant young people

                                Class immigrant young people of a specific ethnic or national
                                group in 362.778

.779 14   *†Displaced young people

                                Class here exiles, refugees, stateless young people

.779 18   *†Nomadic young people

.779 4   *†Unemployed young people

                                Class poverty-stricken and destitute unemployed young people in
                                362.77569

.78   Transgender and intersex young people, young people by sexual
                        orientation, young people in intrafamily relationships

.785   *†Transgender young people and intersex young people

                            Including female-to-male transgender young people, male-to-female
                            transgender young people

                            Class here gender nonconforming young people, transsexual young
                            people

                            Subdivisions are added for transgender young people and intersex young
                            people together, for transgender young people alone

.786   †Young people by sexual orientation

                            Including asexual young people

*Add as instructed under 362–363
†Do not use notation 08 from Table 1 to indicate services rendered by groups of people; class in base
  number

.786 4–.786 6   Young people by specific sexual orientation

> Add to base number 362.786 the numbers following 306.76 in 306.764–306.766, e.g., gay young people 362.7866; then add further as follows:
> | | |
> |---|---|
> | 001–007 | Standard subdivisions |
> | 008 | Groups of people |
> | | Do not use for services rendered by groups of people; class in base number |
> | 009 | History, geographic treatment, biography |
> | 01–08 | Characteristics of problems, social action |
> | | Add to 0 notation 1–8 from table under 362–363, e.g., effects on families of gay young people 362.786603 |

.787   †Young people by intrafamily relationships

> Unless other instructions are given, class a subject with aspects in two or more subdivisions of 362.787 in the number coming last, e.g., divorced young fathers 362.78792 (*not* 362.78742)

.787 2–.787 5   Young people in husband-wife, parent-child, sibling relationships

> Add to base number 362.787 the numbers following 306.87 in 306.872–306.874, e.g., single young mothers 362.787432; then add further as follows:
> | | |
> |---|---|
> | 001–007 | Standard subdivisions |
> | 008 | Groups of people |
> | | Do not use for services rendered by groups of people; class in base number |
> | 009 | History, geographic treatment, biography |
> | 01–08 | Characteristics of problems, social action |
> | | Add to 0 notation 1–8 from table under 362–363, e.g., financial assistance to single young women 362.787432082 |

.787 4   †Parent-child relationship

> Number built according to instructions under 362.7872–362.7875

> Class here young people as parents

.787 43   †Mother-child relationship

> Number built according to instructions under 362.7872–362.7875

> Class here teenage pregnancy

.787 432   †Single motherhood

> Number built according to instructions under 362.7872–362.7875

> Class here single young mothers, unmarried mothers eighteen to twenty

> Class comprehensive works on single motherhood in 362.839532

---

†Do not use notation 08 from Table 1 to indicate services rendered by groups of people; class in base number

.787 8–.787 9   Young people in altered family arrangements

> Add to base number 362.787 the numbers following 306.8 in
> 306.88–306.89, e.g., divorced young mothers 362.78793; then add
> further as follows:
> 001–007   Standard subdivisions
> 008   Groups of people
>   Do not use for services rendered by groups of
>   people; class in base number
> 009   History, geographic treatment, biography
> 01–08   Characteristics of problems, social action
>   Add to 0 notation 1–8 from table under 362–363,
>   e.g., financial assistance to divorced young women
>   362.78793082

.8   Other groups of people

SUMMARY

362.82	**Families**
.83	**Women**
.84	**Ethnic and national groups**
.85	**Working class**
.86	**Veterans of military service**
.87	**Displaced persons**
.88	**Victims of crimes and war**
.89	**Miscellaneous groups of people**

.82   *Families

> Class here parents, family problems focused on the parent

> Class family welfare when synonymous with general welfare in 362; class
> family welfare when synonymous with general welfare of a specific ethnic
> or national group in 362.84. Class a family problem when focused on the
> child with the problem in 362.7, e.g., abused children 362.76

.820 8   Groups of people

> Do not use for services rendered by groups of people; class in 362.82

[.820 83]   Young people by intrafamily relationships

> Do not use for young people through age seventeen; class in
> 362.787

[.820 835]   Young people eighteen to twenty

> Do not use; class in 362.787

.820 86   People by miscellaneous social attributes

[.820 865 3]   Separated parents, divorced parents

> Do not use; class in 362.82

[.820 865 4]   Widowed people

> Do not use; class in 362.8293

*Add as instructed under 362–363

.820 865 5	Married people
	Do not use for married women; class in 362.83952
.828	**Remedial measures, services, forms of assistance**
	Number built according to instructions under 362–363
	Class services and forms of assistance for specific problems in 362.829; class family planning programs in 363.96
.828 2	Financial assistance
	Number built according to instructions under 362–363
	Class aid to families with dependent children (AFDC) in 362.713
.828 3	Provision of food, shelter (temporary housing), household assistance, clothing, other related necessities; recreation
	Number built according to instructions under 362–363
	Including visiting housekeepers
	Class day care in 362.712
.828 6	Counseling and guidance
	Number built according to instructions under 362–363
	Including premarital and marriage counseling
.829	**Specific problems**
	Class a problem not provided for here with the problem, plus notation 3 from table under 362–363, e.g., alcoholism within the family setting 362.2923
.829 2	*†Abuse within the family
	Class here parent, spouse abuse; domestic violence
	Class elder abuse in 362.682; class abused children in 362.76; class abuse as a crime in 364.1555
.829 3	*†Widowed people
	Class here widowers
	Class widowers in late adulthood in 362.6954
	For widows, see 362.83958

---

*Add as instructed under 362–363
†Do not use notation 08 from Table 1 to indicate services rendered by groups of people; class in base
  number

.829 4   *†Single-parent family

                           Class here separated parents, divorced parents

                           Class separated and divorced parents in late adulthood in 362.69653

                               For widowed people, see 362.8293; for unmarried mothers,
                               see 362.839532; for separated women, divorced women, see
                               362.83959

.829 5   *†Parents in prison

.829 7   *†Missing children

                           Class here parental kidnapping

                           Class runaway children in 362.74

.829 8   *†Relationship between adoptees and their biological parents

                           Class adoption in 362.734. Class a specific aspect of children seeking
                           their biological parents with the aspect, e.g., confidentiality of
                           adoption records 362.734, genealogical searching 929.1

.83   *Women

                           Class wife abuse in 362.8292; class rape in 362.883; class transgender and
                           intersex people in 362.897

[.830 8]   Groups of people

                           Do not use; class in 362.839

[.830 83]   Young women

                               Do not use for young women through age seventeen; class in
                               362.7083

[.830 835]   Young women eighteen to twenty

                               Do not use; class in 362.7083

.839   †Groups of people

SUMMARY

362.839 5	Women by intrafamily relationships
.839 6	Women by sexual orientation
.839 8	Women with status defined by changes in residence, retired women, poor women
.839 9	Women by ethnic or national group

*Add as instructed under 362–363
†Do not use notation 08 from Table 1 to indicate services rendered by groups of people; class in base
  number

.839 5	†Women by intrafamily relationships
	Unless other instructions are given, class a subject with aspects in two or more subdivisions of 362.8395 in the number coming last, e.g., divorced mothers 362.83959 (*not* 306.83953)
	Class women by intrafamily relationships and by sexual orientation in 362.8396; class women by intrafamily relationships and with special social status in 362.8398
.839 52	*†Spouses
.839 53	*†Mother-child relationship
.839 532	*†Single motherhood
	Class here single mothers, comprehensive works on single motherhood
	Class comprehensive works on single-parent family in 362.8294
	For single motherhood through age twenty, see 362.787432
.839 55	*†Grandmother-child relationship
.839 57	*†Stepmother-child relationship
.839 58	*†Widows
	Class widows in late adulthood in 362.6954; class comprehensive works on widowed parents in 362.8293
.839 59	*†Separated and divorced women
	Subdivisions are added for either or both topics in heading
	Class comprehensive works on single-parent family in 362.8294
.839 6	†Women by sexual orientation
	Including asexual women

*Add as instructed under 362–363

†Do not use notation 08 from Table 1 to indicate services rendered by groups of people; class in base number

.839 64–.839 68   Women by specific sexual orientation

Add to base number 362.8396 the numbers following 306.76 in 306.764–306.768, e.g., lesbians 362.83966; then add further as follows:

001–007   Standard subdivisions
008   Groups of people
Do not use for services rendered by groups of people; class in base number
009   History, geographic treatment, biography
01–08   Characteristics of problems, social action
Add to 0 notation 1–8 from table under 362–363, e.g., effects on families of lesbians 362.8396603

Class women by specific sexual orientation and with status defined by changes in residence in 362.83981; class retired women by sexual orientation in 362.83984; class poor women by sexual orientation in 362.83985

.839 8   †Women with status defined by changes in residence, retired women, poor women

.839 81   Women with status defined by changes in residence

Class here aliens, expatriates, foreigners

.839 810 01–.839 810 07   Standard subdivisions

.839 810 08   Groups of people

Do not use for services rendered by groups of people; class in 362.83981

.839 810 09   History, geographic treatment, biography

.839 810 1–.839 810 8   Characteristics of problems, social action

Add to base number 362.839810 notation 1–8 from table under 362–363, e.g., effects on families of women expatriates 362.8398103

.839 812   *†Immigrant women

Class immigrant women of a specific ethnic or national group in 362.8399

.839 814   *†Displaced women

Class here exiles, refugees, stateless women

.839 818   *†Nomadic women

.839 84   *†Retired women

.839 85   *†Poor women

Including homeless women

*Add as instructed under 362–363
†Do not use notation 08 from Table 1 to indicate services rendered by groups of people; class in base number

.839 9   Women by ethnic or national group

> Class women of a specific ethnic or national group in intrafamily relationships in 362.8395; class women of a specific ethnic or national group by sexual orientation in 362.8396; class women of a specific ethnic or national group with a specific social status in 362.8398

.839 900 1–.839 900 7   Standard subdivisions

.839 900 8   Groups of people

> Do not use for services rendered by groups of people; class in 362.8399

.839 900 9   History, geographic treatment, biography

.839 905–.839 909   †Women of mixed ancestry with ethnic origins from more than one continent, European women and women of European descent

> Add to base number 362.83990 the numbers following —0 in notation 05–09 from Table 5, e.g., women of European descent 362.839909, women of European descent in Australia 362.839909094

.839 91–.839 99   †Specific ethnic and national groups

> Add to base number 362.8399 notation 1–9 from Table 5, e.g., women of Italian descent 362.839951, women of Italian descent in United States 362.839951073

.84   Ethnic and national groups

.840 01–.840 07   Standard subdivisions

.840 08   Groups of people

> Do not use for services rendered by groups of people; class in 362.84

.840 09   History, geographic treatment, biography

.840 5–.840 9   †People of mixed ancestry with ethnic origins from more than one continent, Europeans and people of European descent

> Add to base number 362.840 the numbers following —0 in notation 05–09 from Table 5, e.g., people of European descent 362.8409, people of European descent in Australia 362.8409094

.841–.849   †Specific ethnic and national groups

> Add to base number 362.84 notation 1–9 from Table 5, e.g., Italians in United States 362.8451073

> Class a social problem of a specific ethnic or national group in a place where the group predominates with the problem, plus notation 093–099 from Table 1, e.g., poor Italians in Rome 362.50945632; class comprehensive works on the social problems of a specific ethnic or national group in a place where the group predominates with the place in 362.9, e.g., social problems of Italians in Italy 362.945

†Do not use notation 08 from Table 1 to indicate services rendered by groups of people; class in base number

.85   *Working class

Including migrant workers

.850 8   Groups of people

Do not use for services rendered by groups of people; class in 362.85

[.850 83]   Young people

Do not use; class in 362.77562

.86   *†Veterans of military service

Class here veterans' rights and benefits

.868 2   Financial assistance

Number built according to instructions under 362–363

Class veterans' pensions in 331.25291355

For veterans' education benefits, see 371.223; for veterans' higher education benefits, see 378.32

.87   *†Displaced persons

Class here exiles, refugees, stateless persons

[.870 82]   Displaced women

Do not use; class in 362.839814

[.870 83]   Displaced young people

Do not use; class in 362.77914

.88   Victims of crimes and war

Standard subdivisions are added for victims of crimes and war together, for victims of crimes alone

Including inmates of concentration or internment camps

Class here victimology

Class services to abused family members, victims of domestic violence in 362.8292; class crime prevention for society as a whole in 364.4; class prevention by individuals in 613.6; class comprehensive works on crimes in 364.1

For works on why people become victims of specific crimes, see 364.1

.880 8   Groups of people

Do not use for services rendered by groups of people; class in 362.88

.880 83   †Young people

Class neglected children in 362.76

*Add as instructed under 362–363
†Do not use notation 08 from Table 1 to indicate services rendered by groups of people; class in base number

.881	Characteristics of problems, social action

> Add to base number 362.881 notation 1–8 from table under 362–363, e.g., effects on families of victims of crime 362.8813

.883	†Rape

> Class rape prevention by individuals in 613.663

.885	†Assault and battery

> Standard subdivisions are added for either or both topics in heading

> Class here victims of abuse

.885 083	†Young people

> Class abused children in 362.76

.885 084	†People in specific stages of adulthood
.885 084 6	†People in late adulthood

> Class elder abuse in 362.682

.89	Miscellaneous groups of people

> Limited to the groups provided for below

.892	*†People by social and economic levels

> Class here social classes

> *For working class, see 362.85*

.896	†People by sexual orientation

> Including asexuals

.896 2	*†Heterosexuals
.896 3	*†Bisexuals
.896 4	*†Gays
.897	*†Transgender people and intersex people

> Including female-to-male transgender people, male-to-female transgender people

> Class here gender nonconforming people, transsexuals

> Subdivisions are added for transgender people and intersex people together, for transgender people alone

.899	People by miscellaneous social attributes

> *For poor people, see 362.5; for unmarried mothers, see 362.839532; for victims of crime and war, see 362.88; for offenders, see 364.3*

---

*Add as instructed under 362–363

†Do not use notation 08 from Table 1 to indicate services rendered by groups of people; class in base number

.899 1   People with status defined by changes in residence

                     Class here aliens, expatriates, foreigners

                     Class retired people with status defined by changes in residence in 362.8994

                     For displaced persons, see 362.87

.899 100 1–.899 100 7   Standard subdivisions

.899 100 8   Groups of people

                           Do not use for services rendered by groups of people; class in 362.8991

.899 100 9   History, geographic treatment, biography

.899 101–.899 108   Characteristics of problems, social action

                           Add to base number 362.89910 notation 1–8 from table under 362–363, e.g., effects on families of expatriates 362.899103

.899 12   *†Immigrants

                     Class here comprehensive works on immigration

                         For immigrants of a specific ethnic or national group, see 362.84; for population problems, see 363.9; for illegal immigration, see 364.137

.899 4   *†Unemployed people

.899 6   *†Retired people

.9   History, geographic treatment, biography

                   Class here comprehensive works on the social problems of a specific ethnic or national group in a place where the group predominates, e.g., social problems of Italians in Italy 362.945

                   Class history, geographic treatment, biography of specific social problems in 362.1–362.8

                       For a social problem of a specific ethnic or national group in a place where the group predominates, see the problem, plus notation 093–099 from Table 1, e.g., poor Italians in Rome 362.50945632

.901–.905   Historical periods

                         Add to base number 362.90 the numbers following —090 in notation 0901–0905 from Table 1, e.g., social welfare in 20th century 362.904

.91–.99   Geographic treatment, biography

                       Add to base number 362.9 notation 1–9 from Table 2, e.g., social welfare in France 362.944

---

*Add as instructed under 362–363
†Do not use notation 08 from Table 1 to indicate services rendered by groups of people; class in base number

363   Other social problems and services

Standard subdivisions are added for comprehensive treatment of environmental and safety problems of society, e.g., assuring a safe and secure environment for Japan 363.0952

Class here public works

For communication facilities, see 384; for transportation facilities, see 388

See Manual at 363 vs. 302–307, 333.7, 570–590, 600; also at 363 vs. 344.02–344.05, 353–354

SUMMARY

.1   Public safety programs

Class here safety measures, interdisciplinary works on safety

Unless other instructions are given, observe the following table of preference, e.g., use of hazardous materials in health care facilities 363.17 (*not* 363.15):

Hazardous materials	363.17
Hazards in sports and recreation	363.14
Transportation hazards	363.12
Hazardous machinery	363.18
Product hazards	363.19
Domestic hazards	363.13
Hazards in health care facilities	363.15
Occupational and industrial hazards	363.11

Class terrorism and responses to terrorism associated with a particular aspect of public safety in 363.325; class managerial response to safety requirements, comprehensive works on safety management in 658.408. Class safety management in a specific industry with the industry, plus notation 0684 from Table 1, e.g., safety management in petroleum industry 665.50684

For police services, see 363.2; for aspects of public safety not provided for here, see 363.3; for personal safety, see 613.6; for survival after accidents, see 613.69. For a specific kind of remedial measure other than rescue operations, see the measure, e.g., medical care for the injured 362.1; for safety technology of a specific subject, see the subject, plus notation 0289 from Table 1, e.g., safety technology in hydraulic engineering 627.0289

See Manual at 363.1; also at 333.7–333.9 vs. 363.1, 363.73, 577; also at 363.1 vs. 600

SUMMARY

363.100 1–.100 9	Standard subdivisions
.101–.108	[General topics of public safety programs]
.11	Occupational and industrial hazards
.12	Transportation hazards
.13	Domestic hazards
.14	Hazards in sports and recreation
.15	Hazards in health care facilities
.17	Hazardous materials
.18	Hazardous machinery
.19	Product hazards

.100 1–.100 9   Standard subdivisions

As modified in notation 01–09 from table under 362–363

.101–.105   General topics of public safety programs

Add to base number 363.10 notation 1–5 from table under 362–363, e.g., public action to promote safety 363.1056

.106   Public control of safety

.106 2   Standards

.106 3   Monitoring, surveillance, reporting

Standard subdivisions are added for any or all topics in heading

.106 4   Inspection and testing

Standard subdivisions are added for either or both topics in heading

.106 5   Investigation of specific incidents

Class here interdisciplinary works on safety investigation

> *For a technical or engineering aspect of the investigation, see the aspect in 600, e.g., safety engineering 620.86, wreckage studies of automobile accidents 629.2826; for accounts of a specific incident that affected general social life and history, see the incident in 900, e.g., San Francisco earthquake of 1906 979.461051*

.106 6   Certification

.107–.108   Measures to prevent, protect against, limit effects of problems; remedial measures, services, forms of assistance

Add to base number 363.10 notation 7–8 from table under 362–363, e.g., alarm and warning systems 363.1072, counseling 363.1086

.11   *Occupational and industrial hazards

Subdivisions are added for either or both topics in heading

.119   Occupational and industrial hazards in specific industries and occupations

*Add as instructed under 362–363

[.119 000 1–.119 000 9]   Standard subdivisions

> Do not use; class in 363.1101–363.1109

.119 001–.119 999   Subdivisions for specific industries and occupations

> Add to base number 363.119 notation 001–999, e.g., school safety programs 363.119371, hazards in coal mining 363.119622334; however, for hazards to transportation workers, see 363.12; for hazards to domestic workers, see 363.13; for hazards to professional athletes, see 363.14; for hazards to workers in health care facilities, see 363.15

.12   Transportation hazards

> Class here accidents, fires resulting from accidents

> Class comprehensive works on fires in transportation facilities in 363.379

> *See Manual at 900: Historic events vs. nonhistoric events*

.120 01–.120 09   Standard subdivisions

> As modified in notation 01–09 from table under 362–363

.120 1–.120 8   Characteristics of transportation hazards, social action

> Add to base number 363.120 notation 1–8 from table under 362–363, e.g., accident prevention 363.1207

.122   *Rail transportation

.123   *Water transportation

> Class here water safety

> Class safety in water sports in 363.14

.124   *Air and space transportation

> Subdivisions are added for either or both topics in heading

.124 1   Causes of air and space accidents

> Number built according to instructions under 362–363

.124 12   Natural factors

> Including birds, clear-air turbulence (CAT)

.124 14   Operator failures

.124 16   Vehicle failures

.124 18   Failures of traffic control

> Class comprehensive works on air traffic control in 387.740426

.124 6   Control of air and space transportation

> Number built according to instructions under 362–363

*Add as instructed under 362–363

.124 65	Investigation of specific air and space accidents
	Number built according to instructions under 362–363
	Class here general investigations of aircraft accidents
	Class wreckage studies in 629.13255
.124 9	Specific types of accidents and accidents in specific types of services
.124 92	Specific types of accidents
	Including midair collisions, takeoff accidents
.124 93	Accidents in specific types of services
	Including air-taxi services, helicopter services
	Class specific types of accidents in specific types of services in 363.12492
.125	*Highway and urban vehicular transportation
	Subdivisions are added for either or both topics in heading
.125 1	Causes of accidents
	Number built according to instructions under 362–363
	Including road rage
	See also 364.147 for traffic offenses as causes of accidents
.125 14	Use of drugs
	Class here drunk driving
.125 6	Control of highway and urban vehicular transportation
	Number built according to instructions under 362–363
	Class traffic control by the police in 363.2332
.125 65	Investigation of specific vehicular and highway accidents
	Number built according to instructions under 362–363
	Class here general investigations of automobile accidents
	Class wreckage studies in 629.2826
.125 9	Hazards in use of specific types of vehicles other than automobiles
	Including bicycles, motorcycles, trucks
.13	*Domestic hazards
.14	*Hazards in sports and recreation
	Subdivisions are added for either or both topics in heading
.15	*Hazards in health care facilities

*Add as instructed under 362–363

.17   *Hazardous materials

Manufacture, transportation, use

Class here interdisciplinary works on hazardous materials, works on the control of such materials in their ordinary commercial setting (manufacture, sale, commercial and industrial use, disposal)

> *For hazardous materials as components of articles that become hazardous products, see 363.19; for hazardous materials as impurities in the water supply, see 363.61; for hazardous wastes, see 363.7287; for hazardous materials as environmental pollutants, see 363.738; for hazardous materials as a cause of disease or injury in an organism, see 571.95; for hazardous materials as an environmental factor affecting the natural ecology, see 577.275; for hazardous materials technology, see 604.7; for chemicals as a cause of injury to people, see 615.9; for radiation hazards as a cause of injury to people, see 616.9897*

.176 3   Monitoring, surveillance, reporting

Number built according to instructions under 362–363

Class here studies on the applicability of both social and technical findings of environmental chemistry and additive toxicology to the monitoring of hazardous materials

.179   Specific types of hazardous materials

Including corrosive materials

.179 1   Toxic chemicals

Including asbestos, lead

Class toxic agricultural chemicals in 363.1792

.179 2   *Agricultural chemicals

Class here pesticides

.179 8   Explosives, fuels, related products

Class here explosions, safety considerations with respect to especially flammable materials

> *See also 363.19 for products, e.g., sweaters, mattresses) that might constitute unsuspected fire hazards; also 363.377 for measures to control accumulation of ordinary combustible materials*

.179 9   *Radioactive materials

Class here nuclear accidents

.18   *Hazardous machinery

.189   Specific kinds of hazardous machinery

Including electrical and x-ray equipment

---

*Add as instructed under 362–363

.19	Product hazards

Adulteration, contamination, safety, adequacy, effectiveness of products offered for human consumption and use

Including household appliances, medical instruments and supplies, textiles, toys

Class here hazards due to containers and applicators that accompany products

.192	*Foods
.192 9	Specific foods

Including beverages, canned goods, dairy products, meats

.194	*Drugs and medicines

Subdivisions are added for either or both topics in heading

.196	*Cosmetics
.2	**Police services**

Class legal aspects of police services in control of factors affecting public morals in 344.05. Class a social service function of police with the function in 362, e.g., counseling of rape victims 362.883; class police committing a crime with the crime in 364.1, e.g., police violation of civil rights 364.1322

[.206 83]	Personnel management (Human resource management)

Do not use; class in 363.22

.22	Personnel

Duties, functions, activities

Class here personnel management (human resource management)

Class specific duties, functions, activities in 363.23–363.25

>	363.23–363.25 Specific aspects of police services

Class specific aspects of services of special kinds of security and law enforcement agencies in 363.28; class comprehensive works in 363.2

.23	Police functions

Class here law enforcement, prevention of crime by police

For detection of crime, see 363.25. For police functions in relation to a type of social conflict, see the type, e.g., control of terrorism 363.32516

See Manual at 363 vs. 344.02–344.05, 353–354: Law enforcement

*Add as instructed under 362–363

.232   Patrol and surveillance

Including pursuit and apprehension of lawbreakers, use of deadly force, undercover work

For highway patrol, see 363.2332

.233   Enforcement of civil laws

Including enforcement of building codes, licensing laws and ordinances, sanitation laws

.233 2   Traffic control

Including highway patrol

Class general investigations of traffic accidents in 363.12565; class investigation of traffic offenses in 363.25; class wreckage studies in 629.2826; class comprehensive works on traffic control in 363.1256

.233 6   Location of missing persons

.24   Auxiliary services

Including communications services, evidence preservation, fingerprint and photograph files, police records

.25   Detection of crime (Criminal investigation)

Class here forensic science (criminalistics); evidence, circumstantial evidence

Class general investigations of transportation accidents in 363.12065

For evidence preservation, see 363.24; for forensic medicine, see 614.1

See also 364.1 for criminal offenses

>   363.252–363.258 **Specific techniques and kinds of evidence**

Class comprehensive works in 363.25; class comprehensive works on detection of a specific kind of crime in 363.259. Class detection of a specific crime with the crime in 364.1, e.g., detection of a murder in New York City 364.1523097471

>   363.252–363.256 **Procurement and analysis of evidence**

Class evidence used in identification of criminals not listed here in 363.258; class comprehensive works in 363.25

.252   Procurement of evidence

Including electronic surveillance, search and seizure, use of informers and secret agents

For interrogation of witnesses, see 363.254

.254   Interrogation of witnesses

Including torture, use of polygraph (lie detector)

Class interdisciplinary works on torture in 364.675

.256	Analysis of evidence

Class here laboratories

Class files resulting from criminal investigations in 363.24

.256 2   Physical evidence

Including analysis of blood and hair, use of ballistics

.256 5   Documentary evidence

Including analysis of handwriting and typewriting

.258   Identification of criminals

Including artists' sketches, fingerprints, lineups, photographs, voice prints

Class files resulting from criminal investigations in 363.24; class interdisciplinary works on biometric identification in 006.248

.259   Detection of specific types of offenses

Add to base number 363.259 the numbers following 364.1 in 364.13–364.18, e.g., investigation of murder 363.259523

Class specific techniques of investigation of specific types of offenses in 363.252–363.258. Class detection of a specific crime with the crime in 364.1, e.g., detection of a murder in New York City 364.1523097471

.28   Services of special kinds of security and law enforcement agencies

Including park police

Class agencies to carry out specific police functions in 363.23; class agencies to investigate specific kinds of crime in 363.259

For military police, see 355.13323; for postal inspectors, see 383.46

.282   Marshals and sheriffs

Standard subdivisions are added for either or both topics in heading

.283   Secret police

.284   Drug enforcement agents

.285   Border patrols

.286   Coast guards and harbor patrols

Standard subdivisions are added for coast guards and harbor patrols together, for coast guards alone

Class here interdisciplinary works on coast guards

For coast guards as a military service, see 359.97; for inland waterway security services, see 363.2872

.287   Transportation security services

For automobile traffic control, see 363.2332; for harbor patrols, see 363.286

See also 363.379 for transportation fire hazards

.287 2   Inland waterway security services

     Class here river security services

.287 4   Railway security services

.287 6   Air transportation security services

     Including airport police, sky marshals

.289   **Private detective and police services**

     Standard subdivisions are added for either or both topics in heading

     Including bodyguards, campus police, store detectives

.289 8   Private military companies

     Class here interdisciplinary works on security measures provided by private military companies

     Class interdisciplinary works on private military companies in 355.34

     For security measures provided as part of military operations, see 355.4; for security measures provided at military installations, see 355.7

.3   **Other aspects of public safety**

     See Manual at 363.1

.31   Censorship

     Class here control of information, press control; censorship as routine governmental function; interdisciplinary works on censorship

     For a specific aspect of censorship not provided for here, see the aspect, e.g., censorship as social control 303.376, legal aspects of censorship 344.0531

     See Manual at 363.31 vs. 303.376, 791.4

.32   Social conflict

     Class here civil disobedience, civil disorder; violence

     Class interdisciplinary works on conflict in 303.6; class interdisciplinary works on civil disorder and disobedience in 303.62

.321   Aspects of social conflict

     Class aspects of a specific kind of civil disorder or disobedience in 363.323–363.325

[.321 01–.321 09]   Standard subdivisions

     Do not use; class in 363.3201–363.3209

.321 1–.321 8   Specific aspects of social conflict

     Add to base number 363.321 notation 1–8 from table under 362–363, e.g., social causes of violence 363.3211

.321 5 Social action

Number built according to instructions under 362–363

Class here conflict resolution

Class interdisciplinary works on conflict resolution in 303.69

.323 *Crowds

Class here crowd control, riot control; demonstrations; riots

[.323 6] Control

Do not use; class in 363.323

.325 Terrorism

Including cyberterrorism

Class here bombing; terrorism and responses to terrorism associated with a particular aspect of public safety; interdisciplinary works on terrorism

Class comprehensive works on data security and cyberterrorism in 005.8; class comprehensive works on aspects of public safety and terrorism and responses to terrorism associated with the aspect in 363.1

For sociology of terrorism, see 303.625; for terrorism as a crime, see 364.1317; for cyberterrorism as a crime, see 364.168

.325 1 Aspects of terrorism

Class aspects of bioterrorism and chemical terrorism in 363.3253; class aspects of nuclear terrorism in 363.3255; class aspects of a specific target of terrorism in 363.3259

[.325 101–.325 109] Standard subdivisions

Do not use; class in 363.32501–363.32509

.325 11–.325 18 Specific aspects of terrorism

Add to base number 363.3251 notation 1–8 from table under 362–363, e.g., social causes of terrorism 363.32511

.325 3 *Bioterrorism and chemical terrorism

Standard subdivisions are added for either or both topics in heading

Class bioterrorism and chemical terrorism against a specific target in 363.3259

.325 5 *Nuclear terrorism

Class nuclear terrorism against a specific target in 363.3259

.325 9 Specific targets of terrorism

Add to base number 363.3259 notation 001–999, e.g., terrorist attacks on food supply 363.32593638, terrorist attacks on nuclear power plants 363.3259621483

*Add as instructed under 362–363

.33   Control of firearms

Class here interdisciplinary works on gun control

Class explosives in 363.1798

For gun control as a civil rights issue, see 323.43

.34   *Disasters

Class survival after disasters in 613.69

For disasters caused by terrorism, see 363.325

See Manual at 900: Historic events vs. nonhistoric events

.348   Remedial measures, services, forms of assistance

Number built according to instructions under 362–363

Class here disaster relief

Class raising funds for mounting and carrying out disaster relief in 363.34570681. Class disaster relief for a specific type of disasters with the type, plus notation 8 from table under 362–363, e.g., disaster relief for flood victims 363.34938

For a specific kind of remedial measure other than those applied immediately at the time and site of the disaster, see the measure, e.g., medical care for the injured 362.1; for a specific form of disaster relief not provided for here, see the form of relief, e.g., long-range planning to replace housing lost due to a volcanic eruption 363.58

.348 1   Rescue operations

Number built according to instructions under 362–363

Forms of assistance applied immediately at time and site of disaster

Class here salvage operations; comprehensive works on rescue and salvage operations for disasters in general

Class rescue and salvage operations for a specific type of disaster with the type, plus notation 81 from table under 362–363, e.g., rescue operations for flood victims 363.349381

.349   Specific kinds of disasters

For epidemics and pandemics, see 362.1; for fires, see 363.37. For a disaster resulting from one of the hazards listed in 363.1, see the hazard, e.g., shipwrecks 363.123, nuclear accidents 363.1799

.349 2   Disasters caused by weather conditions

Class here storms

For floods, see 363.3493

.349 21   Aspects of disasters caused by weather conditions

Class an aspect of disasters caused by a specific weather condition in 363.34922–363.34929

*Add as instructed under 362–363

[.349 210 1–.349 210 9]	Standard subdivisions

Do not use; class in 363.349201–363.349209

.349 211–.349 218	Specific aspects of disasters caused by weather conditions

Add to base number 363.34921 notation 1–8 from table under 362–363, e.g., rescue operations during storms 363.3492181

.349 22–.349 26	Specific kinds of storms

Add to base number 363.3492 the numbers following 551.55 in 551.552–551.556, e.g., ice storms 363.34926; then add further as instructed under 362–363, e.g., rescue operations during ice storms 363.3492681

For dust storms, see 363.34929

.349 29	*Droughts

Including dust storms

.349 3	*Floods

See also 363.3494 for tsunamis

.349 36	Control

Number built according to instructions under 362–363

Class technology of flood control in 627.4

.349 4	*Tsunamis

See also 363.3493 for floods

.349 5	*Earthquakes and volcanoes

Subdivisions are added for earthquakes and volcanoes together, for earthquakes alone

See also 363.3494 for tsunamis

.349 8	*War

For civil defense, see 363.35

See also 303.66 for sociology of war

[.349 87]	Measures to prevent, protect against, limit effects of war

Do not use; class in 327.17

---

*Add as instructed under 362–363

.349 88	Remedial measures, services, forms of assistance

Number built according to instructions under 362–363

Including mine clearing operations by civilians

Class here war relief

Class problems of war refugees when not treated directly in the context of war relief in 362.87; class interdisciplinary works on mine clearing operations in 355.4. Class war relief during a specific war with the war, e.g., relief work of Switzerland during World War II 940.54778494

.35 Civil defense

Measures to defend civilian populations against war

Class comprehensive works on civil defense and emergency preparedness in 363.347

.37 *Fire hazards

Class fire fighting and fire safety technology in 628.92

.377 Measures to prevent, protect against, limit effects of problems

Number built according to instructions under 362–363

Class here fire prevention, measures to control accumulation of ordinary combustible materials

Class safety considerations with respect to especially flammable materials in 363.1798; class safety of products (e.g., sweaters, mattresses) that might constitute unsuspected fire hazards in 363.19

.378 Remedial measures, services, forms of assistance

Number built according to instructions under 362–363

Class here fire fighting

.379 Fire hazards in specific situations

Including fire hazards in high-rise buildings, schools, transportation; forest fires

For fires resulting from transportation accidents, see 363.12

.5 *Housing

Class here housing as a social problem, comprehensive works on housing for poor people, interdisciplinary works on housing

For a specific aspect of housing, see the aspect, e.g., sociological aspects 307.336, economic aspects 333.338, provision of shelter 361.05

See Manual at 363.5, 363.6, 363.8 vs. 338; also at 363.5 vs. 307.336, 307.34; also at 363.5 vs. 643.1

*Add as instructed under 362–363

[.508]   Housing for groups of people

> Do not use; class in 363.59

.51   Social causes

> Number built according to instructions under 362–363

> Class here housing conditions

[.52]   Incidence, extent, severity of housing problems

> Do not use; class in 363.51

.58   Programs and services

> Do not use subdivisions of 8 from the table under 362–363

.582   Financial assistance

> Class here housing allowances, rental subsidies, subsidized housing

.583   Programs and services for specific objectives

> Including home ownership, payment of energy bills, rehabilitation, resettlement, urban homesteading, weatherization

.585   Public operated housing

> Class here council housing

.59   Housing for groups of people

> Add to base number 363.59 the numbers following —08 in notation 081–089 from Table 1, e.g., housing for people in late adulthood 363.5946; however, for extended medical care for older adults, see 362.16; for comprehensive works on homelessness, see 362.5; for residential care for healthy older adults, see 362.61; for comprehensive works on housing for poor people, see 363.5

> Class specific aspects of housing for poor people, of low-income housing in 363.51–363.58

>> *For provision of shelter for a specific group of people, see the group in 362.1–362.8, plus notation 83 from table under 362–363, e.g., shelter for women 362.8383*

.6   Public utilities and related services

> Standard subdivisions are added for public utilities and related services together, for public utilities alone

> Class here problems of allocation among end users, measures to assure abundance of immediately available supplies and services

>> *For electrical utilities, see 333.7932; for communication, see 384; for transportation, see 388*

>> *See Manual at 333.7–333.9 vs. 363.6; also at 363.5, 363.6, 363.8 vs. 338*

.61   Water supply

Class here comprehensive works on water supply, on water-related public works, e.g., a study covering waterworks, treatment plants, canals, flood control, hydroelectric generation

For a specific topic of water supply, see the topic, e.g., flood control 363.34936

See Manual at 363.61

.63   Gas

.68   Park and recreation services

Class here services maintained or proposed after land has been designated for parks, establishment and operation of recreational centers primarily serving the general public

Class park policy and park development in 333.783; class recreational centers in 790.068. Class a specific cultural institution maintained by park and recreation services with the institution, e.g., museums 069, theaters 792

.69   Historic preservation

Including identification and designation of historic buildings and areas

Class here public policies to protect and restore historic buildings and areas and to promote appreciation of them

Class technology of building restoration and preservation in 720.288

See Manual at 913–919: Historic sites and buildings; also at 930–990: Historic preservation

.7   **Environmental problems**

Class here environmental protection; impact of wastes, of pollution, of actions to control waste and pollution

Class interdisciplinary works on the environment in 333.7

See Manual at 333.72 vs. 304.28, 320.58, 363.7

SUMMARY

363.700 1–.700 9	**Standard subdivisions**	
.701–.708	**Characteristics of environmental problems, social action**	
.72	**Sanitation**	
.73	**Pollution**	
.74	**Noise**	
.75	**Disposal of the dead**	
.78	**Pest control**	

.700 1–.700 9   Standard subdivisions

Notation from Table 1 as modified under 01–09, e.g., managerial cost control 363.700681

.701–.708   Characteristics of environmental problems, social action

Add to base number 363.70 notation 1–8 from table under 362–363, e.g., international action to protect the environment 363.70526

.72   *Sanitation

.728   Wastes

> Do not use for other remedial measures, services, forms of assistance; class in 363.72
>
> Class here industrial, municipal wastes; waste disposal, management
>
> Unless other instructions are given, class a subject with aspects in two or more subdivisions of 363.728 in the number coming last, e.g., recycling scrap metal 363.7288 (*not* 363.7282)
>
> Class dangerous wastes still in hands of processors or users in 363.17; class pollution by waste disposal in 363.73; class dangerous wastes which have escaped both safety and sanitary controls in 363.738

.728 2   Recycling

.728 4   *Liquid wastes

> Including urban water runoff; dredging spoil, water reuse planning
>
> Class here wastewater management
>
> *See Manual at 363.61*

.728 49   Specific kinds of liquid wastes

[.728 490 1–.728 490 9]   Standard subdivisions

> Do not use; class in 363.728401–363.728409

.728 493   *Sewage

> Class here biosolids, sewage sludge, wastes from combined sewers

.728 5   *Solid wastes

.728 7   *Hazardous wastes

.728 8   Specific kinds of wastes

> Including agricultural, domestic, medical wastes; beverage containers, garbage, scrap metal
>
> *For radioactive wastes, see 363.7289*

.728 9   *Radioactive wastes

.729   Sanitation in specific environments

.729 1   Streets

.729 2   Recreational areas

> Including swimming pools

.729 3   Common carriers

.729 4   Public toilets

*Add as instructed under 362–363

.729 5	Workplaces
.729 6	Food service establishments
.729 7	Health facilities

Including ambulances

.729 8	Residential buildings

Other than private family dwellings

.729 9	Barbershops, beauty shops, laundries
.73	*Pollution

Class works that discuss waste and sanitation problems as well as pollution in 363.7; class sanitation in 363.72; class noise in 363.74; class management responsibilities and measures with respect to protection and preservation of the environment in 658.408

See Manual at 333.7–333.9 vs. 363.1, 363.73, 577; also at 363.73 vs. 571.95, 577.27

.731	Social causes

Number built according to instructions under 362–363

Including industrial pollution

Class specific pollutants from specific sources in 363.738

.732	Incidence, extent, severity

Number built according to instructions under 362–363

Class incidence, extent, severity of pollution from specific sources in 363.731

.735	Social action

Number built according to instructions under 362–363

Class here remedial measures

.737	Measures to prevent, protect against, limit effects of pollution

Number built according to instructions under 362–363

Class waste disposal as a method of pollution prevention in 363.728; class technology of pollution prevention in 628.5

.738	Pollutants

Do not use for remedial measures; class in 363.735

Class here chemical pollutants

.738 2	*Oil
.738 4	*Toxic chemicals
.738 49	Specific types of toxic chemicals

*Add as instructed under 362–363

.738 492	*Lead
.738 494	*Asbestos
.738 498	*Pesticides

Class here agricultural pollution, agricultural runoff

Class pollution by animal wastes, feedlot runoff, fertilizers in 363.738

.738 6	*Acid rain
.738 7	Fumes, gases, smoke

Class lead emissions in 363.7384

.738 74   *Greenhouse gases

Gases contributing to greenhouse effect (global warming)

Class here interdisciplinary works on greenhouse effect (global warming)

For a specific aspect of greenhouse effect (global warming) not provided for here, see the aspect, e.g., changes in earth's temperature 551.5253, effect on ecology 577.276

.738 75   *Gases contributing to ozone layer depletion

Class here interdisciplinary works on ozone layer depletion

For a specific aspect of ozone layer depletion not provided for here, see the aspect, e.g., chemical changes in earth's ozone layer 551.5142, effect on ecology 577.276

.739   Pollution of specific environments

Class specific pollutants in specific environments in 363.738

.739 2	*Air pollution
.739 4	*Water pollution

Class here comprehensive works on water pollution

For assurance of clean water supply, see 363.61

See Manual at 363.61

.739 6	*Soil pollution
.74	*Noise
.741	Sources of noise

Number built according to instructions under 362–363

Including forms of transportation, e.g., aircraft, automobile traffic; construction equipment, industry

Class effects of specific sources of noise in 363.742

*Add as instructed under 362–363

.742	Incidence, extent, severity

Number built according to instructions under 362–363

Class incidence, extent, severity of noise from specific sources in 363.741

.75	Disposal of the dead

Class here interdisciplinary works on social aspects and services, customs, technology

Class interdisciplinary works on death in 306.9

For death customs, see 393; for technology of disposal of the dead, see 614.6

.78	Pest control

Including dog pounds, rat and mosquito abatement programs, removal of animal carcasses

Class here interdisciplinary works on pest control

For control of disease-carrying pests, see 614.43; for comprehensive works on the technology of pest control, see 628.96; for control of agricultural pests, see 632.9; for control of household pests, see 648.7

.8	***Food supply**

Class here famine, hunger; interdisciplinary works on food supply, on nutrition

Class food stamp programs in 363.882; class food relief in 363.883

For economics of food supply, see 338.19; for problems of malnutrition, see 362.19639; for prevention of malnutrition, see 614.5939

See Manual at 363.5, 363.6, 363.8 vs. 338; also at 363.8 vs. 613.2, 641.3

.808	Groups of people

Do not use for food supply problems of and services to groups of people, other than poor people; class in 362.1–362.8, plus notation 83 from table under 362–363

.82	Incidence, extent, severity of food supply problems

Number built according to instructions under 362–363

Class here nutrition surveys

.85	Social action

Number built according to instructions under 362–363

.856	Governmental action

Number built according to instructions under 362–363

Class here food rationing

---

*Add as instructed under 362–363

.9   **Population problems**

Class here interdisciplinary works on population problems

Class immigration in 362.89912; class interdisciplinary works on population in 304.6

> *For a specific manifestation of a population problem, see the manifestation, e.g., population growth as a cause of poverty 362.51, pressure on food supply leading to famine 363.8*

> *See Manual at 301–307 vs. 361–365*

.91   Population quantity

Overpopulation and underpopulation

Class remedial measures for overpopulation in 363.96

.92   Population quality

Class here interdisciplinary works on eugenics

> *For eugenic measures to reduce crime, see 364.4. For a specific aspect of eugenics, see the aspect, e.g., civil rights 323, involuntary sterilization 363.97*

> *See also 613.94 for family planning techniques*

.96   Birth control

Class here remedial measures for overpopulation; interdisciplinary works on birth control, on family planning programs

Class abortion in 362.19888

> *For sterilization, see 363.97; for personal health aspects of birth control, see 613.94; for comprehensive medical works on birth control, see 618.18*

.97   Sterilization

Including involuntary sterilization

Class here voluntary sterilization

364 Criminology

Crime and its alleviation

Class here comprehensive works on criminology and criminal law, on criminal justice that includes criminology, police services, and criminal law

Unless other instructions are given, observe the following table of preference, e.g., punishment of specific types of offenders 364.6 (*not* 364.3):

Penology	364.6
Discharged offenders	364.8
Offenders	364.3
Prevention of crime and delinquency	364.4
Causes of crime and delinquency	364.2
Criminal offenses	364.1
History, geographic treatment, biography	364.9

Class social services to victims of crimes and crime prevention for the individual in 362.88

For criminal law, see 345; for police services, see 363.2

SUMMARY

364.01–.09	**Standard subdivisions and special topics of criminology**
.1	**Criminal offenses**
.2	**Causes of crime and delinquency**
.3	**Offenders**
.4	**Prevention of crime and delinquency**
.6	**Penology**
.8	**Discharged offenders**
.9	**History, geographic treatment, biography**

.019 Psychological principles

> *For criminal psychology of specific offenses, see 364.1; for criminal psychology of offenders in general, see 364.3*

.04 Special topics of criminology

.042 Extent and incidence of crime

Criminal offenses and offenders

Class criminal offenses in 364.1; class offenders in 364.3

.08 Groups of people

Class works on why people become victims of specific crimes in 364.1

[.086 923] Juvenile delinquents and predelinquents

Do not use for predelinquents; class in 362.74. Do not use for juvenile delinquents; class in 364.36

[.086 927] Offenders

Do not use for offenders; class in 364.3. Do not use for convicts; class in 365.6

.086 949	Victims of war

> Do not use for victims of crimes; class in 362.88

[.09]	History, geographic treatment, biography

> Do not use; class in 364.9

.1 Criminal offenses

Class here conspiracy to and incitement to commit an offense, individuals identified with a specific offense or type of offense, investigation of specific crimes, crimes without victims

Class social services to victims of crimes in 362.88; class investigation of specific types of offenses in 363.259; class crime as an event in history in 900

> *See Manual at 362–363 vs. 364.1; also at 900: Historic events vs. nonhistoric events*

SUMMARY

364.101–.109	**Standard subdivisions and organized crime**
.13	**Political and related offenses**
.14	**Offenses against public health, safety, order, environment**
.15	**Offenses against the person**
.16	**Offenses against property**
.17	**Offenses against public morals**
.18	**Other offenses**

.106	Organized crime

> Do not use for organizations dealing with criminal offenses; class in 364.06

> Class here Mafia

[.106 092]	Biography

> Do not use for organized crime figures not associated with a specific offense; class in 364.1092. Do not use for organized crime figures associated with a specific offense; class in 364.13–364.18 with the offense, e.g., a hired killer 364.1523092

.106 6	Gangsterism

> Engagement of organized groups in piracy, robbery, theft, hijacking

.106 7	Racketeering

> Engagement of organized groups in extortion from legitimate or illegitimate enterprises through intimidation and force

> Including union racketeering

.106 8	Syndicated crime

> Engagement of organized groups in furnishing illegal goods or services

.109 2	Biography

Criminals are classed with the crime for which they are most noted unless they are discussed with relationship to a specific crime, e.g., a general biography of Jesse James, a bank robber, is classed in 364.1552092, but a study of Jesse James' killings is classed in 364.1523092

Class comprehensive works on offenders in 364.3

.13	Political and related offenses
.131	Political offenses

Including espionage, rebellion, seditious libel, subversion, treason

Class genocide in 364.151; class assassination of heads of state and government in 364.1524; class sabotage in 364.164

For war crimes, see 364.138

.131 7	Terrorism

Class interdisciplinary works on terrorism in 363.325

For terrorism as a war crime, see 364.138. For a specific type of terrorism, see the type, e.g., cyberterrorism 364.168

.132	Offenses against proper government

For offenses against administration of justice, see 364.134

.132 2	Denial and violation of civil rights

Standard subdivisions are added for either or both topics in heading

.132 3	Corruption

Including bribery of officials, graft

.132 4	Election offenses

Including bribery of voters, fraudulent reporting of votes, illegal voting, violations of campaign finance laws

.133	Offenses against revenue
.133 2	Bootlegging

Class here production, sale, transportation of alcoholic beverages; illicit distilling; comprehensive works on criminal offenses associated with alcoholic beverages

Class problems of and services to alcoholics in 362.292

For smuggling of alcoholic beverages, see 364.13361; for possession and use of alcoholic beverages, see 364.173

See also 364.1662 for bootlegging of copyrighted property, e.g., software piracy

.133 4   Counterfeiting of mediums of exchange

                     Class here counterfeiting money, comprehensive works on
                     counterfeiting

                     For counterfeiting of merchandise, see 364.1668

.133 6   Smuggling

                     Including smuggling of tobacco products, e.g., cigarettes

                     Class here comprehensive works on importing or exporting items on
                     which duties have not been paid or illegal items

                     *For human smuggling, see 364.137. For a smuggled item not
                     provided for here, see the item, e.g., medicine 364.142*

.133 61   Alcoholic beverages

                     Class bootlegging in 364.1332

.133 65   Drugs

                     Class here narcotics

                     Class comprehensive works on criminal offenses associated with
                     drugs in 364.177

.133 67   Animals

                     Class here wildlife smuggling

                     For violation of animal or plant quarantine, see 364.142

.133 8   Tax evasion

.134   Offenses against administration of justice

                     Including collusion, contempt of court, lynching, perjury, subornation of
                     perjury

.135   International offenses

                     *For a specific international offense, see the offense, e.g., piracy
                     364.164*

.136   Offenses against postal laws

.137   Illegal immigration

                     Class here human smuggling

                     See also 364.1551 for human trafficking

.138   War crimes

                     Class here terrorism as a war crime

                     Class comprehensive works on terrorism in 364.1317

                     For a specific war crime, see the crime, e.g., genocide 364.151

                     See also 341.69 for law of war crimes

.14   Offenses against public health, safety, order, environment

.142	Offenses against public health and safety
	Including adulteration of food and drugs, violations of product and building safety laws
.143	Offenses against public order
	Including carrying concealed weapons, disorderly conduct, rioting, unlawful assembly
.145	Offenses against the environment
	Class here violation of pollution laws
.147	Traffic offenses and misuse of communications facilities
	Class offenses against postal laws in 364.136
.148	Vagrancy
.15	Offenses against the person
	Class here hate crimes
	Class prevention of crimes by individuals in 613.6
.151	Genocide
.152	Homicide
	For lynching, see 364.134; for genocide, see 364.151
.152 2	Suicide
	Class assisted suicide in 364.1523
.152 3	Murder
	Including assisted suicide
	For assassination, see 364.1524
.152 32	Serial murder
.152 34	Mass murder
.152 4	Assassination
.152 5	Manslaughter
.153	Sex offenses
	Including adultery, indecent exposure, seduction, statutory rape
	Class rape in 364.1532; class bigamy in 364.183
.153 2	Rape
	Class social services aspects of rape in 362.883
	See also 364.153 for statutory rape
.153 4	Prostitution
.153 6	Sexual deviations
	Including incest, sodomy

.154   Abduction, kidnapping, taking and holding of hostages

> Class parental kidnapping in 362.8297

.155   Other violent offenses against the person

.155 1   Human trafficking

> Including slave trade

> *For human trafficking associated with a specific crime not provided for here, see the crime, e.g., prostitution 364.1534*

> *See also 364.137 for human smuggling*

.155 2   Robbery

> Thefts including threat of violence or bodily harm, or actual occurrence of violence

> Class here comprehensive works on hijacking

> *For a specific type of hijacking, see the type, e.g., taking hostages 364.154*

.155 5   Assault and battery

> Standard subdivisions are added for either or both topics in heading

> Including elder abuse

> Class elder abuse as a social problem in 362.6

.155 53   Spouse abuse

> Class social services to battered wives, spouse abuse as a social problem in 362.8292

.155 54   Child abuse

> Class here child neglect

> Class child abuse as a social problem in 362.76

> *See also 364.1536 for incest; also 364.174 for pornography*

.156   Offenses against reputation and honor

> Including defamation, invasion of privacy, libel, slander

> Class seditious libel in 364.131

.158   Stalking

.16   Offenses against property

> Class here looting, pillage, plundering

> Class prevention of crimes by individuals in 613.6

.162   Theft

> Class here larceny

> Class robbery in 364.1552; class fraud in 364.163; class identity theft in 364.1633

.162 2	Theft from residential and related buildings

Standard subdivisions are added for theft from residential and related buildings together, for theft from residential buildings alone

Including theft from garages

Class here burglary

Class theft of a specific item from residential or related buildings in 364.1628

For theft from nonresidential buildings, see 364.1623

.162 3	Theft from nonresidential buildings

Class here theft from commercial buildings, employee theft

Class theft of a specific item from nonresidential buildings in 364.1628

.162 32	Shoplifting
.162 4	Embezzlement

Class comprehensive works on business offenses, white collar crime in 364.168

.162 7	Fencing

Class fencing of a specific item in 364.1628

.162 8	Theft of specific items

See also 364.1662 for theft of intellectual property

[.162 800 01–.162 800 09]	Standard subdivisions

Do not use; class in 364.16201–364.16209

.162 800 1–.162 809 9	Theft of computers, books, related objects

Add to base number 364.1628 notation 001–099, e.g., computer theft 364.1628004

.162 81–.162 89	Theft of other specific items

Add to base number 364.1628 notation 100–900, e.g., art thefts 364.16287

.162 859	Theft of animals

Number built according to instructions under 364.16281–364.16289

Class here poaching, comprehensive works on wildlife crimes

For wildlife smuggling, see 364.13367

.162 859 1	Theft of specific nontaxonomic kinds of animals

Number built according to instructions under 364.16281–364.16289

.162 862 904	Transportation vehicle thefts
	Number built according to instructions under 364.16281–364.16289
	Class here theft of the vehicles, theft from the vehicles

> *For theft of a specific item, other than the vehicle, see the item, e.g., theft of computers from motor vehicles 364.1628004*

.163	Fraud

Including welfare fraud, e.g., Medicare fraud

Class mail fraud in 364.136

.163 2	Phishing

Class use of information obtained by phishing for identity theft in 364.1633

.163 3	Identity theft

Class here impersonation (false personation)

.163 5	Forgery

Class product conterfeiting in 364.1668

.164	Violent offenses against property

Including piracy, sabotage

Class robbery, comprehensive works on hijacking in 364.1552; class prevention by individuals of violent offenses against property in 613.66

> *See also 364.1662 for copyright piracy*

.164 2	Arson
.164 4	Vandalism
.165	Extortion

Including blackmail

.166	Intellectual property infringement
.166 2	Copyright infringement

Including bootlegging (making, distribution, or trafficking in copyrighted material); copyright piracy, e.g., software piracy, pirated editions (bootlegged editions)

> *For counterfeiting of copyrighted products, see 364.1668*

> *See also 364.1332 for bootlegging as an offense against revenue*

.166 3	Trademark infringement

> *For counterfeiting of trademarked products, see 364.1668*

.166 8	Product counterfeiting

Class here counterfeiting of copyrighted products, counterfeiting of trademarked products, passing off

Class comprehensive works on counterfeiting in 364.1334

.168	Business, financial, professional offenses

Including criminal usury, cyberterrorism, unfair trade practices; violation of antitrust laws, of laws with respect to securities and their exchange

Class here computer, white collar crime

For embezzlement, see 364.1624; for fraud, see 364.163. For a specific type of computer crime not provided for here, see the type, e.g., tax evasion 364.1338

See also 364.1628004 for theft of computers

.17	Offenses against public morals

For sex offenses, see 364.153

.172	Gambling
.173	Possession and use of alcoholic beverages

Standard subdivisions are added for either or both topics in heading

Including public drunkenness

Class problems of and services to alcoholics in 362.292; class drunk driving in 364.147; class comprehensive works on criminal offenses associated with alcoholic beverages in 364.1332

.174	Obscenity and pornography

Class interdisciplinary works on pornography in 306.771

.177	Drugs

Class here production, sale, possession, use

Class problems of and services to drug addicts in 362.29

For smuggling of drugs, see 364.13365

See also 364.173 for alcoholic beverages

.18	Other offenses

Including illegal adoption

.183	Bigamy
.185	Criminal abortion

Class interdisciplinary works on abortion in 362.19888

.187	Cruelty to animals

.188	Offenses against religion
	Offenses defined and penalized by the state
	Including blasphemy, heresy, sacrilege
	Class offenses against church law in 262.9

.2 **Causes of crime and delinquency**

Class here criminal anthropology

Class victimology in 362.88

.22	Influence of physical environment
	Including climate, seasons, weather

.24	Influence of personal factors
	Including biological factors, e.g., effects of heredity, genetic defects, physical typology; psychological factors

.25	Influence of social factors
	Including leisure and recreation

.253	Influence of family and peer group

.254	Influence of mass media
	Including books, motion pictures, radio, television

.256	Influence of social conflict
	Including class, ethnic group, religion, socioeconomic conditions

.3 **Offenders**

Including recidivists

Class here criminal psychology

Class a specific aspect of the justice system for specific types of offenders with the aspect, e.g., determination of sentences for juvenile offenders 364.650835, offenders as prisoners in 365.6

For individuals chiefly identified with a specific offense or type of offense, see 364.1

[.308 11]	Men
	Do not use; class in 364.373

[.308 2]	Women
	Do not use; class in 364.374

[.308 3]	Young people
	Do not use; class in 364.36

.308 6	People by miscellaneous social attributes

[.308 692 3]	Juvenile delinquents and predelinquents
	Do not use; class in 364.36
[.308 692 7]	Offenders
	Do not use; class in 364.3
[.308 74]	People with mental illnesses and disabilities
	Do not use; class in 364.38
[.308 9]	Ethnic and national groups
	Do not use; class in 364.34

.34   Offenders of ethnic and national groups

Class juvenile delinquents of specific ethnic and national groups in 364.36; class women in 364.374; class offenders with mental illnesses and disabilities in 364.38

.340 01–.340 09   Standard subdivisions

.340 5–.340 9   Offenders of mixed ancestry with ethnic origins from more than one continent, European offenders and offenders of European descent

Add to base number 364.34 notation 05–09 from Table 5, e.g., offenders of European descent 364.3409

.341–.349   Specific ethnic and national groups

Add to base number 364.34 notation 1–9 from Table 5, e.g., Germans as offenders 364.3431

.36   Juvenile delinquents

Including status offenders (juveniles who have broken laws pertaining only to their age group, e.g., curfew laws, drinking below legal age)

Class here comprehensive works on juvenile delinquency, juvenile delinquents, juvenile justice system together

Class comprehensive works on maladjusted young people in 362.74

For legal aspects, see 345

.37   Men and women

Class adult offenders with mental illnesses and disabilities in 364.38. Class men and women with attributes of a specific group with the group, e.g., men and women in late adulthood 364.30846

.373   Men

Works specifically emphasizing male sex

.374   Women

.38   Offenders with mental illnesses and disabilities

Class here offenders with mental retardation

Class juvenile offenders with mental illnesses and disabilities in 364.36

.4   **Prevention of crime and delinquency**

Including curfew, eugenic measures

Class here what society does to prevent crime

Class penalties as a deterrent in 364.601

> *For law enforcement, see 363.23. For a specific aspect of prevention by a potential victim, see the aspect, e.g., prevention of identity theft 332.024, prevention by individuals of crimes 613.6, household security 643.16, business intelligence and security 658.47*

.404   Special topics of prevention of crime and delinquency

.404 5   Social action

Add to base number 364.4045 the numbers following 361 in 361.2–361.8, e.g., social policy 364.404561

.41   Identification of potential offenders

Including genetic screening

.43   Citizen participation

Class individual action in 362.88

.44   Welfare services

Including financial assistance; foster home care; recreational services, e.g., camps, playgrounds

Class preventive police work in 363.23

> *For counseling and guidance, see 364.48*

.48   Counseling and guidance

Standard subdivisions are added for either or both topics in heading

.49   Environmental design

.6   **Penology**

Class here welfare services to offenders, reform of penal system

Class welfare services to prisoners in 365.66; class reform of penal institutions in 365.7

> *For discharged offenders, see 364.8; for institutions for correction of offenders, see 365*

.601   Philosophy and theory

Class here punishment as retribution, deterrent, protection to society, reformation of offenders

.62   Parole and indeterminate sentence

Standard subdivisions are added for parole and indeterminate sentence together, for parole alone

Class services to prisoners to prepare them for parole in 365.66

.63 Probation and suspended sentence

> Standard subdivisions are added for probation and suspended sentence together, for probation alone
>
> Including reprieve
>
> Class here comprehensive works on probation and parole
>
> > *For parole, see 364.62*

.65 Determination of sentence

> Including amnesty, commutation of sentence, pardon
>
> Class a specific punishment with the punishment, e.g., probation 364.63, imprisonment 365

.66 Capital punishment

.67 Corporal punishment

.675 Torture

> Class here interdisciplinary works on torture
>
> > *For ethics of torture, see 179.75; for torture in military intelligence gathering, see 355.3432; for torture in interrogation, see 363.254*

.68 Noninstitutional penalties

> Including community service, deportation, fines, loss of citizenship, loss of vote
>
> > *For capital punishment, see 364.66; for corporal punishment, see 364.67*

.8 Discharged offenders

.9 History, geographic treatment, biography

> *For extent and incidence of crime, see 364.042*

.901–.905 Historical periods

> Add to base number 364.90 the numbers following —090 in notation 0901–0905 from Table 1, e.g., crime and its alleviation in 20th century 364.904

.91–.99 Geographic treatment, biography

> Add to base number 364.9 notation 1–9 from Table 2, e.g., people associated with crime and its alleviation 364.92; however, for victims, see 362.88; for police, see 363.2; for offenders associated with specific kinds of crime, see 364.1; for comprehensive works on offenders, see 364.3; for penologists, see 364.6092; for prisoners, see 365.6

365 Penal and related institutions

Institutions for correction of offenders and for incarceration of other groups considered socially undesirable

Standard subdivisions are added for penal and related institutions together, for penal institutions alone

Class here imprisonment and detention

Unless other instructions are given, class a subject with aspects in two or more subdivisions of 365 in the number coming last, e.g., maximum security prisons for women 365.43 (*not* 365.33)

Class parole and indeterminate sentence in 364.62; class probation and suspended sentence in 364.63

[.068 2]   Plant management

Do not use; class in 365.5

[.09]   History, geographic treatment, biography

Do not use; class in 365.9

.3 Kinds of penal institutions

Class specific institutions in 365.93–365.99

.32   Institutions by level of government

National, state or provincial, local

.33   Institutions by degree of security

.34   Institutions by purpose or type of program

Including jails, penal colonies, penitentiaries, prerelease guidance centers, prison farms, reformatories, work camps

Class penal colonies as a part of history of a place with the place in 930–990, e.g., penal colony of Botany Bay as founding settlement of New South Wales 994.402

.4 Institutions for specific classes of inmates

Including debtors' prisons

Class here personal narratives of specific classes of inmates

Class specific institutions in 365.93–365.99; class comprehensive works on inmates in 365.6

.42   Institutions for juveniles

Including borstals, reformatories; industrial, reform, training schools; halfway houses for the transition from reform school to society

.43   Institutions for adult women

.44   Institutions for adult men

Works specifically emphasizing inmates of the male sex

Class institutions in general, specific kinds of institutions for men in 365.3

.45   Institutions for political prisoners and related groups of people

　　　　　　Standard subdivisions are added for either or both topics in heading

　　　　　　Class here concentration camps

　　　　　　　　For concentration camps associated with a specific war, see the war,
　　　　　　　　e.g., World War II concentration camps 940.5317

.46   Institutions for the criminally insane

.48   Military prisons and prison camps

　　　　　　Institutions whose inmates are military personnel

　　　　　　Class institutions for prisoners of war in 355.1296; class military institutions
　　　　　　for the insane in 365.46

.5   **Prison plant**

　　　　　　Buildings, equipment, grounds

　　　　　　Class prison architecture in 725.6

.6   **Inmates**

　　　　　　Including reception and classification

　　　　　　Class here offenders as inmates; community-based corrections; social aspects of
　　　　　　prison life, e.g., conjugal rights, drug abuse

　　　　　　Class institutions for specific classes of inmates, personal narratives of inmates
　　　　　　in 365.4

.602 1   Tabulated and related materials

　　　　　　　　Class statistics of inmates when used to indicate general statistics of
　　　　　　　　offenders in 364.3021

.609 2   Biography

　　　　　　　　Class a personal narrative of a specific class of inmate with the class
　　　　　　　　of inmate in 365.4, plus notation 092 from Table 1, e.g., a personal
　　　　　　　　narrative of a political prisoner 365.45092

.64   Security, discipline, daily routine, release and discharge

　　　　　　Class here treatment of inmates

.641   Security

　　　　　　Including escapes, riots

.643   Discipline

　　　　　　Rules, rights, privileges

　　　　　　Including furloughs

　　　　　　Class work furloughs in 365.65

　　　　　　　　For punishments, see 365.644

.644   Punishments for infractions of prison discipline

.646		Daily routine

For labor, see 365.65; for services to prisoners, see 365.66

.647		Release and discharge

Class work release in 365.65; class services to prepare prisoners for release in 365.663

.65 Labor

Including chain gangs, contract system, lease system, work furloughs, work release

.66 Services to prisoners

> 365.661–365.663 Counseling, rehabilitation, prerelease programs

Class here how to provide the service, how to perform the service

Class comprehensive works in 365.66

.661 Counseling and rehabilitation

Standard subdivisions are added for either or both topics in heading

Class a specific service providing counseling or rehabilitation with the service, e.g., religious counseling 365.665

.663 Prerelease programs

Class prerelease institutions in 365.34

> 365.665–365.668 Religious, educational, medical, recreational services

How to provide the service is classed here. How to perform the service is classed with the activity in 000–999

Class comprehensive works in 365.66

.665 Religious services

Class care of prisoners by religious leaders in general in 206.1; class Christian pastoral care of prisoners in 259.5

.666 Educational services

Class education of delinquent students in 371.93; class adult education of prisoners in 374.1826927

.667 Health services

Class here medical services

Class technology of medical services in 610; class technology of health services in 613

.667 2 Mental health services

.667 29 Substance abuse treatment

.668	Recreational services

Class recreational arts in 790

.7   **Reform of penal institutions**

Class reform of penal system, reform to eliminate prisons as form of punishment for certain types of crimes in 364.6

.9   **History, geographic treatment, biography**

Class specific aspects of penal institutions in specific times and places, of specific kinds of institutions in 365.3–365.7

.901–.905   Historical periods

Add to base number 365.90 the numbers following —090 in notation 0901–0905 from Table 1, e.g., penal institutions in 20th century 365.904

.91–.99   Geographic treatment, biography

Add to base number 365.9 notation 1–9 from Table 2, e.g., prison administrators 365.92; however, for inmates, see 365.6092

366   Secret associations and societies

Standard subdivisions are added for either or both topics in heading

Class here semisecret associations and societies

Class comprehensive works on associations in 369

For Rosicrucianism, see 135.43; for orders of knighthood, see 929.71. For secret associations and societies not provided for here, see the associations and societies, e.g., student secret associations 371.83

.01–.08   Standard subdivisions

.09   History, geographic treatment, biography

.093–.099   Specific continents, countries, localities

Do not use for specific associations or societies not provided for in 366.1–366.5; class in 366

.1   **Freemasonry**

.108 2   Women in Freemasonry

For Order of the Eastern Star, see 366.18

.12   Rituals

.16   Nobles of the Mystic Shrine (Shriners)

.18   Order of the Eastern Star

.2   **Knights of Pythias**

.3   **Independent Order of Odd Fellows**

.308 2   Women

For International Association of Rebekah Assemblies, see 366.38

.38 International Association of Rebekah Assemblies

.5 **Benevolent and Protective Order of Elks**

367 General clubs

Including social clubs, study clubs

Class here social clubs for specific types of people, e.g., social clubs for actors

Class clubs dealing with a specific subject with the subject, plus notation 06 from Table 1, e.g., pinochle clubs 795.41606

[.09] History, geographic treatment, biography

Do not use; class in 367.9

.9 **History, geographic treatment, biography**

.901–.905 Historical periods

Add to base number 367.90 the numbers following —090 in notation 0901–0905 from Table 1, e.g., general clubs in 20th century 367.904

.91–.99 Geographic treatment, biography

Add to base number 367.9 notation 1–9 from Table 2, e.g., The Lamb (social club in New York City composed chiefly of actors, musicians, and playwrights) 367.97471

368 Insurance

Class here risk, insurance industry

Class risk management as part of management in 658.155

See also 658.153 for managerial decisions on choosing insurance

SUMMARY

368.001–.009	Standard subdivisions and insurance companies
.01–.09	[General principles, specific forms of risk, sales groupings]
.1	Insurance against damage to and loss of property
.2	Insurance against damage to and loss of property in transit
.3	Old-age insurance and insurance against death, illness, injury
.4	Government-sponsored insurance
.5	Liability insurance
.6	Glass insurance
.7	Insurance against industrial casualties (accidents)
.8	Other casualty insurance
.9	Insurance by specific continents, countries, localities in modern world

.001 Philosophy and theory

[.001 51] Mathematical principles

Do not use; class in 368.01

.002–.005 Standard subdivisions

.006 Organizations and management; insurance companies

Notation 06 from Table 1 as modified below

.006 5	Insurance companies

.006 5 Insurance companies

For-profit and nonprofit organizations

Class here interdisciplinary works on insurance companies

Add to base number 368.0065 notation 4–9 from Table 2, e.g., insurance companies of Texas 368.0065764

Class government agencies that provide insurance in 353.54

For credit and loan functions of insurance companies, see 332.38

.007–.008 Standard subdivisions

.009 History, geographic treatment, biography

[.009 4–.009 9] Specific continents, countries, localities in modern world

Do not use; class in 368.9

.01 General principles

Class here actuarial science, finance, mathematical principles

Class investments by insurance companies in 332.672532

.011 Rates

Class here rate making

.012 Underwriting

Risk selection and estimation

.012 2 Reinsurance

.014 Claims

Including adjustment of claims, fraudulent claims, settlement of losses

Class fraudulent claims, insurance fraud as crimes in 364.163

.016 Lapse, persistence, termination

Standard subdivisions are added for any or all topics in heading

.019 Government policies with respect to insurance, insurance industry

> 368.06–368.08 Specific forms of risk

Class comprehensive works in 368

.06 Property risks

Risk of loss from impairment or destruction of property

Class risk of consequential loss in 368.08

.062 Risks to tangible property

.063 Risks to intangible property

.07   Personal risks

> Risk of loss of income or augmented expenditure due to hazards to the person

.08   Other risks

> Including liability risks, risk of consequential loss, risks due to the failure of others, statutory liability risks

.09   Conventional comprehensive sales groupings

> Combinations of different lines of insurance, e.g., property-casualty, property-casualty-life and health

> Class here all-risk, multiple-line coverage

> Class a single line of insurance with the line, e.g., homeowner's liability insurance 368.56

.092   Motor vehicle insurance

> Class here automobile insurance

>> *For motor vehicle transportation insurance as a branch of inland marine insurance, see 368.232; for motor vehicle liability insurance, see 368.572*

.093   Aviation insurance

>> *For air transportation insurance as a branch of inland marine insurance, see 368.24; for aviation liability insurance, see 368.576*

.094   Business insurance

> Broad property and liability coverage

> Class here businessowners insurance, comprehensive business policies; commercial insurance, commercial multi-peril insurance; special multi-peril insurance (SMP)

>> *For a single line of insurance, see the line, e.g., business liability insurance 368.81*

.096   Multi-peril real property insurance

> Coverage of perils associated with land and whatever is growing on or affixed to it

> Class here homeowner's insurance

> **368.1–368.8 Specific kinds of insurance**

Add to each subdivision identified by * as follows:
001–005   Standard subdivisions
006   Organizations and management; insurance companies
                          Notation 06 from Table 1 as modified below
0065   Insurance companies
                          For-profit and nonprofit organizations
                          Add to 0065 notation 4–9 from Table 2, e.g., insurance
                          companies in Great Britain 006541
007–009   Standard subdivisions
01   General principles
                 Add to 01 the numbers following 368.01 in 368.011–368.019,
                 e.g., underwriting 012

Class comprehensive works in 368

.1   *Insurance against damage to and loss of property

Subdivisions are added for either or both topics in heading

Class multi-peril real property insurance in 368.096. Class property damage
(liability) insurance as part of a specific type of liability insurance with the type,
e.g., property damage insurance as part of public liability 368.56

*For insurance against damage to and loss of property in transit, see 368.2;
for casualty insurance, see 368.5–368.8*

.11   *Fire insurance

For extended coverage endorsement, see 368.129

See also 368.12 for allied fire insurance lines

.12   *Allied fire insurance lines and extended coverage endorsement

Perils and losses traditionally associated with fire insurance

Including explosion, smoke damage, vandalism and malicious mischief
(VMM) insurance

Class here commercial property insurance

Subdivisions are added for allied fire insurance lines and extended coverage
endorsement together, for allied fire insurance lines alone

Class business interruption insurance in 368.815

See also 368.56 for livestock liability insurance

.121   *Crop insurance

Class here government-sponsored crop insurance

*Add as instructed under 368.1–368.8

.122   *Disaster insurance

Including insurance against damage and loss from storms

For insurance for damage to crops from storms and other disasters, see 368.121

.122 2   *Flood insurance

.122 6   *Earthquake insurance

.125   *Civil commotion and riot insurance

Subdivisions are added for either or both topics in heading

.129   *Extended coverage endorsement

.14   *War risk insurance

Class ocean marine war risk insurance in 368.22; class war risk life insurance in 368.364

.2   *Insurance against damage to and loss of property in transit

Variant names: Marine insurance, Transportation insurance

Including postal and satellite insurance

Class here insurance against damage to and loss of instrumentalities of transportation

Class a combination of transportation property insurance and transportation liability insurance in 368.09

.22   *Ocean marine insurance

Over-the-sea transportation insurance

Including ocean marine war risk insurance

.23   *Inland marine insurance

Land or over-the-land (including over inland waterways) transportation insurance

For air transportation insurance, see 368.24

.232   *Motor vehicle insurance

Class here automobile insurance

Class comprehensive works on all types of motor vehicle insurance in 368.092

.233   *Railroad insurance

.24   *Air transportation insurance

Class comprehensive works on all types of air transportation and aviation insurance in 368.093

*Add as instructed under 368.1–368.8

.3   ***Old-age insurance and insurance against death, illness, injury**

Class here comprehensive works on private and government-sponsored old-age insurance and insurance against death, illness, injury; comprehensive works on group insurance, on industrial insurance, on old-age and survivors' insurance, on survivors' insurance

Class personnel management of insurance as a fringe benefit in 658.3254; class comprehensive works on insurance as a fringe benefit in 331.255

For government-sponsored insurance, see 368.4. For a specific type of group insurance, of industrial insurance, of old-age and survivors' insurance, of survivors' insurance not provided for here, see the type, e.g., group credit insurance 368.87

.32   *Life insurance

For special fields of life insurance, see 368.36

.322   *Endowment insurance

.323   *Term life insurance

.324   *Universal life insurance

.325   *Variable life insurance

.326   *Whole life insurance

.36   Special fields of life insurance

.362   *Industrial life insurance

.363   *Fraternal insurance

.364   *Life insurance for members of armed services

Including National Service Life Insurance, veterans' life insurance, war risk life insurance

.366   *Burial insurance

.37   *Annuities

Class pensions as an element of personnel management in 658.3253; class comprehensive works on pensions in 331.252

.375   *Variable annuities

.38   *Health insurance, accident insurance, disability income insurance

*Add as instructed under 368.1–368.8

.382   *Health insurance

Including disability insurance; health maintenance organizations, preferred provider plans; long-term care insurance, Medigap (Medicare supplement insurance); reimbursement health insurance (insurance in which the insured first pays the bills)

Class here insurance aspects of managed care, prepaid health insurance (insurance in which the insurer first pays the bills), specific health insurance organizations or plans without regard to type, comprehensive works on health and accident insurance

Class interdisciplinary works on delivery of health care in 362.1

For accident insurance, see 368.384

See also 368.386 for disability income insurance

\>   368.382 2–368.382 7   Basic health insurance coverage for specific kinds of services

Class here policies limited to coverage for specific kinds of services, works that focus on specific types of benefits of broader policies

Class catastrophic health insurance in 368.3828; class comprehensive works in 368.382

.382 2   *Medical and surgical insurance

Subdivisions are added for medical and surgical insurance together, for medical insurance alone

Class major medical insurance in 368.3828

.382 3   *Dental insurance

.382 4   *Pharmaceutical services insurance

.382 5   *Mental health insurance

Including coverage for treatment of substance abuse

.382 7   *Hospital insurance

Class coverage for psychiatric hospitalization in 368.3825; class major medical insurance in 368.3828

.382 8   *Catastrophic health insurance (Major medical insurance)

Insurance providing protection for potentially large health care expenses after basic health care insurance benefits have been exhausted

.384   *Accident insurance

.386   *Disability income insurance

See also 368.382 for disability insurance

---

*Add as instructed under 368.1–368.8

.4   ***Government-sponsored insurance**

  Class here social insurance, social security as a form of social insurance

  Class comprehensive works on social security taxes in 336.249

  For a type of government-sponsored insurance not provided for here, see the type, e.g., crop insurance 368.121, bank deposit insurance 368.854

.400 68   Management

    Class personnel management of insurance for government employees in 352.67

.400 9   History, geographic treatment, biography

.400 973   United States

    Do not use for social security in United States; class in 368.4300973

.41   ***Workers' compensation insurance (Workmen's compensation insurance)**

  Protection against losses incurred through disablements caused on the job

  Class here comprehensive works on workers' compensation insurance and employers' liability insurance

  For employers' liability insurance (insurance of an employer's liability for compensation to his employees in case of accident), see 368.56

.42   ***Health and accident insurance**

  Subdivisions are added for health and accident insurance together, for health insurance alone

  Class comprehensive works on health and accident insurance in 368.382

  For workers' compensation insurance, see 368.41

  See also 362.1042520973 for United States' Medicaid financial benefits; also 362.10973 for United States' Medicaid health services

[.420 084 6]   Accident and health insurance for people in late adulthood

    Do not use; class in 368.426

.420 085 2   Accident and health insurance for mothers

    Do not use for maternity insurance; class in 368.424

.424   ***Maternity insurance**

.426   ***Accident and health insurance for people in late adulthood**

  Class comprehensive works on accident and health insurance for people in late adulthood in 368.38200846

*Add as instructed under 368.1–368.8

.43	*Old-age and survivors' insurance

Class here comprehensive works on government-sponsored old-age and survivors' insurance and government-sponsored accident and health insurance for people in late adulthood

Class supplementary social security for low-income people in 362.582; class comprehensive works on old-age and survivors' insurance in 368.3

For government-sponsored accident and health insurance for people in late adulthood, see 368.426

.430 097 3	United States

Class here social security in United States

.44	*Unemployment insurance
.45	*Paid leave insurance
.452	*Sick leave

Class interdisciplinary works on paid sick leave in 331.25762

.454	*Parental leave

Class here leave for pregnancy, birth, longer-term care of children; adoption leave, parental leave taken by legal guardians

Class interdisciplinary works on paid parental leave in 331.25763

.454 008 51	Fathers

Class here paternity leave, parental leave taken by fathers

.454 008 52	Mothers

Class here maternity leave, parental leave taken by mothers

.454 008 6	People by miscellaneous social attributes
.454 008 664	Gays

Class here parental leave taken by same-sex partners

.48	*Insurance against crimes of violence

Class comprehensive works on crime insurance in 368.82

> **368.5–368.8 Casualty insurance**

Class comprehensive works in 368.5

*Add as instructed under 368.1–368.8

.5 ***Liability insurance**

Including no-fault insurance, umbrella or excess liability insurance

Class here comprehensive works on casualty insurance

Class no-fault insurance, umbrella or excess liability insurance of a specific type with the type, e.g., umbrella personal insurance 368.56, no-fault motor vehicle insurance 368.5728

For glass insurance, see 368.6; for insurance against industrial casualties, see 368.7; for other casualty insurance, see 368.8

.56 Miscellaneous lines of liability insurance

Only those lines named below

Including commercial general, contractual, elevator, employers', homeowners', landlords', owners', tenants' liability insurance; livestock liability insurance; personal liability insurance

Class here public liability insurance

See also 368.121 for crop insurance

.562 ***Product liability insurance**

.563 ***Environmental impairment liability insurance**

Class here pollution liability insurance

.564 ***Professional liability insurance**

Class here errors and omissions insurance, malpractice insurance

.564 2 ***Medical malpractice insurance**

Class here physicians' liability insurance

.57 ***Instrumentalities of transportation**

.572 ***Motor vehicle liability insurance**

Class here automobile liability insurance

Class comprehensive works on all types of motor vehicle insurance in 368.092

.572 8 ***No-fault motor vehicle insurance**

.576 ***Aviation liability insurance**

Class comprehensive works on all types of aviation insurance in 368.093

.6 ***Glass insurance**

Including coverage on plate glass, windows

.7 ***Insurance against industrial casualties (accidents)**

Including boiler and machinery, nuclear (nuclear energy, nuclear hazards), power interruption, power plant insurance

---

*Add as instructed under 368.1–368.8

.8   **Other casualty insurance**

.81   *Business liability insurance

Casualty aspects only

Class comprehensive works on business insurance in 368.094

.815   *Business interruption insurance

Including strike insurance

.82   *Burglary, robbery, theft insurance

Including extortion, kidnap and ransom insurance

Class here comprehensive works on crime insurance

Subdivisions are added for any or all topics in heading

For a specific type of crime insurance not provided for here, see the type, e.g., government-sponsored insurance against crimes of violence 368.48

.83   *Fidelity bonds

Guarantee against loss to employers because of dishonesty of employees

Class here comprehensive works on fidelity and surety bonds

For surety bonds, see 368.84

.84   *Surety bonds

Guarantee against loss due to failure to perform an obligation or fulfill a contract

.85   Guarantees

For a specific guarantee not provided for here, see the guarantee, e.g., surety bonds 368.84

.852   *Mortgage insurance

.853   *Investment guarantees

.854   *Bank deposit insurance

Class here government guaranty of deposits

.87   *Credit insurance

Insurance of creditor against loss due to debtor's insolvency

.88   *Title insurance

.9   **Insurance by specific continents, countries, localities in modern world**

Add to base number 368.9 notation 4–9 from Table 2, e.g., insurance in South America 368.98

For a specific type of insurance in a specific place, see the type, e.g., transportation insurance in South America 368.20098

---

*Add as instructed under 368.1–368.8

369   Associations

Organizations formed for fraternizing or for mutual assistance

Class interdisciplinary works on organizations in 060; class general rules of order in 060.42

For secret associations and societies, see 366; for general clubs, see 367; for orders of knighthood, see 929.71

See also 200 for religious associations; also 368.363 for fraternal insurance

.01–.07	Standard subdivisions
.08	Groups of people
[.083]	Young people

        Do not use; class in 369.4

.089	Ethnic and national groups

        Do not use for ethnic clubs; class in 369.3

.09	History, geographic treatment, biography
.093–.099	Specific continents, countries, localities

        Do not use for specific associations not provided for in 369.1–369.5; class in 369

.1   Hereditary, military, patriotic societies of United States

Standard subdivisions are added for any or all topics in heading

Including state and local societies

(Option: To give local emphasis and a shorter number to hereditary, military, patriotic societies of a specific country, class them in this number; in that case, class hereditary, military, patriotic societies of United States in 369.273)

.11	General societies

        Including military and naval orders, Medal of Honor Legion, Military Order of Foreign Wars of the United States, Veterans of Foreign Wars

.12	Colonial America societies

        Including General Society of Colonial Wars, General Society of Mayflower Descendants, National Society of the Colonial Dames of America

.13	Revolutionary War societies

        Including Society of the Cincinnati, Sons of the American Revolution

.135	**Daughters of the American Revolution**
.14	Societies commemorating events of 1789–1861
.15	Union Civil War societies

        Including Grand Army of the Republic

        Class here comprehensive works on societies of Civil War

        For Confederate Civil War societies, see 369.17

.17	Confederate Civil War societies

Including United Confederate Veterans, United Daughters of the Confederacy

.18	Societies commemorating wars from 1898 to present
.181	Spanish-American War, 1898
.186	World Wars I and II and later wars
.186 1	American Legion
.186 2	American Veterans of World War II, Korea, and Vietnam (AMVETS)
.186 3	Disabled American Veterans

.2   Hereditary, military, patriotic societies

Standard subdivisions are added for any or all topics in heading

Class here nationality clubs

(Option: To give local emphasis and a shorter number to hereditary, military, patriotic societies of a specific country, use one of the following:

(Option A: Place them first by use of a letter or other symbol, e.g., hereditary, military, patriotic societies of France 369.F [preceding 369.1]

(Option B: Class them in 369.1; in that case, class hereditary, military, patriotic societies of United States in 369.273)

[.209 3–.209 9]	Specific continents, countries, localities

Do not use; class in 369.23–369.29

.21	International societies
.23–.29	Specific continents, countries, localities

Add to base number 369.2 notation 3–9 from Table 2, e.g., patriotic societies of Italy 369.245; however, for hereditary, military, patriotic societies of United States, see 369.1
    Notation 09 from Table 1 is added to indicate nationality clubs not located with the nation of interest, e.g., Order Sons of Italy in America 369.2450973

Class clubs of ethnic groups not defined by specific country or locality in 369.3

.3   Ethnic clubs

Class clubs of ethnic groups defined by specific country or locality in 369.23–369.29

.300 1–.300 9	Standard subdivisions
.305–.309	Ethnic clubs for people of mixed ancestry with ethnic origins from more than one continent, ethnic clubs for Europeans and for people of European descent

Add to base number 369.3 notation 05–09 from Table 5, e.g., ethnic clubs for people of European descent 369.309

.31–.39   Specific ethnic and national groups

Add to base number 369.3 notation 1–9 from Table 5, e.g., B'nai B'rith 369.3924

.4   **Young people's societies**

Class a specific aspect of young people's societies with the aspect, e.g., Boy Scout camps 796.5422

[.408 11]   Men

Do not use; class in 369.42

[.408 2]   Women

Do not use; class in 369.46

.42   Boys' societies

Class Boy Scouts in 369.43

.43   Scouting organizations

Class here scouting movement, Boy Scouts, Lone Scouts; comprehensive works on scouting organizations

For girls' scouting organizations, see 369.463

[.430 834]   Children six to eleven

Do not use; class in 369.434

[.430 835]   Young people twelve to twenty

Do not use; class in 369.435

.434   Children six to eleven

Class here Beavers, Cub Scouts

.435   Young people twelve to twenty

Class here Explorers, Rover Scouts, Venture Scouts; Air Scouts, Sea Scouts

For Exploring programs focused on career opportunities in specific vocations or occupational specialties, see the vocation or specialty, plus notation 023 from Table 1, e.g., science career exploring 502.3

.46   Girls' societies

.463   Girls' scouting organizations

Class here Girl Guides, Girl Scouts

Class comprehensive works on scouting organizations in 369.43

[.463 083 4]   Children six to eleven

Do not use; class in 369.4634

[.463 083 5]   Young people twelve to twenty

Do not use; class in 369.4635

.463 4	Children six to eleven
	Class here Rainbows, Brownies, Juniors
.463 5	Young people twelve to twenty
	Class here Pathfinders, Rangers, Seniors
.47	Camp Fire
.5	**Service clubs**
	Including Lions International
.52	Rotary International

370   Education

Class here basic education, public education

Unless other instructions are given, observe the following table of preference, e.g., special education at primary level 371.90472 (*not* 372):

Public policy issues in education	379
Special education	371.9
Specific levels of education	372–374
Higher education	378
Schools and their activities (*except* 371.9)	371
Education for specific objectives	370.11
Curricula	375
Standard subdivisions, educational psychology (*except* 370.11)	370.1–370.9

Class sociology of education in 306.43; class special education in a specific subject in 371.9; class primary education in a specific subject in 372.3–372.8. Class comprehensive works on education in a specific subject and on secondary, higher, and adult education in a specific subject with the subject, plus notation 071 from Table 1, e.g., education in science 507.1

SUMMARY

370.1–.9	Standard subdivisions, education for specific objectives, educational psychology
371	Schools and their activities; special education
.001–.009	Standard subdivisions
.01–.07	Specific kinds of schools
.1	Teachers and teaching, and related activities
.2	School administration; administration of student academic activities
.3	Methods of instruction and study
.4	Student guidance and counseling
.5	School discipline and related activities
.6	Physical plant; materials management
.7	Student welfare
.8	Students
.9	Special education

372	Primary education (Elementary education)
.01–.08	Standard subdivisions, primary education for specific objectives
.1	Organization and activities in primary education
.2	Specific levels of primary education
.3	Knowledge, computer science, library and information sciences, science, technology
.4	Reading
.5	The arts
.6	Language arts (Communication skills)
.7	Mathematics
.8	Other studies
.9	History, geographic treatment, biography of primary education
373	Secondary education
.01–.09	Standard subdivisions, secondary education for specific objectives
.1	Organization and activities in secondary education
.2	Secondary schools and programs of specific kinds, levels, curricula, focus
.3–.9	Secondary education in specific continents, countries, localities
374	Adult education
.001–.008	Standard subdivisions
.01	Adult education for specific objectives
.1	Organization and activities in adult education
.2	Groups, media, computers in adult education
.4	Distance education
.8	Specific kinds of institutions and agencies in adult education
.9	History, geographic treatment, biography
375	Curricula
.000 1–.000 9	Standard subdivisions
.001–.006	[Curriculum development, required and elective courses]
378	Higher education (Tertiary education)
.001–.009	Standard subdivisions
.01–.07	[Higher education for specific objectives, specific kinds of colleges and universities]
.1	Organization and activities in higher education
.2	Academic degrees and related topics
.3	Student aid and related topics
.4–.9	Higher education in specific continents, countries, localities in modern world
379	Public policy issues in education
.1	Specific elements of support and control of public education
.2	Specific policy issues in public education
.3	Public policy issues in private education
.4–.9	Public policy issues in specific continents, countries, localities in modern world

.1 **Philosophy and theory, education for specific objectives, educational psychology**

Notation 01 from Table 1 as modified below

Do not use for philosophical foundations; class in 370.12. Do not use for value; class in 370.13

.11	Education for specific objectives

Do not use for systems; class in 370.1

Class here curricula directed toward specific educational objectives

See also 371 for school systems

.111	Fundamental education

Preparation of educationally disadvantaged students for participation in community life

Class here compensatory education

Class fundamental education of adults in 374.012

.112	Humanistic education (Liberal education)
.113	Vocational education

Class here career education, occupational training, vocational schools

Class on-the-job training, vocational training provided by industry in 331.2592

For vocational education at secondary level, see 373.246; for adult vocational education, see 374.013

See also 331.702 for choice of vocation; also 371.425 for vocational guidance in schools

.114	Moral, ethical, character education

Standard subdivisions are added for any or all topics in heading

Class education for social responsibility in 370.115; class moral and character training of children at home in 649.7

.115	Education for social responsibility

Including critical pedagogy, education for democracy, popular education (education for socioeconomic transformation); social education

Class education for international understanding in 370.116

See also 306.43 for sociology of education

.116	Education for international understanding

Class here educational exchanges, foreign study

.116 2	Exchange of students

Class grants for student exchanges in 371.223

.116 3	Exchange of teachers
.117	Multicultural and bilingual education

Multicultural education: programs to promote mutual understanding among cultures

Standard subdivisions are added for multicultural and bilingual education together, for multicultural education alone

.117 5	Bilingual education
.118	Education for creativity
.119	Education for effective use of leisure

> Class here education for individual fulfillment

.12	Classification and philosophical foundations

> Including idealism, pragmatism, realism

.13	Value of education
.14	Communication
.15	Educational psychology

> Do not use for scientific principles; class in 370.1

> Class here psychology of teaching

> Class interdisciplinary works on psychology in 150. Class psychology of a specific topic in education with the topic, plus notation 019 from Table 1, e.g., psychology of special education 371.9019

> > *See also 153.15 for studies that use students as subjects for research into fundamental processes of learning*

.151	Differential psychology

> Class a specific aspect of psychology of specific groups of people in 370.152–370.158

.152	Conscious mental processes and intelligence

> Subdivisions are added for conscious mental processes and intelligence together, for conscious mental processes alone

> Including critical thinking

> Class here cognition

> > *For emotions, see 370.1534; for perception, see 370.155; for creativity and imagination, see 370.157*

.152 2	Memory
.152 3	Learning

> *For motivation to learn, see 370.154*

.152 4	Reasoning

> Class here problem solving

.152 8	Behavior modification

> Class behavior modification methods of instruction in 371.393

.152 9	Intelligence

> Class here multiple intelligences

> *For emotional intelligence, see 370.1534*

.153	Personality and emotions
	Class behavior modification in 370.1528
.153 2	Personality
.153 4	Emotions
	Class here feelings
.154	Motivation to learn
	Class comprehensive works on learning in 370.1523
.155	Perception, movement, psychological drives
	Including motor skills, sensory perception
	Class emotions in 370.1534
.157	Creativity and imagination
	Standard subdivisions are added for either or both topics in heading
	See also 370.118 for education to promote creativity
.158	Psychological adjustment to education
	Class here effect of school education and environment on students
[.19]	Psychological principles
	Do not use; class in 370.15
.2	**Miscellany**
.28	Auxiliary techniques and procedures
[.284]	Apparatus, equipment, materials
	Do not use; class in 371.67
[.287]	Testing and measurement
	Do not use; class in 371.26
[.288]	Maintenance and repair
	Do not use; class in 371.68
.6	**Organizations**
[.68]	Management
	Do not use; class in 371.2
.7	**Education, research, related topics**
	Class here education, research, related topics in teaching
	Class education, research, related topics at a specific level with the level, e.g., education for teachers at primary level 372.071
.71	Education
	Class here practice teaching

.8 **Groups of people**

Do not use for students; class in 371.8. Do not use for education of specific groups of students; class in 371.82, e.g., education of ethnic minorities 371.829

Class here discrimination in education

.82 Women in education

Do not use for education of women; class in 371.822

.9 **History, geographic treatment, biography**

Class here comparative education

371 Schools and their activities; special education

Standard subdivisions are added for schools and their activities, special education together; for schools and their activities together; for schools alone

Class here school systems, school policy; comprehensive works on schools, school activities, public policy issues in education together

For curricula, see 375; for public policy issues in education, see 379. For schools and their activities in a specific level of education, see the level, e.g., higher education 378

See Manual at 371 vs. 353.8, 371.2, 379

SUMMARY

371.001–.009		**Standard subdivisions**
.01–.07		**Specific kinds of schools**
.1		**Teachers and teaching, and related activities**
.2		**School administration; administration of student academic activities**
.3		**Methods of instruction and study**
.4		**Student guidance and counseling**
.5		**School discipline and related activities**
.6		**Physical plant; materials management**
.7		**Student welfare**
.8		**Students**
.9		**Special education**

.001 Philosophy and theory

.001 1 Systems

The word "systems" as used here refers only to concepts derived from 003, e.g., systems theory, analysis, and design applied to schools and school systems

See also 371.01–371.07 for specific kinds of school systems

.002 Miscellany

[.002 8] Auxiliary techniques and procedures

Do not use; class in 370.28

[.002 84] Apparatus, equipment, materials

Do not use; class in 371.67

[.002 87]	Testing and measurement
	Do not use; class in 371.26
[.002 88]	Maintenance and repair
	Do not use; class in 371.68
.003–.005	Standard subdivisions
.006	Organizations
[.006 8]	Management
	Do not use; class in 371.2
.007	Education, research, related topics
.008	Groups of people
	Do not use for schools for specific groups of people; class in 371.82
.009	History, geographic treatment, biography
.009 4–.009 9	Specific continents, countries, localities in modern world
	Class here specific all-age schools and school systems

> **371.01–371.07 Specific kinds of schools**

Class here specific kinds of school systems; types of education characteristic of specific kinds of schools other than public and community schools

Class comprehensive works in 371. Class a specific topic with respect to a specific kind of school with the topic in 371.1–371.8, e.g., teaching in private schools 371.102; class a specific kind of school defined by a method of instruction or study with the method, e.g., Montessori schools 371.392; class a specific kind of school for a specific group of students with the group in 371.82, e.g., schools for ethnic minorities 371.829, schools for African Americans 371.82996073

See Manual at 371.01–371.8 vs. 372–374, 378

.01   Public schools

Class public education in 370; class public community schools in 371.03; class public alternative schools in 371.04; class publicly supported religious schools in 371.07; class public policy issues concerning public schools in 379

For public schools distinguished by source of funding, locus of control, and mandate, see 371.05

.02   Private schools

Class here publicly supported private schools, schools not under government control

Class private community schools in 371.03; class private alternative schools in 371.04; class public policy issues in private education in 379.3

For religious schools, see 371.07

.03	Community schools
.04	Alternative schools

> Class here experimental schools, free schools

.042	Home schools

> Class here home schooling
>
> *See also 371.39 for home instruction by visiting teachers*

.05	Public schools distinguished by source of funding, locus of control, and mandate

> Class here academy schools, charter schools

.07	Religious schools

> Class religious education to encourage belief and to promote religious life and practice in 207

.071	Christian religious schools

> Add to base number 371.071 the numbers following 28 in 281–289, e.g., Catholic schools 371.0712, Catholic schools in Quebec 371.0712714
>
> Class Christian education to encourage belief and to promote religious life and practice in 268

.072–.079	Other religious schools

> Add to base number 371.07 the numbers following 29 in 292–299, e.g., Islamic schools 371.077

> ### 371.1–371.8 Schools and their activities

Class schools and their activities in special education in 371.9; class public policy issues relating to schools and their activities taken as a whole in 379; class comprehensive works in 371

For comprehensive works on specific kinds of schools, see 371.01–371.07

See Manual at 371.01–371.8 vs. 372–374, 378

.1   Teachers and teaching, and related activities

Standard subdivisions are added for a combination of two or more topics in heading, for teachers alone

.100 1–.100 6	Standard subdivisions
.100 7	Research and related topics
[.100 71]	Education

> Do not use; class in 370.71

.100 8–.100 9	Standard subdivisions

.102	Teaching
	Class here mentoring
	Class substitute teaching in 371.14122; class evaluation of teachers in 371.144; class team teaching in 371.148
	For practice teaching, see 370.71; for methods of instruction, see 371.3
[.102 019]	Psychology of teaching
	Do not use; class in 370.15
[.102 07]	Education, research, related topics
	Do not use; class in 370.7
.102 2	Communication in teaching
.102 3	Teacher-student relations
.102 4	Classroom management
	Class here classroom discipline
	Class classroom techniques of instruction in 371.3; class comprehensive works on school discipline in 371.5
.103	Teacher-parent conferences
	One-on-one teacher-parent relations
	Class comprehensive works on teacher-parent relations in 371.192
.104	Academic status
	Privileges, prerogatives, immunities, responsibilities
	Including academic freedom, sabbatical leave, tenure
	For teacher-community relations, see 371.19
	See also 331.2596 for economic aspects of tenure
.106	Relation of teachers to school administration and nonteaching staff
	Including teacher participation in administration
	Class labor unions in 331.88113711; class collective bargaining in 331.890413711
.12	Professional qualifications of teachers
	Class here teacher certification
.14	Organization of teaching force
	Including teacher turnover
	Class performance contracting in 371.15
.141	Staffing and nonteaching activities

.141 2	Staffing
	Including teacher workload
	For team teaching, see 371.148
.141 22	Substitute teaching
.141 23	Differentiated staffing
	Class use of teacher aides in 371.14124
.141 24	Use of teacher aides (teachers' assistants)
	Paid or volunteer
.141 4	Nonteaching activities
	For teacher participation in management, see 371.106

.144   Evaluation of teachers

Class here accountability, probation

See also 371.15 for performance contracting; also 379.158 for overall educational accountability

.148   Team teaching

Two or more people teaching a class

.15   Performance contracting

See also 371.144 for teacher accountability

.19   Community-school relations

Including teacher-community relations

Class here community involvement in schools, community-school partnerships, school involvement in the community

Class interdisciplinary works on relations of schools and society, teachers and society in 306.432

.192   Parent-school relations

Class here parent participation in schools; comprehensive works on teacher-parent relations

For teacher-parent conferences, see 371.103

.192 06   Organizations and management

Class here home and school associations, parent-teacher associations

.195   Industry-school relations

Class here industry involvement in schools, industry-school partnerships

See also 370.113 for vocational education; also 371.227 for student employment in connection with ongoing academic work

.2 **School administration; administration of student academic activities**

Standard subdivisions are added for either or both topics in heading

See Manual at 371 vs. 353.8, 371.2, 379

SUMMARY

.200 1   Philosophy and theory

.200 2   Miscellany

[.200 28]   Auxiliary techniques and procedures

Do not use; class in 370.28

[.200 284]   Apparatus, equipment, materials

Do not use; class in 371.67

[.200 288]   Maintenance and repair

Do not use; class in 371.68

.200 3–.200 5   Standard subdivisions

.200 6   Organizations

[.200 68]   Management

Do not use; class in 371.2

.200 7–.200 8   Standard subdivisions

.200 9   History, geographic treatment, biography

.200 92   Biography

Class here collected biography of school administrators and biography of specific administrators not associated with a specific level of education or school

Class biography of school administrators best known as leaders in education in 370.92; class biography of administrators best known as leaders in primary education in 372.92; class biography of administrators best known as leaders in adult education in 374.92. Class biography of administrators best known as leaders at a specific level of education other than primary and adult limited to a specific area or school with the geographic area under the specific level, plus notation 092 from Table 1, e.g., a biography of a president of University of California at Berkeley 378.79467092

>   371.201–371.207   School administration

Class comprehensive works in 371.2. Class management of a specific function with the function in 371, plus notation 068 from Table 1, e.g., management of student welfare 371.7068

For plant management, see 371.6; for materials management, see 371.67

.201   Personnel management

Class here staff

For teachers, see 371.1; for support staff, see 371.202

.201 1   School administrators

Role and function

Including school superintendents

Class here leadership, top and middle management

Class education of school administrators in 371.20071; class biography of school administrators in 371.20092

For principals, see 371.2012

.201 2   Principals

.202   Personnel management of support staff

Other than administrators and teachers

Class personnel management of staff providing a specific function with the function, plus notation 0683 from Table 1, e.g., personnel management of school nurses 371.7120683

.202 3   Management of administrative support personnel

.203   School supervision (Instructional supervision)

See also 375.001 for curriculum development

.206   Financial management

Including tuition

Class here financial administration of public schools and school systems

Class financial administration of agencies supporting public education in 353.824; class student aid in 371.22

.207   Executive management

Including internal organization

Class here planning, school improvement programs

Class government policies in 379

For leadership, school administrators, top and middle management, see 371.2011; for school boards, see 379.1531

> 371.21–371.29 **Administration of student academic activities**

Class methods of instruction in 371.3; class student participation in administration in 371.59; class comprehensive works in 371.2

For educational and vocational guidance, see 371.42

.21 Admissions and related topics

Standard subdivisions are added for admissions and related topics, for admissions alone

Class here articulation, matriculation

.216 Admission procedures

.217 Entrance requirements

Class entrance examinations in 371.262; class academic prognosis and placement in 371.264

.218 Credits

Class use of credits in placement in 371.264; class use of credits to determine promotion and failure in 371.28

.219 School enrollment

.219 09 History and biography

Do not use for geographic treatment; class in 371.2191–371.2199

.219 1–.219 9 Geographic treatment of school enrollment

Add to base number 371.219 notation 1–9 from Table 2, e.g., school enrollment in Russia 371.21947

.22 Student aid and cooperative education

Standard subdivisions are added for student aid and cooperative education together, for student aid alone

See also 371.206 for tuition

.223 Scholarships and fellowships

Standard subdivisions are added for either or both topics in heading

Including veterans' education benefits

Class here grants

.224 Student loans

.225 Student employment

Including employment for service to the community

Class here employment of students by their own school, work-study programs

For employment by industry and nonschool agencies in connection with ongoing academic work, see 371.227

.227   Cooperative education

         Student employment by industry and nonschool agencies in connection with ongoing academic work

         Class here apprenticeship programs, work-study plan

         Class apprenticeship programs without school sponsorship, interdisciplinary works on apprenticeship in 331.25922

.23   School year

         Class here school calendar

.232   Summer school

.236   Year-round school

         Class here extended school year

.24   Schedules and school day

         See also 371.294 for school attendance

.242   Schedules

         Including flexible scheduling

         Class here scheduling, school week

.244   School day

         Class here length of school day

         Class scheduling within school day in 371.242

.25   Grouping students for instruction

         Including multigraded classes (mixed-level classrooms, combination of grades)

         Class here school classes

         Class one-room schools in 372.125

.251   Class size

.252   Mixed ability grouping (Heterogeneous grouping)

         Class here mainstreaming outside context of special education

         Class comprehensive works on mainstreaming in 371.9046

.254   Ability grouping (Homogeneous grouping)

         Class here streaming

         Class mainstreaming for ordinary students in 371.252; class nongraded grouping in 371.255

.255   Nongraded grouping

.256   Open classroom grouping

Class here open plan schools

Class open classroom methods of instruction in 371.3941

.26   Examinations and tests; academic prognosis and placement

Standard subdivisions are added for examinations and tests, academic prognosis and placement together; for examinations alone; for tests alone

Including test-taking skills

Class use of examinations and tests in guidance in 371.42

For classroom and school examinations and tests, see 371.271

.260 1   Philosophy and theory, validity and reliability of tests

Notation 01 from Table 1 as modified below

.260 13   Validity and reliability of tests

Including test bias

Class here comprehensive works on validity and reliability of standardized tests

For validity and reliability of specific kinds of standardized tests, see 371.262

.261   Test construction

Class evaluation of tests in 371.26013

.262   Standardized tests

Class here organizations producing standardized tests, comprehensive works on specific kinds of educational tests and their validity and reliability

Class comprehensive works on validity and reliability of standardized tests in 371.26013; class interdisciplinary works on intelligence tests in 153.93; class interdisciplinary works on aptitude tests in 153.94. Class standardized tests for a specific subject in primary school with the subject in 372.3–372.8, plus notation 076 from Table 1, e.g., mathematics tests for primary school 372.7076; class standardized tests for a specific subject at secondary or higher level with the subject in 001–999, plus notation 076 from Table 1, e.g., mathematics tests for secondary school 510.76

For construction of standardized tests, see 371.261; for specific kinds of educational tests devised by individual teachers, see 371.271

See Manual at 371.262 vs. 371.264

.264   Academic prognosis and placement

Including accreditation of prior learning (APL), advanced placement

Class standardized tests, use of specific tests of academic achievement and general education, comprehensive works on specific kinds of educational tests in 371.262

See Manual at 371.262 vs. 371.264

.27   Classroom and school examinations and tests; marking systems

.271   Classroom and school examinations and tests

> Tests devised by individual teacher or school

> Standard subdivisions are added for any or all topics in heading

.272   Marking systems

> Methods used for recording and reporting students achievement

.28   Promotion and failure

> Including educational acceleration, underachievement

.283   Promotion

.285   Failure

> Including grade repetition

.29   Student mobility and school attendance

.291   Student mobility

.291 2   School completion

> Class here graduation; diplomas, other certificates of completion

.291 3   Dropouts (Early school leavers)

> Class student failure in 371.285

.291 4   Transfers

.294   School attendance

> Class compulsory education in 379.23

> *For truancy, school attendance officers, see 371.295*

.295   Truancy

> Class here school attendance officers, truant officers

> Class dropouts in 371.2913

.3   **Methods of instruction and study**

> Class here classroom techniques, creative activities, seatwork

> Class classroom management in 371.1024; class comprehensive works on teaching in 371.102. Class methods of instruction in a specific subject at primary level with the subject in 372.3–372.8, plus notation 044 from table under 372.3–372.8, e.g., methods of teaching mathematics in primary school 372.7044; class methods of instruction in a specific subject at secondary and higher levels with the subject in 001–999, plus notation 071 from Table 1, e.g., methods of teaching mathematics in secondary school 510.712

SUMMARY

371.302 8	**Auxiliary techniques and procedures, techniques of study, lesson plans**
.32	**Use of textbooks**
.33	**Teaching aids, equipment, materials**
.35	**Distance education**
.36	**Project methods (Cooperative learning)**
.37	**Recitation and discussion**
.38	**Methods employed outside classroom**
.39	**Other methods of instruction**

.302 8   Auxiliary techniques and procedures, techniques of study, lesson plans

Notation 028 from Table 1 as modified below

.302 81   Techniques of study

Including book reports, homework, note-taking, reading for content, report writing

Class here techniques for parents, study skills

[.302 84]   Apparatus, equipment, materials

Do not use; class in 371.33

[.302 85]   Computer applications

Do not use; class in 371.334

[.307 8]   Use of apparatus, equipment, materials in study and teaching

Do not use; class in 371.33

.32   Use of textbooks

Including textbook bias

Class public control of textbooks in 379.156. Class textbooks on a specific subject with the subject in 001–999, e.g., textbooks on mathematics 510

.33   Teaching aids, equipment, materials

Class here educational media, educational technology; use of teaching aids, equipment, materials in study and teaching

Class public control of teaching materials in 379.156. Class teaching aids, equipment, materials used in a specific method of instruction with the method, e.g., materials used in Montessori method 371.392

For textbooks, see 371.32

See also 027.7 for instructional materials centers

.333   Audio materials and equipment

Standard subdivisions are added for either or both topics in heading

See also 371.335 for audiovisual materials

.333 1   Radio

.333 2	Sound recordings and their players
	Standard subdivisions are added for either or both topics in heading
.334	Computer science
	Class here data processing, computer-assisted instruction (CAI), electronic programmed instruction
	Unless it is redundant, add to base number 371.334 the numbers following 00 in 004–006, e.g., instructional use of software 371.33453, use of computer graphics in teaching 371.33466
	For computer modeling and simulation, see 371.397
.335	Audiovisual and visual materials and equipment
	Standard subdivisions are added for audiovisual and visual materials or equipment together, for audiovisual materials or equipment alone
	Class audio materials and equipment in 371.333
	See also 371.32 for textbooks
.335 2	Slides and filmstrips, motion pictures and video, pictures
.335 22	Slides and filmstrips
	Standard subdivisions are added for either or both topics in heading
.335 23	Motion pictures and video recordings
	Standard subdivisions are added for either or both topics in heading
.335 6	Bulletin boards
.335 8	Television
	Including videoconferencing
	Class here interactive television
	Class video recordings in 371.33523
.337	Educational games and toys
	Standard subdivisions are added for either or both topics in heading
	See also 371.397 for simulation
.35	Distance education
	Class here extension services, open and distance learning (ODL)
.356	Correspondence courses

.358 Electronic distance education

Including teleconferencing

Class here instructional use of mass media

For distance education by radio, see 371.3331; for distance education by computer, see 371.334; for distance education by television, see 371.3358

.36 Project methods (Cooperative learning)

Methods that emphasize student direction of group projects

Class here group work, unit method

Class group teaching (in which class is divided into groups, but activity is still directed by teacher) in 371.395

.37 Recitation and discussion

Including seminars

.38 Methods employed outside classroom

See also 371.39 for home instruction by visiting teachers

.382 Laboratory method

Class laboratory method with electronic and visual materials and equipment in 371.33

.384 Outdoor education

Class here field trips to indoor locations, open air schools

.39 Other methods of instruction

Including home instruction by educational personnel, monitorial system of education, Morrison plan, rote learning

See also 371.042 for home schooling

.391 Waldorf method

.392 Montessori method

Montessori method is usually limited to primary level in 372.1392. Discussion of advancing it to higher grades is classed with higher level

.393 Behavior modification methods

Including student performance contracting

Class use of behavior modification in classroom discipline in 371.1024

.394 Individualized instruction

Class here tutoring

.394 1 Open classroom instruction

Class grouping students for open classroom instruction in 371.256

.394 2	Honors work

Class here honors programs, honors courses

See also 371.264 for advanced placement

.394 3	Independent study

Class independent honors work in 371.3942

For programmed instruction, see 371.3944

.394 4	Programmed instruction

For electronic programmed instruction, see 371.334

.395	Group teaching

Teaching in which class is divided into groups, but activity is still directed by teacher

Class group work that emphasizes student direction of group projects in 371.36

See also 371.148 for team teaching

.396	Lecture method
.397	Simulation

Class here computer modeling and simulation

Class comprehensive works on instructional use of computers in 371.334

.399	Use of drama

Class here use of theater

.4	**Student guidance and counseling**

Standard subdivisions are added for either or both topics in heading

Class here student personnel services, services of deans of students

For a specific student personnel service not provided for here, see the service, e.g., student employment 371.225

.404	Teachers and students in guidance and counseling
.404 6	Role of teachers in guidance and counseling
.404 7	Peer counseling

Counseling by other students

.42	Educational and vocational guidance
.422	Educational guidance

Other than vocational

.425	Vocational guidance

Class interdisciplinary works on vocational guidance in 331.702. Class vocational guidance in a specific occupation with the occupation, plus notation 023 from Table 1, e.g., guidance in science 502.3

.46 Personal counseling

Counseling of students with emotional, personal, social problems by staff other than psychologists and medical personnel

Including school social workers

Class personal counseling by other students in 371.4047; class student welfare programs in 371.7

.5 School discipline and related activities

Standard subdivisions are added for school discipline and related activities together, for school discipline alone

For classroom discipline, see 371.1024

.51 General regulations for student conduct

Including honor system

.53 Rewards

Class rewards to discourage specific disciplinary problems in 371.58

.54 Punishment

Class punishment for specific discipline problems in 371.58

.542 Corporal punishment

.543 Probation, suspension, expulsion

.58 Specific discipline problems

Class comprehensive works on crime, delinquency, sexual abuse, substance abuse, vandalism, violence in schools in 371.78

For truancy, see 371.295

.59 Student participation in administration

Including monitors, student participation in maintenance of discipline

Class here student government

See also 371.39 for monitorial system of education

.6 Physical plant; materials management

Standard subdivisions are added for physical plant and materials management together; for physical plant alone

Class here plant management, educational buildings, school facilities

See also 727 for architecture of educational buildings

[.602 84] Apparatus, equipment, materials

Do not use; class in 371.67

[.602 88] Maintenance and repair

Do not use; class in 371.68

.61 School grounds, sites, location

.62   Specific kinds of buildings and rooms

> Class here furnishings, apparatus, equipment, supplies for specific kinds of buildings and rooms
>
> Class teaching aids, equipment, materials regardless of kind of building or room in 371.33

.621   Instructional spaces

> Including study facilities
>
> Class here classrooms
>
> *For laboratories, see 371.623*

.623   Laboratories

.625   Noninstructional facilities

> Class facilities for a specific noninstructional objective with the objective, e.g., cafeterias 371.716

.63   School furnishings

> Class furnishings for specific kinds of buildings and rooms in 371.62

.67   Apparatus, equipment, materials

> Class here materials management
>
> Class apparatus, equipment, supplies for specific kinds of buildings and rooms in 371.62
>
> *For teaching aids, equipment, materials, see 371.33; for school furnishings, see 371.63*

.68   Custodial and maintenance services, renovation

> Standard subdivisions are added for a combination of two or more topics in heading, for custodial services alone, for maintenance services alone
>
> Including repair services
>
> *For technical maintenance and repair of a specific facility or piece of equipment, see the facility or piece of equipment, plus notation 0288 from Table 1, e.g., repair of educational computers 371.3340288; for custodial and maintenance services, renovation of a specific noninstructional facility, see the facility, plus notation 0682 from Table 1, e.g., maintenance services for school cafeterias 371.7160682*

.7   **Student welfare**

> Class here school social services
>
> *For a specific provision for student welfare not provided for here, see the provision, e.g., personal counseling 371.46, student housing 371.871*

.71   Student health and related topics

> Standard subdivisions are added for student health and related topics together, for student health alone

.712 School nursing programs

>Class use of school nurses in mental welfare programs in 371.713; class use of school nurses in birth control, pregnancy, sex hygiene programs in 371.714

.713 Mental health services

>Class here school psychologists

>*For substance abuse programs, see 371.784*

.714 Sex hygiene, birth control, pregnancy programs

>Standard subdivisions are added for sex hygiene, birth control, pregnancy programs together; for sex hygiene programs alone

.716 Food services

>Including milk programs, nutrition programs

>Class here school cafeterias, school lunch programs

.78 School programs related to crime, substance abuse, sexual abuse

>Class here crime, substance abuse, sexual abuse problems in schools; assistance to victims of crime and abuse

>Class crime, substance abuse, sexual abuse as school discipline problems in 371.58

.782 Crime prevention and alleviation

>Standard subdivisions are added for either or both topics in heading

>Class here delinquency in schools, school violence

>Class campus police in 363.289; class prevention and alleviation of crime relating to substance abuse in 371.784; class prevention and alleviation of crime related to sexual abuse in 371.786; class interdisciplinary works on victims of crime in 362.88; class interdisciplinary works on crime prevention in 364.4

.784 Substance abuse programs

.786 Sexual abuse programs

.8 **Students**

>Including class reunions

>Class here extracurricular activities, student life

>*For a specific aspect of students not provided for here, see the aspect, e.g., student discipline 371.5*

.801 9 Student psychology

>Class educational psychology in 370.15

.805 Serial publications

>Limited to serials about students, student life, extracurricular activities

>*See also 371.897 for student journalism*

.806   Organizations and management

Do not use for student organizations; class in 371.83

[.808]   Groups of people

Do not use; class in 371.82

.81   Student movements

Student efforts to achieve reform on campus and social change

Including student strikes

Class here student activism, protest, unrest

Class a student movement to achieve a specific objective with the objective, e.g., a movement to achieve electoral reform 324.63

.82   Specific groups of students; schools for specific groups of students

Class here discrimination, group identity, minorities; education of young people; comprehensive works on education of specific groups of students

For a specific aspect of education of specific groups of students, see the aspect, e.g., counseling for women students 371.4082

[.820 1–.820 9]   Standard subdivisions

Do not use; class in 371.801–371.809

>   371.821–371.828 Groups of students by specific attributes

Unless other instructions are given, class a student with aspects in two or more subdivisions of 371.821–371.828 in the number coming last, e.g., poor women 371.826942082 (*not* 371.822086942)

Class comprehensive works on groups of students by specific attributes in 371.82; class comprehensive works on ethnic and national groups in 371.829. Class students of an ethnic or national group with a specific attribute, other than students with status defined by change in residence, with the attribute in 371.821–371.828, e.g., Chinese women 371.822089951

.821   Students by gender or sex

Class here gender identity, gender role, sex role

Subdivisions are added for either or both topics in heading

For women, see 371.822; for transgender and intersex people, see 371.8267

.821 1   Men

Class here males, boys

.822   Women

Class here females, girls

.824   Adults

Add to base number 371.824 the numbers following —084 in notation 0842–0846 from Table 1, e.g., education of middle-aged adults 371.8244

.825–.826	Relatives and students by miscellaneous social attributes

Add to base number 371.82 the numbers following —08 in notation 085–086 from Table 1, e.g., education of immigrants 371.826912

.828	Occupational and religious groups

Add to base number 371.828 notation 001–999, e.g., student farmers 371.82863

.829	Ethnic and national groups

Class here ethnic and national minorities; racial groups, racism

Class students of an ethnic or national group with a specific attribute, other than students with status defined by change in residence, with the attribute in 371.821–371.828, e.g., education of Chinese women 371.822089951

.829 001–.829 009	Forecasting, statistics, illustrations, dictionaries, encyclopedias, concordances, serials, museology, history and geographic treatment

Add to base number 371.82900 the numbers following 0 in notation 01–09 from table under —08, e.g., statistics related to students of ethnic and national groups 371.8290021

.829 05–.829 09	Specific ethnic and national groups with ethnic origins from more than one continent, of European descent

Add to base number 371.8290 the numbers following —0 in notation 05–09 from Table 5, e.g., education of ethnic groups of European descent 371.82909, education of ethnic groups of European descent in Namibia 371.8290906881

.829 1–.829 9	Specific ethnic and national groups

Add to base number 371.829 notation 1–9 from Table 5, e.g., education of groups of Italian descent 371.82951, education of groups of Italian descent in United States 371.82951073

.83	Student organizations

Class here student clubs

Class student movements in 371.81. Class a student organization in a specific field with the field, plus notation 06 from Table 1, e.g., student literary societies 806

For Greek-letter societies, see 371.85

.85	Greek-letter societies

Class here alumni units

Class a Greek-letter society in a specific field with the field, plus notation 06 from Table 1, e.g., a Greek-letter medical society 610.6

.852	Honor societies
.855	Men's Greek-letter social societies

Class here fraternities

.856	Women's Greek-letter social societies

Class here sororities

.87	Housing and transportation of students
.871	Housing
.872	Transportation

Class busing for school integration in 379.263

See also 363.1259 for school bus safety

.89	Miscellaneous student activities

Only those named here or below

Including competitions

For a specific student competition, see the competition, plus notation 079 from Table 1, e.g., a photographic competition 770.79

.895	School assemblies
.897	Student journalism

Class interdisciplinary student journals in 050. Class a student journal on a specific subject with the subject, plus notation 05 from Table 1, e.g., a journal on student life and extracurricular activities 371.805, a student literary journal 805

.897 4	Producing newspapers
.897 5	Producing magazines
.897 6	Producing yearbooks

Class a yearbook of a specific school with the school, e.g., a yearbook of a preparatory school in New York city 373.7471

.9   **Special education**

Class here exceptional students, learning disabilities, underachievers in special education; schools and school activities pertaining to special education

Except for modifications shown under specific entries, add to each subdivision identified by * as follows:

[0284]	Apparatus, equipment, materials	
	Do not use; class in notation 5 from this table	
[0288]	Maintenance and repair	
	Do not use; class in notation 5 from this table	
[0682]	Plant management	
	Do not use; class in notation 5 from this table	
3–7	General topics	

Add to base number the numbers following 371.904 in 371.9043–371.9047, e.g., equipment 5, equipment for students with reading disorders 371.91445

Unless other instructions are given, observe the following table of preference, e.g., emotionally disturbed gifted students 371.95 (*not* 371.94):

Gifted students	371.95
Students with mental disabilities	371.92
Students with emotional disturbances	371.94
Students with physical disabilities	371.91
Delinquent and problem students	371.93

Class comprehensive works on underachievers in 371.28

SUMMARY

371.901–.909	**Standard subdivisions and general topics of special education**
.91	**Students with physical disabilities**
.92	**Students with mental disabilities**
.93	**Delinquent and problem students**
.94	**Students with emotional disturbances**
.95	**Gifted students**

[.902 84]   Apparatus, equipment, materials

Do not use; class in 371.9045

[.902 88]   Maintenance and repair

Do not use; class in 371.9045

.904   General topics of special education

.904 3   Teaching methods

Including academic prognosis and placement

.904 302 8   Auxiliary techniques and procedures, techniques of study, lesson plans

Notation 028 from Table 1 as modified below

.904 302 81	Techniques of study
	Including book reports, homework, note-taking, reading for content, report writing
	Class here techniques for parents, study skills
[.904 302 84]	Apparatus, equipment, materials
	Do not use; class in 371.90433
[.904 302 85]	Computer applications
	Do not use; class in 371.904334
[.904 307 8]	Use of apparatus, equipment, materials in study and teaching
	Do not use; class in 371.90433
.904 32–.904 39	Specific teaching methods
	Add to base number 371.9043 the numbers following 371.3 in 371.32–371.39, e.g., project methods 371.90436
.904 4	Programs in specific subjects
	Class here curricula
	Add to base number 371.9044 the numbers following 372 in 372.3–372.8, e.g., mathematics 371.90447
.904 5	Buildings, rooms, furnishings, apparatus, equipment, supplies
	Including maintenance and repair
	Class here plant management
.904 6	Mainstreaming
	Educating exceptional students in regular school programs
	Including identifying students for special education
	Class here inclusive education
	See also 371.252 for mainstreaming outside the context of special education
.904 7	Special education by level
	Class a specific topic in special education at a specific level with the topic, e.g., teaching at primary level 371.9043
.904 72	Special education at primary level
.904 73	Special education at secondary level
.904 74	Special education at higher level
.904 75	Adult special education
	Other than in colleges and universities
[.906 82]	Plant management
	Do not use; class in 371.9045

.908 Groups of people

Do not use for groups of students requiring special education; class in 371.9

.91 Students with physical disabilities

Including general works on students with brain damage

Unless other instructions are given, observe the following table of preference, e.g., students with blindness and mobility impairments 371.916 (*not* 371.911):

Students with linguistic disorders	371.914
Students with mobility impairments	371.916
Students with blindness and visual impairments	371.911
Students with hearing impairments	371.912

Class students with a specific disorder caused by brain damage with the disorder in 371.911–371.94, e.g., emotional disorders caused by brain damage 371.94

.911 *Students with blindness and visual impairments

Subdivisions are added for either or both topics in heading

.912 Students with hearing impairments

Class here deaf students

[.912 028 4] Apparatus, equipment, materials

Do not use; class in 371.9125

[.912 028 8] Maintenance and repair

Do not use; class in 371.9125

[.912 068 2] Plant management

Do not use; class in 371.9125

.912 3–.912 6 Teaching methods, specific subjects, facilities, mainstreaming

Add to base number 371.912 the numbers following 371.904 in 371.9043–371.9046, e.g., instruction in lipreading 371.91246, teaching methods 371.9123

.912 8 Education by level

Add to base number 371.9128 the numbers following 371.9047 in 371.90472–371.90475, e.g., university education for deaf people 371.91284

.914 Students with linguistic disorders

.914 2 *Students with speaking disorders

Including aphasia, stuttering

*Add as instructed under 371.9

.914 4	*Students with reading disorders
	Class here dyslexia
	See also 372.43 for remedial reading in primary education
.916	*Students with mobility impairments
.92	Students with mental disabilities
	Class here students with developmental disabilities
	Class students with mental illness in 371.94
.926	*Students with moderate mental disabilities
.928	Students with severe mental disabilities
.928 001	Philosophy and theory
.928 002	Miscellany
[.928 002 84]	Apparatus, equipment, materials
	Do not use; class in 371.92805
[.928 002 88]	Maintenance and repair
	Do not use; class in 371.92805
.928 003–.928 005	Standard subdivisions
.928 006	Organizations and management
[.928 006 82]	Plant management
	Do not use; class in 371.92805
.928 007–.928 009	Standard subdivisions
.928 03–.928 07	General topics of students with mental retardation
	Add to base number 371.9280 the numbers following 371.904 in 371.9043–371.9047, e.g., teaching methods 371.92803
.93	*Delinquent and problem students
	Not suffering emotional disturbances
	Including maladjusted students
	Subdivisions are added for either or both topics in heading
	Class delinquent and problem students suffering emotional disturbances in 371.94

*Add as instructed under 371.9

.94   *Students with emotional disturbances

> Including attention-deficit-disordered students, autistic students, hyperactive students

> Class here students with mental illness

> *For delinquent and problem students not suffering severe emotional disturbances, see 371.93*

.95   Gifted students

[.950 284]   Apparatus, equipment, materials

> Do not use; class in 371.955

[.950 288]   Maintenance and repair

> Do not use; class in 371.955

[.950 682]   Plant management

> Do not use; class in 371.955

.952   Mainstreaming

> Educating gifted students in regular school programs

> Including identification

.953   Programs in specific subjects

> Class here curricula

> Add to base number 371.953 the numbers following 372 in 372.3–372.8, e.g., programs in mathematics 371.9537

.955   Buildings, rooms, furnishings, apparatus, equipment, supplies

> Including maintenance and repair

> Class here plant management

.956   Teaching methods

> Including motivating gifted underachievers

.956 028   Auxiliary techniques and procedures, techniques of study, lesson plans

> Notation 028 from Table 1 as modified below

.956 028 1   Techniques of study

> Including book reports, homework, note-taking, reading for content, report writing

> Class here techniques for parents, study skills

[.956 028 4]   Apparatus, equipment, materials

> Do not use; class in 371.9563

*Add as instructed under 371.9

[.956 028 5]		Computer applications
		Do not use; class in 371.95634
[.956 078]		Use of apparatus, equipment, materials in study and teaching
		Do not use; class in 371.9563
.956 2–.956 9		Specific teaching methods

                                Add to base number 371.956 the numbers following 371.3 in 371.32–371.39, e.g., use of computers 371.95634

.957   Education by level

                                Add to base number 371.957 the numbers following 371.9047 in 371.90472–371.90475, e.g., educating gifted students at primary level 371.9572

> ## 372–374 Specific levels of education

Unless other instructions are given, class works treating two sublevels of education that are not subdivisions of the same number with the higher level, e.g., kindergarten and first grade 372.241 (*not* 372.218)

Class special education at any level in 371.9; class public policy issues relating to a specific level of education taken as a whole in 379; class comprehensive works on education and works dealing comprehensively with primary and secondary education, with secondary and higher education in 370; class comprehensive works on schools in 371

For higher education, see 378

See Manual at 371.01–371.8 vs. 372–374, 378

372   Primary education (Elementary education)

Class here elementary schools, primary schools; lower sections of all-age schools

For adult primary education, see 374.012

SUMMARY

372.01–.08	**Standard subdivisions, primary education for specific objectives**
.1	**Organization and activities in primary education**
.2	**Specific levels of primary education**
.3	**Knowledge, computer science, library and information sciences, science, technology**
.4	**Reading**
.5	**The arts**
.6	**Language arts (Communication skills)**
.7	**Mathematics**
.8	**Other studies**
.9	**History, geographic treatment, biography of primary education**

.01   Philosophy and theory; primary education for specific objectives

                Notation 01 from Table 1 as modified below

.011   Primary education for specific objectives

                 Do not use for systems; class in 372.01

                 Class here curricula directed toward specific educational objectives

                 Add to base number 372.011 the numbers following 370.11 in 370.111–370.119, e.g., character education 372.0114

                 Class a specific topic with respect to primary education for a specific objective with the topic in 372.11–372.18, e.g., administration of primary schools 372.12

                     See also 372.1042 for specific kinds of primary school systems

[.028 4]   Apparatus, equipment, materials

                 Do not use; class in 372.167

[.028 7]   Testing and measurement

                 Do not use; class in 372.126

[.028 8]   Maintenance and repair

                 Do not use; class in 372.168

[.068]   Management

                 Do not use; class in 372.12

.08   Groups of people

                 Do not use for students; class in 372.18. Do not use for education of specific groups of students; class in 372.182, e.g., education of ethnic minorities 372.1829

[.09]   History, geographic treatment, biography

                 Do not use; class in 372.9

.1   **Organization and activities in primary education**

                 For comprehensive works on primary education for specific objectives, see 372.011; for comprehensive works on specific levels of primary education, see 372.2

[.101–.103]   Standard subdivisions

                 Do not use; class in 372.01–372.03

.104   Special topics of primary schools

.104 2   Specific kinds of primary schools

> Class here specific kinds of school systems, kinds of primary education (other than public primary education) defined by specific kinds of schools

> Add to base number 372.1042 the numbers following 371.0 in 371.01–371.07, e.g., primary church schools 372.104271, Catholic primary schools 372.1042712

> Class a specific kind of primary schools at a specific level in 372.2; class specific schools regardless of kind in 372.9. Class a specific topic with respect to a specific kind of primary school with the topic in 372.11–372.19, e.g., administration of primary private schools 372.12

[.105–.108]   Standard subdivisions

> Do not use; class in 372.05–372.08

[.109]   History, geographic treatment, biography

> Do not use; class in 372.9

.11–.18   School organization and activities in primary education

> Add to base number 372.1 the numbers following 371 in 371.1–371.8, e.g., administration 372.12; however, for use of drama as a method of instruction, see 372.66

.19   Primary education in subject areas

> Class here curricula

> Class curricula directed toward a specific primary education objective in 372.011

> *For primary education in a specific subject, see 372.3–372.8*

.2   **Specific levels of primary education**

> Class specific schools at a specific level in 372.9. Class a specific topic with respect to primary education at a specific level with the topic in 372.11–372.19, e.g., administration of kindergarten 372.12

[.201–.208]   Standard subdivisions

> Do not use; class in 372.01–372.08

[.209]   History, geographic treatment, biography

> Do not use; class in 372.9

.21   Preschool education

> School-based or center-based pre-primary education

> Class here early childhood education

> Class preschool education by parents in the home as part of child-rearing in 649.68

.218   Kindergarten

.24	Specific levels of primary education

Class primary education covering grades 1–4 in 372

See Manual at 372.24 and 373.23

[.240 1–.240 8]	Standard subdivisions

Do not use; class in 372.01–372.08

[.240 9]	History, geographic treatment, biography

Do not use; class in 372.9

.241	Lower level

Class here grades 1–3

.242	Intermediate level

Class here grades 4–6

Class lower secondary schools, middle schools (grades 5–8), junior high schools (grades 7–9) in 373.236

(Option: Class lower secondary level, grades 7–10 of compulsory primary education in 372.243)

(.243)	Upper level

(Optional number; prefer 373.236)

Class here lower secondary level, grades 7–10 of compulsory primary education

---

> **372.3–372.8 Primary education in specific subjects**

Add to each subdivision identified by * as follows:
```
04        General topics
042         Place of subject in education
043         Curricula
044         Teaching
              Class here methods of instruction, teaching materials
              Class textbooks with the subject in 001–999, e.g., primary
              textbooks on arithmetic 513
(045)       Textbooks
              (Optional number; prefer the subject in 001–999, e.g.,
              primary textbooks on arithmetic 513)
              Including readers (if option at 372.4122 is used)
049         Instruction at specific levels
              Including kindergarten
              Class a specific aspect of instruction at a given level with the
              aspect, e.g., curricula for kindergarten 043
```

Class comprehensive works in 372.19

.3   **Knowledge, computer science, library and information sciences, science, technology**

Including discussion of ideas from many fields, interdisciplinary approach to knowledge

Class interdisciplinary approach to knowledge with a focus on a specific subject with the subject in 372.3–372.8, e.g., environmental studies with components of civics and geography 372.357, writing across the curriculum 372.623

.34   *Computer science; library and information sciences

Class here digital literacy, information literacy

Subdivisions are added for any or all topics in heading

Class use of computers as a method of instruction in 372.1334. Class use of computers as a method of instruction in a specific subject with the subject in 372.3–372.8, plus notation 044 from table under 372.3–372.8, e.g., computer-assisted instruction in arithmetic 372.72044

.35   *Science and technology

Subdivisions are added for science and technology together, for science alone

For mathematics, see 372.7

.357   *Nature study

Class here environmental studies

.358   *Technology (Applied sciences)

Including robots

Class here industrial arts

> *For personal health and safety, home and family management, see 372.37; for physical education, see 372.86*

> *See also 372.5 for manual arts*

.37   *Personal health and safety; social skills

Including comprehensive works on home and family management

Class here life skills

Subdivisions are added for personal health and safety, social skills together; for personal health and safety together; for personal health alone

Class food in 372.373; class social skills in 372.374

> *For sewing, see 372.54; for physical education, see 372.86*

.372   *Sex education

Including human reproductive physiology

*Add as instructed under 372.3–372.8

.373	*Nutrition and food

Including cooking

Subdivisions are added for either or both topics in heading

.374	*Social skills

Class here family life, interpersonal relations

.378	*Substance abuse

.4 **Reading**

Class here reading instruction in home schools

Unless other instructions are given, class a subject with aspects in two or more subdivisions of 372.4 in the number coming last, e.g., vocabulary building by phonetic methods 372.465 (*not* 372.44)

.402 84	Apparatus and equipment

Do not use for materials; class in 372.412

[.402 87]	Testing and measurement

Do not use; class in 372.48

.41	Instructional materials, reading readiness, methods of instruction and study
.412	Instructional materials
(.412 2)	Readers

(Optional number; prefer specific language in 420–490, plus notation 86 from Table 4, e.g., English-language readers 428.6

(If option under this number is chosen, class readers on a specific subject with the subject in 372.3–372.8, plus notation 045 from table under 372.3–372.8, e.g., science readers 372.35045)

.414	Reading readiness
.416	Methods of instruction and study

For a method of instruction or study not provided for here, see the method elsewhere in 372.4, e.g., individualized reading instruction 372.417, word-attack strategies 372.46

.416 2	Small-group reading instruction
.416 4	Whole-class reading instruction
.417	Individualized reading instruction (Personalized reading instruction)

See also 372.454 for independent reading

.42	Reading motivation
.423	Use of national and commercial programs

*Add as instructed under 372.3–372.8

.425	Community-school programs
	Class here parent participation in reading
.427	School-based programs
	Classroom and library programs
.43	Remedial reading
	Including reading failure
	Class reading difficulties treated in special education in 371.9144
.44	Vocabulary development
.45	Reading-skill strategies
	For word-attack strategies, see 372.46; for reading comprehension strategies, see 372.47
.452	Oral reading
.454	Independent reading
.46	Word-attack strategies (Decoding strategies)
.462	Whole-word method (Sight method)
	Class here word-recognition method
.465	Part-word method (Phonetic method)
	Including teaching alphabets
	Class here phonetics in elementary education
	Class pronunciation in a specific communication skill with the skill, e.g., pronunciation in speech 372.622
.47	Reading comprehension strategies
.472	Strategies using standardized materials
	Including cloze procedure
	Class a strategy using standardized materials in a specific subject with the subject in 372.3–372.8, plus notation 044 from table under 372.3–372.8, e.g., cloze procedure in science instruction 372.35044
.474	Cognitive strategies
	Including critical thinking
.475	Whole-language approach
	Class here language experience approach
.476	Reading in content areas
.48	Evaluation of reading skills
	Class here testing and measurement
	Class evaluation of reading readiness in 372.414
.482	Standardized testing

.484	Classroom and school testing

Standard subdivisions are added for either or both topics in heading

.486	Diagnostic testing
.5	***The arts***

For literature, see 372.64; for drama, see 372.66; for dance, see 372.868; for music, see 372.87

.52	*Drawing, painting, design
.53	*Modeling and sculpture

Subdivisions are added for either or both topics in heading

.54	*Sewing

Including weaving

Class here needlework

.55	*Handicrafts

Including paper work

For needlework, see 372.54

.6	***Language arts (Communication skills)***

Including fingerspelling, lipreading, sign languages

Class here literacy education

For reading, see 372.4

(Option: Class here language arts (communication skills) in a language other than English; in that case, class language arts (communication skills) in English in 372.6521)

.61	Grammar

Including language usage, word study

.62	Written and spoken expression

Class here language experience approach, whole-language approach

For whole-language approach in reading, see 372.475. For a specific aspect of language experience in language arts, see the aspect, e.g., listening 372.69

.622	Speech

Including pronunciation

Class oral presentations other than public speaking in 372.66

See also 372.465 for phonetic methods of reading instruction; also 372.66 for drama

---

*Add as instructed under 372.3–372.8

.623	*Composition

Class here comprehensive works on written expression

For spelling and handwriting, see 372.63

.63	Spelling and handwriting
.632	*Spelling (Orthography)

Class fingerspelling in 372.6

.634	*Handwriting (Penmanship)
.64	*Literature appreciation

Class plays taught as theater in 372.66

.65	*Foreign, official, second languages; bilingual instruction

Languages other than the language given preference in 372.6

Subdivisions are added for all topics in heading together, for foreign languages alone, for official languages alone, for second languages alone

.651	*Bilingual instruction

Class comprehensive works on bilingual education in 370.1175

.652–.659	Specific foreign, official, second languages

Subdivisions are added for any or all topics in heading

Add to base number 372.65 notation 2–9 from Table 6, e.g., Spanish 372.6561, English as a second language 372.6521; then add further as follows:

04	General topics
041	Language arts in foreign, official, second languages
	Add to 041 the numbers following 372.6 in 372.61–372.64, e.g., Spanish composition 372.656104123
042	Place of subject in education
043	Curricula
044	Teaching
	Class here methods of instruction, teaching materials
	Class textbooks with the subject in 001–999, e.g., primary textbooks on arithmetic 513
(045)	Textbooks
	(Optional number; prefer the subject in 001–999, e.g., primary textbooks on arithmetic 513)
	Including readers (if option at 372.4122 is used)
049	Instruction at specific levels
	Including kindergarten
	Class a specific aspect of instruction at a given level with the aspect, e.g., curricula for kindergarten 043

*Add as instructed under 372.3–372.8

.66   *Drama (Theater)

        Class here school plays, comprehensive works on oral presentations

        Class plays taught as literature in 372.64

> *For public speaking, see 372.622; for other oral presentations, see 372.67. For use of drama as a method of instruction in a specific subject in elementary education, see the subject in 372.3–372.8, plus notation 044 from table under 372.3–372.8, e.g., use of drama in teaching history 372.89044*

.67   Other oral presentations

        Other than drama and public speaking

        Class here activities related to oral presentations

.672   *Media production and presentation

        Subdivisions are added for either or both topics in heading

        Class media production of a specific dramatic art with the art, e.g., storytelling for media 372.677

.674   *Puppetry

        Limited to instructional use in elementary education

        Class here puppet theater

        Class interdisciplinary works on puppetry in 791.53

.676   *Choral speaking

        Class here readers' theater

.677   *Storytelling

.69   *Listening

.7   ***Mathematics**

        Including measurement

.71   *Algebra

.72   *Arithmetic

        Class here numeracy

.76   *Geometry

.79   *Probabilities and statistical mathematics

        Subdivisions are added for either or both topics in heading

.8   **Other studies**

[.801–.809]   Standard subdivisions

        Do not use; class in 372.1901–372.1909

---

*Add as instructed under 372.3–372.8

.83		*Civics (Citizenship)

Class comprehensive works on social studies in 372.89

.84		*Religion

Class religious education of children under auspices of religious bodies to inculcate religious faith and practice in 207.5; class religious education of children under church auspices to inculcate Christian faith and practice in 268.432

.86		*Physical education and dance

Subdivisions are added for physical education and dance together, for physical education alone

.868		*Dance

Class here movement education

.87		*Music

See also 372.868 for dance

.872		Appreciation
.873		Performance

Including reading music

.874		Composition
.89		History and geography

Standard subdivisions are added for history and geography together, for history alone

Class here civilization, comprehensive works on social studies

For environmental studies, see 372.357; for social skills, see 372.374; for civics, see 372.83

.890 4	General topics of history and geography
.890 42–.890 44	Place of history and geography in education; curricula, teaching

Add to base number 372.8904 the numbers following 04 in notation 042–044 from table under 372.3–372.8, e.g., teaching history 372.89044

(.890 45)	Textbooks

(Optional number; prefer 909)

For textbooks on history and civilization of ancient world, of specific continents, countries, localities, see 372.893–372.899

.890 49	Instruction at specific levels

Class a specific aspect of instruction at a given level with the aspect, e.g., history curricula for primary grades 372.89043

.891	Geography

*Add as instructed under 372.3–372.8

.891 04	General topics of geography
.891 042–.891 044	Place of geography in education; curricula, teaching

> Add to base number 372.89104 the numbers following 04 in notation 042–044 from the table under 372.3–372.8, e.g., using maps in geography 372.891044

(.891 045)	Textbooks

> (Optional number; prefer 910)

> *For textbooks on geography of specific places, see 372.8911–372.8919*

.891 049	Instruction at specific levels

> Class a specific aspect of instruction at a given level with the aspect, e.g., geography curricula for primary grades 372.891043

(.891 1–.891 9)	Textbooks on geography of specific places

> (Optional numbers; prefer 910.91 for geography in general, 913–919 for geography of specific continents, countries, localities)

> Add to base number 372.891 notation 1–9 from Table 2, e.g., geography textbooks on Asia 372.8915

(.893–.899)	Textbooks on history and civilization of ancient world, of specific continents, countries, localities

> (Optional numbers; prefer 930–990)

> Add to base number 372.89 notation 3–9 from Table 2, e.g., textbooks on ancient Egypt 372.8932

> *For textbooks on geography of specific places, see 372.8911–372.8919*

.9 History, geographic treatment, biography of primary education

> Class here specific schools and school systems

.901–.905	Historical periods

> Add to base number 372.9 notation 01–05 from Table 2, e.g., primary education in the 21st century 372.905

.91–.99	Geographic treatment, biography

> Add to base number 372.9 notation 1–9 from Table 2, e.g., primary education in Brazil 372.981

373 Secondary education

> Class here upper sections of all-age schools

> *For secondary education in a specific subject, see the subject, plus notation 0712 from Table 1, e.g., secondary education in agriculture 630.712*

SUMMARY

373.01–.09	**Standard subdivisions, secondary education for specific objectives**
.1	**Organization and activities in secondary education**
.2	**Secondary schools and programs of specific kinds, levels, curricula, focus**
.3–.9	**Secondary education in specific continents, countries, localities**

.01   Philosophy and theory, secondary education for specific objectives

         Notation 01 from Table 1 as modified below

.011   Secondary education for specific objectives

         Do not use for systems; class in 373.01

         Class here curricula directed toward specific educational objectives

         Add to base number 373.011 the numbers following 370.11 in 370.111–370.119, e.g., education for social responsibility in high school 373.0115; however, for vocational education, see 373.246

         Class a specific topic with respect to secondary education for a specific objective with the topic in 373.11–373.18, e.g., professional qualifications for teaching social responsibility in high school 373.112

         See also 373.21–373.22 for specific kinds of secondary school systems

.02   Miscellany

[.028 4]   Apparatus, equipment, materials

         Do not use; class in 373.167

[.028 7]   Testing and measurement

         Do not use; class in 373.126

[.028 8]   Maintenance and repair

         Do not use; class in 373.168

.06   Organizations

[.068]   Management

         Do not use; class in 373.12

.08   Groups of people

         Do not use for students; class in 373.18. Do not use for schools and education for specific groups of students; class in 373.182, e.g., secondary schools for ethnic minorities 373.1829

.082   Women in secondary education

         Do not use for secondary education of young women; class in 373.1822

.09   History, geographic treatment, biography

[.093–.099]   Specific continents, countries, localities

         Do not use; class in 373.3–373.9

.1   **Organization and activities in secondary education**

> *For comprehensive works on secondary education for specific objectives, see 373.011; for comprehensive works on schools and programs of specific kinds, levels, curricula, focus, see 373.2*

[.101–.109]   Standard subdivisions

> Do not use; class in 373.01–373.09

.11–.18   School organization and activities in secondary education

> Add to base number 373.1 the numbers following 371 in 371.1–371.8, e.g., evaluation of teachers 373.1144, secondary education of young women 373.1822; however, for cooperative education, see 373.28

.19   Curricula

> Class curricula directed toward specific secondary educational objectives in 373.011; class education in secondary schools identified by specific types of curricula in 373.24–373.26

.2   **Secondary schools and programs of specific kinds, levels, curricula, focus**

> Class here types of education (other than public education in general) provided by schools and programs of specific kinds, levels, curricula, focus

> Unless other instructions are given, class a subject with aspects in two or more subdivisions of 373.2 in the number coming last, e.g., public senior vocational schools 373.246 (*not* 373.224 or 373.238)

> Class a specific topic relating to schools and programs of a specific kind, level, curriculum, focus in 373.11–373.18; class a specific school regardless of kind, level, curriculum, focus in 373.3–373.9; class continuation schools in 374.8; class folk high schools in 374.83

SUMMARY

373.21	Community, alternative, religious secondary schools; public secondary schools distinguished by source of funding, locus of control, and mandate
.22	Private and public secondary schools
.23	Specific levels of secondary education
.24	Academic, military, vocational schools
.25	Comprehensive secondary schools
.26	General secondary schools
.27	Apprenticeship programs in secondary education
.28	Cooperative education

[.201–.209]   Standard subdivisions

> Do not use; class in 373.01–373.09

>   373.21–373.22   Specific kinds of schools

> Class comprehensive works in 373

.21   Community, alternative, religious secondary schools; public secondary schools distinguished by source of funding, locus of control, and mandate

> Add to base number 373.21 the numbers following 371.0 in 371.03–371.07, e.g., public secondary schools distinguished by source of funding, locus of control, and mandate 373.215

.22   Private and public secondary schools

> Class private and public community, alternative, religious secondary schools in 373.21

.222   Private secondary schools (Preparatory schools)

> Class here public schools (private secondary schools), comprehensive works on boarding schools
>
> Class private schools (other than academic schools) identified by type of curriculum in 373.24–373.26
>
> > *For a specific kind of boarding school (other than private secondary schools), see the kind, e.g., private primary boarding schools 372.10422, military boarding schools 373.243*

.224   Public secondary schools

> Class comprehensive works on public secondary education in 373
>
> > *For specific levels of public secondary schools, see 373.23; for public secondary schools distinguished by source of funding, locus of control, and mandate, see 373.215; for public secondary schools identified by a specific type of curriculum, see 373.24–373.26*

.23   Specific levels of secondary education

> Class private schools regardless of level in 373.222; class schools identified by a specific type of curriculum regardless of level in 373.24–373.26; class comprehensive works on levels of secondary schools, four-year high schools not of a specific type in 373
>
> > *See Manual at 372.24 and 373.23*

[.230 1–.230 9]   Standard subdivisions

> Do not use; class in 373.01–373.09

.236   Lower level

> Including grades above 6 in primary schools
>
> Class here middle schools (grades 5–8), junior high schools (grades 7–9); grades 7–10 of compulsory primary education
>
> > *For lower grades of middle schools, see 372.242*
>
> (Option: Class lower secondary level, grades 7–10 of compulsory primary education in 372.243)

.238 Upper level

Including high school equivalency programs

Class here senior high schools (grades 10–12); high school postgraduate programs

---

> 373.24–373.26 Secondary schools identified by type of curriculum

Class here private schools (other than academic schools) identified by type of curriculum

Class comprehensive works in 373

.24 Academic, military, vocational schools

.241 Academic schools

Schools preparing for higher education

Class here classical schools, comprehensive works on magnet schools (specialist schools)

Class private academic schools in 373.222; class preparing for higher education in military schools in 373.243; class preparing for higher education in comprehensive secondary schools in 373.25; class comprehensive works on secondary schools preparing for higher education in 373

> *For a specific type of magnet school, see the type, e.g., magnet public primary schools 372.10421, magnet vocational schools 373.246, magnet secondary schools for science 507.12, magnet secondary schools for arts 700.712*

.243 Military schools

Secondary schools offering professional military education but remaining basically academic in nature

Class here naval schools

Class schools concentrating on professional military education in 355.0071

.246 Vocational schools

Class here technical secondary schools, vocational education

Class vocational education in comprehensive secondary schools in 373.24; class comprehensive works on vocational education in 370.113

.25 Comprehensive secondary schools

Schools offering academic, vocational, general programs when considered distinct from undifferentiated secondary schools

.26 General secondary schools

Schools offering nonvocational, general terminal education when considered distinct from undifferentiated secondary schools

.27   Apprenticeship programs in secondary education

> Class apprenticeship programs offered by industry in 331.25922; class work-study plan in 373.28; class apprenticeship training as part of personnel management in 658.3124

.28   Cooperative education

> Class here work-study plan

.3–.9   Secondary education in specific continents, countries, localities

> Class here specific schools and school systems

> Add to base number 373 notation 3–9 from Table 2, e.g., secondary schools of Australia 373.94

> *For a specific school devoted primarily to a specific discipline, see the discipline, plus notation 0712 from Table 1, e.g., a science high school 507.12*

374   Adult education

> Class here continuing, further, lifelong, permanent, recurrent education

> Class on-the-job training in 331.2592; class adult high school equivalency programs in 373.238

> *For adult education in a specific subject, see the subject, plus notation 0715 from Table 1, e.g., sculpture courses for adults 730.715*

.001   Philosophy and theory

.002   Miscellany

[.002 84]   Apparatus, equipment, materials

> Do not use; class in 374.167

[.002 87]   Testing and measurement

> Do not use; class in 374.126

[.002 88]   Maintenance and repair

> Do not use; class in 374.168

.003–.005   Standard subdivisions

.006   Organizations

[.006 8]   Management

> Do not use; class in 374.12

.007   Education, research, related topics

.008   Groups of people

> Do not use for students; class in 374.18. Do not use for education of specific groups of students; class in 374.182, e.g., adult education of ethnic minority students 374.1829

[.009]   History, geographic treatment, biography

Do not use; class in 374.9

.01   Adult education for specific objectives

Class here curricula directed toward specific adult educational objectives, kinds of agencies promoting specific objectives

Class specific agencies for adult education regardless of objective in 374.94–374.99. Class a specific topic with respect to a specific adult educational objective with the topic in 374.11–374.18, e.g., testing in adult basic education 374.126

.012   Adult basic education

Class here adult primary, fundamental, remedial education

.012 4   Literacy programs

Limited to general discussion of programs to promote ability of adults to read and write up to a sixth-grade level

Class comprehensive works on literacy programs in 379.24; class adult education in effective composition (writing) in 808.00715. Class adult education in standard usage of a specific language with the language, plus notation 800715 from Table 4, e.g., a course in basic English for adults 428.00715

.013–.019   Vocational, moral, ethical, character education; education for social responsibility, for international understanding; multicultural and bilingual education; education for creativity, for effective use of leisure

Add to base number 374.01 the numbers following 370.11 in 370.113–370.119, e.g., adult education for effective use of leisure 374.019

.1   **Organization and activities in adult education**

For groups, media, computers in adult education, see 374.2; for comprehensive works on adult education for specific objectives, see 374.01; for comprehensive works on distance education, see 374.4; for comprehensive works on specific kinds of institutions and agencies, see 374.8

[.101–.108]   Standard subdivisions

Do not use; class in 374.001–374.008

[.109]   History, geographic treatment, biography

Do not use; class in 374.9

.11–.18   School organization and activities in adult education

Add to base number 374.1 the numbers following 371 in 371.1–371.8, e.g., testing 374.126; however, for use of media and computers, electronic distance education, see 374.26; for distance education, correspondence schools and courses, see 374.4

.2   **Groups, media, computers in adult education**

.22 Groups in adult education

> Class here discussion, reading, special-interest, study groups
>
> Class self-help groups in 361.4
>
> *See also 374.182 for specific groups of people as students*

.26 Use of mass media and computers

> Subdivisions are added for either or both topics in heading
>
> Class here electronic distance education
>
> Add to base number 374.26 the numbers following 371.33 in 371.333–371.337, e.g., use of radio in adult education 374.2631; online adult education 374.264

.4 Distance education

> Class here correspondence schools and courses, open and distance learning (ODL), open learning
>
> *For electronic distance education, see 374.26*

.8 Specific kinds of institutions and agencies in adult education

> Including community centers for adult education; continuation, evening, vacation schools
>
> Class here specific kinds of schools
>
> Class adult education role of libraries in 021.24; class specific institutions and agencies regardless of kind in 374.94–374.99. Class a specific topic with respect to a specific kind of institution or agency in adult education with the topic in 374.11–374.18, e.g., vacation school students 374.18
>
> *For kinds of agencies promoting adult education for specific objectives, see 374.01; for correspondence schools, see 374.4; for alternative colleges and universities as agencies for adult education, see 378.03; for university extension services as agencies for adult education, see 378.175*

[.801–.808] Standard subdivisions

> Do not use; class in 374.001–374.008

[.809] History, geographic treatment, biography

> Do not use; class in 374.9

.83 Folk high schools

.830 9 History, geographic treatment, biography

> Class specific folk high schools in 374.9

.9 History, geographic treatment, biography

.901–.905 Historical periods

> Add to base number 374.9 notation 01–05 from Table 2, e.g., adult education in the 21st century 374.905

.91–.99	Geographic treatment, biography

Add to base number 374.9 notation 1–9 from Table 2, e.g., adult education in Sweden 374.9485

375   Curricula

For curricula of a specific subject at the primary level, see 372.3–372.8. For curricula of a specific subject for a specific level other than primary level and for more than one level, see the subject, plus notation 071 from Table 1, e.g., curricula for health 613.071; for curricula for a specific level, see the level, e.g., secondary-school curricula 373.19

.000 1–.000 9	Standard subdivisions
.001	Curriculum development

Class here curriculum planning

Class comprehensive works on curriculum development and instructional supervision in 371.203

For curriculum evaluation and change, see 375.006

.002	Required courses

Class here core curriculum

.004	Elective courses
.006	Evaluation and change
(.01–.03)	Curricula and courses in bibliography, library and information sciences, encyclopedias

(Optional numbers; prefer 010–030, plus notation 071 from Table 1)

Add to base number 375 notation 010–030, e.g., curricula in cataloging and classification 375.0253

(.04)	Curricula and courses in knowledge, systems study, computer science

(Optional number; prefer 001–006, plus notation 071 from Table 1)

Add to base number 375.04 the numbers following 00 in 001–006, e.g., curricula in computer science 375.044

(.05–.09)	Curricula and courses of study in general serial publications; general organizations and museology; documentary media, educational media, news media; journalism; publishing; general collections; manuscripts, rare books, other rare printed materials

(Optional numbers; prefer 050–090, plus notation 071 from Table 1)

Add to base number 375 notation 050–090, e.g., journalism curricula 375.0704

(.1–.9)	**Curricula and courses of study in other specific subjects**

(Optional numbers; prefer 100–900, plus notation 071 from Table 1)

Add to base number 375 notation 100–900, e.g., history curricula 375.9

[376] **[Unassigned]**

Most recently used in Edition 20

[377] **[Unassigned]**

Most recently used in Edition 20

378 **Higher education (Tertiary education)**

Class here college education, university education; universities

Class four-year colleges in 378.1542

> *For higher education in a specific subject, see the subject, plus notation 0711 from Table 1, e.g., medical schools 610.711*

> *See Manual at 371.01–371.8 vs. 372–374, 378*

SUMMARY

378.001–.009	Standard subdivisions	
.01–.07	[Higher education for specific objectives, specific kinds of colleges and universities]	
.1	Organization and activities in higher education	
.2	Academic degrees and related topics	
.3	Student aid and related topics	
.4–.9	Higher education in specific continents, countries, localities in modern world	

.001 Philosophy and theory

.001 1 Systems

The word "systems" as used here refers only to concepts derived from 003, e.g., systems theory, analysis, and design applied to schools and school systems

> *See also 378.03–378.07 for specific kinds of college and university systems*

.002 Miscellany

[.002 84] Apparatus, equipment, materials

Do not use; class in 378.1967

[.002 87] Testing and measurement

Do not use; class in 378.166

[.002 88] Maintenance and repair

Do not use; class in 378.1968

.003–.005 Standard subdivisions

.006 Organizations

[.006 8] Management

Do not use; class in 378.101

.007 Education, research, related topics

.008	Groups of people

> Do not use for students; class in 378.198. Do not use for higher education of specific groups of student; class in 378.1982, e.g., higher education of ethnic minorities 378.19829

.008 2	Women in higher education

> Do not use for higher education of women; class in 378.19822. Do not use for higher education of young women; class in 378.1982422

.009	History, geographic treatment, biography
.009 2	Biography

> Class here administrators

> Class persons associated with specific colleges and universities in 378.4–378.9

[.009 4–.009 9]	Specific continents, countries, localities in modern world

> Do not use; class in 378.4–378.9

.01	Higher education for specific objectives

> Class here curricula directed toward specific higher educational objectives

> Add to base number 378.01 the numbers following 370.11 in 370.111–370.119, e.g., professional education 378.013

> Class professional schools in 378.155. Class a specific topic with respect to a specific higher educational objective with the topic in 378.101–378.198, e.g., seminars in professional education 378.177

> 378.03–378.07 **Specific kinds of colleges and universities**

> Class here specific kinds of higher education (other than public higher education) characteristic of specific kinds of colleges and universities, specific kinds of college and university systems

> Class a specific kind of college and university at a specific level in 378.15; class schools for specific groups of students in 378.1982; class specific institutions in 378.4–378.9; class comprehensive works in 378. Class a specific topic with respect to a specific kind of college or university with the topic in 378.1, e.g., graduate school fraternities 378.19855

.03	Alternative colleges and universities

> Standard subdivisions are added for either or both topics in heading

> Class here experimental schools of higher education, free universities, open universities, universities without walls

> *See also 378.175 for extension services*

> 378.04–378.05 **Private and public colleges and universities**

> Class public and private alternative colleges and universities in 378.03; class public and private colleges and universities related to religious bodies in 378.07; class comprehensive works in 378

.04 Private colleges and universities

Standard subdivisions are added for either or both topics in heading

.05 Public colleges and universities

Standard subdivisions are added for either or both topics in heading

Class two-year public colleges in 378.1543; class comprehensive works on public higher education in 378

.052 Municipal colleges and universities

Standard subdivisions are added for either or both topics in heading

Class here county, regional colleges and universities

.053 State and provincial colleges and universities

Standard subdivisions are added for either state or provincial colleges and universities

> *For municipal colleges supported by state and provincial governments, see 378.052*

.07 Colleges and universities related to religious bodies

Add to base number 378.07 the numbers following 371.07 in 371.071–371.079, e.g., church-related universities 378.071, Jewish universities 378.076
Subdivisions are added for either or both topics in heading

.1 Organization and activities in higher education

Including university autonomy

> *For academic degrees and related topics, see 378.2; for student aid and related topics, see 378.3; for comprehensive works on higher education for specific objectives, see 378.01; for comprehensive works on specific kinds of colleges and universities, see 378.03–378.07*

SUMMARY

378.101–.107	**[Administration, community relations, cooperation]**
.11	**Personnel management**
.12	**Faculty and teaching**
.15	**Specific levels of higher education**
.16	**Administration of student academic activities**
.17	**Methods of instruction and study**
.19	**Guidance, discipline, physical plant, welfare, students, curricula**

[.100 1–.100 9] Standard subdivisions

Do not use; class in 378.001–378.009

.101 College and university administration

Standard subdivisions are added for either or both topics in heading

Class administrators in 378.111

> *For financial management, see 378.106; for executive management, see 378.107; for personnel management, see 378.11; for plant and materials management, see 378.196*

.101 1   Governing bodies

.101 2   Policies and regulations

.103   Community relations

        Including volunteer student service (for credit or not for credit)

        Class interdisciplinary works on relations of colleges and universities with society in 306.432

.103 5   Industry relations

        Class here industry involvement in higher education, industry-school partnerships

        Class technology transfer in 338.926

        See also 378.37 for cooperative education

.104   Cooperation in higher education

        Class here consortia in higher education

        Class a specific instance of cooperation with the instance, e.g., cooperation in computer networking 004.6

.106   Financial management

        Including tuition

        For student aid and related topics, see 378.3

.107   Executive management

        Class here planning

        For governing bodies, see 378.1011; for administrators, leadership, top and middle management, see 378.111

.11   Personnel management

        Class here staff

        For faculty, see 378.12

.111   Administrators

        Including leadership, top and middle management

        For biography of administrators, see 378.0092. For administrators of a specific function, see the function, e.g., directors of admissions 378.161

.112   Staff personnel

        Other than administrators and faculty

        For a specific kind of staff personnel, see the kind, e.g., counselors 378.194

.12   Faculty and teaching

        Standard subdivisions are added for faculty and teaching together, for faculty alone

[.120 71]	Education of faculty
	Do not use; class in 378.0071
.121	Academic status
	Privileges, prerogatives, immunities, responsibilities
	Including sabbatical leave
.121 3	Academic freedom
.121 4	Tenure
.122	Organization of teaching force
	Including hierarchy
	Add to base number 378.122 the numbers following 371.14 in 371.141–371.148, e.g., faculty workload 378.12212, evaluation of faculty 378.1224
.124	Professional qualifications
.125	Teaching
	For methods of instruction and study, see 378.17
[.125 07]	Education, research, related topics in teaching
	Do not use; class in 378.007
.15	Specific levels of higher education
	Class specific institutions in 378.4–378.9. Class a specific topic of higher education with respect to a specific level of higher education with the topic in 378.1, e.g., teaching at the graduate level 378.125
[.150 1–.150 9]	Standard subdivisions
	Do not use; class in 378.001–378.009
.154	Undergraduate level
	Institutions conferring degrees or their equivalent at the undergraduate level within the national qualification structure for higher education
.154 2	Programs leading to a bachelor's degree
	Class here four-year colleges, three-year institutions conferring the equivalent of a bachelor's degree, undergraduate departments and schools of universities
.154 3	Programs leading to degrees below the bachelor's degree
	Class here institutions conferring degrees below the bachelor's level, two-year colleges

.155 Graduate level

Including postdoctoral programs

Class here independent institutions conferring advanced degrees, graduate departments and schools of universities, comprehensive works on professional schools

Class comprehensive works on professional education in 378.013

For professional schools at undergraduate level, see 378.154

.16 Administration of student academic activities

Add to base number 378.16 the numbers following 371.2 in 371.21–371.29, e.g., admissions and related topics 378.161, standardized tests at college level 378.1662; however, for academic degrees and related topics, see 378.2; for student aid and related topics, see 378.3

Class methods of instruction in 378.17; class student participation in management in 378.1959

.17 Methods of instruction and study

.170 28 Auxiliary techniques and procedures, techniques of study, lesson plans

Notation 028 from Table 1 as modified below

.170 281 Techniques of study

Including book reports, homework, note-taking, reading for content, report writing

Class here techniques for parents, study skills

[.170 284] Apparatus, equipment, materials

Do not use; class in 378.173

[.170 285] Computer applications

Do not use; class in 378.1734

[.170 78] Use of apparatus, equipment, materials in study and teaching

Do not use; class in 378.173

.172–.179 Specific methods of instruction and study

Add to base number 378.17 the numbers following 371.3 in 371.32–371.39, e.g., extension services 378.175, seminars 378.177

.19 Guidance, discipline, physical plant, welfare, students, curricula

.194–.198 Guidance, discipline, physical plant, welfare, students

Add to base number 378.19 the numbers following 371 in 371.4–371.8, e.g., school discipline 378.195, higher education of specific kinds of students 378.1982

.199 Curricula

Class curricula directed toward specific educational objectives in 378.01

.2	**Academic degrees and related topics**

Standard subdivisions are added for academic degrees and related topics together, for academic degrees alone

.24	Requirements for earned degrees

.241	Course, residence, subject requirements

Class here college majors

.242	Thesis and dissertation requirements

Class preparation of theses and dissertations in 808.066378

.25	Honorary degrees

.28	Academic costume

.3	**Student aid and related topics**

Standard subdivisions are added for student aid and related topics together, for student aid alone

For student aid in a specific field, see the field, plus notation 079 from Table 1, e.g., student aid in medical education 610.79

.32	Veterans' higher education benefits

.33	Fellowships and grants

Class comprehensive works on student exchanges in higher education in 378.0162

.34	Scholarships

.36	Loans and employment

.362	Student loans

.365	Student employment

Including employment for service to the community

Class here employment of students by their own schools, work-study programs

For volunteer student service to community, see 378.103; for employment in connection with fellowships, see 378.33; for employment by industry and nonschool agencies in connection with ongoing academic work, see 378.37

.37	Cooperative education

Student employment by industry and nonschool agencies in connection with ongoing academic work

Class here work-study plan

Class general work-study programs for student employment in 378.365

.38	Costs and expenditures

Standard subdivisions are added for either or both topics in heading

.4–.9   Higher education in specific continents, countries, localities in modern world

Class here specific schools

Add to base number 378 notation 4–9 from Table 2, e.g., higher education in Mexico 378.72
(Option: If it is desired to give local emphasis and a shorter number to a specific college or university, place it first by use of a letter or other symbol, e.g., University of South Africa 378.S [preceding 378.4])

For a school or department of a college or university devoted to a specific subject, see the subject, plus notation 0711 from Table 1, e.g., Harvard Law School 340.07117444

See Manual at 378.4–378.9 vs. 355.00711

379   Public policy issues in education

Public policy issues at any level of education

Class public administration of education in 353.8; class school administration in 371.2

For public policy issues on a topic not provided for here, see the topic, e.g., policy on school admissions 371.21, on medical schools 610.711

See Manual at 371 vs. 353.8, 371.2, 379

SUMMARY

379.1	**Specific elements of support and control of public education**
.2	**Specific policy issues in public education**
.3	**Public policy issues in private education**
.4–.9	**Public policy issues in specific continents, countries, localities in modern world**

[.094–.099]   Specific continents, countries, localities in modern world

Do not use; class in 379.4–379.9

.1   Specific elements of support and control of public education

Class support and control of activities involved in specific policy issues in public education in 379.2

SUMMARY

379.11	**Support of public education**
.12	**Support by specific level of government, international support**
.13	**Revenue sources**
.15	**Control of public education**

[.101–.109]   Standard subdivisions

Do not use; class in 379.01–379.09

.11   Support of public education

Class here financial support; comprehensive works on financial support of education

For support by specific levels of government, international support, see 379.12; for revenue sources, see 379.13; for financial support of private education, see 379.32

See also 353.824 for financial administration of agencies supporting public education

.111   Educational vouchers

Regardless of level of government

Class here school choice

Class educational vouchers for a specific level of education in 379.112–379.118; class educational vouchers for special education in 379.119

For use of educational vouchers in private education, see 379.32

.112   Support of public primary education

.112 2   Support of public preschool education

.113   Support of public secondary education

.114   Public support of adult education

.118   Support of public higher education

.119   Public support of special education

.12   Support by specific level of government, international support

Class educational vouchers regardless of level of government providing them in 379.111; class revenue sources of specific levels of government in 379.13

[.120 1–.120 9]   Standard subdivisions

Do not use; class in 379.01–379.09

.121   Support by national governments

.121 2   National support of primary education

.121 22   National support of preschool education

.121 3   National support of secondary education

.121 4   National support of higher education

.121 5   National support of adult education

.121 6   National support of special education

.122   Support by state, provincial, regional governments

Add to base number 379.122 the numbers following 379.121 in 379.1212–379.1216, e.g., state support of adult education 379.1225

.123   Local support

.128   Support by regional intergovernmental organizations

.128 2–.128 9   Support by specific regional intergovernmental organizations

> Add to base number 379.128 the numbers following 341.24 in 341.242–341.249, e.g., support by European Union 379.12822

.129   International support

> Class here international multicultural educational aid

.129 09   History, geographic treatment, biography

> Do not use for geographic treatment by recipient area; class in 379.1291–379.1299

.129 1–.129 9   Geographic treatment by recipient area

> Add to base number 379.129 notation 1–9 from Table 2, e.g., educational aid to Asia 379.1295; then, for area providing support, add 0*, and again add notation 1–9 from Table 2, e.g., French educational aid to Asia 379.1295044

.13   Revenue sources

> Class here school taxes

> Class financial assistance from higher levels of government in 379.12

.15   Control of public education

> Class here autonomy

>   379.151–379.154   Control by specific governmental level

> Class control of specific aspects of education regardless of level in 379.155–379.158; class comprehensive works in 379.15

.151   Control by national governments

.152   Control by state, provincial, regional governments

.153   Control by local governments

.153 1   School boards

.153 5   School districts

> Including centralization and consolidation of schools, changing school attendance boundaries

.154   Control by specific regional intergovernmental organizations

.154 2–.154 9   Control by specific regional intergovernmental organizations

> Add to base number 379.154 the numbers following 341.24 in 341.242–341.249, e.g., control by European Commission 379.1542226

---

*Add 00 for standard subdivisions; see instructions at beginning of Table 1

>   379.155–379.158 Control of specific aspects of education

        Class comprehensive works in 379.15

>   *For control of a specific aspect of education not provided for here, see the aspect, e.g., control of school discipline 371.5*

.155   Control of curriculum

>   *See also 379.28 for place of religion in public education*

.156   Control of teaching materials

        Class here control of textbooks

.157   Control of teachers and administrators

        Class control of specific aspects of teachers and teaching in 371.1; class control of specific aspects of school administrators in 371.2011

.158   School standards and accreditation

        Standard subdivisions are added for either or both topics in heading

        Class here educational evaluation, school accountability

>   *See also 353.8284 for government commissions on standards and accreditation; also 371.26 for examinations and tests*

.2   **Specific policy issues in public education**

        Not otherwise provided for

[.201–.209]   Standard subdivisions

        Do not use; class in 379.01–379.09

.23   Compulsory education

        Including school-leaving age

.24   Literacy policies

        Class here right to read

.26   Educational equalization (Equal educational opportunity)

        Class here affirmative action, right to education

        Class discrimination in education in 370.8

.263   School desegregation

.28   Place of religion in public schools

        Regardless of faith or denomination

        Including teaching creationism in public schools

.3   **Public policy issues in private education**

.32   Public support of private education

Class here educational vouchers, financial support

Class comprehensive works on financial support of education in 379.11

.322   Public support of private primary education

.322 2   Public support of private preschool education

.323   Public support of private secondary education

.324   Public support of private higher education

.326   Public support of private adult education

.328   Public support of private special education

.34   Public control of private education

Add to base number 379.34 the numbers following 379.32 in 379.322–379.328, e.g., public control of private primary education 379.342

.4–.9   **Public policy issues in specific continents, countries, localities in modern world**

Add to base number 379 notation 4–9 from Table 2, e.g., public educational policies in United States 379.73

380   Commerce, communications, transportation

Except for modifications shown under specific entries, add to each subdivision identified by * as follows:

> 025   Directories of persons and organizations
> 06   Organizations and management; business enterprises
>   Notation 06 from Table 1 as modified below
> 065   Business enterprises
>   Including individual proprietorships, partnerships, companies, public and private corporations, combinations
>   Add to 065 notation 3–9 from Table 2, e.g., business enterprises of France 06544
>   Class directories of business enterprises, membership lists with directory information in notation 025 from this table; class organizations whose members are business enterprises, e.g., trade associations and chambers of commerce, in notation 06 from this table
>   *See Manual at T1—025 vs. T1—0601–T1—0609; also at 380: Add table: 09 vs. 065*
> 068   Management
>   Public and private
> 09   History, geographic treatment, biography
>   Class specific business enterprises in notation 065 from this table
>   *See Manual at 380: Add table: 09 vs. 065*

Class public regulation and control in 354.7

See Manual at 380

SUMMARY

380.1–.9	**Standard subdivisions**
381	**Commerce (Trade)**
382	**International commerce (Foreign trade)**
383	**Postal communication**
384	**Communications**
385	**Railroad transportation**
386	**Inland waterway and ferry transportation**
387	**Water, air, space transportation**
388	**Transportation**
389	**Metrology and standardization**

381   *Commerce (Trade)

Class here internal commerce (domestic trade), warehousing, interdisciplinary works on marketing

Unless other instructions are given, observe the following table of preference, e.g., retail trade in rice 381.41318 (*not* 381.1):

Specific products and services	381.4
Marketing channels	381.1
Wholesale trade	381.2
Interregional and interstate commerce	381.5
Commercial policy	381.3

Class supply and demand in 338.1–338.5; class restrictive practices in business organizations engaged in commerce in 338.82; class comprehensive works on warehousing in 388.044; class interdisciplinary works on consumption in 339.47. Class cooperative, labor, finance, land, energy economics in relation to commerce with the branch of economics in 330, e.g., cooperative marketing 334.6

For international commerce, see 382; for management of marketing, see 658.8

See Manual at T1—025 vs. T1—029

SUMMARY

381.029	**Commercial miscellany**
.1	**Marketing channels**
.2	**Wholesale trade**
.3	**Commercial policy**
.4	**Specific products and services**
.5	**Interregional and interstate commerce**

*Add as instructed under 380

.029   Commercial miscellany

> Do not use for evaluation and purchasing manuals; class in 381.33

> Notation 029 from Table 1 is seldom used with the subdivisions of 381

> Class here interdisciplinary works on commercial miscellany

>> *For commercial miscellany with respect to a specific product or service, see the noncommercial number for the product or service, plus notation 029 from Table 1, e.g., buyers' guides for passenger automobiles 629.222029*

>> *See Manual at T1—025 vs. T1—029*

.1   ***Marketing channels**

> Including exhibitions, trade fairs (trade shows)

> Class here retail trade; markets, shops, stores

> Class street fairs in 381.186; class consumer problems and their alleviation in 381.3; class interdisciplinary works on exhibitions, on fairs in 907.4. Class marketing channels and marketing enterprises limited to or predominantly for a specific product or service with the product or service in 381.4, e.g., food supermarkets, comprehensive works on food and grocery trade 381.456413

> Management of marketing channels limited to or predominantly for a specific product or service is classed with the product or service in 381.4, e.g., management of chain bookstores 381.45002068, management of food supermarkets 381.4564130068. Management of marketing channels not limited to or predominantly for a specific product or service is classed in 658.87, e.g., management of all kinds of chain stores 658.8702, management of supermarkets that are not predominantly food stores 658.879

>> *For consumer cooperatives, see 334.5; for producer cooperatives, see 334.6*

.106   Organizations, business enterprises

> Notation 06 from Table 1 as modified in notation 06 from table under 380

[.106 8]   Management

> Do not use; class in 658.87

.11   †Shopping centers

.12   †Chain stores

> Class chain stores with a specific merchandising pattern in 381.14

.13   †Franchise businesses

> Class franchise businesses with a specific merchandising pattern in 381.14

.14   Retail channels by merchandising pattern

>> *For factory outlets, see 381.15; for outdoor and street markets, see 381.18*

---

*Add as instructed under 380

†Add as instructed under 380, except observe special instructions for management at 381.1

.141   †Department stores

> Class department stores that are discount stores in 381.149

.142   †Teleshopping

> Class here catalog shopping, mail-order shopping, online shopping, telephone and television shopping; comprehensive works on electronic commerce

> *For online auctions, see 381.177*

[.142 028 5]   Computer applications

> Do not use; class in 381.142

.147   †Convenience stores

> Including forecourt sales

> Class convenience stores that are mainly grocery stores in 381.456413

.149   †Discount stores

> Including customer clubs, warehouse clubs, wholesale clubs

> Class here supermarkets that are not predominantly food stores, hypermarkets, superstores

> Class food retailing in supermarkets in 381.456413

.15   †Outlet stores

> Class here discount stores that are outlet stores, factory outlets, manufacturers' outlets, wholesale outlet stores

.17   †Auctions

[.170 285]   Computer applications

> Do not use; class in 381.177

.177   †Online auctions

.18   †Outdoor and street markets

> Class here street vending

> Subdivisions are added for either or both topics in heading

> *For outdoor and street markets for secondhand goods, see 381.19*

.186   †Street fairs

> *See also 381.457451 for antique fairs; also 381.45790132 for collectors' fairs*

---

†Add as instructed under 380, except observe special instructions for management at 381.1

.19   †Outlets for secondhand goods

Including estate sales; charity, thrift shops

Class outdoor and street markets selling both new and secondhand goods in 381.18. Class a specific kind of estate sale with the kind, e.g., estate yard sales 381.195

For auctions of second hand goods, see 381.17

.192   †Flea markets

.195   †Garage, rummage, and related sales

Sales held over a short time period of goods owned or contributed by individuals who no longer need them

Standard subdivisions are added for any or all topics in heading

Class here car boot, jumble, tag, white elephant, yard sales

.2   **Wholesale trade**

Class wholesale trade through specific marketing channels in 381.1

.206   Organizations, business enterprises

Notation 06 from Table 1 as modified below

.206 5   Business enterprises

Including individual proprietorships, partnerships, companies, public and private corporations, combinations

Add to 381.2065 notation 3–9 from Table 2, e.g., wholesale trade business enterprises of France 381.206544

Class organizations whose members are business enterprises, e.g., trade associations, in 381.206

See Manual at 380: Add table: 09 vs. 065

[.206 8]   Management

Do not use for comprehensive works on management of wholesale trade; class in 658.86. Do not use for management of wholesale trade limited to or predominantly in a specific product or service; class with the product or service in 381.4, e.g., management of wholesale trade in food 381.4564130068

.209   History, geographic treatment, biography

Class specific business enterprises in 381.2065

See Manual at 380: Add table: 09 vs. 065

.3   **Commercial policy**

Class here consumer problems and their alleviation, consumerism

---

†Add as instructed under 380, except observe special instructions for management at 381.1

.32   Consumer movements

Class specific activities of consumer movements in 381.33–381.34

.33   Consumer information

Including consumer information aspects of product labeling; research, testing of products

Class here consumer education, comprehensive works on evaluation of products and services to be purchased, interdisciplinary evaluation and purchasing manuals

For evaluation and purchasing guides and consumer education for household and personal products and services, see 640.73. For evaluation and purchasing manuals for a specific product or service, see the product or service, plus notation 029 from Table 1, e.g., manual on evaluating passenger automobiles 629.222029

.34   Consumer protection

Class product hazards in 363.19; class fraud in 364.163

.347   Better business bureaus

.4   Specific products and services

Class here works discussing consumption as a measure of the volume, value, or kind of trade in specific products; management of enterprises selling specific products and services

Class interdisciplinary works on consumption of specific products and services in 339.48

[.401–.409]   Standard subdivisions

Do not use; class in 381.01–381.09

.41   *Products of agriculture

Class here farmers' markets, produce trade

See also 381.45637 for commerce of dairy and related products

[.410 29]   Commercial miscellany

Do not use; class in 630.209

.413–.416   Specific products of culture of plants, of domestic mammals, of domestic birds

Add to base number 381.41 the numbers following 63 in 633–636, e.g., rice 381.41318

.418   Specific products of insect culture

Add to base number 381.418 the numbers following 638 in 638.1–638.5, e.g., honey 381.41816

.42   *Products of mineral industries

*Add as instructed under 380

[.420 29]	Commercial miscellany
	Do not use; class in 553.029
.422–.429	Specific products

Add to base number 381.42 the numbers following 553 in 553.2–553.9, e.g., oil 381.42282

.43　　　*Products of other extractive industries

[.430 29]	Commercial miscellany
	Do not use; class in 639.029

.431　　　*Products of culture of invertebrates and cold-blooded vertebrates

Class products of insect culture in 381.418

[.431 029]	Commercial miscellany
	Do not use; class in 639.029
.431 3–.431 7	Specific products

Add to base number 381.431 the numbers following 639 in 639.3–639.7, e.g., oysters 381.43141

.432–.439　　　Products of fishing, whaling, hunting, trapping

Add to base number 381.43 the numbers following 59 in 592–599, e.g., fur 381.4397, comprehensive works on products of both finfishing and shellfishing industries 381.437

.44　　　*Slave trade

Limited to works that emphasize economic aspects of slave trade

Class interdisciplinary works on slave trade in 306.362

.45　　　Products of secondary industries and services

Standard subdivisions are added for either or both topics in heading

.450 001–.450 009　　　Standard subdivisions

Notation from Table 1 as modified in notation 02–09 from table under 380, e.g., companies 381.4500065

.450 01–.459 99　　　Specific products and services

Add to base number 381.45 notation 001–999, e.g., clothing 381.45687; then add further as instructed under 380, e.g., clothing stores 381.45687065
Subdivisions are added for either or both topics in heading

See Manual at 709.2 vs. 381.457092

---

*Add as instructed under 380

.456 413   *Food trade

Number built according to instructions under
381.45001–381.45999

Class here food retailing in supermarkets; grocery stores

Class supermarkets that are not predominantly food stores in
381.149

*For produce trade, see 381.41; for trade in commercially
processed foods, see 381.45664. For trade in a specific
food, see the food in 381.41–381.45, e.g., oysters 381.43141*

.5   *Interregional and interstate commerce

Commerce between parts of a single jurisdiction

Standard subdivisions are added for either or both topics in heading

382   *International commerce (Foreign trade)

Class here trade between nations and their colonies, protectorates, trusts

Unless other instructions are given, observe the following table of preference, e.g.,
import trade in rice 382.41318 (*not* 382.5):

Specific products and services	382.4
Tariff policy	382.7
Import and export trade	382.5–382.6
General topics of international commerce	382.1
Trade agreements	382.9
Commercial policy	382.3

Class interdisciplinary works on international finance in 332.042; class
interdisciplinary works on international economics in 337

SUMMARY

382.01–.09	**Standard subdivisions and business enterprises**
.1	**General topics of international commerce**
.3	**Commercial policy**
.4	**Specific products and services**
.5	**Import trade**
.6	**Export trade**
.7	**Tariff policy**
.9	**Trade agreements**

.01   Philosophy and theory

Do not use for theories of international commerce; class in 382.104

.06   Organizations and management; business enterprises

Notation 06 from Table 1 as modified in notation 06 from table under 380.
Do not use for organizations associated with trade agreements; class in 382.9
e.g., World Trade Organization 382.92

.09   History, geographic treatment, biography

*Add as instructed under 380

.091　　　　International commerce of areas, regions, places in general

> Add to base number 382.091 the numbers following —1 in notation
> 11–19 from Table 2, e.g., international commerce of developing
> countries 382.091724; then, for commerce between an area, region, or
> place and another area, region, place or a continent, country, locality,
> add 0† and add notation 1–9 from Table 2, e.g., commerce between
> developing countries and United Kingdom 382.091724041
> Do not follow add instructions under —091 in Table 1

> Give priority in notation to the region, area, place emphasized. If
> emphasis is equal, give priority to the one coming first in Table 2
> > (Option: Give priority in notation to the region, area, place requiring
> > local emphasis, e.g., libraries in United States class trade between
> > developing nations and United States in 382.097301724)

.093–.099　　　International commerce in specific continents, countries, localities

> Add to base number 382.09 notation 3–9 from Table 2, e.g., international
> commerce of United Kingdom 382.0941; then, for commerce between
> two continents, countries, localities or between a continent, country,
> locality and a region, area, place, add 0† and add notation 1–9 from
> Table 2, e.g., commerce between United Kingdom and communist bloc
> 382.094101717
> Do not use add table under —093–099 in Table 1

> Give priority in notation to the continent, country, locality emphasized. If
> emphasis is equal, give priority to the one coming first in Table 2
> > (Option: Give priority in notation to the continent, country, locality
> > requiring local emphasis, e.g., libraries in United States class trade
> > between United Kingdom and United States in 382.0973041)

.1　　General topics of international commerce

.104　　Theories

.104 2　　Specialization and comparative advantage

> Standard subdivisions are added for either or both topics in heading

> Class comprehensive works on specialization and comparative
> advantage in 338.6046

.17　　Balance of payments

> Class here balance of trade

.3　　Commercial policy

> Class economic imperialism in 337

.4　　Specific products and services

> Class here works discussing consumption as a measure of the volume, value, or
> kind of trade in specific products

> Class interdisciplinary works on consumption of specific products and services
> in 339.48

---

†Add 00 for standard subdivisions; see instructions at beginning of Table 1

[.401–.409]   Standard subdivisions

>   Do not use; class in 382.01–382.09

.41–.45   Specific products and services

>   Add to base number 382.4 the numbers following 381.4 in 381.41–381.45,
>   e.g., foreign trade in products of agriculture 382.41, of rice 382.41318
>   Subdivisions are added for either or both topics in heading

.5   *Import trade

>   Class here nontariff trade barriers

>   Class the combined import and export trade of a country, the trade between two
>   countries in 382.09; class agreements on nontariff trade barriers in 382.9

.52   Import quotas

.53   Embargoes on imports

.54   Licensing of imports

.6   *Export trade

>   Class the combined import and export trade of a country, the trade between two
>   countries in 382.09

.609   History, geographic treatment, biography

>>   Do not use for the area to which goods are being exported; class in
>>   382.6109

.61   Export trade by export market area

.610 9   History, geographic treatment, biography

>>   Class here the area to which goods are being exported

>>   Class the area doing the exporting in 382.609

.63   Export policy

>   Including subsidies, export trade promotion

>   *For export controls and restrictions, see 382.64*

.64   Export controls and restrictions

>   Standard subdivisions are added for either or both topics in heading

>   Including inspection, licensing

.7   Tariff policy

>   Including drawbacks

>   Class here interdisciplinary works on customs duties

>   Class international agreements on tariffs in 382.9

>>   *For a specific aspect of customs duties, see the aspect, e.g., law 343.056*

---

*Add as instructed under 380

.71   Free trade

> Class international free trade agreements in 382.9

.72   Revenue tariffs

.73   Protectionism

> Class here protective and prohibitive tariffs, comprehensive works on trade barriers and restrictions

> *For nontariff trade barriers, see 382.5; for single and multiple column tariffs, see 382.75*

.75   Single and multiple column tariffs

.752   Single column tariffs

> Single rates for each product

.753   Multiple column tariffs

> Varying rates on the same product designed to favor certain countries of origin

> Including generalized system of preference (GSP)

.78   Tariff exemptions (Duty-free importation)

> Including educational, scientific, tourist exemptions

.9   Trade agreements

> Class here agreements on nontariff trade barriers, on tariffs

> Class general economic cooperation and international arrangements for this purpose in 337; class texts of treaties on tariffs in 343.0560261; class texts of treaties on international commerce in 343.0870261

.906   Organizations and management

> Do not use for organizations associated with multilateral agreements; class in 382.91–382.92. Do not use for organizations associated with bilateral agreements; class in 382.93–382.99

.909   History, geographic treatment, biography

> Do not use for multilateral agreements; class in 382.91. Do not use for bilateral agreements; class in 382.93–382.99

.91   Multilateral agreements

> Class here customs unions

> Class bilateral agreements in 382.93–382.99; class interdisciplinary works on intergovernmental organizations in 341.2

> *For World Trade Organization, see 382.92*

[.910 91]   Area, regions, places in general

> Do not use; class in 382.911

[.910 94–.910 99]   Specific continents, countries, localities in modern world

> Do not use; class in 382.914–382.919

.911   Multilateral agreements in areas, regions, places in general

> Add to base number 382.911 the numbers following —1 in notation
> 11–19 from Table 2, e.g., western bloc nations 382.911713

>   382.914–382.919 Multilateral agreements in specific continents, countries,
                        localities in modern world

Class comprehensive works in 382.91

.914   Multilateral agreements in Europe

.914 2   European Union

> Class here European Common Market, European Community,
> European Economic Community

.914 3   European Free Trade Association (EFTA)

.914 7   Multilateral agreements in Eastern Europe

.915–.919   Multilateral agreements in other continents and regions

> Add to base number 382.91 notation 5–9 from Table 2, e.g., southeast
> Asia 382.9159

.92   World Trade Organization (WTO)

Class here General Agreement on Tariffs and Trade (GATT)

.93–.99   Trade agreements by specific countries

> Add to base number 382.9 notation 3–9 from Table 2, e.g., trade agreements
> of United Kingdom 382.941; then, for bilateral agreements, add 0† and again
> add notation 3–9 from Table 2, e.g., agreements between United Kingdom
> and France 382.941044
> Do not use add table under —093–099 in Table 1

> Give priority in notation to the country emphasized. If emphasis is equal,
> give priority to the one coming first in Table 2
> (Option: Give priority in notation to the country requiring local emphasis,
> e.g., libraries in United States class agreements between United Kingdom
> and United States in 382.973041)

>   **383–388 Communications and transportation**

Class comprehensive works on communications in 384; class comprehensive
works on communications and transportation together, on transportation alone
in 388

Comprehensive works on the activities, services, and facilities of a system
are classed in the number for the system, e.g., radio broadcasting activities,
services, and facilities 384.54, not 384.544

---

†Add 00 for standard subdivisions; see instructions at beginning of Table 1

383   **Postal communication**

Class comprehensive works on communications in 384

See also 769.56 for philately

.06   Organizations and management

Do not use for postal organizations; class in 383.4

[.09]   History, geographic treatment, biography

Do not use; class in 383.49

.1   **Mail handling**

.12   Classes of mail

Class a specific mode of transportation for a specific class of mail in 383.141–383.144. Class a specific service for a specific class of mail with the service, e.g., special delivery of letters 383.183

.120 01–.120 09   Standard subdivisions

>   383.120 2–383.120 5 Special classes

Class comprehensive works in 383.12

.120 2   Free mail

Including franking privileges

.120 5   Nonmailable matter

Including obscene and subversive material

.122   Letters, postcards, sealed material

Class here first-class mail

.123   Newspapers and periodicals

Class here second-class mail

.124   Printed material

Not provided for elsewhere

Including books, catalogs, circulars; bulk mailings

Class here third-class mail

.125   Parcels

Class here fourth-class mail

Class printed matter in 383.124

.14   Transportation systems, collection, delivery

Standard subdivisions are added for transportation systems, collection, delivery together; for transportation systems alone

> 383.141–383.144 Transportation systems

Class comprehensive works in 383.14

.141 Facsimile transmission

.142 Sea mail

.143 Overland mail

Including inland waterway, railroad mail; star routes

.144 Air mail

Including mail carried through space

.145 Collection and delivery

Including postal zones

Class collection and delivery of mail within the military services in 355.69; class star routes in 383.143; class special delivery in 383.183

.145 5 Postal codes

Class here zip code

.18 Other services

Including express mail

.182 Insured and registered mail

Standard subdivisions are added for either or both topics in heading

.183 Special delivery and special handling

Standard subdivisions are added for either or both topics in heading

.184 Cash on delivery (Collect on delivery, COD)

.186 Dead letter services

.2 Economic aspects of production

Class economic aspects of mail handling in 383.1

See also 330 for other economic aspects, e.g., postal workers' unions 331.8811383

.23 Rates and costs

Including use of postage stamps

.24 Efficiency of operation

Including use of mechanization and automation

.4 Postal organization

[.409] History, geographic treatment, biography

Do not use; class in 383.49

.41 International systems and conventions

.42   Post offices

.46   Internal services

Including postal inspection

.49   History, geographic treatment, biography of postal communication, of postal organizations and systems

Add to base number 383.49 notation 1–9 from Table 2, e.g., postal communication in Europe 383.494

384   *Communications

Including recordings, visual signaling

Class here interdisciplinary works on telecommunication

Class sociology of communication in 302.2; class services designed to facilitate communication by people with disabilities in 362.40483; class services designed to facilitate communication by people in late adulthood in 362.63; class comprehensive works on communications and transportation in 388

For postal communication, see 383. For a specific aspect of telecommunication, see the aspect, e.g., telecommunication engineering 621.382

SUMMARY

384.04	**Special topics of communications**	
.1	**Telegraphy**	
.3	**Computer communication**	
.5	**Wireless communication**	
.6	**Telephony**	
.8	**Motion pictures**	

.04   Special topics of communications

.041   Economic aspects of production

Class economic aspects of facilities in 384.042; class economic aspects of activities and services in 384.043

See also 330 for other economic aspects, e.g., telecommunication workers' unions 331.8811384

.042   Facilities

Including stations

Class use of facilities in specific activities and services in 384.043

.043   Activities and services

Standard subdivisions are added for either or both topics in heading

---

>   **384.1–384.6 Telecommunication**

Class comprehensive works in 384

*Add as instructed under 380

.1   *Telegraphy

Class here submarine cable telegraphy

For radiotelegraphy, see 384.52

.102 84   Materials

Do not use for apparatus and equipment; class in 384.15

.13   Economic aspects of production

Class economic aspects of activities and services in 384.14; class economic aspects of facilities in 384.15

See also 330 for other economic aspects, e.g., telegraphy workers' unions 331.88113841

.14   *Activities and services

Including Morse and other code telegraphy, printing telegraphy; stock tickers, teletype, telex; comprehensive works on facsimile transmission

Subdivisions are added for either or both topics in heading

Class comprehensive works on electronic mail in 384.34

For postal facsimile transmission, see 383.141

.15   Facilities

Class use of facilities in specific activities and services in 384.14

.3   *Computer communication

Transfer of computer-based information by any of various media (e.g., coaxial cable or radio waves) from one computer to another or between computers and terminals

Class here computer communications networks, links between computers via telephone lines

Class interdisciplinary works on computer communications in 004.6

See Manual at 004.6 vs. 384.3

.302 85   Computer applications

Class here computer science applied to economic and related aspects of providing computer communication to the public

.31   Economic aspects of production

Class economic aspects of production of computer communication hardware and software and comprehensive works on production and sale in 338.470046; class sale of computer communication hardware and software in 381.450046; class economic aspects of facilities in 384.32; class economic aspects of activities and services in 384.33

See also 330 for other economic aspects, e.g., computer communication workers' unions 331.88113843

*Add as instructed under 380

.32 Facilities

> Class use of facilities in specific activities and services in 384.33

.33 Activities and services

> Standard subdivisions are added for either or both topics in heading

> Including Internet telephony, network neutrality, services of value-added networks, videotex

> Class here social media

>> *For electronic mail, point-to-point communications, see 384.34; for discussion groups, broadcast communications, see 384.36; for computer communications in multimedia systems, see 384.38*

>> *See Manual at 004.678 vs. 006.7, 025.042, 384.33*

.334 Internet governance

.34 *Electronic mail

> Class here point-to-point communications, comprehensive works on electronic mail

> Class interdisciplinary works on electronic mail in 004.692; class e-mail lists in 384.36

>> *For a specific kind of electronic mail, see the kind, e.g., postal facsimile transmission 383.141*

.36 *Discussion groups

> Class here chat groups, electronic bulletin boards, Internet forums, e-mail lists, newsgroups; broadcast communications

> Class electronic mail in 384.34

.38 *Computer communications in multimedia systems

> Including blogs, wikis, online social networks

.5 *Wireless communication

SUMMARY

384.51	**Satellite communication**
.52	**Radiotelegraphy**
.53	**Radiotelephony**
.54	**Radiobroadcasting**
.55	**Television**

.51 *Satellite communication

>> *For a specific form of satellite communication, see the form, e.g., television transmission by satellite 384.552*

.52 *Radiotelegraphy

---

*Add as instructed under 380

.523–.525   Economic aspects, activities and services, facilities

> Add to base number 384.52 the numbers following 384.1 in 384.13–384.15, e.g., apparatus 384.525

.53   *Radiotelephony

> Including ship-to-shore communication, citizens band radio

> Class here mobile telephones

.533–.535   Economic aspects, activities and services, facilities

> Add to base number 384.53 the numbers following 384.6 in 384.63–384.65, e.g., transmitting and receiving equipment 384.535

.54   *Radiobroadcasting

> Class here digital audio broadcasting, public broadcasting (noncommercial broadcasting), public aspects of amateur radio, interdisciplinary works on radiobroadcasting and television broadcasting

> *For television broadcasting, see 384.55*

> *See Manual at 384.54, 384.55, 384.8 vs. 791.4*

.540 65   Business enterprises

> Number built according to instructions under 380

> Including network affiliates, public (noncommercial) networks and stations

> Class here stations and networks

> *See Manual at 384.54, 384.55, 384.8 vs. 791.4*

.543   Economic aspects of production

> Class economic aspects of activities and services in 384.544; class economic aspects of facilities in 384.545

> *See also 330 for other economic aspects, e.g., radiobroadcasting workers' unions 331.881138454*

.544   *Activities and services

> Subdivisions are added for either or both topics in heading

.544 2   Scheduling

> Including sale of time

.544 3   Programs

> Class techniques of producing programs in 791.44. Class a specific type of program with the type, e.g., news broadcasts 070.43

.545   Facilities

> Class use of facilities in specific activities and services in 384.544

---

*Add as instructed under 380

.545 2	Broadcasting channels
	Class listings of stations by channel (assigned frequency) in 384.5453025
.545 24	Frequency allocation
.545 3	Stations
	Including AM, FM stations
	Class stations as business enterprises in 384.54065
.545 5	Networks
	Class networks as business enterprises in 384.54065
.545 6	Satellites
.55	*Television

Including low power television (LPTV) stations (stations that rebroadcast the programs of full-service stations, originate programming that often includes pay television, and are usually limited in power to 10–1000 watts and a 10–mile to 15–mile broadcasting radius)

Class here interactive television

Unless other instructions are given, class a subject with aspects in two or more subdivisions of 384.55 in the number coming last, e.g., economic aspects of cable television and controlled transmission television 384.5561 (*not* 384.5551)

See Manual at 384.54, 384.55, 384.8 vs. 791.4

.550 65	Business enterprises

Number built according to instructions under 380

Enterprises engaged in two or more aspects of television, e.g., pay television enterprises that produce video products

Including network affiliates; nonaffiliated commercial, private television

Class here stations and networks

See Manual at 384.54, 384.55, 384.8 vs. 791.4

.551	Economic aspects of production of television in general

See also 330 for other economic aspects, e.g., television workers' unions 331.881138455

.552	Facilities and channels of television in general

Class here direct broadcast satellite (DBS) systems, satellites, satellite dishes

.552 1	Broadcasting channels

Including frequency allocation

*Add as instructed under 380

.552 2		Stations
		Class stations as business enterprises in 384.55065
.552 3		Networks
		Class networks as business enterprises in 384.55065
.553		*Activities and services of television in general
		Subdivisions are added for either or both topics in heading
.553 1		Scheduling
		Including sale of time
.553 2		Programs
		Class technique of producing programs in 791.45. Class a specific type of program with the type, e.g., news broadcasts 070.43
.554		*General broadcasting (Free television)
		Transmitting signals over the air for use by the general public
		Including translator stations (low-power stations for transmitting the signals of television broadcast stations to areas where reception is unsatisfactory)
		Class here public television (noncommercial television)
		Class works combining both general broadcasting and cable television in 384.55
.554 3		Economic aspects of production
		See also 330 for other economic aspects, e.g., public television workers' unions 331.8811384554
.554 4		*Activities and services
		Subdivisions are added for either or both topics in heading
.554 42		Scheduling
		Including sale of time
.554 43		Programs
		Including local programming
		Class techniques of producing programs in 791.45. Class a specific type of program with the type, e.g., news broadcasts 070.43
.554 5		Facilities and channels
		Class here direct broadcast satellite (DBS) systems, satellites, satellite dishes
		Class use of facilities and channels in specific activities and services in 384.5544
.554 52		Broadcasting channels

*Add as instructed under 380

.554 53	Stations
	Class stations as business enterprises in 384.554065
.554 55	Networks
	Class networks as business enterprises in 384.554065
.554 6	*Community antenna television systems (CATV systems)
	Systems that provide television reception to remote communities, using a tall antenna, usually limited to no more than 12 channels
.554 61–.554 63	Economic aspects, activities and services, facilities
	Add to base number 384.5546 the numbers following 384.55 in 384.551–384.553, e.g., networks 384.554623

.555 ***Pay television**

Systems that receive and distribute signals to customers who pay for the service

Class here cable television

Class works combining general broadcasting and cable television in 384.55; class pay television in Canada in 384.5554; class use of cable television in closed-circuit television in 384.556

.555 1–.555 3	Economic aspects, facilities and channels, activities and services
	Add to base number 384.555 the numbers following 384.55 in 384.551–384.553, e.g., networks 384.55523
.555 4	*Premium television (Subscription television)
	Systems that scramble signals that are decoded for a fee
	Class here pay-cable, pay television in Canada
	See also 384.55 for low power television (LPTV) stations
.555 41–.555 43	Economic aspects, activities and services, facilities
	Add to base number 384.5554 the numbers following 384.55 in 384.551–384.553, e.g., facilities 384.55542

.556 ***Television systems whose signals are transmitted to a specific audience**

Including telepresence, theater television

Class here closed-circuit television, videoconferencing, videotelephony; industrial uses, e.g., surveillance, monitoring of hazardous industrial processes

See also 384.5554 for pay-per-view television

.556 1–.556 3	Economic aspects, activities and services, facilities
	Add to base number 384.556 the numbers following 384.55 in 384.551–384.553, e.g., rates 384.5561

*Add as instructed under 380

.558   *Video production

         Including camcorders, video recorders, laser optical discs

         Class video production associated with a specific aspect of television communication with the aspect, e.g., video production in cable television 384.555

.6   *Telephony

         Class here comprehensive works on wire and cable communication

         Class mobile telephones in 384.53

         For Internet telephony, see 384.33; for telegraphy, see 384.1; for radiotelephony, see 384.53; for cable television, see 384.555; for videotelephony, see 384.556

.602 5   Directories of persons and organizations

         See also 914–919, plus notation 0025 from table under 913–919, for telephone directories, e.g., New York City telephone directory 917.4710025

.63   Economic aspects of production

         Class economic aspects of activities and services in 384.64; class economic aspects of facilities in 384.65

         See also 330 for other economic aspects, e.g., telephone workers' unions 331.88113846

.64   *Activities and services

         Including caller ID telephone service; conference calls; emergency services; local, long-distance, overseas service

         Subdivisions are added for either or both topics in heading

.646   *Audiotex

         Including dial-a-message telephone calls

.65   Facilities

         Including stations, lines, switchboards, dialing systems, transmitting and receiving equipment

         Class use of facilities in specific activities and services in 384.64

.8   *Motion pictures

         See Manual at 384.54, 384.55, 384.8 vs. 791.4

.83–.85   Economic aspects, activities and services, facilities

         Add to base number 384.8 the numbers following 384.1 in 384.13–384.15, e.g., activities 384.84

---

*Add as instructed under 380

385   *Railroad transportation

Class here standard-gage and broad-gage railways

Class comprehensive works on transportation, on ground transportation in 388

For local rail transit systems, see 388.42

See Manual at 629.046 vs. 388

.065   Business enterprises

Number built according to instructions under 380

Class here railroad companies

> *See also 385.5065 for narrow-gage and special-duty railroad companies; also 385.6065 for inclined and mountain railroad companies*

> ### 385.1–385.3 Specific aspects

Class specific aspects of narrow-gage and special-duty railroads in 385.5; class specific aspects of inclined and mountain railroads in 385.6; class comprehensive works in 385

.1   **Economic aspects of production**

Class economic aspects of activities and services in 385.2; class economic aspects of facilities in 385.3

See also 330 for other economic aspects, e.g., railroad workers' unions 331.8811385

.2   **Activities and services**

Standard subdivisions are added for either or both topics in heading

.204   Special topics of activities and services

.204 2   Basic activities

Including dispatching, routing, scheduling, traffic control

For operation of rolling stock, see 385.2044

.204 4   Operation of rolling stock

> ### 385.22–385.24 Transportation activities and services

Class comprehensive works in 385.2

.22   *Passenger services

Including baggage, meal, sleeper services

.23   *Express transportation of goods

---

*Add as instructed under 380

.24   *Freight services

       Class unitized cargo services in 385.72

       For express transportation of goods, see 385.23

.26   Activities and services of terminals and stations

       Standard subdivisions are added for either or both topics in heading

       Including fueling

.262   *Passenger services

       Including passenger amenities, reservation systems

.264   *Freight services

       Including freight handling, warehousing, storage

       For railroad mail, see 383.143

.3   Facilities and vehicles

       Class use of facilities and vehicles in specific activities and services in 385.2

.31   Stationary facilities

.312   The way

       Including bridges, grade crossings, tracks, tunnels

       Class comprenensive works on tunnels in 388.13; class comprehensive works on bridges in 388.132

.314   Terminals and stations

       Including yards, roundhouses, train sheds, shop buildings

.316   Communications facilities

       Including signals

.32–.34   Cars

       Add to base number 385.3 the numbers following 625.2 in 625.22–625.24, e.g., dining cars 385.33

       Class comprehensive works in 385.37

.36   Locomotives

       Add to base number 385.36 the numbers following 625.26 in 625.261–625.266, e.g., steam locomotives 385.361

.37   Rolling stock

       For cars, see 385.32–385.34; for locomotives, see 385.36; for rolling stock of local rail transit systems, see 388.42

---

*Add as instructed under 380

.5	***Narrow-gage and special-purpose railroads**

For inclined and mountain railroads, see 385.6; for special-purpose railroads located entirely within a metropolitan region, see 388.42–388.46

.52	*Narrow-gage railroads

Class narrow-gage industrial railroads in 385.54

.54	*Industrial railroads

Subdivisions are added for any purpose of the railroad, e.g., lumber railroads in Georgia 385.5409758, mine railroads in Colorado 385.5409788

.6	***Inclined and mountain railroad systems**

Including cable, funicular, rack railroads

.7	**Railroad combined with other transportation systems**

.72	*Unitized cargo services

Including piggyback transportation (trucks, trailers, buses, private automobiles on flatcars)

For container-ship operations, see 387.5442

.77	*Ship railroads

Rail transportation of vessels overland between bodies of water

386   ***Inland waterway and ferry transportation**

Subdivisions are added for inland waterway and ferry transportation together, for inland waterway transportation alone

Class comprehensive works on water transportation in 387; class comprehensive works on transportation in 388

See Manual at 629.046 vs. 388

.1	**Economic aspects of production**

Class economic aspects of facilities in 386.2; class economic aspects of activities and services in 386.24; class economic aspects of specific kinds of inland water and ferry transportation in 386.3–386.6

See also 330 for other economic aspects, e.g., inland-waterway transportation workers' unions 331.8811386

.2	**Activities, services, facilities, ships**

Class activities and facilities (*except* for ships and ports) of specific types of inland water systems in 386.3–386.6; class activities, services, facilities of ports in 386.8

*Add as instructed under 380

.22		Ships

> Including air-cushion vehicles
>
> Add to base number 386.22 the numbers following 623.82 in 623.821–623.829, e.g., tugboats 386.2232
>
> Class use of ships in specific activities and services in 386.24

.24   Activities and services

> Standard subdivisions are added for either or both topics in heading

.240 4   Special topics of activities and services

.240 42   Basic activities

> Including dispatching, routing, scheduling, traffic control
>
> *For operation of ships, see 386.24044*

.240 44   Operation of ships

.242   *Passenger services

> Including baggage, meal, sleeper services

.244   *Freight services

> *For inland waterway mail, see 383.143*

> **386.3–386.6 Specific kinds of inland water and ferry transportation**

Class here activities, services, facilities

Class ships for specific kinds of inland water transportation in 386.22; class ports for specific kinds of inland water transportation in 386.8; class comprehensive works in 386

> **386.3–386.5 Specific kinds of waters**

Class ferry transportation on specific kinds of waters in 386.6; class comprehensive works in 386

.3   *River transportation

Class here transportation by canalized rivers

Class combined river, lake, canal systems in 386.5

.32   The way

.35   Activities and services

> Standard subdivisions are added for either or both topics in heading

.350 4   Special topics of activities and services

*Add as instructed under 380

.350 42	Basic activities

Including dispatching, routing, scheduling, traffic control

For operation of ships, see 386.35044

.350 44	Operation of ships
.352	*Passenger services

Including baggage, meal, sleeper services

.354	*Freight services

For inland waterway mail, see 383.143

.4   *Canal transportation

Class canalized rivers in 386.3; class combined river, lake, canal systems in 386.5

.404	Special topics of canal transportation
.404 2	Activities and services

Standard subdivisions are added for either or both topics in heading

.404 204	Special topics of activities and services
.404 204 2	Basic activities

Including dispatching, routing, scheduling, traffic control

For operation of ships, see 386.4042044

.404 204 4	Operation of ships
.404 22	*Passenger services

Including baggage, meal, sleeper services

.404 24	*Freight services

For inland waterway mail, see 383.143

>   386.42–386.48 Specific canals and kinds of canals

Existing and proposed

Class comprehensive works in 386.4

.42	Interoceanic canals

For canals connecting specific oceans, see 386.43–386.45

>   386.43–386.45 Canals connecting specific oceans

Class comprehensive works in 386.42

*Add as instructed under 380

.43	Canals connecting Indian and Atlantic Oceans

Class here Suez Canal

.44	Canals connecting Atlantic and Pacific Oceans

Class here Panama Canal

.445	Proposed Nicaragua Canal
.447	Proposed Tehuantepec Canal
.45	Canals connecting Pacific and Indian Oceans
.46	Noninteroceanic canals

Including canals connecting parts of one ocean

For kinds of noninteroceanic canals, see 386.47–386.48

>   386.47–386.48 Kinds of noninteroceanic canals

Class here specific canals

Class comprehensive works in 386.46

.47	*Ship canals
.48	*Small craft and barge canals

Subdivisions are added for either or both topics in heading

.5	***Lake transportation**

Class here transportation on combined river, lake, canal systems, e.g., Saint Lawrence Seaway 386.509714

.52	The way
.54	Activities and services

Standard subdivisions are added for either or both topics in heading

.540 4	Special topics of activities and services
.540 42	Basic activities

Including dispatching, routing, scheduling, traffic control

For operation of ships, see 386.54044

.540 44	Operation of ships
.542	*Passenger services

Including baggage, meal, sleeper services

.544	*Freight services

For inland waterway mail, see 383.143

---

*Add as instructed under 380

.6   ***Ferry transportation**

> Oceanic and inland

.8   ***Ports**

> Class here ports on nontidal waters

.82–.86   Physiographic location, facilities, activities, services; free ports

> Add to base number 386.8 the numbers following 387.1 in 387.12–387.16, e.g., freight terminals 386.853

387   Water, air, space transportation

> Class here comprehensive works on water transportation

> Class comprehensive works on transportation in 388

> *For inland waterway and ferry transportation, see 386*

SUMMARY

387.01–.09	Standard subdivisions of water transportation
.1	Ports
.2	Ships
.5	Ocean transportation (Marine transportation)
.7	Air transportation
.8	Space transportation

.01–.09   Standard subdivisions of water transportation

> Notation from Table 1 as modified in notation 02–09 from table under 380, e.g., water transportation business enterprises 387.065; however, do not use for water, air, space transportation together; class in 388.01–388.09

.1   **Ports**

> Class here ports on tidal waters

> *For inland ports, see 386.8*

.12   Physiographic location of ports

> Including ports on tidal rivers, roadsteads

> Class facilities of specific types of ports in 387.15; class activities and services of specific types of ports in 387.16

.120 9   History, geographic treatment, biography

> Class a specific port in 387.109

.13   Free ports

> Class facilities of free ports in 387.15; class activities and services of free ports in 387.16

.130 9   History, geographic treatment, biography

> Class a specific free port in 387.109

---

*Add as instructed under 380

.15 Port facilities

> Including docks, marinas, piers, quays
>
> Class use of port facilities in specific activities and services in 387.16

.152 Passenger terminals

.153 Freight terminals

.155 Navigational aids

> Class here lighthouses, lightships
>
> Class piloting in 387.166

.16 Activities and services

> Standard subdivisions are added for either or both topics in heading
>
> Including port maintenance

.162 *Passenger services

> Including booking services

.164 *Freight services

> Including freight handling, warehousing, storage, connection with land transportation

.166 Operational services

> Including piloting, ship-to-shore communication, towing, tug services

.168 Auxiliary services

> Including fueling

.2 **Ships**

> Including air-cushion vehicles
>
> Class use of ships in inland waterway transportation in 386.22; class use of ships in specific activities and services in 387.54
>
> *See Manual at 629.046 vs. 388*

.204 General types

> Add to base number 387.204 the numbers following 623.820 in 623.8202–623.8205, e.g., sailing craft 387.2043

.21–.29 Specific types

> Add to base number 387.2 the numbers following 623.82 in 623.821–623.829, e.g., cargo ships 387.245

.5 ***Ocean transportation (Marine transportation)**

> *For seaports, see 387.1; for ships, see 387.2*
>
> *See Manual at 629.046 vs. 388*

*Add as instructed under 380

.51   Economic aspects of production

Class economic aspects of ships in 387.2; class economic aspects of routes and kinds of routes in 387.52; class economic aspects of activities and services in 387.54; class economic aspects of facilities in 387.58

See also 330 for other economic aspects, e.g., ocean transportation workers' unions 331.88113875

.52   Routes and kinds of routes

Class here specific routes

Class activities and services on routes and kinds of routes in 387.54; class use of facilities on routes and kinds of routes in 387.58

.522   Intercoastal routes

.523   Auxiliary, irregular, tramp routes

.524   Coastwise routes

.54   Activities and services

Standard subdivisions are added for either or both topics in heading

Class activities and services of ports in 387.16

.540 4   Special topics of activities and services

.540 42   Basic activities

Including dispatching, routing, scheduling, traffic control

For operation of ships, see 387.54044

.540 44   Operation of ships

Including life and activities of marine personnel at sea

.542   *Passenger services

Including baggage, meal, sleeper services

.544   *Freight services

.544 2   *Container-ship operations

Class unitized cargo in 385.72; class carriage of specific kinds of cargo in container-ship operations in 387.5448

.544 8   Carriage of specific kinds of cargo

Including dry cargo, fertilizer, petroleum

For sea mail, see 383.142

.55   *Salvage

---

*Add as instructed under 380

.58   Facilities

Class facilities of ports in 387.15; class ships in 387.2; class use of facilities in specific activities and services in 387.54

For lighthouses, see 387.155

.7   ***Air transportation**

See Manual at 629.046 vs. 388

.71   Economic aspects of production

Class economic aspects of routes in 387.72; class economic aspects of facilities in 387.73; class economic aspects of activities and services in 387.74

See also 330 for other economic aspects, e.g., air transportation workers' unions 331.88113877

.712   Rates and fares

.72   Routes

Including helicopter routes to and from airports

Class use of facilities on routes and kinds of routes in 387.73; class activities and services on routes in 387.74

.73   Aircraft and facilities

Standard subdivisions are added for aircraft and facilities together, for aircraft alone

.732–.733   Specific types of aircraft

Add to base number 387.73 the numbers following 629.133 in 629.1332–629.1333, e.g., helicopters 387.73352

Class use of aircraft in specific activities and services in 387.74

.736   Airports

Class here landing fields

.736 2   Facilities

Including hangars, runways, terminal buildings; access to airports

Class use of facilities in specific activities and services in 387.7364

.736 4   Activities and services

Standard subdivisions are added for either or both topics in heading

Including booking, fueling, passenger services

.74   Activities and services

Standard subdivisions are added for either or both topics in heading

Class activities and services of airports and landing fields in 387.7364

---

*Add as instructed under 380

.740 4		Special topics of activities and services
.740 42		Basic activities

Including dispatching, routing, scheduling; airport noise and its alleviation

For operation of aircraft, see 387.74044

.740 426   Air traffic control

See Manual at 629.1366 vs. 387.740426

.740 44   Operation of aircraft

Class here operating personnel, flight crews

Class maintenance and maintenance personnel in 387.73

.742   *Passenger services

Including baggage, meal, sleeper services

.742 2   *Reservation systems

.742 8   *Charter services

.744   *Freight services

Including all-cargo plane services

For air mail, see 383.144

.8   *Space transportation

See Manual at 629.046 vs. 388

388   *Transportation

Class here ground transportation, comprehensive works on communications and transportation, interdisciplinary works on transportation

Comprehensive works on the activities, services, and facilities of a system are classed in the number for the system, e.g., seaport activities, services, and facilities 387.1, not 387.15 nor 387.16

Class services designed to facilitate the use of transportation by people with disabilities in 362.40483; class services designed to facilitate the use of transportation by people in late adulthood in 362.63; class transportation of students in 371.872

For transportation safety and safety measures, see 363.12; for transportation security, see 363.287; for postal transportation, see 383.14; for communications, see 384; for railroad transportation, see 385; for water, air, space transportation, see 387; for transportation technology, see 629.04

See also 385.7 for railroad combined with other transportation systems

See Manual at 629.046 vs. 388

*Add as instructed under 380

SUMMARY

388.04	**Special topics of transportation**
.1	**Roads**
.3	**Vehicular transportation**
.4	**Local transportation**
.5	**Pipeline transportation**

.04   Special topics of transportation

Including facilities, vehicles

.041   Activities and services

Standard subdivisions are added for either or both topics in heading

Including routing, scheduling, dispatching, traffic control

Class specific kinds of services in 388.042–388.044

.042   *Passenger services

Including baggage, reservation, meal, sleeper services

Class here mass transportation

.044   *Freight services

Including handling, storage; comprehensive works on warehousing

Class unitized cargo services in 385.72

For commerce aspects of warehousing, see 381

.047   Comparative studies of kinds of transportation

Class a comparative study of a specific kind of transportation with the kind, e.g., comparative study of local transportation 388.4

.049   Economic aspects of transportation

Class economic aspects of activities and services in 388.041; class economic aspects of passenger services in 388.042; class economic aspects of freight services in 388.044

See also 330 for other economic aspects, e.g., transportation workers' unions 331.8811388

.1   ***Roads**

Class here highways

For highway services and use, see 388.31; for urban roads, see 388.411

.102 23   Diagrams

Do not use for maps and plans; class in 912

*Add as instructed under 380

.11   Economic aspects of production

Class economic aspects of kinds of roads in 388.12; class economic aspects of special road features in 388.13. Class economic effects of roads on a specific aspect of an economic activity with the activity, e.g., effect on business location 338.6042

See also 330 for other economic aspects, e.g., road transportation workers' unions 331.88113881

.112   Costs

.114   Finance

Including user charges, tolls

.12   Kinds of roads

Including primary and secondary roads, bicycle paths, pedestrian paths

Class special features of kinds of roads in 388.13

For access roads, see 388.13

.120 223   Diagrams

Do not use for maps and plans; class in 912

.122   Expressways

Variant names: beltways, freeways, motorways, parkways, throughways, tollways, turnpikes

.122 022 3   Diagrams

Do not use for maps and plans; class in 912

.13   Special road features

Including access roads, grade separations, intersections, interdisciplinary works on tunnels

Class signs and signals for traffic control in 388.3122

For railroad tunnels, see 385.312. For a specific aspect of tunnels, see the aspect, e.g., tunnel engineering 624.193

.132   Bridges

Class here interdisciplinary works on bridges

For railroad bridges, see 385.312. For a specific aspect of bridges, see the aspect, e.g., bridge engineering 624.2

.3   ***Vehicular transportation**

Class urban vehicular transportation in 388.41

.31   Traffic flow and maintenance

**Add as instructed under 380

.312	Highway services

Including lighting, roadside park facilities, snow removal

For traffic control by police, see 363.2332; for speed limits, see 388.3144

.312 2	Traffic control through signs and signals

Standard subdivisions are added for either or both topics in heading

.312 4	Driver information

Information supplied en route

Including information on traffic patterns via commercial radio

.314	Highway use
.314 2	Traffic volume

Class peak hours in 388.3143

.314 3	Traffic patterns

Including patterns by origin, by destination; peak hours; use by specific kinds of vehicles

.314 4	Speed limits
.32	*Vehicular activities and services

Subdivisions are added for either or both topics in heading

See also 388.34 for vehicles

See Manual at 629.046 vs. 388

.321	*Services of private passenger automobiles

Including limousine services

.322	*Bus services

Class here passenger services

Class services of terminals, stations, stops in 388.33

.322 04	Special topics of bus services
.322 042	Basic activities

Including dispatching, routing, scheduling, traffic control

For operation of vehicles, see 388.322044

.322 044	Operation of vehicles
.322 1	Routes

Intercity and trunk

Class services offered on specific routes and kinds of routes in 388.3222

*Add as instructed under 380

.322 2   Types of services

Including charter, baggage, meal, small package and express services; tourism

.322 8   *Stagecoach services

Class stagecoach routes in 388.3221

For types of stagecoach services, see 388.3222

.324   *Trucking services

Class services of terminals in 388.33

.324 04   Special topics of trucking services

.324 042   Basic activities

Including dispatching, routing, scheduling, traffic control

For operation of vehicles, see 388.324044

.324 044   Operation of vehicles

.324 2   Routes

Including long-haul, line-haul, intercity routes

.324 3   Kinds of carriers

Including common (for-hire), contract, private carriers

.33   Terminals, stations, stops

Including activities, services, facilities (e.g., vehicle sheds, docks, booking facilities)

.34   Vehicles

Class here interdisciplinary works on land vehicles

Class use of vehicles in specific services, vehicle operation in 388.32. Class flexible fuel vehicles with the fuel that predominates, e.g., automobiles powered by fossil fuels with biofuel additives 388.342

For railroad rolling stock, see 385.37; for air-cushion vehicles, see 388.35; for rolling stock of local rail transit systems, see 388.42. For a specific aspect of vehicles, see the aspect, e.g., engineering of motor land vehicles 629.2

See Manual at 629.046 vs. 388

.341   Nonmotor land vehicles

Class here specific types of nonmotor land vehicles

Class cycles in 388.347

*Add as instructed under 380

.342–.348   Vehicles powered by fossil fuels and human-powered vehicles

        Class here comprehensive works on a specific type of vehicle regardless of source of power, e.g., comprehensive works on trucks 388.344

        Add to base number 388.34 the numbers following 629.22 in 629.222–629.228, e.g., buses 388.34233, bicycles 388.3472

        For rickshaws, see 388.341; for natural gas vehicles, see 388.34973

.349   Vehicles powered by other sources and vehicles powered by natural gas

        Class here alternative fuel vehicles

        Add to base number 388.349 the numbers following 629.229 in 629.2292–629.2297, e.g., electric-powered vehicles 388.3493

        Class comprehensive works on vehicles powered by fossil fuels in 388.34; class comprehensive works on a specific type of vehicle regardless of source of power in 388.342–388.348, e.g., comprehensive works on trucks 388.344

.35   Air-cushion vehicles

        Class here comprehensive works on air-cushion vehicles

        For air-cushion ships for inland waterways, see 386.22; for air-cushion ships for ocean transportation, see 387.2

.4   ***Local transportation**

        Class here urban and suburban transportation, rapid transit, mass transit, commuter services

.404   Special topics of local transportation

.404 2   Economic aspects of production

        See also 330 for other economic aspects, e.g., local transportation workers' unions 331.88113884

>   **388.41–388.46 Specific kinds of local transportation**

        Class terminals and parking facilities for specific kinds of transportation in 388.47; class comprehensive works in 388.4

        See Manual at 629.046 vs. 388

.41   Vehicular and pedestrian traffic

        Including moving sidewalks

        Class vehicles in 388.34–388.35

*Add as instructed under 380

.411	Urban roads

Including parkways, expressways, arterial and side streets, sidewalks, bicycle paths (bikeways); intersections, traffic circles (roundabouts)

Class here streets

Class operation, services, use of urban roads in 388.4131

.411 022 3	Diagrams

Do not use for maps and plans; class in 912

.413	Activities and services

Standard subdivisions are added for either or both topics in heading

.413 1	Traffic flow and maintenance

Add to base number 388.4131 the numbers following 388.31 in 388.312–388.314, e.g., peak hours 388.413143

.413 2	Vehicular services
.413 21	*Services by private passenger automobiles
.413 212	*Car and van pools

Class here ridesharing

Subdivisions are added for either or both topics in heading

.413 214	*Taxicabs and limousines
.413 22	*Bus services

Including animal-drawn omnibuses

For guided-way systems, see 388.42

.413 223	*Trolleybus services
.413 24	*Trucking services
.42	*Local rail transit systems

Including guided-way systems, monorail systems

Class here rolling stock; elevated rail transit systems, underground systems; comprehensive works on local rail transit systems with multiple transit modes

Class rail terminals and stations in 388.472

For light rail transit systems, see 388.46

See also 388.34 for trolleybuses; also 388.413223 for trolleybus services

.46	*Light rail transit systems

Class here interurban railroads (streetcar lines running between urban areas or from urban to rural areas); streetcar systems, tramways, trolley-car systems

---

*Add as instructed under 380

.47	Terminals, stations, parking facilities
.472	Rail terminals and stations
.473	Truck and bus stations and terminals

> Including bus stops

.474 Parking facilities

> Including on-street and off-street parking facilities, facilities located above and below street level

> Class here interdisciplinary works on parking

> > *For a specific aspect of parking, see the aspect, e.g., city planning 711.73*

.5 ***Pipeline transportation**

.55 *Oil (Petroleum)

.56 *Natural gas

.57 *Coal

> Class here coal slurry

389 Metrology and standardization

.1 **Metrology**

> Class interdisciplinary works on measurement in 530.8

.15 Systems of measurement

> Including metric system (système international, SI), imperial (British) system

> Class adoption of metric system in 389.16; class mathematical tables of conversion from one system to another in 530.81

.16 Adoption of metric system (système international, SI)

> > *See also 658.4062 for management measures for coping with conversion to metric system*

.17 Time systems and standards

> Including conversion tables; daylight saving, standard, universal time; time zones

> Class interdisciplinary works on chronology in 529

---

*Add as instructed under 380

.6   Standardization

Class here interdisciplinary works on standards

For law of standardization and standards, see 343.075; for public administration aspects of standardization and standards, see 352.83; for production management aspects of standardization and standards, see 658.562. For standardization and standards of a specific topic, see the topic, plus notation 0218 from Table 1, e.g., technical standards 602.18

.62   Standardization of quantity and size

Class here standardization for interchangeability

.63   Standardization of quality

Class here performance standards

390   Customs, etiquette, folklore

Standard subdivisions are added for customs, etiquette, folklore together; for customs alone

Class here folkways; interdisciplinary works on ceremonies, on rites

For customs of military life, see 355.1. For a type of ceremony or rite not provided for here, see the type, e.g., religious rites 203.8, military ceremonies 355.17

SUMMARY

390.01–.09	Standard subdivisions of customs, etiquette, folklore together; standard subdivisions of customs
.1–.4	Customs of specific economic, social, occupational classes
391	Costume and personal appearance
392	Customs of life cycle and domestic life
393	Death customs
394	General customs
395	Etiquette (Manners)
398	Folklore
399	Customs of war and diplomacy

.01–.07   Standard subdivisions

.08   Groups of people

.086   People by miscellaneous social attributes

[.086 2]   People by social and economic levels

Do not use for people by economic status; class in 390.1. Do not use for people by social class; class in 390.2

.088   Religious groups

Do not use for occupational groups; class in 390.4

.09   History, geographic treatment, biography

>   **390.1–390.4 Customs of specific economic, social, occupational classes**

            Class comprehensive works in 390

.1   **Customs of people by economic status**

            Class customs of slaves and serfs in 390.25

.2   **Customs of people by social class**

.22   Customs of royalty

.23   Customs of nobility

.24   Customs of common people

            Class customs of common people of specific economic statuses in 390.1; class customs of specific occupations in 390.4

.25   Customs of slaves and serfs

.4   **Customs of people by occupation**

            Add to base number 390.4 notation 001–999, e.g., customs of lawyers 390.434; however, for customs of military personnel, see 355.1; for customs of diplomats, see 399

>   **391–394 Customs**

            Class comprehensive works in 390

            For customs of specific economic, social, occupational classes, see 390.1–390.4; for customs of war and diplomacy, see 399

391   **Costume and personal appearance**

            Standard subdivisions are added for costume and personal appearance together, for costume alone

            Class here interdisciplinary works on costume, clothing (apparel, garments), fashion; casual wear (sportswear)

            Class costume and clothing associated with a specific occasion with the occasion in 392–394, e.g., wedding clothes 392.54

            For fashion design, see 746.92; for interdisciplinary works on stage costumes, see 792.026. For a specific aspect of costume and clothing, see the aspect, e.g., clothing construction 646.4

            See Manual at 391 vs. 646.3, 746.92

.001–.007   Standard subdivisions

.008   Groups of people

.008 1   People by gender or sex

[.008 11]   Men

            Do not use; class in 391.1

| [.008 2] | Women |
| | Do not use; class in 391.2 |

.008 3   Young people

Do not use for children under twelve; class in 391.3

.008 4   People in specific stages of adulthood

Do not use for clothing for men in specific stages of adulthood; class in 391.1. Do not use for clothing for women in specific stages of adulthood; class in 391.2

.008 6   People by miscellaneous social attributes

[.008 62]   People by social and economic levels

Do not use for people by economic status; class in 391.01. Do not use for people by social class; class in 391.02

.008 8   Religious groups

Do not use for occupational groups; class in 391.04

.009   History, geographic treatment, biography

.01–.04   Costume of economic, social, occupational groups

Add to base number 391.0 the numbers following 390 in 390.1–390.4, e.g., costume of royalty 391.022; however, for military costume, see 355.14; for costume of diplomats, see 399

\>   **391.1–391.3 Costume of men, women, children**

Class costume for men, women, children by specific economic, social, occupational groups in 391.01–391.04; class kinds of garments for men, women, children in 391.4; class accessories for men, women, children in 391.44; class comprehensive works in 391

.1   **Costume of men**

.2   **Costume of women**

.3   **Costume of children**

.4   **Kinds of garments; accessories; buttons**

Class comprehensive works on garments in 391

[.401–.409]   Standard subdivisions

Do not use; class in 391.001–391.009

.41   Gloves, mittens, footwear, neckwear

Including scarves, ties

.412   Gloves and mittens

Standard subdivisions are added for either or both topics in heading

.413	Footwear

Class here shoes and boots

.42	Undergarments, hosiery, sleepwear, loungewear

.423	Undergarments and hosiery

Standard subdivisions are added for undergarments and hosiery together, for undergarments alone

See also 391.473 for vests (waistcoats); also 391.476 for pants (trousers)

.426	Sleepwear and loungewear

Variant name for sleepwear: nightclothes

Standard subdivisions are added for either or both topics in heading

.43	Headwear

Including headscarves, helmets, protective headwear

Class here bonnets, caps, hats

.434	Masks

.44	Accessories

Including canes, combs, eyeglasses, fans, flowers, handbags, muffs, parasols

For gloves, mittens, footwear, neckwear, see 391.41; for headwear, see 391.43; for jewelry, see 391.7

.45	Buttons

.46	Outerwear

Including capes, cloaks, stoles, sweaters

Class here overcoats, topcoats, raincoats; comprehensive works on coats and jackets

Class garments for specific purposes in 391.48

For suit jackets, sport coats, see 391.473

.47	Specific kinds of garments

Not provided for elsewhere

Class garments for specific purposes in 391.48

.472	Dresses

.473	Suits

Class here jackets, sport coats, vests (waistcoats)

Class skirts in 391.477; class outerwear, comprehensive works on coats and jackets in 391.46

For pants (trousers), see 391.476

See also 391.423 for vests (undergarments)

.475	Shirts, blouses, tops

Standard subdivisions are added for any or all topics in heading

.476	Pants (Trousers)

See also 391.423 for pants (undergarments)

.477	Skirts

.48	Garments for special purposes

Including activewear (clothing for athletic and outdoor sports), costumes, maternity garments

Class headwear for special purposes in 391.43; class accessories for special purposes in 391.44

For sleepwear and loungewear, see 391.426; for wedding clothes, see 392.54

See also 391 for casual wear (sportswear)

.486	Evening and formal dress

Standard subdivisions are added for either or both topics in heading

.5 Hairstyles

Including beards, wigs

.6 Personal appearance

For hairstyles, see 391.5

.62	Body contours

.63	Use of cosmetics and perfume

.64	Personal cleanliness and hygiene

Including bathing

.65	Tattooing and scarification

Standard subdivisions are added for tattooing and scarification together, for tattooing alone

See also 391.7 for body piercing

.7 Jewelry

Including body piercing

Class here interdisciplinary works on jewelry

For jewelry making, see 739.27

.72	Finger rings

392 Customs of life cycle and domestic life

For death customs, see 393

.1 Customs of birth, puberty, majority

.12   Birth customs

       Including baptism, couvade, infanticide, name giving

.13   Child-rearing customs

.14   Customs relating to attainment of puberty

       Including initiation rites

.15   Customs relating to attainment of majority

       Including debuts

.3   Customs relating to dwelling places and domestic arts

.36   Dwelling places

       Class here furnishings, heating, lighting, sanitation

.37   Cooking

       Class comprehensive works on food and meals in 394.12

.4   Courtship and engagement customs

       Standard subdivisions are added for courtship and engagement customs together, for courtship customs alone

       Including bride purchase, bundling, infant betrothal, matchmaking

.5   Wedding and marriage customs

       Standard subdivisions are added for either or both topics in heading

       See also 395.22 for etiquette of weddings

.54   Wedding clothes

.6   Customs of sexual relations

       Including chaperonage

       For courtship and engagement customs, see 392.4; for wedding and marriage customs, see 392.5

393   Death customs

       Customs relating to disposal of the dead and to mourning

.1   Burial

       Including entombment

.2   Cremation

.3   Embalming

.4   Exposure

.9   Mourning

       Including wakes

.93   Funerals

Including sati

394   General customs

Including kissing, swearing

Class etiquette in 395

SUMMARY

.1   Eating, drinking; using drugs

Situations and methods of use, prohibited uses

.12   Eating and drinking

Class here food

Class table manners in 395.54

For cooking, see 392.37; for drinking of alcoholic beverages, see 394.13; for customs of tea, see 394.15; for food taboos, see 394.16

.125   Meals

.125 2   First meal of the day

Class here breakfasts, brunches

.125 3   Light meals

Class here snacks; dinners, lunches, suppers, teas as light meals

Class breakfasts, brunches in 394.1252; class dinners, lunches, suppers, teas as main meals in 394.1254

See also 394.15 for Japanese tea ceremony

.125 4   Main meal of the day

Class here dinners; lunches, suppers, teas as main meals

Class breakfasts, brunches in 394.1252; class dinners, lunches, suppers, teas as light meals in 394.1253

.13   Drinking of alcoholic beverages

.14   Use of drugs

Including marijuana, narcotics, tobacco

For alcoholic beverages, see 394.13

.15	Customs of tea

> Class here tea ceremonies
>
> *See also 394.1253 for teas as a light meal*

.16	Food taboos
.2	**Special occasions**

> Including anniversaries, birthdays, celebrations, fast days
>
> Class official ceremonies in 394.4; class pageants, processions, parades in 394.5

.25	Carnival

> Pre-Lenten festival
>
> Class here Mardi Gras; festivals of pre-Lenten origin
>
> *See also 394.26 for carnivals other than pre-Lenten festivals*

.26	Holidays

> Class here carnivals other than pre-Lenten festivals, festivals; independence days; patriotic, seasonal, secular holidays
>
> Class a season associated with a holiday with the holiday, e.g., the Christmas season 394.2663; class a technology or craft associated with holidays with the technology or craft, e.g., making fireworks 662.1, decorating Easter eggs 745.5944
>
> *For Carnival, Mardi Gras, see 394.25*

[.260 9]	History, geographic treatment, biography

> Do not use; class in 394.269

> **394.261–394.264 Secular holidays**
>
> Class here patriotic holidays, seasonal holidays
>
> Class religious holidays of a specific season in 394.265; class comprehensive works in 394.26

.261	Holidays of December, January, February

> Class here wintertime holidays of the northern hemisphere, summertime holidays of the southern hemisphere

.261 2	Kwanzaa
.261 4	New Year
.261 8	Valentine's Day
.262	Holidays of March, April, May

> Class here springtime holidays of the northern hemisphere, autumn holidays of the southern hemisphere

.262 7	May Day

> Class here May Day as a springtime festival, as a labor holiday

.262 8	Mother's Day
	Class here Mothering Sunday
.263	Holidays of June, July, August
	Class here summertime holidays of the northern hemisphere, wintertime holidays of the southern hemisphere
.263 4	Fourth of July
.263 5	Bastille Day
.264	Holidays of September, October, November
	Class here autumn holidays of the northern hemisphere, springtime holidays of the southern hemisphere
.264 4	Oktoberfest
.264 6	Halloween
.264 9	Thanksgiving
.265	Religious holidays
	Add to base number 394.265 the numbers following 29 in 292–299 for the religion only, e.g., Hindu holidays 394.26545; however, for Jewish holidays, see 394.267
	Class secular holidays with a religious or quasi-religious origin in 394.261–394.264
	For Christian holidays, see 394.266
	See Manual at 203.6, 263.9, 292–299 vs. 394.265–394.267
.266	Christian holidays
	Holidays of the church year
	For pre-Lenten festivals, see 394.25
.266 3	Christmas
.266 7	Easter
.267	Jewish holidays
.269	History, geographic treatment, biography
	Class history, geographic treatment, biography of specific holidays and of specific kinds of holidays in 394.261–394.267
.269 01–.269 05	Historical periods
	Add to base number 394.2690 the numbers following —090 in notation 0901–0905 from Table 1, e.g., holidays in 20th century 394.26904
.269 1–.269 9	Geographical treatment, biography
	Add to base number 394.269 notation 1–9 from Table 2, e.g., holidays of Mexico 394.26972

.3   **Recreational customs**

>   Including dances, gambling, games, toys

.4   **Official ceremonies and observances**

>   Including coronations, inaugurations, jubilees, state visits, triumphs

>   *For military ceremonies, see 355.17*

.5   **Pageants, processions, parades**

>   Class planning, promoting, staging of pageants, processions, parades in 791.6.
>   Class pageants, processions, parades associated with a specific activity with the
>   activity, e.g., Thanksgiving Day parades 394.2649

.6   **Fairs**

.7   **Customs of chivalry**

.8   **Dueling and suicide**

>   Standard subdivisions are added for dueling and suicide together, for dueling
>   alone

.88   Suicide

.9   **Cannibalism**

395   **Etiquette (Manners)**

>   Prescriptive and practical works on social behavior

>   Unless other instructions are given, class a subject with aspects in two or more
>   subdivisions of 395 in the number coming last, e.g., table manners for children
>   395.54 (*not* 395.122)

>   Class customs in 391–394

>   *For protocol of diplomacy, see 327.2*

[.081–.084]   People by gender or sex; age groups

>   Do not use; class in 395.1

.1   **Etiquette for people by gender or sex; for age groups**

.12   Etiquette for age groups

.122   Children

>   From birth through age eleven

.123   Young people twelve to twenty

>   Variant names: adolescents, teenagers, young adults, youth

>   Class comprehensive works on young adults in 395.124

.123 2   Males twelve to twenty

.123 3   Females twelve to twenty

.124	People in early adulthood

Class here comprehensive works on young adults

For young adults under twenty-one, see 395.123

.124 1	Young men
.124 2	Young women
.126	Adults aged sixty-five and over
.14	Etiquette for people by gender or sex

Class etiquette for age groups regardless of gender or sex in 395.12

.142	Male
.144	Female
.2	**Etiquette for stages in life cycle**
.22	Engagements and weddings
.23	Funerals
.24	Occasions associated with birth, puberty, majority

Including christening, confirmation, bar mitzvah, debut

.3	**Etiquette for social occasions**

Including dances

Class here hospitality and entertainment

Class etiquette for stages in life cycle in 395.2; class invitations in 395.4

.4	**Social correspondence**

Including invitations and announcements

Class here written and spoken styles and forms of address and greeting

.5	**Etiquette by situations**

Including online, school, sports etiquette

.52	Business and office etiquette
.53	Public behavior

Including etiquette in church, at theater, in stores and shops

.54	Table manners
.59	Conversation

Class here telephone etiquette

[396]	**[Unassigned]**

Most recently used in Edition 16

[397]   [Unassigned]

Most recently used in Edition 16

398   Folklore

See also 201.3 for religious mythology; also 800 for belles-lettres by identifiable authors, anonymous literary classics

SUMMARY

398.09	History, geographic treatment, biography of folklore
.2	Folk literature
.3	Real phenomena as subjects of folklore
.4	Paranatural and legendary phenomena as subjects of folklore
.6	Riddles
.7	Jokes and jests
.8	Rhymes and rhyming games
.9	Proverbs

.09   History, geographic treatment, biography of folklore

For history, geographic treatment, biography of folk literature, see 398.209

.2   **Folk literature**

Folklore as literature

Standard subdivisions may be added to subdivisions of this number for any topic even if the subject of the work does not approximate the whole, e.g., 18th century folktales about elves 398.2109033

Class here fairy tales, literary appraisal and criticism of folk literature; interdisciplinary works on mythology

Class an anonymous classic or a work by a known author with the classic or work in 800, e.g., Icelandic sagas 839.63, fairy tales by Hans Christian Andersen 839.8136

For religious mythology, see 201.3; for riddles, see 398.6; for jokes and jests, see 398.7; for rhymes and rhyming games, see 398.8; for proverbs, see 398.9; for folk poetry other than rhymes and rhyming games, see 808.81; for folk drama, see 808.82

See Manual at 398.2; also at 398.2 vs. 201.3, 230, 270, 292–299; also at 398.2 vs. 398.3–398.4; also at 800 vs. 398.2

.204   Folk literature by language

Add to base number 398.204 notation 1–9 from Table 6, e.g., folk tales from French-speaking areas of the world 398.20441; however, for tales of a specific language from an area where that language predominates, see the area in 398.209, e.g., French folk tales from France 398.20944, from Quebec 398.209714

.208   Groups of people

.208 9   Ethnic and national groups

Class here individual tales, collections of tales, lore on a specific topic

Class collections of tales or lore by ethnic and national groups from a specific continent, country, locality where they predominate with the continent, country, locality in 398.2093–398.2099, e.g., French tales and lore from France 398.20944, from Quebec 398.209714; class individual tales, collections of tales, lore on a specific topic by ethnic and national groups from a specific continent, country, locality where they predominate with the continent, country, locality in 398.2093–398.2099, plus the notation for the topic from table under 398.2093–398.2099, e.g., French tales and lore from France about witches 398.2094401, from Quebec about witches 398.20971401

.209   History, geographic treatment, biography

.209 3–.209 9   Specific continents, countries, localities

Class here individual tales, collections of tales, lore on a specific topic from a specific continent, country, locality; collections of tales and lore from a specific continent, country, locality; works consisting equally of the tales and lore and criticism of them

Unless other instructions are given in the add table below, observe the following table of preference, e.g., periodicals of statistics 0021 (*not* 005):

Tales and lore on a specific topic	01–08
Forecasting and forecasts	001
Museums, collections, exhibits	0074
Collecting folk literature	0075
Illustrations	0022
Statistics	0021
Serial publications	005

Add to base number 398.209 notation 3–9 from Table 2, e.g., folk literature of France 398.20944; then add further as follows (*not* as instructed under notation 093–099 from Table 1):

001	Forecasting and forecasts
002	Statistics and illustrations
0021	Statistics
0022	Illustrations
	Including cartoons, drawings, pictures, pictorial charts and designs, sketches; graphs; maps, plans, diagrams
	Class statistical drafts in notation 0021 from this table; class humorous cartoons in 398.2093–398.2099 without adding from this table
005	Serial publications
	Regardless of form (print or electronic) or frequency
	Class here house organs, magazines, newspapers, yearbooks
007	Museums, collections, exhibits; collecting objects
0074	Museums, collections, exhibits
	Class here exhibitions, fairs, festivals; catalogs, lists regardless of whether or not articles are offered for sale; guidebooks, history and description
	Add to 0074 notation 4–9 from Table 2, e.g., museums in Germany 007443
0075	Collecting folk literature
	Class here collectibles, memorabilia, price trends for collectors

.209 3–.209 9 Specific continents, countries, localities

01–08 Tales and lore on a specific topic

Class here literary criticism

Add to 0 the numbers following 398.2 in 398.21–398.28, e.g., animal tales 045

Class comprehensive works in the base number for the specific continent, country, locality in 398.2093–398.2099. Class comprehensive works on history and criticism of a specific topic with the topic in 398.3–398.4, e.g., history and criticism of tales and lore about witches 398.45

See Manual at 398.2 vs. 398.3–398.4

09 History and geographic treatment

Class here literary criticism

09005 Serial publications

0901–0905 Historical periods

Class here literary criticism

Add to 090 the numbers following —090 in notation 0901–0905 from Table 1, e.g., folk literature of Middle Ages 0902

091 Areas, regions, places in general

Add to 091 the numbers following —1 in notation 11–19 from Table 2, e.g., folk literature of urban regions 091732

093–099 Specific continents, countries, localities

Add to 09 notation 3–9 from Table 2, e.g., folk literature of United States 0973

Use to add notation for a specific continent, country, locality when first area notation is used to specify area of origin of the tales and lore, while second one identifies area in which the tales and lore are discussed or modified, e.g., French tales 398.20944, Haitian version of French tales 398.20944097294

(Option: Class individual tales, collections of tales, lore on a specific topic from a specific continent, country, locality in 398.21–398.28)

> 398.21–398.28 Tales and lore on a specific topic

Add to each subdivision identified by * as follows:
01–07 Standard subdivisions
08 Groups of people
[089] Individual tales, collections of tales, lore on a specific topic by ethnic and national groups
Do not use; class in 398.2089
(Option: Continue to use 089; prefer 398.2089)
09 History, geographic treatment, biography
Class here literary criticism
Class comprehensive works on history and criticism of a specific topic with the topic in 398.3–398.4, e.g., history and criticism of tales and lore about witches 398.45
See Manual at 398.2 vs. 398.3–398.4
[093–099] Individual tales, collections of tales, lore on a specific topic from a specific continent, country, locality
Do not use; class in 398.2093–398.2099
(Option: Continue to use 093–099; prefer 398.2093–398.2099)

Class comprehensive works in 398.2

.21 *Tales and lore of paranatural beings of human and semihuman form

For werewolves, see 398.2454; for ghosts, see 398.25

See also 398.2 for comprehensive works on fairy tales (tales of paranatural beings)

.22 *Tales and lore of persons without paranormal powers

Class here legendary or mythological persons

.23 *Tales and lore of places and times

Class historical and quasi-historical events in 398.27

.232 *Real places

Class tales of real places at special times in 398.236

See also 398.209 for tales originating in specific places

.232 1–.232 9 Specific places

Add to base number 398.232 notation 1–9 from Table 2, e.g., tales about India 398.23254; then add further as instructed under 398.21–398.28, e.g., 18th century tales about India 398.2325409033

.234 *Legendary places

.236 *Times

Class here holidays, seasons

*Add as instructed under 398.21–398.28

.24   *Tales and lore of plants and animals

             Class here agriculture

             Class comprehensive works on tales and lore involving science in 398.26

.242   *Plants

             Real and legendary

.245   *Animals

             See Manual at 800, T3C—362 vs. 398.245, 590, 636

.245 2   *Real animals

.245 22–.245 29   Specific animals

             Add to base number 398.2452 the numbers following 59 in 592–599, e.g., cats 398.24529752; then add further as instructed under 398.21–398.28, e.g., 18th century tales about cats 398.2452975209033

.245 4   *Legendary animals

.25   *Ghost stories

.26   *Tales and lore involving physical and natural phenomena

             Real and legendary

             Class here comprehensive works on tales and lore involving scientific and technical themes

             For tales and lore of plants and animals, see 398.24; for tales and lore involving technical themes, see 398.27

.27   *Tales and lore of humanity and human existence

             For tales and lore of persons without paranormal powers, see 398.22; for tales and lore of agriculture, see 398.24

.273–.278   Specific human, social, technical, artistic, recreational, literary, historical, political, military themes

             Add to base number 398.27 the numbers following —35 in notation 353–358 from Table 3C, e.g., tales of everyday life 398.275, of historical events 398.278; then add further as instructed under 398.21–398.28, e.g., 18th century tales about everyday life 398.27509033

.28   *Tales and lore of other topics

             Tales and lore not provided for elsewhere

*Add as instructed under 398.21–398.28

> ## 398.3–398.4 History and criticism of specific subjects of folklore

Standard subdivisions may be added to subdivisions of 398.3–398.4 for any topic even if the subject of the work does not approximate the whole, e.g., history and criticism of folktales from France about elves 398.450944

Limited to works without extended text of folk tales

Class here origin, role, function of themes and subjects of folklore as cultural and social phenomena

Class comprehensive works in 398.09. Class literary criticism of individual tales, collections of tales, lore on a specific topic by a specific ethnic or national group with the group in 398.2089, e.g., literary criticism of Navajo tales and lore about witches 398.20899726; class literary criticism of individual tales, collections of tales, lore on a specific topic from a specific continent, country, locality with the continent, country, locality in 398.2093–398.2099, plus the notation for the topic from table under 398.2093–398.2099, plus notation 09 from table under 398.21–398.28, e.g., literary criticism of French tales and lore about witches 398.209440109; class comprehensive treatment of literary criticism of tales or lore on a specific topic with the topic in 398.2, plus notation 09 from table under 398.21–398.28, e.g., literary criticism of tales and lore about witches 398.2109

See Manual at 398.2 vs. 398.3–398.4

.3   **Real phenomena as subjects of folklore**

.32   Places

.322   Physiographic regions

.329   Specific places

                Class historical and political themes, historical events in specific places in 398.358

[.329 01–.329 09]   Standard subdivisions

                Do not use; class in 398.3201–398.3209

.329 3–.329 9   Specific continents, countries, localities

                Add to base number 398.329 notation 3–9 from Table 2, e.g., London as a subject for folklore 398.329421

.33   Times

                Class here holidays, seasons

.35   Humanity and human existence

.352   Persons without paranormal powers

.353–.358   Specific human, social, technical, artistic, recreational, literary, historical, political, military themes

> Add to base number 398.35 the numbers following —35 in notation 353–358 from Table 3C, e.g., tales of historical events 398.358

> Class specific human, social, technical, artistic, recreational, literary, historical, political, military themes related to a specific kind of person without paranomal powers in 398.352; class specific human, social, technical, artistic, recreational, literary, historical, political, military themes related to paranatural beings of human and semihuman form in 398.45; class agriculture, comprehensive works on scientific and technical themes in 398.36

.36   Scientific themes

> Class here agriculture, nature, physical phenomena, comprehensive works on scientific and technical themes

> *For technical themes, see 398.356*

.362   Heavenly bodies

.363   Weather

.364   Fire and water

.365   Minerals

.368   Plants

> Add to base number 398.368 the numbers following 58 in 582–588, e.g., flowers 398.368213

.369   Animals

> Add to base number 398.369 the numbers following 59 in 592–599, e.g., rabbits 398.369932

.4   Paranatural and legendary phenomena as subjects of folklore

> Class here magic

> *See also 133.43 for magic in occultism*

.41   Folk beliefs

> Class here superstitions

.42   Legendary places

.45   Paranormal beings of human and semihuman form

> *For ghosts, see 398.47*

.46   Legendary minerals, plants, animals

.465   Minerals

> Class here philosopher's stone

.468   Plants

.469   Animals

.47   Ghosts

> Class here haunted places

.6   **Riddles**

> Class riddles as a type of puzzle similar to logic puzzles in 793.735; class riddles as jokes by known authors; interdisciplinary works on riddles in 808.882

> *See Manual at T3A—8 + 02, T3B—802, T3B—8 + 02 vs. 398.6, 793.735*

.7   **Jokes and jests**

> Standard subdivisions are added for either or both topics in heading

> Class here jokebooks, jestbooks

> Class jokes and jests by known authors, interdisciplinary works on jokes and jests in 808.882

> *See Manual at 800 vs. 398.2*

.8   **Rhymes and rhyming games**

> Standard subdivisions are added for either or both topics in heading

> Including jump rope rhymes, lullabies, tongue twisters

> Class here anonymous children's rhymes from the oral tradition, nursery rhymes

> Class interdisciplinary works on tongue twisters in 808.882. Class forms of folk poetry not provided for here with the form in 800, e.g., medieval metrical romances 808.8133

> *See Manual at 800 vs. 398.2*

[.808 3]   Young people

> Do not use; class in 398.8

.84   Counting-out rhymes (Counting rhymes)

.87   Street cries and songs

.9   **Proverbs**

> Class here folk aphorisms

> Add to base number 398.9 notation 1–9 from Table 6, e.g., French proverbs 398.941

> *See Manual at 800 vs. 398.2*

399   **Customs of war and diplomacy**

> Including dances, peace pipe

> Class protocol of diplomacy in 327.2; class customs of military life in 355.1; class cannibalism in 394.9

400

<hr>

400 Language

Class here interdisciplinary works on language and literature

> *For government policy on language, see 306.449; for literature, see 800; for rhetoric, see 808. For the language of a specific subject, see the subject, plus notation 014 from Table 1, e.g., language of science 501.4*

(Option A: To give local emphasis or a shorter number to a specific language, class in 410, where full instructions appear

(Option B: To give local emphasis or a shorter number to a specific language, place before 420 through use of a letter or other symbol. Full instructions appear under 420–490)

SUMMARY

401–409	**Standard subdivisions, international languages, special topics of languages**
410	**Linguistics**
420	**English and Old English (Anglo-Saxon)**
430	**German and related languages**
440	**French and related Romance languages**
450	**Italian, Dalmatian, Romanian, Rhaetian, Sardinian, Corsican**
460	**Spanish, Portuguese, Galician**
470	**Latin and related Italic languages**
480	**Classical Greek and related Hellenic languages**
490	**Other languages**

401 Philosophy and theory; international languages

Notation 01 from Table 1 as modified below

Class interdisciplinary works on philosophy of language in 121.68

.3 International languages

Class here universal languages; general discussions of international languages, e.g., diplomatic languages, lingua francas

Class artificial languages in 499.99. Class a specific international sign language with the language in 419, e.g., American Sign Language as a universal language 419.7; class other specific international languages with the language in 420–490, e.g., Latin as a diplomatic language 470, Swahili as a lingua franca 496.392

.4 **Communication; semantics, pragmatics, languages for special purposes**

Notation 014 from Table 1 as modified below

Class here lexicology, interdisciplinary works on terminology

Class interdisciplinary works on communication, content analysis, semiotics in 302.2. Class the semiotics of a specific subject with the subject, plus notation 014 from Table 1, e.g., semiotics of biology 570.14

For dictionaries of linguistics, see 410.3; for general polyglot dictionaries, see 413; for lexicography, see 413.028; for applied linguistics treatment of terminology, see 418. For terminology (including pronunciation and spelling) of a specific subject, see the subject, plus notation 014 from Table 1, e.g., terminology of linguistics 410.14, terminology of engineering 620.0014

See also 121.68 for semiotics as a topic in philosophy

.41 Discourse analysis

Including pragmatics in discourse analysis

Class discourse analysis of languages for special purposes in 401.47; class interdisciplinary works on pragmatics in 401.45. Class discourse analysis of a specific subject with the subject, plus notation 014 from Table 1, e.g., discourse analysis of political science 320.014

[.42] Etymology

Do not use; class in 412

.43 Semantics

For history of word meanings, see 412

See also 121.68 for semantics as a topic in philosophy; also 149.94 for general semantics as a philosophical school

See Manual at 401.43 vs. 306.44, 401.45, 401.9, 412, 415

.430 1 Philosophy and theory

Notation 01 from Table 1 as modified below

Do not use for schools and theories of semantics; class in 401.43018

See also 121.68 for semantics as a topic in philosophy; also 149.94 for general semantics as a philosophical school

.430 18 Schools, theories, methodologies

.430 182 Formal linguistics

Including generative semantics

.430 183 Functional linguistics

.430 183 5 Cognitive semantics

Class here frame semantics

.430 285 Computer applications

| .430 285 635 | Natural language processing |
| | Class here word sense disambiguation |

.45   **Pragmatics**

Class here interdisciplinary works on pragmatics

For pragmatics in sociolinguistics, see 306.44; for pragmatics in discourse analysis, see 401.41; for pragmatics in psycholinguistics, see 401.9

See Manual at 401.43 vs. 306.44, 401.45, 401.9, 412, 415

.452   **Speech acts**

Class here illocutionary acts

.454   **Presupposition**

Class here implication, entailment

Class presupposition, implication, entailment in logic in 160

.456   **Reference**

Class here anaphora, deixis; comprehensive works on reference

Class reference in philosophy of language in 121.68

.47   **Languages for special purposes**

Class here sublanguages, discourse analysis of languages for special purposes

Class teaching of languages for special purposes as second languages in 418.0071; class translation of languages for special purposes in 418.03. Class dictionaries of languages for special purposes with the purpose, plus notation 03 from Table 1, e.g., medical dictionaries 610.3

[.48]   **Abbreviations, acronyms, symbols**

Do not use for abbreviations, acronyms, symbols as part of writing systems; class in 411. Do not use for dictionaries of abbreviations, acronyms, symbols; class in 413.15

.5   **Scientific principles**

.51   **Mathematical principles**

Class mathematical linguistics in 410.151

.59   **Zoological principles**

Class here biolinguistics

Class evolutionary psychology of language in 401.9; class language acquisition from the viewpoint of psycholinguistics in 401.93. Class biolinguistics of a specific linguistic topic with the topic in 410, plus notation 0159 from Table 1, e.g., biolinguistics of grammar 415.0159

For medical aspects of biolinguistics, see the aspect in 610, e.g., neurolinguistics 612.82336

.9 **Psychological principles, language acquisition, speech perception**

Notation 019 from Table 1 as modified below

Including speech errors

Class here psycholinguistics

Class biolinguistics in 401.59; class speech errors in language acquisition in 401.93; class psychology of bilingualism in 404.2019

See also 306.44 for sociolinguistics

See Manual at 401.43 vs. 306.44, 401.45, 401.9, 412, 415

.93 Language acquisition

Class language acquisition from the viewpoint of biolinguistics in 401.59

See also 418.0071 for study and teaching of language; also 418.4019 for psychology of reading

See Manual at 407.1, T1—071 vs. 401.93, T4—019, 410.71, 418.0071, T4—80071

.95 Speech perception

See also 152.15 for auditory perception

402 Miscellany

.85 Computer applications

Class computational linguistics in 006.35

403 Dictionaries, encyclopedias, concordances

For dictionaries, encyclopedias, concordances of linguistics, see 410.3; for general polyglot dictionaries, see 413; for dictionaries, encyclopedias, concordances of literature, see 803

404 Special topics of language

.2 **Bilingualism**

Class here multilingualism

Specific instances of bilingualism are classed with the language dominant in the country in which the linguistic interaction occurs, e.g., a discussion of Spanish-English bilingualism in Los Angeles 420.42610979494. If neither language is dominant, class with the one coming later in 420–490 (if both languages are sign languages, class with the one coming later in 419)

See also 306.446 for sociology of bilingualism and multilingualism

405 Serial publications

406 Organizations and management

407   Education, research, related topics

See Manual at 407.1, T1—071 vs. 401.93, T4—019, 410.71, 418.0071,
T4—80071

.1   Education

See Manual at 407.1, T1—071 vs. 401.93, T4—019, 410.71, 418.0071,
T4—80071

.2   Research

.21   Research methods

Class corpus-based research methods in 410.188

408   Groups of people

See also 306.44 for sociology of language

.9   Treatment of language with respect to ethnic and national groups

Class ethnolinguistics in 306.44

409   Geographic treatment and biography

Do not use for language history not limited by area; class in 417.7

Class specific sign languages and groups of sign languages in 419; class other
specific languages and groups of languages in 420–490

See also 410.9 for geographic treatment and biography of linguistics

410   Linguistics

Class here descriptive, synchronic linguistics; comprehensive works on Eurasiatic
languages, on Indo-European languages, on Indo-Germanic languages, on
Indo-Hittite languages; interdisciplinary works on language documentation

Class linguistics of specific sign languages in 419; class linguistics of other specific
languages in 420–490

For sociolinguistics, language documentation as a response to endangerment of
languages,, see 306.44; for lexicology, semiotics, see 401.4; for semantics, see
401.43; for specific Indo-European languages other than east Indo-European
languages and Celtic languages, see 420–480; for east Indo-European and
Celtic languages, see 491

See Manual at 410

(Option A: To give local emphasis and a shorter number to a specific language,
e.g., Russian, class it here and add to base number 41 as instructed under 420–490;
in that case class linguistics in 400, its subdivisions in 401–409, standard
subdivisions of language and of linguistics in 400.1–400.9. Option B is described
under 420–490)

SUMMARY

410.1–.9	**Standard subdivisions**
411	**Writing systems of standard forms of languages**
412	**Etymology of standard forms of languages**
413	**Dictionaries of standard forms of languages**
414	**Phonology and phonetics of standard forms of languages**
415	**Grammar of standard forms of languages**
417	**Dialectology and historical linguistics**
418	**Applied linguistics**
419	**Sign languages**

.1   **Philosophy and theory**

Notation 01 from Table 1 as modified below

Do not use for philosophy and theory of language and languages; class in 401. Do not use for schools and theories of linguistics; class in 410.18

.151   Mathematical principles

Class here mathematical linguistics

.159   Zoological principles

Class biolinguistics in 401.59

.18   Schools, theories, methodologies

Add to base number 410.18 the numbers following —018 in notation 0181–0184 from Table 4, e.g., cognitive linguistics 410.1835

For works on schools, theories, methodologies that stress semantics, see 401.43018; for works on schools, theories, methodologies that stress phonology, see 414.018; for works on schools, theories, methodologies that stress syntax, or syntax and phonology, see 415.018

.188   Corpus linguistics

Including language data samples collected as corpora to support corpus-based analysis, corpus linguistics applied to texts in a specific subject

Class corpus linguistics applied to a specific topic in linguistics with the topic, e.g., corpus-based analysis of noun phrases 415.5; class corpus linguistics applied to a specific work or the works of a specific author with the work or author, e.g., versions of the Bible 220.4, Shakespeare's works 822.33

.19   Psychological principles

Class psycholinguistics in 401.9

.2   **Miscellany**

Do not use for miscellany of language and languages; class in 402

.285 Computer applications

> Class computational linguistics in 006.35; class computer applications in corpus linguistics in 410.188. Class a computational linguistics application of a linguistic process with the process, plus notation 0285635 from Table 1, e.g., part-of-speech tagging 415.0285635

> *See Manual at 006.35 vs. 410.285*

.3–.9 **Standard subdivisions**

> Do not use for standard subdivisions of language and languages; class in 403–409

> *See Manual at 407.1, T1—071 vs. 401.93, T4—019, 410.71, 418.0071, T4—80071*

411 Writing systems of standard forms of languages

> Including alphabets, ideographs, syllabaries; braille; abbreviations, acronyms, capitalization, punctuation, spelling, transliteration

> Class dictionaries of abbreviations and acronyms in 413.15; class writing systems of geographic variations, of modern nongeographic variations of languages in 417.2; class manual alphabets, fingerspelling in 418

> *See also 652 for practical works on how to write by hand or machine, e.g., penmanship 652.1*

.7 **Paleography and epigraphy**

> Study of ancient and medieval handwriting and inscriptions

> Standard subdivisions are added for either or both topics in heading

> *See also 417.7 for paleography covering all aspects of early writings*

412 Etymology of standard forms of languages

> Class etymology of geographic variations, of modern nongeographic variations of languages in 417.2; class comprehensive works on historical linguistics in 417.7; class interdisciplinary works on onomastics in 929.97. Class a specific aspect of etymology with the aspect, e.g., phonetic development of words 414

> *See Manual at 401.43 vs. 306.44, 401.45, 401.9, 412, 415*

413 Dictionaries of standard forms of languages

> Class here polyglot dictionaries

> Class dictionaries of geographic variations, of modern nongeographic variations of languages in 417.2

> *For bilingual dictionaries, see the language, plus notation 32–39 from Table 4, e.g., French-English dictionary 443.21*

.028 Auxiliary techniques and procedures; apparatus, equipment, materials

> Class here basic techniques and procedures; lexicography

.1   **Specialized dictionaries**

Including synonym dictionaries

Class dictionaries of eponyms, etymological dictionaries in 412.03. Class subject dictionaries with the subject, plus notation 03 from Table 1, e.g., dictionary of medicine 610.3

For crossword-puzzle dictionaries, see 793.73203

.15   Dictionaries of abbreviations, acronyms, symbols

Standard subdivisions are added for any or all topics in heading

Class subject dictionaries of abbreviations, acronyms, symbols with the subject, plus notation 0148 from Table 1, e.g., dictionary of scientific abbreviations and acronyms 501.48

.17   Picture dictionaries

Limited to dictionaries with pictures of what words represent

See also 419.03 for dictionaries with pictures of sign-language signs

.2–.9   **Polyglot dictionaries with entry words or definitions in only one language**

Add to base number 413 notation 2–9 from Table 6, e.g., a dictionary with terms in English, French, and German, but with definitions only in English 413.21

414   **Phonology and phonetics of standard forms of languages**

Standard subdivisions are added for phonology and phonetics together, for phonology alone

Class here consonants, vowels; morphophonology, morphophonemics, phonemics

Class phonology and phonetics of geographic variations, of modern nongeographic variations of languages in 417.2; class comprehensive works on phonology, morphology, syntax; on phonology and morphology; on phonology and syntax in 415

.01   Philosophy and theory

Notation 01 from Table 1 as modified below

Do not use for schools and theories of phonology; class in 414.018

.018   Schools, theories, methodologies

.018 2   Formal linguistics

Including generative phonology

.018 3   Functional linguistics

Including cognitive phonology

.6   **Suprasegmental features**

Phonology and phonetics of vocal effects extending over more than one sound element

Including juncture (pauses), pitch, stress

Class here intonation

.8   **Phonetics**

For phonetic aspects of suprasegmental features, see 414.6

415   Grammar of standard forms of languages

Class here grammatical categories, sentences, syntax, topic and comment; word order; comprehensive works on phonology, morphology, syntax; on phonology and morphology; on phonology and syntax

Class grammar of geographic variations, of modern nongeographic variations of languages in 417.2

Unless other instructions are given, class a subject with aspects in two or more subdivisions of 415 in the number coming last, e.g., number expressed by verbs 415.6 (*not* 415.5)

For phonology, see 414; for prescriptive grammar, see 418

See Manual at 401.43 vs. 306.44, 401.45, 401.9, 412, 415

.01   Philosophy and theory

Notation 01 from Table 1 as modified below

Do not use for schools and theories of grammar; class in 415.018

.018   Schools, theories, methodologies

Add to base number 415.018 the numbers following —5018 in notation 50181–50184 from Table 4, e.g., cognitive grammar 415.01835

.02   Miscellany

.028 5   Computer applications

.028 563 5   Natural language processing

Class here part-of-speech tagging, parsing

>   **415.5–415.7 Word classes**

Class here parts of speech

Class comprehensive works in 415

.5   **Nouns, pronouns, adjectives, articles**

Including case, gender, number, person

Class here noun phrases

.54   Nouns

.55   Pronouns

.6   **Verbs**

Including modality, mood, voice; comprehensive works on words derived from verbs, on infinitives, on participles

Class here verb phrases

Class works that treat a specific function (other than the verb function) of words derived from verbs with the function, e.g., gerunds as nouns 415.54

.62   Tense

.63   Aspect

.7   **Miscellaneous word classes**

Including conjunctions, interjections, particles, prepositions, prepositional phrases

Class clitics in 415.92

.76   Adverbs

Including adverbials

.9   **Morphology**

Class morphophonology, morphophonemics in 414

For morphology of specific word classes, see 415.5–415.7

.92   Word formation

Including affixes (infixes, prefixes, suffixes), clitics; formation of compound words

Class here derivational morphology

Class etymology in 412

.95   Inflection

For inflectional schemata designed for use as aids in learning a language, see 418

[416]   **[Unassigned]**

Most recently used in Edition 18

417   **Dialectology and historical linguistics**

.2   **Dialectology**

Including argot, cant, jargon, slang

Class here dialects, patois, provincialisms

Works on writing systems, etymology, dictionaries, phonology, phonetics, grammar, applied linguistics are classed here when applied to geographic variations, to modern nongeographic variations, e.g., morphology of geographic variations

.22 Pidgins, creoles, mixed languages

> Standard subdivisions are added for any or all topics in heading
>
> *See Manual at T4—7*

.7 **Historical linguistics (Diachronic linguistics)**

> Study of development of language over time
>
> Class here language history not limited by area, language change, paleography covering all aspects of early writings
>
> Class endangered languages in 306.44
>
>> *For change in and history of a specific element of language, see the element, e.g., paleography limited to study of ancient and medieval handwriting 411.7, grammar 415*
>>
>> *See also 409 for geographic treatment of language history; also 410.9 for history of linguistics*
>>
>> *See Manual at 410*

418 Applied linguistics

> Including prescriptive linguistics; comprehensive works on instruction in lipreading with respect to multiple languages, comprehensive works on use of signs and fingerspelling for manual coding of multiple standard spoken languages
>
> Class descriptive linguistics in 411–415; class dictionaries in 413; class lexicography in 413.028; class applied linguistics applied to geographic variations, to modern nongeographic variations of languages in 417.2
>
>> *For use of signs and fingerspelling for manual coding of a specific spoken language, see the language, plus notation 891 from Table 4, e.g., use of signs and fingerspelling to represent standard English 428.91, use of British Sign Language signs to represent standard English 428.9141; for lipreading a specific language, see the language, plus notation 8954 from Table 4, e.g., lipreading English 428.954; for a specific aspect of applied linguistics provided for elsewhere, see the aspect, e.g., language for special purposes 401.47, rhetoric 808.04*

.001–.006 Standard subdivisions

.007 Education, research, related topics

.007 1 Education

> Class here second language teaching
>
>> *See Manual at 407.1, T1—071 vs. 401.93, T4—019, 410.71, 418.0071, T4—80071*

.008–.009 Standard subdivisions

.02 Translating

> Class here interpreting
>
>> *For translating materials on specific subjects, see 418.03; for translating literature (belles-lettres) and rhetoric, see 418.04*

.020 285 Computer applications

.020 285 635		Natural language processing

Class here machine translation

.03   Translating materials on specific subjects

Class here interpreting materials on specific subjects

Add to base number 418.03 three-digit numbers 001–999 (but stop before any zero that follows a non-zero number), e.g., translating natural history materials 418.035 (*not* 418.03508), translating medical materials 418.0361

Class translating a specific work or the works of a specific author with the work, translations of the work, or author, e.g., translating the Bible 220, translating the Bible into English 220.52, translating the works of Aristotle 185

For translating literature (belles-lettres) and rhetoric, see 418.04

.04   Translating literature (belles-lettres) and rhetoric

Class here interpreting literature and rhetoric, translating works about literature, rhetoric

Class translating a specific work or works of a specific author with the work or author, e.g., translating the Aeneid 873.01, translating the works of Shakespeare 822.33

.041–.048   Translating specific forms of literature

Add to base number 418.04 one-digit notation 1–8 from Table 3B, e.g., translating poetry 418.041, translating tragedy 418.042 (*not* 418.0420512)

.07   Multilingual phrase books

.4   Reading

419   Sign languages

Class here comprehensive works on fingerspelling, use of fingerspelling as part of sign languages

Class nonlinguistic (nonstructured) communication (e.g., use of gestures) in 302.222

For comprehensive works on use of signs and fingerspelling for manual coding of multiple standard spoken languages, see 418; for use of signs and fingerspelling for manual coding of specific standard spoken languages, see notation 891 from Table 4

.03   Dictionaries, encyclopedias, concordances

Class a dictionary of a specific sign language with the language, e.g., dictionary of American Sign Language 419.703

.09   History, geographic treatment, biography

[.094–.099]   Specific continents, countries, localities in modern world

> Do not use for sign languages used primarily for purposes other than communication among deaf people or between hearing and deaf people; class in 419.1. Do not use for sign languages used primarily for communication among deaf people or between hearing and deaf people; class in 419.4–419.9. Do not use for comprehensive works on all types of sign languages; class in 419

.1   **Sign languages used primarily for purposes other than communication of deaf people**

> Including monastic sign languages, sign languages used as lingua francas among hearing people

> (Option: To give local emphasis and a shorter number to a specific sign language used primarily for purposes other than communication of deaf people, class it in 419.3. Prefer 419.1)

(.3)   **Specific sign language**

> (Optional number; prefer 419.1 or 419.4–419.9)

.4–.9   **Sign languages used primarily for communication among deaf people or between hearing and deaf people**

> Class here indigenous sign languages of deaf communities, comprehensive works on methods of communication of deaf-blind people

> Add to base number 419 notation 4–9 from Table 2, e.g., British Sign Language 419.41, Spanish Sign Language 419.46, Catalonian Sign Language 419.467, American Sign Language 419.7; then for a specific sign language add 0 and to the result add further as instructed at beginning of Table 4, e.g., grammar of British Sign Language 419.4105, grammar of Spanish Sign Language 419.4605, grammar of Catalonian Sign Language 419.46705, grammar of American Sign Language 419.705

> Class sign languages used primarily for purposes other than communication of deaf people in 419.1

> *For braille, see 411*

> (Option: To give local emphasis and a shorter number to a specific sign language used primarily for communication among deaf people or between hearing and deaf people, class it in 419.3. Prefer 419.4–419.9)

> ## 420–490 Specific languages

Class here comprehensive works on specific languages and their literatures

Except for modifications shown under specific entries, add to base number for each language identified by * as instructed at beginning of Table 4, e.g., grammar of Japanese 495.65. The base number is the number given for the language unless the schedule specifies a different number
> (Option: For any group of languages, add notation 04 to the base number and then add as instructed at beginning of Table 4, e.g., grammar of Celtic languages 491.6045)

The numbers used in this schedule for individual languages do not necessarily correspond exactly with those in 810–890 or with notation in Table 6. Use notation from Table 6 only when so instructed, e.g., at 494

Class language documentation as a response to endangerment of languages in 306.44; class polyglot dictionaries in 413; class comprehensive works on specific languages, interdisciplinary works on language documentation in 410

For specific sign languages, see 419; for literatures of specific languages, see 810–890

See Manual at 420–490

(Option B: To give local emphasis and a shorter number to a specific language, place it first by use of a letter or other symbol, e.g., Arabic language 4A0 [preceding 420], for which the base number is 4A. Option A is described under 410)

> ## 420–480 Specific Indo-European languages other than east Indo-European languages and Celtic languages

Class comprehensive works on Indo-European languages in 410

420   English and Old English (Anglo-Saxon)

.1–.9   Standard subdivisions of English

Notation from Table 1 as modified under —01–09 in Table 4, e.g., semantics of English 420.143

421–428 Subdivisions of English

Class here comprehensive works on English and Old English (Anglo-Saxon)

Except for modifications shown under specific entries, add to base number 42 notation 1–8 from Table 4, e.g., phonology of English 421.5

For Old English (Anglo-Saxon), see 429

421   Writing system, phonology, phonetics of standard English

Number built according to instructions under 421–428

.52	Spelling (Orthography) and pronunciation

Number built according to instructions under 421–428

Including standard Canadian spelling and pronunciation

For standard American (U.S.) spelling and pronunciation, see 421.54; for standard British spelling and pronunciation, see 421.55

.54	Standard American (U.S.) spelling and pronunciation
.55	Standard British spelling and pronunciation

422 Etymology of standard English

Number built according to instructions under 421–428

423 Dictionaries of standard English

Number built according to instructions under 421–428

[424] [Unassigned]

Most recently used in Edition 16

425 Grammar of standard English

Number built according to instructions under 421–428

[426] [Unassigned]

Most recently used in Edition 18

427 Historical and geographic variations, modern nongeographic variations of English

Number built according to instructions under 421–428

For Old English (Anglo-Saxon), see 429

.001–.008	Standard subdivisions
.009	History, geographic treatment, biography
[.009 02]	6th–15th centuries, 500–1499

Do not use for Middle English; class in 427.02

[.009 4–.009 9]	Specific continents, countries, localities in modern world

Do not use; class in 427.9

.02	Middle English, 1100–1500

See also 429 for Old English (Anglo-Saxon)

.9	**Geographic variations**
[.901–.909]	Standard subdivisions

Do not use; class in 427.001–427.009

.91 Geographic variations in areas, regions, places in general

> Add to base number 427.91 the numbers following —1 in notation 11–19 from Table 2, e.g., dialects of the British empire 427.9171241

.94–.99 Geographic variations in specific continents, countries, localities in modern world

> Add to base number 427.9 notation 4–9 from Table 2, e.g.,slang of British Isles 427.941, geographic variations in England 427.942, dialects of Canada 427.971, Tok Pisin 427.9953

> *For geographic variations of Middle English, see 427.02094–427.02099*

428 Standard English usage (Prescriptive linguistics)

> Number built according to instructions under 421–428

> Class here Basic English

429 *Old English (Anglo-Saxon)

> *See also 427.02 for Middle English*

430 German and related languages

> Class here Germanic languages

> *For English and Old English (Anglo-Saxon), see 420*

.01–.03 Standard subdivisions of Germanic languages

> Notation from Table 1 as modified under —01–03 in Table 4, e.g., semantics of Germanic languages 430.0143

.04 Special topics of Germanic languages

> Add to base number 430.04 notation 1–8 from Table 4, e.g., grammar of Germanic languages 430.045

.05–.09 Standard subdivisions of Germanic languages

.1–.9 Standard subdivisions of German

> Notation from Table 1 as modified under —01–09 in Table 4, e.g., semantics of German 430.143

431–438 Subdivisions of German

> Except for modifications shown under specific entries, add to base number 43 notation 1–8 from Table 4, e.g., phonology of German 431.5

431 Writing systems, phonology, phonetics of standard German

> Number built according to instructions under 431–438

432 Etymology of standard German

> Number built according to instructions under 431–438

---

*Add to base number as instructed under 420–490

433   **Dictionaries of standard German**

Number built according to instructions under 431–438

[434]   **[Unassigned]**

Most recently used in Edition 16

435   **Grammar of standard German**

Number built according to instructions under 431–438

.6   **German language — verbs**

[436]   **[Unassigned]**

Most recently used in Edition 18

437   **Historical and geographic variations, modern nongeographic variations of German**

Number built according to instructions under 431–438

Class Low German in 439.4

.001–.008   Standard subdivisions

.009   History, geographic treatment, biography

[.009 02]   6th-15th centuries, 500–1499

Do not use for Old High German; class in 437.01. Do not use for Middle High German and Early New High German; class in 437.02

[.009 4–.009 9]   Specific continents, countries, localities in modern world

Do not use; class in 437.9

.01   Old High German to 1100

.02   Middle High German and Early New High German, 1100–1500

Standard subdivisions are added for either or both topics in heading

.9   **Geographic variations**

See also 439.1 for Yiddish

[.901–.909]   Standard subdivisions

Do not use; class in 437.001–437.009

.91   Geographic variations in areas, regions, places in general

Add to base number 437.91 the numbers following —1 in notation 11–19 from Table 2, e.g., dialects of rural regions 437.91734

.94–.99   Geographic variations in specific continents, countries, localities in modern world

> Add to base number 437.9 notation 4–9 from Table 2, e.g., geographic variations in Germany 437.943, German dialects of Alsace 437.94439

> *For geographic variations of Old High German, see 437.01094–437.01099; for geographic variations of Middle High German and Early New High, see 437.02094–437.02099*

438   Standard German usage (Prescriptive linguistics)

> Number built according to instructions under 431–438

439   Other Germanic languages

.1   *Yiddish

>   **439.2–439.4 Low Germanic languages**

> Class here West Germanic languages

> Class comprehensive works in 439

.2   ***Frisian**

> Including Old Frisian

.3   **Netherlandish languages**

.31   *Dutch

> Including Old Low Franconian

> Class here Flemish

.36   *Afrikaans

.4   ***Low German (Plattdeutsch)**

> Including Old Low German, Old Saxon

.5   **North Germanic languages**

> Including proto-Scandinavian language

> Class here comprehensive works on east Scandinavian languages, comprehensive works on west Scandinavian languages, comprehensive works on modern west Scandinavian languages; comprehensive works on languages in the Nordic countries

> *For specific North Germanic languages, see 439.6–439.8; for Finnish, see 494.541; for Sámi, see 494.57*

>   **439.6–439.8 Specific North Germanic languages**

> Class comprehensive works in 439.5

*Add to base number as instructed under 420–490

.6   **Old Norse (Old Icelandic), Icelandic, Faroese**

Class comprehensive works on west Scandinavian languages in 439.5

.601–.609   Standard subdivisions of Old Norse (Old Icelandic), Icelandic,
                Faroese together; of Old Norse (Old Icelandic) alone

> Notation from Table 1 as modified under —01–09 in Table 4, e.g.,
> semantics of Old Norse 439.60143

.61–.68   Subdivisions of Old Norse (Old Icelandic)

> Add to base number 439.6 notation 1–8 from Table 4, e.g., grammar of Old
> Norse 439.65

.69   Icelandic and Faroese

> Icelandic ca. 1500–

> Class comprehensive works on modern west Scandinavian languages in
> 439.5

.690 1–.690 9   Standard subdivisions of Icelandic and Faroese together; of Icelandic
                alone

> Notation from Table 1 as modified under —01–09 in Table 4, e.g.,
> semantics of Icelandic 439.690143

.691–.698   Subdivisions of Icelandic

> Add to base number 439.69 notation 1–8 from Table 4, e.g., grammar of
> Icelandic 439.695

.699   *Faroese

.7   ***Swedish**

.77   Historical and geographic variations, modern nongeographic variations

> Number built according to instructions under 420–490

.770 01–.770 09   Standard subdivisions

[.770 090 1]   To 499 A.D.

> Do not use; class in 439.5

[.770 090 2]   6th-15th centuries, 500–1499

> Do not use for proto-Nordic language; class in 439.5. Do
> not use for Old Swedish; class in 439.7701

[.770 094–.770 099]   Specific continents, countries, localities in modern world

> Do not use; class in 439.779

.770 1   Old Swedish to 1526

.779   Geographic variations

[.779 01–.779 09]   Standard subdivisions

> Do not use; class in 439.77001–439.77009

*Add to base number as instructed under 420–490

.779 1	Geographic variations in areas, regions, places in general
	Add to base number 439.7791 the numbers following —1 in notation 11–19 from Table 2, e.g., dialects of rural regions 439.7791734
.779 4–.779 9	Geographic variations in specific continents, countries, localities in modern world
	Add to base number 439.779 notation 4–9 from Table 2, e.g., geographic variations in Sweden 439.779485, dialects of Finland 439.7794897

.8 Danish and Norwegian

.81	*Danish
	Class Dano-Norwegian in 439.82
.817	Historical and geographic variations, modern nongeographic variations
	Number built according to instructions under 420–490
.817 001–.817 009	Standard subdivisions
[.817 009 01]	To 499 A.D.
	Do not use; class in 439.5
[.817 009 02]	6th-15th centuries, 500–1499
	Do not use for proto-Nordic language; class in 439.5. Do not use for Old Danish; class in 439.81701
[.817 009 4–.817 009 9]	Specific continents, countries, localities in modern world
	Do not use; class in 439.8179
.817 01	Old Danish to 1500
.817 9	Geographic variations
[.817 901–.817 909]	Standard subdivisions
	Do not use; class in 439.817001–439.817009
.817 91	Geographic variations in areas, regions, places in general
	Add to base number 439.81791 the numbers following —1 in notation 11–19 from Table 2, e.g., dialects of rural regions 439.81791734
.817 94–.817 99	Geographic variations in specific continents, countries, localities in modern world
	Add to base number 439.8179 notation 4–9 from Table 2, e.g., geographic variations in Denmark 439.8179489, dialects of Germany 439.817943
.82	*Norwegian
	Class here Bokmål, Dano-Norwegian, Riksmål; New Norse, Landsmål

*Add to base number as instructed under 420–490

.827   Historical and geographic variations, modern nongeographic variations

> Number built according to instructions under 420–490

.827 001–.827 009   Standard subdivisions

[.827 009 01]   To 499 A.D.

> Do not use; class in 439.5

[.827 009 02]   6th-15th centuries, 500–1499

> Do not use for proto-Nordic language; class in 439.5.
> Do not use for Old Norse; class in 439.6. Do not use for
> Middle Norwegian; class in 439.82702

.827 009 03   Modern period, 1500–

> Do not use for Middle Norwegian; class in 439.82702

[.827 009 4–.827 009 9]   Specific continents, countries, localities in modern world

> Do not use; class in 439.8279

.827 02   Middle Norwegian, 1350–1525

.827 9   Geographic variations

[.827 901–.827 909]   Standard subdivisions

> Do not use; class in 439.827001–439.827009

.827 91   Geographic variations in areas, regions, places in general

> Add to base number 439.82791 the numbers following —1
> in notation 11–19 from Table 2, e.g., dialects of rural regions
> 439.82791734

.827 94–.827 99   Geographic variations in specific continents, countries, localities in modern world

> Add to base number 439.8279 notation 4–9 from Table 2, e.g.,
> geographic variations in Norway 439.8279481, dialects of United
> States 439.827973

.9   **East Germanic languages**

> Including Burgundian, Gothic, Vandalic

440   French and related Romance languages

Class here Romance languages

Class comprehensive works on Italic languages in 470

> *For Italian, Dalmatian, Romanian, Rhaetian, Sardinian, Corsican, see 450; for
> Spanish, Portuguese, Galician, see 460*

.01–.03   Standard subdivisions of Romance languages

> Notation from Table 1 as modified under —01–03 in Table 4, e.g., semantics
> of Romance languages 440.0143

.04	Special topics of Romance languages

> Add to base number 440.04 notation 1–8 from Table 4, e.g., grammar of Romance languages 440.045

.05–.09	Standard subdivisions of Romance languages
.1–.9	**Standard subdivisions of French**

> Notation from Table 1 as modified under —01–09 in Table 4, e.g., semantics of French 440.143

441–448   Subdivisions of French

> Except for modifications shown under specific entries, add to base number 44 notation 1–8 from Table 4, e.g., phonology of French 441.5

441   Writing systems, phonology, phonetics of standard French

> Number built according to instructions under 441–448

442   Etymology of standard French

> Number built according to instructions under 441–448

443   Dictionaries of standard French

> Number built according to instructions under 441–448

[444]   [Unassigned]

> Most recently used in Edition 16

445   Grammar of standard French

> Number built according to instructions under 441–448

.6	**French language — verbs**

[446]   [Unassigned]

> Most recently used in Edition 18

447   Historical and geographic variations, modern nongeographic variations of French

> Number built according to instructions under 441–448

> *See also 449 for Occitan, Franco-Provençal*

.001–.008	Standard subdivisions
.009	History, geographic treatment, biography
[.009 02]	6th-15th centuries, 500–1499

> Do not use for Old French; class in 447.01. Do not use for Middle French; class in 447.02

[.009 031]	16th century, 1500–1599

> Do not use; class in 447.02

[.009 4–.009 9]	Specific continents, countries, localities in modern world

Do not use; class in 447.9

.01   Old French to 1400

.02   Middle French, 1400–1600

.9   Geographic variations

[.901–.909]   Standard subdivisions

Do not use; class in 447.001–447.009

.91   Geographic variations in areas, regions, places in general

Add to base number 447.91 the numbers following —1 in notation 11–19 from Table 2, e.g., dialects of the overseas regions of the French Republic 447.9171244

.94–.99   Geographic variations in specific continents, countries, localities in modern world

Add to base number 447.9 notation 4–9 from Table 2, e.g., geographic variations in France 447.944, dialects of Quebec 447.9714, Haitian Creole 447.97294

For geographic variations of Old French, see 447.01094–447.01099; for geographic variations of Middle French, see 447.02094–447.02099

See also 449.709449 for Provençal dialect of Occitan; also 459.984 for Corsican

448   Standard French usage (Prescriptive linguistics)

Number built according to instructions under 441–448

.2

449   Occitan, Catalan, Franco-Provençal

Class here Langue d'oc; Provençal (Occitan)

Class Provençal (dialect of Occitan) in 449.709449

.01–.09   Standard subdivisions of Occitan, Langue d'oc

Notation from Table 1 as modified under —01–09 in Table 4, e.g., semantics of Occitan 449.0143
Subdivisions are added for either or both topics in heading

.1–.8   Subdivisions of Occitan, Langue d'oc

Add to base number 449 notation 1–8 from Table 4, e.g., grammar of Occitan 449.5
Subdivisions are added for either or both topics in heading

.709 449   Provençal dialect

Number built according to instructions under 449.1–449.8

Class Provençal (Occitan) in 449

See also 449 for Franco-Provençal

.9   ***Catalan**

450   Italian, Dalmatian, Romanian, Rhaetian, Sardinian, Corsican

> Class Dalmatian in 457.94972; class comprehensive works on Romance languages in 440; class comprehensive works on Italic languages in 470

.1–.9   Standard subdivisions of Italian

> Notation from Table 1 as modified under —01–09 in Table 4, e.g., semantics of Italian 450.143

451–458 Subdivisions of Italian

> Except for modifications shown under specific entries, add to base number 45 notation 1–8 from Table 4, e.g., phonology of Italian 451.5

451   Writing systems, phonology, phonetics of standard Italian

> Number built according to instructions under 451–458

452   Etymology of standard Italian

> Number built according to instructions under 451–458

453   Dictionaries of standard Italian

> Number built according to instructions under 451–458

[454]   [Unassigned]

> Most recently used in Edition 16

455   Grammar of standard Italian

> Number built according to instructions under 451–458

[456]   [Unassigned]

> Most recently used in Edition 18

457   Historical and geographic variations, modern nongeographic variations of Italian

> Number built according to instructions under 451–458

.001–.008   Standard subdivisions

.009   History, geographic treatment, biography

[.009 02]   6th-15th centuries, 500–1499

> Do not use for Old Italian; class in 457.01. Do not use for Middle Italian; class in 457.02

[.009 031]   16th century, 1500–1599

> Do not use; class in 457.02

---

*Add to base number as instructed under 420–490

[.009 4–.009 9]	Specific continents, countries, localities in modern world

> Do not use; class in 457.1–457.9

.01	Old Italian to 1300
.02	Middle Italian, 1300–1600

.9   Geographic variations

[.901–.909]	Standard subdivisions

> Do not use; class in 457.001–457.009

.91	Geographic variations in areas, regions, places in general

> Add to base number 457.91 the numbers following —1 in notation 11–19 from Table 2, e.g., dialects of rural regions 457.91734

.94–.99	Geographic variations in specific continents, countries, localities in modern world

> Add to base number 457.9 notation 4–9 from Table 2, e.g., geographic variations in Italy 457.945, Dalmatian language 457.94972

> *For geographic variations of Old Italian, see 457.01094–457.01099; for geographic variations of Middle Italian, see 457.02094–457.02099*

458   Standard Italian usage (Prescriptive linguistics)

> Number built according to instructions under 451–458

459   Romanian, Rhaetian, Sardinian, Corsican

.01–.09	Standard subdivisions of Romanian

> Notation from Table 1 as modified under —01–09 in Table 4, e.g., semantics of Romanian 459.0143

.1–.8   Subdivisions of Romanian

> Add to base number 459 notation 1–8 from Table 4, e.g., grammar of Romanian 459.5

.9   Rhaetian languages; Sardinian, Corsican

.92	*Friulian language
.94	*Ladin language

> *See also 467.9496 for Judeo-Spanish (Ladino)*

.96	*Romansch language
.98	Sardinian and Corsican
.982	*Sardinian
.982 7	Historical and geographic variations, modern nongeographic variations

> Number built according to instructions under 420–490

*Add to base number as instructed under 420–490

| [.982 709 459 1–.982 709 459 4] | Treatment by localities in Sardinia |
| | Do not use; class in 459.98271–459.98274 |

.982 71   Geographic variations in Cagliari province of Sardinia

.982 72   Geographic variations in Nuoro province of Sardinia

.982 73   Geographic variations in Sassari province of Sardinia

.982 74   Geographic variations in Oristano province of Sardinia

.984   *Corsican

460   Spanish, Portuguese, Galician

Class comprehensive works on Romance languages in 440

.01–.09   Standard subdivisions of comprehensive works on Spanish, Portuguese, Galician

.1–.9   Standard subdivisions of Spanish

Notation from Table 1 as modified under —01–09 in Table 4, e.g., semantics of Spanish 460.143

461–468 Subdivisions of Spanish

Except for modifications shown under specific entries, add to base number 46 notation 1–8 from Table 4, e.g., phonology of Spanish 461.5

461   Writing systems, phonology, phonetics of standard Spanish

Number built according to instructions under 461–468

462   Etymology of standard Spanish

Number built according to instructions under 461–468

463   Dictionaries of standard Spanish

Number built according to instructions under 461–468

[464]   [Unassigned]

Most recently used in Edition 16

465   Grammar of standard Spanish

Number built according to instructions under 461–468

[466]   [Unassigned]

Most recently used in Edition 18

467   Historical and geographic variations, modern nongeographic variations of Spanish

Number built according to instructions under 461–468

*Add to base number as instructed under 420–490

.001–.008	Standard subdivisions
.009	History, geographic treatment, biography
[.009 02]	6th-15th centuries, 500–1499

> Do not use for Old Spanish; class in 467.01. Do not use for Middle Spanish; class in 467.02

[.009 031]	16th century, 1500–1599

> Do not use; class in 467.02

[.009 4–.009 9]	Specific continents, countries, localities in modern world

> Do not use; class in 467.9

.01	Old Spanish to 1100
.02	Middle Spanish, 1100–1600
.9	**Geographic variations**
[.901–.909]	Standard subdivisions

> Do not use; class in 467.001–467.009

.91	Geographic variations in areas, regions, places in general

> Add to base number 467.91 the numbers following —1 in notation 11–19 from Table 2, e.g., dialects of rural regions 467.91734

.94–.99	Geographic variations in specific continents, countries, localities in modern world

> Add to base number 467.9 notation 4–9 from Table 2, e.g., geographic variations in Spain 467.946, Judeo-Spanish (Ladino) 467.9496, Papiamento 467.972986, Latin American dialects 467.98

> *For geographic variations of Old Spanish, see 467.01094–467.01099; for geographic variations of Middle Spanish, see 467.02094–467.02099*

468 Standard Spanish usage (Prescriptive linguistics)

> Number built according to instructions under 461–468

469 Portuguese

.01–.09	Standard subdivisions of Portuguese

> Notation from Table 1 as modified under —01–09 in Table 4, e.g., semantics of Portuguese 469.0143

.1–.5 Subdivisions of Portuguese

> Except for modifications shown under specific entries, add to base number 469 notation 1–5 from Table 4, e.g., phonology of Portuguese 469.15

.7 Historical and geographic variations, modern nongeographic variations

> Number built according to instructions under 420–490

.700 1–.700 8	Standard subdivisions

.700 9	History, geographic treatment, biography

[.700 902]   6th-15th centuries, 500–1499

> Do not use for Old Portuguese; class in 469.701. Do not use for Middle Portuguese; class in 469.702

[.700 903 1]   16th century, 1500–1599

> Do not use; class in 469.702

[.700 94–.700 99]   Specific continents, countries, localities in modern world

> Do not use; class in 469.79

.701   Old Portuguese to 1100

.702   Middle Portuguese, 1100–1600

.79   Geographic variations

Class here pidgins, creoles

[.790 1–.790 9]   Standard subdivisions

> Do not use; class in 469.7001–469.7009

.791   Geographic variations in areas, regions, places in general

> Add to base number 469.791 the numbers following —1 in notation 11–19 from Table 2, e.g., dialects of the Portuguese Empire 469.791712469

.794–.799   Geographic variations in specific continents, countries, localities in modern world

> Add to base number 469.79 notation 5–7 from Table 2, e.g., geographic variations in Spain 469.7946, geographic variations in Portugal 469.79469, Crioulo 469.796658, geographic variations in Brazil 469.7981, dialects of São Paulo 469.798161

> *For geographic variations of Old Portuguese, see 469.701094–469.701099; for geographic variations of Middle Portuguese, see 469.702094–469.702099*

> *See also 467.972986 for Papiamento*

.8   Standard Portuguese usage (Prescriptive linguistics)

> Add to base number 469.8 the numbers following —8 in notation 8001–8955 from Table 4, e.g., reading Portuguese 469.84

.9   *Galician*

Class here Gallegan

---

*Add to base number as instructed under 420–490

470 Latin and related Italic languages

Class here Italic languages

Class comprehensive works on Latin and Greek in 480

For Romance languages, see 440

.01–.09   Standard subdivisions of Italic languages

.1–.9   Standard subdivisions of Latin

Notation from Table 1 as modified under —01–09 in Table 4, e.g., semantics of Latin 470.143

471–478 Subdivisions of Latin

Except for modifications shown under specific entries, add to base number 47 notation 1–8 from Table 4, e.g., phonology of Latin 471.5

See Manual at 471–475, 478 vs. 477

471 Writing systems, phonology, phonetics of classical Latin

Number built according to instructions under 471–478

472 Etymology of classical Latin

Number built according to instructions under 471–478

473 Dictionaries of classical Latin

Number built according to instructions under 471–478

[474] [Unassigned]

Most recently used in Edition 16

475 Grammar of classical Latin

Number built according to instructions under 471–478

[476] [Unassigned]

Most recently used in Edition 18

477 Old, postclassical, Vulgar Latin

Standard subdivisions are added for any or all topics in heading

Variant name for Old Latin: preclassical Latin

Number built according to instructions under 471–478

478 Classical Latin usage (Prescriptive linguistics)

Number built according to instructions under 471–478

Class here classical-revival Latin usage during medieval or modern times

479 Other Italic languages

.4–.9   **Specific languages**

> Add to base number 479 the numbers following —79 in notation 794–799 from Table 6, e.g., Umbrian 479.9

480   Classical Greek and related Hellenic languages

> Classical Greek: the Greek that flourished between 750 and 350 B.C.
>
> Class here Hellenic languages, comprehensive works on classical (Greek and Latin) languages
>
> *For Latin, see 470*

.01–.09   Standard subdivisions of classical (Greek and Latin) languages

.1–.9   **Standard subdivisions of Hellenic languages, of classical Greek**

481–488 Subdivisions of classical, preclassical, postclassical Greek

> Except for modifications shown under specific entries, add to base number 48 notation 1–8 from Table 4, e.g., phonology of classical Greek 481.5
>
> Dialects of classical Greek are classed in the numbers for classical Greek (480.1–480.9, 481–485, 488)
>
> *For standard subdivisions of classical Greek, see 480.1–480.9*

481   Writing systems, phonology, phonetics of classical Greek

> Number built according to instructions under 481–488

482   Etymology of classical Greek

> Number built according to instructions under 481–488

483   Dictionaries of classical Greek

> Number built according to instructions under 481–488

[484]   [Unassigned]

> Most recently used in Edition 16

485   Grammar of classical Greek

> Number built according to instructions under 481–488

[486]   [Unassigned]

> Most recently used in Edition 18

487   Preclassical and postclassical Greek

> Number built according to instructions under 481–488

.1   **Preclassical Greek**

> Including Mycenaean Greek, Linear B
>
> *See also 492.6 for Linear A*

488   Classical Greek usage (Prescriptive linguistics)

Number built according to instructions under 481–488

489   Other Hellenic languages

490   Other languages

SUMMARY

491   East Indo-European and Celtic languages

Class comprehensive works on Indo-European languages in 410

SUMMARY

*Add to base number as instructed under 420–490

.1   **Indo-Iranian languages**

Class here comprehensive works on languages of south Asia

For Indo-Aryan languages, see 491.2–491.4; for Iranian languages, see 491.5; for Dravidian languages and miscellaneous languages of south Asia, see 494.8; for languages of south Asia closely related to languages of east and southeast Asia, see 495; for Andamanese languages, see 495.9

>   **491.2–491.4 Indo-Aryan languages**

Class comprehensive works in 491.1

.2   ***Sanskrit**

.29   Vedic (Old Indo-Aryan)

.3   **Middle Indo-Aryan languages**

Class here comprehensive works on Prakrit languages

For modern Prakrit languages, see 491.4

.37   *Pali

.4   **Modern Indo-Aryan languages**

Class here modern Prakrit languages

Class comprehensive works on Prakrit languages in 491.3

.41   Sindhi and Lahnda

.410 1–.410 9   Standard subdivisions of Sindhi

         Notation from Table 1 as modified under —01–09 in Table 4, e.g., semantics of Sindhi 491.40143

.411–.418   Subdivisions of Sindhi

         Add to base number 491.41 notation 1–8 from Table 4, e.g., grammar of Sindhi 491.415

.419   *Lahnda

.42   *Panjabi

.43   Western Hindi languages

Class here comprehensive works on Hindi languages

For languages of east central zone of Indo-Aryan languages (Eastern Hindi languages), see 491.492

.430 1–.430 9   Standard subdivisions of Western Hindi languages together, of Hindi alone

         Notation from Table 1 as modified under —01–09 in Table 4, e.g., semantics of Hindi 491.430143

---

*Add to base number as instructed under 420–490

.431–.438	Subdivisions of Hindi
	Add to base number 491.43 notation 1–8 from Table 4, e.g., grammar of Hindi 491.435
.439	*Urdu
.44	*Bengali
	Class here comprehensive works on Bengali and Assamese
	For Assamese, see 491.451
.45	Assamese, Bihari, Oriya
.451	*Assamese
.454	*Bihari
.454 7	Historical and geographic variations, modern nongeographic variations
	Number built according to instructions under 420–490
	Including Bhojpuri, Magahi, Maithili
.456	*Oriya
.46	Marathi and Konkani
.460 1–.460 9	Standard subdivisions of Marathi
	Notation from Table 1 as modified under —01–09 in Table 4, e.g., semantics of Marathi 491.460143
.461–.468	Subdivisions of Marathi
	Add to base number 491.46 notation 1–8 from Table 4, e.g., grammar of Marathi 491.465
.467	Historical and geographic variations, modern nongeographic variations of Marathi
	Number built according to instructions under 491.461–491.468
	For Konkani, see 491.469
.469	*Konkani
.47	Gujarati, Bhili, Rajasthani
.470 1–.470 9	Standard subdivisions of Gujarati
	Notation from Table 1 as modified under —01–09 in Table 4, e.g., semantics of Gujarati 491.470143
.471–.478	Subdivisions of Gujarati
	Add to base number 491.47 notation 1–8 from Table 4, e.g., grammar of Gujarati 491.475
.479	*Rajasthani

*Add to base number as instructed under 420–490

.479 7	Historical and geographic variations, modern nongeographic variations

Number built according to instructions under 420–490

Including Jaipuri, Marwari

.48	Sinhalese-Maldivian languages

Class here Sinhalese (Sinhala)

.480 1–.480 9	Standard subdivisions of Sinhalese (Sinhala)

Notation from Table 1 as modified under —01–09 in Table 4, e.g., semantics of Sinhalese 491.480143

.481–.488	Subdivisions of Sinhalese (Sinhala)

Add to base number 491.48 notation 1–8 from Table 4, e.g., grammar of Sinhalese 491.485

.489	*Divehi (Maldivian)

.49	Other Indo-Aryan languages

Including Nuristani (Kafiri)

See also 494.8 for Dravidian languages; also 495.4 for Tibeto-Burman languages; also 495.95 for Munda languages

.492	Languages of east central zone of Indo-Aryan languages (Eastern Hindi languages)

Including Awadhi, Bagheli, Chattisgarhi, Fijian Hindustani (Fiji Hindi)

Class comprehensive works on Hindi languages in 491.43

.495	*Nepali language

.496	Pahari languages

Including Garhwali

Class here languages of northern zone of Indo-Aryan languages

For Nepali, see 491.495

.497	*Romani

.499	Dardic (Pisacha) languages

Including Kashmiri, Khowar, Kohistani, Shina

.5	**Iranian languages**

.51	*Old Persian

Class here ancient west Iranian languages

See also 491.52 for Avestan language

.52	*Avestan

Class here ancient east Iranian languages

*Add to base number as instructed under 420–490

.53	Middle Iranian languages
	Including Khotanese (Saka), Pahlavi (Middle Persian), Sogdian
.55	*Modern Persian (Farsi)
	Class Tajik in 491.57
.56	*Dari
.57	*Tajik
.59	Other modern Iranian languages
	Including Pamir languages; Osetin (Ossetic)
.593	*Pashto (Afghan)
.597	Kurdish languages
	Including central and southern Kurdish
	Class here Kurdish (Kurmanji, northern Kurdish)
.597 01–.597 09	Standard subdivisions of Kurdish (Kurmanji)
	Notation from Table 1 as modified under —01–09 in Table 4, e.g., semantics of Kurdish 491.5970143
.597 1–.597 8	Subdivisions of Kurdish (Kurmanji)
	Add to base number 491.597 notation 1–8 from Table 4, e.g., grammar of Kurdish 491.5975
.598	*Baluchi
.6	**Celtic languages**
	Including Gaulish
.62	*Irish Gaelic
.63	*Scottish Gaelic
.64	*Manx
.66	*Welsh (Cymric)
.67	*Cornish
.68	*Breton
.7	**Russian and related East Slavic languages**
	Class here East Slavic languages
	Class comprehensive works on Slavic (Slavonic) languages in 491.8
.700 1–.700 9	Standard subdivisions of East Slavic languages

*Add to base number as instructed under 420–490

.701–.709   Standard subdivisions of Russian

> Notation from Table 1 as modified under —01–09 in Table 4, e.g., semantics of Russian 491.70143

.71–.75   Writing systems, phonology, phonetics, etymology, dictionaries, grammar of Russian

> Add to base number 491.7 notation 1–5 from Table 4, e.g., grammar of Russian 491.75

.77   Historical and geographic variations, modern nongeographic variations of Russian

.770 01–.770 08   Standard subdivisions

.770 09   History, geographic treatment, biography

[.770 090 2]   6th-15th centuries, 500–1499

> Do not use; class in 491.7701

[.770 090 31]   16th century, 1500–1599

> Do not use for Old Russian; class in 491.7701. Do not use for Middle Russian; class in 491.7702

[.770 090 32]   17th century, 1600–1699

> Do not use; class in 491.7702

.770 090 33   18th century, 1700–1799

> Do not use for Middle Russian; class in 491.7702

[.770 094–.770 099]   Specific continents, countries, localities in modern world

> Do not use; class in 491.774–491.779

.770 1   Old Russian to 1550

.770 2   Middle Russian, 1550–1750

.774–.779   Geographic variations

> Add to base number 491.77 notation 4–9 from Table 2, e.g., dialects of Far Eastern Siberia 491.77577
>
> *For geographic variations of Old Russian, see 491.7701094–491.7701099; for geographic variations in Middle Russian, see 491.7702094–491.7702099*

.78   Standard Russian usage (Prescriptive linguistics)

.780 01–.780 09   Standard subdivisions

.780 2–.780 4   Translating

> Add to base number 491.78 the numbers following —8 in notation 802–804 from Table 4, e.g., translating Russian literature (belles-lettres) and rhetoric 491.7804

.781–.786   Words, approaches to expression, reading, readers

> Add to base number 491.78 the numbers following —8 in notation 81–86 from Table 4, e.g., reading Russian 491.784

.79	Ukrainian and Belarusian

.790 1–.790 9   Standard subdivisions of Ukrainian

> Notation from Table 1 as modified under —01–09 in Table 4, e.g., semantics of Ukrainian 491.790143

.791–.798   Subdivisions of Ukrainian

> Add to base number 491.79 notation 1–8 from Table 4, e.g., grammar of Ukrainian 491.795

.799   *Belarusian

.8   Slavic (Slavonic) languages

> Including Common Slavic

> Class here comprehensive works on Balto-Slavic languages

> *For East Slavic languages, see 491.7; for Baltic languages, see 491.9*

.801–.803   Standard subdivisions

> Notation from Table 1 as modified under —01–03 in Table 4, e.g., semantics of Slavic languages 491.80143

.804   Special topics of Slavic languages

> Add to base number 491.804 notation 1–8 from Table 4, e.g., grammar of Slavic languages 491.8045

.805–.809   Standard subdivisions

.81   Bulgarian and related South Slavic languages

> Class here South Slavic languages

> *For Serbian, see 491.82; for Croatian and Bosnian, see 491.83; for Slovenian, see 491.84*

.810 1–.810 9   Standard subdivisions of South Slavic languages and Bulgarian together, of Bulgarian alone

> Notation from Table 1 as modified under —01–09 in Table 4, e.g., semantics of Bulgarian 491.810143

.811–.815   Writing systems, phonology, phonetics, etymology, dictionaries, grammar of Bulgarian

> Add to base number 491.81 notation 1–5 from Table 4, e.g., phonology of Bulgarian 491.8115

.817   Historical and geographic variations, modern nongeographic variations of Bulgarian

.817 001–.817 008   Standard subdivisions

.817 009   History, geographic treatment, biography

> Do not use for Old Bulgarian; class in 491.81701

.817 01   *Old Bulgarian (Church Slavic)

*Add to base number as instructed under 420–490

.818	Standard Bulgarian usage (Prescriptive linguistics)
.818 001–.818 009	Standard subdivisions
.818 02–.818 04	Translating

> Add to base number 491.818 the numbers following —8 in notation 802–804 from Table 4, e.g., translating Bulgarian literature (belles-lettres) and rhetoric 491.81804

.818 1–.818 6	Words, approaches to expression, reading, readers

> Add to base number 491.818 the numbers following —8 in notation 81–86 from Table 4, e.g., reading Bulgarian 491.8184

.819	*Macedonian
.82	*Serbian

> Class here Serbo-Croatian (languages of Serbs, Croats, and Bosnians treated together as a single language)

.83	*Croatian and Bosnian

> Subdivisions are added for Croatian and Bosnian together, for Croatian alone

.839	*Bosnian
.84	*Slovenian
.85	Polish and related West Slavic languages

> Including Kashubian

> Class here West Slavic languages

> *For Czech, see 491.86; for Slovak, see 491.87; for Wendish, see 491.88; for Polabian, see 491.89*

.850 1–.850 9	Standard subdivisions of West Slavic languages and Polish together, of Polish alone

> Notation from Table 1 as modified under —01–09 in Table 4, e.g., semantics of Polish 491.850143

.851–.858	Subdivisions of Polish

> Add to base number 491.85 notation 1–8 from Table 4, e.g., grammar of Polish 491.855

.86	*Czech
.867	Historical and geographic variations, modern nongeographic variations

> Number built according to instructions under 420–490

> Including Moravian dialects

.87	*Slovak
.88	*Wendish (Lusatian, Sorbian)

*Add to base number as instructed under 420–490

.89 *Polabian

.9 Baltic and other Indo-European languages

> 491.91–491.93 Baltic languages

Class comprehensive works in 491.9

.91 Old Prussian

.92 *Lithuanian

.93 *Latvian (Lettish)

.99 Other Indo-European languages

Add to base number 491.99 the numbers following —9199 in notation 91991–91998 from Table 6, e.g., Albanian 491.991, Phrygian 491.993; then to the number given for each language listed below add further as instructed at beginning of Table 4, e.g., grammar of Albanian 491.9915

491.991 Albanian

491.992 Armenian

491.994 Tocharian

491.998 Hittite

492 Afro-Asiatic languages

Class here Semitic languages

For non-Semitic Afro-Asiatic languages, see 493

.01–.03 Standard subdivisions

Notation from Table 1 as modified under —01–03 in Table 4, e.g., semantics of Semitic languages 492.0143

.04 Special topics of Afro-Asiatic and Semitic languages

Add to base number 492.04 notation 1–8 from Table 4, e.g., grammar of Semitic languages 492.045

.05–.09 Standard subdivisions

.1 East Semitic languages

Including Assyrian, Babylonian

Class here Akkadian (Assyro-Babylonian)

For Eblaite, see 492.6

See also 499.95 for Sumerian

---

*Add to base number as instructed under 420–490

.101–.109   Standard subdivisions of Akkadian (Assyro-Babylonian)

> Notation from Table 1 as modified under —01–09 in Table 4, e.g.,
> semantics of Akkadian 492.10143

.11–.18   Subdivisions of Akkadian (Assyro-Babylonian)

> Add to base number 492.1 notation 1–8 from Table 4, e.g., grammar of
> Akkadian 492.15; dialects of Assyrian, Babylonian 492.17

> ### 492.2–492.9 West Semitic languages

> Class comprehensive works in 492

.2   Aramaic languages

> *For Eastern Aramaic languages, see 492.3*

.29   Western Aramaic languages

> Including Biblical Aramaic (Chaldee) and Samaritan

.3   Eastern Aramaic languages

> Class here Syriac

.301–.309   Standard subdivisions of Syriac

> Notation from Table 1 as modified under —01–09 in Table 4, e.g.,
> semantics of Syriac 492.30143

.31–.38   Subdivisions of Syriac

> Add to base number 492.3 notation 1–8 from Table 4, e.g., grammar of
> Syriac 492.35

.4   *Hebrew

.6   Canaanite languages

> Including Ammonite, Eblaite, Moabite, Phoenician; Linear A and its language
>
> Class here comprehensive works on Canaanitic languages
>
> *For Hebrew, see 492.4*
>
> *See also 487.1 for Linear B*
>
> *See Manual at T6—926*

.67   *Ugaritic

.7   Arabic and Maltese

> Class here Classical Arabic, modern standard Arabic
>
> *See also 492.9 for South Arabian languages*

*Add to base number as instructed under 420–490

.701–.709   Standard subdivisions of Arabic

> Notation from Table 1 as modified under —01–09 in Table 4, e.g., semantics of Arabic 492.70143

.71–.78   Subdivisions of Arabic

> Add to base number 492.7 notation 1–8 from Table 4, e.g., grammar of Arabic 492.75

> Class Maltese in 492.79

.79   *Maltese

.8   Ethiopian languages

> Including Gurage, Harari

> Class here comprehensive works on South Semitic languages

> *For South Arabian languages, see 492.9*

.81   *Ge'ez language

.82   *Tigré

.83   *Tigrinya

.87   *Amharic

.877   Historical and geographic variations, modern nongeographic variations

> Number built according to instructions under 420–490

.9   South Arabian languages

> Including Mahri, Sokotri

> Class comprehensive works on South Semitic languages in 492.8

> *See also 492.7 for Arabic*

---

*Add to base number as instructed under 420–490

493   Non-Semitic Afro-Asiatic languages

Add to base number 493 the numbers following —93 in notation 931–937 from Table 6, e.g., Afar 493.5, Oromo 493.55; then to the number for each language listed below add further as instructed at beginning of Table 4, e.g., grammar of Oromo 493.555

493.1 Egyptian

493.2 Coptic

493.33 Tamazight

493.34 Kabyle

493.38 Tamashek

493.54 Somali

493.55 Oromo

493.72 Hausa

494   Altaic, Uralic, Hyperborean, Dravidian languages, miscellaneous languages of south Asia

Add to base number 494 the numbers following —94 in notation 941–948 from Table 6, e.g., Mongolian 494.23, Altai 494.33; then to the number for each language listed below add further as instructed at beginning of Table 4, e.g., grammar of Mongolian 494.235

494.23 Mongolian proper, Halh Mongolian (Khalkha Mongolian)

494.315 Chuvash

494.323 Uighur

494.325 Uzbek

494.332 Yakut

494.345 Kazakh

494.347 Kyrgyz

494.35 Turkish, Osmanli, Ottoman Turkish

494.361 Azerbaijani

494.364 Turkmen

494.387 Tatar

494.388 Crimean Tatar

494.511 Hungarian (Magyar)

494.541 Finnish (Suomi)

494.543 Kven Finnish

494.545 Estonian

494.5722 South Sámi

494.5743 Lule Sámi

494.5745 North Sámi

494.811 Tamil

494.812 Malayalam

494.814 Kannada (Kanarese)

494.823 Gondi

494.824 Kui (Khond, Kandh)

494.827 Telugu

494 Altaic, Uralic, Hyperborean, Dravidian languages, miscellaneous languages of south Asia

494.83 Brahui

494.892 Burushaski

For Japanese, see 495.6; for Korean, see 495.7

See also 497.1 for Inuit, Yupik, Aleut languages

495 Languages of east and southeast Asia

Including Karen

Here are classed languages of south Asia closely related to the languages of east and southeast Asia

Class here Sino-Tibetan languages

For Austronesian languages of east and southeast Asia, see 499.2

.1 *Chinese

Class here Beijing dialect; Mandarin (Putonghua) (standard written Chinese)

.17 Historical and geographic variations, modern nongeographic variations of Chinese

Number built according to instructions under 420–490

Class Mandarin Chinese in 495.1

[.170 94–.170 99] Specific continents, countries, localities in modern world

Do not use; class in 495.179

.179 Geographic variations

[.179 01–.179 09] Standard subdivisions

Do not use; class in 495.17001–495.17009

.179 1 Geographic variations in areas, regions, places in general

Add to base number 495.1791 the numbers following —1 in notation 11–19 from Table 2, e.g., dialects of rural regions 495.1791734

.179 4–.179 9 Geographic variations in specific continents, countries, localities in modern world

Add to base number 495.179 notation 4–9 from Table 2, e.g., geographic variations in China 495.17951, Chinese dialects in Malaysia 495.179595, Yue (Cantonese) dialects as spoken in North America 495.1797

*Add to base number as instructed under 420–490

.4   **Tibetan and related Tibeto-Burman languages**

       Including Baric, Bodish, Loloish languages

       Class here Tibeto-Burman languages

       Class Karen in 495

       For Burmese, see 495.8

.401–.409   Standard subdivisions of Tibeto-Burman languages and Tibetan together, of Tibetan alone

       Notation from Table 1 as modified under —01–09 in Table 4, e.g., semantics of Tibetan 495.40143

.41–.48   Subdivisions of Tibetan

       Add to base number 495.4 notation 1–8 from Table 4, e.g., grammar of Tibetan 495.45

.49   Eastern Himalayan languages

       Including Chepang, Limbu, Magari, Sunwar; Newari

       Class here Kiranti languages, Mahakiranti languages

       See also 491.495 for Nepali

.6   ***Japanese**

.7   ***Korean**

.8   ***Burmese**

.9   **Miscellaneous languages of southeast Asia; Munda languages**

       Only those languages provided for below

       Including Andamanese languages, Kadai languages, Kam-Sui languages

       Class here Daic languages

       Class Austroasiatic languages in 495.93

       For Austronesian languages, see 499.2

.91   Thai (Siamese) and related Tai languages

       Class here Tai languages

.910 1–.910 9   Standard subdivisions of Tai languages and Thai (Siamese) together, of Thai (Siamese) alone

       Notation from Table 1 as modified under —01–09 in Table 4, e.g., semantics of Thai 495.910143

.911–.918   Subdivisions of Thai (Siamese)

       Add to base number 495.91 notation 1–8 from Table 4, e.g., grammar of Thai 495.915

---

*Add to base number as instructed under 420–490

.919	Other Tai languages

Including Shan

For Viet-Muong languages, see 495.92

.919 1	*Lao
.92–.97	Viet-Muong, Austroasiatic, Munda, Hmong-Mien (Miao-Yao) languages

Add to base number 495.9 the numbers following —959 in notation 9592–9597 from Table 6, e.g., Vietnamese 495.922, Khasi 495.93; then to the number for each language listed below add further as instructed at beginning of Table 4, e.g., grammar of Vietnamese 495.9225

495.922 Vietnamese

495.932 Khmer (Cambodian)

495.972 Hmong (Miao)

495.978 Yao

496 African languages

Class Afrikaans in 439.36; class Malagasy in 499.3. Class an African creole having a non-African primary source language with the source language, plus notation 7 from Table 4, e.g., Krio 427.9664

For Ethiopian languages, see 492.8; for non-Semitic Afro-Asiatic languages, see 493

.1	**Khoisan languages**

Including Khoikhoi, San

.3	**Niger-Congo languages**

Including Ijoid, Kordofanian languages; Dogon

.32	West Atlantic languages
.321	Senegambian languages

Including Serer (Serer-Sine)

For Fula, see 496.322

.321 4	*Wolof
.322	*Fula (Fulani)

*Add to base number as instructed under 420–490

.33   Igboid, Defoid, Edoid, Idomoid, Nupoid, Akpes, Oko, Ukaan
             languages; Kwa languages; Kru languages

             Igboid, Defoid, Edoid, Idomoid, Nupoid, Akpes, Oko, Ukaan languages,
             formerly considered Kwa languages, are now considered Benue-Congo
             languages

             Add to base number 496.33 the numbers following —9633 in notation
             96332–96338 from Table 6, e.g., Yoruba 496.333, Baoulé 496.338; then
             to the number for each language listed below add further as instructed at
             beginning of Table 4, e.g., grammar of Yoruba 496.3335

             496.332 Ibo (Igbo)

             496.333 Yoruba

             496.3374 Ewe

             496.3378 Gã

             496.3385 Akan, Fante, Twi

             Class comprehensive works on Benue-Congo languages in 496.36

.34   Mande languages

.345   Manding-Mokole languages

                 Class here Mandekan languages

.345 2   *Bambara

.348   Mende-Bandi languages

                 Including Bandi (Gbandi)

                 Class here Mende

.348 01–.348 09   Standard subdivisions of Mende

                         Notation from Table 1 as modified under —01–09 in Table 4, e.g.,
                         semantics of Mende 496.3480143

.348 1–.348 8   Subdivisions of Mende

                         Add to base number 496.348 notation 1–8 from Table 4, e.g.,
                         grammar of Mende 496.3485

.35   Gur (Voltaic) languages

             Including Dagomba, Moré, Senufo

             Class Dogon in 496.3

---

*Add to base number as instructed under 420–490

.36   Benue-Congo and Adamawa-Ubangi languages

               Standard subdivisions are added for Benue-Congo and Adamawa-Ubangi
               languages together, for Benue-Congo languages alone

               Including Bamileke

               Class here Bantoid languages

               Class Mbam languages (from zone A) in 496.396

                    *For Igboid, Defoid, Edoid, Idomoid, Nupoid, Akpes, Oko, Ukaan
                    languages, see 496.33; for Bantu languages, see 496.39*

.361   Adamawa-Ubangi languages

               Including Gbaya, Zande

.361 6   *Sango

.364   Cross River languages

               Including Ibibio

.364 2   *Efik

.39   Bantu languages

               Bantu proper (Narrow Bantu)

               See also 496.36 for Bantoid languages other than Bantu proper

               See Manual at T6—9639

.390 1–.390 3 Standard subdivisions

                    Notation from Table 1 as modified under —01–03 in Table 4, e.g.,
                    semantics of Bantu languages 496.390143

.390 4   Special topics of Bantu languages

                    Add to base number 496.3904 notation 1–8 from Table 4, e.g.,
                    grammar of Bantu languages 496.39045

.390 5–.390 9 Standard subdivisions

---

*Add to base number as instructed under 420–490

.391–.399   Specific Bantu languages and language families

> Add to base number 496.39 the numbers following —9639 in notation 96391–96399 from Table 6, e.g., Ewondo 496.396, Zulu 496.3986; then to the number for each language listed below add further as instructed at beginning of Table 4, e.g., grammar of Zulu 496.39865

496.3915 Bemba

496.3918 Nyanja, Chichewa (Chewa)

496.392 Swahili

496.3931 Kongo (Koongo)

496.3932 Mbundu (Kimbundu)

496.39461 Rwanda (Kinyarwanda)

496.39465 Rundi

496.3954 Kikuyu

496.3957 Ganda (Luganda)

496.3962 Duala

496.39686 Lingala

496.3975 Shona

496.3976 Venda (Tshivenda)

496.39771 Northern Sotho

496.39772 Southern Sotho

496.39775 Tswana

496.3978 Tsonga

496.3985 Xhosa

496.3986 Zulu

496.3987 Swazi (siSwati)

496.3989 Ndebele (South Africa)

.5   **Nilo-Saharan languages**

> Add to base number 496.5 the numbers following —965 in notation 9653–9658 from Table 6, e.g., Maasai 496.55226, Zarma 496.58; then to the number for each language listed below add further as instructed at beginning of Table 4, e.g., grammar of Maasai 496.552265

496.55226 Maasai

496.55842 Dholuo (Luo of Kenya and Tanzania)

497   North American native languages

Class here comprehensive works on North and South American native languages

For South American native languages, see 498

.1–.2   Inuit, Yupik, Aleut, Na-Dene languages

Add to base number 497 the numbers following —97 in notation 971–972 from Table 6, e.g., Na-Dene languages 497.2, Navajo 497.26; then to the number for each language listed below add further as instructed at beginning of Table 4, e.g., grammar of Navajo 497.265

497.124 Eastern Canadian Inuktitut

497.19 Aleut

497.256 Mescalero-Chiricahua Apache (Chiricahua, Mescalero)

497.26 Navajo (Diné)

497.27 Tlingit

497.28 Haida

.3   Algic and Muskogean languages

Standard subdivisions are added for Algic and Muskogean languages together, for Algic languages alone

Including Lumbee, Yurok

Class here Algonquian languages

.31–.38   Specific Algic and Muskogean languages and language families

Add to base number 497.3 the numbers following —973 in notation
9731–9738 from Table 6, e.g., Cree 497.323, Muskogean languages 497.38;
then to the number for each language listed below add further as instructed
at beginning of Table 4, e.g., grammar of Cree 497.3235

497.312 Kickapoo

497.313 Menomini

497.314 Mesquakie, Fox

497.315 Miami

497.316 Potawatomi

497.317 Shawnee

497.323 Cree

497.333 Ojibwa, Chippewa

497.336 Ottawa

497.343 Micmac

497.344 Mohegan, Narragansett

497.345 Unami (Delaware, Lenni Lenape)

497.347 Powhatan

497.348 Wampanoag

497.352 Blackfoot, Siksika

497.353 Cheyenne

497.354 Arapaho

497.385 Muskogee (Creek)

497.3859 Seminole

497.386 Chickasaw

497.387 Choctaw

.4   **Penutian, Mayan, Mixe-Zoque, Uto-Aztecan, Kiowa-Tanoan
languages**

.41–.49   Specific Penutian, Mayan, Mixe-Zoque, Uto-Aztecan, Kiowa-Tanoan languages and language families

> Add to base number 497.4 the numbers following —974 in notation 9741–9749 from Table 6, e.g., Uto-Aztecan languages 497.45, Nahuatl 497.452; then to the number for each language listed below add further as instructed at beginning of Table 4, e.g., grammar of Nahuatl 497.4525

> 497.4122 Klamath, Modoc

> 497.4124 Nez Percé

> 497.4127 Yakama

> 497.4128 Tsimshian

> 497.4133 Miwok

> 497.422 Cakchikel

> 497.423 Quiché

> 497.427 Maya, Yucatec Maya

> 497.4287 Tzotzil

> 497.452 Nahuatl (Aztec)

> 497.4542 Yaqui

> 497.4544 Huichol

> 497.4546 Tarahumara

> 497.4552 Tohono O'odham

> 497.45529 Akimel O'odham

.5   **Siouan, Iroquoian, Hokan, Chumash, Yuki languages**

> Class Keresan languages in 497.9; class Caddoan languages in 497.93

> *See also 497.9 for Yuchi*

.52–.58 Specific Siouan, Iroquoian, Hokan, Chumash, Yuki languages and language families

Add to base number 497.5 the numbers following —975 in notation 9752–9758 from Table 6, e.g., Iroquoian languages 497.55, Cherokee 497.557; then to the number for each language listed below add further as instructed at beginning of Table 4, e.g., grammar of Cherokee 497.5575

497.522 Mandan

497.5243 Dakota

497.5244 Lakota

497.5253 Omaha

497.52539 Ponca

497.5254 Osage

497.526 Winnebago

497.5272 Crow

497.5274 Hidatsa

497.5542 Mohawk

497.5543 Oneida

497.5546 Seneca

497.555 Wyandot, Huron

497.557 Cherokee

497.5722 Mohave

497.5724 Havasupai, Walapai, Yavapai

497.576 Washo

.6–.9   **Oto-Manguean, Chibchan languages of North America, Misumalpan, other North American languages**

Add to base number 497 the numbers following —97 in notation 976–979 from Table 6, e.g., Oto-Manguean languages 497.6, Zapotec 497.68; then to the number for each language listed below add further as instructed at beginning of Table 4, e.g., grammar of Zapotec 497.685

497.63 Mixtec

497.68 Zapotec

497.83 San Blas Kuna (San Blas Cuna)

497.882 Mískito

497.922 Taino

497.932 Arikara

497.933 Pawnee

497.9435 Kalispel, Pend d'Oreille

497.953 Kwakiutl

497.955 Nootka

497.96 Purépecha (Tarasco)

497.992 Kutenai

497.994 Zuni

498   South American native languages

Add to base number 498 the numbers following —98 in notation 982–989 from Table 6, e.g., Quechua 498.323, Tucanoan languages 498.35; then to the number for each language listed below add further as instructed at beginning of Table 4, e.g., grammar of Quechua 498.3235

498.323 Quechua (Kechua)

498.324 Aymara

498.372 Shuar

498.3822 Paraguayan Guaraní

498.3832 Tupí (Nhengatu)

498.422 Carib (Galibi)

498.72 Mapudungun (Mapuche)

498.92 Yanomamo

499   Non-Austronesian languages of Oceania, Austronesian languages, miscellaneous languages

Add to base number 499 the numbers following —99 in notation 991–999 from Table 6, e.g., Polynesian languages 499.4, Maori 499.442; then to the number for each language listed below add further as instructed at beginning of Table 4, e.g., grammar of Maori 499.4425; however, for sign languages, see 419

499.211 Tagalog (Filipino)

499.221 Indonesian (Bahasa Indonesia)

499.222 Javanese

499.2232 Sunda (Sundanese)

499.2234 Madura (Madurese)

499.2238 Bali (Balinese)

499.2242 Aceh (Achinese)

499.2244 Minangkabau

499.22462 Batak Toba

499.22466 Batak Dairi

499.2248 Lampung

499.2256 Banjar (Banjarese)

499.2262 Bugis (Buginese)

499.2264 Makasar

499.28 Malay (Bahasa Malaysia, Standard Malay)

499.3 Malagasy

499.42 Hawaiian

499.442 Maori

499.444 Tahitian

499.462 Samoan

499.482 Tongan (Tonga)

499.484 Niue (Niuean)

499.59 Fijian

499.92 Basque

499.95 Sumerian

499   Non-Austronesian languages of Oceania, Austronesian languages, miscellaneous languages

499.9623 Abkhaz

499.9625 Adyghe

499.969 Georgian

499.992 Esperanto

499.993 Interlingua

500

500 Natural sciences and mathematics

Natural sciences: sciences that deal with matter and energy, or with objects and processes observable in nature

Class here interdisciplinary works on natural and applied sciences

Class natural history in 508. Class scientific principles of a subject with the subject, plus notation 015 from Table 1, e.g., scientific principles of photography 770.15

For government policy on science, see 338.926; for applied sciences, see 600

See Manual at 231.7652 vs. 213, 500, 576.8; also at 338.926 vs. 352.745, 500; also at 500 vs. 001

SUMMARY

530	Physics
.01–.09	Standard subdivisions
.1–.8	[Theories, mathematical physics, states of matter, instrumentation, measurement]
531	Classical mechanics
532	Fluid mechanics
533	Pneumatics (Gas mechanics)
534	Sound and related vibrations
535	Light and related radiation
536	Heat
537	Electricity and electronics
538	Magnetism
539	Modern physics
540	Chemistry and allied sciences
.1–.9	Standard subdivisions
541	Physical chemistry
542	Techniques, procedures, apparatus, equipment, materials
543	Analytical chemistry
546	Inorganic chemistry
547	Organic chemistry
548	Crystallography
549	Mineralogy
550	Earth sciences
551	Geology, hydrology, meteorology
552	Petrology
553	Economic geology
554–559	Earth sciences by specific continents, countries, localities in modern world; extraterrestrial worlds
560	Paleontology
.1–.9	Standard subdivisions; stratigraphic paleontology; special topics of paleontology and paleozoology
561	Paleobotany; fossil microorganisms
562	Fossil invertebrates
563	Miscellaneous fossil marine and seashore invertebrates
564	Fossil Mollusca and Molluscoidea
565	Fossil Arthropoda
566	Fossil Chordata
567	Fossil cold-blooded vertebrates
568	Fossil Aves (birds)
569	Fossil Mammalia
570	Biology
.1–.9	Standard subdivisions
571	Physiology and related subjects
572	Biochemistry
573	Specific physiological systems in animals, regional histology and physiology in animals
575	Specific parts of and physiological systems in plants
576	Genetics and evolution
577	Ecology
578	Natural history of organisms and related subjects
579	Natural history of microorganisms, fungi, algae

580		**Plants**
	.1–.9	Standard subdivisions
581		Specific topics in natural history of plants
582		Plants noted for specific vegetative characteristics and flowers
583		Eudicots and Ceratophyllales
584		Monocots, basal angiosperms, Chloranthales, magnoliids
585		Pinophyta
586		Cryptogamia
587		Pteridophyta
588		Bryophyta
590		**Animals**
	.1–.9	Standard subdivisions
591		Specific topics in natural history of animals
592		Invertebrates
593		Miscellaneous marine and seashore invertebrates
594		Mollusca and Molluscoidea
595		Arthropoda
596		Chordata
597		Cold-blooded vertebrates
598		Aves
599		Mammalia

.2 **Physical sciences**

> *For astronomy and allied sciences, see 520; for physics, see 530; for chemistry and allied sciences, see 540; for earth sciences, see 550*

.5 **Space sciences**

> *For astronomy, see 520; for earth sciences in other worlds, see 550. For space sciences aspects of a specific subject, see the subject, plus notation 0919 from Table 1, e.g., chemical reactions in space 541.390919*
>
> *See Manual at 520 vs. 500.5, 523.1, 530.1, 919.9*

.8 **Groups of people**

> Add to base number 500.8 the numbers following —08 in notation 081–089 from Table 1, e.g., women in science 500.82

501 Philosophy and theory

> Class scientific method as a general research technique in 001.42; class scientific method applied in the natural sciences in 507.21

502 Miscellany

.8 **Auxiliary techniques and procedures; apparatus, equipment, materials**

> Notation 028 from Table 1 as modified below

.82   Microscopy

Including photomicrography, stereology

Class here microscopes; interdisciplinary works on microscopy

Class interdisciplinary works on photomicrography in 778.31

> *For manufacture of microscopes, see 681.413. For microscopy in a specific subject, see the subject, plus notation 028 from Table 1, e.g., microscopy in archaeology 930.1028*

.823   Compound microscopy

Class stereology with compound microscopes in 502.82

.825   Electron microscopy

Class stereology with electron microscopes in 502.82

.84   Apparatus, equipment, materials

Do not use for microscopes; class in 502.82

503   Dictionaries, encyclopedias, concordances

[504]   [Unassigned]

Most recently used in Edition 16

505   Serial publications

506   Organizations and management

507   Education, research, related topics

.2   **Research**

Class research covering the sciences in the broad sense of all knowledge in 001.4

> *See Manual at 500 vs. 001*

.21   Research methods

Class scientific method as a general research technique in 001.42

.8   **Use of apparatus and equipment in study and teaching**

Class here science fair projects, science projects in schools

508   Natural history

Do not use for groups of people; class in 500.8

Class here description and surveys of phenomena in nature

Class natural history of organisms in 578

> *See Manual at 333.7–333.9 vs. 508, 913–919, 930–990; also at 578 vs. 304.2, 508, 910*

.09 History and biography

> Do not use for geographic treatment; class in 508.3–508.9

.2 Seasons

> Class here interdisciplinary works on seasons

> *For a specific aspect of seasons, see the aspect, e.g., effect of seasons on organisms 577.23*

.3 Areas, regions, places in general; specific continents, countries, localities in ancient world

.31 Areas, regions, places in general

> Add to base number 508.31 the numbers following —1 in notation 11–19 from Table 2, e.g., natural history of the sea 508.3162

.33 Specific continents, countries, localities in ancient world

> Add to base number 508.33 the numbers following —3 in notation 31–39 from Table 2, e.g., natural history of ancient Greece 508.338

.4–.9 Specific continents, countries, localities in modern world

> Add to base number 508 notation 4–9 from Table 2, e.g., natural history of Brazil 508.81

509 History, geographic treatment, biography

> Class history, geographic treatment, biography of natural phenomena in 508

510 Mathematics

> Class here pure mathematics

> *See Manual at 510; also at 510, T1—0151 vs. 003, T1—011; also at 510, T1—0151 vs. 004–006, T1—0285*

SUMMARY

510.1	**Philosophy and theory**
511	**General principles of mathematics**
512	**Algebra**
513	**Arithmetic**
514	**Topology**
515	**Analysis**
516	**Geometry**
518	**Numerical analysis**
519	**Probabilities and applied mathematics**

.1 Philosophy and theory

> Including metamathematics

> Class mathematical logic in 511.3

511 General principles of mathematics

> Class general principles applied to a specific branch of mathematics with the branch, e.g., finite geometry 516.11

SUMMARY

.1   Finite mathematics

Class here discrete mathematics

> *For a specific aspect of finite mathematics, see the aspect, e.g., finite groups 512.23*

> *See Manual at 004.0151 vs. 511.1, 511.35*

.3   Mathematical logic (Symbolic logic)

Including logic operators, truth tables; axiom of choice, completeness theorem, decidability, formal languages, Gödel's theorem, type theory; combinatory logic, intermediate logic

Class here formal logic, propositional calculus (sentential calculus), predicate calculus; first-order logic, higher-order logic; axioms, hypotheses; interdisciplinary works on logic

Class formal logic, propositional calculus (sentential calculus), predicate calculus, first-order logic, logic operators, truth tables from the perspective of philosophical logic in 160

> *For philosophical logic, see 160; for category theory, see 512.62*

.31   Nonclassical logic

Including abduction; default, defeasible, nonmonotonic logic; linear, paraconsistent, relevance, substructural logic

Unless other instructions are given, class a subject with aspects in two or more subdivisions of 511.31 in the number coming last, e.g., conditional probability 511.318 (*not* 511.317)

> *For intuitionistic logic, see 511.36*

.312   Many-valued logic (Multiple-valued logic)

.313   Fuzzy logic

Class here fuzzy mathematics, fuzzy systems

Class fuzzy sets in 511.3223

.314   Modal logic

Including alethic, deontic, dynamic, epistemic, provability, temporal logic; possible worlds

.317   Conditional logic

Including counterfactuals

.318   Probabilistic logic

       *See also 161 for induction; also 519.2 for applied mathematical
       probabilities*

.32   Sets

       For point sets, see 511.33; for partially ordered sets, see 511.332

.322   Set theory

       Including axiomatic set theory, cardinal numbers, combinatorial set
       theory, continuum hypothesis, transfinite numbers

       For natural numbers, see 512.72

.322 3   Fuzzy sets

.324   Set algebra

       Class here Boolean algebra

.326   Functions and relations

       Including automorphisms, equations, isomorphisms, variables

       Class here mappings, transformations

.33   Order, lattices, ordered algebraic structures

       Standard subdivisions are added for any or all topics in heading

       Including point sets

       See also 511.326 for functions and relations

.332   Partially ordered sets

.34   Model theory

       See also 511.8 for mathematical models

.35   Recursion theory

       Including cellular automata, lambda calculus, Petri nets, recursive functions

       Class here automata theory, machine theory, sequential machines, Turing
       machines

       Class computer mathematics in 004.0151

       See Manual at 004.0151 vs. 511.1, 511.35

.352   Recursive functions

       Including NP-complete problems

       Class here computability, computable functions, computational
       complexity

.36   Proof theory and constructive mathematics

       Standard subdivisions are added for either or both topics in heading

       Including intuitionistic logic, intuitionistic mathematics

.4	**Approximations and expansions**

Class numerical approximation in 518.5; class stochastic approximation in 519.623

.42	Methods

Including curve fitting, least squares

.422	Interpolation
.422 3	Splines
.43	Error analysis

.5	**Graph theory**

Including network theory

Class interdisciplinary works on network theory in 003.72; class matching theory in 511.66

See also 518.23 for nomography

.52	Trees
.54	Directed graphs (Digraphs)

Including tournaments

.56	Coloring of graphs

Class here map coloring

.6	**Combinatorics (Combinatorial analysis)**

Including algebraic combinatorics; combinatorial configurations and designs; matroids

Class graph theory in 511.5; class design of experiments in 519.57

.62	Enumeration
.64	Permutations and combinations

Including Latin and magic squares

.65	Choice

See also 511.3 for axiom of choice; also 519.3 for decision making in game theory

.66	Extremal combinatorics

Including matching theory

Class here maxima, minima

.8	**Mathematical models (Mathematical simulation)**

See also 511.34 for model theory

512   Algebra

Class here universal algebra, modern algebra (abstract algebra combined with number theory)

Class foundations of algebra in 512.9

For numerical algebra, see 518.42

SUMMARY

512.001–.009	**Standard subdivisions**
.02	**Abstract algebra**
.1	**Algebra combined with other branches of mathematics**
.2	**Groups and group theory**
.3	**Fields**
.4	**Rings**
.5	**Linear algebra**
.6	**Category theory, homological algebra, K-theory**
.7	**Number theory**
.9	**Foundations of algebra**

.001–.009   Standard subdivisions

.02   Abstract algebra

For subdivisions of abstract algebra, see 512.2–512.5

.1   Algebra combined with other branches of mathematics

For arithmetic and algebra, see 513.12

See Manual at 510: Combination of topics

.12   Algebra and Euclidean geometry

.13   Algebra and trigonometry

.14   Algebra and analytic geometry

.15   Algebra and calculus

> ## 512.2–512.5 Subdivisions of abstract algebra

Class comprehensive works in 512.02

.2   Groups and group theory

Standard subdivisions are added for either or both topics in heading

Class here cosets, subgroups

For Brauer groups, see 512.46; for topological and related algebras and groups, see 512.55; for groups, semigroups, groupoids viewed as categories, see 512.62; for algebraic topology, see 514.2

.21   Permutation groups

.22   Representations of groups

.23	Finite groups

For finite Abelian groups, see 512.25

.25	Abelian groups (Commutative groups)

Including cyclic groups

Class here finite Abelian groups

.27	Semigroups
.28	Groupoids

.3   Fields

Class here field theory

Class linear algebra in 512.5; class differential algebras in 512.56; class number theory in 512.7

.32	Galois theory

.4   Rings

Including algebras based on group properties, flexible algebras, free algebras, subrings; extension theory

Class here integral domains, radical theory

Class algebras defined by dimension of space in 512.5; class topological algebras in 512.55

For fields, see 512.3

.42	Modules and ideals
.44	Commutative rings

Class here commutative algebras

.46	Associative rings

Including Brauer groups

Class here associative algebras, noncommutative algebras, noncommutative rings

.48	Nonassociative rings

Including Jordan algebras

Class here nonassociative algebras

.482	Lie algebras and groups

.5   Linear algebra

Including Cayley algebra, multidimensional algebra, multilinear algebra, quaternions

Class here linear algebra combined with analytic geometry; vector algebra

Class foundations of algebra in 512.9; class analysis combined with linear algebra in 515.14; class numerical linear algebra in 518.43

.52	Vector spaces

Class bilinear forms in 512.944; class topological vector spaces in 515.73

.55	Topological and related algebras and groups

Standard subdivisions are added for topological and related algebras and groups together, for topological algebras alone, for topological groups alone

Including Fréchet, Hopf, reductive, Stein, uniform algebras and their groups

For Lie algebras and groups, see 512.482; for differential algebras, see 512.56; for factor algebras, see 512.57; for homological algebra, see 512.64

See also 512.62 for category theory; also 512.66 for algebraic K-theory; also 514.2 for algebraic topology

.554	Banach algebras

.556	Self-adjoint operator algebras

Including C*-algebras, Von Neumann algebras, W*-algebras

Class here operator algebras

.56	Differential algebras

Class here difference algebras

.57	Factor algebras

Including Clifford, exterior, spinor, tensor algebras

.6	**Category theory, homological algebra, K-theory**

.62	Category theory

Including Abelian categories; functors, morphisms, toposes

.64	Homological algebra

.66	K-theory

Including algebraic K-theory

For topological K-theory, see 514.23

.7	**Number theory**

Class numerical methods in 518.47

For theory of equations, see 512.94

.72	Elementary number theory

Including congruences, continued fractions, Diophantine equations, divisibility, factorization, Fibonacci numbers, integers, natural numbers, operations, power residues, quadratic residues, residues, roots, sequences of integers

.723	Prime numbers

.73	Analytic number theory

Including Diophantine approximations, distribution theory of prime numbers, functions, L-functions, modular forms, multiplicative properties, number theoretic functions, partitions, Riemann hypothesis, sieves, transcendental numbers, Zeta function

.74	Algebraic number theory

Including algebraic function theory, class groups, class numbers, discriminants, Fermat's last theorem, field extensions, fields, ideals, p-adic numbers, quadratic forms, reciprocity, rings, unit theory

For factorization, see 512.72

.75	Geometry of numbers
.76	Probabilistic number theory
.78	Specific fields of numbers
.782	Rational numbers

Including specific rational numbers which are not integers

Class rational functions in 512.96

.784	Algebraic numbers

Including specific algebraic numbers which are not rational numbers

.786	Real numbers

Class transcendental numbers in 512.73; class real functions in 515.8

.788	Complex numbers

Class here imaginary numbers

Class complex functions in 515.9

.9	**Foundations of algebra**

Class algebra combined with other branches of mathematics in 512.1

.92	Algebraic operations

Class here addition, subtraction, multiplication, division

.922	Exponents and logarithms
.923	Root extraction

Including factorization

.924	Approximation, ratio, proportion
.94	Theory of equations
.942	Specific types and systems of equations
.942 2	Polynomial equations

Including binomial, cubic, quartic equations

.942 22	Quadratic equations

.942 6	Simultaneous equations
.943	Determinants and matrices
.943 2	Determinants
.943 4	Matrices

> Class determinants of matrices in 512.9432
>
> *For eigenvalues and eigenvectors, see 512.9436*

.943 6	Eigenvalues and eigenvectors

> Standard subdivisions are added for either or both topics in heading

.944	Theory of forms and algebraic invariant theory

> Standard subdivisions are added for either or both topics in heading

.96	Algebra of non-equation functions

> Including rational functions
>
> *For inequalities, see 512.97*

.97	Inequalities

513   Arithmetic

Including numeracy

Class numerical methods in 518.45

.1	**Arithmetic combined with other branches of mathematics**

> *See Manual at 510: Combination of topics*

.12	Arithmetic and algebra
.13	Arithmetic and geometry
.14	Arithmetic, algebra, geometry
.2	**Arithmetic operations**

> *For approximations, see 511.4*

.21	Basic operations
.211	Addition

> Including counting

.212	Subtraction
.213	Multiplication
.214	Division
.22	Exponents and logarithms
.23	Root extraction

> Including factorization; square root, cube root

.24	Ratio and proportion
.245	Percentage
.26	Fractions

> *For ratio, see 513.24; for percentage, see 513.245*
>
> *See also 512.782 for rational numbers*

.265	Decimal fractions

.5   Numeration systems

Including base 3, 5, 20 systems

.52	Binary system (Base 2 system)
.55	Decimal system (Base 10 system)

Class decimal fractions in 513.265

.6   Modular arithmetic

.9   Rapid calculations

Class here mental arithmetic, ready reckoners, shortcuts

514   Topology

Class here analysis situs, homeomorphisms, homogeneous spaces, mappings

Class topology combined with analysis in 515.13; class topology combined with geometry in 516

> *For topological vector spaces, see 515.73*

.2   Algebraic topology

> *See also 512.55 for topological algebras*

.22	Combinatorial topology
.223	Combinatorial elements

Including simplexes, complexes, nets

.224	Structures and spaces

Standard subdivisions are added for either or both topics in heading

Including braids, fiber bundles, fiber spaces, links, path spaces, sheaves, vector bundles

.224 2	Knots
.23	Homology and cohomology theories

Standard subdivisions are added for either or both topics in heading

Including topological K-theory

Class homological algebra in 512.64; class K-theory in 512.66

> *See also 512.55 for topological groups*

SUMMARY

.1 **Analysis and calculus combined with other branches of mathematics**

> *For algebra and calculus, see 512.15*

> *See Manual at 510: Combination of topics*

.13 Analysis and topology

.14 Analysis and linear algebra

.15 Calculus and analytic geometry

.16 Calculus and trigonometry

.2 **General aspects of analysis**

Class a specific application with the application, e.g., operations on functions of real variables 515.823

.22 Properties of functions

.222 Continuity, dimension, limit

Class here continuous functions

.23 Operations on functions

> *For differentiation, see 515.33; for integration, see 515.43*

.24 Sequences and series

Standard subdivisions are added for sequences and series together, for sequences alone

Including algebraic progressions, arithmetic progressions, geometric progressions

Class here infinite processes

.243 Series

Including summability

Class here infinite series

Class number theory of continued fractions in 512.72

.243 2 Power series

.243 3	Fourier and harmonic analysis

> Standard subdivisions are added for either or both topics in heading
>
> Including wavelets
>
> Class here Fourier series
>
> Class Fourier transforms in 515.723
>
> *For abstract harmonic analysis, see 515.785*

.25	Equations and functions

> Standard subdivisions are added for either or both topics in heading

.252	Equations and functions by degree

> Including linear, nonlinear, quadratic equations

.253	Equations and functions by property

> Including homogeneous, indeterminate, reciprocal equations

.26	Inequalities

.3   Differential calculus and equations

> Class differential topology in 514.72; class differential operators in 515.7242; class differential geometry in 516.36; class comprehensive works on differential and integral calculus and equations in 515

.33	Differential calculus

> Including ordinary, partial, total differentiations; total and directional derivatives, mean value theorems
>
> Class vector differentiation in 515.63; class numerical differentiation in 518.53; class probability calculus in 519.2

.35	Differential equations

> Class here Cauchy problem; orders, degrees; comprehensive works on boundary-value problems
>
> Class mixed equations in 515.38; class numerical solutions in 518.63
>
> *For dynamical systems, see 515.39 For boundary-value problems of finite differences, see 515.62*

.352	Ordinary differential equations
.353	Partial differential equations
.353 3	Elliptic equations
.353 4	Parabolic equations
.353 5	Hyperbolic equations
.354	Linear differential equations

> Class linear ordinary differential equations in 515.352; class linear partial differential equations in 515.353

.355	Nonlinear differential equations

Class nonlinear ordinary differential equations in 515.352; class nonlinear partial differential equations in 515.353

.357	Inverse problems

Class inverse problems of specific kinds of equations in 515.352–515.355

.36	Differential inequalities
.37	Differential forms
.38	Mixed equations

Including differential-difference and integro-differential equations

.39	Dynamical systems

Including chaos theory, Hamiltonian systems

.392	Stability theory

Including bifurcation theory, perturbation theory

.4	**Integral calculus and equations**

Class special functions in 515.5; class integral transforms in 515.723; class integral geometry in 516.362

.42	Theory of measure and integration

Standard subdivisions are added for either or both topics in heading

Class here abstract measure theory

For functionals, see 515.7

.43	Integral calculus

Including integration, summation, arc length, convolutions, cubature, quadrature; Cauchy, definite, Denjoy, Green, Haar, improper, Lebesgue, line, Poisson, Poisson-Stieltjes, proper, Riemann, Stokes', surface integrals

Class vector integration in 515.63; class numerical integration in 518.54; class probability integration in 519.2

.45	Integral equations

Class mixed equations in 515.38; class numerical solutions in 518.66

.46	Integral inequalities
.48	Ergodic theory
.5	**Special functions**
.52	Eulerian integrals

Including beta and gamma functions

.53	Harmonic functions

Including Bessel, Hankel, Laplace, Legendre, Neumann functions

.54	Mathieu functions

.55	Orthogonal polynomials

Including Chebyshev, Hermite, hypergeometric, Jacobi, Lagrange, Laguerre, Legendre polynomials

.56	Zeta function

Class application of Riemann zeta function with respect to prime number theory in 512.73

.6 Other analytic methods

For functional analysis, see 515.7

.62	Calculus of finite differences

Class here boundary-value problems when either limit has a numerical value

.625	Difference equations

Class difference-differential equations in 515.38

.63	Vector, tensor, spinor analysis

Standard subdivisions are added for vector, tensor, spinor analysis together; for vector analysis alone; for tensor analysis alone

Including vector and tensor calculus

Class algebraic vector analysis in 512.52; class geometric vector analysis in 516.182

.64	Calculus of variations

.642	Control theory

Class here optimal control

Class optimization in 519.6

See also 003.5 for interdisciplinary works on control theory; also 629.8312 for control theory in engineering

.7 Functional analysis

Class here comprehensive works on real-valued, complex-valued, vector-valued functions

Class theory of measure and integration in 515.42; class potential theory in 515.9

For topological algebras, see 512.55; for functions of real variables, see 515.8; for functions of complex variables, see 515.9

.72	Operational calculus

Class a specific application with the application, e.g., differential operators in topological vector spaces 515.73

.722	Spectral and representation theories

.722 2	Spectral theory

Class spectral theory of a specific kind of operator with the kind of operator, e.g., spectral theory of differential operators 515.7242

.722 3	Representation theory

Class abstract harmonic analysis in 515.42

.723	Transforms (Integral operators, integral transforms)

Including Fourier, Hilbert, Laplace, Legendre, Radon, Z transforms

.724	Operator theory

For integral operators, see 515.723

.724 2	Differential operators

Including elliptic operators

.724 6	Linear operators

Class linear integral operators in 515.723; class linear differential operators in 515.7242

.724 8	Nonlinear operators

Class here nonlinear functional analysis

Class nonlinear integral operators in 515.723; class nonlinear differential operators in 515.7242

.73	Topological vector spaces

Including spaces of analytic functions; spaces of continuous functions; spaces of measurable functions, e.g., L^p spaces, Orlicz spaces; Hermitian (unitary) and Riesz spaces

Class here linear topological spaces

For functionals, see 515.7

.732	Banach spaces

Class here normed linear spaces

For Hilbert spaces, see 515.733

.733	Hilbert spaces

Class here inner product spaces

.75	Functional equations

Class difference equations in 515.625

.78	Special topics of functional analysis
.782	Distribution theory

Including duality, Sobolev spaces

Class here generalized functions

.785   Abstract harmonic analysis

         Including Fourier analysis on groups

.8   **Functions of real variables**

         Class here real analysis

         Class combined treatment of functions of real and complex variables in 515.9

         See also 512.786 for real numbers

.82   General aspects of functions of real variables

         Add to base number 515.82 the numbers following 515.2 in 515.22–515.26, e.g., expansion of functions 515.823

         Class a specific application with the application, e.g., expansion of functions of several real variables 515.84

.83   Functions of one real variable

         Including fractional calculus

.84   Functions of several real variables

.88   Specific types of real variable functions

         Including real variable analytic functions

.882   Convex functions

         Class here convex analysis

.9   **Functions of complex variables**

         Class here automorphic functions, complex analysis, conformal mapping

         See also 512.788 for complex numbers

.92   General aspects of functions of complex variables

         Add to base number 515.92 the numbers following 515.2 in 515.22–515.26, e.g., expansion of functions 515.923

         Class a specific application with the application, e.g., expansion of functions of several complex variables 515.94

.93   Functions of one complex variable

         Including Riemann surfaces

.94   Functions of several complex variables

         Including singularities in functions of several complex variables, Teichmüller spaces

         Class comprehensive works on singularities in 514.746

.942   Analytic spaces

         Generalization of Riemann surfaces to n-dimensional spaces

.946   Complex manifolds

.96   Potential theory

> *For a specific application of potential theory, see the application, e.g., harmonic analysis and potential theory 515.2433*

.98   Specific types of complex variable functions

> Including entire, holomorphic, pseudoanalytic functions

.982   Meromorphic functions

.983   Elliptic functions

> Class special elliptic functions in 515.5

.984   Theta function

516   Geometry

> Class here geometry combined with topology

> Class algebra combined with geometry in 512.1; class arithmetic combined with geometry in 513.13; class analysis combined with geometry in 515.1; class geometric probability in 519.2

> *For topology, see 514*

SUMMARY

516.001–.009	**Standard subdivisions**
.02–.08	**[Classical and modern geometry; manifolds, convex sets]**
.1	**General aspects of geometry**
.2	**Euclidean geometry**
.3	**Analytic geometries**
.4	**Affine geometry**
.5	**Projective geometry**
.6	**Abstract descriptive geometry**
.9	**Non-Euclidean geometries**

.001–.009   Standard subdivisions

.02   Classical geometry

.04   Modern geometry

.07   Manifolds

> *For topological manifolds, see 514.34*

.08   Convex sets

> Class here convex geometry

.1   General aspects of geometry

> Including symmetry

> Class here automorphisms, metric geometry, transformations

> Class general aspects applied to a specific geometry with the geometry, e.g., conic sections in Euclidean geometry 516.2152

.11	Finite geometry
	Class here discrete geometry
.12	Incidence geometry
.13	Combinatorial geometry
.132	Tilings
	Class here tessellations
.15	Geometric configurations

.15 Geometric configurations

Including mensuration, patterns, sizes, space

Class here measures, shapes

Class geometric configurations in a specific subject with the subject, e.g., measuring the sphere in solid geometry 516.23

.152 One-dimensional configurations

Including angles, circles, conic sections, lines, spirals

Class here curves

.154 Two-dimensional configurations

Including cones, cylinders, disks, polygons, spheres, squares, triangles

Class here planes, surfaces

See also 516.22 for plane geometry

.156 Three-dimensional configurations

Including balls, cubes, polyhedra, prisms, pyramids

Class here solids

See also 516.23 for solid geometry

.158 Four-dimensional and higher-dimensional configurations

Including hypercubes, polytopes

.16 Coordinate systems

Including Cartesian, curvilinear, homogeneous systems

.18 Nonpoint base geometries

.182 Vector geometry

Class vector algebra in 512.5

.183 Line geometry

.2 Euclidean geometry

Class here congruences, similarity, metric geometry

Class a specific type of Euclidean geometry with the type, e.g., Euclidean analytic geometry 516.3

.200 1–.200 9 Standard subdivisions

.204		Famous problems

> Including trisecting an angle, squaring the circle, doubling the cube

.21		General aspects of Euclidean geometry

> Add to base number 516.21 the numbers following 516.1 in 516.12–516.18, e.g., conic sections 516.2152

> Class a specific application with the application, e.g., conic sections in plane geometry 516.22

.22		Plane geometry

> Including Pythagorean theorem

.23		Solid geometry
.24		Trigonometry
.242		Plane trigonometry
.244		Spherical trigonometry
.246		Trigonometric functions

> Class analytic trigonometry in 516.34

.3   **Analytic geometries**

> Class linear algebra combined with analytic geometry in 512.5; class analytic affine geometry in 516.4; class analytic projective geometry in 516.5

.32		Plane analytic geometry
.33		Solid analytic geometry
.34		Analytic trigonometry

> Plane and spherical

.35		Algebraic geometry

> Geometries based on linear algebra

> Including enumerative geometry, lattice point geometry, singularities

> Class here birational and conformal transformations, connections, dual geometries, intersections; bilinear and sesquilinear forms; complex multiplication

> Class comprehensive works in singularities in 514.746

.352		Curves and surfaces on projective and affine planes

> Standard subdivisions are added for either or both topics in heading

> Including Mordell conjecture

> Class here theory of curves

.353		Algebraic varieties of higher dimensions

> Including Abelian varieties

.36 Differential and integral geometry

Standard subdivisions are added for differential and integral geometry together, for differential geometry alone

Including symplectic manifolds

Class here curves, differentiable manifolds, surfaces, torsion

For metric differential geometries, see 516.37

.362 Integral geometry (Global differential geometry)

Including arc length, curvature, evolutes, geodesics, involutes, tangent space at a point; analytic, convex, developable, minimal, ruled surfaces; analytic, asymptotic, minimal curves; Riemannian manifolds, symmetric spaces

Class here modern differential geometry

For fiber bundles, fiber spaces, see 514.224

.37 Metric differential geometries

.373 Riemannian geometry

Including Sasakian geometry

.374 Minkowski geometry

Including Einstein geometry

.375 Finsler geometry

.376 Cartan geometry

.4 **Affine geometry**

Class affine differential geometry in 516.36

.5 **Projective geometry**

Class projective differential geometry in 516.36

.6 **Abstract descriptive geometry**

See also 604.2015166 for descriptive geometry in technical drawing

.9 **Non-Euclidean geometries**

Including Bolyai, elliptic, Gauss, hyperbolic, inversive, Lobachevski geometries; imbeddings of non-Euclidean spaces in other geometries

Class a specific type of non-Euclidean geometry with the type, e.g., non-Euclidean analytic geometries 516.3

[517] **[Unassigned]**

Most recently used in Edition 17

518   Numerical analysis

Class here applied numerical analysis, numerical calculations, numerical mathematics

Class approximations and expansions in 511.4

For numerical statistical mathematics, see 519.5

.1   **Algorithms**

.2   **Specific numerical methods**

Class specific numerical methods applied to a particular field in 518.4–518.6

.23   Graphic methods

Including nomography

.25   Finite element analysis

Class here finite strip method, finite volume method

.26   Iterative methods

.28   Probabilistic methods

Class here statistical methods, stochastic methods

.282   Monte Carlo method

.4   **Numerical methods in algebra, arithmetic, number theory**

.42   Numerical methods in algebra

Class here numerical algebra

For numerical linear algebra, see 518.43

.43   Numerical linear algebra

.45   Numerical methods in arithmetic

.47   Numerical methods in number theory

.5   **Numerical approximation**

.53   Numerical differentiation

.54   Numerical integration

.6   **Numerical methods in analysis**

Class here numerical methods in calculus

Class numerical approximation in 518.5

.63   Numerical solutions of ordinary differential equations

Including Galerkin method, relaxation methods, Runge-Kutta method

.64   Numerical solutions of partial differential equations

.66   Numerical solutions of integral equations

519 Probabilities and applied mathematics

Standard subdivisions are added for probabilities and applied mathematics together; for applied mathematics alone

Class a specific application with the application, e.g., statistics in physics 530.1595, game theory in gambling 795.01

SUMMARY

519.2	**Probabilities**
.3	**Game theory**
.5	**Statistical mathematics**
.6	**Mathematical optimization**
.7	**Programming**
.8	**Special topics of applied mathematics**

.2   **Probabilities**

Class here conditional probabilities, geometric probability, probability calculus

Class probabilistic methods of numerical analysis in 518.28; class probabilities applied to statistical mathematics in 519.5

.22   Stochastic analysis

.23   Random processes (Stochastic processes)

For queuing processes, see 519.82

.232   Stationary processes

Including time series

.233   Markov processes

Including Markov chains

.234   Branching processes

.236   Martingales

.24   Probability distribution

Including binomial distribution, Poisson distribution

.27   Games of chance (Stochastic games)

Class here gambling

See Manual at 795.015192 vs. 519.27

.28   Special topics of probabilities

.282   Random walks

.287   Expectation and prediction

Standard subdivisions are added for either or both topics in heading

Including estimation, reliability, renewal theories; Markov risk

.3   **Game theory**

Class games of chance in 519.27

.32	Differential games
.5	**Statistical mathematics**

Class here parametric and nonparametric methods

See Manual at 519.5, T1—015195 vs. 001.422, T1—0727

.52	Theory of sampling
.53	Descriptive statistics, multivariate analysis, analysis of variance and covariance

Including cluster analysis

.532	Frequency distributions
.533	Measures of central tendency

Including median, mean, mode

Class here averaging

.534	Measures of deviation

Including standard deviation

.535	Multivariate analysis

Including latent structure analysis

For regression analysis, see 519.536; for correlation analysis, see 519.537

.535 4	Factor analysis

Including principal components analysis

.536	Regression analysis

Including autoregression

.537	Correlation analysis (Association analysis)

Including autocorrelation

.538	Analysis of variance and covariance

Standard subdivisions are added for either or both topics in heading

.54	Statistical inference

Including bootstrap methods, confidence regions, expectation, nonparametric inference, parametric inference, prediction, resampling methods, sequential analysis

.542	Decision theory

Including Bayesian statistical decision theory

.544	Estimation theory
.546	Survival analysis

Class here censored observations

.55	Time-series analysis
.56	Hypothesis testing

Including chi-square test, goodness-of-fit tests

.57	Design of experiments

Including factorial experiment designs

.6 **Mathematical optimization**

Class control theory in 515.642

For a specific mathematical optimization technique, see the technique, e.g., mathematical programming 519.7

See also 511.65 for choice and decision making in combinatorial analysis

.62	Stochastic optimization
.623	Stochastic approximation
.625	Genetic algorithms
.64	Combinatorial optimization

.7 **Programming**

.700 1–.700 9	Standard subdivisions
.702	Single-stage programming
.703	Multistage programming

Including dynamic programming

.72	Linear programming
.76	Nonlinear programming

Including convex and quadratic programming

Class integer programming in 519.77

.77	Integer programming

.8 **Special topics of applied mathematics**

.82	Queuing

Including congestion

Class here queuing processes

.83	Inventory and storage
.84	Success runs
.85	Epidemics and fluctuations
.86	Quality control

520 Astronomy and allied sciences

See Manual at 520 vs. 500.5, 523.1, 530.1, 919.9; also at 520 vs. 523.1, 523.112, 523.8

SUMMARY

521	**Celestial mechanics**
522	**Techniques, procedures, apparatus, equipment, materials**
523	**Specific celestial bodies and phenomena**
525	**Earth (Astronomical geography)**
526	**Mathematical geography**
527	**Celestial navigation**
528	**Ephemerides**
529	**Chronology**

[.153]   Physical principles

Do not use; class in 523.01

[.154]   Chemical principles

Do not use; class in 523.02

[.28]   Auxiliary techniques and procedures; apparatus, equipment, materials

Do not use; class in 522

> ## 521–525 Astronomy

Class comprehensive works in 520

For geodetic astronomy, see 526.6

521 Celestial mechanics

Including equilibrium, problems of three and n bodies

Class here motion

Class applications to specific celestial bodies and phenomena in 523

.1   **Gravitation**

.3   **Orbits**

Class here Kepler's laws

.4   **Perturbations**

.9   **Precession**

Including nutation

Class corrections of precession in 522.9

522 Techniques, procedures, apparatus, equipment, materials

Class here astrometry, positional and practical astronomy

Class positional astronomy as an aspect of mathematical geography in 526.6

[.028]	Auxiliary techniques and procedures; apparatus, equipment, materials

> Do not use for general works; class in 522. Do not use for specific auxiliary techniques and procedures; class in 522.8

> ### 522.1–522.6 Practical astronomy

Class comprehensive works in 522

For corrections, see 522.9; for practical astronomy of specific celestial bodies and phenomena, see 523

.1	**Observatories**

Optical and nonoptical

.109	History and biography

> Do not use for geographic treatment; class in 522.19

.19	Geographic treatment

> Add to base number 522.19 notation 1–9 from Table 2, e.g., space observatories 522.1919, observatories in China 522.1951

.2	**Astronomical instruments**

Class here movable nonspace telescopes; comprehensive works on telescopes

For auxiliary instruments, see 522.5; for astronomical instruments used in nonoptical astronomy, see 522.68; for sextants, see 527.0284

.29	Fixed-location and space telescopes
.290 9	History and biography

> Do not use for geographic treatment; class in 522.291–522.299

.291–.299	Geographic treatment

> Add to base number 522.29 notation 1–9 from Table 2, e.g., fixed location telescopes in Chile 522.2983

.5	**Auxiliary instruments**

Including chronographs, chronometers

For auxiliary instruments in special methods of observation, see 522.6

.6	**Special methods of observation**
.62	Photometry
.622	Photographic photometry
.623	Photoelectric photometry
.63	Photography

For photographic photometry, see 522.622

.65	Polarimetry

| .67 | Spectroscopy |

Class spectroscopy of a specific celestial body with the body, plus notation 0287 from Table 1, e.g., spectroscopy of planets 523.40287

| .68 | Nonoptical astronomy |

Class here nonoptical telescopes

For nonoptical observatories, see 522.1

| .682 | Radio astronomy |

| .683 | Infrared astronomy |

| .686 | Particle methods of observation |

| .686 2 | Gamma-ray astronomy |

| .686 3 | X-ray astronomy |

| **.7** | **Spherical astronomy** |

Including celestial reference systems

Class comprehensive works on geodetic coordinates in 526.6

| **.8** | **Specific auxiliary techniques and procedures** |

Add to base number 522.8 the numbers following —028 in notation 0285–0289 from Table 1, e.g., testing and measurement 522.87

Class spectroscopy in 522.67

| **.9** | **Corrections** |

Corrections of aberration, astronomical refraction, parallax, precession; of instrumental errors

523   Specific celestial bodies and phenomena

Including zodiac

Class phenomena of celestial bodies directly comparable to terrestrial phenomena with the terrestrial phenomena in 550, e.g., volcanic activity on Mars 551.21099923

See Manual at 523 vs. 550

SUMMARY

523.01–.02	**[Astrophysics and cosmochemistry]**
.1	**The universe, galaxies, quasars**
.2	**Planetary systems**
.3	**Moon**
.4	**Planets, asteroids, trans-Neptunian objects of solar system**
.5	**Meteors, solar wind, zodiacal light**
.6	**Comets**
.7	**Sun**
.8	**Stars**
.9	**Satellites and rings; eclipses, transits, occultations**

[.001–.009]	Standard subdivisions

Do not use; class in 520.1–520.9

.01	Astrophysics

For celestial mechanics, see 521

.013	Heat

Add to base number 523.013 the numbers following 536 in 536.1–536.7, e.g., heat transfer 523.0132

.015	Light and related radiation

Standard subdivisions are added for light and related radiation together, for light alone

.015 01	Infrared and ultraviolet radiation; philosophy and theory of light and related radiation

Class here radiation of nonvisible spectral regions

Add to base number 523.01501 the numbers following 535.01 in 535.012–535.019, e.g., infrared radiation 523.015012

Class a specific element of infrared and ultraviolet radiation in 523.0152–523.0156

.015 1–.015 8	Specific aspects of light and related radiation

Add to base number 523.015 the numbers following 535 in 535.1–535.8, e.g., polarization 523.01552

.018	Electricity and magnetism

Add to base number 523.018 the numbers following 53 in 537–538, e.g., magnetism 523.0188

.019	Molecular, atomic, nuclear physics

Add to base number 523.019 the numbers following 539 in 539.1–539.7, e.g., cosmic rays 523.0197223

.02	Cosmochemistry
.1	**The universe, galaxies, quasars**

Standard subdivisions are added for the universe, galaxies, quasars together; for the universe alone

Class here cosmology

See also 523.8875 for black holes

See Manual at 520 vs. 500.5, 523.1, 530.1, 919.9; also at 520 vs. 523.1, 523.112, 523.8

.11	Galaxies and quasars
.112	Galaxies

For Milky Way, see 523.113

See Manual at 520 vs. 523.1, 523.112, 523.8: Stars and galaxies

.112 5	Interstellar and intergalactic matter

Standard subdivisions are added for interstellar and intergalactic matter together, for interstellar matter alone

Class here cosmic dust

See also 523.1126 for dark matter

.112 6	Dark matter
.113	Milky Way
.113 5	Interstellar matter

Including diffuse and planetary nebulas

For dark matter, see 523.1126

.115	Quasars
.12	Cosmogony

For expanding universe theories, see 523.18

.18	Expanding universe theories

Class here big bang theory

.19	End of universe theories
.2	**Planetary systems**

Class here solar system

For specific parts of solar system, see 523.3–523.7

.24	Extrasolar systems

Class here extrasolar planets

>   **523.3–523.7 Specific parts of solar system**

Class comprehensive works in 523.2

.3	**Moon**
.31	Constants and dimensions

Including gravity, size, mass

.32	Optical, electromagnetic, radioactive, thermal phenomena

Including phases

.33	Orbit and motions

Including librations, sidereal month

.38	Eclipses

.4	**Planets, asteroids, trans-Neptunian objects of solar system**

Standard subdivisions are added for planets, asteroids, trans-Neptunian objects of solar system together, for planets of solar system alone

Class here comprehensive works on planets, satellites, rings of solar system

Add to notation for each number identified by * the numbers following 523.3 in 523.31–523.33, e.g., orbit of Jupiter 523.453

For meteors, see 523.51; for satellites and rings, see 523.98; for transits, occultations, see 523.99; for earth, see 525

See also 523.24 for extrasolar planets

.41	*Mercury
.42	*Venus
.43	*Mars
.44	Asteroids (Planetoids)

Including Ceres

Class comprehensive works on meteors and asteroids in 523.5

.45	*Jupiter
.46	*Saturn
.47	*Uranus
.48	*Neptune
.49	Trans-Neptunian objects
.492	Kuiper belt objects
.492 2	*Pluto
.494	Scattered disk objects
.497	Oort cloud objects

.5	**Meteors, solar wind, zodiacal light**

Class here interplanetary matter, comprehensive works on meteors and asteroids

For asteroids, see 523.44

.51	Meteors

Class here meteoroids, meteorites

For meteor showers, see 523.53

.53	Meteor showers

Including radiant points

.58	Solar wind

*Add as instructed under 523.4

.59	Zodiacal light

Including counterglow (gegenschein)

.6 **Comets**

.63 Motion and orbits

Class motion and orbits of specific comets in 523.64

.64 Specific comets

[.640 1–.640 9] Standard subdivisions

Do not use; class in 523.601–523.609

.642 Halley's comet

.66 Physical phenomena and constitution

Class physical phenomena and constitution of specific comets in 523.64

.7 **Sun**

.702 1 Tabulated and related materials

Class sun tables indicating orbits and motions of earth in 525.38

.71 Constants and dimensions

Including gravity, size, mass

.72 Optical, electromagnetic, radioactive, thermal phenomena

Class here solar energy, solar radiation

For phenomena of photosphere, see 523.74; for phenomena of chromosphere and corona, see 523.75

See also 523.59 for zodiacal light

.73 Motions

Including apparent motion, rotation

.74 Photosphere

Including faculae, solar granulation, sunspots

.75 Chromosphere and corona

Including solar flares and prominences

See also 523.58 for solar wind

.76 Solar interior

.78 Eclipses

.8   **Stars**

> Class here comprehensive works on stars and galaxies
>
> *For galaxies, see 523.112; for sun, see 523.7*
>
> *See also 523.115 for quasars; also 523.24 for extrasolar systems*
>
> *See Manual at 520 vs. 523.1, 523.112, 523.8: Stars and galaxies*

[.802 87]   Testing and measurement

> Do not use; class in 523.87

>   **523.81–523.83 Properties and phenomena**
>
> Class comprehensive works in 523.8
>
> *For physical constitution, see 523.86. For properties and phenomena of a specific kind of star or aggregation of stars, see the kind or aggregation, e.g., properties of supernovas 523.84465, properties of spectral types 523.87*

.81   Constants and dimensions

> Including gravity, size, mass, parallax

.82   Optical, electromagnetic, radioactive, thermal phenomena

> Class here stellar radiation

.822   Magnitudes

.83   Motion

> Including velocity

.84   Aggregations and variable stars

> Standard subdivisions are added for aggregations and variable stars together, for aggregations alone
>
> Class here comprehensive works on binary stars and clusters
>
> *For clusters, see 523.85*
>
> *See also 523.112 for galaxies*

.841   Binary and multiple stars

> Standard subdivisions are added for binary and multiple stars together, for binary stars alone
>
> Including optical and visual binaries
>
> Class here astrometric binaries
>
> *For spectroscopic binaries, see 523.842; for eclipsing binaries, see 523.8444*

.842   Spectroscopic binaries

.844   Variable stars

.844 2	Intrinsic variables

For eruptive variables, see 523.8446

.844 25	Pulsating variables

Class here Cepheids

For long-period and semiregular variables, see 523.84426; for pulsars, see 523.8874

.844 26	Long-period and semiregular variables
.844 4	Eclipsing binaries (Extrinsic variables)
.844 6	Eruptive variables

Including flare stars, novas

.844 65	Supernovas
.85	Clusters
.852	Open clusters
.855	Globular clusters
.86	Physical constitution

Class physical constitution of a specific kind or aggregation of star with the kind or aggregation, e.g., constitution of neutron stars 523.8874

.87	Spectral types

Class here spectroscopy, testing and measurement

Class spectral types representative of specific stages in the evolution of stars in 523.88. Class spectroscopy of a specific kind or aggregation of star with the kind or aggregation, plus notation 0287 from Table 1, e.g., spectroscopy of neutron stars 523.88740287

.88	Kinds of stars characteristic of stages of stellar evolution

Including giant (R, N, or S spectral type), main sequence, red dwarf, Wolf-Rayet stars; star formation

Class here stellar evolution

For intrinsic variables, see 523.8442

.887	Terminal stages

Including white dwarfs

.887 4	Neutron stars

Class here pulsars

.887 5	Black holes
.9	**Satellites and rings; eclipses, transits, occultations**
.91	Transits of Mercury
.92	Transits of Venus

.98 Satellites and rings

Variant name for satellites: moons

Add to base number 523.98 the numbers following 523.4 in 523.43–523.48, e.g., satellites of Jupiter 523.985, orbits of Jovian satellites 523.9853

Subdivisions are added for either or both topics in heading

For earth's moon, see 523.3

.99 Eclipses, transits, occultations

For transits of Mercury, see 523.91; for transits of Venus, see 523.92. For eclipses of a specific celestial body, see the body, e.g., eclipses of the moon 523.38

[524] [Unassigned]

Most recently used in Edition 14

525 Earth (Astronomical geography)

For magnetic properties, see 538.7

.1 Constants and dimensions

Including size, shape

Class determination of size and shape in 526.1

For gravity, see 531.14

.2 Optical, radioactive, thermal properties

.3 Orbit and motions

.35 Rotation

.36 Foucault's pendulum

.38 Sun tables

Class here sunrise and sunset tables

.5 Seasons and zones of latitude

Standard subdivisions are added for seasons and zones of latitude together, for seasons alone

Limited to astronomical causes of seasons and zones of latitude

Class climatology in 551.6; class interdisciplinary works on seasons in 508.2

.7 Twilight

Class here dawn

526   Mathematical geography

Class here cartography, map drawing, map making

Class map making for a specific purpose with the purpose, e.g., military map making 623.71

For astronomical geography, see 525

See also 912.014 for map reading

.1   Geodesy

For geodetic surveying, see 526.3; for geodetic astronomy and geographic positions, see 526.6; for gravity determinations, see 526.7

.3   Geodetic surveying

Surveying in which curvature of earth is considered

.31   Reconnaissance surveys

.32   Bench marks

.320 9   History and biography

Do not use for geographic treatment; class in 526.321–526.329

.321–.329   Geographic treatment

Add to base number 526.32 notation 1–9 from Table 2, e.g., bench marks in California 526.32794

.33   Triangulation, trilateration, traversing

Standard subdivisions are added for triangulation, trilateration, traversing together; for triangulation alone

Including base lines, nets

.36   Leveling

Class here spirit leveling

For bench marks, see 526.32; for barometric leveling, see 526.37; for trigonometric leveling, see 526.38

.37   Barometric leveling

.38   Trigonometric leveling

.6   Geodetic astronomy and geographic positions

Standard subdivisions are added for geodetic astronomy and geographic positions together, for geodetic astronomy alone

Class here geodetic aspects of positional astronomy; comprehensive works on geodetic coordinates

Class comprehensive works on positional astronomy in 522

For coordinates in spherical astronomy, see 522.7

.61   Latitude

> *For latitude in celestial navigation, see 527.1*

.62   Longitude

> *For longitude in celestial navigation, see 527.2*

.63   Azimuth

.64   Geographic positions

> Including effect of irregularities of earth's surface on determining geographic positions

.7   Gravity determinations

.8   Map projections

> Class map reading in 912.014

.82   Conformal projections (Orthomorphic projections)

.85   Equal-area projections (Equivalent projections)

.9   Surveying

> Class here plane surveying (surveying in which curvature of earth is disregarded), land surveying
>
> Class work of chartered surveyors (United Kingdom), interdisciplinary works on land surveys in 333.08; class engineering surveys in 622–629
>
> *For geodetic surveying, see 526.3*

.98   Topographic surveying

.981   Contour surveying

.982   Photogrammetry

> Class here aerial and space surveying

.982 5   Ground photogrammetry (Terrestrial photogrammetry)

.99   Hydrographic surveying

527   Celestial navigation

> *For celestial navigation of specific craft, see the craft, e.g., navigation of nautical craft 623.89*

.028 4   Apparatus, equipment, materials

> Including sextants

.1   Latitude

.2   Longitude

.3   **Position determination**

         Including Sumner's method

            For determination of latitude, see 527.1; for determination of longitude, see 527.2

528   **Ephemerides**

         Variant names: astronomical, nautical almanacs

         Class tables of specific celestial bodies in 523

.093–.099   Treatment in ancient world, treatment by specific continent

            Do not use for treatment by specific country or locality; class in 528.1–528.8

.1–.8   **Ephemerides of specific countries and localities**

            Add to base number 528 the numbers following 06 in 061–068, e.g., ephemerides of England 528.2

.9   **Ephemeris making**

529   **Chronology**

.1   **Days**

         Including apparent and mean days, equation of time, sidereal and solar days

.2   **Intervals of time**

         Including years, months, weeks

            For sidereal month, see 523.33; for days, see 529.1

            See also 525.5 for seasons

.3   **Calendars**

            For western calendars, see 529.4; for calendar reform, see 529.5

.32   Calendars of specific religions and traditions

            Add to base number 529.32 the numbers following 29 in 292–299, e.g., Jewish calendar 529.326; however, for Julian calendar, see 529.42

            For Christian calendars, see 529.4

.4   **Western calendars**

         Class here Christian calendars

.42   Julian calendar

.43   Gregorian calendar

.44   Christian church calendar

         Including determination of movable feasts and fast days

.5   **Calendar reform**

.7   **Horology**

Finding and measuring time

Class time systems and standards in 389.17

For manufacture of instruments for measuring time, see 681.11

530   Physics

Class here energy, matter, antimatter, classical physics; comprehensive works on classical and quantum mechanics

Class quantum mechanics, energy in quantum mechanics in 530.12; class classical mechanics in 531; class energy in classical mechanics in 531.6; class physical chemistry in 541

For astrophysics, see 523.01

SUMMARY

530.01–.09	Standard subdivisions	
.1	Theories and mathematical physics	
.4	States of matter	
.7	Instrumentation	
.8	Measurement	
531	Classical mechanics	
.015 195		Statistical mathematics
.1	Dynamics, statics, mass and gravity, particle mechanics	
.2	Solid statics	
.3	Solid dynamics	
.4	Friction and viscosity of solids	
.5	Mass and gravity of solids; projectiles	
.6	Energy	
532	Fluid mechanics	
.001–.009	Standard subdivisions	
.02–.05	Fluid statics and dynamics	
.2	Hydrostatics	
.4	Mass, density, specific gravity of liquids	
.5	Hydrodynamics	
533	Pneumatics (Gas mechanics)	
.1	Statics; mass, density, specific gravity	
.2	Dynamics	
.5	Vacuums	
.6	Aeromechanics	
.7	Kinetic theory of gases	
534	Sound and related vibrations	
.1	Generation of sound	
.2	Transmission of sound	
.3	Characteristics of sound	
.5	Vibrations related to sound	

535		**Light and related radiation**
	.01–.09	**Infrared and ultraviolet radiation; standard subdivisions**
	.1	**Theories**
	.2	**Physical optics**
	.3	**Transmission, absorption, emission of light**
	.4	**Dispersion of light**
	.5	**Beams**
	.6	**Color**
	.8	**Special developments of light and related radiation**
536		**Heat**
	.01	**Philosophy and theory**
	.1	**Theories**
	.2	**Heat transfer**
	.3	**Radiation**
	.4	**Effects of heat on matter**
	.5	**Temperature**
	.6	**Specific heat**
	.7	**Thermodynamics**
537		**Electricity and electronics**
	.01	**Philosophy and theory**
	.1	**Theories**
	.2	**Electrostatics**
	.5	**Electronics**
	.6	**Electrodynamics (Electric currents) and thermoelectricity**
538		**Magnetism**
	.3	**Magnetic properties and phenomena**
	.4	**Magnetic substances and their characteristic phenomena**
	.6	**Magnetohydrodynamics**
	.7	**Geomagnetism and related phenomena**
539		**Modern physics**
	.01	**Philosophy and theory**
	.1	**Structure of matter**
	.2	**Radiation (Radiant energy)**
	.6	**Molecular physics**
	.7	**Atomic and nuclear physics**

.01   Philosophy and theory

> Do not use for theories; class in 530.1

[.015 1]   Mathematical physics

> Do not use; class in 530.15

.02   Miscellany

.028 4   Materials

> Do not use for apparatus and equipment; class in 530.7

[.028 7]   Testing and measurement

> Do not use; class in 530.8

.03–.09   Standard subdivisions

.1	**Theories and mathematical physics**

Standard subdivisions are added for theories and mathematical physics together, for theories alone

Including space

Class applications to specific states of matter in 530.4

See Manual at 520 vs. 500.5, 523.1, 530.1, 919.9

.11	Relativity theory

Including fourth dimension

Class here conservation of mass-energy, equivalence of mass-energy ($E=mc^2$), space-time

Class specific relativistic theories in 530.12–530.14

.12	Quantum mechanics (Quantum theory)

Class here relativistic, nonrelativistic quantum mechanics

For quantum statistics, see 530.133; for quantum kinetic theories, see 530.136; for quantum field theory, see 530.143; for quantum electronics, see 537.5

See Manual at 530.475 vs. 530.12, 531.16

.122	Matrix mechanics (Heisenberg representation)
.124	Wave mechanics

Waves considered as a fundamental property of matter

Class here Schrödinger wave mechanics

See also 530.141 for waves in electromagnetic theory; also 531.1133 for waves in classical physics

.13	Statistical mechanics

Class here relativistic, nonrelativistic statistical mechanics

Including percolation theory

.132	Classical statistical mechanics (Boltzmann statistics)
.133	Quantum statistics (Quantum statistical mechanics)
.136	Kinetic theories

Class here quantum, combined quantum-classical kinetic theories

For classical kinetic theory, see 531.113

.138	Transport theory

.14   Field and wave theories

            Classical, quantum, relativistic, nonrelativistic theories accounting for
            fundamental particles and interactions

            Standard subdivisions are added for field and wave theories together, for
            field theories alone

            Including problem of few bodies, theory of continuum physics

                *For wave mechanics, see 530.124; for string and superstring theories,
                see 539.7258*

.141   Electromagnetic theory

            Electromagnetic fields and waves considered in terms of fundamental
            structure of matter

            Including Maxwell's equations

            Class electromagnetic spectrum and waves in 539.2

                *See also 537.1 for theories of electricity; also 538.01 for theories of
                magnetism*

.142   Unified field theory

            Class here grand unified theory

.142 3   Supergravity

                Class here comprehensive works on supergravity and supersymmetry

                For supersymmetry, see 539.725

.143   Quantum field theory

.143 3   Quantum electrodynamics

.143 5   Gauge fields

.144   Problem of many bodies

.15   Mathematical physics

            Add to base number 530.15 the numbers following 51 in 511–519, e.g.,
            statistics 530.1595

            Class mathematical description of physical phenomena according to a
            specific theory with the theory in 530.1, e.g., statistical mechanics 530.13

.4   States of matter

            Class here quantum mechanics of specific states of matter; sound, light, heat,
            electricity, magnetism as properties of a specific state of matter

            Unless other instructions are given, class a subject with aspects in two or more
            subdivisions of 530.4 in the number coming last, e.g., tunneling in thin films
            530.4175 (*not* 530.416)

                For superconductivity and superconductors, see 537.623

.41 Solid-state physics

Class here physics of condensed matter

For liquid-state physics, see 530.42; for crystallography, see 548

See Manual at 548 vs. 530.41

.411 Structure

Including electron arrangement, lattice dynamics

.412 Properties

Including elastic, electrical, magnetic, optical, thermal properties

.413 Kinds

Including amorphous, crystalline and noncrystalline, metallic and nonmetallic, ordered and disordered, organic, porous solids; polymers; solid particles

For dielectric matter, see 537.24; for semiconductors, see 537.622; for crystals, see 548

.414 Phase transformations

Transformations between different phases of condensed matter, between solid and gas phases

.415 Diffusion and mass transfer

Standard subdivisions are added for either or both topics in heading

Class transport theory in 530.138

.416 Responsive behavior and energy phenomena

Including bombardment, collisions, emission, excitation, excited states, excitons, field effects, internal friction, ion implantation, Jahn-Teller effect, Josephson effect, oscillation, phonons, radiation effect, relaxation, scattering, sputtering, tunneling, vibration

Class responsive behavior and energy phenomena in semiconductors in 537.622

See Manual at 530.416 vs. 539.75

.417 Surface physics

Class here interface with other states of matter

Class surface physics of semiconductors in 537.622

.417 5 Thin films

Class comprehensive works on thin films in 530.4275

.42 Liquid-state physics

Including superfluidity

Class here fluid-state physics

For gaseous-state physics, see 530.43

.424   **Phase transformations**

Transformations between different fluid phases

Including critical points

Class phase transformations between fluids and solids in 530.414

.425   **Diffusion and mass transfer**

Standard subdivisions are added for either or both topics in heading

Including Brownian motion in liquids, osmosis

See Manual at 530.475 vs. 530.12, 531.16

.427   **Surface physics**

Including capillarity, drops, surface tension

Class here interface with gases

Class interface with solids in 530.417; class surface tension of thin films in 530.4275

.427 5   Thin films

Class here bubbles

.429   **Liquid crystals**

Including liquid polymers

.43   **Gaseous-state physics**

Class interface with solids in 530.417; class interface with liquids in 530.427; class ionization of gases in 530.444

For plasma physics, see 530.44

.435   **Diffusion and mass transfer**

Standard subdivisions are added for either or both topics in heading

.44   **Plasma physics**

Physics of ionized gases

Add to base number 530.44 the numbers following 530.41 in 530.412–530.416, e.g., optical properties of plasmas 530.442, ionization of gases 530.444

See also 537.532 for ionization of gases in electronics

.47   **Generalities of states of matter**

For generalities of specific states of matter, see 530.41–530.44

.474   Phase transformations

Variant names: phase changes, phase transitions

Including critical phenomena, e.g., critical points; phase diagrams, equilibria, stability; triple points

Class here analysis of phase transformations to matter at the molecular and submolecular level; changes of state

Class phase transformations between different phases of condensed matter, between solids and gases in 530.414; class phase transformations between fluid phases in 530.424; class phase transformations between plasmas and other states of matter in 530.444

.475   Diffusion and mass transfer

Standard subdivisions are added for either or both topics in heading

Variant name for mass transfer: mass transport

Class here Brownian motion

For heat transfer, see 536.2

See Manual at 530.475 vs. 530.12, 531.16

.7   **Instrumentation**

Instrumentation for measurement, control, recording

.8   **Measurement**

Including dimensional analysis, testing

Class here interdisciplinary works on measurement, on mensuration

Class instrumentation for measurement in 530.7

For horology, see 529.7. For measurement, mensuration in a specific subject, see the subject, plus notation 0287 from Table 1, e.g., psychological measurement 150.287

See also 516.15 for geometric mensuration

.801   Philosophy and theory

Class here measurement theory

.802   Miscellany

[.802 1]   Tabulated and related material

Do not use; class in 530.81

.81 Physical units and constants

> Standard subdivisions are added for physical units and constants together, for physical units alone

> Including dimensions, interdisciplinary works on size

> Class here conversion tables between systems, systems of measurement, tabulated and related materials, weights and measures

> Class units of dimension and size in metric system in 530.812; class units of dimension and size in British system in 530.813

> *For social aspects of systems of measurement, see 389.1. For a specific aspect of size, see the aspect, e.g., size of business enterprise 338.64*

[.810 21] Tabulated and related material

> Do not use; class in 530.81

.812 Metric system (Système international, SI)

.813 British system

> Variant names: English, Imperial system

> Class here United States customary units

531 Classical mechanics

> Variant names: mechanics, continuum mechanics, Newtonian mechanics

> Class here solid mechanics

> *For fluid mechanics, see 532*

.015 195 Statistical mathematics

> Class classical statistical mechanics in 530.132

.1 Dynamics, statics, mass and gravity, particle mechanics

> Including pressure, mechanics of points

[.101–.109] Standard subdivisions

> Do not use; class in 531.01–531.09

.11 Dynamics

> *For particle dynamics, see 531.163; for solid dynamics, see 531.3*

.112 Kinematics

> Motion considered apart from mass and force

> Including linear and relative motion, velocity, acceleration, vector quantities; search for a moving target

.113 Kinetics

> Including centrifugal and centripetal forces, rotational motion

> Class comprehensive works on motion in 531.11

.113 3		Waves

Waves observable in matter of classical physics

Including shock waves

> *See also 530.124 for waves considered as a fundamental property of matter*

.113 4		Rheology (Deformation and flow)

Including viscosity and friction

Most works on deformation are limited to solids and are classed in 531.38; most works on flow are limited to fluids and are classed in 532.051

.12	Statics

Including graphic statics

> *For particle statics, see 531.16; for solid statics, see 531.2*

.14	Mass and gravity

Including density, gravity of earth, specific gravity

Class geodetic gravity determinations in 526.7

> *For gravity in celestial mechanics, see 521.1*

> *See also 539.754 for fundamental gravitational interaction*

.16	Particle mechanics

Class here mechanics of solid particles

Class mechanics of molecular, atomic, and subatomic particles (quantum mechanics) in 530.12

> *See also 620.43 for fine particle technology*

> *See Manual at 530.475 vs. 530.12, 531.16*

.163	Dynamics

> **531.2–531.5 Mechanics of solids**

Class here mechanics of rigid bodies

Class comprehensive works in 531

> *For mechanics of solid particles, see 531.16*

.2	**Solid statics**

Including graphic statics

.3   **Solid dynamics**

       Including solid kinematics

       Class here solid kinetics

       For friction and viscosity, see 531.4; for ballistics, see 531.55

.32   Vibrations

       Class here oscillations

.324   Pendulum motion

.33   Waves

       Including shock waves

.34   Rotational motion (Spin)

       Class here gyrodynamics

       For centrifugal and centripetal forces, see 531.35

.35   Centrifugal and centripetal forces

       Standard subdivisions are added for either or both topics in heading

.38   Deformation; stresses and strains

       Standard subdivisions are added for deformation, stresses, strains together; for deformation alone

.381   Stresses and strains

       Standard subdivisions are added for either or both topics in heading

       Including elastic constants, Poisson's ratio, yield point

       Class application to elasticity in 531.382; class application to plasticity in 531.385

.382   Elasticity

       Variant names: elastic, temporary deformation

       Including elastic limit, coefficient of restitution

       Class here Hooke's law

       Class elastic vibrations in 531.32

.385   Plasticity

       Variant names: permanent, plastic deformation

.4   **Friction and viscosity of solids**

       Standard subdivisions are added for either or both topics in heading

.5   **Mass and gravity of solids; projectiles**

       Including laws of falling bodies

.54	Density and specific gravity

Standard subdivisions are added for either or both topics in heading

.55	Projectiles

Class here ballistics

.6   Energy

Including momentum, work

Class comprehensive works on energy in physics in 530; class interdisciplinary works on energy in 333.79

.62	Conservation of energy

See also 333.7916 for programs to conserve energy; also 530.11 for conservation of mass-energy

.68	Transformation

Change in form of energy

For a specific transformation, see the resultant form, e.g., transformation of light to heat 536

532   Fluid mechanics

Class here hydraulics (hydromechanics), liquid mechanics

For pneumatics, see 533

.001–.009	Standard subdivisions

>	532.02–532.05 Fluid statics and dynamics

Class comprehensive works in 532

.02	Statics

Including buoyancy

For liquid statics, see 532.2

.05	Dynamics

Including kinematics, vibrations

Class here kinetics

For liquid dynamics, see 532.5

.051	Flow

Including boundary layers

Class waves and vortex motion in 532.059

For types of flow, see 532.052; for flow properties, see 532.053

.052	Types of flow

        Class properties of specific types of flow in 532.053

        For viscous flow, see 532.0533; for rotational flow, see 532.0595

.052 5	Laminar flow
.052 6	Transitional flow
.052 7	Turbulent flow
.053	Flow properties
.053 2	Velocity
.053 3	Viscosity and friction

        Standard subdivisions are added for either or both topics in heading

        Class here viscous flow

.053 5	Elasticity and compressibility

        Standard subdivisions are added for either or both topics in heading

.059	Waves and vortex motion
.059 3	Waves

        Including shock waves

.059 5	Vortex motion

        Including centrifugal and centripetal forces

        Class here rotational flow

> **532.2–532.5 Hydraulics**

    In sense of liquid mechanics

    Class comprehensive works in 532

.2	**Hydrostatics**

    In sense of liquid statics

    See also 532.02 for hydrostatics in sense of fluid statics

.25	Buoyancy

    Class here floating, sinking

.4	**Mass, density, specific gravity of liquids**

.5	**Hydrodynamics**

        In sense of liquid dynamics

        Including kinematics

        Class here kinetics

        See also 532.05 for hydrodynamics in sense of fluid dynamics

.51	Flow

        Class waves and vortex motion in 532.59

        For flow variations, see 532.52–532.56; for flow properties, see 532.58; for rotational flow, see 532.595

.515	Laminar flow
.516	Transitional flow
.517	Turbulent flow

>   **532.52–532.56 Flow variations**

        Class comprehensive works in 532.51

.52	Flow through openings
.53	Flow over and around obstacles

        Standard subdivisions are added for either or both topics in heading

.54	Flow through open and closed channels

        Standard subdivisions are added for either or both topics in heading

.55	Flow through bends and irregular enclosures

        Standard subdivisions are added for either or both topics in heading

.56	Flow when pressure is variable

        Including flow over and around submerged bodies, multiphase flow

.57	Flow velocity
.58	Flow properties

        Including elasticity and compressibility, viscosity and friction, viscous flow

        For flow velocity, see 532.57

        See also 536.413 for expansion and contraction of liquids as a result of heating and cooling

.59	Waves, vortex motion, cavitation
.593	Waves

        Including shock waves

.595	Vortex motion

        Class here rotational flow

.597   Cavitation

533   Pneumatics (Gas mechanics)

>   **533.1–533.5 Specific aspects of pneumatics (gas mechanics)**

            Class comprehensive works in 533

.1   **Statics; mass, density, specific gravity**

            For vacuums, see 533.5

.12   Statics

            Including buoyancy

            For aerostatics, see 533.61

.15   Mass, density, specific gravity

.2   **Dynamics**

            Including kinematics

            Class here kinetics

            For aerodynamics, see 533.62; for kinetic theory of gases, see 533.7

.21   Flow

            Class waves and vortex motion in 533.29

            For flow at specific speeds, see 533.27; for flow properties, see 533.28; for rotational flow, see 533.295

.215   Laminar flow

.216   Transitional flow

.217   Turbulent flow

.27   Flow at specific speeds

            Class here velocity

.273   Subsonic flow

.274   Transonic flow

.275   Supersonic flow

            For hypersonic flow, see 533.276

.276   Hypersonic flow

.28   Flow properties

            Including elasticity and compressibility, viscosity and friction, viscous flow

            Class flow properties at specific speeds in 533.27

            See also 536.412 for expansion and contraction of gases resulting from heating and cooling

.29   Waves and vortex motion

.293   Waves

           Including shock waves

.295   Vortex motion

           Class here rotational flow

.5   **Vacuums**

.6   **Aeromechanics**

       Including mass, density, specific gravity of air

       For vacuums, see 533.5

.61   Aerostatics

       Including buoyancy

.62   Aerodynamics

.7   **Kinetic theory of gases**

>   **534–538 Specific forms of energy**

       Class here transformation into specific forms of energy

       Class specific forms of energy as properties of specific states of matter in 530.4; class comprehensive works in 530; class comprehensive works on transformation of energy in 531.68

       For mechanical energy, see 531.6

534   **Sound and related vibrations**

       Standard subdivisions are added for sound and related vibrations together, for sound alone

---

>   **534.1–534.3 Sound**

       Class comprehensive works in 534

.1   **Generation of sound**

.2   **Transmission of sound**

.200 1–.200 9   Standard subdivisions

.202   Velocity

.204   Reflection (Echoes)

.208   Absorption (Damping)

.22   Transmission in solids

.23   Transmission in liquids

.24	Transmission in gases

.3   Characteristics of sound

Including Doppler effect

.5   Vibrations related to sound

Class here vibrations that can not be heard by the human ear

.52	Subsonic vibrations
.55	Ultrasonic vibrations

535   Light and related radiation

Standard subdivisions are added for light and related radiation together, for light alone

Class here optics

See also 537.56 for electron and ion optics

.01   Infrared and ultraviolet radiation; philosophy and theory of light and related radiation

Notation 01 from Table 1 as modified below

Class here radiation of nonvisible spectral regions

Class a specific element of infrared and ultraviolet radiation in 535.2–535.6

.010 1–.010 9   Standard subdivisions of infrared and ultraviolet radiation

.012   Infrared radiation

Class heat radiation in 536.3

.014   Ultraviolet radiation

.019   Philosophy and theory of light and related radiation

Add to base number 535.019 the numbers following —01 in notation 011–019 from Table 1, e.g., abbreviations, acronyms, symbols in optics 535.01948

Class theories in 535.1

.02   Miscellany

.028   Auxiliary techniques and procedures; apparatus, equipment, materials

Class spectroscopy in 535.84

.1   Theories

See also 539.7217 for photons

.12	Corpuscular theory
.13	Mechanical wave theory
.14	Electromagnetic theory

.15 Quantum theory

> **535.2–535.6 Specific elements of light**

Class comprehensive works in 535

For spectroscopy, see 535.84

.2 **Physical optics**

Including coherent and nonlinear optics

For dispersion of light, see 535.4; for beams, see 535.5

.22 Intensity of light

.220 287 Testing and measurement

Class here photometry

.24 Velocity of light

.3 **Transmission, absorption, emission of light**

.32 Geometrical optics

.323 Reflection

.324 Refraction

.326 Absorption

.35 Luminescence

.352 Fluorescence

Class fluorescence by source of exciting energy in 535.355–535.357

.353 Phosphorescence

Class phosphorescence by source of exciting energy in 535.355–535.357

> 535.355–535.357 Luminescence by source of exciting energy

Class comprehensive works in 535.35

For chemiluminescence, see 541.35; for bioluminescence, see 572.4358

.355 Photoluminescence

.356 Thermoluminescence

.357 Electroluminescence

.4 **Dispersion of light**

Including shadows

Class comprehensive works on beams and their dispersion in 535.5

See also 774.0153 for physical properties of holography

.42 Diffraction

.420 284		Apparatus, equipment, materials

Class here interdisciplinary works on prisms

> *For a specific aspect of prisms, see the aspect, e.g., geometry of prisms 516.156*

.43	Scattering
.47	Interference

.5   Beams

.52	Polarization

.6   Color

.8   Special developments of light and related radiation

.84	Optical, infrared, ultraviolet spectroscopy

Class here comprehensive works on spectroscopy in physics

Class interdisciplinary works on spectroscopy in 543.5

> *For a specific kind of spectroscopy in physics other than optical, infrared, or ultraviolet, see the kind, e.g., radiofrequency spectroscopy 537.534*

.842	Infrared spectroscopy
.843	Light spectroscopy
.844	Ultraviolet spectroscopy
.845	Vacuum ultraviolet spectroscopy
.846	Raman spectroscopy

Including Raman effect

536   Heat

.01	Philosophy and theory

Do not use for theories; class in 536.1

.1   Theories

.2   Heat transfer

> *For radiation, see 536.3*

.200 1–.200 9	Standard subdivisions
.201	Heat-transfer properties of matter

Class specific heat in 536.6

> *For heat-transfer properties of matter at low temperatures, see 536.56; for heat-transfer properties of matter at high temperatures, see 536.57*

> *See also 620.11296 for thermal properties of engineering materials*

.201 2		Thermal conductivity
.201 4		Thermal diffusivity
.23		Conduction

Class here heat transfer in solids

Class thermal conductivity in 536.2012

For conduction in fluids, see 536.25

.25	Convection

Class here heat transfer in fluids

.3 **Radiation**

Class here absorption, scattering

.4 **Effects of heat on matter**

Class here effects of heat that can be readily observed or measured with simple instruments

.41	Expansion and contraction

Class here coefficients of expansion

Class expansion and contraction in fusion and solidification in 536.42; class expansion and contraction in vaporization and condensation in 536.44

.412	Gases

For liquefaction and solidification of gases at low temperatures, see 536.56

.413	Liquids
.414	Solids
.42	Fusion (Melting) and solidification

Including freezing and melting points, latent heat of fusion and solidification

Class comprehensive works on fusion and solidification (536.42) and vaporization and condensation (536.44) in 536.4

.44	Vaporization and condensation

Including boiling points, dew points, latent heat of evaporation and condensation, liquefaction of gases

For liquefaction of gases at low temperatures, see 536.56

.5 **Temperature**

Class here absolute temperature

.502 87   Testing and measurement

               Including resistance thermometry

               Class here thermometry

               For measurement at a specific range of temperature, see 536.51–536.54

>   536.51–536.54   Measurement at a specific range of temperature

               Class comprehensive works in 536.50287

.51   Measurement of normal-range temperatures

               Including liquid-in-glass thermometry

.52   Measurement of high temperatures (Pyrometry)

               Including thermocouples

.54   Measurement of low temperatures (Cryometry)

.56   Cryogenics and low temperatures

               Standard subdivisions are added for either or both topics in heading

               Including liquefaction and solidification of gases at low temperatures, properties of matter at low temperatures

               Class a specific property of matter at low temperature with the property, e.g., conduction of electricity at low temperatures 537.62

.560 287   Testing

               Do not use for measurement; class in 536.54

.57   High temperatures

               Including properties of matter at high temperature

               Class a specific property of matter at high temperature with the property, e.g., conduction of electricity 537.62

.570 287   Testing

               Do not use for measurement; class in 536.52

.6   **Specific heat**

               Class here calorimetry, heat capacity

               Class heat of transformation in fusion and solidification in 536.42; class heat of transformation in vaporization and condensation in 536.44

.63   Solids and liquids

.65   Gases

.7   **Thermodynamics**

.701   Philosophy and theory

               Do not use for theories; class in 536.71

.71	Theories

> Including Carnot cycle, Joule's law, Maxwell's thermodynamic formulas

> Class here laws of thermodynamics

.73	Entropy

537 Electricity and electronics

> Standard subdivisions are added for electricity and electronics together, for electricity alone

> Class here electromagnetism

> Class interdisciplinary works on electricity in 333.7932

> *For magnetism, see 538*

.01	Philosophy and theory

> Do not use for theories; class in 537.1

.1	**Theories**
.12	Wave theories

> Class electromagnetic theory of matter in 530.141

.2	**Electrostatics**
.21	Electric charge and potential

> Standard subdivisions are added for either or both topics in heading

> Including triboelectricity

.24	Dielectrics

> Including electrets, electrocapillarity, electrostriction

.243	Dipole moments
.244	Piezoelectricity and ferroelectricity

> *See also 548.85 for electrical properties of crystals*

.244 6	Piezoelectricity
.244 8	Ferroelectricity
.5	**Electronics**

> Including exploding wire phenomena

> Class here quantum electronics

> *For semiconductors, see 537.622*

.52	Disruptive discharges

> Including coronas, electric arcs

> Class discharge through rarefied gases and vacuums in 537.53

.53	Discharge through rarefied gases and vacuums

.532	Ionization of gases

Class comprehensive works on ionization of gases in 530.444

.534	Radio wave and microwave electronics

Standard subdivisions are added for radio wave and microwave electronics together, for radio wave electronics alone

Class here spectroscopy

.534 2	Long waves

.534 3	Short waves

.534 4	Microwaves and ultrahigh-frequency waves

.535	X-ray and gamma-ray electronics

.535 2	Spectroscopy

Including Mössbauer spectroscopy and effect

Class a specific application of spectroscopy with the application, e.g., X-ray spectroscopy in chemical analysis 543.62

.54	Photoelectric phenomena

Including photoconductivity, photoemission, photovoltaic effect

.56	Electron and ion optics

Standard subdivisions are added for electron and ion optics together, for electron optics alone

.6	**Electrodynamics (Electric currents) and thermoelectricity**

Standard subdivisions are added for electrodynamics and thermoelectricity together, for electrodynamics alone

For quantum electrodynamics, see 530.1433

.62	Electric conductivity and resistance

For dielectrics, see 537.24

.622	Semiconductivity

Class here solid-state physics of semiconductors

.622 1	Structure of semiconductors

Class structure of specific kinds of semiconductors in 537.6223

.622 3	Kinds of semiconductors

Class diffusion and mass transfer in specific kinds of semiconductors in 537.6225; class interactions in and specific properties of specific kinds of semiconductors in 537.6226

.622 5	Diffusion and mass transfer in semiconductors

Standard subdivisions are added for either or both topics in heading

.622 6	Interactions in and specific properties of semiconductors

Including effects of beams and electromagnetic fields, Hall effects; adsorption, instabilities, resistivity, tunneling

.623   Superconductivity

Class here solid-state physics of superconductors

Add to base number 537.623 the numbers following 537.622 in 537.6221–537.6226, e.g., ternary superconductors 537.6233

.624   Thermal effects of currents

.65   Thermoelectricity

538   Magnetism

.3   Magnetic properties and phenomena

Standard subdivisions are added for either or both topics in heading

Including hysteresis, magnetic moment and relaxation

Class specific magnetic substances and their characteristic phenomena in 538.4

.36   Magnetic resonance

.362   Nuclear magnetic resonance (NMR)

Including nuclear quadrupole resonance (NQR), electron-nuclear double resonance (ENDOR)

.364   Electron paramagnetic resonance (EPR)

Variant name: electron spin resonance (ESR)

.4   Magnetic substances and their characteristic phenomena

Standard subdivisions are added for either or both topics in heading

Class here magnetic induction, natural magnets

Class comprehensive works on specific magnetic phenomena in 538.3

.42   Diamagnetism

.43   Paramagnetism

.44   Ferromagnetism

.45   Ferrimagnetism

.6   Magnetohydrodynamics

.7   Geomagnetism and related phenomena

Standard subdivisions are added for geomagnetism and related phenomena together, for geomagnetism alone

.709   History, geographic treatment, biography

Do not use for geographic treatment of magnetic surveys; class in 538.78. Do not use for geographic treatment of magnetic observations at observatories; class in 538.79

.72	Magnetic fields of solid earth

Class here secular variations

Class transient variations in magnetism of solid earth in 538.74; class observations of magnetic fields of solid earth at observatories in 538.79

For magnetic surveys, see 538.78

.727	Paleomagnetism

Class here geomagnetic reversals, paleomagnetic observations at observatories, paleomagnetic surveys

.74	*Transient magnetism

For auroras, see 538.768

.742	*Diurnal variations
.744	*Magnetic storms
.746	*Sunspot effects
.748	*Earth currents
.76	Magnetosphere, ionosphere, auroras
.766	Magnetosphere

Including Van Allen radiation belts

Class transient magnetism of magnetosphere in 538.74

.767	Ionosphere

Class here atmospheric ionization

.767 2	D region
.767 3	E region

Variant name: Kennelly-Heaviside layers

.767 4	F region

Variant name: Appleton layers

.768	Auroras

Class here northern lights

.78	Magnetic surveys

For paleomagnetic surveys, see 538.727

.780 9	History and biography

Do not use for geographic treatment; class in 538.781–538.789

---

*Do not use notation 09 from Table 1 for magnetic observations at permanent observatories; class in 538.79

.781–.789   Geographic treatment

> Add to base number 538.78 notation 1–9 from Table 2, e.g., surveys of Ireland 538.78415

.79   Magnetic observations at observatories

> *For paleomagnetic observations at observatories, see 538.727*

.790 9   History and biography

> Do not use for geographic treatment; class in 538.791–538.799

.791–.799   Geographic treatment

> Add to base number 538.79 notation 1–9 from Table 2, e.g., findings from observatories in Russia 538.7947

539   Modern physics

Class here quantum physics

> *For theories of modern physics, see 530.1; for states of matter, see 530.4; for modern physics of specific forms of energy, see 534–538*

SUMMARY

539.01	**Philosophy and theory**
.1	**Structure of matter**
.2	**Radiation (Radiant energy)**
.6	**Molecular physics**
.7	**Atomic and nuclear physics**

.01   Philosophy and theory

> Do not use for theories; class in 530.1

[.015 1]   Mathematical principles

> Do not use; class in 530.15

.1   Structure of matter

> *For structure of specific states of matter, see 530.4*

.12   Molecular structure

> Use 539.12 only for studies of molecular structure without reference to chemical characteristics. Prefer 541.22 if there is discussion of chemical phenomena

.14   Atomic structure

> *For nuclear structure, see 539.74*

.2   Radiation (Radiant energy)

Class here electromagnetic radiation, spectrum, waves

> *For a specific kind of radiation, see the kind, e.g., ultraviolet radiation 535.014, ionizing radiation 539.722*

.6 **Molecular physics**

Atom-atom and molecule-molecule relationships

Including molecular and vibrational spectra

For molecular structure, see 539.12

.602 87 Testing and measurement

Class here comprehensive works on mass spectrometry in physics

Class interdisciplinary works on mass spectrometry in 543.65

For spectrometry of a specific nonmolecular particle, see the particle, e.g., atomic spectrometry 539.7

.7 **Atomic and nuclear physics**

Standard subdivisions are added for either or both topics in heading

For atomic structure, see 539.14

SUMMARY

539.72	**Particle physics; ionizing radiation**
.73	**Particle acceleration**
.74	**Nuclear structure**
.75	**Nuclear activities and interactions**
.76	**High-energy physics**
.77	**Detecting and measuring particles and radioactivity**

.72 Particle physics; ionizing radiation

Standard subdivisions are added for particle physics and ionizing radiation together, for particle physics alone

Class here antiparticles, relativistic particles

For field and wave theories accounting for fundamental particles, see 530.14; for particle acceleration, see 539.73; for nuclear activities and interactions, see 539.75; for detection and measurement of particles and radioactivity, see 539.77

[.720 287] Testing and measurement

Do not use; class in 539.77

.721 Specific kinds of subatomic particles

Including bosons, fermions, Regge poles

Class subatomic particles considered as a cosmic ray in 539.7223

[.721 01–.721 09] Standard subdivisions

Do not use; class in 539.7201–539.7209

.721 1 Leptons

For neutrinos, see 539.7215; for photons, see 539.7217

.721 12	Electrons
	Including beta particles
	For beta positrons, see 539.7214
	See also 537.5 for electronics
.721 14	Muons (Mu-mesons)
.721 2	Nucleons
	For neutrons, see 539.7213
.721 23	Protons
	Class here antiprotons
	Class protons considered as cosmic rays in 539.7223
.721 3	Neutrons
.721 4	Positrons
.721 5	Neutrinos
.721 6	Hadrons
	Class here strange particles and strangeness
.721 62	Mesons
	Including pions (pi-mesons), kaons (K-mesons)
	For mu-mesons, see 539.72114
.721 64	Baryons
	Including hyperons
	For nucleons, see 539.7212
.721 67	Quarks
	Including quantum flavor
	See also 539.7548 for quantum chromodynamics
.721 7	Photons
	See also 539.756 for photonuclear reactions
.722	Ionizing radiation
	For a specific kind of ionizing radiation not provided for here, see the kind, e.g., alpha particles 539.7232
	See also 537.532 for ionization of gases by electron discharge
.722 2	X and gamma rays
	Including bremsstrahlung (secondary X rays), gamma particles
	See also 537.535 for X-ray and gamma-ray electronics

.722 3	Cosmic rays
	Class here any particle considered as a cosmic ray
.723	Nuclei and atoms considered as particles
.723 2	Nuclei
	Including alpha particles, deuterons
	Class component particles of nuclei in 539.721; class nuclei considered as cosmic rays in 539.7223; class nuclear structure in 539.74
.723 4	Heavy ions
.725	Particle characteristics
	Including angular momentum, charge, energy levels, orbits, spin, symmetry, supersymmetry
	Class characteristics of a specific particle with the particle, e.g., orbits of electrons 539.72112, strangeness of strange particles 539.7216
	For supergravity, comprehensive works on supergravity and supersymmetry, see 530.1423; for magnetic properties, see 538.3
.725 8	String theory
	Class here superstring theory
.73	Particle acceleration
	Including bombardment, particle beams
.732	High-voltage accelerators
	Including Van de Graaff electrostatic generators
.733	Resonance accelerators
	Including cyclotrons, linear accelerators
.734	Induction accelerators
	Including betatrons
.735	Synchronous accelerators
	Including synchro-cyclotrons and synchrotrons (betatron-synchrotrons)
.736	Supercolliders
	Class here superconducting supercolliders
.737	Acceleration of specific particles
	Class acceleration of specific particles in specific accelerators in 539.732–539.736
[.737 01–.737 09]	Standard subdivisions
	Do not use; class in 539.7301–539.7309

.737 1–.737 7	Specific particles

Add to base number 539.737 the numbers following 539.721 in 539.7211–539.7217, e.g., proton acceleration 539.73723

.74	Nuclear structure

Class here isotope and nuclide structure, nuclear models

.742	Liquid-drop model
.743	Shell model
.744	Interpretation through spectroscopy
.75	Nuclear activities and interactions

Standard subdivisions are added for either or both topics in heading

Including annihilation, capture, coupling, creation

For ionizations of gases, see 530.444; for high-energy physics, see 539.76

See Manual at 530.416 vs. 539.75

.752	Natural radioactivity

Including half-life

Class here decay schemes, radioactive substances (radioelements), radioisotopes, radionuclides; comprehensive works on radioactivity

For artificial radioactivity, see 539.753

[.752 028 7]	Testing and measurement

Do not use; class in 539.77

.752 2	Alpha decay
.752 3	Beta decay
.752 4	Gamma decay
.753	Artificial radioactivity

Including radioactive fallout

See also 363.738 for pollution from radioactive fallout

[.753 028 7]	Testing and measurement

Do not use; class in 539.77

.754	Fundamental interactions

Including gravitational interaction, gravitational waves

Class field theories covering fundamental interactions in 530.14

See also 531.14 for gravity

.754 4	Weak interaction

For beta decay, see 539.7523

.754 6	Electromagnetic interaction
.754 8	Strong interaction
	Including quantum chromodynamics
.756	Photonuclear reactions
.757	Collision
.758	Scattering
.76	High-energy physics
	Class high-energy levels of particles in 539.725
.762	Nuclear fission
.764	Nuclear fusion (Thermonuclear reaction)
.77	Detecting and measuring particles and radioactivity
	Class here radiation measurement
.772	Ionization chambers
.773	Proportional counters
.774	Geiger-Müller counters
.775	Scintillation counters
.776	Crystal conduction counters
.777	Wilson cloud chambers
.778	Photography

540 Chemistry and allied sciences

Standard subdivisions are added for chemistry and allied sciences together, for chemistry alone

Class cosmochemistry in 523.02

SUMMARY

540.1–.9	**Standard subdivisions**
541	**Physical chemistry**
542	**Techniques, procedures, apparatus, equipment, materials**
543	**Analytical chemistry**
546	**Inorganic chemistry**
547	**Organic chemistry**
548	**Crystallography**
549	**Mineralogy**

.1	**Philosophy and theory**
	Do not use for theoretical chemistry; class in 541.2
.11	Alchemy and systems
.112	Alchemy

.113	Systems

Add to base number 540.113 the numbers following 003 in 003.1–003.8, e.g., computer modeling and simulation 540.1133

[.28]	Auxiliary techniques and procedures; apparatus, equipment, materials

Do not use; class in 542

.7	**Education, research, related topics**
.72	Research

Do not use for laboratories; class in 542.1

> **541–547 Chemistry**

Class comprehensive works in 540

541 Physical chemistry

Inorganic and combined inorganic-organic chemistry

Class physical crystallography in 548

For physical chemistry of specific kinds of inorganic chemicals, see 546; for physical chemistry of organic compounds, see 547

See Manual at 541 vs. 546

SUMMARY

541.04	**Special topics of physical chemistry**
.2	**Theoretical chemistry**
.3	**Miscellaneous topics in physical chemistry**
.7	**Optical activity**

.04	Special topics of physical chemistry
.042	Chemistry of states of matter

Add to base number 541.042 the numbers following 530.4 in 530.41–530.44, e.g., solid-state chemistry 541.0421

.2	**Theoretical chemistry**
.22	Molecular structure

For molecular structure studied without reference to chemical characteristics, see 539.12; for quantum chemistry, see 541.28

.222	Molecular weights
.223	Stereochemistry

Class comprehensive works on stereochemistry in 547.1223

For structural variations, see 541.225

.224	Chemical bonds, valence, radicals

Standard subdivisions are added for chemical bonds, valence, radicals together; for chemical bonds alone; for valence alone

Class bond angles and distances in 541.223

.224 2	Coordination chemistry

Including ligands

Class chelates in 547.59044242

.225	Structural variations
.225 2	Isomers

Class here tautomerism

Class comprehensive works on isomers in 547.12252

.225 4	Polymers

Class comprehensive works on polymerization in 547.28; class comprehensive works on polymers in 547.7

.226	Intermolecular forces

Class here supramolecular chemistry

Class comprehensive works on supramolecular chemistry in 547.1226

.24	Atomic structure

For periodic law, see 546.8

.242	Atomic weight

Class here atomic mass and number

.26	Stoichiometry
.28	Quantum chemistry

Including molecular and atomic orbitals

Class radiochemistry in 541.38

.3	**Miscellaneous topics in physical chemistry**

Limited to topics named below

SUMMARY

541.33	**Surface chemistry**
.34	**Solution chemistry**
.35	**Photochemistry**
.36	**Thermochemistry and thermodynamics**
.37	**Electrochemistry and magnetochemistry**
.38	**Radiochemistry**
.39	**Chemical reactions**

[.301–.309]	Standard subdivisions

Do not use; class in 541.01–541.09

.33   Surface chemistry

                 Including absorption, adhesion

                 Class surface chemical reactions in 541.39

.335   Adsorption

                 Including chemisorption

.34   Solution chemistry

                 For electrolytic solutions, see 541.372

.341   Properties of solutions

.341 3   Mechanical properties

.341 4   Optical properties

.341 5   Colligative properties

                     Including effect of osmotic pressure

.341 6   Thermal properties

.342   Solutions by type of solvent

                 Class here solubility

                 Class properties of specific type of solvent in 541.341

.342 2   Aqueous solutions

.342 3   Nonaqueous solutions

.345   Colloid chemistry

.345 1   Specific types of colloids

[.345 101–.345 109]   Standard subdivisions

                         Do not use; class in 541.34501–541.34509

.345 13   Matter dispersed in solids

                     Including gels, solid foams

.345 14   Hydrosols

                     Including emulsions, foams, froths, lathers

                     Class solid foams in 541.34513

.345 15   Aerosols

                     Including fogs, mists, smokes

.348   Solution components

.348 2   Solvents

.348 3   Solutes

.348 5   Precipitates

                     Including Liesegang rings

.35   Photochemistry

Including chemiluminescence

For bioluminescence, see 572.4358

.351   Energy transformations

.353   Photochemical reactions due to specific radiation

[.353 01–.353 09]   Standard subdivisions

Do not use; class in 541.3501–541.3509

.353 2   Infrared radiation

.353 3   Visible light

.353 4   Ultraviolet radiation

.36   Thermochemistry and thermodynamics

Standard subdivisions are added for thermochemistry and thermodynamics together, for thermochemistry alone

---

>   541.361–541.368 Thermochemistry

Class comprehensive works in 541.36

.361   Combustion

Including explosion, flame, ignition

.362   Exothermic and endothermic reactions

Including latent heat

For combustion, see 541.361

.363   Changes of state (Phase transformations)

Including Gibbs' phase rule

Class interdisciplinary works on phase transformations in 530.474

For latent heat, see 541.362

See also 541.042 for chemistry of specific states of matter

.364   Thermal dissociation

.368   Reactions under temperature extremes

.368 6   Low temperatures

Reactions below -100C

.368 7   High temperatures

.369   Thermodynamics

.37   Electrochemistry and magnetochemistry

Standard subdivisions are added for electrochemistry and magnetochemistry together, for electrochemistry alone

> 541.372–541.377 Electrochemistry

Class comprehensive works in 541.37

.372 Electrolytic solutions

Including electrodialysis, electrolyte conductivity, electrophoresis

Class here ions

For nonelectrical properties, see 541.374

.372 2 Ionization (Electrolytic dissociation)

.372 3 Ion exchange and ionic equilibriums

Standard subdivisions are added for either or both topics in heading

.372 4 Electrodes and electrode phenomena

Standard subdivisions are added for either or both topics in heading

.372 8 Hydrogen-ion concentration

Class here pH

.374 Nonelectrical properties of electrolytic solutions

Add to base number 541.374 the numbers following 541.341 in 541.3413–541.3416, e.g., optical properties 541.3744

.377 Semiconductors

.378 Magnetochemistry

.38 Radiochemistry

Class here nuclear chemistry

Class quantum chemistry in 541.28

.382 Radiation chemistry

Class here radiolysis

.388 Isotopes

.388 4 Radioisotopes

.39 Chemical reactions

Including addition, condensation, hydrolysis, polymerization, substitution

Class here synthesis

Class thermochemistry of reactions in 541.36; class comprehensive works on polymerization in 547.28

.392 Chemical equilibrium

.393 Oxidation-reduction reaction (Redox reaction)

Class here oxidation, reduction

.394   Reaction kinetics

Class kinetics of oxidation-reduction reaction in 541.393

For catalysis, see 541.395

.395   Catalysis

.7   **Optical activity**

Including optical rotation

542   **Techniques, procedures, apparatus, equipment, materials**

Of inorganic and combined inorganic-organic chemistry

Standard subdivisions are added for any or all topics in heading

Class techniques, procedures, apparatus, equipment, materials used in a specific application with the application, e.g., techniques and equipment for chemical analysis 543

.1   **Laboratories**

Class containers and accessory equipment in 542.2; class specific techniques and procedures of laboratories in 542.3–542.8

.2   **Containers and accessory equipment**

Standard subdivisions are added for containers and accessory equipment together, for containers alone

Including crucibles, test tubes

Class containers and accessory equipment for specific techniques and procedures in 542.3–542.8

\>   **542.3–542.8 Specific techniques and procedures**

Class here apparatus, equipment, materials used in specific techniques and procedures

Class comprehensive works in 542

.3   **Testing and measuring**

Standard subdivisions are added for either or both topics in heading

For gas measuring, see 542.7; for analytical chemistry, see 543

.4   **Heating and distilling**

Standard subdivisions are added for heating and distilling together, for heating alone

Including blowpipes

.6   **Filtering and dialysis**

Standard subdivisions are added for either or both topics in heading

Class dialysis in chemical analysis in 543.2

.7	**Gas production, processing, measuring**	

.8   **Auxiliary techniques and procedures, electrical and electronic equipment**

> Add to base number 542.8 the numbers following —028 in notation 0284–0289 from Table 1, e.g., electrical and electronic equipment 542.84; however, for comprehensive works on apparatus, equipment, materials, see 542; for testing and measurement, see 542.3

543   Analytical chemistry

> Of inorganic or organic chemicals in general
>
> Class here analytical chemistry of metals in general
>
> Unless other instructions are given, class a subject with aspects in two or more subdivisions of 543 in the number coming last, e.g., chromatography in organic chemical analysis 543.8 (*not* 543.17)
>
> *For analytical chemistry of specific elements, compounds, mixtures, groupings (other than metals and metallic compounds in general), see 546; for analytical chemistry of specific organic compounds, see 547*

.028 4   Materials

> Including reagents
>
> Do not use for apparatus and equipment; class in 543.19

.1   **General topics in analytical chemistry**

> Including qualitative analysis, quantitative analysis

.17   Analytical organic chemistry

.19   Techniques of general application

> Including sample preparation
>
> Class here instrumentation

>   **543.2–543.8 Specific methods**

> Class comprehensive works in 543

.2   **Classical methods**

> Not provided for elsewhere
>
> Including diffusion methods, gravimetric analysis

.22   Microchemistry (Microanalysis)

> Including microscopic analysis, spot tests

.24   Volumetric analysis

> Class here titration

.26   Thermal analysis

> Including thermogravimetry

.4	**Electrochemical analysis**

Including coulometry, electrophoresis, polarography

.5	**Optical spectroscopy (Spectrum analysis)**

Class here atomic and ultraviolet spectroscopy, interdisciplinary works on spectroscopy

For spectroscopy in physics, see 535.84; for spectroscopic interpretation of chemical structure, see 541.2; for nonoptical spectroscopy, see 543.6

.52	Atomic emission spectroscopy

Including flame emission spectroscopy

.54	Molecular spectroscopy
.55	Spectrophotometry

Class here colorimetry

.56	Luminescence spectroscopy

Class here fluorescence spectroscopy

.57	Infrared and Raman spectroscopy

Standard subdivisions are added for infrared and Raman spectroscopy together, for infrared spectroscopy alone

.59	Methods based on refraction, interference, scattering

Including interferometry, polariscopic analysis, refractometry

For Raman spectroscopy, see 543.57

.6	**Nonoptical spectroscopy**

Including gamma-ray, microwave spectroscopy

Class here nuclear spectroscopy

.62	X-ray and electron spectroscopy

Standard subdivisions are added for X-ray and electron spectroscopy together, for X-ray spectroscopy alone

.63	Radiochemical analysis

Including nuclear activation analysis

.65	Mass spectrometry (Mass spectroscopy)
.66	Nuclear magnetic resonance spectroscopy
.67	Electron paramagnetic resonance spectroscopy

Variant name: electron spin resonance spectroscopy

.8	**Chromatography**
.82	Ion-exchange chromatography

.84 Liquid chromatography

Including paper and thin-layer chromatography

.85 Gas chromatography

.86 Supercritical fluid chromatography

Variant name: supercritical gas chromatography

[544] [Unassigned]

Most recently used in Edition 21

[545] [Unassigned]

Most recently used in Edition 21

546 Inorganic chemistry

Class here general topics of chemistry applied to specific elements, compounds, mixtures, groupings; comprehensive works on inorganic and organic chemistry of specific elements, compounds, mixtures, groupings

Specific compounds are classed with the first element named, except that hydrogen is disregarded for acids

Add to each subdivision identified by * as follows:
>1–3   The element, compounds, mixtures
             Class theoretical, physical, analytical chemistry of the element, compounds, mixtures in notation 4–6 from this table; class comprehensive works in base number for the element in 546.3–546.7
     1   The element
     2   Compounds
             Names of compounds usually end in -ide or one of the suffixes listed in 22 and 24 below
                 For organo compounds, see 547.01–547.08
     22   Acids and bases
             Names of acids usually end in -ic or -ous
     24   Salts
             Names of salts frequently end in -ate or -ite
     25   Complex compounds
     3   Molecular and colloidal mixtures
             Class here alloys
     4   Theoretical chemistry
             Add to 4 the numbers following 541.2 in 541.22–541.28, e.g., molecular structure 42
             Class comprehensive works on physical chemistry in 5 from this table
     5   Physical chemistry
             Add to 5 the numbers following 541.3 in 541.33–541.39, e.g., radiochemistry 58
                 For theoretical chemistry, see 4 from this table
     6   Analytical chemistry
Class physical chemistry applied to inorganic chemistry as a whole in 541

For organic chemistry of specific elements, compounds, mixtures, groupings, see 547

See Manual at 541 vs. 546; also at 549 vs. 546

SUMMARY

.2   **Hydrogen and its compounds**

Standard subdivisions are added for hydrogen and its compounds together, for hydrogen compounds alone

Class here hydrogen chemistry

Class the element hydrogen studied by itself in 546.21

.21   The element

.212   Deuterium

.213   Tritium

>   546.22–546.24 Hydrogen compounds

Class comprehensive works in 546.2

For bases, see 546.32

.22   Water

Including deuterium oxide (heavy water)

.224   Theoretical chemistry

Class comprehensive works on physical chemistry in 546.225

.225   Physical chemistry

For theoretical chemistry, see 546.224

.226   Analytical chemistry

.24   Acids

For a specific acid, see the distinguishing element, plus notation 22 from table under 546, e.g., hydrochloric acid 546.73222

.25   Theoretical chemistry of hydrogen

Class comprehensive works on physical chemistry of hydrogen in 546.26

.26   Physical chemistry of hydrogen

For theoretical chemistry of hydrogen, see 546.25

.3   **Metals, metallic compounds, alloys**

Standard subdivisions are added for any or all topics in heading

Class analytical chemistry of metals in general in 543; class metallic elements studied collectively in 546.31; class physical and chemical metallurgy in 669.9; class interdisciplinary works on metals in 669

> *For metals of groups other than 1 and 2, see 546.4–546.7; for organometallic compounds, see 547.05*

.31   Metallic elements

> *For a specific metal treated as an element, see the metal in 546.38–546.7, plus notation 1 from table under 546, e.g., the element iron 546.6211*

.32   Bases

> *For bases of a specific metal, see the metal in 546.38–546.7, plus notation 22 from table under 546, e.g., bases of iron 546.62122*

.34   Salts

> *For salts of a specific metal, see the metal in 546.38–546.7, plus notation 24 from table under 546, e.g., salts of iron 546.62124*
>
> *See also 546.38224 for table salt*

>   546.38–546.39   Alkali and alkaline-earth metals

Class comprehensive works in 546.38

.38   Alkali metals (Group 1)

Class here comprehensive works on alkali and alkaline-earth metals

> *For alkaline-earth metals, see 546.39*

.381   *Lithium

.382   *Sodium

.383   *Potassium

.384   *Rubidium

.385   *Cesium

.386   *Francium

.39   Alkaline-earth metals (Group 2)

.391   *Beryllium

.392   *Magnesium

.393   *Calcium

.394   *Strontium

---

*Add as instructed under 546

| .395 | *Barium |
| .396 | *Radium |

.4   Group 3

.400 1–.400 9	Standard subdivisions
.401	*Scandium
.403	*Yttrium
.41	Rare earth elements (Lanthanide series)
.411	*Lanthanum
.412	*Cerium
.413	Praseodymium and neodymium
.414	*Promethium
.415	Samarium and europium
.416	Gadolinium and terbium
.417	Dysprosium and holmium
.418	Erbium and thulium
.419	Ytterbium and lutetium
.42	Actinide series

> *For uranium, see 546.431; for transuranium elements, see 546.44*

.421	*Actinium
.422	*Thorium
.424	*Protactinium
.43	Uranium, neptunium, plutonium
.431	*Uranium
.432	*Neptunium
.434	*Plutonium
.44	Transuranium elements

> *For neptunium, see 546.432; for plutonium, see 546.434; for rutherfordium, see 546.51; for dubnium, see 546.52; for seaborgium, see 546.53; for bohrium, see 546.54; for darmstadtium, hassium, meitnerium, see 546.62; for roentgenium, see 546.65; for nihonium, see 546.67; for moscovium, see 546.71; for tennessine, see 546.73; for oganesson, see 546.75*

| .441 | Americium |
| .442 | Curium |

*Add as instructed under 546

.444	Berkelium
.448	Californium
.449	Other transuranium elements

Including einsteinium, fermium, lawrencium, mendelevium, nobelium

.5	**Groups 4, 5, 6, 7**
.51	Titanium group (Group 4)

Including rutherfordium

.512	*Titanium
.513	*Zirconium
.514	*Hafnium
.52	Vanadium group (Group 5)

Including dubnium

.522	*Vanadium
.524	*Niobium (Columbium)
.526	*Tantalum
.53	Chromium group (Group 6)

Including seaborgium

.532	*Chromium
.534	*Molybdenum
.536	*Tungsten
.54	Manganese group (Group 7)

Including bohrium

.541	*Manganese
.543	*Technetium
.545	*Rhenium
.6	**Groups 8, 9, 10, 11, 12, 13, 14**

Class here comprehensive works on transition metals

For group 3, see 546.4; for groups 4, 5, 6, 7, see 546.5

.62	Groups 8, 9, 10

Standard subdivisions are added for any or all topics in heading

Including darmstadtium, hassium, meitnerium

For platinum metals, see 546.63

*Add as instructed under 546

.621	*Iron
.623	*Cobalt
.625	*Nickel
.63	Platinum metals

For osmium, iridium, platinum, see 546.64

.632	*Ruthenium
.634	*Rhodium
.636	*Palladium
.64	Osmium, iridium, platinum
.641	*Osmium
.643	*Iridium
.645	*Platinum

Class comprehensive works on platinum metals in 546.63

.65	Group 11

Including roentgenium

.652	*Copper
.654	*Silver
.656	*Gold
.66	Group 12

Including copernicium

.661	*Zinc
.662	*Cadmium
.663	*Mercury
.67	Group 13

Including nihonium

.671	*Boron
.673	*Aluminum
.675	*Gallium
.677	*Indium
.678	*Thallium
.68	Group 14
.681	*Carbon

*Add as instructed under 546

.681 2	Carbon compounds

Number built according to instructions under 546

Use this number for carbon oxides, carbonates, metal carbonyls, carbon halides when treated as inorganic compounds. Class other carbon compounds, comprehensive works on carbon compounds, in 547

.683	*Silicon
.684	*Germanium
.686	*Tin
.688	*Lead

.7	**Groups 15, 16, 17, 18**

Class here nonmetals

For a specific nonmetallic element not provided for here, see the element, e.g., silicon 546.683

.71	Group 15

Including moscovium

.711	*Nitrogen
.712	*Phosphorus
.715	*Arsenic
.716	*Antimony
.718	*Bismuth
.72	Chalcogens (Group 16)
.721	*Oxygen
.723	*Sulfur
.724	*Selenium
.726	*Tellurium
.728	*Polonium
.73	Halogens (Group 17)

Including tennessine

.731	*Fluorine
.732	*Chlorine
.733	*Bromine
.734	*Iodine
.735	*Astatine

*Add as instructed under 546

.75   Noble gases (Group 18)

> Variant names: inert, rare gases

> Including oganesson

.751   *Helium

.752   *Neon

.753   *Argon

.754   *Krypton

.755   *Xenon

.756   *Radon

.8   **Periodic law and periodic table**

> Class here periodicity

> Class comprehensive works on atomic structure in 541.24

547   Organic chemistry

Class here biochemicals when not considered in their biological context

Add to each subdivision identified by * as follows:
```
04          Special topics
044            Theoretical chemistry
                  Add to 044 the numbers following 541.2 in 541.22–541.28, e.g.,
                  molecular structure 0442
                  Class comprehensive works on physical chemistry in notation
                  045 from this table
045            Physical chemistry
0453–0458      Specific topics of physical chemistry
                  Add to 045 the numbers following 541.3 in 541.33–541.38,
                  e.g., solution chemistry 0454
                     For theoretical chemistry, see notation 044 from this table
046            Analytical chemistry
```
Unless other instructions are given, observe the following table of preference, e.g., aromatic compounds and aromatization 547.6 (*not* 547.27):

Organic chemical reactions (*except* 547.27)	547.2
Other organic substances	547.8
Macromolecules and related compounds	547.7
Kinds of compounds identified by structure	547.4–547.6
Kinds of compounds identified by component elements	547.01–547.08
Reactions producing specific kinds of organic compounds	547.27
Physical and theoretical chemistry	547.1

Class interdisciplinary works on biochemicals in 572

For biochemistry, see 572

---

*Add as instructed under 546

SUMMARY

547.001–.009	**Standard subdivisions**
.01–.08	**Kinds of compounds identified by component elements**
.1	**Physical and theoretical chemistry**
.2	**Organic chemical reactions**
.4	**Aliphatic compounds**
.5	**Cyclic compounds**
.6	**Aromatic compounds**
.7	**Macromolecules and related compounds**
.8	**Other organic substances**

.001   Philosophy and theory

> Do not use for theoretical organic chemistry; class in 547.12

.002–.009   Standard subdivisions

>   547.01–547.08 Kinds of compounds identified by component elements

> Unless other instructions are given, class a subject with aspects in two or more subdivisions of 547.01–547.08 in the number coming last, e.g., sulfonamides 547.067 (*not* 547.042)

> Class comprehensive works in 547

.01   *Hydrocarbons

.02   *Halocarbons

.03   *Oxy and hydroxy compounds

.031   *Alcohols

.035   *Ethers

.036   *Aldehydes and ketones

> Subdivisions are added for either or both topics in heading

.037   *Acids

.038   *Esters

.04   *Organonitrogen compounds

.041   *Nitro and nitroso compounds

.042   *Amines and amides

> Subdivisions are added for either or both topics in heading

.043   *Azo compounds

.044   *Nitriles and isonitriles

> Subdivisions are added for either or both topics in heading

.05   *Organometallic compounds

*Add as instructed under 547

.053–.057   Specific organometallic compounds

> Add to base number 547.05 the numbers following 546 in 546.3–546.7 for the element only, e.g., organozinc compounds 547.05661; then add further as instructed under 547, e.g., analytic chemistry of organozinc compounds 547.05661046; however, for organophosphorus compounds, see 547.07; for organosilicon compounds, see 547.08

.06   *Organosulfur compounds

.061   *Sulfides

.063   *Hydrosulfides

.064   *Thio acids

.065   Oxy derivatives of sulfides

> Including sulfones, sulfoxides, thioaldehydes, thioketones

.066   *Sulfinic acids

.067   *Sulfonic acids

.07   *Organophosphorus compounds

.08   *Organosilicon compounds

.1   Physical and theoretical chemistry

> Add to base number 547.1 the numbers following 541 in 541.2–541.3, e.g., stereochemistry 547.1223; however, for organic chemical reactions, see 547.2

.2   Organic chemical reactions

> Class here chemical reactions of compounds; addition, synthesis

.21   General topics in chemical reactions

.212   Chemical equilibrium

.214   Reaction kinetics

> *For catalysis, see 547.215*

.215   Catalysis

.23   Oxidation-reduction reaction (Redox reaction)

> Including hydrogenation
>
> Class here oxidation, reduction

.27   Reactions producing specific kinds of organic compounds

> Including amination, aromatization, diazotization, esterification, halogenation, nitration, nitrosation, saponification, sulfonation
>
> *For polymerization, see 547.28*

.28   Polymerization

> Class comprehensive works on polymers and polymerization in 547.7

*Add as instructed under 547

.29   Fermentation

>   **547.4–547.6 Kinds of compounds identified by structure**

Class comprehensive works in 547

.4   ***Aliphatic compounds**

Unless other instructions are given, class a subject with aspects in two or more subdivisions of 547.4 in the number coming last, e.g., aliphatic sulfonamides 547.467 (*not* 547.442)

Class aliphatic macromolecular compounds in 547.7

.41   *Hydrocarbons

.411   *Paraffins (Alkanes)

See also 547.77 for paraffin wax

.412   *Olefins (Alkenes)

.413   *Acetylenes (Alkynes)

.42–.48   Other compounds

Add to base number 547.4 the numbers following 547.0 in 547.02–547.08, e.g., carboxylic acids 547.437

For proteins, see 547.7

.5   ***Cyclic compounds**

Class here alicyclic compounds

For aromatic compounds, see 547.6

>   547.51–547.58 Alicyclic compounds

Unless other instructions are given, class a subject with aspects in two or more subdivisions of 547.51–547.58 in the number coming last, e.g., alicyclic sulfonamides 547.567 (*not* 547.542)

Class comprehensive works in 547.5

.51   *Alicyclic hydrocarbons

.511   *Cycloparaffins

.512   *Cycloolefins

.513   *Cycloacetylenes

.52–.58   Other alicyclic compounds

Add to base number 547.5 the numbers following 547.0 in 547.02–547.08, e.g., alicyclic halocarbons 547.52

.59   *Heterocyclic compounds

*Add as instructed under 547

.592	*Hetero oxygen compounds

> Including furans, oxazoles, pyrans

.593	*Hetero nitrogen compounds

> Including chlorophylls, diazines, imidazoles, porphyrins, pyrazoles, pyridines, pyrroles

.594	*Hetero sulfur compounds

> Including thiazoles, thiophenes

.595	Compounds with two or more different hetero atoms

> Including oxazines, oxdiazines, oxdiazoles

.596	*Fused heterocyclic compounds

> Including purines, quinolines

.6   *Aromatic compounds

> Unless other instructions are given, class a subject with aspects in two or more subdivisions of 547.6 in the number coming last, e.g., aromatic sulfonamides 547.667 (*not* 547.642)

.61	*Hydrocarbons
.611	*Benzenes
.613	*Polyphenyl hydrocarbons

> Including diphenyl hydrocarbons

.615	*Fused hydrocarbons

> Including naphthalenes
>
> *For anthracenes, see 547.616*

.616	*Anthracenes
.62	*Halogenated compounds
.63	*Oxy and hydroxy compounds

> Subdivisions are added for either or both topics in heading

.631	*Alcohols

> Class phenols in 547.632

.632	*Phenols

> Including monohydric hydroxy aromatics

.633	*Polyhydroxy aromatics

> Including dihydroxy and trihydroxy aromatics, catechols, hydroquinones, resorcinols

.635	*Ethers

*Add as instructed under 547

.636	*Aldehydes and ketones

Subdivisions are added for either or both topics in heading

.637	*Acids

.638	*Esters

.64–.68	Other aromatic compounds

Add to base number 547.6 the numbers following 547.0 in 547.04–547.08, e.g., aromatic amines 547.642

.7   *Macromolecules and related compounds

Including alkaloids, antibiotics, hormones, nucleic acids, proteins, steroids, vitamins

Class here macromolecules when not considered in their biological context; comprehensive works on polymers

Subdivisions are added for macromolecules and related compounds, for macromolecules alone

Class interdisciplinary works on macromolecules in 572

> *For inorganic polymers, see 541.2254; for fossil substances, see 547.82; for comprehensive works on high polymers, see 547.84; for dyes and pigments, see 547.86*

> *See also 668.9 for synthetic polymers*

.71	Terpenes and essential oils

Including camphors

.77	*Lipids

Including waxes

Class here fats

Class steroids in 547.7

> *For essential oils, see 547.71*

> *See also 547.411 for paraffin hydrocarbons*

.78	*Carbohydrates

Including sugars, starches, gums

.8   Other organic substances

.82	*Fossil substances

Including coal tar

Class a specific compound derived from a fossil substance with the compound, e.g., synthetic rubber 678.72

> *For petroleum, see 547.83*

*Add as instructed under 547

.83	*Petroleum	

.84   *High polymers

> Class high polymers of a specific chemical group with the group, e.g., starches 547.78

.842   *Elastomers

.842 5   *Latexes

.842 6   *Rubber

.843   *Flexible polymers

.843 4   *Resins

.86   *Dyes and pigments

> Standard subdivisions are added for dyes and pigments together, for dyes alone

.869   *Pigments

548   Crystallography

> Class crystallographic mineralogy in 549.18; class comprehensive works on solid-state physics in 530.41

> *See Manual at 548 vs. 530.41; also at 549 vs. 548*

.015 1   Mathematical principles

> Do not use for mathematical crystallography; class in 548.7

.3   Chemical crystallography

> Relationship between structure and bonding

> Including isomorphism, polymorphism, pseudomorphism

.5   Crystallization

> Class here crystal growth

.7   Mathematical crystallography

> Measurement and calculation of angles

> Class geometric crystallography in 548.81

.8   Physical and structural crystallography

> Standard subdivisions are added for physical and structural crystallography together, for physical crystallography alone

*Add as instructed under 547

.81   Structural crystallography

Class here crystal lattices, geometrical crystallography

Class structural crystallography of a specific substance with the substance, e.g., structural chemistry of silicates 549.6

For diffraction methods, see 548.83

.810 151   Mathematical principles

Do not use for mathematical crystallography; class in 548.7

.83   Diffraction crystallography

Including crystallograms

Class optical methods of crystal study in 548.9

>   **548.84–548.86 Physical properties of crystals**

Class comprehensive works in 548.8

For optical properties, see 548.9

.84   Mechanical properties

.842   Stresses, deformation, strength properties

Including elasticity, plasticity; dislocation, fracture, hardness

.85   Electrical, electronic, magnetic properties

Including conductivity, dielectricity

.86   Thermal properties

Including fusibility

.9   **Optical crystallography**

Optical properties of crystals and optical methods of crystal study

549   Mineralogy

Occurrence, description, classification, identification of naturally occurring minerals

Class crystallography in 548; class economic geology in 553

See Manual at 549 vs. 546; also at 549 vs. 548

SUMMARY

549.09	**History, geographic treatment, biography**
.1	**Determinative mineralogy**
.2	**Native elements**
.3	**Sulfides, antimonides, arsenides, selenides, tellurides; sulfosalts**
.4	**Halides**
.5	**Oxides**
.6	**Silicates**
.7	**Other minerals**
.9	**Geographic treatment of minerals**

.09   History, geographic treatment, biography

           Do not use for geographic treatment of minerals; class in 549.9

.1   **Determinative mineralogy**

           Class determinative mineralogy of specific minerals in 549.2–549.7

.11   Minerals in specific kinds of formations

.112   Meteorite minerals

           Class here petrology of meteorites

           Class comprehensive works on meteorites in 523.51

.114   Minerals in rocks

           Add to base number 549.114 the numbers following 552 in 552.1–552.5, e.g., determinative mineralogy in sedimentary rocks 549.1145

           Class comprehensive works on rocks in 552

.116   Minerals in pegmatite dikes

           Class comprehensive works on dikes in 551.88

.12   Physical mineralogy

.121   Mechanical properties

           Including cleavage, fracture, hardness

.125   Optical properties

           Including color, fluorescence, luminescence

.127   Electrical, electronic, magnetic properties

.13   Chemical mineralogy

.131   Composition, properties, reactivity

.133   Analysis

.18   Crystallographic mineralogy

           Study of crystalline structure and properties of minerals

---

>   **549.2–549.7   Specific minerals**

           Class comprehensive works in 549

.2   **Native elements**

           Use 549.7 for mineral compounds of specific elements not provided for elsewhere in 549.3–549.6

.23   Metals

           Native metals only

           Class interdisciplinary works on physico-chemical characteristics of metals in 669.9

.25   Semimetals

            Including antimony, arsenic, bismuth, boron, selenium, tellurium

.27   Nonmetals

            Including graphite (carbon)

.3   **Sulfides, antimonides, arsenides, selenides, tellurides; sulfosalts**

            Class sulfates in 549.75

.32   Sulfides, antimonides, arsenides, selenides, tellurides

            Including chalcocite, cinnabar, galena, molybdenite, pyrite, sphalerite

.35   Sulfosalts (Double sulfides)

            Including tetrahedrite

.4   **Halides**

            Including carnallite, cryolite, fluorite (fluorspar), halite, rock salt

.5   **Oxides**

.52   Simple and multiple oxides

            Standard subdivisions are added for either or both topics in heading

.522   Cuprite, ice, zincite

.523   Hematite group

            Including corundum, ilmenite

.524   Rutile group

            Including cassiterite

.525   Goethite group

            Including diaspore

.526   Spinel group

            Including chromite, magnetite

.528   Other groups of oxides

            Including uraninite

.53   Hydroxides

            Including bauxite, limonite

.6   **Silicates**

            Class here clay

.62   Nesosilicates

            Including andalusite, cyanite, garnet, kyanite, sillimanite, staurolite, topaz, zircon

.63	Sorosilicates	

Including epidote

.64	Cyclosilicates	

Including beryl, chrysocolla, cordierite, tourmaline

.66	Inosilicates	

Including amphiboles, pyroxenes, spodumene, wollastonite

.67	Phyllosilicates	

Including chlorite, glauconite, kaolinite, mica, pyrophyllite, serpentine, talc

.68	Tectosilicates	

Including feldspar, leucite, opal, quartz, scapolite, zeolite

.7   Other minerals

[.701–.709]   Standard subdivisions

Do not use; class in 549.01–549.09

.72   Phosphates, arsenates, vanadates

Including apatite, monazite, turquoise

.73   Nitrates and borates

.732   Nitrates

Including saltpeter (niter), Chile saltpeter (soda niter)

.735   Borates

Including borax, colemanite

.74   Molybdates and tungstates

Including scheelite, wolframite

.75   Sulfates and chromates

Standard subdivisions are added for sulfates and chromates together, for sulfates alone

.752   Chromates and anhydrous sulfates

Including anhydrite, barite, celestite

.755   Hydrous and basic sulfates

Including alunite, gypsum

.78   Carbonates

.782   Calcite group

Including dolomite, magnesite, siderite

.785   Aragonite group

Including malachite

.9   **Geographic treatment of minerals**

Add to base number 549.9 notation 1–9 from Table 2, e.g., minerals of Greenland 549.9982

550   Earth sciences

Class here geophysics; phenomena of celestial bodies directly comparable to terrestrial phenomena, e.g., volcanic activity on Mars 551.21099923

Use 550 and its standard subdivisions for works that deal comprehensively with geology, hydrology, and meteorology; for works on geology in the sense of all earth sciences. Use 551 and its standard subdivisions for works on geology in the sense limited to properties and phenomena of the solid earth

See Manual at 523 vs. 550; also at 550 vs. 910

SUMMARY

551	**Geology, hydrology, meteorology**
552	**Petrology**
553	**Economic geology**
554–559	**Earth sciences by specific continents, countries, localities in modern world; extraterrestrial worlds**

[.154]   Chemical principles

Do not use; class in 551.9

[.94–.99]   Specific continents, countries, localities in modern world; extraterrestrial worlds

Do not use; class in 554–559

551   Geology, hydrology, meteorology

Geology: science that deals with properties and phenomena of the solid earth (lithosphere)

Use 550 and its standard subdivisions for works that deal comprehensively with geology, hydrology, and meteorology; for works on geology in the sense of all earth sciences. Use 551 and its standard subdivisions for works on geology in the sense limited to properties and phenomena of the solid earth

For astronomical geography, see 525; for geodesy, see 526.1; for petrology, see 552; for economic geology, see 553; for physical geography, see 910.02

See also 363.34 for disasters; also 904.5 for history of events of natural origin

SUMMARY

551.01–.09	**Standard subdivisions of geology**
.1	**Gross structure and properties of the earth**
.2	**Volcanoes, earthquakes, thermal waters and gases**
.3	**Surface and exogenous processes and their agents**
.4	**Geomorphology and hydrosphere**
.5	**Meteorology**
.6	**Climatology and weather**
.7	**Historical geology**
.8	**Structural geology**
.9	**Geochemistry**

.01 Philosophy and theory of geology

[.015 4] Chemical principles

Do not use; class in 551.9

.02–.08 Standard subdivisions of geology

.09 History, geographic treatment, biography of geology

[.091 62–.091 68] Treatment in oceans and seas

Do not use; class in 551.4608

[.094–.099] Geology by specific continents, countries, localities in modern world; extraterrestrial worlds

Do not use; class in 554–559

.1 Gross structure and properties of the earth

For geomagnetism, see 538.7

.11 Interior of the earth

For properties, see 551.12

.112 Core

.116 Mantle

.12 Properties of interior

Including heat, temperature ranges

.13 Crust

Including magma

For properties, see 551.14; for structural geology, see 551.8

.136 Plate tectonics (Continental drift)

Including sea-floor spreading

Class comprehensive works on tectonics in 551.8

.14 Properties of crust

Including elasticity, heat, temperature ranges

.2 Volcanoes, earthquakes, thermal waters and gases

.21 Volcanoes

Class here comprehensive works on craters

Class volcanic thermal waters and gases in 551.23; class petrology of volcanic rocks in 552.2

For meteorite craters, see 551.397

.22   Earthquakes

> Class here seismology
>
> Class seismic sea waves in 551.463

.220 287   Testing and measurement

> Class here seismography

.23   Thermal waters and gases

> Standard subdivisions are added for thermal waters and gases together, for thermal waters alone
>
> Including volcanic volatiles
>
> Class here surface manifestations, e.g., fumaroles, hot springs

.3   Surface and exogenous processes and their agents

> Standard subdivisions are added for any or all topics in heading
>
> Class here sedimentology as study of surface processes
>
> Class comprehensive works on landforms in 551.41; class comprehensive works on sedimentology in 552.5

.300 1–.300 9   Standard subdivisions

> \>   551.302–551.307 Erosion and weathering, sediments and sedimentation, soil formation, mass movement
>
> Class comprehensive works in 551.3
>
> *See Manual at 551.302–551.307 vs. 551.35*

.302   Erosion and weathering

> Class here soil erosion, interdisciplinary works on erosion
>
> Class role of weathering in soil formation in 551.305
>
> > *For a specific aspect of erosion, see the aspect, e.g., erosion engineering 627.5, control of agricultural soil erosion 631.45*

.303   Transporting and depositing of materials

> Standard subdivisions are added for either or both topics in heading
>
> Class here sedimentation

.304   Transported materials (Sediments)

.305   Soil formation

> Class here role of water in soil formation

.307   **Mass movement (Mass wasting)**

Including avalanches, creep, mud flows, rockfalls; subsidence

Class here landslides, slope failure, work of water in mass movement

See also 363.349 for disasters resulting from avalanches and other mass movements

.31   **Glaciology**

Class here geologic work of ice; interdisciplinary works on ice

For ice in water and other forms of ice, see 551.34; for geologic work of frost, see 551.38. For a specific aspect of ice, see the aspect, e.g., ice manufacture 621.58

.312   **Glaciers**

For icebergs, shelf ice, growlers, see 551.342

.313   **Glacial action**

Including work of glaciers in erosion, soil formation, weathering

.314   **Material transported by glaciers**

Class here glacial drift and till, moraines regarded as materials

Class glacial drift and till, moraines regarded as landforms in 551.315

.315   **Landforms created by glaciers**

Including cirques, drumlins, kames, kettles, roches moutonnées

Class here glacial drift and till, moraines regarded as landforms

.34   **Ice in water and other forms of ice**

Standard subdivisions are added for ice in water and other forms of ice together, for ice in water alone

For snow, see 551.5784; for hail, see 551.5787

.342   **Ice in the sea**

Including icebergs, shelf ice, growlers

For sea ice, see 551.343

.343   **Sea ice (Frozen seawater)**

.344   **Anchor and frazil ice**

.345   **Lake and river ice**

Class here ice cover

For anchor and frazil ice, see 551.344

.35	Geologic work of water

Work of precipitation, of surface and subsurface waters

For role of water in soil formation, see 551.305; for geologic work of marine waters, see 551.36

See Manual at 551.302–551.307 vs. 551.35

.352	Erosion and weathering

Standard subdivisions are added for erosion and weathering together, for erosion alone

.353	Transporting and depositing materials

Standard subdivisions are added for either or both topics in heading

Class here sedimentation in water

For role of water in mass movement, see 551.307

.354	Transported materials (Sediments)
.355	Landforms created by water

For specific landforms created by water, see 551.42–551.45

.36	Geologic work of marine waters

Including wave action, beach erosion

For specific landforms created by marine waters, see 551.42–551.45

.37	Geologic work of wind
.372	Erosion

Class here weathering

.373	Transporting and depositing materials

Standard subdivisions are added for either or both topics in heading

.374	Transported materials
.375	Landforms created by wind

Class here dunes

.38	Geologic work of frost

Class here nivation; work of frost in erosion, in soil formation, in weathering; comprehensive works on frost

For frost as a cold spell, see 551.5253; for condensation of frost, see 551.5744

.382	Fragmentation of rocks
.384	Permafrost
.39	Geologic work of other agents

Including temperature changes

.397   Meteorites

         Class here meteorite craters

.4   **Geomorphology and hydrosphere**

SUMMARY

551.41	**Geomorphology**
.42	**Islands and reefs**
.43	**Elevations**
.44	**Depressions and openings**
.45	**Plane and coastal regions**
.46	**Oceanography and submarine geology**
.48	**Hydrology**
.49	**Groundwater (Subsurface water)**

.41   Geomorphology

         Creation and modification of topographic landforms by erosional and depositional processes

         Class here geomorphology of continents, comprehensive works on landforms

         For landforms created by water, see 551.355; for specific landforms, see 551.42–551.45; for submarine geomorphology, see 551.4683

         See also 551.136 for continental drift

[.410 916 2–.410 916 8]   Treatment in oceans and seas

         Do not use; class in 551.4683

.415   Arid-land geomorphology

         Class here desert geomorphology

.417   Wetland geomorphology

>   551.42–551.45 Specific landforms

         Class here specific land formations created by water; comprehensive works on specific kinds of topographical features, on present and past examples of specific landforms

         Class comprehensive works in 551.41

         For a specific landform created by plutonic action, see the landform in 551.2, e.g., volcanic mountains 551.21; for a specific landform created primarily by exogenous agents other than water or living organisms, see the landform in 551.3, e.g., glacial moraines 551.315; for a specific landform created by tectonic deformations, see the landform in 551.8, e.g., rift valleys 551.872

.42   Islands and reefs

         Standard subdivisions are added for islands and reefs together, for islands alone

.423	Barrier islands
	Class barrier reefs in 551.424
.424	Reefs
	Including atolls
.43	Elevations
	Including slopes
	Class slopes of specific kinds of elevations in 551.432–551.436; class orogeny in 551.82
.432	Mountains
.434	Plateaus
.436	Hills
.44	Depressions and openings
	Including sedimentary basins
	For craters, see 551.21
.442	Valleys
	Including canyons, gorges, ravines; floodplains; river beds
	For deltas, see 551.456; for rift valleys, see 551.872
.447	Caves and related features
	Standard subdivisions are added for caves and related features together, for caves alone
	Including karst formations, sink holes
.45	Plane and coastal regions
.453	Plane regions
	Class here pampas, plains, prairies, steppes, tundras; comprehensive works on grasslands
	For floodplains, see 551.442; for deltas, see 551.456. For a specific kind of grassland not in a plane region, see the kind, e.g., alpine meadows 551.432
.456	Deltas
.457	Coastal regions
	Including beaches
	For deltas, see 551.456; for shorelines, see 551.458
.458	Shorelines
	Marine and lake
	Class here changes in sea and lake levels

.46   Oceanography and submarine geology

Standard subdivisions are added for oceanography and submarine geology together, for oceanography alone

Class here hydrography, hydrosphere; physical oceanography, seawater; interdisciplinary works on marine science, on oceans and seas

Class ice in 551.31; class geologic work of water in 551.35; class ocean-atmosphere interactions in 551.5246; class interdisciplinary works on water in 553.7

> *For hydrology, see 551.48. For a specific aspect of marine science, of oceans and seas, not provided for here, see the aspect, e.g., international law of ocean and sea waters 341.45, marine biology 578.77*
>
> *See Manual at 578.76–578.77 vs. 551.46, 551.48*

.460 9   History, geographic treatment, biography

[.460 916 3–.460 916 7]   Treatment in specific oceans and seas

Do not use; class in 551.4613–551.4617

[.460 916 8]   Special oceanographic forms and inland seas

Do not use for coastal water saltwater bodies; class in 551.4618. Do not use for inland seas; class in 551.4829

.461   Specific oceans and seas, coastal saltwater bodies

Class treatment of a specific topic in oceanography in specific oceans and seas in 551.462–551.468

.461 3–.461 7   Specific oceans and seas

Add to base number 551.461 the numbers following —16 in notation 163–167 from Table 2, e.g., Atlantic Ocean 551.4613

.461 8   Coastal saltwater bodies

Including fjords, saltwater lagoons

Class here estuaries

> *For coastal saltwater bodies in a specific ocean or sea, see the ocean or sea in 551.4613–551.4617, e.g., estuaries in Atlantic Ocean 551.4613*
>
> *See also 551.4829 for salt lakes and inland seas*

> 551.462–551.468 Specific topics in oceanography; submarine geology

Except for modifications shown under specific entries, add to each subdivision identified by * as follows:

01–09   Standard subdivisions
                    As modified under 551.46
1   Specific oceans and seas, coastal saltwater bodies
13–17   Specific oceans and seas
                    Add to 1 the numbers following —16 in notation 163–167 from
                    Table 2, e.g., Atlantic Ocean 13
18   Coastal saltwater bodies
                    Including fjords, saltwater lagoons
                    Class here estuaries
                            *For coastal saltwater bodies in a specific ocean or sea, see
                            the ocean or sea in notation 13–17 from this table, e.g.,
                            estuaries in Atlantic Ocean 13*

Unless other instructions are given, class a subject with aspects in two or more subdivisions of 551.462–551.468 in the number coming last, e.g., physical properties of sediments 551.4686 (*not* 551.465)

Class comprehensive works in 551.46

.462   *Ocean circulation

Including eddies, mixing, turbulence, upwelling

Class here dynamic oceanography, ocean currents

.463   *Waves

Including seiches, storm surges

Class here wind waves

Class comprehensive works on ocean-atmosphere interactions in 551.5246

See also 551.36 for geologic work of waves

.463 7   *Tsunamis

Variant names: seismic sea waves, tidal waves

.464   *Tides

Class here tidal currents

See also 551.36 for geologic work of tides

.465   *Physical properties of seawater

.465 3   *Temperature

.465 4   *Acoustical properties

.465 5   *Optical properties

.466   *Chemical oceanography

*Add as instructed under 551.462–551.468

.466 4	*Salinity
.466 43	*Temperature-salinity relationships
.468	*Submarine geology

Class here ocean floor

For sea-floor spreading, see 551.136

.468 3	*Submarine geomorphology

Class here topography of ocean floor

.468 6	*Sediments
.48	Hydrology

Class here hydrological cycle, limnology, water balance

Class comprehensive works on oceanography and hydrology in 551.46; class water resources, interdisciplinary works on water in 553.7

For fumaroles, see 551.23; for groundwater, see 551.49; for hydrometeorology, see 551.57

See also 551.417 for wetland geomorphology

See Manual at 578.76–578.77 vs. 551.46, 551.48

.482	Lakes and inland seas

Class here freshwater lakes, freshwater ponds, freshwater lagoons

.482 9	Salt lakes and inland seas

Standard subdivisions are added for either or both topics in heading

Class interdisciplinary works on a specific inland sea or salt lake in 940–990, e.g., Caspian Sea 947.5

.483	Rivers and streams

Standard subdivisions are added for either or both topics in heading

For waterfalls, see 551.484; for floods, see 551.489

.484	Waterfalls
.488	Runoff
.489	Floods
.49	Groundwater (Subsurface water)

Class here aquifers

For thermal waters, see 551.23

.492	Water table

---

*Add as instructed under 551.462–551.468

.498   Surface manifestations

> Including springs, wells

> *For hot springs, see 551.23*

.5   **Meteorology**

> Class here atmosphere

> Class forecasting and forecasts of specific phenomena in 551.64; class forecasts of specific phenomena in specific areas in 551.65; class micrometeorology in 551.66

> *For climatology and weather, see 551.6*

> *See Manual at 551.5 vs. 551.6*

SUMMARY

551.51	Composition, regions, dynamics of atmosphere
.52	Thermodynamics, atmosphere interactions with earth's surface, temperatures, radiation
.54	Atmospheric pressure
.55	Atmospheric disturbances and formations
.56	Atmospheric electricity and optics
.57	Hydrometeorology

[.501 12]   Forecasting and forecasts

> Do not use; class in 551.63

.51   Composition, regions, dynamics of atmosphere

.511   Composition

> Class here chemistry, photochemistry of atmosphere

.511 2   Gases

.511 3   Aerosols and dust

> Class dust storms in 551.559

> 551.513–551.514   Atmospheric regions

> Class comprehensive works in 551.51. Class a specific aspect with the aspect, e.g., upper-atmosphere temperatures 551.5257

.513   Troposphere

.514   Upper atmosphere

> Including magnetosphere, mesosphere

> Class magnetic phenomena in magnetosphere, comprehensive works on magnetosphere in 538.766

.514 2   Stratosphere

> Class here ozone layer

.514 5   Ionosphere

.515   Dynamics

              Including gravity waves

              Class here mechanics

              For circulation, see 551.517

.515 1   Kinematics

.517   Circulation

              For wind, see 551.518; for atmospheric disturbances and formations, see 551.55

.518   Wind

              Class wind in atmospheric disturbances and formations in 551.55

>   551.518 3–551.518 5   Wind systems in troposphere

            Class comprehensive works in 551.518

.518 3   Planetary wind systems

              Including jet streams, trade winds, westerlies

.518 4   Monsoons

.518 5   Local wind systems

              Including land and sea breezes; mountain and valley winds, e.g., chinooks, foehns

.518 7   Winds in upper atmosphere

.52   Thermodynamics, atmosphere interactions with earth's surface, temperatures, radiation

.522   Thermodynamics

              Class thermodynamics in microclimatology in 551.66

.523   Land-atmosphere interactions

              Class here earth temperatures affecting atmosphere

.524   Atmosphere interactions with earth's surface

              Class here water-atmosphere interactions, water temperatures affecting atmosphere

              For land-atmosphere interactions, see 551.523

[.524 091 62–.524 091 68]   Treatment in oceans and seas

              Do not use; class in 551.5246

[.524 091 69]   Fresh and brackish waters

              Do not use; class in 551.5248

.524 6   Ocean-atmosphere interactions

[.524 609 163–.524 609 167]	Treatment in specific oceans and seas

Do not use; class in 551.52463–551.52467

.524 63–.524 67   Specific oceans and seas

Add to base number 551.5246 the numbers following —16 in notation 163–167 from Table 2, e.g., temperatures of Indian Ocean 551.52465

.524 8   Lake and river interactions with atmosphere

.525   Temperatures

Class here air temperatures, energy budget, energy flow

For earth temperatures affecting atmosphere, see 551.523; for water temperatures affecting atmosphere, see 551.524; for radiant energy, see 551.527

See also 333.79 for economic aspects of energy budgets

.525 091 732   Urban regions

Class here urban heat islands

For specific urban heat islands, see 551.525093–551.525099

.525 3   Variations over time at earth's surface

Including maximums, minimums, frosts

Class comprehensive works on frost in 551.38

.525 4   Vertical distribution in troposphere

.525 7   Upper-atmosphere temperatures

.527   Radiation

For optical phenomena, see 551.565

.527 1   Solar radiation

.527 2   Terrestrial radiation

For radiation originating in atmosphere, see 551.5273

.527 3   Radiation originating in atmosphere

.527 6   Cosmic radiation

Including cosmic noise

Class here cosmic rays

.54   Atmospheric pressure

.543   Variations over time at earth's surface

.543 09   History and biography

Do not use for geographic treatment; class in 551.5409

.547   Upper-atmosphere pressures

.55	Atmospheric disturbances and formations

Standard subdivisions are added for atmospheric disturbances and formations together, for atmospheric disturbances alone

Class here storms

Class precipitation from storms in 551.577

See also 363.3492 for storms as disasters

.551	Atmospheric formations
.551 2	Air masses and fronts
.551 3	Cyclones

See also 551.552 for hurricanes; also 551.553 for tornadoes

.551 4	Anticyclones

>   551.552–551.559 Atmospheric disturbances

Class comprehensive works in 551.55

.552	Hurricanes

Variant names: typhoons, baguios, tropical cyclones, willy-willies

.553	Tornadoes

Variant names: cyclones, twisters

Including waterspouts

.554	Thermal convective storms

Including hailstorms

Class here thunderstorms

For tornadoes, see 551.553

.555	Snowstorms

Class here blizzards

.556	Ice storms
.559	Dust storms
.56	Atmospheric electricity and optics
.561	Electricity in stable atmosphere

Including conductivity, ionization

.563	Atmospheric electricity

Class magnetic phenomena in 538.7

For electricity in stable atmosphere, see 551.561

.563 2	Lightning

> *For ball lightning, see 551.5634*

.563 4	Ball lightning
.565	Atmospheric optics

Class here optical phenomena produced by refraction, e.g., mirages, scintillation

Class visibility in 551.568

> *For optical phenomena produced by absorption and scattering, see 551.566; for optical phenomena produced by condensation products, see 551.567*

.566	Optical phenomena produced by absorption and scattering

Including sky color, twilight, night skies

.567	Optical phenomena produced by condensation products

Including cloud colors, rainbows

.568	Visibility
.57	Hydrometeorology
.571	Humidity
.571 3	Variations of humidity over time
.572	Evapotranspiration

Class here evaporation

.574	Condensation of moisture

> *For condensation of moisture in a specific form, see the form, e.g., clouds 551.576*

.574 1	Condensation processes

Class here atmospheric nucleation, formation of particles on which moisture condenses

Class condensation processes on earth's surface in 551.5744; class comprehensive works on atmospheric aerosols and dust in 551.5113

.574 4	Condensations on earth's surface

Including dew, glaze, hoarfrost

Class comprehensive work on frost in 551.38

.575	Fog and mist

Standard subdivisions are added for fog and mist together, for fog alone

.576	Clouds

Class cloud colors in 551.567

.577	Precipitation
	Class here liquid precipitation, rain, rainfall
	Class geologic work of precipitation in 551.35
	For frozen precipitation, see 551.578
.577 09	History and biography
	Do not use for geographic treatment; class in 551.5772
.577 1	Properties
	Including composition, temperature; meteorology of acid rain
	Class interdisciplinary works on acid rain in 363.7386
.577 2	Geographic distribution of precipitation
	Add to base number 551.5772 notation 1–9 from Table 2, e.g., rainfall in Nigeria 551.5772669
	Class geographic distribution of variations over time in 551.5773
.577 3	Variations over time
	Including droughts, maximums, minimums
	See also 551.489 for floods
.577 5	Factors affecting precipitation
	Including bodies of water, cities, topography, vegetation
	Class comprehensive works on atmosphere interactions with earth's surface in 551.524
.578	Frozen precipitation
.578 4	Snow
	Class snowstorms in 551.555
.578 409	History and biography
	Do not use for geographic treatment; class in 551.57842
.578 41–.578 43	Properties, geographic distribution, variations over time
	Add to base number 551.5784 the numbers following 551.577 in 551.5771–551.5773, e.g., variations in snow and snowfall over time 551.57843
.578 46	Snow cover
	For snow surveys, see 551.579
.578 464	Ablation
	Class here melting
.578 47	Snow formations
	Including drifts
	For avalanches, see 551.57848

.578 48		Avalanches
.578 7		Hail and graupel

          Standard subdivisions are added for hail and graupel together, for hail alone

          Class hailstorms in 551.554

.579   Snow surveys

.579 09   History and biography

          Do not use for geographic treatment; class in 551.5791–551.5799

.579 1–.579 9   Geographic treatment

          Add to base number 551.579 notation 1–9 from Table 2, e.g., snow surveys in Nevada 551.579793

.6   **Climatology and weather**

          Standard subdivisions are added for either or both topics in heading

          See Manual at 551.5 vs. 551.6

[.601 12]   Forecasting and forecasts

          Do not use; class in 551.63

.609   History, geographic treatment, biography

          Do not use for geographic treatment of weather; class in 551.65. Do not use for geographic treatment of climate, of climate and weather taken together; class in 551.69

.62   General types of climate

.620 9   History and biography

          Do not use for geographic treatment; class in 551.69

.63   Weather forecasting and forecasts, reporting and reports

          Standard subdivisions are added for weather forecasting and forecasts, reporting and reports together; for weather forecasting alone; for weather forecasts alone

          For forecasting and forecasts of specific phenomena, see 551.64

.630 284   Materials

          Do not use for apparatus and equipment; class in 551.635

.630 9   History and biography

          Do not use for geographic treatment; class in 551.65

.631   Historical methods of forecasting

          Class here weather lore

.632	Reporting and reports

Standard subdivisions are added for either or both topics in heading

Class reports of specific weather phenomena in 551.5

For instrumentation in reporting, see 551.635

.632 09	History, geographic treatment, biography

Do not use for geographic treatment of weather reports; class in 551.65

.633	Statistical forecasting
.634	Numerical forecasting
.635	Instrumentation in reporting and forecasting

Standard subdivisions are added for either or both topics in heading

.635 2	Radiosondes
.635 3	Radar
.635 4	Weather satellites
.636	Short-range and long-range forecasts

Class a specific aspect of short-range and long-range forecasts with the aspect, e.g., satellites in long-range forecasts 551.6354

.636 2	Short-range forecasts

Forecasts for a maximum of a week

.636 5	Long-range forecasts

Forecasts more than a week in advance

.64	Forecasting and forecasts of specific phenomena
[.640 1–.640 9]	Standard subdivisions

Do not use; class in 551.6301–551.6309

.641–.647	Specific meteorological phenomena

Class here methods of forecasting specific phenomena for specific areas

Add to base number 551.64 the numbers following 551.5 in 551.51–551.57, e.g., hurricane warnings 551.6452

Class flood forecasting and forecasts in 551.4890112; class forecasts of specific phenomena for specific areas in 551.65

.65	Geographic treatment of weather

Class here geographic treatment of weather forecasts and reports, of forecasts of specific phenomena

Class geographic treatment of climate and weather taken together in 551.69

[.650 1–.650 9]	Standard subdivisions

Do not use; class in 551.601–551.609

.651–.659	Specific regions and areas

Class here forecasts of specific phenomena for specific regions and areas

Add to base number 551.65 notation 1–9 from Table 2, e.g., forecasts for South Africa 551.6568

.66	Microclimatology

Small-scale interactions of atmosphere with land and water

Class here micrometeorology

Class specific meteorological phenomena other than thermodynamics in 551.5; class comprehensive works on atmosphere interactions with earth's surface in 551.524

.68	Artificial modification and control of weather

Add to base number 551.68 the numbers following 551.5 in 551.51–551.57, e.g., cloud seeding 551.6876

Subdivisions are added for either or both topics in heading

.69	Geographic treatment of climate

Class here paleoclimatology of specific areas, geographic treatment of climate and weather taken together

Add to base number 551.69 notation 1–9 from Table 2, e.g., climate of Australia 551.6994

Class general types of climate in 551.62; class microclimatology of specific areas in 551.6609; class comprehensive works on paleoclimatology in 551.60901

For geographic treatment of weather, see 551.65

[.690 1–.690 9]	Standard subdivisions

Do not use; class in 551.601–551.609

.7	**Historical geology**

Class here paleogeography, stratigraphy

Class history of a specific kind of geologic phenomenon with the kind, e.g., history of Jurassic volcanism in Pacific Northwest 551.210979509012, Devonian reefs 551.42409012, Paleozoic orogeny 551.8209012

For paleontology, see 560

See Manual at 551.7 vs. 560

.700 1–.700 8	Standard subdivisions

.700 9	History, geographic treatment, biography

Do not use for geographic treatment of historical geology during a specific geological era or period; class in 551.71–551.79

[.700 94–.700 99]	Historical geology of specific continents, countries, localities in modern world; extraterrestrial worlds

Do not use; class in 554–559

.701   Geologic time and age measurements

Standard subdivisions are added for either or both topics in heading

---

>   551.71–551.79   Specific geological periods

Class comprehensive works in 551.7

.71   Precambrian era

Variant name: Cryptozoic eon

.712   Archean era

Variant names: Archeozoic, Lower Precambrian era

.715   Proterozoic era

Variant names: Algonkian, Upper Precambrian era

.72   Paleozoic era

For Ordovician and Silurian periods, see 551.73; for Devonian period, see 551.74; for Carboniferous and Permian periods, see 551.75

.723   Cambrian period

Standard subdivisions are added for the period as a whole and for specific epochs, stages, or formations

.73   Ordovician and Silurian periods

.731   Ordovician period

Standard subdivisions are added for the period as a whole and for specific epochs, stages, or formations

Former name: Lower Silurian epoch

.732   Silurian period

Standard subdivisions are added for the period as a whole and for specific epochs, stages, or formations

Former name: Upper Silurian epoch

.74   Devonian period

Standard subdivisions are added for the period as a whole and for specific epochs, stages, or formations

.75   Carboniferous and Permian periods

Standard subdivisions are added for Carboniferous and Permian periods together, for Carboniferous period alone

---

>   551.751–551.752   Carboniferous period

Class comprehensive works in 551.75

.751   Mississippian period (Lower Carboniferous period)

> Standard subdivisions are added for the period as a whole and for specific epochs, stages, or formations

.752   Pennsylvanian period (Upper Carboniferous period)

> Standard subdivisions are added for the period as a whole and for specific epochs, stages, or formations

.756   Permian period

> Standard subdivisions are added for the period as a whole and for specific epochs, stages, or formations

.76   Mesozoic era

> *For Cretaceous period, see 551.77*

.762   Triassic period

> Standard subdivisions are added for the period as a whole and for specific epochs, stages, or formations

.766   Jurassic period

> Standard subdivisions are added for the period as a whole and for specific epochs, stages, or formations

.77   Cretaceous period

> Standard subdivisions are added for the period as a whole and for specific epochs, stages, or formations

.78   Cenozoic era

> Class here Tertiary period

> *For Quaternary period, see 551.79*

.782   Paleogene period

> *For Paleocene epoch, see 551.783; for Eocene epoch, see 551.784; for Oligocene epoch, see 551.785*

.783   Paleocene epoch

> Standard subdivisions are added for the epoch as a whole and for specific stages or formations

.784   Eocene epoch

> Standard subdivisions are added for the epoch as a whole and for specific stages or formations

.785   Oligocene epoch

> Standard subdivisions are added for the epoch as a whole and for specific stages or formations

.786   Neogene period (Neocene period)

> Class Quaternary period in 551.79

> *For Miocene epoch, see 551.787; for Pliocene epoch, see 551.788*

.787   Miocene epoch

> Standard subdivisions are added for the epoch as a whole and for specific stages or formations

.788   Pliocene epoch

> Standard subdivisions are added for the epoch as a whole and for specific stages or formations

.79   Quaternary period

.792   Pleistocene epoch (Ice age)

> Standard subdivisions are added for the epoch as a whole and for specific stages or formations

.793   Holocene epoch

> Standard subdivisions are added for the epoch as a whole and for specific stages or formations

> Variant names: postglacial, recent epoch

.8   **Structural geology**

> Class here deformation, diastrophism, epeirogeny, tectonics

> Class geomorphology in 551.41

> *For plate tectonics, see 551.136*

.81   Stratifications

.810 9   History, geographic treatment, biography

> Do not use for geographic treatment of stratifications during a specific geologic era or period; class in 551.71–551.79

[.810 94–.810 99]   Stratifications by specific continents, countries, localities in modern world; extraterrestrial worlds

> Do not use; class in 554–559

.82   Orogeny

> Class here lateral compression of earth's crust, specific orogenies

> Class comprehensive works on elevations (e.g., mountains, plateaus, hills) in 551.43. Class a specific aspect of orogeny with the aspect, e.g., volcanism 551.21

.84   Joints and cleavages

> Standard subdivisions are added for either or both topics in heading

.85   Dips, outcrops, strikes

.86   Anticlines and synclines

.87   Faults and folds

.872		Faults

Including nappes, rift valleys

Class here dislocations

Class nappes produced by folding in 551.875

.875   Folds

For anticlines and synclines, see 551.86

.88   Intrusions

Including dikes, laccoliths, necks, sills, veins

Class volcanoes in 551.21

.9   **Geochemistry**

For geochemistry of a specific subject in earth sciences or mineralogy, see the subject, e.g., organic geochemistry 553.2

552   Petrology

Class here petrography, lithology, rocks

Class structural geology in 551.8

For mineralogy, see 549; for petrology of geologic materials of economic utility other than structural and sculptural stone, see 553

.001–.008   Standard subdivisions

.009   History, geographic treatment, biography

Do not use for geographic distribution of rocks; class in 552.09

.03   Petrogenesis

Class here diagenesis

.06   Properties, composition, analysis, structure of rocks

Class comprehensive works on geochemistry in 551.9

.09   Geographic distribution of rocks

Add to base number 552.09 notation 1–9 from Table 2, e.g., rocks of Sahara Desert 552.0966

Class rocks studied in their stratigraphic setting in 554–559

>   **552.1–552.5 Specific kinds of rocks**

Class comprehensive works in 552

.1   **Igneous rocks**

For volcanic rocks, see 552.2; for plutonic rocks, see 552.3

.2   **Volcanic rocks**

Class here aphanite

See also 551.23 for volcanic volatiles

.22   Lava

Including felsite, obsidian, rhyolite

Class pyroclastic felsite in 552.23

For basalt, see 552.26

.23   Pyroclastic rocks

Including andesite, pumice, tuff, volcanic ash

Class andesitic lava in 552.22

.26   Basalt

Including pillow lava

Class basaltic pyroclastic rocks in 552.23

.3   **Plutonic rocks**

Including diorite, dolerite, gabbro, granite, norite, peridotite, porphyry, syenite

Class here phanerite

.4   **Metamorphic rocks**

Including gneiss, marble, quartzite, schist, serpentinite, slate

.5   **Sedimentary rocks**

Including gypsum, sandstone, shale, tufa; clay, diatomaceous earth, sand, silt, soil

Class here comprehensive works on sedimentology

Class pyroclastic tufa (tuff) in 552.23

For sedimentology as study of surface processes, see 551.3

.58   Carbonate rocks

Including chalk, dolomite, limestone, oolite

.8   **Microscopic petrology**

Class microscopic petrology of specific kinds of rocks in 552.1–552.5

553 Economic geology

Quantitative occurrence and distribution of geologic materials of economic utility

Class here interdisciplinary works on nonmetallic geologic materials

Class economic aspects other than reserves of geologic materials in 333.7; class interdisciplinary works on metals in 669

> *For a specific aspect of nonmetallic geologic materials other than economic geology, see the aspect, e.g., mining 622*

SUMMARY

.1 Formation and structure of deposits

Class formation and structure of deposits of specific materials in 553.2–553.9

.13 Placer deposits

.14 Stratified layers and beds

.16 Pegmatite dikes

.19 Veins and lodes

> ### 553.2–553.9 Specific materials

Class comprehensive works in 553

.2 Carbonaceous materials

Class here fossil fuels, nonrenewable fuels, organic geochemistry; comprehensive works on fuels

Class interdisciplinary works on fuels in 662.6

> *For nuclear fuels, see 553.493; for diamonds, see 553.82; for jet, see 553.87; for amber, see 553.879*

> ### 553.21–553.25 Coal

Class comprehensive works in 553.24

.21 Peat

Including peat coal

.22 Lignite (Brown coal)

.23 Cannel coal

.24 Bituminous and semibituminous coal

> Standard subdivisions are added for bituminous and semibituminous coal together, for bituminous coal alone

> Class here comprehensive works on coal

>> *For peat, see 553.21; for lignite, see 553.22; for cannel coal, see 553.23; for anthracite, see 553.25; for jet, see 553.87*

.25 Anthracite

.26 Graphite

> Variant names: black lead, plumbago

> Class graphitic anthracite coal in 553.25

.27 Solid and semisolid bitumens

> Standard subdivisions are added for either or both topics in heading

> Including ozokerite

> Class here asphalt (pitch)

> Class liquid bitumens (oil) in 553.282; class rocks and sands impregnated with solid or semisolid bitumens in 553.283

.28 Oil, oil shales, tar sands, natural gas

> Class here petroleum geology

> Use 553.28 for petroleum covering oil and gas, use 553.282 for petroleum limited to oil

.282 Oil

.283 Oil shale and tar sands

> Variant names for oil shale: bituminous shale, black shale; for tar sands: bituminous sands, oil sands

.285 Natural gas

.29 Fossil resins and gums

> Standard subdivisions are added for fossil resins and gums together, for fossil resins alone

>> *For amber, see 553.879*

.3 Iron

.4 Metals and semimetals

> Standard subdivisions are added for metals and semimetals together, for metals alone

>> *For iron, see 553.3*

.41 Gold

.42	Precious metals
	For gold, see 553.41
.421	Silver
.422	Platinum
.43	Copper
.44	Lead
.45	Zinc, tin, mercury
.452	Zinc
.453	Tin
.454	Mercury
.46	Metals used in ferroalloys
	For cobalt and nickel, see 553.48
.462	Titanium, vanadium, manganese
.462 3	Titanium
.462 6	Vanadium
.462 9	Manganese
.464	Chromium, molybdenum, tungsten
.464 3	Chromium
.464 6	Molybdenum
.464 9	Tungsten
.465	Zirconium and tantalum
.47	Antimony, arsenic, bismuth
.48	Cobalt and nickel
.483	Cobalt
.485	Nickel
.49	Other metals
.492	Light metals
.492 3	Beryllium
.492 6	Aluminum
.492 9	Magnesium
.493	Fissionable metals
	Including radium, thorium
	Class here nuclear fuels
.493 2	Uranium

.494	Rare-earth metals

Class here lanthanide series

.494 2	Scandium
.494 3	Cerium group
.494 7	Yttrium group
.495	Platinum metals

For platinum, see 553.422

.499	Metals not provided for elsewhere

Including barium, indium, lithium, niobium, sodium, tellurium

Class here semimetals

For antimony, arsenic, bismuth, see 553.47

.5	**Structural and sculptural stone**

Standard subdivisions are added for either or both topics in heading

Class petrology of structural and sculptural stone in 552

For semiprecious sculptural stone, see 553.87

.51	Marble and limestone
.512	Marble

For verd antique and onyx marble, see 553.55

.516	Limestone

Including dolomite, travertine

.52	Granite and syenite

Standard subdivisions are added for granite and syenite together, for granite alone

.53	Sandstone

Including bluestone, flagstones

For flagstones of a specific stone other than sandstone, see the stone, e.g., slate 553.54

.54	Slate
.55	Serpentine, soapstone (steatite), and their variants

Including verd antique and onyx marble

See also 553.87 for onyx

.6   **Other economic materials**

Including diatomaceous earth

Class here earthy materials, industrial minerals

For inorganic gases, see 553.9; for soils, see 631.4

.61   Clay

Including bentonite, diaspore clay, kaolin; fuller's earth

Class here comprehensive works on ceramic materials

For fireclay, see 553.67. For a specific nonclay ceramic material, see the material, e.g., glass sands 553.622

.62   Sand and gravel

Class here aggregates

.622   Sand

Including glass sand

.626   Gravel

.63   Salts

For saltpeter, see 553.64; for mineral waters, see 553.73

.632   Rock salt (Sodium chloride)

.633   Borates

Including borax

.635   Gypsum

Including alabaster

.636   Potash salts

Class here potassium minerals

.64   Nitrates and phosphates

Including apatites, saltpeter

Class here mineral fertilizers

.65   Abrasives

Including corundum, flint, industrial diamonds

Class comprehensive works on abrasives that are also gems in 553.8

For sand, see 553.622

.66   Mineral pigments and sulfur

.662   Mineral pigments

Including barite

.668   Sulfur

.67	Refractory materials

Including alumina, fireclay

For soapstone, see 553.55

.672	Asbestos
.674	Mica
.676	Talc
.678	Vermiculite
.68	Cement materials

Including chalk, lime, marl

For gypsum, see 553.635

.7	**Water**

Including ice

Class interdisciplinary works on thermal waters in 333.88; class interdisciplinary works on ice in 551.31

For geology of thermal waters, see 551.23

See Manual at 363.61

.72	Saline water
.73	Mineral waters

For saline water, see 553.72

.78	Surface water
.79	Groundwater (Subsurface water)
.8	**Gems**

Class here comprehensive works on stones that are both gems and abrasives

For gemstones treated as abrasives, see 553.65

>	553.82–553.86 Precious stones

Class comprehensive works in 553.8

.82	Diamonds

For industrial diamonds, see 553.65

.84	Rubies and sapphires
.86	Emeralds
.87	Semiprecious stones

Including agates, amethysts, garnet, jet, tourmaline, turquoise

.873	Opals

.876		Jade
		Class here jadite, nephrite
.879		Amber

.9   **Inorganic gases**

.92	Hydrogen
.93	Nitrogen
.94	Oxygen
.95	Chlorine and fluorine
.97	Noble gases

> Variant name: inert, rare gases
>
> Including radon

.971   Helium

554–559   Earth sciences by specific continents, countries, localities in modern world; extraterrestrial worlds

Class here geology, geological surveys, stratifications

Add to base number 55 notation 4–9 from Table 2, e.g., geology of Japan 555.2, of moon 559.91

Class historical geology and stratifications of specific continents, countries, localities during a specific era or period in 551.71–551.79; class geological surveys of specific areas emphasizing materials of economic importance in 553.094–553.099; class comprehensive works on earth sciences in 550; class comprehensive works on geology in 551. Class a specific geologic topic (other than historical geology taken as a whole) in a specific area with the topic, e.g., volcanoes in Japan 551.210952, geomorphology of Japan 551.410952

554   Earth sciences of Europe

Number built according to instructions under 554–559

555   Earth sciences of Asia

Number built according to instructions under 554–559

556   Earth sciences of Africa

Number built according to instructions under 554–559

557   Earth sciences of North America

Number built according to instructions under 554–559

558   Earth sciences of South America

Number built according to instructions under 554–559

559 **Earth sciences of Australasia, Pacific Ocean islands, Atlantic Ocean islands, Arctic islands, Antarctica, extraterrestrial worlds**

> Number built according to instructions under 554–559

.9 **Earth sciences of extraterrestrial worlds**

> Number built according to instructions under 554–559
>
> *See Manual at 523 vs. 550; also at 629.43, 629.45 vs. 559.9, 919.904*

560 Paleontology

> Including organisms of uncertain status as plant or animal, as chordate or invertebrate
>
> Class here paleozoology
>
> Class the analysis of paleontological evidence to determine geological time and age in 551.701; class the analysis of paleontological evidence to determine a specific geological age in 551.71–551.79; class comprehensive works on paleontology and historic geology in 551.7
>
> *See Manual at 551.7 vs. 560; also at 576.8 vs. 560*

SUMMARY

560.1–.9	Standard subdivisions; stratigraphic paleontology; special topics of paleontology and paleozoology
561	Paleobotany; fossil microorganisms
562	Fossil invertebrates
563	Miscellaneous fossil marine and seashore invertebrates
564	Fossil Mollusca and Molluscoidea
565	Fossil Arthropoda
566	Fossil Chordata
567	Fossil cold-blooded vertebrates
568	Fossil Aves (birds)
569	Fossil Mammalia

.1 **Philosophy and theory; stratigraphic paleontology**

.17 Stratigraphic paleontology

> Class here stratigraphic paleozoology
>
> Add to base number 560.17 the numbers following 551.7 in 551.71–551.79, e.g., Precambrian paleontology 560.171
>
> Class fossils of specific kinds of organisms in 561–569

.4 **Special topics of paleontology and paleozoology**

.41 Fossilization (Taphonomy)

.43 Trace fossils

> Class here fossil footprints, ichnology

.45 Paleoecology and fossils of specific environment

> Class here zoological paleoecology and fossil animals of specific environments

> Subdivisions are added for either or both topics in heading

.450 1–.450 8 Standard subdivisions

> Notation from Table 1 as modified under 578.01–578.08, e.g., microscopy 560.450282

.450 9 History, geographic treatment, biography

[.450 914–.450 919] Areas, regions, places in general other than polar, temperate, tropical regions

> Do not use; class in 560.453–560.457

.451–.457 Specific aspects of paleoecology and fossils of specific environment

> Add to base number 560.45 the numbers following 577 in 577.1–577.7, e.g., marine paleoecology 560.457

.47 Micropaleontology

> Class here microfossils

> Class a specific kind of microfossil with the kind, e.g., fossil microorganisms 561.9

.9 History, geographic treatment, biography

> Class stratigraphic paleontology and paleozoology in 560.17

[.914–.919] Areas, regions, places in general other than polar, temperate, tropical regions

> Do not use; class in 560.45

561 Paleobotany; fossil microorganisms

> Standard subdivisions are added for paleobotany and fossil microorganisms together, for paleobotany alone

> Including plantlike fossils of uncertain taxonomic position

> Class here fossil Spermatophyta; taxonomic paleobotany

> Class fernlike fossils of uncertain taxonomic position in 561.597

.09 History, geographic treatment, biography

> *For geographic treatment of fossil plants, see 561.19*

[.091 4–.091 9] Areas, regions, places in general other than polar, temperate, tropical regions

> Do not use; class in 561.1

.1 General topics of paleobotany

> Including botanical paleoecology, plant fossils of specific environments

> Class general topics of specific plants and groups of plants in 561.3–561.9

.11   Stratigraphic paleobotany

> Add to base number 561.11 the numbers following 551.7 in 551.71–551.79, e.g., Carboniferous paleobotany 561.115

.13   Fossil pollen and spores

> Standard subdivisions are added for either or both topics in heading

> Class here paleopalynology

> Class comprehensive works on palynology, comprehensive works on pollen in 571.8452; class comprehensive works on spores in 571.847

.14   Fossil fruits and seeds

> Standard subdivisions are added for either or both topics in heading

.15   Fossil leaves

.16   Trees and petrified wood

> Standard subdivisions are added for either or both topics in heading

.19   Geographic treatment of fossil plants

> Add to base number 561.19 notation 1–9 from Table 2, e.g., plant fossils of West Indies 561.19729; however, for treatment by areas, regions, places in general other than polar, temperate, tropical regions, see 561.1

>   **561.3–561.9 Specific plants and groups of plants**

> Class comprehensive works in 561

.3   **Fossil eudicots and fossil Ceratophyllales**

> Standard subdivisions are added for fossil eudicots and fossil Ceratophyllales together, for fossil eudicots alone

> Class here fossil angiosperms, fossil core eudicots, fossil flowering plants

> *For fossil monocots, fossil basal angiosperms, fossil Chloranthales, fossil magnoliids, see 561.4*

.4   **Fossil monocots, fossil basal angiosperms, fossil Chloranthales, fossil magnoliids**

> Standard subdivisions are added for fossil monocots, fossil basal angiosperms, fossil Chloranthales, fossil magnoliids together; for fossil monocots alone

.45   Arecidae

> Class here Arecales (Palmales), Arecaceae (Palmae, palm family)

.49   Poales

> Variant names: Graminales, grasses

.5	**Fossil Pinophyta and fernlike fossils of uncertain taxonomic position**

Standard subdivisions are added for fossil Pinophyta and fernlike fossils of uncertain taxonomic position together, for fossil Pinophyta alone

Variant name for fossil Pinophyta: fossil gymnosperms

Class here Coniferales (conifers)

.52–.58	Pinophyta (Gymnosperms)

Add to base number 561.5 the numbers following 585 in 585.2–585.8, e.g., fossil Pinaceae 561.52

For Cycadales, Cycadeoidales, Pteridospermales, Cordaitales, see 561.59

.59	Cycadales, Cycadeoidales, Pteridospermales, fernlike fossils of uncertain taxonomic position, Cordaitales
.591	Cycadales (True cycads)
.592	Cycadeoidales (Bennettitales)

Including Cycadeoidaceae, Williamsoniaceae

.595	Pteridospermales

Variant names: Cycadofilicales, seed ferns

Including Calamopityaceae, Lyginopteridaceae, Medullosaceae

.597	Fernlike fossils of uncertain taxonomic position

Including Archaeopteris, Callipteris, Glossopteris, Mariopteris, Megalopteris, Neuropteris, Odontopteris, Pecopteris, Sphenopteris

.6	**Fossil Cryptogamia**

For Pteridophyta, see 561.7; for Bryophyta, see 561.8; for microorganisms, fungi, algae, see 561.9

.7	**Fossil Pteridophyta**

Class fernlike fossils of uncertain taxonomic position in 561.597

.72	Sphenopsida

Including Calamitales, Equisetales, Hyeniales, Pseudoborniales, Sphenophyllales

.73	Polypodiopsida (Filicopsida)

Including Coenopteridales, Filicales, Marattiales, Ophioglossales

.74	Psilopsida

Including Psilophytales, Psilotales

.79	Lycopsida (Club mosses)

Including Isoetales, Lepidodendrales, Pleuromeiales, Protolepidodendrales

.8	**Fossil Bryophyta**

.9 **Fossil microorganisms, fungi, algae**

Class comprehensive works on micropaleontology in 560.47

.91 Prokaryotes

Class here bacteria

.92 Fungi

.93 Algae

Add to base number 561.93 the numbers following 579.8 in 579.82–579.89, e.g., fossil diatoms 561.935

.99 Protozoa

.992 Zoomastigophorea

.994 Foraminifera

.995 Radiolaria

> ## 562–569 Specific taxonomic groups of animals

Class here taxonomic paleozoology

Class comprehensive works in 560

562 Fossil invertebrates

For Protozoa, see 561.99; for miscellaneous marine and seashore invertebrates, see 563; for Mollusca and Molluscoidea, see 564; for Arthropoda, see 565

.2 **Conodonts**

.3–.7 **Worms and related animals**

Add to base number 562 the numbers following 592 in 592.3–592.7, e.g., Annelida 562.6

Class comprehensive works in 562.3

563 Miscellaneous fossil marine and seashore invertebrates

[.01–.09] Standard subdivisions

Do not use; class in 562.01–562.09

.4 **Porifera (Sponges) and Archaeocyatha**

Standard subdivisions are added for Porifera and Archaeocyatha together, for Porifera alone

Class here Parazoa

.47 Archaeocyatha

.5 **Cnidaria (Coelenterata)**

Including Scyphozoa

For Anthozoa, see 563.6

.55 Hydrozoa

Including Graptolitoidea

.58 Stromatoporoidea

.6 **Anthozoa**

Class here corals

Class Archaeocyatha in 563.47

.8 **Ctenophora**

.9 **Echinodermata and Hemichordata**

Standard subdivisions are added for Echinodermata and Hemichordata together, for Echinodermata alone

> 563.92–563.96 Echinodermata

Class comprehensive works in 563.9

.92 Crinozoa, Blastozoa, Homalozoa

Standard subdivisions are added for Crinozoa, Blastozoa, Homalozoa together; for Crinozoa alone

Including Camerata, Flexibilia, Inadunata; carpoids

.93 Asterozoa (Starfish)

For Ophiuroidea, see 563.94

.94 Ophiuroidea

.95 Echinozoa

Including Cystoidea

For Holothurioidea, see 563.96

.96 Holothurioidea

Including Arthrochirotida

.99 Hemichordata

Including Enteropneusta, Planctosphaeroidea

Class here Pterobranchia

564 **Fossil Mollusca and Molluscoidea**

> **564.2–564.5 Mollusca (Mollusks)**

Class comprehensive works in 564

.2–.4 Specific Mollusca other than Cephalopoda

Add to base number 564 the numbers following 594 in 594.2–594.4, e.g., Bivalvia 564.4

.5 Cephalopoda

.52 Nautiloidea

.53 Ammonoidea

.56 Octopoda

.58 Decapoda

.6 Molluscoidea

Including Entoprocta

.67 Bryozoa

.68 Brachiopoda (Lamp shells)

565 Fossil Arthropoda

.3 Crustacea and Trilobita

Standard subdivisions are added for Crustacea and Trilobita together, for Crustacea alone

Including Bradoriida, Phosphatocopida

.32–.38 Specific kinds of Crustacea

Add to base number 565.3 the numbers following 595.3 in 595.32–595.38, e.g., Ostracoda 565.33

.39 Trilobita

.4 Chelicerata

Including Architarbi

Class here Arachnida

.49 Merostomata and Pycnogonida

Standard subdivisions are added for Merostomata and Pycnogonida together, for Merostomata alone

.492 Xiphosura (Horseshoe crabs)

.493 Eurypterida

.6 Myriapoda

.7 Insecta

Class here Uniramia, Hexapoda, Pterygota

Add to base number 565.7 the numbers following 595.7 in 595.72–595.79, e.g., Coleoptera 565.76

For Myriapoda, see 565.6

566 Fossil Chordata

Including Cephalochordata, Urochordata (Tunicata)

Class here Vertebrata (Craniata, vertebrates), Tetrapoda (land vertebrates)

For fossil cold-blooded vertebrates, see 567; for fossil Aves, see 568; for fossil Mammalia, see 569

567 Fossil cold-blooded vertebrates

Including Leptolepis

Class here Pisces (fishes); Actinopterygii, Osteichthyes, Teleostei

Class specific kinds of Actinopterygii, Osteichthyes, Teleostei in 567.4–567.7

> ### 567.2–567.7 Fossil Pisces (fishes)

Class comprehensive works in 567

.2 Agnatha, Acanthodii, Placodermi

Including Cyclostomata

.3 Chondrichthyes and Sarcopterygii

Standard subdivisions are added for Chondrichthyes and Sarcopterygii together, for Chondrichthyes alone

Including Bradyodonti, Cladoselachii, Pleuracanthodii

Class here Elasmobranchii, Selachii; sharks

Add to base number 567.3 the numbers following 597.3 in 597.33–597.39, e.g., Sarcopterygii 567.39

.4–.7 Specific fossil Actinopterygii

Class here Osteichthyes, Teleostei

Add to base number 567 the numbers following 597 in 597.4–597.7, e.g., Salmoniformes 567.5

Class fossil Actinopterygii not traceable to surviving superorders, e.g., Leptolepis; comprehensive works on Actinopterygii, Osteichthyes, Teleostei in 567

For Sarcopterygii, see 567.39

.8 Amphibia

Including Anura, Gymnophiona, Labyrinthodontia, Lepospondyli, Urodela

.9   **Reptilia**

Class here Archosauria, Diapsida, Dinosaurs

.91   Specific dinosaurs and other Archosauria

Including Thecodontia

For Crocodilia, see 567.98. For a "dinosaur" of an order not assigned to Archosauria, see the order, e.g., Ichthyosauria 567.937

[.910 1–.910 9]   Standard subdivisions

Do not use; class in 567.901–567.909

>   567.912–567.915 Specific dinosaurs

Class comprehensive works in 567.9

.912   Saurischia

Including Allosaurus, Baryonyx, Coelophysis, Deinonychus, Oviraptor

Class here Theropoda (carnivorous dinosaurs)

For Sauropodomorpha, see 567.913

.912 9   Tyrannosaurus

.913   Sauropodomorpha (Herbivorous Saurischia)

Including Diplodocus, Seismosaurus

.913 8   Apatosaurus (Brontosaurus)

.914   Ornithischia

Including Hadrosauridae (duck-billed dinosaurs); Anatosaurus, Corythosaurus, Hypsilophodon, Iguanodon, Maiasaura, Pachycephalosaurus, Parasaurolophus

Class here Ornithopoda

For Stegosauria, Ankylosauria, Ceratopsia, see 567.915

.915   Stegosauria, Ankylosauria, Ceratopsia (horned dinosaurs)

Including Protoceratops

Class here armored dinosaurs

.915 3   Stegosaurus

.915 8   Triceratops

.918   Pterosauria (Flying reptiles)

Including Pteranodon, Pterodactylus

Class comprehensive works on flying and marine reptiles in 567.937

.92	Anapsida

Including Chelonia (Testudines), Cotylosauria

For Mesosauria, see 567.937

.93	Euryapsida, Synapsida; Mesosauria

Including Araeoscelidia, Pelycosauria, Placodontia, Therapsida

.937	Marine reptiles

Including Ichthyosauria, Mesosauria, Sauropterygia (Nothosauria and Plesiosauria)

For Mosasauridae, see 567.95

.94	Lepidosauria

Including Eosuchia

Class here Squamata

For Sauria, see 567.95; for Serpentes, see 567.96

.945	Rhynchocephalia
.95	Sauria

Including Mosasauridae (marine lizards)

Class comprehensive works on Sauria and Serpentes in 567.94

.96	Serpentes
.98	Crocodilia

568 Fossil Aves (birds)

Class here Neornithes

.2	**Archaeornithes, Hesperornithiformes, Ichthyornithiformes**
.22	Archaeornithes
.23	Hesperornithiformes and Ichthyornithiformes
.3	**Charadriiformes, Ciconiiformes, Diatrymiformes, Gruiformes, Phoenicopteriformes**
.4	**Water birds**

Including Anseriformes, Gaviiformes, Pelecaniformes, Podicipediformes, Procellariiformes, Sphenisciformes

For Hesperornithiformes and Ichthyornithiformes, see 568.23; for Charadriiformes, Ciconiiformes, Diatrymiformes, Gruiformes, Phoenicopteriformes, see 568.3

.5	**Palaeognathae**

Including Aepyornithiformes, Apterygiformes, Caenagnathiformes, Casuariiformes, Rheiformes, Struthioniformes, Tinamiformes

Class here ratites

.6   **Galliformes and Columbiformes**

> Standard subdivisions are added for Galliformes and Columbiformes together, for Galliformes alone

.7   **Miscellaneous land birds**

> Limited to those named herein
>
> Including Apodiformes, Coliiformes, Coraciiformes, Cuculiformes, Piciformes, Psittaciformes, Trogoniformes
>
> Class comprehensive works on land birds in 568

[.701–.709]   Standard subdivisions

> Do not use; class in 568.01–568.09

.8   **Passeriformes**

.9   **Falconiformes, Caprimulgiformes, Strigiformes**

> Standard subdivisions are added for Falconiformes, Caprimulgiformes, Strigiformes, together; for Falconiformes alone

569   Fossil Mammalia

.2   **Metatheria and Prototheria**

> Standard subdivisions are added for Metatheria and Prototheria together, for Metatheria alone
>
> Including Trituberculata
>
> Class here Marsupialia

.29   Prototheria

> Including Allotheria, Eotheria
>
> Class here Monotremata

\>   **569.3–569.9 Eutheria**

> Class comprehensive works in 569

.3   **Miscellaneous orders of Eutheria**

> Limited to those named below

[.301–.309]   Standard subdivisions

> Do not use; class in 569.01–569.09

.31   Edentata, Palaeanodonta, Pholidota, Taeniodontia, Tillodontia, Tubulidentata

.32–.37   Dermoptera, Insectivora, Lagomorpha, Macroscelidea, Rodentia, Scandentia

> Add to base number 569.3 the numbers following 599.3 in 599.32–599.37, e.g., Insectivora 569.33

.4 **Chiroptera (Bats)**

Including Megachiroptera

Class here Microchiroptera

.5 **Cetacea, Desmostylia, Sirenia**

Standard subdivisions are added for Cetacea, Desmostylia, Sirenia together; for Cetacea alone

Including Archaeoceti

Class here Mysticeti, Odontoceti; marine mammals, whales

For Pinnipedia, see 569.79

.6 **Ungulates**

Class Desmostylia, Sirenia in 569.5

.62 Extinct orders of ungulates

Including Astrapotheria, Condylarthra, Dinocerata, Embrithopoda, Litopterna, Notoungulata, Pantodonta, Pyrotheria, Xenungulata

Class extinct members of surviving orders in 569.63–569.68

.63–.68 Surviving orders of ungulates

Add to base number 569.6 the numbers following 599.6 in 599.63–599.68, e.g., Proboscidea 569.67

.7 **Carnivores**

Including Creodonta

Class here Fissipedia

Add to base number 569.7 the numbers following 599.7 in 599.74–599.79, e.g., Pinnipedia 569.79

.8 **Primates**

Class here Anthropoidea, monkeys

Add to base number 569.8 the numbers following 599.8 in 599.83–599.88, e.g., Hominidae 569.88

Class Tupaiidae in 569.338

For Homo and related genera, see 569.9

.9 **Homo and related genera**

Humans and forebears, including species and genera that are more closely related to the species Homo sapiens than to any other living species, e.g., Ardipithecus

Including Piltdown forgery

.93	Australopithecus

Including Paranthropus, Plesianthropus

Class here australopithecines

Class australopithecines not assigned to genus Australopithecus in 569.9

.97	Homo erectus

Including Heidelberg man, Java man, Peking man

.98	Homo sapiens

Including Cro-Magnon man, Kabwe (Rhodesian) man

.986	Homo sapiens neanderthalis (Neanderthals)

570 Biology

Class here life sciences, information processing in nature

For paleontology, see 560; for plants, see 580; for animals, see 590; for medical sciences, see 610. For information processing associated with a specific natural phenomenon, see the phenomenon, e.g., cellular computing 571.6, gene regulatory networks 572.865

See also 006.384 for computing with natural materials

See Manual at 363 vs. 302–307, 333.7, 570–590, 600; also at 578 vs. 304.2, 508, 910

SUMMARY

570.1–.9	**Standard subdivisions**
571	**Physiology and related subjects**
.01–.09	Standard subdivisions
.1	Animals
.2	Plants and microorganisms
.3	Anatomy and morphology
.4	Biophysics
.5	Tissue biology and regional physiology
.6	Cell biology
.7	Biological control and secretions
.8	Reproduction, development, growth
.9	Diseases
572	**Biochemistry**
.3	General topics of biochemistry
.4	Metabolism
.5	Miscellaneous chemicals
.6	Proteins
.7	Enzymes
.8	Biochemical genetics

573		Specific physiological systems in animals, regional histology and physiology in animals
	.1	Circulatory system
	.2	Respiratory system
	.3	Digestive system
	.4	Endocrine and excretory systems
	.5	Integument
	.6	Reproductive system
	.7	Musculoskeletal system
	.8	Nervous and sensory systems
	.9	Miscellaneous systems and organs in animals, regional histology and physiology in animals
575		Specific parts of and physiological systems in plants
	.4	Stems
	.5	Roots and leaves
	.6	Reproductive organs
	.7	Circulation, food storage, excretion
	.8	Transpiration
	.9	Animal-like physiological processes
576		Genetics and evolution
	.01–.09	Standard subdivisions
	.5	Genetics
	.8	Evolution
577		Ecology
	.01–.09	Standard subdivisions
	.1	Specific ecosystem processes
	.2	Specific factors affecting ecology
	.3	Forest ecology
	.4	Grassland ecology
	.5	Ecology of miscellaneous environments
	.6	Aquatic ecology
	.7	Marine ecology
	.8	Synecology and population biology
578		Natural history of organisms and related subjects
	.01–.09	Standard subdivisions
	.4	Adaptation
	.6	Miscellaneous nontaxonomic kinds of organisms
	.7	Organisms characteristic of specific kinds of environments
579		Natural history of microorganisms, fungi, algae
	.01–.09	Standard subdivisions
	.1	Specific topics in natural history of microorganisms, fungi, algae
	.2	Viruses and subviral organisms
	.3	Prokaryotes
	.4	Protozoa
	.5	Fungi
	.6	Mushrooms
	.7	Lichens
	.8	Algae

.1   **Philosophy and theory**

Class here nature of life, differences between living and nonliving substances

Class origin of life, conditions needed for life to begin in 576.83

.12   Classification

Class taxonomic classification in 578.012

.15	Scientific principles
.151 95	Statistical mathematics
	Class here biometrics, biostatistics
	See Manual at 519.5, T1—015195 vs. 001.422, T1—0727
.2	**Miscellany**
.28	Auxiliary techniques and procedures; apparatus, equipment, procedures
	Notation 028 from Table 1 as modified below
.282	Microscopy
	Including photomicrography, stereology
	Class here microscopes
	Class interdisciplinary works on microscopy in 502.82
.282 3	Light microscopy
	Including magnifying glasses (simple microscopes)
	Class here compound microscopes
	Class stereology with compound microscopes in 570.282
.282 5	Electron microscopy
	Class stereology with electron microscopes in 570.282
.282 7	Slide preparation
	Including fixation, staining; microtomy
.284	Apparatus, equipment, materials
	Do not use for microscopes; class in 570.282
.288	Maintenance and repair
	Do not use for preservation of biological specimens; class in 570.752
.7	**Education, research, related topics**
.72	Research
.724	Experimental research
	Class here experimental biology
	Class tissue and organ culture in 571.538; class cell culture in 571.638
.75	Museum activities and services
.752	Preserving biological specimens
.9	**History, geographic treatment, biography**
	Do not use for geographic treatment of organisms; class in 578.09
.919	Space
	Do not use for space biology; class in 571.0919

.999 Extraterrestrial worlds

Do not use for extraterrestrial life; class in 576.839

> ## 571–575 Internal biological processes and structures

Class here internal biological processes and structures in plants and animals

Unless other instructions are given, class a subject with aspects in two or more subdivisions of 571–575 in the number coming last, e.g., cytology of animal circulatory system 573.136 (*not* 571.1 or 571.6)

Class comprehensive works in 571

See Manual at 571–575 vs. 630; also at 579–590 vs. 571–575

> ## 571–572 General internal processes common to all organisms

Add to each subdivision identified by * as follows:
01–08   Standard subdivisions
Notation from Table 1 as modified under 570.1–570.8, e.g., microscopy 0282
09   History, geographic treatment, biography
Notation from Table 1 as modified under 571.09, e.g., space biology 0919
1–2   Specific kinds of organisms
Add the numbers following 571 in 571.1–571.2, e.g., the subject in animals 1, the subject in plants and microorganisms 2
Class comprehensive works in 571

See Manual at 571–573 vs. 610

571   Physiology and related subjects

Standard subdivisions are added for physiology and related subjects, for physiology alone

Class here comprehensive works on internal biological processes

For biochemistry, see 572; for specific physiological systems in animals, regional histology and physiology in animals, see 573; for specific parts of and physiological systems in plants, see 575; for genetics, see 576.5

See Manual at 571–575 vs. 630

SUMMARY

571.01–.09	Standard subdivisions
.1	Animals
.2	Plants and microorganisms
.3	Anatomy and morphology
.4	Biophysics
.5	Tissue biology and regional physiology
.6	Cell biology
.7	Biological control and secretions
.8	Reproduction, development, growth
.9	Diseases

.01–.08   Standard subdivisions

> Notation from Table 1 as modified under 570.1–570.8, e.g., microscopy in physiology 571.0282

.09   History, geographic treatment, biography

.091 9   Space

> Class here space biology

.099 9   Extraterrestrial worlds

> Class extraterrestrial life in 576.839

.1   Animals

Class here comparative physiology

Class comprehensive works on animals in 590

> *For comparative physiology of plants and microorganisms, see 571.2; for physiology of Protozoa, see 571.294*

.101–.109   Standard subdivisions

> Notation from Table 1 as modified under 590.1–590.9, e.g., microscopy in animal physiology 571.10282

.11–.19   Specific kinds of animals

> Add to base number 571.1 the numbers following 59 in 591–599, e.g., marine animals 571.1177, mammals 571.19; however, for physiology and related subjects in humans, see 612; for physiology and related subjects in domestic animals, see 636.0892

.2   Plants and microorganisms

Standard subdivisions are added for plants and microorganisms together, for plants alone

Class here comparative physiology of plants and microorganisms, physiology of agricultural plants

Class comprehensive works on plants in 580

.201–.209   Standard subdivisions

> Notation from Table 1 as modified under 580.1–580.9, e.g., microscopy in plant physiology 571.20282

.21–.28   Specific kinds of plants

> Add to base number 571.2 the numbers following 58 in 581–588, e.g., aquatic plants 571.2176, monocotyledons 571.24

> *For physiology of fungi, see 571.295; for physiology of algae, see 571.298*

.29 Microorganisms, fungi, algae

> Subdivisions are added for microorganisms, fungi, algae together, for microorganisms alone

> Class comprehensive works on microorganisms, fungi, algae in 579

> *See Manual at 571.629 vs. 571.29*

.290 1–.290 9 Standard subdivisions

>> Notation from Table 1 as modified under 579.01–579.09, e.g., microscopy in microorganism physiology 571.290282

.291–.298 Specific kinds of microorganisms, fungi, algae

> Add to base number 571.29 the numbers following 579 in 579.1–579.8, e.g., marine microorganisms 571.29177, Protozoa 571.294

.3 ***Anatomy and morphology**

> Class here comparative anatomy

> Subdivisions are added for either or both topics in heading

> *For anatomy and morphology of microorganisms, see 571.63329*

.4 ***Biophysics**

> Class here effects of physical forces on organisms

> Class comprehensive works on biophysics and biochemistry in 572

> *For bioenergetics, physical biochemistry, see 572.43*

.43 *Biomechanics and effects of mechanical forces

> Class here biodynamics, solid biomechanics

> Subdivisions are added for either or both topics in heading

> Class biomechanics of locomotion in 573.79343

.435 *Gravity

.437 *Pressure

.44 *Effects of mechanical vibrations, sound, related vibrations

.443 *Mechanical vibrations

> Class here subsonic vibrations

.444 *Sound

.445 *Ultrasonic vibrations

.45 *Radiobiology

.453 *Radio waves and microwaves

> Subdivisions are added for either or both topics in heading

---

*Add as instructed under 571–572

.454	*Infrared radiation
.455	*Light
.456	*Ultraviolet radiation
.457	*X rays
.459	*Particle radiation

> Including beta, gamma, neutron radiation; cosmic rays
>
> *For X rays, see 571.457*

.46	*Effects of temperature
.464	*Low temperatures
.464 5	*Cryogenic temperatures (Cryobiology)
.467	*High temperatures
.47	*Effects of electricity and magnetism

> Subdivisions are added for effects of electricity and magnetism together, for effects of electricity alone, for effects of electromagnetism alone

| .49 | *Environmental biophysics |

> Effects of combinations of physical forces characteristic of unusual environments
>
> Including effects of climate, of high altitudes
>
> Class effects of a specific physical force with the force in 571.43–571.47

| .499 | *Extraterrestrial biophysics |

> Class here bioastronautics

*Add as instructed under 571–572

>   **571.5–571.9 Tissue biology, regional physiology, cell biology, biological control and secretions, reproduction, development, growth, diseases**

> Except for modifications shown under specific entries, add to each subdivision identified by † as follows:
>
> 01–08   Standard subdivisions
> > Notation from Table 1 as modified under 570.1–570.8, e.g., microscopy in physiology 0282
>
> 09   History, geographic treatment, biography
> > Notation from Table 1 as modified under 571.09, e.g., space biology 0919
>
> 1–2   Specific kinds of organisms
> > Add the numbers following 571 in 571.1–571.2, e.g., the subject in animals 1, the subject in plants 2
>
> 3   Anatomy and application of processes to other processes
>
> [301–309]   Standard subdivisions
> > Do not use; class in notation 01–09 from this table
>
> 33–38   Anatomy and application of specific processes to other processes
> > Add to 3 the numbers following 571 in 571.3–571.8, e.g., anatomy 33, biophysics 34, cell biology 36

Class comprehensive works in 571.5

.5   ***Tissue biology and regional physiology**

Class here histology, histophysiology; comprehensive works on tissue and cell biology

Subdivisions are added for tissue biology and regional physiology together, for tissue biology alone

Class biophysics of tissues in general in 571.4; class biophysics of specific tissues in 571.55–571.58

For cell biology, see 571.6; for histogenesis, see 571.835

.52

.53   Tissue anatomy, morphology, culture

[.530 1–.530 9]   Standard subdivisions

> Do not use; class in 571.501–571.509

.533   *Tissue anatomy and morphology

Subdivisions are added for either or both topics in heading

.538   *Tissue culture

Class here organ culture, comprehensive works on tissue and cell culture

For cell culture, see 571.638

---

*Add as instructed under 571–572

>   571.55–571.57   Specific tissues in animals

       Class comprehensive works in 571.51

         For tissues of a specific physiological system, see the system in 573, plus notation 35 from table under 573, e.g., tissues of circulatory system 573.135

.55   †Epithelial tissues

.555   †Endothelium

.56   †Connective tissues

         For adipose tissues, see 571.57

.57   †Adipose tissues

.58   Specific tissues in plants

       Class comprehensive works in 571.52

         For tissues of a specific part or physiological system, see the part or physiological system in 575, plus notation 35 from table under 575, e.g., tissues of leaves 575.5735

[.580 1–.580 9]   Standard subdivisions

         Do not use; class in 571.5201–571.5209

.585   †Parenchyma

         Class here pith, sclerenchyma

.59   Regional histology and physiology

       Standard subdivisions are added for either or both topics in heading

         For regional histology and physiology of animals, see 573.99; for regional physiology of plants, see 575.4; for regional histology of plants, see 575.4359

.590 1–.590 9   Standard subdivisions

         Notation from Table 1 as modified under 570.1–570.9, e.g., microscopy in regional physiology 571.590282

.592   Fungi and algae

.592 9   Specific fungi and algae

         Add to base number 571.5929 the numbers following 579 in 579.5–579.8, e.g., regional physiology of mushrooms 571.59296

.6   ***Cell biology**

       Class here cell physiology, cytology, eukaryotic cells, protoplasm

         For reproduction and growth of cells, see 571.84; for cytopathology, see 571.936; for cytochemistry, see 572; for cell digestion, metabolism, nutrition, see 572.4; for cell respiration, see 572.47

*Add as instructed under 571–572
†Add as instructed under 571.5–571.9

.629 Microorganisms, fungi, algae

Number built according to instructions under 571–572

See Manual at 571.629 vs. 571.29

.63 Cell anatomy, morphology, biophysics, culture

[.630 1–.630 9] Standard subdivisions

Do not use; class in 571.601–571.609

.633 *Cell anatomy and morphology

Class here ultrastructure

Subdivisions are added for either or both topics in heading

.634 *Cell biophysics

.634 3–.634 9 Specific topics of cell biophysics

Add to base number 571.634 the numbers following 571.4 in 571.43–571.49, e.g., effect of high temperatures on cells 571.63467

.638 *Cell culture

Class comprehensive works on tissue and cell culture in 571.538

.64 †Membranes

Class here biological transport

Class lipid membranes and their chemistry in 572.577; class protein membranes and their chemistry in 572.696

For membranes of specific cellular components, see 571.65–571.68; for ion transport, see 572.3

.65 †Cytoplasm

Class here endoplasmic reticulum, organelles

.654 †Cytoskeleton

Class here microfilaments, microtubules

.655 †Vacuoles

Including peroxisomes

Class here lysosomes, vesicles

.656 †Golgi apparatus

.657 †Mitochondria

.658 †Ribosomes

.659 †Plastids

*Add as instructed under 571–572
†Add as instructed under 571.5–571.9

.659 2   Plants and microorganisms

> Number built according to instructions under 571.5–571.9

> Class here chloroplasts

.66   †Nucleus

> Including linin network, nuclear envelope, nuclear membrane, nucleolus

> Class here nucleoplasm

> Class nucleic acids in 572.8

> *For chromosomes, see 572.87*

.67   †Cell movement

> Including basal body

> Class here cilia, flagella, irritability, pseudopoda

.68   †Cell walls

.7   **†Biological control and secretions**

> Biological control: control of an organism's own physiological processes

> Subdivisions are added for biological control and secretions together, for biological control alone

> *See also 632.96 for biological control of agricultural pests*

.71   Animals

> Number built according to instructions under 571.5–571.9

> Class here comprehensive works on endocrine and nervous systems

>> *For endocrine system, see 573.4; for nervous and sensory systems, see 573.8*

.72   Plants and microorganisms

> Number built according to instructions under 571.5–571.9

>> *See also 575.9 for animal-like physiological processes in plants*

.74   †Biochemistry of control

> Class here comprehensive works on hormones

> *For animal hormones, see 573.44*

> *See Manual at 573.44 vs. 571.74*

.75   †Homeostasis and physiological balance

> Including electrolytic balance, fluid balance

> Subdivisions are added for either or both topics in heading

†Add as instructed under 571.5–571.9

.76	†Body temperature

Class here homoiothermy, poikilothermy

.77	†Periodicity

Class here biorhythms, chronobiology

.78	†Dormancy
.785	†Diapause
.786	†Aestivation
.787	†Hibernation

Class comprehensive works on hibernation in 591.565

.79	†Secretion

Other than hormones

Class here exocrine glands, comprehensive works on glands

Class excretory system of animals in 573.49

> *For endocrine glands, see 573.4. For secretions of a specific organ or system, or ones related to a specific process, see the organ, system or process in 571.5–571.9 or 573–575, plus notation 379 from table under 571.5–571.9, notation 379 from table under 573, or notation 379 from table under 575, e.g., digestive secretions 573.3379*

.8	**†Reproduction, development, growth**

Class here physiology of life cycle, sexual reproduction

Subdivisions are added for any or all topics in heading

See Manual at 571.8 vs. 573.6, 575.6

.81	Animals

Number built according to instructions under 571.5–571.9

Class comprehensive works on life cycle of animals in 591.56

> *For reproduction, sexual reproduction in animals, see 573.6*

.82	Plants and microorganisms

Number built according to instructions under 571.5–571.9

> *For reproduction, sexual reproduction in plants, see 575.6*

.829	Fungi and algae

Number built according to instructions under 571.5–571.9

Class reproduction and development of unicellular microorganisms in 571.8429; class sexual reproduction of unicellular microorganisms in 571.84529

---

†Add as instructed under 571.5–571.9

.835   Histogenesis

Number built according to instructions under 571.5–571.9

Class here cell differentiation, tissue differentiation

Class cell differentiation in embryology, cell determination in 571.8636

[.836]   Cell biology

Do not use for cell differentiation; class in 571.835. Do not use for cell reproduction and growth; class in 571.84

.84   †Reproduction and growth of cells

Subdivisions are added for reproduction and growth together, for reproduction alone

Class chromosome recombination in 572.877

For cell differentiation, see 571.835

.844   †Cell division

Including centromeres, chromatids

Class here mitosis

.845   †Gametogenesis

Including egg cells

Class here meiosis; germ, haploid, sex cells

For maturation and fertilization of gametes, see 571.864

.845 2   Plants

Number built according to instructions under 571.5–571.9

Class here comprehensive works on palynology

.847   †Reproduction by asexual spores

Class here asexual spores, sporulation

Class sexual spores (gametes) in 571.845

.849   †Cell growth

Class cell differentiation in 571.835

See also 571.936 for cell pathology and death

.85   †Developmental genetics

.86   †Embryology

Class comprehensive works on developmental biology in 571.8

---

†Add as instructed under 571.5–571.9

.864   †Fertilization

                  Including maturation of gametes

                  Class here zygotes

.864 2   Fertilization in plants and microorganisms

                        Number built according to instructions under 571.5–571.9

                        Class here pollination

                        For coevolution of pollination, see 576.875

.865   †Early cell division

                  Class here blastulas, gastrulation

.87   †Development after embryo

                  Class here maturation

                  Class comprehensive works on development in 571.8

.876   †Development in distinct stages

                  Including larvae

                  Class here comprehensive works on metamorphosis

                  For embryo stage, see 571.86

.878   †Aging

                  Class pathological aging and death in 571.939

.879   †Longevity

.88   Miscellaneous topics in reproduction

                  Limited to topics named below

[.880 1–.880 9]   Standard subdivisions

                        Do not use; class in 571.801–571.809

.882   †Sex differentiation

                  For gametogenesis, see 571.845

.882 157 9   Sex differentiation in Hymenoptera

                        Number built according to instructions under 571.5–571.9

                        Class here physiology of caste differentiation among social insects

.884   †Alternation of generations (Metagenesis)

.886   †Hermaphroditism

.887   †Parthenogenesis

                  Class comprehensive works on asexual reproduction in 571.89

†Add as instructed under 571.5–571.9

.889   †Regeneration

.89   †Vegetative reproduction

> Class here asexual reproduction
>
> *For asexual reproduction of microorganisms, see 571.8429; for parthenogenesis, see 571.887*

.892   Microorganisms, fungi, algae

> Number built according to instructions under 571.5–571.9
>
> Do not use for vegetative reproduction of plants; class in 575.49

.892 9   Specific microorganisms, fungi, algae

> Number built according to instructions under 571.5–571.9
>
> Add to base number 571.8929 the numbers following 579 in 579.2–579.8, e.g., vegetative reproduction of fungi 571.89295

.9   ***Diseases**

> Class here pathology, histopathology, pathogenicity, pathophysiology; noncommunicable diseases
>
> *For human diseases, results of experimental research on human diseases in animals, see 616; for comprehensive works on agricultural diseases, see 632. For diseases of a specific physiological system in animals, see the system in 573, plus notation 39 from table under 573, e.g., bone diseases 573.7639; for diseases of specific parts of and physiological systems in plants, see the part or system in 575, plus notation 39 from table under 575, e.g., diseases of leaves 575.5739*

.91   Animal diseases

> Number built according to instructions under 571–572
>
> *For diseases of domestic animals, see 636.0896*

.92   Plant diseases

> Number built according to instructions under 571–572
>
> *For diseases of domestic plants, see 632.3*

.93   Generalities of diseases

[.930 1–.930 9]   Standard subdivisions

> Do not use; class in 571.901–571.909

.933–.938   General topics of disease

> Add to base number 571.93 the numbers following 571 in 571.3–571.8, e.g., physical causes of diseases 571.934; however, for pathological aging, see 571.939
>
> Class comprehensive works in 571.9

---

*Add as instructed under 571–572

†Add as instructed under 571.5–571.9

.939 †Pathological aging and death

> Subdivisions are added for either or both topics in heading

> Class comprehensive works on physiology and pathology of aging in 571.878

.94 *Pathological biochemistry

.943–.948 Specific topics of pathological biochemistry

> Add to base number 571.94 the numbers following 572 in 572.3–572.8, e.g., protein deficiency 571.946

.95 †Toxicology

> Class here diseases and stress caused by pollutants, by water pollution; ecotoxicology, environmental diseases, poisons

> *For environmental diseases induced by physical stresses, see 571.934*

> *See Manual at 363.73 vs. 571.95, 577.27*

.954 Specific elements and groups of elements

[.954 01–.954 09] Standard subdivisions

> Do not use; class in 571.9501–571.9509

.954 3–.954 7 Specific elements and groups of elements

> Add to base number 571.954 the numbers following 546 in 546.3–546.7 for the element or group of elements only, e.g., metal toxicology 571.9543, mercury toxicology 571.954663

.956 †Air pollutants

> Class here toxicology of combustion gases

.957 †Organic compounds

> Including toxins

> Class organic pesticides in 571.959

.959 †Pesticides

.96 †Immunity

> Class here disease resistance, immune system, immunology, leukocytes, lymphocytes

> Class allergies in 571.972; class autoimmunity in 571.973; class immune deficiency diseases in 571.974

> *For immunity in relation to diseases in humans, see 616.079*

.964 †Immunochemistry and immune response

> Subdivisions are added for immunochemistry and immune response together, for immunochemistry alone

---

*Add as instructed under 571–572
†Add as instructed under 571.5–571.9

.964 4   †Interferons

.964 5   †Antigens

                Class blood groups in 573.154

                See also 573.154 for blood groups

.964 6   †Immune response

                Including clonal selection

                Class here antigen recognition

                Class antigen-antibody reactions in 571.9677

.964 8   †Immunogenetics

                Including transduction, transfection, transformation

.966   †T cells (T lymphocytes)

                Class here cell-mediated (cellular) immunity, cytotoxic T cells

                See also 571.968 for killer cells

.967   †B cells (B lymphocytes)

                Class here antibodies (immunoglobulins)

                *For maternally acquired antibodies, see 571.9638; for
                antibody-dependent immune mechanisms, see 571.968*

.967 7   †Antigen-antibody reactions

.968   †Phagocytes and complement

                Including granulocytes, killer cells

                Class here antibody-dependent immune mechanisms

                Subdivisions are added for phagocytes and complement together, for
                phagocytes alone

                See also 571.966 for cytotoxic T cells

.968 5   †Macrophages

.968 8   †Complement

                Class activation of macrophages by complement in 571.9685

.97   Miscellaneous diseases

                Limited to those named below

[.970 1–.970 9]   Standard subdivisions

                Do not use; class in 571.901–571.909

.972   †Allergies

---

†Add as instructed under 571.5–571.9

.973 †Autoimmunity

Class here autoimmune diseases

.974 †Immune deficiency diseases

.975 †Injuries and wounds

Subdivisions are added for either or both topics in heading

.976 †Deformities

Class here teratology

.978 †Tumors

Class here cancer

.98 †Communicable diseases

Class here diseases caused by living organisms, by microorganisms

Class poisons in 571.95; class comprehensive works on immunity to communicable diseases in 571.96

For specific communicable diseases, see 571.99

.986 †Disease vectors

.99 Specific communicable diseases

[.990 1–.990 9] Standard subdivisions

Do not use; class in 571.9801–571.9809

.992–.995 Diseases caused by microorganisms and fungi

Add to base number 571.99 the numbers following 579 in 579.2–579.5 for the organism only, e.g., protozoan diseases 571.994; then add 1 and to the result add further the numbers following 571 in 571.1–571.2, e.g., protozoan diseases in animals 571.99411, protozoan diseases in plants 571.99412

Do not add notation 12 (derived from 571.2) to 571.9928 (diseases caused by plant viruses) except for viral diseases of specific kinds of plants. Do not add notation 1293 (derived from 571.293) to 571.9926 (diseases caused by bacterial viruses) except for viral diseases of specific kinds of bacteria

Class comprehensive works in 571.98

.999 †Parasitic diseases

Class here diseases caused by animals, by endoparasites, by worms, comprehensive works on parasitism

For protozoan diseases, see 571.994; for ecology of parasitism, see 577.857

†Add as instructed under 571.5–571.9

572   *Biochemistry

Class here cytochemistry, histochemistry; comprehensive works on biochemistry of nonmetallic elements and their compounds; comprehensive works on biochemistry and biophysics; interdisciplinary works on biochemicals, on macromolecules

For chemistry of biochemicals, see 547; for chemistry of macromolecules, see 547.7; for biophysics, see 571.4; for biochemistry of control processes, see 571.74; for pathological biochemistry, see 571.94; for immunochemistry, see 571.964; for biogeochemistry, see 577.14; for industrial biochemistry, see 660.63. For biochemistry of a specific physiological system in animals, see the system in 573, plus notation 4 from table under 573, e.g., chemistry of circulatory fluids in animals 573.154; for biochemistry of a reproductive organ or physiological system in plants, see the organ or system in 575.6–575.9, plus notation 4 from table under 575.6–575.9, e.g., chemistry of circulatory fluids in plants 575.754

SUMMARY

572.3	**General topics of biochemistry**
.4	**Metabolism**
.5	**Miscellaneous chemicals**
.6	**Proteins**
.7	**Enzymes**
.8	**Biochemical genetics**

.3   General topics of biochemistry

Including ion transport

[.301–.309]   Standard subdivisions

Do not use; class in 572.01–572.09

.33   *Molecular structure

Class here bonds, conformation, sequences of polymers and other component units of large molecules, theoretical chemistry

Class structure-activity relationships in 572.4; class molecular biology (biochemical genetics) in 572.8

.36   *Analytical biochemistry

.38   *Biochemical evolution

Class comprehensive works on molecular evolution in 572.838

For biochemistry of origin of life, see 576.83

.39   *Nutritional requirements

Class conditions needed for life to begin in 576.83

For a specific kind of chemical requirement, see the chemical in 572.5–572.8, plus notation 39 from table under 572.5–572.8, e.g., vitamin requirements 572.5839

---

*Add as instructed under 571–572

.4   *Metabolism

> Class here cell digestion and metabolism, structure-activity relationships, comprehensive biological works on nutrition
>
> Class molecular structure in 572.33; class interdisciplinary works on human nutrition in 363.8
>
>> *For metabolism of a specific chemical, see the chemical in 572.5–572.8, plus notation 4 from table under 572.5–572.8, e.g., metabolism of enzymes 572.74, enzyme kinetics 572.744; for a specific aspect of biology of nutrition, see the aspect, e.g., nutritional requirements 572.39, digestive system 573.3*

.41   Animal metabolism

> Number built according to instructions under 571–572
>
> Class comprehensive works on animal digestion in 573.3

.43   *Energy metabolism

> Class here biochemical interactions, reactions; bioenergetics, energy phenomena in organisms, physical biochemistry
>
> Class effects of physical agents on organisms, comprehensive works on biophysics in 571.4
>
>> *For bonds, see 572.33*

.435   *Photobiochemistry and bioluminescence

> Subdivisions are added for photobiochemistry and bioluminescence together, for photobiochemistry alone
>
> *For photosynthesis, see 572.46*

.435 8   *Bioluminescence

> *For bioluminescent organs, see 573.95*

.436   *Thermodynamics

> Class here thermobiology, thermochemistry

.437   *Bioelectrochemistry

> *For electric organs, see 573.97*

.44   *Reaction kinetics

.45   *Biosynthesis (Anabolism)

> *For photosynthesis, see 572.46*

.46   *Photosynthesis

> Class here chlorophylls

.47   *Cell respiration

> Class here tissue respiration, comprehensive works on respiration

---

*Add as instructed under 571–572

.471   Cell respiration in animals

                 Number built according to instructions under 571–572

                 Class comprehensive works on respiration in animals in 573.2

.472   Cell respiration in plants and microorganisms

                 Number built according to instructions under 571–572

                 For gas exchange from surface tissues of plants, see 575.8

.475   *Tricarboxylic acid cycle

                 Variant names: citric acid cycle, Krebs cycle

                 Class here adenosine triphosphate

.478   *Anaerobic respiration

.48   *Catabolism

.49   *Fermentation

>   **572.5–572.8 Specific biochemicals and biochemical genetics**

Except for modifications shown under specific entries, add to each subdivision identified by † as follows:
01–08   Standard subdivisions
             Notation from Table 1 as modified under 570.1–570.8, e.g., microscopy in physiology 0282
09   History, geographic treatment, biography
             Notation from Table 1 as modified under 571.09, e.g., space biology 0919
1–2   Specific kinds of organisms
             Add the numbers following 571 in 571.1–571.2, e.g., the subject in animals 1, the subject in plants 2
3   General topics in biochemistry
[301–309]   Standard subdivisions
             Do not use; class in notation 01–09 from this table
33–39   Anatomy and application of specific processes to other processes
             Add to 3 the numbers following 572.3 in 572.33–572.39, e.g., molecular structure 33, nutritional requirements 39
4   Metabolism and genetic aspects
             Subdivisions are added for either or both topics in heading
401–408   Standard subdivisions
             Notation from Table 1 as modified under 570.1–570.8, e.g., microscopy 40282
409   History, geographic treatment, biography
             Notation from Table 1 as modified under 571.09, e.g., space biology 40919
41–49   Specific aspects of metabolism
             Add to 4 the numbers following 572.4 in 572.41–572.49, e.g., biosynthesis 45

Class comprehensive works in 572

---

*Add as instructed under 571–572

.5 **Miscellaneous chemicals**

Not provided for elsewhere

[.501–.509]   Standard subdivisions

Do not use; class in 572.01–572.09

.51   †Bioinorganic chemistry

Class here biomineralization, coordination biochemistry, metals in biochemistry

For bioinorganic chemistry of metals other than calcium, iron, copper, see 572.52; for bioinorganic chemistry of nonmetallic elements, see 572.53–572.55

.511   Animals

Number built according to instructions under 572.5–572.8

For biomineralization in animals, see 573.76451

.515   †Trace elements

Class here micronutrients

For a specific trace element, see the element in 572.51–572.55, e.g., iron 572.517

.516   †Calcium

.517   †Iron

.518   †Copper

.52   Bioinorganic chemistry of metals other than calcium, iron, copper

[.520 1–.520 9]   Standard subdivisions

Do not use; class in 572.5101–572.5109

.523–.527   Specific metals

Add to base number 572.52 the numbers following 546 in 546.38–546.72, e.g., magnesium 572.52392; however, for calcium, see 572.516; for iron, see 572.517; for copper, see 572.518

> 572.53–572.55   Nonmetallic elements and their compounds in biochemistry

Class comprehensive works in 572

.53   †Oxygen

For oxygen in respiration, see 572.47

.539   †Water

Class fluid balance in 571.75

---

†Add as instructed under 572.5–572.8

.54   †Nitrogen

> *For biogeochemical nitrogen cycle, see 577.145*

.545   †Nitrogen fixation

.548   †Amines

> *For alkaloids, see 572.549; for amino acids, see 572.65*

.549   †Alkaloids

.55   Other nonmetallic elements and their compounds in biochemistry

> Class carbon, hydrogen in 572

[.550 1–.550 9]   Standard subdivisions

> Do not use; class in 572.01–572.09

.553   †Phosphorus

.554   †Sulfur

.555   †Selenium

.556   †Halogens

.56   †Carbohydrates

> Class here saccharides

.565   †Sugars

> Including insulin
>
> Class here monosaccharides, oligosaccharides

[.565 49]   Fermentation

> Do not use; class in 572.49

.566   †Polysaccharides

.566 8   †Structural polysaccharides

> Class cellulose in 572.56682; class chitin in 573.774

.567   †Conjugated carbohydrates

> Including glycosides

.567 2   Plants and microorganisms

> Number built according to instructions under 572.5–572.8
>
> Including gums

.57   †Lipids

> Including waxes
>
> Class here fats, fatty acids

---

†Add as instructed under 572.5–572.8

.577	†Membrane lipids
	Class here bilayer lipid membranes
.579	†Steroids
.579 5	†Sterols
	Class here cholesterol
.58	†Vitamins
.59	†Pigments
	Class chlorophyll in 572.46

.6   †Proteins

> *For hormones, see 571.74; for antibodies, see 571.967; for enzymes, see 572.7; for nucleoproteins, see 572.84; for prions, see 579.29*

.633	Molecular structure
	Number built according to instructions under 572.5–572.8
	Class here amino acid sequence
.645	Biosynthesis (Anabolism)
	Number built according to instructions under 572.5–572.8
	Class here genetic translation
.65	†Components of proteins
	Class here amino acids, peptides, polypeptides
	Class amino-acid sequence in 572.633
.66	†Simple proteins
	Including albumins, globulins, histones
.67	†Structural proteins
	Class here collagen, scleroproteins
.68	†Conjugated proteins
	Including chromoproteins, glycoproteins, lipoproteins, phosphoproteins
.69	†Bioactive proteins
.696	†Carrier and transport proteins
	Including cell receptors
	Class here membrane proteins
	Subdivisions are added for either or both topics in heading

†Add as instructed under 572.5–572.8

.7 †**Enzymes**

Class here coenzymes, cofactors

For enzymes performing a specific physiological function, see the physiological function, e.g., enzymes in cellular respiration 572.47, digestive enzymes 573.347

.75–.78 Enzymes catalyzing reactions of specific chemicals

Add to base number 572.7 the numbers following 572 in 572.5–572.8, e.g., proteolytic enzymes 572.76; however, for oxidases, see 572.791

Class comprehensive works on classes of enzymes named according to the reaction they catalyze in 572.79

.79 Classes of enzymes named according to specific kind of reaction they catalyze

Including isomerases, ligases, lyases

For enzymes catalyzing specific kinds of chemicals, see 572.75–572.78

[.790 1–.790 9] Standard subdivisions

Do not use; class in 572.701–572.709

.791 †Oxidoreductases

Oxidizing and reducing enzymes

Including catalases, dehydrogenases, oxidases, zymases

Class cellular respiration in 572.47

.792 †Transferases

.793 †Hydrolases

.8 †**Biochemical genetics**

Class here cytogenetics, molecular biology, molecular genetics, physiological genetics; nucleic acids

Class developmental genetics in 571.85; class comprehensive works on genetics in 576.5. Class genetic aspects of a specific biochemical with the specific biochemical in 572.5–572.7, plus notation 4 from table under 572.5–572.8, e.g., genetic regulation of enzymes 572.74

See Manual at 576.5 vs. 572.8

.829

†Add as instructed under 572.5–572.8

.838   Molecular evolution

Number built according to instructions under 572.5–572.8

Including mutagenesis, radiogenetics

Class here evolutionary genetics, genetic evolution

Class molecular evolution of a specific biochemical with the biochemical, plus notation 38 from table under 572.5–572.8, e.g., biochemical evolution of enzymes 572.738

For molecular evolution during origin of life, see 576.83

.84   Metabolism

Number built according to instructions under 572.5–572.8

Class here nucleic-acid hybridization, nucleic acid-protein interactions, comprehensive works on nucleoproteins

For nucleoproteins in a specific situation, see the situation, e.g., nucleoproteins in chromosomes 572.87

.85   †Nucleotides

Class here nucleosides

.86   †DNA (Deoxyribonucleic acid)

Class here chromosomal DNA, codons, genes, genomes

Class genetic transfection and transformation in 571.9648; class DNA as a component of chromosomes in 572.87

.863 3   Molecular structure

Number built according to instructions under 572.5–572.8

Class here DNA topology, double helix, genetic code; chromosome, gene, genome mapping; base, gene, nucleotide sequences

Class amino acid sequence in 572.633

For use of DNA fingerprinting in biometric identification, see 006.2482; for base and nucleotide sequence in RNA, see 572.8833

.864 5   Biosynthesis

Number built according to instructions under 572.5–572.8

Class here DNA replication

Class genetic transcription in 572.8845

.864 59   *DNA repair

.865   †Gene expression

Class here genetic regulation, regulation of gene expression

*Add as instructed under 571–572
†Add as instructed under 572.5–572.8

.869   †Extrachromosomal DNA

Including plasmid DNA, plasmids, transposons

Class here chloroplastic DNA, cytoplasmic inheritance, mitochondrial DNA

Class viruses in 579.2

For transduction, transfection, transformation, see 571.9648

See also 572.877 for genetic recombination

.87   †Chromosomes

Class here chromatin, chromosome numbers, nucleosomes

.873 3   Molecular structure

Number built according to instructions under 572.5–572.8

For chromosome mapping, nucleotide sequences in chromosomes, see 572.8633

.877   †Genetic recombination

Including aneuploidy, crossing over, inversion, translocation

Class somatic variation resulting from genetic recombination in 576.54; class recombinant DNA in 660.65

.88   †RNA (Ribonucleic acid)

For viroids, see 579.29

.884 5   Biosynthesis

Number built according to instructions under 572.5–572.8

Class here genetic transcription

Class genetic translation, protein synthesis in 572.645

.886   †Transfer RNA

†Add as instructed under 572.5–572.8

573 **Specific physiological systems in animals, regional histology and physiology in animals**

> Class here comprehensive works on specific physiological systems

> Except for modifications shown under specific entries, add to each subdivision identified by * as follows:
>
> 01–08   Standard subdivisions
> > Notation from Table 1 as modified under 570.1–570.8, e.g., microscopy 0282
>
> 09   History, geographic treatment, biography
> > Notation from Table 1 as modified under 571.09, e.g., space biology 0919
>
> 1   Comparative physiology of the system
> > Add to 1 the numbers following 59 in 591–599, e.g., the system in mammals 19
>
> 2   Operation of one physiological system within another system
> > Class hormones in notation 374 from this table
>
> 21   Circulation in the system
>
> 2101–2108   Standard subdivisions
> > Notation from Table 1 as modified under 570.1–570.8, e.g., microscopy 210282
>
> 2109   History, geographic treatment, biography
> > Notation from Table 1 as modified under 571.09, e.g., space biology 210919
>
> 211   Comparative physiology of circulation in the system
> > Add to 211 the numbers following 59 in 591–599, e.g., circulation in the system in mammals 2119
>
> 213   Anatomy and general biological processes of circulation
> > Add to 213 the numbers following 571 in 571.3–571.9, e.g., anatomy of circulation 2133, development of circulation 2138
>
> 25   Integument of the system
> > Class here membranes enveloping an organ even if not an integral part of the organ, e.g., pericardium 573.1725
>
> 2501–2508   Standard subdivisions
> > Notation from Table 1 as modified under 570.1–570.8, e.g., microscopy 250282
>
> 2509   History, geographic treatment, biography
> > Notation from Table 1 as modified under 571.09, e.g., space biology 250919
>
> 251   Comparative physiology of integument in the system
> > Add to 251 the numbers following 59 in 591–599, e.g., integument of the system in mammals 2519
>
> 253   Anatomy and general biological processes of integument
> > Add to 253 the numbers following 571 in 571.3–571.9, e.g., cytology of integument of an organ 2536
>
> 27   Muscles of the system
>
> 2701–2708   Standard subdivisions
> > Notation from Table 1 as modified under 570.1–570.8, e.g., microscopy 270282
>
> 2709   History, geographic treatment, biography
> > Notation from Table 1 as modified under 571.09, e.g., space biology 270919
>
> 271   Comparative physiology of muscles of the system
> > Add to 271 the numbers following 59 in 591–599, e.g., muscles of the system in mammals 2719

573   **Specific physiological systems in animals, regional histology and physiology in animals**

> 273   Anatomy and general biological processes of muscles
> > Add to 273 the numbers following 571 in 571.3–571.9, e.g., biophysics of muscles 2734
> 28   Innervation of the system
> 2801–2808   Standard subdivisions
> > Notation from Table 1 as modified under 570.1–570.8, e.g., microscopy 280282
> 2809   History, geographic treatment, biography
> > Notation from Table 1 as modified under 571.09, e.g., space biology 280919
> 281   Comparative physiology of innervation of the system
> > Add to 281 the numbers following 59 in 592–599, e.g., innervation of the system in mammals 2819
> 283   Anatomy and general biological processes of innervation
> > Add to 283 the numbers following 571 in 571.3–571.9, e.g., diseases of innervation of an organ 2839
> 3   Anatomy and general biological processes of the system or region
> > Class anatomy of, or a specific biological process within, a specific physiological subsystem in notation 2 from this table
> [301–309]   Standard subdivisions
> > Do not use; class in notation 01–09 from this table
> 33–39   Anatomy and specific biological processes of the system or region
> > Add to 3 the numbers following 571 in 571.3–571.9, e.g., anatomy 33, biophysics 34, cell biology 36
> 4   Biochemistry
> 401–408   Standard subdivisions
> > Notation from Table 1 as modified under 570.1–570.8, e.g., microscopy 40282
> 409   History, geographic treatment, biography
> > Notation from Table 1 as modified under 571.09, e.g., space biology 40919
> 41   Biochemistry of the system in specific kinds of animals
> > Add to 41 the numbers following 59 in 591–599, e.g., biochemistry of the system in mammals 419
> 43–48   Specific topics of biochemistry
> > Add to 4 the numbers following 572 in 572.3–572.8, e.g., enzymes 47, biochemical genetics 48

Class biometric identification based on physiological aspects in 006.2483; class comprehensive works on physiological systems in 571

For specific physiological systems in plants, see 575; for specific physiological systems in humans, see 612; for specific physiological systems in domestic animals, see 636.0892

See Manual at 571–573 vs. 610

SUMMARY

[.01–.09]   Standard subdivisions

> Do not use; class in 571.101–571.109

.1   ***Circulatory system**

> Class here cardiovascular system

> *For circulation in a specific system or organ, see the system or organ, plus notation 21 from table under 573, e.g., circulation in brain 573.8621*

.15   ***Circulatory fluids**

> Class here blood

> *For lymph, see 573.16*

.153 6   Cell biology

> Number built according to instructions under 573

> Class here blood cells, erythrocytes

> *For leukocytes, see 571.96; for platelets, see 573.159*

.154   Biochemistry

> Number built according to instructions under 573

> Including blood groups

.155   ***Hematopoiesis**

> Class here hematopoietic (blood-forming) system

.155 5   ***Spleen**

.155 6   ***Bone marrow**

.156   ***Plasma**

.159   ***Blood coagulation**

> Class here blood coagulation factors, platelets (thrombocytes)

*Add as instructed under 573

.16   *Lymphatic system

      Class here lymph

        For role of lymphatic system in immunity, see 571.96; for spleen, see 573.1555

.163 6   Cell biology

        Number built according to instructions under 573

          For leukocytes, lymphocytes, see 571.96

>   573.17–573.18 Circulatory organs

        Class comprehensive works in 573.1

.17   *Pumping mechanisms

      Class here heart

.18   *Blood vessels

.185   *Arteries

.186   *Veins

.187   *Capillaries

.2   *Respiratory system

      Class here aerobic respiration, comprehensive works on respiration in animals

      For cell and tissue respiration in animals, see 572.471

.25   *Lungs

.26   *Organs accessory to lungs

      Including diaphragm, nasal sinuses, nose, trachea

      Class olfactory nerves in 573.877; class use of accessory respiratory organs in vocal communication in 573.92

        For larynx, see 573.925

.28   *Gills

.3   *Digestive system

      Class here digestion

      Class comprehensive works on biology of nutrition in 572.4; class interdisciplinary works on human nutrition in 363.8

      For cell digestion, see 572.4

.35   *Mouth and esophagus

      Class here physiology of eating, ingestion

      Subdivisions are added for mouth and esophagus together, for mouth alone

*Add as instructed under 573

.355   *External mouth parts

         Class here beak, bill, cheeks, lips; feeding appendages and tentacles

.356   *Teeth

         See also 591.47 for fangs and tusks

.357   *Tongue

.359   *Esophagus

.36   *Stomach

         Including pylorus

.37   *Intestine

.377   *Pancreas

         Including islands of Langerhans

         Class insulin in 572.565

.378   *Small intestine

         Including duodenum, ileum, jejunum

.379   *Large intestine

         Including colon, rectum

.38   *Biliary tract

         Including bile ducts, gallbladder

         Class here liver

.383 79   Bile

         Number built according to instructions under 573

         Including bile acids

.4   ***Endocrine and excretory systems**

         Class here endocrinology

         Subdivisions are added for endocrine and excretory systems together, for endocrine system alone

         Class comprehensive works on animal endocrine and nervous systems in 571.71

---

*Add as instructed under 573

.44   Biochemistry

Number built according to instructions under 573

Class here comprehensive works on animal hormones

> *For hormones of a specific endocrine gland, see the gland, plus notation 4 from table under 573, e.g., pituitary hormones 573.454, estrogen 573.6654; for hormones controlling a specific function in 571.5–571.9, see the function, plus notation 374 from table under 571.5–571.9, e.g., growth hormones 571.8374; for hormones controlling a specific animal physiological system, see the function in 573, plus notation 374 from table under 573, e.g., gastrointestinal hormones 573.3374*

> *See Manual at 573.44 vs. 571.74*

>   573.45–573.47   Specific endocrine glands

Class comprehensive works in 573.4

> *For islands of Langerhans, see 573.377; for testes, see 573.655; for ovaries, see 573.665; for nervous system, see 573.8*

.45   *Pituitary gland and hypothalamus

Subdivisions are added for pituitary gland and hypothalamus together, for pituitary gland alone

Class comprehensive works on neurohormones in 573.8374

.459   *Hypothalamus

.46   *Adrenal glands

.47   *Thyroid and parathyroid glands

Subdivisions are added for thyroid and parathyroid glands together, for thyroid gland alone

.478   *Parathyroid glands

.49   *Excretory system

Class here excretion, urinary system

.496   *Kidneys

.5   ***Integument**

Including physiology of color

Class here skin

Class color of hair, fur, scales, feathers, horns, related topics in 573.58–573.59; class exoskeleton in 573.77; class comprehensive works on color of animals in 591.472

> *For integument of a specific system or organ, see the system or organ, plus notation 25 from table under 573, e.g., pericardium 573.1725, meninges 573.8625*

---

*Add as instructed under 573

.58	*Hair and fur

> Subdivisions are added for either or both topics in heading

.59	*Scales, feathers, horns, related topics

> Including claws, nails

.595	*Scales
.597	*Feathers

.6   *Reproductive system

> Class here genital organs, reproduction, sexual reproduction, comprehensive works on urogenital system
>
> Class comprehensive works on reproduction, development, growth of animals in 571.81
>
> *For urinary system, see 573.49*
>
> *See Manual at 571.8 vs. 573.6, 575.6*

.65	*Male reproductive system
.655	*Testes

> Class sperm in 571.8451

.656	*Penis
.658	*Prostate
.66	*Female reproductive system

> Class pregnancy and lactation in 573.67

.665	*Ovaries

> Class egg cells in 571.845; class eggs in 573.68; class plant ovaries in 575.665

.667	*Uterus
.67	*Pregnancy and lactation

> Subdivisions are added for pregnancy and lactation together, for pregnancy alone

.679	*Lactation

> Class here mammary glands

.68	*Eggs

> *For embryology of animals, see 571.861*

.7   *Musculoskeletal system

> Class here physiology of movement

---

*Add as instructed under 573

.735 6   Connective tissues

Number built according to instructions under 573

For tendons, see 573.75356; for cartilage, see 573.76356; for ligaments, see 573.78356

.75   *Muscles

For muscles of a specific system or organ, see the system or organ, plus notation 27 from table under 573, e.g., heart muscles 573.1727

.76   *Bones

Class here comprehensive works on skeleton

For bone marrow, see 573.1556; for horns, see 573.59; for exoskeleton, see 573.77

.764 51   Bioinorganic chemistry

Number built according to instructions under 573

Class here comprehensive works on biomineralization in animals

For biomineralization in a specific system or organ, see the system or organ, plus notation 451 from table under 573, e.g., biomineralization in teeth 573.356451

.77   *Exoskeleton

.78   *Joints

.79   *Locomotion and related activities

Including rest

Class here crawling, running, walking, work

Subdivisions are added for locomotion and related activities together, for locomotion alone

Class behavioral aspects of locomotion in 591.57

.798   *Flying

Class here physiology of wings

Class comprehensive works on wings in 591.479

.8   *Nervous and sensory systems

Subdivisions are added for nervous and sensory systems together, for nervous system alone

Class comprehensive works on regulation and control in animals, on endocrine and nervous systems in 571.71

*Add as instructed under 573

.85   *Nerves and nerve fibers

       Class here irritability, peripheral nerves

       Subdivisions are added for either or both topics in heading

       Class comprehensive works on nerves, nerve fibers, central nervous system in 573.8

         For cell irritability, see 571.67; for nerves and nerve fibers in central nervous system, see 573.86. For innervation of a specific system or organ, see the system or organ, plus notation 28 from table under 573, e.g., innervation of muscles 573.7528

.86   *Central nervous system

       Class here brain

.868   *Physiology of sleep

         Class sleep behavior in 591.56; class interdisciplinary works on sleep in 154.6

.869   *Spinal cord

.87   *Sense organs

       Including physiology of navigation

       Class here sensation, senses

       Class migration in 591.568

         For eyes, see 573.88; for ears, see 573.89

.875   *Touch

.877   *Chemical senses

       Class here olfaction, olfactory nerves, smell

         For taste, see 573.878

.878   *Taste

       Class here taste buds

.88   *Eyes

       Including light sensing by pineal gland

       Class here sight, vision

.89   *Ears

       Class here hearing

.9   **Miscellaneous systems and organs in animals, regional histology and physiology in animals**

       Limited to topics provided for below

*Add as instructed under 573

[.901–.909]   Standard subdivisions

>Do not use; class in 571.101–571.109

.92   *Communication systems

>Class here vocal communication

>Class comprehensive works on animal communication in 591.59

>>*For receiving sensory systems, see 573.87; for bioluminescent communication, see 573.95; for communication involving electric organs, see 573.97*

.925   *Larynx

>Class here vocal cords

.927   *Nonvocal sound communication

>Class here physiology of stridulation

.929   *Chemical communication

>Production of chemicals that arouse behavioral responses

.95   *Bioluminescent organs

>Class here bioluminescent communication

.97   *Electric organs

.99   *Regional histology and physiology in animals

>Subdivisions are added for either or both topics in heading

.995   *Head

.996   *Thorax

.997   *Abdomen

.998   *Appendages

>Class locomotor functions of appendages in 573.79

[574]   [Unassigned]

>Most recently used in Edition 20

---

*Add as instructed under 573

575   Specific parts of and physiological systems in plants

Except for modifications shown under specific entries, add to each subdivision identified by † as follows:

01–09   Standard subdivisions

> Notation from Table 1 as modified under 570.1–570.9, e.g., microscopy 0282

2   Specific kinds of plants

> Class here comparative physiology, evolution of the part or system
> Add to 2 the numbers following 58 in 581–588, e.g., monocotyledons 24

> > *For physiological systems in fungi and algae, see 571; for specific parts of fungi and algae, see 571.5929*

3   Generalities of parts or processes

[301–309]   Standard subdivisions

> Do not use; class in notation 01–09 from this table

33–39   Generalities of specific parts or processes

> Add to 3 the numbers following 571 in 571.3–571.9, e.g., histology 35, pathology 39

For external description of parts and organs and their configurations, see 581.4

SUMMARY

575.4	**Stems**
.5	**Roots and leaves**
.6	**Reproductive organs**
.7	**Circulation, food storage, excretion**
.8	**Transpiration**
.9	**Animal-like physiological processes**

[.01–.09]   Standard subdivisions

> Do not use; class in 571.201–571.209

.4   †**Stems**

> Class here comprehensive works on regional physiology, on shoots

> *For regional physiology of roots, see 575.54; for leaves, see 575.57*

.435 9   Regional histology

> Number built according to instructions under 575

> Class here comprehensive works on regional histology of plants

> > *For regional histology of roots, see 575.54359; for regional histology of leaves, see 575.57359*

.45   Special features of stems

> Limited to those named below

[.450 1–.450 9]   Standard subdivisions

> Do not use; class in 575.401–575.409

†Add as instructed under 575

.451   †Primary epidermis

        Including physiology of color

        Class here comprehensive works on epidermis of plants

        Class comprehensive works on color of plants in 581.47

           For bark, see 575.452; for transpiration from primary epidermis, see 575.8. For color of a specific organ or part, see the organ or part, e.g., color of leaves 575.57

.452   †Bark

        Class here phloem

        For circulation in phloem, see 575.7

.454   †Nodes

.457   †Thorns

.46   †Wood

        Class here xylem

        For circulation in phloem, see 575.7

.48   †Growing points and layers

        Class here meristem

        Subdivisions are added for either or both topics in heading

.485   †Apical meristem

.486   †Buds

.488   †Cambium

.49   †Stems specialized for reproduction

        Class here asexual reproduction, vegetative reproduction, underground stems

        Class food storage in specialized stems in 575.78; class comprehensive works on reproduction of plants in 575.6

.495   †Bulbs

.496   †Corms

.497   †Rhizomes

.498   †Tubers

.499   †Runners (Stolons)

.5   **Roots and leaves**

---

†Add as instructed under 575

.54   †Roots

> *For absorption of water and nutrients by roots, see 575.76*

> *See also 575.49 for underground stems*

.545–.548   Specific aspects of roots

> Add to base number 575.54 the numbers following 575.4 in 575.45–575.48, e.g., xylem in roots 575.546

.57   †Leaves

> *For transpiration from leaves, see 575.8*

> ## 575.6–575.9 Reproductive organs and physiological systems in plants

> Except for modifications shown under specific entries, add to each subdivision identified by * as follows:
> 01–09   Standard subdivisions
>   Notation from Table 1 as modified under 570.1–570.9, e.g., microscopy 0282
> 2–3   Specific kinds of plants; generalities of organs and systems
>   Add as instructed under 575, e.g., the organ or process in monocotyledons 24, histology 35
> 4   Biochemistry
> 401–408   Standard subdivisions
>   Notation from Table 1 as modified under 570.1–570.8, e.g., microscopy 40282
> 409   History, geographic treatment, biography
>   Notation from Table 1 as modified under 571.09, e.g., space biology 40919
> 42   Biochemistry in specific kinds of plants
>   Add to 42 the numbers following 58 in 581–588, e.g., biochemistry of the organ or process in monocotyledons 42
> 43–48   Specific topics of biochemistry
>   Add to 4 the numbers following 572 in 572.3–572.8, e.g., enzymes 47, biochemical genetics 48

> Class comprehensive works in 571.2

.6   ***Reproductive organs**

> Class here flowers, reproduction, sexual reproduction, sporangia

> Class pollination in 571.8642; class comprehensive works on reproduction, development, growth of plants in 571.82; class interdisciplinary works on flowers in 582.13

> *For asexual reproduction, vegetative reproduction, see 575.49*

> *See Manual at 571.8 vs. 573.6, 575.6*

---

*Add as instructed under 575.6–575.9
†Add as instructed under 575

.65   *Male reproductive organs

       Class here anthers, microsporangia, stamens

       Class pollen (microspores) in 571.8452

.66   *Female reproductive organs

       Class here pistils

       Class fruits in 575.67

.665   *Ovaries

       Class here carpels, megasporangia

       Class egg cells (megaspores) in 571.845; class seeds in 575.68

.67   *Fruits

       Including nuts

       For seeds, see 575.68

.68   *Seeds

       For embryology of plants (including germination of seeds), see 571.862

.69   *Other flower parts

       Class here petals, sepals

.7   ***Circulation, food storage, excretion**

       Subdivisions are added for circulation, food storage, excretion together; for circulation alone

       Class transpiration in 575.8

       For a specific circulatory tissue, see the tissue, e.g., phloem 575.452, xylem 575.46

.75   *Circulatory fluids

       Class here sap

.76   *Absorption of water and nutrients

       Subdivisions are added for either or both topics in heading

.78   *Food and water storage

       Subdivisions are added for food and water storage together, for food storage alone

.79   *Excretion

       Class here internal isolation of unusable substances

*Add as instructed under 575.6–575.9

.8   ***Transpiration**

Class here gas exchange from surface tissues

For a specific tissue or organ of transpiration, see the tissue or organ, e.g., leaves 575.57

.9   ***Animal-like physiological processes**

Class here behavior of plants

.97   *Movement

For movement that is a direct result of growth, see 571.82

.98   *Sensitivity

Class here irritability

.99   *Physiology of predatory activity

Trapping mobile organisms

Class comprehensive works on carnivorous plants in 583.887

>   **576–578 General and external biological phenomena**

Class general and external biological phenomena of microorganisms, fungi, algae in 579; class general and external biological phenomena of plants in 580; class general and external biological phenomena of animals in 590; class comprehensive works in 578

576   Genetics and evolution

Except for modifications shown under specific entries, add to each subdivision identified by † as follows:
01–09   Standard subdivisions
          Notation from Table 1 as modified under 570.1–570.9, e.g., microscopy 0282

.01–.09   Standard subdivisions

Notation from Table 1 as modified under 570.1–570.9, e.g., microscopy in study of genetics and evolution 576.0282

.5   **†Genetics**

Class here heredity, experimental works on genetics of specific organisms; interdisciplinary works on genetics

For biochemical, molecular, physiological genetics; cytogenetics, see 572.8; for genetics of microorganisms, fungi, algae, see 579.135; for genetics of plants, see 581.35; for genetics of animals, see 591.35. For a specific aspect of genetics, see the aspect, e.g., eugenics 363.92, medical genetics 616.042, genetic engineering 660.65

See Manual at 576.5 vs. 572.8

---

*Add as instructed under 575.6–575.9

†Add standard subdivisions as instructed under 576

.52	†Laws of genetics

Class here Mendel's laws

.53	†Genetic makeup

Class here genotypes, phenotypes

Class biochemical aspects of genetic makeup in 572.8

.54	†Variation

Class here factors affecting heredity and variation

> *For genetic recombination as a factor affecting heredity and variation, see 572.877*

> *See also 571.9648 for transduction, transformation; also 572.869 for transposons*

.542	†Environmental factors (Mutagens)

Class here chemical mutagens

Class toxic aspects of mutagens in 571.95; class mutagenesis, radiogenetics in 572.838

.544	†Breeding patterns

Class here inbreeding

.549	†Mutation

Class biochemistry of mutation (mutagenesis) in 572.838

.58	†Population genetics

Class here ecological genetics, gene pools, role of populations as vehicles of evolution

Class role of species in evolution in 576.86; class comprehensive works on population biology in 577.88

.8	**†Evolution**

Including homoplasy

Class creationism in 231.7652

> *For evolution of microorganisms, see 579.138; for evolution of plants, see 581.38; for evolution of animals, see 591.38. For evolution of a specific internal process or structure, see the process or structure, e.g., molecular evolution 572.838, evolution of circulatory system 573.1*

> *See Manual at 231.7652 vs. 213, 500, 576.8; also at 576.8 vs. 560*

.801	Philosophy and theory

Do not use for theories; class in 576.82

---

†Add standard subdivisions as instructed under 576

.82   †Theories of evolution

             Including punctuated equilibrium

             Class here Darwinism, natural selection

             Class sexual selection in 591.562

.827   †Lamarckian theories

             Class here inheritance of acquired characteristics

.83   †Origin of life

             Including spontaneous generation

             Class here conditions needed for life to begin, biochemistry of forms of life
             before achievement of full self-replication

             Class comprehensive works on molecular evolution in 572.838

.839   †Extraterrestrial life

             Including theory of extraterrestrial origin of life on earth

             Class here astrobiology

             Class extraterrestrial civilization, extraterrestrial intelligence in 999

             See also 571.0919 for space biology

.84   †Evolutionary cycles

             Class here catastrophes, extinction, radiation

.85   †Factors affecting evolution

             Including symbiosis

             Class here genotype-environment interaction

             Class comprehensive works on symbiosis in 577.85

             *For role of genetics in evolution, see 576.5; for natural selection, see
             576.82*

.855   †Sexual factors

             Class here evolution of sexes

             Class sexual selection in 591.562

.86   †Speciation

             Class here role of species in evolution

             Class role of populations in evolution in 576.58; class comprehensive works
             on species in 578.012

.87   †Coevolution

             Class symbiosis as a factor affecting evolution in 576.85

†Add standard subdivisions as instructed under 576

.875 †Coevolution of flowering plants and insects

Class here coevolution of flowering plants with insect-like pollinators

.88 †Phylogeny

577 Ecology

Including ecotones

Class here biomes, ecosystems, terrestrial ecology

Except for modifications shown under specific entries, add to each subdivision identified by * as follows:

01–08 Standard subdivisions
Notation from Table 1 as modified under 578.01–578.08, e.g., microscopy 0282

09 History, geographic treatment, biography

[0914–0919] Areas, regions, places in general other than polar, temperate, tropical regions
Do not use; class in 577.3–577.7

Unless other instructions are given, class a subject with aspects in two or more subdivisions of 577 in the number coming last, e.g., grassland swamps 577.684 (*not* 577.4)

For paleoecology, see 560.45; for ecology of microorganisms, fungi, algae, see 579.17; for plant ecology, see 581.7; for animal ecology, see 591.7

See Manual at 333.7–333.9 vs. 363.1, 363.73, 577; also at 577.3–577.7 vs. 578.73–578.77

SUMMARY

577.01–.09	**Standard subdivisions**
.1	**Specific ecosystem processes**
.2	**Specific factors affecting ecology**
.3	**Forest ecology**
.4	**Grassland ecology**
.5	**Ecology of miscellaneous environments**
.6	**Aquatic ecology**
.7	**Marine ecology**
.8	**Synecology and population biology**

.01–.08 Standard subdivisions

Notation from Table 1 as modified under 578.01–578.08, e.g., microscopy 577.0282

.09 History, geographic treatment, biography

[.091 4–.091 9] Areas, regions, places in general other than polar, temperate, tropical regions

Do not use; class in 577.3–577.7

.1 **Specific ecosystem processes**

[.101–.109] Standard subdivisions

Do not use; class in 577.01–577.09

†Add standard subdivisions as instructed under 576

.13   *Ecological bioenergetics

Class here energy budget, energy flow, physics in ecology

.14   *Environmental chemistry

Class here biogeochemical cycles, biogeochemistry

Class eutrophication in 577.63158; class comprehensive works on biochemistry and biogeochemistry in 572

For ecological bioenergetics, see 577.13; for environmental chemistry of pollution, see 577.27

.144   *Carbon cycle

Including carbon dioxide sinks

.145   *Nitrogen cycle

.15   *Biological productivity

Class here primary productivity

Class eutrophication in 577.63158

.16   *Food chains

Class here ecological pyramids, multitrophic reactions

.18   *Ecological succession

Including biological invasions

See also 578.62 for nonnative species

.2   Specific factors affecting ecology

For effect of a specific kind of microorganism, fungi, algae on the ecology, see the organism in 579.2–579.8, plus notation 17 from table under 579.2–579.8, e.g., effect of red algae on ecology 579.8917; for effect of a specific kind of plant on the ecology, see the plant in 583–588, plus notation 17 from table under 583–588, e.g., effect of grasses on ecology 584.9217; for effect of a specific kind of animal on the ecology, see the animal in 592–599, plus notation 17 from table under 592–599, e.g., effect of wolves on ecology 599.77317

[.201–.209]   Standard subdivisions

Do not use; class in 577.01–577.09

.22   *Biometeorology (Bioclimatology)

Including effect of droughts, micrometeorology

Class acclimatization and temperature adaptation in 578.42

See also 571.95 for diseases caused by climate and weather

.23   *Seasons

Class seasonal adaptation in 578.43

---

*Add standard subdivisions as instructed under 577

.24 *Fire ecology

.26 *Autecology

> *For autecology of a specific kind of microorganism, fungi, algae, see the kind of organism in 579.2–579.8, plus notation 17 from table under 579.2–579.8, e.g., autecology of fungi 579.517; for autecology of a specific kind of plant, see the kind of plant in 583–588, plus notation 17 from table under 583–588, e.g., autecology of orchids 584.7217; for autecology of a specific kind of animal, see the kind of animal in 592–599, plus notation 17 from table under 592–599, e.g., autecology of insects 595.717*

.27 *Effects of humans on ecology

> Class here effects of pollution on ecology

> Including fragmented landscapes

> Class comprehensive works on ecotoxicology, on environmental toxicology in 571.95; class interdisciplinary works on pollution in 363.73

>> *For soil pollution, see 577.5727; for water pollution, see 577.627*

>> *See also 304.28 for social consequences of pollution; also 577.55 for natural ecology of environments made by humans*

>> *See Manual at 363.73 vs. 571.95, 577.27*

.272 *Engineering works

> Including dams, land reclamation, roads

.272 6 *Thermal pollution

> Thermal pollution is primarily about water pollution; class comprehensive works in 577.62726

> Class interdisciplinary work on thermal pollution in 363.7394

.273 *Agricultural pollution

> Class land reclamation in 577.272

.274 *War

.275 Pollution by acids, by specific elements and groups of elements

[.275 01–.275 09] Standard subdivisions

> Do not use; class in 577.2701–577.2709

.275 2 *Pollution by acids

> Class here acidification

*Add standard subdivisions as instructed under 577

| .275 3–.275 7 | Pollution by specific elements and groups of elements |

Add to base number 577.275 the numbers following 546 in 546.3–546.7 for the element or group of elements only, e.g., influence of metals on ecology 577.2753, influence of mercury 577.275663; then to the result add standard subdivision notation as modified under 577.01–577.09, e.g., microscopy in study of pollution by metals 577.27530282

Class comprehensive works in 577.27

| .276 | *Air pollution |

Including pollution by gases contributing to greenhouse effect (global warming), to ozone layer depletion

Class here pollution by combustion gases

| .277 | *Radioactive pollution |

Class here radioecology

| .278 | *Pollution by organic compounds |

| .279 | *Pesticide pollution |

> ## 577.3–577.6 Ecology of specific nonmarine environments

Add to each subdivision identified by † as follows:
01–08   Standard subdivisions
        Notation from Table 1 as modified under 578.01–578.08, e.g., microscopy 0282
09   History, geographic treatment, biography
[0914–0919]   Areas, regions, places in general other than polar, temperate, tropical regions
        Do not use; class in 577.3–577.7
1   Specific ecosystem processes
        Add to 1 the numbers following 577.1 in 577.13–577.18, e.g., food chains 16
2   Specific factors affecting ecology
        Add to 2 the numbers following 577.2 in 577.22–577.27, e.g., effects of pollution 27; however,
        do not add notation 26 derived from 577.26 for autecology; class in number for the environment in 577.3–577.6 without use of notation 26

Class terrestrial ecology, comprehensive works on ecology in 577; class comprehensive works on biology of specific environments in 578.7

See Manual at 577.3–577.7 vs. 578.73–578.77; also at 577.3–577.7 vs. 579–590

| .3 | †Forest ecology |

Class here ecology of exploited forests, of woodlands

For forest wetland ecology, see 577.683

---

*Add standard subdivisions as instructed under 577
†Add as instructed under 577.3–577.6

.309 13   Torrid zone (Tropics)

                              Class tropical rain forest ecology in 577.34

.34   †Rain forest ecology

                    Including cloud forest ecology

                    Class here ecology of jungles, tropical rain forests

[.340 913]   Torrid zone (Tropics)

                              Do not use; class in 577.34

.37   †Taiga ecology

                    Class here ecology of boreal forests, taiga wetlands

.38   †Shrubland ecology

                    Class here chaparral, heath (dry moor) ecology, Mediterranean-type
                    ecosystems

                    Class comprehensive works on ecosystems of Mediterranean region in
                    577.091822; class bog ecology, comprehensive works on moor ecology in
                    577.687

.4   †Grassland ecology

                    Class here ecology of agricultural grasslands, of rangelands, of temperate zone
                    grasslands

                    Class alpine grassland ecology in 577.538

                    See also 333.74 for management of grasslands by society

[.409 12]   Temperate zones (Middle latitude zones)

                              Do not use; class in 577.4

[.409 13]   Torrid zone (Tropics)

                              Do not use; class in 577.48

.44   †Prairie ecology

[.440 912]   Temperate zones (Middle latitude zones)

                              Do not use; class in 577.44

.46   †Meadow ecology

[.460 912]   Temperate zones (Middle latitude zones)

                              Do not use; class in 577.46

.48   †Savanna ecology

                    Class here tropical grassland ecology

[.480 913]   Torrid zone (Tropics)

                              Do not use; class in 577.48

†Add as instructed under 577.3–577.6

.5 **Ecology of miscellaneous environments**

Only those named below

Including upland ecology

Class ecology of atmosphere in 579.175

For ecology of a specific upland environment, see the environment, e.g., upland forest ecology 577.3

[.501–.509] Standard subdivisions

Do not use; class in 577.01–577.09

.51 †Coastal ecology

For ecology of a specific environment in coastal zone, see the environment, e.g., coastal forest ecology 577.3, saltwater wetland ecology 577.69, sublittoral ecology 577.78

.52 †Island ecology

Class island forest ecology in 577.3; class island grassland ecology in 577.4

.53 †Mountain ecology

Class mountain forest ecology in 577.3; class mountain grassland ecology other than alpine grassland ecology in 577.4

.538 †Alpine ecology

Ecology above timber line

Including alpine grassland ecology, paramo ecology

.54 †Desert ecology

Class here ecology in arid lands, in semiarid lands

For sand dune ecology, see 577.583

.55 †Ecology of environments made by humans

Including roadside ecology

Class here agricultural ecology

Class meadow ecology in 577.46

For ecology of exploited forests, see 577.3; for ecology of agricultural grasslands, of rangelands, see 577.4; for urban ecology, see 577.56

See also 577.27 for effects of humans on ecology

.554 †Garden and household ecology

Class here backyard ecology

Subdivisions are added for garden and household ecology together, for garden ecology alone

.555 †Hedgerow ecology

†Add as instructed under 577.3–577.6

| .56 | †Urban ecology |

Class here suburban ecology

| .57 | †Soil ecology |

Including rhizosphere

Class sand dune ecology in 577.583

| .58 | †Ecology of hostile land environments |

Not provided for elsewhere

Including cliff ecology

Class here extreme environments

| .583 | †Sand dune ecology |

Desert or seashore dune ecology

| .584 | †Cave ecology |

| .586 | †Tundra, permafrost, glacier, snow cover ecology |

Subdivisions are added for tundra, permafrost, glacier, snow cover ecology together; for tundra ecology alone; for permafrost ecology alone

| **.6** | **†Aquatic ecology** |

Class here biological limnology, freshwater ecology

Class interdisciplinary works on limnology in 551.48

For marine ecology, see 577.7

| .63 | †Lake and pond ecology |

Class here ecology of freshwater lagoons, reservoirs

Subdivisions are added for lake and pond ecology together, for lake ecology alone

Class comprehensive works on ecology of lakes, ponds, rivers, streams in 577.6; class comprehensive works on lagoons in 577.78

| .631 5 | Biological productivity |

Number built according to instructions under 577.3–577.6

| .631 58 | *Eutrophication |

Class social measures to control eutrophication in 363.73946; class engineering measures to control eutrophication in 628.112. Class eutrophication of a specific environment with the environment in 577.6, plus notation 15 from table under 577.3–577.6, e.g., eutrophication of swamps 577.6815

| .636 | †Pond ecology |

*Add standard subdivisions as instructed under 577
†Add as instructed under 577.3–577.6

| .639 | †Salt lake ecology |
| | Class here ecology of inland seas |

.64 †River and stream ecology

Subdivisions are added for either or both topics in heading

.66 †Floodplain ecology

Class ecology of a specific environment on a floodplain with the specific environment, e.g., ecology of floodplain grasslands 577.4

.68 †Wetland ecology

Including riparian ecology

Class here marsh, swamp ecology

For saltwater wetland ecology, see 577.69

.683 †Forest wetland ecology

For taiga, see 577.37

.684 †Grass wetland ecology

.687 †Peat bog ecology

Class here bog, peatland, wet moor ecology; comprehensive works on moor ecology

For heath (dry moor) ecology, see 577.38

.69 †Saltwater wetland and seashore ecology

Class here ecology of coastal wetlands, salt and tide marshes

Subdivisions are added for saltwater wetland and seashore ecology together, for saltwater wetland ecology alone

.694 †Sea grass wetland ecology

.697 †Forest saltwater wetland ecology

[.697 091 3] Torrid zone (Tropics)

Do not use; class in 577.698

.698 †Mangrove swamp ecology

Class here tropical saltwater wetland forest ecology

.699 †Seashore ecology

Including ecology of rock pools, sea caves, tidal flats, tide pools

For sand dune ecology, see 577.583

†Add as instructed under 577.3–577.6

.7   **Marine ecology**

Class here saltwater ecology

Class comprehensive works on marine biology in 578.77

> *For salt lake ecology, see 577.639; for saltwater wetland and seashore ecology, see 577.69*
>
> *See Manual at 577.3–577.7 vs. 578.73–578.77; also at 577.3–577.7 vs. 579–590*

.701–.708   Standard subdivisions

> Notation from Table 1 as modified under 578.01–578.08, e.g., microscopy in marine ecology 577.70282

.709   History, geographic treatment, biography

[.709 162]   Oceans and seas

> Do not use; class in 577.7

[.709 163–.709 165]   Atlantic, Pacific, Indian Oceans

> Do not use; class in 577.73–577.75

.71–.72   Specific ecosystem processes; specific factors affecting marine ecology

> Add to base number 577.7 the numbers following 577 in 577.1–577.2, e.g., marine food chains 577.716, marine pollution 577.727; however, for autecology, see 577.7

.73–.75   Ecology of specific oceans and seas

> Add to base number 577.7 the numbers following —16 in notation 163–165 from Table 2, e.g., Atlantic Ocean ecology 577.73; then add 0 and to the result add the numbers following 577 in 577.01–577.2, e.g., food chains in Atlantic Ocean 577.73016; however, for Sargasso Sea ecology, see 577.76362
>
> *For Antarctic Ocean, see 577.709167*

>   **577.76–577.79 Specific kinds of marine environments**

Add to each subdivision identified by ‡ as follows:
     01–08   Standard subdivisions
           Notation from Table 1 as modified under 578.01–578.08, e.g., microscopy 0282
     09   History, geographic treatment, biography
     [09162]   Oceans and seas
           Do not use; class in base number
     [09163–09165]   Atlantic, Pacific, Indian Oceans
           Do not use; class in notation 3–5 from this table
     1–5   Specific ecosystem processes; specific factors affecting marine ecology; ecology of specific oceans and seas
           Add to base number the numbers following 577.7 in 577.71–577.75, e.g., food chains 16, pollution 27, the environment in Atlantic Ocean 3

Class comprehensive works in 577.7

| .76 | ‡Surface regions |
| | Class here ecology of plankton |

For freshwater plankton ecology, see 577.6

| .763 62 | Sargasso Sea |

Number built according to instructions under 577.76–577.79

| .77 | ‡Marine benthic ecology |
| | Relating to floor of oceans and seas |

Class benthic ecology of abyssal, bathyal, hadal zones in 577.79

| .78 | ‡Nearshore ecology |
| | Including saltwater lagoons, comprehensive works on lagoons |

Class here sublittoral ecology

For freshwater lagoons, see 577.63; for saltwater wetland and seashore ecology, see 577.69

| .786 | ‡Estuarine ecology |
| .789 | ‡Reef ecology |

Class here coral reef ecology

| .79 | ‡Deep sea ecology |

Including ecology of bathyal and hadal zones

Class here ecology of abyssal zone

| .799 | Hydrothermal vent ecology |

.8   Synecology and population biology

Standard subdivisions are added for synecology and population biology together, for synecology alone

Class here ecological aspects of sociobiology, animal-plant relationships

Except for modifications shown under specific entries, add to each subdivision identified by † as follows:
| 01–08 | Standard subdivisions |

Notation from Table 1 as modified under 578.01–578.08, e.g., microscopy 0282
| 09 | History, geographic treatment, biography |

Class ecological succession in 577.18; class rhizosphere in 577.57; class behavioral aspects of sociobiology in 591.5; class predation in 591.53; class comprehensive works on synecology of a specific environment in 577.3–577.7; class interdisciplinary works on sociobiology in 304.5. Class a general relationship between a small taxonomic group and a larger taxonomic group with the smaller group, e.g., plant-microbial relationships 579.178 (*not* 581.78), relationships between mushrooms and dicotyledons 579.6178 (*not* 583.178), between ferns and flowering plants 587.3178 (*not* 581.78)

‡Add as instructed under 577.76–577.79

.801–.808   Standard subdivisions

Notation from Table 1 as modified under 578.01–578.08, e.g., microscopy in study of synecology 577.80282

.809   History, geographic treatment, biography

.82   †Ecological communities

Including ecological niches

Class biomes in 577. Class plant associations characteristic of a specific environment with the environment in 577.3–577.7, e.g., prairie grass associations 577.44

.83   †Competition

.85   †Symbiosis

Class symbiosis as a factor affecting evolution in 576.85; class symbiosis in the sense limited to mutually beneficial relationships in 577.852

.852   †Mutualism

Including commensalism

.857   †Parasitism

Class parasites in 578.65; class pathology of parasitism, comprehensive works on parasitism in 571.999

When classifying parasitism of specific kinds of organisms in 579 or 580–590, prefer the number for the parasite. Emphasis on the host organism usually indicates that the work should be classed as a disease in 571.999

.88   †Population biology

Class here population dynamics

See also 576.58 for population genetics

---

†Add standard subdivisions as instructed under 577.8

578 Natural history of organisms and related subjects

Standard subdivisions are added for natural history of organisms and related subjects together, for natural history of organisms alone

Class here descriptive biology, specific nontaxonomic kinds of organisms, comprehensive works on general and external biological phenomena, comprehensive works on taxonomic biology

Except for modifications shown under specific entries, add to each subdivision identified by * as follows:

01–08 Standard subdivisions

Notation from Table 1 as modified under 578.01–578.08, e.g., microscopy 0282

09 History, geographic treatment, biography

For internal biological processes of specific kinds of organisms, see 571–575; for genetics and evolution, see 576; for ecology, see 577; for natural history of microorganisms, fungi, algae, see 579; for natural history of plants, see 580; for natural history of animals, see 590

See Manual at 578 vs. 304.2, 508, 910

.012 Classification

Including chemotaxonomy, cladistic analysis, cytotaxonomy, numerical taxonomy, species

Class here systematics, taxonomy

Class speciation in 576.86; class taxonomic nomenclature in 578.014; class comprehensive works on taxonomic biology in 578

.02 Miscellany

.028 Auxiliary techniques and procedures; apparatus, equipment, materials

Notation from Table 1 as modified under 570.28, e.g., microscopy in descriptive biology 578.0282

.028 8 Maintenance and repair

Do not use for preservation of biological specimens; class in 578.0752

.07 Education, research, related topics

.073 Collections and exhibits of living organisms

Class here history and description, guidebooks; bioparks

Add to base number 578.073 notation 1–9 from Table 2 for area in which collections, exhibits are found, e.g., collections of living plants and animals in China 578.07351

.074 Museums, collections, exhibits

Do not use for collections and exhibits of living organisms; class in 578.073

.075 Museum activities and services

.075 2 Preserving biological specimens

.09 History, geographic treatment, biography

[.091 4–.091 9]	Areas, regions, places in general other than polar, temperate, tropical regions

> Do not use; class in 578.73–578.77

.099 9   Extraterrestrial worlds

> Class extraterrestrial life in 576.839

.4   *Adaptation

> Class here organisms illustrating specific kinds of adaptation
>
> Class adaptation of miscellaneous nontaxonomic kinds of organisms in 578.6

.41   *Size, weight, shape of organisms

.42   *Acclimatization and temperature adaptation

> Standard subdivisions are added for acclimatization and temperature adaptation together, for acclimatization alone
>
> Including phenology
>
> Class climate and weather as factors influencing ecology in 577.22
>
> *For seasonal adaptation, see 578.43*

.43   *Seasonal adaptation

> Class seasonal variation as a factor influencing ecology in 577.23

.46   *Reproductive adaptation

> Class reproductive physiology in 571.8

.47   *Protective adaptation, color

> Standard subdivisions are added for protective adaptation and color together, for protective adaptation alone
>
> Including mimicry
>
> Class color of a specific adaptation with the adaptation, e.g., color of reproductive adaptation 578.46
>
> *For camouflage, see 591.472*

.6   *Miscellaneous nontaxonomic kinds of organisms

> Not provided for elsewhere
>
> Class here economic biology

.62   *Nonnative species

> Class here alien, exotic, introduced, invasive, naturalized species

.63   *Beneficial organisms

> *See Manual at 630 vs. 579–590, 641.3*

---

*Add standard subdivisions as instructed under 578

.65   *Harmful organisms

               Including parasites

               When classifying parasites under a specific kind of organism in 579 or
               580–590, prefer number for the parasite. Emphasis on host organism usually
               indicates that the work should be classed as a disease in 571.999

.68   *Rare and endangered species

               Standard subdivisions are added for either or both topics in heading

               Including recently extinct species

.7   **Organisms characteristic of specific kinds of environments**

               Class here biology of specific kinds of environments

               Class specific kinds of adaptation characteristic of specific kinds of
               environment in 578.4; class miscellaneous nontaxonomic kinds of organisms
               characteristic of specific kinds of environments in 578.6

               For ecology of specific kinds of environments, see 577

[.701–.709]   Standard subdivisions

               Do not use; class in 578.01–578.09

.73–.75   Specific kinds of nonaquatic environments

               Add to base number 578.7 the numbers following 577 in 577.3–577.5 for the
               environment only, e.g., organisms characteristic of grasslands 578.74; then
               to the result add standard subdivisions as instructed under 578.01–578.09,
               e.g., collections of living grassland plants and animals 578.74073

               Class comprehensive works on terrestrial environments in 578

               For space biology, see 571.0919; for extraterrestrial life, see 576.839

               See Manual at 577.3–577.7 vs. 578.73–578.77

.76–.77   Aquatic environments

               Add to base number 578.7 the numbers following 577 in 577.6–577.7 for the
               environment only, e.g., marine organisms, marine biology 578.77; then to
               the result add standard subdivisions as instructed under 578.01–578.09, e.g.,
               collections of living marine plants and animals 578.77073

               *See Manual at 577.3–577.7 vs. 578.73–578.77; also at 578.76–578.77 vs.
               551.46, 551.48*

*Add standard subdivisions as instructed under 578

579   Natural history of microorganisms, fungi, algae

Standard subdivisions are added for microorganisms, fungi, algae together; for microorganisms alone

Class here Protista, Thallobionta (Thallophyta)

Class here microbiology, protophytes; descriptive biology of microorganisms, fungi, algae; taxonomic biology of microorganisms, fungi, algae; comprehensive works on biology of microorganisms, fungi, algae; interdisciplinary works on microorganisms, fungi, algae

> *For internal biological processes of microorganisms, fungi, algae, see 571.29. For a specific aspect of microorganisms, fungi, algae, see the aspect, e.g., microbiology of human body 612.001579, cooking mushrooms 641.658*

> *See Manual at 577.3–577.7 vs. 579–590; also at 579–590; also at 579–590 vs. 571–575; also at 630 vs. 579–590, 641.3*

SUMMARY

579.01–.09	**Standard subdivisions**
.1	**Specific topics in natural history of microorganisms, fungi, algae**
.2	**Viruses and subviral organisms**
.3	**Prokaryotes**
.4	**Protozoa**
.5	**Fungi**
.6	**Mushrooms**
.7	**Lichens**
.8	**Algae**

.01–.08   Standard subdivisions

Notation from Table 1 as modified under 578.01–578.08, e.g., collections of living microorganisms 579.073

.09   History, geographic treatment, biography

> *For history, geographic treatment, biography in specific kinds of environment, see 579.17*

[.091 4–.091 9]   Areas, regions, places in general other than polar, temperate, tropical regions

Do not use; class in 579.17

.1   **Specific topics in natural history of microorganisms, fungi, algae**

Class here specific nontaxonomic kinds of organisms

Except for modifications shown under specific entries, add to each subdivision identified by † as follows:
01–08   Standard subdivisions
              Notation from Table 1 as modified under 578.01–578.08, e.g., microscopy 0282
09   History, geographic treatment, biography

Unless other instructions are given, observe the following table of preference, e.g., beneficial marine microorganisms 579.163 (*not* 579.177):

Miscellaneous nontaxonomic kinds of organisms   579.16
Adaptation   579.14
Genetics and evolution   579.13
Organisms characteristic of specific environments,
      ecology   579.17

Class a specific topic in natural history of microorganisms, fungi, algae with respect to a specific taxonomic group with the group, plus notation 1 as instructed under 579.2–579.8, e.g., useful fungi 579.5163

[.101–.109]   Standard subdivisions

Do not use; class in 579.01–579.09

.13   †Genetics and evolution

.135   †Genetics

Class here works on genetic constitution of microorganisms, fungi, algae that elucidate their total function

Class experimental works on genetics of microorganisms, fungi, algae; comprehensive works on genetics in 576.5

For biochemical genetics in microorganisms, fungi, algae, see 572.829

.138   †Evolution

Class here phylogeny

.14   †Adaptation

.141–.147   Specific kinds of adaptation

Add to base number 579.14 the numbers following 578.4 in 578.41–578.47, e.g., seasonal adaptation 579.143

.16   †Miscellaneous nontaxonomic kinds of organisms

Not provided for elsewhere

Including nonnative, rare, endangered species

Class here economic microbiology

Class food microbiology in 664.001579

†Add standard subdivisions as instructed under 579.1

.163   †Beneficial organisms

                  Including edible organisms

.165   †Harmful organisms

                  Class here pathogenic and poisonous organisms

                  See Manual at 579.165 vs. 616.9041

.17   Ecology, organisms characteristic of specific environments

                  Standard subdivisions are added for either or both topics in heading

                  Class here autecology, biology of specific environments

                  Class aerial microorganisms, ecology of atmosphere in 579.175

.170 1–.170 8   Standard subdivisions

                  Notation from Table 1 as modified under 578.01–578.08, e.g.,
                  microscopy in study of ecology of microorganisms 579.170282

.170 9   History, geographic treatment, biography

[.170 914–.170 919]   Areas, regions, places in general other than polar, temperate,
                  tropical regions

                  Do not use; class in 579.173–579.177

.171–.178   Specific topics in ecology, specific environments

                  Add to base number 579.17 the numbers following 577 in 577.1–577.8,
                  e.g., effect of pollution on microorganisms 579.1727, marine
                  microorganisms, marine botany 579.177, effect of pollution on marine
                  microorganisms 579.17727

                  Class comprehensive works on terrestrial microorganisms, fungi, algae in
                  579

.175   Ecology of miscellaneous environments

                  Number built according to instructions under 579.171–579.178

                  Including aerial microorganisms, ecology of atmosphere

†Add standard subdivisions as instructed under 579.1

> **579.2–579.8 Specific taxonomic groups of microorganisms, fungi, algae**

Except for modifications shown under specific entries, add to each subdivision identified by * as follows:
01–08   Standard subdivisions
          Notation from Table 1 as modified under 578.01–578.08, e.g., collections of living organisms 073
09   History, geographic treatment, biography
[0914–0919]   Areas, regions, places in general other than polar, temperate, tropical regions
          Do not use; class in notation 173–176 from this table
1   General topics of natural history of microorganisms, fungi, algae
          Add to 1 the numbers following 579.1 in 579.13–579.17, e.g., beneficial organisms 163

Class comprehensive works in 579

For internal biological processes of specific kinds of microorganisms, fungi, algae, see 571–575

.2   ***Viruses and subviral organisms**

Class here animal viruses, vertebrate viruses, virology

Subdivisions are added for viruses and subviral organisms together, for viruses alone

See also 579.327 for rickettsias

.23   *Invertebrate viruses

For specific kinds of invertebrate viruses, see 579.24–579.25

> **579.24–579.25 Specific kinds of viruses**

Class comprehensive works in 579.2

For specific kinds of bacterial viruses, see 579.26; for specific kinds of fungal viruses, see 579.27; for specific kinds of plant viruses, see 579.28

See Manual at 579.24–579.25

.24   *DNA viruses

.243   *Double-stranded, enveloped DNA viruses

.243 2   *Poxviridae

.243 4   *Herpesviridae

.243 6   *Baculoviridae

.244   *Double-stranded, nonenveloped DNA viruses

.244 3   *Adenoviridae

---

*Add as instructed under 579.2–579.8

.244 5	*Papovaviridae

Including Papillomavirus, Polyomavirus, Simian virus 40

.247	*Single-stranded, nonenveloped DNA viruses

Class here Parvoviridae

.25	*RNA viruses

.254	*Double-stranded, nonenveloped RNA viruses

Including Reoviridae

.256	*Single-stranded, enveloped RNA viruses

Including Arenaviridae, Filoviridae, Paramyxoviridae

.256 2	*Togaviridae

Class here arboviruses

.256 6	*Rhabdoviridae

Including Lyssavirus

.256 9	*Retroviridae

Class here oncoviruses, comprehensive works on oncogenic viruses

For a specific nonretrovirus oncogenic virus, see the virus, e.g., oncogenic papovaviruses 579.2445

.257	*Single-stranded, nonenveloped RNA viruses

.257 2	*Picornaviridae

Including Poliovirus

.26	*Bacterial viruses (Bacteriophages)

.27	*Fungal viruses

.28	*Plant viruses

.29	*Subviral organisms

Including prions

Class here viroids

.3	***Prokaryotes**

Variant names: Monera, Schizomycetes, Schizophyta

Class here Eubacteriales

Class here bacteria, bacteriology, comprehensive works on bacteria and viruses

Class bacteria culture for biological research in 571.638293

For viruses, see 579.2

See Manual at 579.3

*Add as instructed under 579.2–579.8

.314	Adaptation
	Number built according to instructions under 579.2–579.8
.314 9	†Anaerobic bacteria
.32	Minor kinds of bacteria
	Not provided for elsewhere
	Including Myxobacteria, Spirochetes
	Including chemolithotrophic bacteria, colorless sulfur bacteria
	Class comprehensive works on minor kinds of bacteria in 579.3
	See Manual at 579.3
[.320 1–.320 9]	Standard subdivisions
	Do not use; class in 579.301–579.309
.321	*Archaeobacteria
	Including Halobacteriaceae
	Including halophilic bacteria, methanogenic bacteria
.323	*Aerobic-microaerophilic, motile, helical-vibrioid gram-negative bacteria
	Including Aquaspirillum, Azospirillum
.325	*Anaerobic gram-negative straight, curved, and helical rods
	Including Bacteroides
.327	*Rickettsias and Chlamydias
.328	*Mycoplasmas
	Variant names: Mollicutes, Tenericutes
.33	*Gram-negative aerobic rods and cocci
	Including Acetobacter, Brucella, Legionella, Neisseria
	For Halobacteriaceae, see 579.321
.332	*Pseudomonas
	Subdivisions are added for the genus as a whole and for individual species
.334	*Rhizobium
	Subdivisions are added for the genus as a whole and for individual species

*Add as instructed under 579.2–579.8
†Add standard subdivisions as instructed under 579.1

.34   *Facultatively anaerobic gram-negative rods

Including Erwinia, Pasteurella, Photobacterium, Shigella, Yersinia

Class here Enterobacteriaceae

.342   *Escherichia

Subdivisions are added for the genus as a whole and for individual species

.344   *Salmonella

Subdivisions are added for the genus as a whole and for individual species

.35   *Gram-positive cocci

Class here lactic acid bacteria

For Lactobacillus, see 579.37

.353   *Staphylococcus

Subdivisions are added for the genus as a whole and for individual species

.355   *Streptococcus

Class here Lactococcus (lactic acid Streptococcus)

Subdivisions are added for the genus as a whole and for individual species

.36   *Endospore-forming gram-positive rods and cocci

.362   *Bacillus

Subdivisions are added for the genus as a whole and for individual species

.364   *Clostridium

Subdivisions are added for the genus as a whole and for individual species

.37   *Actinomycetes and related bacteria

Including Frankia, Lactobacillus, Listeria, Nocardia

Subdivisions are added for Actinomycetes and related bacteria together, for Actinomycetes alone

See Manual at 579.3

.373   *Irregular, nonsporing, gram-positive rods

Including Arthrobacter, Bifidobacterium, Corynebacterium

.374   *Mycobacteria

*Add as instructed under 579.2–579.8

.378 ***Streptomycetes and related genera**

Class here Streptomyces

.38 ***Anoxygenic phototrophic bacteria**

Including green bacteria

Class here purple bacteria; comprehensive works on photosynthetic bacteria, on sulfur bacteria

For colorless sulfur bacteria, see 579.32; for oxygenic photosynthetic bacteria, see 579.39

.385 ***Purple nonsulfur bacteria**

Including Rhodobacter, Rhodopseudomonas

.39 ***Cyanobacteria and Prochlorales**

Oxygenic photosynthetic bacteria

Variant name for Cyanobacteria: Cyanophyta

Including Chroococcales, Nostocales, Oscillatoriales

Class here blue-green algae

Subdivisions are added for Cyanobacteria and Prochlorales together, for Cyanobacteria alone

.4 ***Protozoa**

Class here Sarcomastigophora

For a specific group or organism that may be regarded as either protozoa or algae, see the group or organism in 579.8, e.g., Euglenophyta (Euglenida) 579.84

\> 579.42–579.45 Sarcomastigophora

Class comprehensive works in 579.4

.42 ***Zoomastigophorea**

Class here zooflagellates

Class phytoflagellates, comprehensive works on flagellates in 579.82

.43 ***Rhizopodea**

Including Arcellinida

Class here Sarcodina

For Foraminifera, see 579.44

.432 ***Amoebida**

Class here amoebas

.44 ***Foraminifera**

*Add as instructed under 579.2–579.8

.45   *Actinopoda

          Class here Radiolaria

          The term Radiolaria is sometimes limited to one of several subtaxa of Actinopoda

.47   *Sporozoa

.48   *Cnidospora

          Including Microsporida

.49   *Ciliophora

          Class here Ciliatea

          Class here ciliates

.495   *Hymenostomatida

          Including Paramecium

.5   ***Fungi**

          Class here Eumycophyta

          Class here mycology; filamentous fungi, true fungi

          Class comprehensive works on molds, on mildew in 579.53

          For lichens, see 579.7; for comprehensive works on mushrooms, on macrofungi, see 579.6

.52   *Myxomycotina

          Variant names: Mycetozoa, Myxomycetes, Myxomycophyta, Myxomycota

          Including Acrasia, Physarales, Stemonitales, Trichiales

          Including cellular slime molds

          Class here Myxogastromycetidae

          Class here slime molds

          For Plasmodiophoromycetes, see 579.53

>   579.53–579.59 Eumycophyta

          Class comprehensive works in 579.5

*Add as instructed under 579.2–579.8

.53   *Miscellaneous fungi

        Not provided for elsewhere

        Including Chytridiomycetes, Hyphochytridiomycetes, Plasmodiophoromycetes, Rhizopus, Trichomycetes, Zygomycetes

        Including bread molds, uniflagellate molds

        Class here Mastigomycotina, Phycomycetes

        Class here comprehensive works on molds, on mildew

        Class slime molds in 579.52

           For Oomycetes, see 579.54; for ascomycete molds and mildew, see 579.56

.54   *Oomycetes

        Former name: Biflagellates

.542   *Saprolegniales

.546   *Peronosporales

        Including Phytophthora

        Class here downy mildew

.55   *Deuteromycotina

        Variant name: Deuteromycetes, Fungi Imperfecti

        Including Coelomycetes, Hyphomycetes, Melanconiales, Moniliales, Mycelia Sterilia, Sphaeropsidales

        Including sterile fungi

        Class here imperfect fungi

        When sexual reproduction of some members of a specific genus of imperfect fungi has been established with a specific kind of sexually reproducing fungi, class the genus with the kind of the sexually reproducing fungi, e.g., Penicillium 579.5654, Fusarium 579.5677. If, however, members of the genus are assigned to different families of fungi, class them here, e.g., Septoria 579.55

.56   *Ascomycotina

        Class here Ascomycetes

        For Discomycetes, see 579.57

*Add as instructed under 579.2–579.8

.562   *Hemiascomycetes

        Including Protomycetales, Taphrinales; comprehensive works on Saccharomycetaceae

        Including comprehensive works on yeasts

        Class here Endomycetales

            For Saccharomyces, see 579.563. For a specific kind of yeasts not in family Saccharomycetaceae, see the kind, e.g., basidiomycete yeasts 579.59

.563   *Saccharomyces

        Class here common yeasts

        Subdivisions are added for the genus as a whole and for individual species

        Class comprehensive works on Saccharomycetaceae in 579.562

.564   *Loculoascomycetes

        Including Asterinales, Dothideales, Melanommatales, Mycrothyriales, Myriangiales, Pleosporales

.565   *Plectomycetes

        Including Gymnascales, Microascales, Onygenales

        Class here Eurotiales

.565 4   *Penicillium

          Subdivisions are added for the genus as a whole and for individual species

.565 7   *Aspergillus

          Subdivisions are added for the genus as a whole and for individual species

.567   *Pyrenomycetes

        Including Chaetomiales, Clavicipitales, Diaporthales, Erysiphales, Laboulbeniales, Sordariales, Xylariales

.567 7   *Hypocreales

          Including Fusarium, Nectria, Trichoderma

.57   *Discomycetes

        Including Helotiales, Ostropales, Phacidiales, Tuberales

        Including truffles

        Class here cup fungi

---

*Add as instructed under 579.2–579.8

.578   *Pezizales

        Including Ascobolus

        Including morels, saddle fungi

.59   *Basidiomycotina

        Including Exobasidiales, Tremellales

        Including basidiomycete yeasts, jelly fungi

        Class here Basidiomycetes, Heterobasidiomycetes, Homobasidiomycetes

        For Agaricales, comprehensive works on mushrooms, see 579.6

.592   *Uredinales

        Class here rusts

.593   *Ustilaginales

        Class here smuts

.597   *Polyporales

        Variant name: Aphyllophorales

        Including bracket fungi, club fungi, coral fungi, pore fungi, shelf fungi

.599   *Gasteromycetes

        Including Lycoperdales, Nidulariales, Phallales

        Including bird's-nest fungi, puffballs, stinkhorns

.6   ***Mushrooms**

        Including Boletaceae, Hydnaceae, Thelephoraceae

        Including boletes, leather fungi, spine fungi

        Class here Agaricales, Agaricaceae

        Class here gill fungi, macrofungi, toadstools

        Class comprehensive works on Basidiomycotina in 579.59

        For mushrooms, macrofungi of a specific order other than Agaricales, see the order in 579.5, e.g., morels 579.578

.616 3   Beneficial mushrooms

        Number built according to instructions under 579.2–579.8

.616 32   Edible mushrooms

.7   ***Lichens**

---

*Add as instructed under 579.2–579.8

.8   ***Algae**

Class here algology, phycology

For blue-green algae, see 579.39; for lichens, see 579.7

.82   **Minor divisions of algae*

Including Chloromonadophyta, Cryptophyta, Xanthophyta

Including yellow-green algae

Class here Phytomastigophorea

Class here phytoflagellates; comprehensive works on flagellates, on organisms that may be regarded as either protozoa or algae

For a specific kind of flagellate, see the kind, e.g., Zoomastigophorea 579.42, Oomycetes 579.54, dinoflagellates 579.87; for a specific organism that may be regarded as either protozoa or algae, see the kind in 579.8, e.g., euglenoids 579.84

.83   **Chlorophyta*

Including Chaetophorales, Prasinophyceae, Siphonocladales

Class here Chlorophyceae

Class here green algae, green seaweeds

.832   **Volvocales*

Including Chlamydomonadaceae, Dunaliellaceae

.833   **Chlorococcales*

.835   **Caulerpales*

Variant names: Bryopodales, Codiales, Siphonales

.836   **Dasycladales*

Including Acetabularia

.837   **Zygnematales*

Variant name: Conjugales

Including Desmidiaceae

Including desmids

.839   **Charophyceae*

Class here Charales

Class here stoneworts

.84   **Euglenophyta*

Variant name: Euglenida

Class here euglenoids

---

*Add as instructed under 579.2–579.8

.85   *Bacillariophyceae

        Class here diatoms

.86   *Chrysophyta

        Including Haptophyceae

        Class here Chrysophyceae

        Class here golden algae

.87   *Pyrrophyta

        Including Desmophyceae, Pfiesteriaceae

        Including red tide

        Class here Dinophyceae

        Class here dinoflagellates

.88   *Phaeophyta

        Class here Phaeophyceae

        Class here brown algae, comprehensive works on seaweeds

          For green seaweeds, see 579.83; for red seaweeds, see 579.89

.887   *Laminariales

        Including Macrocystis, Saccorhiza, Undaria

        Class here comprehensive works on kelps

          For kelps of order Fucales, see 579.888

.888   *Fucales

        Including Ascophyllum, Fucus, Sargassum

        Class here rockweeds

.89   *Rhodophyta

        Including Bangiophycideae

        Including red seaweeds

        Class here Florideophycideae, Rhodophyceae

        Class here red algae

        Class red tide in 579.87

*Add as instructed under 579.2–579.8

> ## 580–590 Natural history of plants and animals

Class comprehensive works on biology of plants and animals in 570; class comprehensive works on natural history of plants and animals in 578

For internal biological processes of specific kinds of plants and animals, see 571–575; for natural history of microorganisms, fungi, algae, see 579

580   Plants

Class here botany; Embryophyta, vascular plants (tracheophytes), Spermatophyta (seed plants); natural history of plants; descriptive biology of plants; taxonomic biology of plants; comprehensive works on biology of plants; interdisciplinary works on plants

Class angiosperms (flowering plants) in 583; class interdisciplinary works on plants of agricultural importance in 630; class interdisciplinary works on food from plants in 641.303

For paleobotany, see 561; for internal biological processes and structures of plants, see 571.2; for fungi, see 579.5; for algae, see 579.8. For a specific aspect of plants, see the aspect, e.g., plant cultivation 631.5

See Manual at 363 vs. 302–307, 333.7, 570–590, 600; also at 577.3–577.7 vs. 579–590; also at 579–590; also at 579–590 vs. 571–575; also at 630 vs. 579–590, 641.3

SUMMARY

580.1–.9	**Standard subdivisions**
581	**Specific topics in natural history of plants**
582	**Plants noted for specific vegetative characteristics and flowers**
583	**Eudicots and Ceratophyllales**
584	**Monocots, basal angiosperms, Chloranthales, magnoliids**
585	**Pinophyta**
586	**Cryptogamia**
587	**Pteridophyta**
588	**Bryophyta**

.1–.6   **Standard subdivisions**

Notation from Table 1 as modified under 578.01–578.06, e.g., microscopy of plants 580.282

.7   **Education, research, related topics**

.73   Collections and exhibits of living plants

Class here botanical gardens

Add to base number 580.73 notation 1–9 from Table 2 for area in which collections and exhibits are found, e.g., botanical gardens of Germany 580.7343

.74   Museums, collections, exhibits

Do not use for collections and exhibits of living organisms; class in 580.73

Class here herbariums, collections of dried plants

.75	Museum activities and services
.752	Preserving botanical specimens

.8 Groups of people

.9 History, geographic treatment, biography

[.914–.919]   Areas, regions, places in general other than polar, temperate, tropical regions

> Do not use; class in 581.73–581.76

.93–.99   Botany by specific continents, countries, localities

> Class plants by specific continents, countries, localities in 581.9

581 Specific topics in natural history of plants

> Class here specific nontaxonomic kinds of plants

> Except for modifications shown under specific entries, add to each subdivision identified by † as follows:
> 01–08   Standard subdivisions
> Notation from Table 1 as modified under 580.1–580.8, e.g., preservation of botanical specimens 0752
> 09   History, geographic treatment, biography
> Unless other instructions are given, observe the following table of preference, e.g., beneficial aquatic plants 581.63 (*not* 581.76):

Miscellaneous nontaxonomic kinds of plants	581.6
Adaptation	581.4
Genetics, evolution, age characteristics	581.3
Plant ecology, plants characteristic of specific environments	581.7
Plants by specific continents, countries, localities	581.9

> Class a specific topic in natural history of plants with respect to a specific taxonomic group with the group, plus notation 1 from table under 583–588, e.g., useful monocotyledons 584.163

> *For plants noted for specific vegetative characteristics and flowers, see 582*

[.01–.09]   Standard subdivisions

> Do not use; class in 580.1–580.9

.3 †Genetics, evolution, age characteristics

> Standard subdivisions are added for genetics, evolution, age characteristics together, for genetics and evolution alone

---

†Add standard subdivisions as instructed under 581

.35   †Genetics

          Class here works on genetic constitution of plants that elucidate their total function

          Class experimental works on plant genetics, comprehensive works on genetics in 576.5

          For biochemical genetics in plants, see 572.82

.38   †Evolution

          Class here phylogeny

.39   †Age characteristics

          Class here age determination

.4   **†Adaptation**

          Class here plants noted for specific kinds of adaptation

.41   †Size, weight, shape

          Including silhouettes

.42   †Acclimatization and temperature adaptation

          Standard subdivisions are added for acclimatization and temperature adaptation together, for acclimatization alone

          For seasonal adaptation, see 581.43

.43   †Seasonal adaptation

>   581.46–581.49 Adaptation of specific parts of plants

          Class comprehensive works in 581.4

          For physiology of specific parts of plants, see 575

.46   †Reproductive adaptation

          Including buds, stems specialized for reproduction

          For comprehensive works on flowers and their adaptations, see 582.13

.464   †Fruits

          Including nuts

          For seeds, see 581.467

.467   †Seeds

†Add standard subdivisions as instructed under 581

.47	†Protective adaptation, color

> Subdivisions are added for protective adaptation and color together, for protective adaptation alone

> Including mimicry, thorns

> Class here bark

> Class color of a specific adaptation with the adaptation, e.g., color of flowers 582.13

.48	†Leaves and fronds

> Standard subdivisions are added for either or both topics in heading

> Including tendrils

.49	†Stems and roots
.495	†Stems

> *For stems specialized for reproduction, see 581.46*

.498	†Roots
.6	**†Miscellaneous nontaxonomic kinds of plants**

> Not provided for elsewhere

> Class here economic botany

> Class carnivorous plants in 583.887

.62	†Nonnative plants

> Class here alien, exotic, introduced, invasive, naturalized plants

.63	†Beneficial plants

> Class here herbs

.632	†Edible plants
.634	†Medicinal plants
.636	†Plants of industrial and technological value

> Other than medicinal plants

.65	†Harmful plants
.652	†Weeds

> Class interdisciplinary works on weeds in 632.5

.657	†Allergenic plants
.659	†Poisonous plants

†Add standard subdivisions as instructed under 581

.68 †Rare and endangered plants

> Standard subdivisions are added for either or both topics in heading
>
> Including recently extinct species

.7 **Plant ecology, plants characteristic of specific environments**

> Standard subdivisions are added for either or both topics in heading
>
> Class here autecology, botany of specific environments
>
> Class plants characteristic of specific environments noted for specific vegetative characteristics and flowers, ecology of such plants in 582

.701–.708 Standard subdivisions

> Notation from Table 1 as modified under 580.1–580.8, e.g., microscopy 581.70282

.709 History, geographic treatment, biography

[.709 14–.709 19] Areas, regions, places in general other than polar, temperate, tropical regions

> Do not use; class in 581.73–581.76

.71–.76 Specific topics in plant ecology, specific environments

> Add to base number 581.7 the numbers following 577 in 577.1–577.6, e.g., aquatic plants 581.76, aquatic gardens 581.76073
>
> Class marine botany in 579.177
>
> *For synecology and population biology, see 581.78*

.78 †Synecology and population biology

.782–.788 Specific topics of synecology and population biology

> Add to base number 581.78 the numbers following 577.8 in 577.82–577.88, e.g., parasitism 581.7857

.9 **Plants by specific continents, countries, localities**

> Add to base number 581.9 notation 3–9 from Table 2, e.g., plants in Argentina 581.982

582 **Plants noted for specific vegetative characteristics and flowers**

> Class genetics and evolution, adaptation and parts other than flowers, miscellaneous kinds of plants noted for vegetative characteristics and flowers in 581
>
> *For a specific taxonomic group of plants noted for either specific vegetative characteristics or flowers, see the group in 583–588, e.g., lilies noted for their flowers 584.6*

†Add standard subdivisions as instructed under 581

[.01–.09]   Standard subdivisions

>   Do not use; class in 580.1–580.9

.1   Herbaceous and woody plants, plants noted for their flowers

>   Except for modifications shown under specific entries, add to each subdivision
>   identified by ‡ as follows:
>   01–08   Standard subdivisions
>   >   Notation from Table 1 as modified under 580.1–580.8, e.g.,
>   >   botanical gardens 073
>   09   History, geographic treatment, biography
>   [0914–0919]   Areas, regions, places in general other than polar, temperate,
>   >   tropical regions
>   >   >   Do not use; class in notation 7 from this table
>   3–7   Specific topics of natural history of plants
>   >   Add the numbers following 581 in 581.3–581.7, e.g., genetics 35,
>   >   seeds 467, rare and endangered plants 68, aquatic plants 76, aquatic
>   >   gardens 76073

>   *See Manual at 635.9 vs. 582.1*

[.101–.109]   Standard subdivisions

>   Do not use; class in 580.1–580.9

.12   ‡Herbaceous plants

>   Including biennials

>   Class here annuals, forbs

>   Class herbaceous plants noted for their flowers in 582.13

>   *For herbaceous vines, see 582.189*

.13   ‡Plants noted for their flowers

>   Class here wild flowers, interdisciplinary works on flowers

>   Class woody plants noted for their flowers in 582.16; class vines noted
>   for their flowers in 582.18; class comprehensive works on Angiospermae
>   (flowering plants) in 580

>   >   *For physiology of flowers, see 575.6. For a specific aspect of flowers, see
>   >   the aspect, e.g., flower gardening 635.9, flower arrangement 745.92*

>   >   *See Manual at 580 vs. 582.13*

.16   ‡Trees

>   Class here dendrology; comprehensive works on perennials, on woody
>   plants

>   Class forest ecology in 577.3

>   >   *For herbaceous perennials, see 582.12; for shrubs, see 582.17; for
>   >   woody vines, see 582.18*

.17   ‡Shrubs

---

‡Add as instructed under 582.1

.18 ‡Vines

Class here woody vines

.189 ‡Herbaceous vines

> ## 583–588 Specific taxonomic groups of plants

Except for modifications shown under specific entries, add to each subdivision identified by * as follows:

01–08 Standard subdivisions

Notation from Table 1 as modified under 580.1–580.8, e.g., collections of living plants 073

09 History, geographic treatment, biography

[0914–0919] Areas, regions, places in general other than polar, temperate, tropical regions

Do not use; class in notation 173–176 from this table

1 General topics of natural history of plants

Add to 1 the numbers following 581 in 581.3–581.7, e.g., aquatic plants 176

Class comprehensive works in 580

> ## 583–584 Angiosperms

583 ***Eudicots and Ceratophyllales**

Subdivisions are added for eudicots and Ceratophyllales together, for eudicots alone

Class here angiosperms (flowering plants), core eudicots

For monocots, basal angiosperms, Chloranthales, magnoliids, see 584

See Manual at 583–585 vs. 600; also at 583–584; also at 583 vs. 582.13

SUMMARY

583.2	**Ceratophyllales**
.3	**Ranunculales, Sabiaceae, Proteales, Trochodendrales, Buxales**
.4	**Miscellaneous core eudicots**
.6	**Fabids**
.7	**Malvids and Vitales**
.8	**Berberidopsidales, Santalales, Caryophyllales**
.9	**Asterids**

*Add as instructed under 583–588
‡Add as instructed under 582.1

SUMMARY

583.2	**Magnoliidae**
.3	**Ranunculidae**
.4	**Hamamelididae**
.5	**Caryophyllidae**
.6	**Dilleniidae**
.7	**Rosidae**
.8	**Other orders of Rosidae**
.9	**Asteridae**

.176 98   Mangrove swamp ecology

> Number built according to instructions under 583–588

> Class here comprehensive works on mangroves

> *For mangroves of a specific order or family, see the order or family, e.g., mangroves of family Combretaceae 583.73*

.2   *Ceratophyllales

> Class here Ceratophyllaceae

> Class here hornworts

> **583.3–583.9 Eudicots**

> Class comprehensive works in 583

.3   *Ranunculales, Sabiaceae, Proteales, Trochodendrales, Buxales

.34   *Ranunculales

> Including Berberidaceae, Eupteleaceae, Menispermaceae, Ranunculaceae

> Including aconites, anemones, barberries, buttercups, Christmas roses, clematises, columbines, delphiniums, hellebores, larkspurs, lesser celandine, mandrake, mayapple, mayflower, monkshoods, moonseeds, wolfsbanes

> *For Fumariaceae, Papaveraceae, Pteridophyllaceae, see 583.35*

> *See also 583.9593 for mandrakes of family Solanaceae*

.35   *Fumariaceae, Papaveraceae, Pteridophyllaceae

> Including bleeding hearts, bloodroot, celandines, Dutchman's breeches, fumitories, poppies

> *See also 583.34 for lesser celandine*

.37   *Sabiaceae

---

*Add as instructed under 583–588

.38   *Proteales

         Including Nelumbonaceae, Persoonia, Platanaceae, Telopea

         Including banksias, grevilleas, hakeas, lotuses, macadamias, plane trees, proteas, spider flowers, sycamores, waratahs

         Class here Proteaceae

           See also 583.73 for spiderflowers of family Melastomataceae; also 583.78 for spiderflowers of family Cleomaceae

.39   *Trochodendrales and Buxales

.393   *Trochodendrales

.395   *Buxales

         Including Buxaceae, Didymelaceae

         Including boxwoods

           See also 583.648 for West Indian boxwood

>   **583.4–583.9 Core eudicots**

         Class comprehensive works in 583

.4   ***Miscellaneous core eudicots**

         Only those provided for below

.42   *Gunnerales

         Including Gunneraceae, Myrothamnaceae

         Including gunneras

.43   *Dilleniaceae

.44   *Saxifragales

         Including Cercidiphyllaceae, Crassulaceae, Grossulariaceae, Hamamelidaceae, Paeoniaceae, Peridiscaceae, Ribes, Saxifragaceae

         Including currants, gooseberries, houseleeks, ironwoods, katsura trees, live-forevers, orpines, peonies, pickaback plants, saxifrages, sedums, stonecrops, sweet gums, Virginia willow, witch hazels

         Class comprehensive works on ironwoods in 583.65

.47   *Cynomoriaceae

.6   ***Fabids**

         Class here eurosids I, rosids

         For malvids and Vitales, see 583.7

*Add as instructed under 583–588

.62   *Zygophyllales

>   Including Krameriaceae, Zygophyllaceae

>   Including creosote bush, lignum vitae

.63   *Fabales

>   Including Melilotus, Polygalaceae, Quillajaceae, Stylobasium, Surianaceae, Trifolium

>   Including alfalfa, beans, beggar's lice, bluebonnet, carob, clovers, groundnuts, honey bush, indigo plants, kudzu, lentils, lespedezas, locoweeds, locusts, lucernes, lupines, milkworts, peanuts, peas, Scotch broom, shamrocks, smoke trees, sojas, soyas, soybeans, tamarind, trefoils, vetches, wisterias

>   Class here Fabaceae, Faboideae

>   Class here legumes

>>   *See also 583.68 for shamrock of family Oxalidaceae; also 583.75 for smoke trees of family Anacardiaceae*

.633   *Mimosoideae

>   Including acacias, mesquite, sensitive plants, silk tree, wattles

>   Class here mimosas

.634   *Caesalpinioideae

>   Including redbuds, sennas

.64   *Rosales

.642   *Rosaceae

>   Including Rubus

>   Including almonds, apples, apricots, blackberries, cane fruits, cherries, chokeberries, cinquefoils, dewberries, drupaceous fruits, fire thorns, hawthorns, juneberries, loquats, medlars, mountain ashes, peaches, pears, plums, pomaceous fruits, pyracanthas, quinces, raspberries, rowan trees, serviceberries, spireas, stone fruits, strawberries

>   Class here rose family

>>   *See also 583.732 for rose apples; also 583.75 for hog plums of family Anacardiaceae*

>>   *For Rosa, see 583.644*

.644   *Rosa

>   Subdivisions are added for the genus as a whole and for individual species

>   Class here roses

---

*Add as instructed under 583–588

.646   *Barbeyaceae, Dirachmaceae, Elaeagnaceae, Rhamnaceae

Including buckthorns, ironwoods, jujubes, oleasters

Class comprehensive works on ironwoods in 583.65

.648   *Cannabaceae, Moraceae, Ulmaceae, Urticaceae

Including banyan, breadfruits, China grass plant, elms, figs, hackberries, hops, India rubber tree, marijuana, mulberries, nettles, osage orange, pileas, ramie, rubber plant, West Indian boxwood; comprehensive works on hemps

> *For hemps of a specific family other than Cannabaceae, see the family, e.g., aloe hemp 584.79*

> *See also 583.395 for boxwoods of family Buxaceae; also 583.96 for dead nettles*

.65   *Fagales

Including Betulaceae, Casuarinaceae, Juglandaceae, Myricaceae

Including alders, bayberries, beeches, beefwoods, birches, bog myrtle, butternuts, candleberry, chestnuts, chinquapins, cork oak, filberts, hazelnuts, hickories, hornbeams, oaks, pecans, sweet gale, walnuts, wax myrtles; comprehensive works on ironwoods

Class here Fagaceae

Class Jamaica bayberry, comprehensive works on myrtles in 583.732

> *For ironwoods of a specific order or family other then Fagales, see the order or family, e.g., ironwoods of family Rhamnaceae 583.646*

> *See also 583.983 for bog myrtle of family Menyanthaceae*

.66   *Cucurbitales

Including Anisophylleaceae, Begoniaceae, Coriariaceae, Datiscaceae

Including begonias, cucumbers, melons, pepos, pumpkins, squashes, watermelons

Class here Cucurbitaceae

Class here gourds

.67   *Celastrales

Including bittersweet, brexias, khat, staff trees

Class here Celastraceae

> *See also 583.9593 for bittersweet of family Solanaceae*

.68   *Oxalidales

Including Brunelliaceae, Cephalotaceae, Connaraceae, Cunoniaceae, Elaeocarpaceae, Oxalidaceae

Including shamrock, wood sorrels

---

*Add as instructed under 583–588

.69   *Malpighiales

Including Achariaceae, Balanopaceae, Bonnetiaceae, Caryocaraceae, Clusiaceae, Dichapetalaceae, Elatinaceae, Erythroxylaceae, Euphorbiaceae, Guttiferae, Humiriaceae, Hypericaceae, Ixonanthaceae, Lacistemataceae, Linaceae, Malpighiaceae, Ochnaceae, Passifloraceae, Podostemaceae, Populus, Rafflesiaceae, Rhizophoraceae, Salicaceae, Salix, Violaceae

Including aspens, cassavas, castor-oil plant, cocas, copperleaves, cottonwoods, crotons, crown of thorns, dika, flax, garcinias, granadillas, heveas, mammee apple, manchineels, mangosteen, maniocs, maypop, mercuries, pansies, passionflowers, poinsettias, poplars, riverweeds, rubber tree, rose of Sharon, snow-on-the-mountain, spurges, tallow tree, tung tree, violets, wild mango, willows

See also 583.648 for India rubber tree; also 583.96 for African violets; also 584.286 for yellow poplar

.7   *Malvids and Vitales

Subdivisions are added for malvids and Vitales together, for malvids alone

Class here eurosids II

.72   *Geraniales

Including Geraniaceae, Melianthaceae

Including erodiums, geraniums, pelargoniums

.73   *Myrtales

Including Combretaceae, Lythraceae, Melastomataceae, Onagraceae, Vochysiaceae

Including Brazilian spiderflower, button mangrove, cigar flower, clarkias, crape myrtle, evening primroses, fireweeds, fuchsias, loosestrifes, meadow beauties, pomegranate, white mangrove

Class comprehensive works on mangroves in 583.17698

See also 583.38 for spider flowers of family Proteaceae; also 583.78 for spiderflowers of family Cleomaceae; also 583.93 for loosestrifes of family Primulaceae; also 583.983 for fireweeds of family Asteraceae

.732   *Myrtaceae

Including allspice, bay rum tree, clove, guavas, Jamaica bayberry, pimento, rose apples, water chestnuts; comprehensive works on myrtles

For Eucalyptus, see 583.733. For myrtle of a specific family other than Myrtaceae, see the family, e.g., wax myrtles 583.65, crape myrtle 583.73, Oregon myrtle 584.288

See also 583.9593 for pimientos of family Solanaceae; also 584.94 for Chinese water chestnut

*Add as instructed under 583–588

.733   *Eucalyptus

Subdivisions are added for the genus as a whole and for individual species

Class here gum trees

.74   *Crossosomatales and Picramniales

.742   *Crossosomatales

Including Stachyuraceae, Staphyleaceae, Strasburgeriaceae

Including bladdernuts

Class here Crossosomataceae

.745   *Picramniales

.75   *Sapindales

Including Anacardiaceae, Burseraceae, Hippocastanaceae, Leitneria, Meliaceae, Rutaceae, Sapindaceae, Simaroubaceae

Including ailanthuses, buckeyes, cashews, chinaberry tree, citrus fruits, cork trees, hog plums, hop tree, hopbushes, horse chestnuts, incense trees, litchis, mahoganies, mangoes, maples, orange jessamine, oranges, pistachios, poison ivies, poison oaks, rues, smoke trees, soapberries, Spanish plums, sugar maple, sumacs, tree of heaven, varnish trees; comprehensive works on balms

Class comprehensive works on ivies in 583.988

For balm of a specific family other than Burseraceae, see the family, e.g., bee balms 583.96

See also 583.63 for smoke trees of family Fabaceae; also 583.642 for hog plums of family Rosaceae; also 583.65 for cork oak; also 583.963 for jasmines

.76   *Huerteales

Including Dipentodontaceae, Gerrardinaceae, Petenaeaceae, Tapisciaceae

.77   *Malvales

Including Bixaceae, Cistaceae, Cytinaceae, Dipterocarpaceae, Sphaerosepalaceae, Thymelaeaceae

Including annatto tree, daphnes, mezereum, rockroses, spurge laurel

.775   *Malvaceae

Including Bombacoideae, Sterculia, Tilia

Including balsa, baobabs, basswood, cacao, cotton, hibiscuses, hollyhock, jute, kapok, kenaf, kola nuts, lime trees, lindens, okra, silk cotton tree; comprehensive works on rose of Sharon

Class here mallows

For roses of Sharon of a specific family other than Malvaceae, see the family, e.g., roses of Sharon of family Hypericaceae 583.69

*Add as instructed under 583–588

.78   *Brassicales

Including Capparaceae, Caricaceae, Cleomaceae, Matthiola, Moringaceae, Resedaceae, Tropaeolaceae

Including alyssums, cabbages, candytufts, capers, cresses, crucifixion thorns, mignonettes, mustard, nasturtiums, papaws, papayas, radishes, rapes, rutabagas, shepherd's purse, spiderflowers, stocks, turnips, wallflowers, watercresses

Class here Brassicaceae, Cruciferae

See also 583.38 for spider flowers of family Proteaceae; also 583.73 for spiderflowers of family Melastomataceae; also 584.286 for papaws of family Annonaceae; also 584.442 for skunk cabbages

.79   *Vitales

Including Vitaceae

Including Boston ivy, grapes, Virginia creeper

.8   *Berberidopsidales, Santalales, Caryophyllales

.82   *Berberidopsidales

Including Aextoxicaceae

Class here Berberidopsidaceae

.85   *Santalales

Including Balanophoraceae, Loranthaceae, Olacaceae, Opiliaceae, Santalaceae

Including mistletoes, sandalwood

.88   *Caryophyllales

Including Anacampserotaceae, Asteropeiaceae, Frankeniaceae, Limeaceae, Plumbaginaceae, Tamaricaceae

Including alkali heath, leadworts, sea lavenders, tamarisk, thrifts

.883   *Caryophyllaceae and related families

Including Achatocarpaceae, Aizoaceae, Amaranthaceae, Barbeuiaceae, Basellaceae, Didiereaceae, Molluginaceae, Nyctaginaceae, Phytolaccaceae, Portulacaceae, Stegnospermataceae

Including amaranths, beets, bougainvilleas, carnations, carpetweeds, four-o'clock, goosefoots, ice plants, lithops, living stones, Madeira vine, pinks, pokeweed, purslanes, sea figs, spinach

.885   *Cactaceae

Class here cacti

*Add as instructed under 583–588

.887   *Nepenthaceae and related families

> Including Ancistrocladaceae, Dioncophyllaceae, Droseraceae, Drosophyllaceae

> Including sundews, Venus's flytrap; Old World pitcher plants; comprehensive works on pitcher plants

> Class here comprehensive works on carnivorous plants

> *For Cephalotaceae, see 583.68; for New World pitcher plants, see 583.93; for Byblidaceae, Lentibulariaceae, see 583.96*

.888   *Polygonaceae

> Including buckwheat, canaigre, dock, rhubarb, sorrel

.9   *Asterids

.92   *Cornales

> Including Cornaceae, Hydrangeaceae, Hydrostachyaceae, Loasaceae

> Including deutzias, dogwoods, hydrangeas, mock oranges, sour gums, syringas, tupelos

.93   *Ericales

> Including Balsaminaceae, Clethraceae, Diapensiaceae, Ebenaceae, Ericaceae, Fouquieriaceae, Lecythidaceae, Marcgraviaceae, Pentaphylacaceae, Polemoniaceae, Primulaceae, Sapotaceae, Sarraceniaceae, Stewartia, Styracaceae, Symplocaceae, Tetrameristaceae, Theaceae

> Including auriculas, azaleas, balsams, blueberries, Brazil nut, camellias, candlewood, Chinese gooseberry, coralberry, cranberries, crowberries, cyclamens, ebonies, galax, heather, heaths, huckleberries, impatiens, Indian pipes, Jacob's ladders, jewelweeds, kalmias, kiwi, loosestrifes, mountain laurel, New World pitcher plants, ocotillo, pepperbushes, persimmons, phloxes, primroses, primulas, rhododendrons, sapodilla, shooting stars, sourwood, star apples, storaxes, sweetleaf, tea, touch-me-nots, wintergreens

> Class evening primroses in 583.73; class comprehensive works on carnivorous plants, on pitcher plants in 583.887; class comprehensive works on laurels in 584.288

> *See also 583.73 for loosestrifes of family Lythraceae*

.95   *Lamiids

> Class here euasterids I

> *For Lamiales, see 583.96*

.952   *Oncothecaceae

.953   *Metteniusaceae

.954   *Icacinaceae

.955   *Garryales

> Including Eucommiaceae, Garryaceae

*Add as instructed under 583–588

.956   *Gentianales

> Including Apocynaceae, Cynocrambe, Gentianaceae, Loganiaceae, Plumeria, Rubiaceae, Theligonum

> Including buttonbushes, carrion flowers, cinchonas, coffee, dogbanes, gardenias, gentians, Indian hemps, Indian sarsaparilla, madders, milkweeds, oleanders, partridgeberry, periwinkles, rauwolfias, stephanotises

>> *See also 584.6 for carrion flowers and sarsaparillas of family Smilacaceae*

.957   *Vahliaceae

.958   *Boraginaceae

> Including baby blue-eyes, bluebells, borage, comfreys, forget-me-nots, heliotropes, honeyworts, hound's tongues, Virginia cowslip, waterleafs

>> *See also 583.983 for bluebells of family Campanulaceae; also 584.79 for bluebells of family Asparagaceae*

.959   *Solanales

> Including Convolvulaceae, Sphenocleaceae

> Including dichondras, dodders, morning glories, sweet potatoes, yams

>> *See also 584.52 for yams of family Dioscoreaceae*

.959 3   *Solanaceae

> Including belladonna, bittersweet, butterfly flowers, capsicums, cayenne pepper, daturas, eggplants, henbanes, jimsonweed, mandrakes, nightshades, paprika, petunias, pimientos, potatoes, red peppers, schizanthuses, sweet peppers, tobacco, tomatoes; comprehensive works on peppers

>> *For peppers of family Piperaceae, see 584.284*

>> *See also 583.34 for mandrake of family Berberidaceae; also 583.67 for bittersweet of family Celastraceae; also 583.732 for pimento of family Myrtaceae*

---

*Add as instructed under 583–588

.96   *Lamiales

Including Acanthaceae, Bignoniaceae, Byblidaceae, Gesneriaceae, Hippuris, Lentibulariaceae, Martyniaceae, Orobanchaceae, Pedaliaceae, Plantaginaceae, Scrophulariaceae, Verbenaceae

Including acanthuses, African violets, basils, bee balms, black mangrove, bladderworts, broomrapes, butterfly bushes, calabash tree, catalpas, catnip, Chinese artichoke, dead nettles, figworts, foxglove, gloxinias, ground ivy, horehounds, hyssop, lavenders, lopseed, mare's tails, marjoram, mint, mulleins, penstemon, plantagos, plantains, rosemary, sage, sesames, snapdragons, teak, thymes, trumpet creepers, unicorn plants, verbenas, vervains

Class here Labiatae, Lamiaceae

Class comprehensive works on mangroves in 583.17698; class comprehensive works on balms in 583.75; class comprehensive works on carnivorous plants in 583.887

See also 583.983 for artichokes, sagebrushes; also 584.88 for plantains of family Musaceae

.963   *Oleales

Including ashes, forsythias, jasmines, lilacs, olives, privets

Class here Oleaceae

See also 583.75 for orange jessamine

.98   *Campanulids

Class here euasterids II

.982   *Aquifoliales

Including Cardiopteridaceae

Including maté

Class here Aquifoliaceae, Ilex

Class here holly

*Add as instructed under 583–588

.983   *Asterales

Including Calyceraceae, Campanula, Campanulaceae, Goodeniaceae, Menyanthaceae, Stylidiaceae

Including artichokes, asters, bellflowers, black-eyed Susans, bluebells, bog myrtle, buckbean, chamomiles, chicory, chrysanthemums, cornflower, cosmos, dahlias, daisies, dandelions, endive, everlastings, fireweed, fleabanes, gerberas, goldenrods, groundsels, guayule, Indian tobacco, lettuce, marigolds, ragweeds, ragworts, safflower, sagebrushes, salsify, sunflowers, thistles, wormwoods, zinnias

Class here Asteraceae, Compositae

See also 583.65 for bog myrtle of family Myricaceae; also 583.73 for fireweed of family Onagraceae; also 583.958 for bluebells of family Boraginaceae; also 583.96 for Chinese artichoke; also 584.79 for bluebells of family Asparagaceae

.984   *Escalloniales

Class here Escalloniaceae

Class here escallonias

.985   *Bruniales

Including Bruniaceae, Columelliaceae

.986   *Paracryphiales

Class here Paracryphiaceae

.987   *Dipsacales

Including Caprifoliaceae

Including elders, honeysuckles, snowballs, teasels, valerians, viburnums

.988   *Apiales

Including Araliaceae, Pittosporaceae, Torricelliaceae

Including ginsengs, hedge laurel, wild sarsaparilla; comprehensive works on ivies

For ivies of a specific family other than Araliaceae, see the family, e.g., poison ivies 583.75

See also 584.6 for sarsaparilla of family Smilacaceae

.988 2   *Apiaceae

Variant name: Umbelliferae

Including anise, caraway, carrots, celery, dills, parsley, parsnips, poison hemlocks, Queen Anne's lace

*Add as instructed under 583–588

584   *Monocots, basal angiosperms, Chloranthales, magnoliids

Subdivisions are added for monocots, basal angiosperms, Chloranthales, magnoliids together; for monocots alone

See Manual at 583–585 vs. 600; also at 583–584

SUMMARY

584.2	**Basal angiosperms, Chloranthales, magnoliids**
.4	**Acorales, Alismatales, Petrosaviales**
.5	**Dioscoreales and Pandanales**
.6	**Liliales**
.7	**Asparagales**
.8	**Commelinids**
.9	**Poales**

.2   *Basal angiosperms, Chloranthales, magnoliids

Standard subdivisions are added for basal angiosperms, Chloranthales, magnoliids together; for basal angiosperms alone

.22   *Amborellales

Class here Amborellaceae

.23   *Nymphaeales

Including Cabombaceae, Hydatellaceae, Nymphaeaceae

Including water lilies

.24   *Austrobaileyales

Including Austrobaileyaceae, Schisandraceae, Trimeniaceae

Including magnolia vine, star anise

.26   *Chloranthales

Class here Chloranthaceae

.28   *Magnoliids

.282   *Canellales

Including Canellaceae, Winteraceae

Including wild cinnamon, winter's barks

.284   *Piperales

Including Aristolochiaceae, Hydnoraceae, Saururaceae

Including birthwort, black pepper, lizard's-tails, peperomias

Class here Piperaceae

Class here peppers

Class comprehensive works on peppers in 583.9593

---

*Add as instructed under 583–588

.286   *Magnoliales

Including Annonaceae, Magnoliaceae, Myristicaceae

Including cherimoya, cucumber tree, custard apples, lancewoods, mace, magnolias, michelias, nutmegs, papaws, tulip tree, yellow poplar

See also 583.78 for papaws of family Caricaceae

.288   *Laurales

Including Atherospermataceae, Calycanthaceae, Hernandiaceae, Monimiaceae, Siparunaceae

Including avocados, bay laurel, California laurel, cinnamon, Oregon myrtle, sassafras, sweet bay; comprehensive works on laurels

Class here Lauraceae

Class comprehensive works on myrtles in 583.732

For spurge laurel, see 583.77; for laurels of family Ericaceae, see 583.93; for hedge laurel, see 583.988

See Manual at 579–590

>   **584.4–584.9 Monocots**

Class comprehensive works in 584

.4   ***Acorales, Alismatales, Petrosaviales**

.42   *Acorales

.44   *Alismatales

Including Alismataceae, Aponogetonaceae, Butomaceae, Cymodoceaceae, Juncaginaceae, Posidoniaceae, Ruppiaceae, Scheuchzeriaceae, Tofieldiaceae, Zosteraceae

Including arrow grass, arrowheads, eelgrass, lattice plant, water plantains, water poppy, widgeon grass

.442   *Araceae

Including Lemnoideae

Including anthuriums, arums, caladiums, calla lilies, Chinese evergreen, dieffenbachias, duckweeds, elephant's ears, jack-in-the-pulpits, monsteras, philodendrons, skunk cabbages, taro, watermeals

Class comprehensive works on lilies in 584.6

See also 583.78 for cabbages of family Brassicaceae

.445   *Hydrocharitaceae

Including Najas

Including frogbit, naiads, turtle grass

---

*Add as instructed under 583–588

.447   *Potamogetonaceae

Class here pondweeds

.48   *Petrosaviales

.5   *Dioscoreales and Pandanales

.52   *Dioscoreales

Including Burmanniaceae, Dioscoreaceae, Nartheciaceae

Including yams

See also 583.959 for yams of family Convolvulaceae

.55   *Pandanales

Including Cyclanthaceae, Pandanaceae, Stemonaceae, Triuridaceae, Velloziaceae

Including hala, jipijapa, Panama hat palm, screw pines, tree lily

Class comprehensive works on lilies in 584.6

.6   *Liliales

Including Alstroemeriaceae, Colchicaceae, Corsiaceae, Melanthiaceae, Petermanniaceae, Philesiaceae, Smilacaceae

Including carrion flowers, cat briers, Easter lily, greenbriers, Peruvian lily, sarsaparillas, trilliums

Class here comprehensive works on lilies

For a specific lily not provided for here, see the lily, e.g., calla lilies 584.442, tree lilies 584.55, African lilies 584.78

See also 584.23 for water lilies

.69   *Liliaceae

Including tulips

Class here lilies

.7   *Asparagales

Including Asteliaceae, Blandfordiaceae, Boryaceae, Cyanastraceae, Doryanthaceae, Hypoxidaceae, Ixioliriaceae, Lanariaceae, Tecophilaeaceae, Xeronemataceae

.72   *Orchidaceae

Including vanillas

Class here orchids

---

*Add as instructed under 583–588

.75   *Iridaceae

> Including blackberry lily, crocuses, freesias, gladiolus, saffron, sword lilies, tigerflowers
>
> Class here irises

.77   *Xanthorrhoeaceae

> Including aloes, asphodels, day lilies

.78   *Amaryllidaceae

> Including Agapanthoideae, Allioideae
>
> Including African lilies, atamasco lilies, chives, daffodils, garlic, jonquils, leeks, narcissus, onions, shallots, spider lilies
>
> Class here Amaryllidoideae
>
> Class here amaryllises

.79   *Asparagaceae

> Including Agavoideae, Aphyllanthoideae, Brodiaeoideae, Lomandroideae, Nolinoideae
>
> Including agaves, aloe hemp, asparagus, bluebells, century plants, dracaenas, hostas, hyacinths, lily of the valley, plantain lilies, sansevierias, sisal, snake plants, tequila, yuccas
>
> Class comprehensive works on hemps in 583.648
>
> > *See also 583.958 for bluebells of family Boraginaceae; also 583.983 for bluebells of family Campanulaceae; also 584.86 for water hyacinths*

.8   ***Commelinids**

> *For Poales, see 584.9*

.82   *Dasypogonaceae

.84   *Arecales

> Including coconuts, dates, mangrove, nipa palm, palmettos, rattans
>
> Class here Arecaceae, Palmae
>
> Class here palms

.86   *Commelinales

> Including Haemodoraceae, Hanguanaceae, Philydraceae, Pontederiaceae
>
> Including bloodworts, boat lily, spiderworts, wandering Jews, water hyacinths
>
> Class here Commelinaceae

*Add as instructed under 583–588

.88   *Zingiberales

> Including Cannaceae, Costaceae, Heliconiaceae, Marantaceae, Musaceae, Zingiberaceae
>
> Including abaca, arrowroot, bananas, cannas, cardamoms, ginger, ginger lily, heliconias, Manila hemp, plantains, prayer plant, turmeric, zebra plant
>
> Class comprehensive works on hemps in 583.648
>
> *See also 583.96 for plantains of family Plantaginaceae*

.9   *Poales

> Including Anarthriaceae, Centrolepidaceae, Ecdeiocoleaceae, Flagellariaceae, Joinvilleaceae, Rapateaceae, Restionaceae, Xyridaceae
>
> Including yellow-eyed grass

.92   *Poaceae

> Variant name: Gramineae
>
> Including Anomochloeae, Arundinoideae, Chloridoideae, Eragrosteae, Leptureae, Oryzeae, Pappophoreae, Sporobolus, Streptochaeteae, Thysanolaena, Zoysieae
>
> Including pampas grass, rice
>
> Class here grasses

.922   *Bambusoideae

> Including Bambuseae, Olyreae, Parianeae, Phareae
>
> Including bamboos

.924   *Panicoideae

> Including Andropogoneae, Arundinella, Maydeae, Paniceae
>
> Including citronella, corn, crabgrasses, gama grass, lemongrass, maize, millets, milos, panic grasses, proso, sorghums, Sudan grass, sugarcane, thatch grasses

.926   *Pooideae

> Including Agrostis, Festuca, Hordeum, Lygeum, Nardeae, Phalaris, Stipeae, Triticeae
>
> Including barley, bent grasses, bluegrasses, bromegrasses, canary grass, cocksfoot, espartos, fescues, oats, orchard grass, rye, timothy, wheat

*Add as instructed under 583–588

.94   *Cyperaceae

Including beak rushes, Chinese water chestnut, cotton grasses, papyrus, spike rushes, umbrella plant; comprehensive works on bulrushes

Class here sedges

Class comprehensive works on rushes in 584.95

For bulrushes of family Typhaceae, see 584.99

.95   *Juncaceae, Mayacaceae, Thurniaceae

Standard subdivisions are added for Juncaceae, Mayacaceae, Thurniaceae together; for Juncaceae alone

Class here comprehensive works on rushes

For rushes of family Cyperaceae, see 584.94; for rushes of family Typhaceae, see 584.99

.96   *Eriocaulaceae

Including pipeworts

.98   *Bromeliaceae

Including black moss, pineapples, Spanish moss

Class here bromeliads

.99   *Typhaceae

Including Sparganium, Typha

Including bulrushes, bur reeds, cattails

Class comprehensive works on bulrushes in 584.94

585   *Pinophyta

Class here Coniferales, Pinicae

Class here conifers, gymnosperms

See Manual at 583–585 vs. 600

>   **585.2–585.5 Coniferales**

Class comprehensive works in 585

.2   ***Pinaceae**

Including firs, hemlocks, larches, piñons, spruces, tamaracks, true cedars; comprehensive works on cedars

Class here comprehensive works on pines

For dammar pine, Huon pine, New Zealand red pine, see 585.3; for cedars of the cypress family, cypress pine, see 585.4; for China fir, Japanese cedar, Tasmanian cedar, see 585.5

*Add as instructed under 583–588

.3   **Podocarpaceae, Araucariaceae, Cephalotaxaceae**

Including dammar pine, Huon pine, kauris, New Zealand red pine, plum-yews, podocarpuses, Prince Albert's yew, yellowwoods

Subdivisions are added for Podocarpaceae, Araucariaceae, Cephalotaxaceae together; for Podocarpaceae alone

.4   **Cupressaceae**

Including arborvitaes, Chilean cedar, cypress pine, incense cedar, junipers, red cedars

Class here comprehensive works on cypresses

For bald cypresses, see 585.5

.5   **Taxodiaceae**

Including bald cypresses, China fir, Japanese cedar, redwood, sequoias, Tasmanian cedars

.6   **Taxales**

Class here Taxaceae

Class here comprehensive works on yews

For plum-yew and Prince Albert's yew, see 585.3

.7   **Ginkgoales**

Class here Ginkgoaceae

Class here ginkgo, maidenhair tree

.8   **Gneticae**

Including Ephedrales, Gnetales, Gnetum, Welwitschiales

Including ephedras, Mormon tea, tumboa plant

.9   **Cycadales**

Class here Cycadaceae

Class here cycads

586   **Cryptogamia**

Class here seedless plants

For fungi, see 579.5; for algae, see 579.8; for Pteridophyta, see 587; for Bryophyta, see 588

587   **Pteridophyta**

Variant names: vascular cryptogams, vascular seedless plants

---

*Add as instructed under 583–588

.2 ***Sphenopsida**

 Variant names: Articulatae, horsetails

 Class here Equisetales, Equisetaceae, Equisetum

.3 ***Polypodiopsida**

 Variant name: Filicopsida

 Including Marsiliales, Salviniales

 Including bracken, brakes, maidenhair fern, royal fern, spleenworts, staghorn fern, water spangles, waterclovers

 Class here Filicales, Polypodiales

 Class here ferns

 See also 587.4 for whisk ferns

.33 ***Marattiales and Ophioglossales**

 Variant name for Marattiales: giant ferns

 Including adder's-tongues, moonworts; grape, rattlesnake ferns

.4 ***Psilopsida**

 Class here Psilotales

 Class here whisk ferns

.9 ***Lycopsida**

 Including Isoetales, Lycopodiales, Selaginellales

 Including club mosses, quillworts, resurrection plants, spike mosses

 Class here club mosses covering Lycopsida

588 ***Bryophyta**

.2 ***Bryopsida**

 Variant name: Musci

 Including Andreaeales

 Including granite mosses, rock mosses

 Class here Bryales

 Class here true mosses, comprehensive works on mosses

 For club mosses and spike mosses, see 587.9; for bog mosses and peat mosses, see 588.29; for scale mosses, see 588.3

---

*Add as instructed under 583–588

.29 *Sphagnales

> Including Sphagnaceae
>
> Including bog mosses, peat mosses

.3 *Hepatopsida

> Including Anthocerotidae, Marchantiales
>
> Including great liverworts, horned liverworts, hornworts
>
> Class here Hepaticae, Hepatidae, Jungermanniales
>
> Class here leafy liverworts, liverworts, scale mosses
>
> *See also 583.2 for hornworts of family Ceratophyllaceae*

[589]   [Unassigned]

> Most recently used in Edition 20

590   Animals

> Class here natural history of animals; descriptive biology of animals; taxonomic biology of animals; zoology; comprehensive works on biology of animals, interdisciplinary works on animals
>
> Class interdisciplinary works on food from animals in 641.306
>
> *For paleozoology, see 560; for internal biological processes and structures in animals, see 571.1. For a specific aspect of animals, see the aspect, e.g., animal husbandry 636*
>
> *See Manual at 363 vs. 302–307, 333.7, 570–590, 600; also at 577.3–577.7 vs. 579–590; also at 579–590; also at 579–590 vs. 571–575; also at 630 vs. 579–590, 641.3; also at 800, T3C—362 vs. 398.245, 590, 636*

SUMMARY

590.1–.9	**Standard subdivisions**
591	**Specific topics in natural history of animals**
.3	Genetics, evolution, age characteristics
.4	Physical adaptation
.5	Behavior
.6	Miscellaneous nontaxonomic kinds of animals
.7	Animal ecology, animals characteristic of specific environments
.9	Animals by specific continents, countries, localities
592	**Invertebrates**
.3	Worms
.4	Platyhelminthes
.5	Aschelminthes
.6	Annelida
.7	Oncopods

*Add as instructed under 583–588

593		Miscellaneous marine and seashore invertebrates
	.4	Porifera
	.5	Cnidaria
	.6	Anthozoa
	.8	Ctenophora
	.9	Echinodermata and Hemichordata
594		Mollusca and Molluscoidea
	.2	Minor classes of Mollusca
	.3	Gastropoda
	.4	Bivalvia
	.5	Cephalopoda
	.6	Molluscoidea
595		Arthropoda
	.3	Crustacea
	.4	Chelicerata
	.6	Myriapoda
	.7	Insecta
596		Chordata
	.2	Urochordata
	.4	Cephalochordata
597		Cold-blooded vertebrates
	.073	Collections and exhibits of living fishes
	.176 36	Pond ecology
	.2	Agnatha
	.3	Selachii, Holocephali, Sarcopterygii
	.4	Miscellaneous superorders of Actinopterygii
	.5	Protacanthopterygii
	.6	Scopelomorpha, Paracanthopterygii, Acanthopterygii
	.7	Perciformes
	.8	Amphibia
	.9	Reptilia
598		Aves
	.072 3	Descriptive research
	.163–.176	[Beneficial and aquatic birds]
	.3	Gruiformes, Charadriiformes, Ciconiiformes, Phoenicopteriformes
	.4	Miscellaneous orders of water birds
	.5	Palaeognathae
	.6	Galliformes and Columbiformes
	.7	Miscellaneous orders of land birds
	.8	Passeriformes
	.9	Falconiformes, Strigiformes, Caprimulgiformes
599		Mammalia
	.144–.163	[Head and beneficial mammals]
	.2	Marsupialia and Monotremata
	.3	Miscellaneous orders of Eutheria
	.4	Chiroptera
	.5	Cetacea and Sirenia
	.6	Ungulates
	.7	Carnivora
	.8	Primates
	.9	Homo sapiens

.1–.6   Standard subdivisions

> Notation from Table 1 as modified under 578.01–578.06, e.g., microscopy of animals 590.282

.7   Education, research, related topics

.723   Descriptive research

.723 2   Animal marking and census taking

                    Standard subdivisions are added for either or both topics in heading

.723 4   Animal watching

[.723 409 4–.723 409 9]   Specific continents, countries, localities in modern world

                    Do not use; class in 590.72344–590.72349

.723 44–.723 49   Specific continents, countries, localities in modern world

                    Add to base number 590.7234 notation 4–9 from Table 2, e.g.,
                    animal watching in East Africa 590.7234676

.73   Collections and exhibits of living animals

                    Class here general zoos; zoos limited to vertebrates in general, to land
                    vertebrates in general, to mammals in general

                    Add to base number 590.73 notation 1–9 from Table 2 for area in which
                    collections and exhibits are found, e.g., zoos of Germany 590.7343

                    Class zoos limited to other groups of animals with the group, e.g., insect
                    zoos 595.7073, aquariums for marine vertebrates 596.177073

.74   Museums, collections, exhibits

                    Do not use for collections and exhibits of living organisms; class in 590.73

.75   Museum activities and services

.752   Preserving zoological specimens

.8   Groups of people

.9   History, geographic treatment, biography

[.914–.919]   Areas, regions, places in general other than polar, temperate, tropical
                    regions

                    Do not use; class in 591.73–591.77

.93–.99   Zoology by specific continents, countries, localities

                    Class animals by specific continents, countries, localities in 591.9

591   Specific topics in natural history of animals

Class here specific nontaxonomic kinds of animals

Except for modifications shown under specific entries, add to each subdivision identified by † as follows:

01–08   Standard subdivisions

           Notation from Table 1 as modified under 590.1–590.8, e.g.,
           preservation of zoological specimens 0752

09   History, geographic treatment, biography

Unless other instructions are given, observe the following table of preference, e.g., social behavior of beneficial animals 591.56 (*not* 591.63):

Behavior	591.5
Miscellaneous nontaxonomic kinds of animals	591.6
Physical adaptation	591.4
Genetics, evolution, age characteristics	591.3
Animal ecology, animals characteristic of specific environments	591.7
Animals by specific continents, countries, localities	591.9

Class a specific topic in natural history of animals with respect to a specific taxonomic group of animals with the group of animals, plus notation 1 from table under 592–599, e.g., beneficial mammals 599.163

SUMMARY

591.3	Genetics, evolution, age characteristics
.4	Physical adaptation
.5	Behavior
.6	Miscellaneous nontaxonomic kinds of animals
.7	Animal ecology, animals characteristic of specific environments
.9	Animals by specific continents, countries, localities

[.01–.09]   Standard subdivisions

Do not use; class in 590.1–590.9

.3   †Genetics, evolution, age characteristics

Standard subdivisions are added for genetics, evolution, age characteristics together, for genetics and evolution alone

.35   †Genetics

Class here works on genetic constitution of animals that elucidate their total function

Class experimental works on animal genetics, comprehensive works on genetics in 576.5

For biochemical genetics in animals, see 572.81

.38   †Evolution

Class here phylogeny

Class sexual selection in 591.562

†Add standard subdivisions as instructed under 591

.39   †Age characteristics

Class here age determination

.392   †Young animals

.4   †Physical adaptation

Class here animals noted for specific kinds of physical adaptation, comprehensive works on animal adaptation

For behavioral adaptation, see 591.5

.41   †Size, weight, shape

Including silhouettes

.42   †Acclimatization and temperature adaptation

Standard subdivisions are added for acclimatization and temperature adaptation together, for acclimatization alone

For seasonal adaptation, see 591.43

.43   †Seasonal adaptation

.44   †Head

Including ears, eyes, mouth

Class nose in 599.144

For fangs, horns, tusks, see 591.47

.46   †Reproductive adaptation

Class here sex characteristics, secondary sexual characteristics

Class reproductive physiology in 573.6

.468   †Eggs

For physiology of eggs, see 573.68

.47   †Protective and locomotor adaptations, color

Standard subdivisions are added for protective and locomotor adaptations, color together; for protective adaptation alone

Including animal weapons, claws, fangs, horns, tusks; integument

Class here animal defenses

Class physiology of musculoskeletal system in 573.7

For protective behavior, see 591.566

†Add standard subdivisions as instructed under 591

.472	†Camouflage and color
	Standard subdivisions are added for either or both topics in heading
	Class here protective coloration
	Class physiology of color in 573.5; class mimicry in 591.473
.473	†Mimicry
.477	†Protective covering
	Class here exoskeletons, shells, armored animals
.479	†Locomotor adaptation
	Including legs, tracks, wings

.5   †Behavior

Class here animal psychology, behavioral adaptation, ethology

Class comparative psychology of humans and animals in 156; class physiology of nervous system in 573.8; class comprehensive works on animal adaptation in 591.4

See Manual at 302–307 vs. 156

.51	General topics in behavior
	Limited to those named below
	Class general topics related to specific behaviors in 591.53–591.59; class play in 591.563
.512	†Instinct
.513	†Intelligence
.514	†Learning
.518	†Nocturnal behavior
	Class here nocturnal animals
.519	†Sleep
	Class hibernation in 591.565
	For physiology of sleep, see 573.868

> 591.53–591.54 Feeding behavior

Class comprehensive works in 591.53

---

†Add standard subdivisions as instructed under 591

.53 †Predation

    Including food storing and hoarding

    Class here food habits, predator-prey relations; carnivorous animals, predatory animals; comprehensive works on feeding behavior

    Class physiology of eating in 573.35

    For herbivorous feeding, see 591.54

.54 †Herbivorous feeding

    Class here browsing, grazing; herbivorous animals

.56 †Behavior relating to life cycle

    Class here reproductive behavior, social behavior, comprehensive works on life cycle of animals

    Class reproductive physiology in 573.6; class physical reproductive adaptation in 591.46; class interdisciplinary works on sociobiology in 304.5

    For physiology of life cycle of animals, see 571.81; for communication, see 591.59

.562 †Sexual behavior

    Including sexual selection

    Class here courtship, mating

    Class grooming in 591.563

.563 †Family behavior

    Including grooming, kin recognition, play (regardless of kinship)

    Class here maternal behavior, parental behavior

.564 †Making habitations

    Class here nesting, nests

.564 8 †Burrowing

    Class here burrowing animals

    Class comprehensive works on soil animals in 591.757

.565 †Hibernation

    Class physiology of hibernation in 571.787

.566 †Territoriality

    Class here comprehensive works on fighting, on protective behavior

    For fighting during mating, see 591.562; for fighting, protective behaviors during parenting, see 591.563

†Add standard subdivisions as instructed under 591

.568	†Migration

Class here migratory animals

Class physiology of navigation in 573.87

.57	†Locomotion

Including flying, swimming

.59	†Communication

For physiology of communication, see 573.92

.594	†Acoustical communication

Class here animal sounds

Class stridulation in 595.71594; class vocalization in 596.1594

.6	**†Miscellaneous nontaxonomic kinds of animals**

Not provided for elsewhere

Class here economic zoology

See Manual at 630 vs. 579–590, 641.3

.62	†Nonnative animals

Class here alien, exotic, introduced, invasive, naturalized animals

.63	†Beneficial animals

Including game animals

For animals as food source, see 641.306

.65	†Harmful animals

Class here dangerous and poisonous animals, pests

.68	†Rare and endangered animals

Standard subdivisions are added for either or both topics in heading

Including recently extinct, threatened, vanishing species

.7	**Animal ecology, animals characteristic of specific environments**

Standard subdivisions are added for either or both topics in heading

Class here autecology, zoology of specific environments

.701–.708	Standard subdivisions

Notation from Table 1 as modified under 590.1–590.8, e.g., microscopy 591.70282

.709	History, geographic treatment, biography

†Add standard subdivisions as instructed under 591

[.709 14–.709 19] Areas, regions, places in general other than polar, temperate, tropical regions

Do not use; class in 591.73–591.77

.71–.78 Specific topics in animal ecology; specific environments

Add to base number 591.7 the numbers following 577 in 577.1–577.8, e.g., effect of pollution on animals 591.727, marine animals 591.77, effect of pollution on marine animals 591.7727

Class comprehensive works on terrestrial animals in 590

.788 Population biology

Number built according to instructions under 591.71–591.78

For animal marking and census taking, see 590.7232

.9 **Animals by specific continents, countries, localities**

Add to base number 591.9 notation 3–9 from Table 2, e.g., animals in Brazil 591.981

> **592–599 Specific taxonomic groups of animals**

Except for modifications shown under specific entries, add to each subdivision identified by * as follows:
01–08 Standard subdivisions
            Notation from Table 1 as modified under 590.1–590.8, e.g., collections of living animals 073
09   History, geographic treatment, biography
[0914–0919] Areas, regions, places in general other than polar, temperate, tropical regions
            Do not use; class in notation 173–177 from this table
1   General topics of natural history of animals
            Add to 1 the numbers following 591 in 591.3–591.7, e.g., beneficial animals 163, marine animals 177
            Do not add notation from 591.3–591.7 when redundant or nearly so, e.g., marine sponges 593.4 (*not* 593.4177); however, it is not redundant to add notation to specify area, e.g., marine sponges of Atlantic Ocean 593.41773
Class comprehensive works in 590

592 *Invertebrates

For Protozoa, see 579.4; for miscellaneous marine and seashore invertebrates, see 593; for Mollusca and Molluscoidea, see 594; for Arthropoda, see 595

---

*Add as instructed under 592–599

.3 ***Worms**

    Including Echiurida, Phoronida, Pogonophora, Priapulida

    Including beardworms, horseshoe worms, spoonworms

    Class here helminthology

        For Platyhelminthes, see 592.4; for Aschelminthes, see 592.5; for Annelida, see 592.6

        See also 592.7 for oncopods

.32 ***Nemertea**

    Variant names: Nemertina, Rhynchocoela

    Class here bootlace worms, proboscis worms, ribbon worms

.33 ***Acanthocephala**

    Class here spiny-headed worms

.35 ***Sipuncula**

    Class here peanut worms

.38 ***Chaetognatha**

    Class here Sagitta

    Class here arrowworms

.4 ***Platyhelminthes**

    Including Aspidobothria, Aspidocotylea

    Class here flatworms

.42 ***Turbellaria**

    Including Acoela, Alloecoela, Rhabdocoela

    Including planarians

.44 ***Monogenea**

.46 ***Cestoda**

    Class here Eucestoda

    Class here tapeworms

.48 ***Trematoda**

    Including Aspidogastrea

    Class here Digenea

    Class here flukes

*Add as instructed under 592–599

.5	***Aschelminthes**

Class here Nemathelminthes

.52	*Rotifera

Class here rotifers

.53	*Gastrotricha
.55	*Kinorhyncha

Class here Echinodera

See also 593.9 for Echinodermata

.57	*Nematoda

Variant name: Nemata

Including Adenophorea, Secernentea

Class here roundworms

.59	*Nematomorpha

Variant names: hairworms, horsehair worms

Class here Gordioida

.6	***Annelida**

Class here segmented worms

.62	*Polychaeta

Including Archiannelida, Myzostomida, Phyllodocida

.64	*Oligochaeta

Including Haplotaxia, Lumbriculida, Moniligastrida

Class here earthworms, night crawlers

.66	*Hirudinea

Including Arhynchobdellida, Rhynchobdellida

Class here leeches

.7	***Oncopods**

Class here Pararthropoda

.72	*Tardigrada

Class here water bears

.74	*Onychophora
.76	*Pentastomida

Including Linguatula

*Add as instructed under 592–599

593   Miscellaneous marine and seashore invertebrates

Limited to phyla provided for below

See also 592.3177 for marine and seashore worms; also 594 for Mollusca and Molluscoidea; also 595.3 for Crustacea

[.01–.09]   Standard subdivisions

Do not use; class in 592.01–592.09

.4   *Porifera

Class here Parazoa

Class here sponges

.42   *Calcispongiae

Including Calcaronea, Calcinea

Class here Calcarea

.44   *Hyalospongiae

Class here Hexactinellida

Class here glass sponges

.46   *Demospongiae

Including Haplosclerida, Spongillidae

.5   *Cnidaria

Class here Coelenterata

For Anthozoa, see 593.6

.53   *Scyphozoa

Including Coronatae, Cubomedusae, Rhizostomeae, Semaeostomeae, Stauromedusae

Class here comprehensive works on jellyfishes, medusae

For hydrozoan jellyfishes and medusae, see 593.55

.55   *Hydrozoa

Including Chondrophora, Hydroida, Milleporina, Pteromedusae, Siphonophora, Stylasterina, Trachylina

Including hydras, Portuguese man-of-war

Class here hydroids

*Add as instructed under 592–599

.6   ***Anthozoa**

> Including Alcyonaria, Zoantharia (Hexacorallia)
>
> Including fans, pens, sea anemones
>
> Class here corals

.8   ***Ctenophora**

> Including Nuda, Tentaculata
>
> Including sea walnuts
>
> Class here comb jellies

.9   ***Echinodermata and Hemichordata**

> Subdivisions are added for Echinodermata and Hemichordata together, for Echinodermata alone
>
> *See also 592.55 for Echinodera*

>   593.92–593.96 Echinodermata

> Class comprehensive works in 593.9

.92   ***Crinozoa**

> Class here Articulata, Crinoidea
>
> Class here sea lilies

.93   ***Asterozoa**

> Including Concentricycloidea, Forcipulata, Phanerozonia, Spinulosa, Stelleroidea
>
> Class here Asteroidea
>
> Class here starfish
>
> *For Ophiuroidea, see 593.94*

.94   ***Ophiuroidea**

> Including Phrynophiurida
>
> Including basket stars
>
> Class here Ophiurida
>
> Class here brittle stars

*Add as instructed under 592–599

.95   *Echinozoa

> Including Perischoechinoidea
>
> Including sand dollars, sea urchins
>
> Class here Echinoidea, Euechinoidea
>
> *For Holothurioidea, see 593.96*

.96   *Holothurioidea

> Including Apodacea, Aspidochirotacea, Dendrochirotacea
>
> Class here sea cucumbers

.99   *Hemichordata

> Including Enteropneusta, Planctosphaeroidea, Pterobranchia

594   *Mollusca and Molluscoidea

Class here malacology, comprehensive works on shellfish

Subdivisions are added for Mollusca and Molluscoidea together, for Mollusca alone

For crustacean shellfish, see 595.3

>   **594.2–594.5 Mollusca**

Class comprehensive works in 594

.2   *Minor classes of Mollusca

> Including Aplacophora, Caudofoveata, Monoplacophora, Solenogastres

.27   *Polyplacophora

> Variant name: Amphineura
>
> Class here chitons

.29   *Scaphopoda

> Variant names: tooth shells, tusk shells

.3   *Gastropoda

> Including slugs
>
> Class here snails

*Add as instructed under 592–599

.32   *Prosobranchia

        Variant name: Streptoneura

        Including Archaeogastropoda, Mesogastropoda, Neogastropoda

        Including abalones, cowries, whelks; comprehensive works on limpets

         For pulmonate limpets, see 594.38

.34   *Opisthobranchia

        Including Acochlidacea, Cephalaspidea, Gymnosomata, Notaspidea, Philinoglossacea, Pyramidellacea, Thecosomata

        Class here sea slugs

         For Sacoglossa, see 594.35; for Nudibranchia, sea slugs in the sense of Nudibranchia, see 594.36; for Anaspidea, see 594.37

.35   *Sacoglossa

.36   *Nudibranchia

.37   *Anaspidea

        Variant name: Tectibranchia

        Including Pteropoda

        Class here sea hares

.38   *Pulmonata

        Including Basommatophora, Systellommatophora

        Including land slugs

        Class here Stylommatophora

        Class here land snails

.4   ***Bivalvia**

        Including Protobranchia

        Including mussels, oysters, scallops, shipworms

        Class here Lamellibranchia

        Class here clams

.5   ***Cephalopoda**

        Class here Coleoidea

.52   *Nautiloidea

.55   *Vampyromorpha

.56   *Octopoda

        Class here octopuses

---

*Add as instructed under 592–599

.58   *Decapoda

        Including Sepioidea

        Including cuttlefish

        Class here Teuthoidea

        Class here squid

        See also 595.38 for crustacean Decapoda

.6   ***Molluscoidea**

        See also 592.3 for Phoronida

.66   *Entoprocta

.67   *Bryozoa

        Variant names: Ectoprocta, Polyzoa

        Including Cyclostomata, Stenolaemata

        Class here moss animals

.676   *Gymnolaemata

        Including Ctenostomata

        Class here Cheilostomata

.68   *Brachiopoda

        Class here lamp shells

595   *Arthropoda

        Class Pararthropoda in 592.7

SUMMARY

595.3	**Crustacea**	
.4	**Chelicerata**	
.6	**Myriapoda**	
.7	**Insecta**	

.3   ***Crustacea**

.32   *Branchiopoda

        Including Anostraca, Cladocera, Conchostraca, Notostraca

        Including brine shrimps, clam shrimps, fairy shrimps, tadpole shrimps, water fleas

.33   *Ostracoda

        Variant names: mussel shrimps, seed shrimps

        Including Cladocopa, Myodocopa, Platycopa, Podocopa

*Add as instructed under 592–599

.34	*Copepoda

Including Calanoida, Caligoida, Cyclopoida, Harpacticoida, Lernaeopodoida, Monstrilloida, Notodelphyoida

Including cyclops

Class here copepods

.35   *Cirripedia

Including Acrothoracica, Ascothoracica, Rhizocephala, Thoracica

Class here barnacles

.36   *Branchiura, Cephalocarida, Mystacocarida

Including Arguloida

Including fish lice, horseshoe shrimps, mustache shrimps

.37   *Malacostraca

Class here Peracarida

For Eucarida, see 595.38

>   595.372–595.378 Peracarida

Class comprehensive works in 595.37

.372   *Isopoda

Including pill bugs, sow bugs, wood lice

.373   *Thermosbaenacea

.374   *Tanaidacea

.375   *Mysidacea

Class here opossum shrimps

.376   *Cumacea

.378   *Amphipoda

Including beach hoppers, sand fleas, scuds, well shrimps, whale lice

.379   *Phyllocarida, Hoplocarida, Syncarida

.379 2   *Phyllocarida

Class here Leptostraca (Nebaliacea)

.379 6   *Hoplocarida

Class here Stomatopoda

Class here mantis shrimps

*Add as instructed under 592–599

.38 ***Eucarida**

Class here Decapoda, Reptantia

See also 594.58 for cephalopod Decapoda

> 595.384–595.388 Decapoda

Class comprehensive works in 595.38

.384 ***Macrura**

Including crayfishes, lobsters

.386 ***Brachyura**

Class here crabs

See also 595.387 for hermit crabs, king crabs; also 595.492 for horseshoe crabs

.387 ***Anomura**

Including hermit crabs, king crabs

.388 ***Natantia**

Including prawns

Class here Caridea

Class here shrimps

.389 ***Euphausiacea**

Class here krill

.4 ***Chelicerata**

Class here Arachnida

> 595.42–595.48 Arachnida

Class comprehensive works in 595.4

.42 ***Acari**

Variant names: Acarida, Acarina

Including Opilioacariformes

Including chiggers

Class here Acariformes

Class here mites

.429 ***Parasitiformes**

Including ticks

*Add as instructed under 592–599

.43	*Opiliones

        Variant name: Phalangida

        Including daddy longlegs

        Class here harvestmen

.44	*Araneida

        Variant name: Araneae

        Class here spiders

.45	*Minor orders of Arachnida

        Including Schizomida

.452	*Palpigradi
.453	*Uropygi and Amblypygi
.453 2	*Uropygi

        Class here whip scorpions

.453 6	*Amblypygi

        Class here tailless whip scorpions

.455	*Ricinulei
.46	*Scorpiones

        Class here scorpions

.47	*Pseudoscorpiones

        Class here book scorpions

.48	*Solpugida

        Variant name: Solifugae

        Class here sun spiders, weasel spiders, wind scorpions

.49	*Xiphosura and Pycnogonida
.492	*Xiphosura

        Class here horseshoe crabs

.496	*Pycnogonida

        Class here sea spiders

.6	***Myriapoda**
.62	*Chilopoda

        Class here centipedes

.63	*Symphyla

*Add as instructed under 592–599

.64   *Pauropoda

.66   *Diplopoda

> Class here millipedes

.7   *Insecta

> Class here Endopterygota (Holometabola), Hexapoda, Pterygota, Uniramia
>
> Class here entomology, insects
>
> *For Myriapoda, see 595.6*

SUMMARY

595.72	**Apterygota; Orthoptera and related orders**
.73	**Exopterygota**
.74	**Mecoptera, Trichoptera, Neuroptera, Megaloptera, Raphidiodea**
.75	**Homoptera, Heteroptera, Anoplura, Mallophaga, Thysanoptera**
.76	**Coleoptera**
.77	**Diptera and Siphonaptera**
.78	**Lepidoptera**
.79	**Hymenoptera**

.72   *Apterygota; Orthoptera and related orders

> Subdivisions are added for Apterygota, Orthoptera and related orders together; for Apterygota alone

---

>   595.722–595.725   Apterygota

> All orders of Apterygota except Thysanura are sometimes regarded as classes coordinate with Insecta
>
> Class comprehensive works in 595.72

.722   *Protura

.723   *Thysanura

> Including Microcoryphia
>
> Including silverfish
>
> Class here bristletails

.724   *Diplura

> Class here Entotrophi

.725   *Collembola

> Class here springtails

>   595.726–595.729   Orthoptera and related orders
>
> Class comprehensive works in 595.726

*Add as instructed under 592–599

.726	*Orthoptera and Grylloblattodea

Including crickets, grasshoppers, ice bugs, katydids, locusts

Class here comprehensive works on Orthoptera and related orders

Subdivisions are added for Orthoptera and Grylloblattodea together, for Orthoptera alone

> *For Mantodea, see 595.727; for Blattaria, see 595.728; for Phasmida, see 595.729*

.727	*Mantodea

Class here mantises

.728	*Blattaria

Class here comprehensive works on Dictyoptera

Class here cockroaches

> *For Mantodea, see 595.727*

.729	*Phasmida

Including leaf insects, stick insects, walkingsticks

Class here Phasmatodea

.73	*Exopterygota

Class here Hemimetabola

> *For Orthoptera and related orders, see 595.726–595.729; for Homoptera, Heteroptera, Anoplura, Mallophaga, Thysanoptera, see 595.75*

.732	*Psocoptera

Variant name: Corrodentia

Class here book lice

.733	*Odonata

Including damselflies

Class here dragonflies

.734	*Ephemeroptera

Class here mayflies

.735	*Plecoptera

Class here stone flies

.736	*Isoptera

Class here termites

.737	*Embioptera

*Add as instructed under 592–599

.738   *Zoraptera

.739   *Dermaptera

                  Class here earwigs

.74   *Mecoptera, Trichoptera, Neuroptera, Megaloptera, Raphidiodea

.744   *Mecoptera

                  Class here scorpion flies

.745   *Trichoptera

                  Class here caddisflies

.747   *Neuroptera, Megaloptera, Raphidiodea

                  Megaloptera consist of Corydalidae and Sialidae

                  Including alderflies, ant lions, dobsonflies, snakeflies

                  Class here lacewings

                  Subdivisions are added for Neuroptera, Megaloptera, Raphidiodea
                  together; for Neuroptera alone

.75   *Homoptera, Heteroptera, Anoplura, Mallophaga, Thysanoptera

.752   *Homoptera

                  Including aphids, cicadas, hoppers, plant lice, scale insects, whiteflies

                  Class comprehensive works on Homoptera and Heteroptera (sometimes
                  regarded as a single order Hemiptera) in 595.754

.754   *Heteroptera

                  Including bedbugs, water striders

                  Class here Hemiptera whether regarded as a synonym of Heteroptera or
                  as an order including Homoptera and Heteroptera

                  Class here true bugs

                      For Homoptera, see 595.752

.756   *Anoplura

                  Variant name: Siphunculata

                  Class here comprehensive works on Phthiraptera

                  Class here sucking lice, true lice; comprehensive works on apterous
                  insects

                      For Mallophaga, see 595.757

                      See also 595.732 for book lice; also 595.752 for plant lice

.757   *Mallophaga

                  Variant names: bird lice, biting lice, chewing lice

*Add as instructed under 592–599

.758   *Thysanoptera

Class here thrips

>   595.76–595.79 Endopterygota

Class comprehensive works in 595.7

For Mecoptera, Trichoptera, Neuroptera, Megaloptera, Raphidiodea, see 595.74

.76   *Coleoptera

Including Strepsiptera

Class here Polyphaga

Class here beetles

.762   *Adephaga, Archostemata, Myxophaga

Including Carabidae, Cicindelidae, Cupedidae, Dytiscidae, Gyrinidae, Hydroscaphidae

Including ground beetles, reticulated beetles, skiff beetles, tiger beetles, true water beetles, whirligig beetles

Subdivisions are added for Adephaga, Archostemata, Myxophaga together; for Adephaga alone

---

>   595.763–595.769 Polyphaga

Class comprehensive works in 595.76

.763   *Minor superfamilies of Polyphaga

Including Bostrychoidea, Buprestoidea, Byrrhoidea, Cleroidea, Dascilloidea, Dermestoidea, Histeroidea, Hydrophiloidea, Lymexyloidea, Rhipiceroidea

Including checkered beetles, death watch beetles, hister beetles, metallic wood-boring beetles, pill beetles, pine beetles, powder post beetles, ship timber beetles, skin beetles, soft-winged flower beetles, spider beetles, water scavenger beetles

.764   *Staphylinoidea, Cantharoidea, Dryopoidea, Chrysomeloidea, Scarabaeoidea

.764 2   *Staphylinoidea

Including Pselaphidae, Silphidae

Including burying beetles, carrion beetles, mammal nest beetles

Class here Staphylinidae

Class here rove beetles

---

*Add as instructed under 592–599

.764 4   *Cantharoidea

        Including Cantharidae, Lampyridae, Lycidae

        Including fireflies, glowworms, net-winged beetles, soldier beetles

.764 5   *Dryopoidea

        Including Elminidae

        Including riffle beetles

.764 8   *Chrysomeloidea

        Including Cerambycidae, Chrysomelidae, Diabrotica

        Including flea beetles, leaf beetles, wood boring beetles

.764 9   *Scarabaeoidea

        Including Lucanidae

        Including chafers, dung beetles, Japanese beetles, June beetles, pinching bugs, stag beetles, tumble bugs

        Class here Lamellicornia, Scarabaeidae

.765   *Elateroidea

        Including wireworms

        Class here Elateridae

        Class here click beetles, snapping beetles

.768   *Curculionoidea

        Including Anthribidae, Scolytidae

        Including bark beetles, fungus weevils

        Class here Curculionidae

        Class here snout beetles, weevils

.769   *Cucujoidea

        Including Coccinellidae, Colydiidae, Meloidea, Mordellidae, Nitidulidae, Tenebrionidae

        Including blister beetles, cylindrical bark beetles, darkling beetles, flour beetles, ladybugs, mealworms, oil beetles, sap beetles, tumbling flower beetles

.77   *Diptera and Siphonaptera

        Class here flies

        Subdivisions are added for Diptera and Siphonaptera together, for Diptera alone

        Class maggots in 595.771392

---

*Add as instructed under 592–599

> 595.772–595.774 Diptera

Class comprehensive works in 595.77

.772 *Nematocera

Including Bibionidae, Cecidomyiidae, Chironomidae, Culicidae, Psychodidae, Sciaridae, Simuliidae, Tipulidae

Including blackflies, buffalo gnats, crane flies, gall gnats, gall midges, gnats, leatherjackets, March flies, midges, mosquitoes, moth flies

Class here long-horned flies

See also 595.773 for March flies of family Tabanidae

.773 *Brachycera

Variant name: Brachycera-Orthorrhapha

Including Asilidae, Bombyliidae, Dolichopodidae, Empididae, Rhagionidae, Stratiomyidae, Tabanidae, Therevidae

Including bee flies, dance flies, deerflies, horseflies, long-legged flies, March flies, mydas flies, robber flies, snipe flies, soldier flies, stiletto flies

See also 595.772 for March flies of family Bibionidae

.774 *Cyclorrhapha

Variant name: Brachycera-Cyclorrhapha

Including Agromyzidae, Braulidae, Calliphoridae, Chamaemyiidae, Chyromyiidae, Diopsidae, Drosophilidae, Ephydridae, Glossinidae, Hippoboscidae, Muscidae, Oestridae, Phoridae, Piophilidae, Sarcophagidae, Scatophagidae, Sciomyzidae, Syrphidae, Tachinidae, Trypetidae

Including aphid flies, bat flies, beach flies, bee lice, blowflies, botflies, coffin flies, dung flies, flesh flies, flower flies, houseflies, hover flies, humpbacked flies, large fruit flies, leaf miner flies, louse flies, marsh flies, rust flies, shore flies, skipper flies, small fruit flies, stable flies, stalk-eyed flies, tsetse flies, vinegar flies, warble flies

.775 *Siphonaptera

Class here fleas

.78 *Lepidoptera

Including Bombycoidea, Geometroidea, Heliothis, Noctuoidea, Pyralidoidea, Tineoidea, Tortricoidea

Including armyworms, budworms, cutworms

Class here moths

Class caterpillars in 595.781392

*Add as instructed under 592–599

.788   *Hesperioidea

>   Class here skippers

.789   *Papilionoidea

>   Class here butterflies

.79   *Hymenoptera

>   Including Chalcidoidea, Ichneumonoidea, Scolioidea, Symphyta
>
>   Including sawflies
>
>   Class here Apocrita
>
>   Class here wasps, social insects
>
>   Class true wasps of superfamily Vespoidea in 595.798

.796   *Formicidae

>   Class here ants

.798   *Vespoidea and Sphecoidea

>   Class here true wasps
>
>   Subdivisions are added for Vespoidea and Sphecoidea together, for Vespoidea alone
>
>   Class wasps of superfamilies other than Vespoidea and Sphecoidea in 595.79

.799   *Apoidea

>   Class here bees

596   *Chordata

> Class here Tetrapoda, Vertebrata (Craniata)
>
> Class here amniotes, land vertebrates, vertebrates
>
> *For cold-blooded vertebrates, see 597; for Aves, see 598; for Mammalia, see 599*

[.073]   Collections and exhibits of living vertebrates

>   Do not use; class in 590.73

.2   *Urochordata

>   Including Ascidiacea, Larvacea, Thaliacea
>
>   Including sea squirts
>
>   Class here Tunicata

.4   *Cephalochordata

>   Class here lancelets

---

*Add as instructed under 592–599

597 *Cold-blooded vertebrates

Class here Actinopterygii, Osteichthyes, Pisces, Teleostei

Class here bony fishes, fishes, ray-finned fishes; ichthyology

Class specific kinds of Osteichthyes in 597.39 or 597.4–597.7; class specific kinds of Actinopterygii in 597.4–597.7; class specific kinds of Teleostei in 597.43–597.49 or 597.5–597.7

SUMMARY

597.073	**Collections and exhibits of living fishes**
.176 36	**Pond ecology**
.2	**Agnatha**
.3	**Selachii, Holocephali, Sarcopterygii**
.4	**Miscellaneous superorders of Actinopterygii**
.5	**Protacanthopterygii**
.6	**Scopelomorpha, Paracanthopterygii, Acanthopterygii**
.7	**Perciformes**
.8	**Amphibia**
.9	**Reptilia**

.073 Collections and exhibits of living fishes

Class here interdisciplinary works on aquariums

For fish culture in aquariums, see 639.34

.176 36 Pond ecology

Number built according to instructions under 592–599

Class fishpond ecosystems in 577.636

> **597.2–597.7 Pisces**

Class comprehensive works in 597

.2 *Agnatha

Class here Cyclostomata

Class here hagfishes, jawless fishes, lampreys

.3 *Selachii, Holocephali, Sarcopterygii

Class here Carcharhiniformes, Chondrichthyes, Elasmobranchii, Lamniformes covering most sharks

Class here cartilaginous fishes, sharks

Subdivisions are added for Selachii, Holocephali, Sarcopterygii together; for Selachii alone

Class typical sharks of family Carcharhinidae in 597.34; class cartilaginous ganoids in 597.42

*Add as instructed under 592–599

>   597.33–597.36 Selachii

        Class comprehensive works in 597.3

.33   *Lamnidae

        Variant name: Isuridae

        Including mako sharks

        Class here Carcharodon carcharias

        Class here great white shark, mackerel sharks

        Class comprehensive works on Lamniformes in 597.3

.34   *Carcharhinidae

        Variant name: typical sharks

        Including Australian school shark, blacktip shark, bull shark, great blue shark, lemon shark, soupfin shark, tiger shark, tope, whitetip sharks

        Class comprehensive works on Carcharhiniformes in 597.3

.35   *Rajiformes

        Including guitarfishes, sawfishes, skates, torpedoes

        Class here Batoidei

        Class here rays

.36   *Dogfishes

        Including Dalatiidae, Oxynotidae, Triakidae

        Class here Squalidae, Squaliformes

.38   *Holocephali

        Class here Chimaerae, Chimaeriformes

        Class here chimeras, ghost sharks

.39   *Sarcopterygii

        Including Crossopterygii, Dipnoi

        Including barramunda, coelacanths, lungfishes

        Class here fleshy-finned fishes

>   **597.4–597.7 Actinopterygii**

        Class comprehensive works in 597

---

*Add as instructed under 592–599

.4   **Miscellaneous superorders of Actinopterygii**

> Limited to those named below
>
> Class comprehensive works on Actinopterygii in 597

[.401–.409]   Standard subdivisions

> Do not use; class in 597.01–597.09

.41   *Holostei

> Including Amiiformes, Semionotiformes
>
> Including bowfins, gars, river dogfishes
>
> Class here bony ganoids
>
>> See also 597.66 for garfish of order Atheriniformes

.42   *Chondrostei

> Including Polypteriformes
>
> Including bichirs, reedfishes
>
> Class here Acipenseriformes, comprehensive works on Ganoidei
>
> Class here cartilaginous ganoids, paddlefishes, sturgeons
>
>> For bony ganoids, see 597.41

.43   *Elopomorpha

> Including Elopiformes, Notacanthiformes, Saccopharyngidae
>
> Including congers, morays, swallowers, tarpons
>
> Class here Anguilliformes
>
> Class here comprehensive works on eels
>
>> For a specific kind of nonanguilliform eel, see the kind, e.g., electric eels 597.48, swamp eels 597.64
>>
>> See also 597.7 for swallowers of family Chiasmodontidae

.432   *Anguillidae

> Class here Anguilla
>
> Class here freshwater eels
>
> Subdivisions are added for the family as a whole and for individual species

---

*Add as instructed under 592–599

.45   *Clupeomorpha

         Including anchovies, menhadens, pilchards, sardines, shads

         Class here Clupeidae, Clupeiformes

         Class here herrings

         Class sardines in sense of young bristling and herring in 597.452

.452   *Clupea

         Class here bristling, common herring, sprat

         Young bristling and common herring are often called sardines

         Class true sardine in 597.45

.47   *Osteoglossomorpha

         Including Mormyriformes, Osteoglossiformes

         Including elephant fishes, freshwater butterfly fishes

         See also 597.72 for marine butterfly fishes

\>   597.48–597.49 Ostariophysi

         Class Gonorhynchiformes in 597.5; class comprehensive works in 597.48

.48   *Cypriniformes

         Including Characidae, Citharinidae, Gasteropelecidae, Gymnotidae

         Including characins, electric eels, freshwater hatchetfishes, headstanders, knifefishes, loaches, moonfishes, pencil fishes, piranhas, suckers, tetras, tigerfishes

         Class here Characiformes, comprehensive works on Ostariophysi

         For Siluriformes, see 597.49

         See also 597.5 for marine hatchetfishes; also 597.66 for Cyprinodontoidei; also 597.7 for moonfishes of order Perciformes

.482   *Cyprinidae

         Including barbels, barbs, bighead carp, bream, chubs, daces, danios, freshwater zebra fishes, grass carp, roach, shiners, squawfishes, tench

         Class here carps, minnows

         For Cyprinus carpio, see 597.483; for Carassius, see 597.484

         See also 597.68 for marine zebra fishes

.483   *Cyprinus carpio

         Class here common carp

         Class koi in 639.37483; class interdisciplinary works on carp in 641.392

---

*Add as instructed under 592–599

.484   *Carassius

       Class here goldfish

       Class interdisciplinary works on goldfish in 639.37484

.49   *Siluriformes

       Class here catfishes

.492   *Ictaluridae

       Including Noturus

       Including madtoms

       Class here Ictalurus

       Class here blue catfish, bullheads, channel catfish, North American freshwater catfishes

       Subdivisions are added for Ictaluridae as a whole and for individual species of Ictalurus

.5   ***Protacanthopterygii**

       Including Gonorhynchiformes, Sternoptychidae, Stomiiformes (Stomiatiformes)

       Including marine hatchetfishes, milkfish, mudminnows, smelts, stomiatoid dragonfishes, viperfishes

       Class here Salmoniformes

       Class Myctophiformes in 597.61

         See also 597.48 for freshwater hatchetfishes; also 597.64 for dragonfishes of order Pegasiformes

>   597.55–597.59 Salmoniformes

       Class comprehensive works in 597.5

.55   *Salmonidae

       Including Australian grayling, whitefishes, whitings

       Class brook trout, Dolly Varden trout, lake trout, speckled trout in 597.554

         For salmon, see 597.56; for trout of genus Salmo, see 597.57

         See also 597.633 for whitings of genus Gadus; also 597.72 for rock whiting; also 597.725 for whiting of family Sciaenidae

.554   *Salvelinus

       Class here brook trout, chars, Dolly Varden trout, lake trout, speckled trout

       Subdivisions are added for the genus as a whole and for individual species

---

*Add as instructed under 592–599

.559   *Thymallus

    Class here graylings

    Subdivisions are added for the genus as a whole and for individual species

    Class Australian grayling in 597.55

.56   *Salmon

    Class here Salmo salar, comprehensive works on Oncorhynchus

    Class here Atlantic salmon, Pacific salmon

    Subdivisions are added for salmon as a whole and for individual species of salmon

    For Rhabdofario, see 597.57

    See also 597.7 for Australian salmon

.57   *Trout

    Species of subgenus Rhabdofario and genus Salmo other than Salmo salar

    Class here comprehensive works on Salmo

    Subdivisions are added for trout as a whole and for individual species

    For Salmo salar, comprehensive works on Oncorhynchus, see 597.56

    See also 597.554 for brook trout, Dolly Varden trout, lake trout, speckled trout

.59   *Esocidae

    Class here Esox

    Class here muskellunge, muskie, pickerels, pikes

    Subdivisions are added for the family as a whole and for individual species

    Class comprehensive works on Esociformes in 597.5

    See also 597.758 for walleyed pike

.6   Scopelomorpha, Paracanthopterygii, Acanthopterygii

    Class comprehensive works in 597

[.601–.609]   Standard subdivisions

    Do not use; class in 597.01–597.09

.61   *Scopelomorpha

    Including Myctophidae, Synodontidae

    Including lantern fishes, lizard fishes, spiderfishes

    Class here Myctophiformes

*Add as instructed under 592–599

.62 *Paracanthopterygii

Including Batrachoidiformes, Gobiesociformes, Percopsiformes, Polymixiiformes

Including anglerfishes, batfishes, beard fishes, cavefishes, clingfishes, frogfishes, goosefishes, toadfishes, trout-perches

Class here Lophiiformes

> *For cave fishes of superorder Ostariophysi, see 597.48; for Gadiformes, see 597.63*

.63 *Gadiformes

Including Carapidae (Carapodidae), Macrouridae, Moridae, Ophidiidae, Zoarcidae

Including brotulas, cusk eels, deep sea cods, eelpouts, grenadiers, pearlfishes

.632 *Gadidae, Merluciidae, Pycidae

Including arctic cod, burbots, haddocks, hakes, Merlucciid hakes, Phycid hakes, pollocks

Class here Gadoidei

Subdivisions are added for Gadidae, Merluciidae, Pycidae together, for Gadidae alone

> *For Gadus, see 597.633*

.633 *Gadus

Class here Atlantic cod, cods, Greenland cod, Pacific cod, whitings

> *See also 597.55 for whitings of family Salmonidae; also 597.63 for deep sea cods; also 597.632 for arctic cod; also 597.72 for rock whitings; also 597.725 for whiting of family Sciaenidae*

.64 *Acanthopterygii

Including Beryciformes, Channiformes, Dactylopteriformes, Lampridiformes, Pegasiformes, Synbranchiformes, Tetraodontiformes, Zeiformes

Including alfonsinos, boar fishes, boxfishes, cowfishes, dragonfishes, filefishes, John Dories, lantern-eyed fishes, oarfishes, ocean sunfishes, opah, orange roughy, pinecone fishes, porcupine fishes, puffer fishes, seamoths, snakeheads, soldierfishes, squirrelfishes, swamp eels, triggerfishes, unicorn fishes, whale fishes

Class here spiny-rayed fishes

> *For Atheriniformes, see 597.66; for Gasterosteiformes, see 597.67; for Scorpaeniformes, see 597.68; for Pleuronectiformes, see 597.69; for Perciformes, see 597.7*

> *See also 597.2 for lampreys; also 597.5 for stomiatoid dragonfishes*

---

*Add as instructed under 592–599

.66	*Atheriniformes

Including Cyprinodontoidei, Exocoetidae

Including flying fishes, garfish, halfbeaks, needlefishes, silversides, topminnows

Class Cyprinodontidae and topminnows of families Cyprinodontidae and Poeciliidae in 597.665–597.667

See also 597.41 for gars of order Semionotiformes; also 597.48 for Cypriniformes

.665	*Cyprinodontidae

Class here killifishes

.667	*Poeciliidae

Including guppies, mollies, platy, swordtail

Class here live-bearers

.67	*Gasterosteiformes

Including ghost pipefishes, trumpet fishes

.672	*Gasterosteidae

Class here sticklebacks

Subdivisions are added for the family as a whole and for individual genera and species

.679	*Syngnathidae

Class here pipefishes

Subdivisions are added for the family as a whole and for individual species of pipefishes

Class ghost pipefishes in 597.67

.679 8	*Sea horses

Class here Hippocampus

Subdivisions are added for sea horses as a whole and for individual genera and species

.68	*Scorpaeniformes

Including gurnards, marine zebra fishes, rockfishes, scorpion fishes

See also 597.482 for freshwater zebra fishes

*Add as instructed under 592–599

.69 ***Pleuronectiformes**

Variant name: Heterosomata

Including California halibut, soles, turbots

Class here flatfishes, flounders

Class turbot of family Pleuronectidae in 597.694

.694 ***Pleuronectidae**

Including Greenland halibut, plaice, winter flounder

Class here right-eyed flounders

For Hippoglossus, see 597.695

.695 ***Hippoglossus**

Class here halibuts

Subdivisions are added for the genus as a whole and for individual species

See also 597.69 for California halibut; also 597.694 for Greenland halibut

.7 ***Perciformes**

Including Chiasmodontidae, Mugilidae

Including Australian salmon, barracudas, betta, big game fishes, cardinal fishes, goatfishes, gobies, grunts, halfmoons, labyrinth fishes, moonfishes, mullets, parrotfishes, Siamese fighting fish, spiny eels, stargazers, swallowers, wrasses

Class here Percoidei

See also 597.43 for swallowers of family Saccopharyngidae; also 597.48 for moonfishes of family Citharinidae

.72 ***Percoidea**

Including Centropomidae, Chaetodontidae, Latidae, Lethrinidae, Lutjanidae, Pomacanthidae, Pomacentridae, Sparidae

Including damselfishes, dolphinfishes, garibaldi, giant perches, jacks, marine butterfly fishes, porgies, robalos, rock whiting, scups, sea breams, snappers, snooks; comprehensive works on angelfishes

For basses and related fishes, see 597.73; for Cichlidae, angelfishes of cichlid family, see 597.74; for Percidae, see 597.75

See also 597.47 for freshwater butterfly fishes

*Add as instructed under 592–599

.725   *Sciaenidae

    Variant names: croakers, drums

    Including Sciaenops

    Including channel bass, kingfish, red drum, weakfish, whiting

     See also 597.55 for whitings of family Salmonidae; also 597.633 for whitings of genus Gadus; also 597.72 for rock whiting

.73   *Basses and related fishes

    Including Grammatidae, Percichthyidae

    Including Australian bass, basslets, macquarie perch, perch trout, temperate basses

    Subdivisions are added for basses and related fishes together, for basses alone

    For channel bass, see 597.725

.732   *Moronidae

    Class here Morone

    Class here striped bass, white bass, white perch

.736   *Serranidae

    Including graysby, groupers

    Class here sea basses

.738   *Centrarchidae

    Including calico basses, crappies, rock bass

    Class here sunfishes

.738 8   *Micropterus

    Class here black basses, largemouth bass, smallmouth bass

    Subdivisions are added for the genus as a whole and for individual species

.74   *Cichlidae

    Including Pterophyllum, Symphysodon

    Including angelfishes, discus fishes, tilapias

    Class comprehensive works on angelfishes in 597.72

.75   *Percidae

    Including perches

    Class here darters

    See also 597.72 for giant perches; also 597.732 for white perch

---

*Add as instructed under 592–599

.758   *Stizostedion

    Variant name: Lucioperca

    Class here pike perches, sauger, walleye, walleyed pike, zander

.77   *Blennioidei

    Class here blennies

.78   *Scombroidei

    Including Gempylidae, Istiophoridae, Trichiuridae, Xiphiidae

    Including billfishes, cutlass fishes, marlins, sailfishes, spearfishes, swordfish

.782   *Scombridae

    Class here mackerel

    For tunas, see 597.783

.783   *Tunas

    Class here Thunnus

    Class here albacore, bonito, skipjack

    Subdivisions are added for tunas as a whole and for individual species

.8   ***Amphibia**

    Class here Anura, Salientia

    Class here amphibians

    Class herpetology, comprehensive works on Amphibia and Reptilia in 597.9

.82   *Gymnophiona

    Variant names: Apoda, Caecilians

.85   *Urodela

    Variant name: Caudata

    Including Sirenidae

    Including congo eels, hellbender, mud puppies, newts, sirens

    Class here salamanders

.858   *Ambystomatidae

    Class here Ambystoma

    Class here axolotl, mole salamanders

    Subdivisions are added for the genus Ambystoma and for individual species of Ambystoma

.859   *Plethodontidae

    Class here lungless salamanders

*Add as instructed under 592–599

.859 2   *Plethodon

              Subdivisions are added for the genus as a whole and for individual species

---

\>   597.86–597.89 Anura

          Class comprehensive works in 597.8

.86   *Pipoidea, Discoglossoidea, Pelobatoidea

          Including fire-bellied toads, midwife toads, spadefoots

          Class comprehensive works on toads in 597.87; class comprehensive works on frogs in 597.89

.865   *Pipoidea

          Including burrowing toads, Surinam toad

          Class here Pipidae

          Class here tongueless frogs

.865 4   *Xenopus

            Class here African clawed frog

            Subdivisions are added for the genus as a whole and for individual species

.87   *Bufonoidea

          Including Centrolenidae, Rhinodermatidae

          Including leaf frogs, mouth-breeding frogs

          Class here Bufonidae

          Class here comprehensive works on toads

          Class comprehensive works on frogs and toads in 597.8

            For a specific kind of toad of a superfamily other than Bufonoidea, see the kind, e.g., midwife toads 597.86

.872   *Bufo

          Subdivisions are added for the genus as a whole and for individual species

.875   *Leptodactylidae

.875 4   *Eleutherodactylus

            Subdivisions are added for the genus as a whole and for individual species

.877   *Dendrobatidae

          Class here poison arrow frogs

*Add as instructed under 592–599

.878	*Hylidae

Class here tree frogs

.878 2	*Hyla

Subdivisions are added for the genus as a whole and individual species

.89	*Ranoidea

Including Microhylidae

Class here Ranidae

Class here comprehensive works on frogs

> *For a specific kind of frog of a superfamily other than Ranoidea, see the kind, e.g., tree frogs 597.878*

.892	*Rana

Class here bullfrogs

Subdivisions are added for the genus as a whole and for individual species

.9	***Reptilia**

Class here comprehensive works on Amphibia and Reptilia

Class here herpetology, reptiles

> *For Amphibia, see 597.8*

SUMMARY

597.92	**Chelonia**
.94	**Lepidosauria**
.95	**Sauria**
.96	**Serpentes**
.98	**Crocodilia**

.92	*Chelonia

Variant name: Testudines

Class here Testudinoidea

Class here turtles

[.921 77]	Marine turtles

Do not use; class in 597.928

.922	*Chelydridae

Class here snapping turtles

Subdivisions are added for the family as a whole and for individual genera and species

*Add as instructed under 592–599

.923   *Kinosternidae

     Including musk turtles

     Class here Kinosternon

     Class here mud turtles

     Subdivisions are added for the genus Kinosternon as a whole and for individual species of Kinosternon

.924   *Testudinidae

     Variant names: terrestrial turtles, tortoises

.924 6   *Geochelone

     Including Galapagos tortoise

.925   *Emydidae

     Including Terrapene

     Including North American box turtles

     Class here terrapins

.925 7   *Clemmys

     Class here bog turtle, spotted turtle, wood turtle

     Subdivisions are added for the genus as a whole and for individual species

.925 9   *Chrysemys, Pseudemys, Deirochelys, Graptemys, Malaclemys, Trachemys

     Including chicken turtle, diamond-backed terrapin, map turtles, sliders

.925 92   *Chrysemys

     Class here painted turtle

.925 94   *Pseudemys

     Class here cooters, red-bellied turtles

     Subdivisions are added for the genus as a whole and for individual species

.926   *Trionychidae, Carettochelyidae, Dermatemydidae, Platysternidae

     Including New Guinea plateless turtle

     Class here soft-shelled turtles

     Subdivisions are added for Trionychidae, Carettochelyidae, Dermatemydidae, Platysternidae together; for Trionychidae alone

*Add as instructed under 592–599

.928   *Chelonioidea

              Class here Cheloniidae

              Class here marine turtles, sea turtles

              Subdivisions are added for the family Cheloniidae and for individual genera and species of Cheloniidae

.928 9   *Dermochelyidae

              Class here leatherback turtle

.929   *Pleurodira

              Including Chelyidae, Pelomedusidae

              Including snake-necked turtles

              Class here side-necked turtles

.94   *Lepidosauria

              Class here Squamata

              Class here scaly reptiles

              For Sauria, see 597.95; for Serpentes, see 597.96

.945   *Rhynchocephalia

              Class here Sphenodontidae

              Class here beaked reptiles, tuatara

.948   *Amphisbaenia

              Class here Amphisbaenidae

              Class here worm lizards

.95   *Sauria

              Class here lizards

              Class comprehensive works on Sauria and Serpentes in 597.94

.952   *Gekkonidea

              Including Anelytropsidae, Dibamidae, Pygopodidae

              Including flap-footed lizards

              Class here Gekkonidae

              Class here geckos

.954   *Iguanidae

              Class here Iguanioidea

              For Agamidae, see 597.955

.954 2   *Iguanas

*Add as instructed under 592–599

.954 8   *Anolis

    Class here anoles, false chameleons, New World chameleons

.955   *Agamidae

    Including Draco

    Including flying lizards

.956   *Chamaeleontidae

    Class here Rhiptoglossidea

    Class here chameleons

    Subdivisions are added for the family as a whole and for individual genera and species

      See also 597.9548 for false chameleons, New World chameleons

.957   *Scincidae

    Class here Scincomorphoidea

    Class here skinks

      For Teiidae, Cordylidae, Lacertidae, see 597.958

.957 3   *Eumeces

.958   *Teiidae, Cordylidae, Lacertidae

    Including girdle-tailed lizards, Old World runners

.958 2   *Teiidae

    Including Ameiva

    Class here New World runners

.958 25   *Cnemidophorus

    Variant names: racerunners, whiptails

    Subdivisions are added for the genus as a whole and for individual species

.959   *Anguinomorphoidea

    Including Anniellidae, Xenosauridae

    Including California legless lizards

.959 2   *Anguidae

    Including alligator lizards, glass lizards

.959 5   *Helodermatidae

    Including beaded lizard

    Class here Heloderma

---

*Add as instructed under 592–599

.959 52	*Heloderma suspectum
	Class here Gila monster
.959 6	*Varanidae and Lanthanotidae
	Including earless monitor lizard
	Class here Varanus
	Class here monitor lizards
	Subdivisions are added for Varanidae and Lanthanotidae together, for Varanidae alone
.959 68	*Varanus komodoensis
	Class here Komodo dragon
.959 8	*Xantusiidae
	Class here night lizards
.96	*Serpentes
	Class here Colubroidea
	Class here snakes
[.961 77]	Marine snakes
	Do not use; class in 597.965
.962	*Colubridae
	Including egg-eating snakes, false coral snakes
	Class here Colubrinae
	See also 597.967 for false coral snake of family Aniliidae
.963	*Viperidae
	Class here adders, vipers
	Class death adders in 597.964
.963 6	*Vipera
	Class here asp, common adder, Lebanese adder, Portuguese adder, sand adder
	Subdivisions are added for the genus as a whole and for individual species
.963 8	*Crotalus and Sistrurus
	Including pigmy rattlesnakes
	Class here rattlesnakes
	Subdivisions are added for Crotalus and Sistrurus together, for Crotalus alone, for individual species of Crotalus

*Add as instructed under 592–599

.964   *Elapidae

    Including death adders

.964 2   *Cobras

    Class here Naja

    Subdivisions are added for the genus Naja and for individual species of Naja

.964 4   *Coral snakes

    Class here Micrurus

    Subdivisions are added for the genus Micrurus and for individual species of Micrurus

        See also 597.962 for false coral snakes of family Colubridae; also 597.967 for false coral snake of family Aniliidae

.965   *Hydrophiidae

    Class here marine snakes, sea snakes

.967   *Booidea

    Including Acrochordidae, Aniliidae, Uropeltidae, Xenopeltidae

    Including anacondas, false coral snake, pipe snakes, shieldtail snakes, sunbeam snakes, wart snakes, wood snakes

    Class here Boidae, Boinae, Henophidia

    Class here boas

        See also 597.962 for false coral snake of family Colubridae

.967 8   *Pythoninae

    Class here Python

    Class here pythons

    Subdivisions are added for the genus Python and for individual species of Python

.969   *Typhlopoidea

    Including Leptotyphlopidae, Typhlopidae

    Including blind snakes, slender blind snakes, worm snakes

    Class here Scolecophidia

.98   *Crocodilia

    Including gavial

    Class here crocodilians

---

*Add as instructed under 592–599

.982   *Crocodilidae

>   Class here Crocodylus
>
>   Class here crocodiles
>
>   Subdivisions are added for the genus Crocodylus and for individual species of Crocodylus

.984   *Alligatoridae

>   Including caimans
>
>   Class here Alligator mississippiensis
>
>   Class here alligators

598   *Aves

>   Class here birds, land birds; ornithology
>
>   Class specific kinds of land birds in 598.5–598.9; class comprehensive works on warm-blooded vertebrates in 599; class interdisciplinary works on species of domestic birds in 636.5

SUMMARY

598.072 3	**Descriptive research**
.163–.176	**[Beneficial and aquatic birds]**
.3	**Gruiformes, Charadriiformes, Ciconiiformes, Phoenicopteriformes**
.4	**Miscellaneous orders of water birds**
.5	**Palaeognathae**
.6	**Galliformes and Columbiformes**
.7	**Miscellaneous orders of land birds**
.8	**Passeriformes**
.9	**Falconiformes, Strigiformes, Caprimulgiformes**

.072 3   Descriptive research

.072 32   Bird marking and census taking

>   Number built according to instructions under 592–599
>
>   Class here birdbanding

[.072 340 94–.072 340 99]   Specific continents, countries, localities in modern world

>   Do not use; class in 598.072344–598.072349

.072 344–.072 349   Specific continents, countries, localities in modern world

>   Add to base number 598.07234 notation 4–9 from Table 2, e.g., bird watching in East Africa 598.07234676

.163   Beneficial birds

>   Number built according to instructions under 592–599
>
>   Including game birds, wildfowl
>
>   Class lowland game birds, waterfowl in 598.41; class upland game birds in 598.6

---

*Add as instructed under 592–599

.176 Aquatic birds

> Number built according to instructions under 592–599

> Class here water birds

> Class waterfowl in 598.41

> *For specific kinds of water birds, see 598.3–598.4*

> **598.3–598.4 Water birds**

> Class comprehensive works in 598.176

.3 ***Gruiformes, Charadriiformes, Ciconiiformes, Phoenicopteriformes**

> Class here wading birds

.32 *Gruiformes

> Including Gruidae, Otididae, Psophiidae, Rallidae, Turnicidae

> Including bustards, button quails, coots, cranes, gallinules, rails, trumpeters

.33 *Charadriiformes

> Including Alcidae, Charadriidae, Haematopodidae, Jacanidae, Phalaropodidae, Scolopacidae

> Including auks, jacanas, lapwings, murres, oystercatchers, phalaropes, plovers, puffins, sandpipers, snipes, turnstones, woodcocks

> Class here Charadrii

> Class here shore birds

.338 *Lari

> Including Rynchopidae, Stercorariidae

> Including jaegers, skimmers, skuas

> Class here Laridae

> Class here gulls, terns

.34 *Ciconiiformes

> Including Ardeidae, Ciconiidae, Threskiornithidae

> Including bitterns, egrets, herons, ibis, spoonbills, storks

> Class Charadriiformes in 598.33

---

*Add as instructed under 592–599

.35   *Phoenicopteriformes

        Class here Phoenicopteridae

        Class here flamingos

        Subdivisions are added for the genus Phoenicopterus and for individual species of Phoenicopterus

.4   Miscellaneous orders of water birds

        Limited to those named below

        Class comprehensive works on water birds in 598.176

[.401–.409]   Standard subdivisions

        Do not use; class in 598.17601–598.17609

.41   *Anseriformes

        Including Anhimidae

        Including screamers

        Class here Anatidae

        Class here ducks, waterfowl; comprehensive works on lowland game birds

        For a specific kind of lowland game bird, see the kind, e.g., murres 598.33

>   598.412–598.415 Ducks

        Class comprehensive works in 598.41

.412   *Aix

        Including mandarin duck

.412 3   *Aix sponsa

        Class here wood duck

.413   *Anas

        Including black duck, blue-winged teal

.413 4   *Anas platyrhynchos

        Class here mallard

.414   *Aythya

        Including canvasback

.415   *Mergini

        Including eiders, goldeneyes, mergansers

---

*Add as instructed under 592–599

.417 *Anserini

    Class here geese

.417 3 *Anser

    Including greylag goose, white-fronted geese

.417 5 *Chen

    Class here blue goose, snow goose

.417 8 *Branta

    Class here Canada goose

.418 *Cygninae

    Class here Cygnus

    Class here swans

.418 4 *Cygnus buccinator

    Class here trumpeter swan

.418 7 *Cygnus olor

    Class here mute swan

.42 *Procellariiformes

    Including Diomedeidae, Hydrobatidae, Pelecanoididae, Procellariidae

    Including albatrosses, diving petrels, fulmars, shearwaters, storm petrels

.43 *Pelecaniformes

    Including Fregatidae, Pelecanidae, Phaethontidae, Phalacrocoracidae, Sulidae

    Including boobies, cormorants, frigate birds, pelicans, tropic birds

.44 *Gaviiformes and Podicipediformes

    Class here Colymbiformes

.442 *Gaviiformes

    Class here loons

.443 *Podicipediformes

    Class here Podicipedidae

    Class here grebes

.47 *Sphenisciformes

    Class here penguins

*Add as instructed under 592–599

> **598.5–598.9 Land birds**

Class comprehensive works in 598

.5 ***Palaeognathae**

Class here ratites

.52 *Rheiformes and Struthioniformes

.522 *Rheiformes

Subdivisions are added for the genus Rhea as a whole and for individual species of Rhea

.524 *Struthioniformes

Class here ostrich

.53 *Casuariiformes

Including emu

Class here Casuariidae

Class here cassowaries

Subdivisions are added for the genus Casuarius and for individual species of Casuarius

.54 *Apterygiformes

Class here kiwis

Subdivisions are added for the genus Apteryx and for individual species of Apteryx

Sometimes classed with extinct moas as Dinornithiformes

.55 *Tinamiformes

Class here Tinamidae

Class here tinamous

.6 ***Galliformes and Columbiformes**

Class here Galli

Class here poultry; comprehensive works on upland game birds

Subdivisions are added for Galliformes and Columbiformes together, for Galliformes alone

Class interdisciplinary works on domestic poultry in 636.5

For a specific kind of upland game bird, see the kind, e.g., crows 598.864

---

*Add as instructed under 592–599

>   598.62–598.64 Galliformes

Class comprehensive works in 598.6

.62   *Phasianidae

.623   *Partridges

Including francolins

.623 2   *Perdix perdix

Variant names: common partridge, gray partridge, Hungarian partridge

.625   *Pheasants

Including Gallus

Including chickens, jungle fowl

Class results of experimental studies in internal biological processes using chickens in 571–573, plus notation 18625 from add instructions in 571–573, e.g., embryology in domestic chickens 571.8618625; class interdisciplinary works on chickens in 636.5

.625 2   *Phasianus colchicus

Class here ring-necked pheasant

.625 8   *Pavo

Class here peafowl

Subdivisions are added for the genus as a whole, and for individual species

.627   *Quails

Including Gambel's quail

See also 598.32 for button quails

.627 2   *Coturnix

Including common quail, Japanese quail

See also 598.6273 for bobwhites

.627 3   *Colinus

Class here bobwhites

Subdivisions are added for the genus as a whole and for individual species

.63   *Tetraonidae

Class here grouse

See also 598.65 for sand grouse

*Add as instructed under 592–599

.633   *Lagopus

        Class here ptarmigans

        Subdivisions are added for the genus as a whole and for individual species

.634   *Tetrao

        Including black grouse, capercaillies

.635   *Bonasa

        Class here ruffed grouse

.636   *Centrocercus

        Class here sage grouse

.637   *Tympanuchus

        Subdivisions are added for either of both species of prairie chickens

.637 8   *Tympanuchus phasianellus

        Class here sharp-tailed grouse

.64   *Other families of Galliformes

        Including Cracidae, Megapodiidae, Numididae

        Including brush turkeys, chachalacas, curassows, guans, Guinea fowl, mound builders

.645   *Meleagrididae

        Class here Meleagris gallopavo

        Class here turkeys, wild turkeys

        Class interdisciplinary works on turkeys in 636.592

.65   *Columbiformes

        Including Pteroclididae

        Including dodos, sand grouse

        Class here Columbidae

        Class here doves, pigeons

.7   **Miscellaneous orders of land birds**

        Limited to those named below

        Class comprehensive works on land birds in 598

[.701–.709]   Standard subdivisions

        Do not use; class in 598.01–598.09

---

*Add as instructed under 592–599

.71   *Psittaciformes

 Including budgerigars, cockatoos, kakapo, lories, macaws, parakeets, rosellas

 Class here Psittacidae

 Class here parrots

.72   *Piciformes

 Including Bucconidae, Capitonidae, Galbulidae, Indicatoridae, Picidae, Ramphastidae

 Including barbets, honey guides, jacamars, puffbirds, toucans, woodpeckers

 Class here Pici

.73   *Trogoniformes

 Including quetzals

 Class here Trogonidae

 Class here trogons

.74   *Cuculiformes

 Including Cuculidae, Musophagidae, Opisthocomidae

 Including anis, cuckoos, hoatzin, roadrunners, touracos

.75   *Coliiformes

 Class here Coliidae

 Class here mousebirds

.76   *Apodiformes

.762   *Apodi

 Including Hemiprocnidae

 Including tree swifts

 Class here Apodidae

 Class here swifts, true swifts

.764   *Trochili

 Class here Trochilidae

 Class here hummingbirds

.78   *Coraciiformes

 Including Alcedinidae, Bucerotidae, Corcaciidae, Meropidae

 Including bee eaters, hornbills, kingfishers, rollers

*Add as instructed under 592–599

.8 ***Passeriformes**

Including bell magpies, cuckoo shrikes, honey eaters, magpie larks, vanga shrikes, wattled crows, wood shrikes, wood swallows

Class here Oscines, Passeres

Class here perching birds, songbirds

See Manual at 598.824–598.88

.82 *Nonoscine Passeriformes, Paridae, Alaudidae, Hirundinidae, Certhiidae, Sittidae

Including creepers, nuthatches

.822 *Nonoscine Passeriformes

Including Cotingidae, Dendrocolaptidae, Eurylaimidae, Menuridae, Pipridae, Pittidae

Including broadbills, cotingas, lyrebirds, manakins, pittas, woodcreepers

For Tyrannidae, see 598.823

.822 5 *Furnariidae

Class here ovenbirds

.822 6 *Formicariidae

Class here antbirds

.823 *Tyrannidae

Variant names: New World flycatchers, tyrant flycatchers

See also 598.848 for Old World flycatchers

.824 *Paridae

Including chickadees

Class here titmice

.825 *Alaudidae

Class here larks

Class magpie larks in 598.8

See also 598.874 for meadowlarks

.826 *Hirundinidae

Including martins

Class here swallows

Class wood swallows in 598.8

.83 *Cinclidae, Troglodytidae, Timaliidae, Chamaeidae

---

*Add as instructed under 592–599

.832	*Cinclidae

> Variant names: dippers, water ouzels

.833	*Troglodytidae

> Class here wrens

.834	*Timaliidae and Chamaeidae

> Including wren-tit

> Class here babblers

> Subdivisions are added for Timaliidae and Chamaeidae together, for Timaliidae alone

.84	*Turdidae, Sylviidae, Mimidae, Muscicapidae
.842	*Turdidae

> Including bluebirds, nightingales, Old World blackbird, robins

> Class here thrushes

.843	*Sylviidae

> Including kinglets

> Class here Old World warblers

.844	*Mimidae

> Including catbirds, mockingbirds, thrashers

.848	*Muscicapidae

> Class here Old World flycatchers

> *See also 598.823 for New World flycatchers*

.85	*Bombycillidae, Ptilogonatidae, Motacillidae
.852	*Bombycillidae

> Class here waxwings

.853	*Ptilogonatidae

> Class here silky flycatchers

.854	*Motacillidae

> Including wagtails

> Class here pipits

.86	*Laniidae, Sturnidae, Corvidae, Paradisaeidae

*Add as instructed under 592–599

.862   *Laniidae

Class here shrikes

Class cuckoo shrikes, vanga shrikes, wood shrikes in 598.8

See also 598.878 for pepper-shrikes and shrike-vireos

.863   *Sturnidae

Including mynas, oxpeckers

Class here starlings

.864   *Corvidae

Including crows, jays, magpies, ravens, rooks

Class bell magpies, magpie larks, wattled crows in 598.8

.865   *Paradisaeidae

Class here birds of paradise

.87   *Parulidae, Icteridae, Thraupidae, Tersinidae, Vireonidae, Cyclarhidae, Vireolaniidae

.872   *Parulidae

Class here New World warblers

.874   *Icteridae

Including cowbirds, grackles, meadowlarks, New World blackbirds, orioles

See also 598.825 for larks of family Alaudidae

.875   *Thraupidae and Tersinidae

Including swallow-tanager

Class here tanagers

Subdivisions are added for Thraupidae and Tersinidae together, for Thraupidae alone

.878   *Vireonidae, Cyclarhidae, Vireolaniidae

Including greenlets, pepper-shrikes, shrike-vireos

Class here vireos

Subdivisions are added for Vireonidae, Cyclarhidae, Vireolaniidae together; for Vireonidae alone

.88   *Finches and related birds

Including Catamblyrhynchidae

Including plush-capped finch

Subdivisions are added for finches and related birds together, for finches alone

*Add as instructed under 592–599

.883   *Fringillidae

     Including Emberizidae, Emberizinae

     Including buntings, cardinals, Darwin's finches, grosbeaks, juncos, towhees; comprehensive works on sparrows

     Class here New World seedeaters

     For sparrows of genus Passer, see 598.887

.885   *Carduelidae

     Including bullfinches, canaries, crossbills, goldfinches, hawfinches, redpolls, rosefinches, siskins

.886   *Estrildidae

     Including weaver finch

     Class here waxbills

     Class comprehensive works on weaver finches in 598.887

.887   *Ploceidae

     Variant names: weaverbirds, weavers

     Including queleas; sparrows of genus Passer, e.g., English sparrow, house sparrow

     Class here comprehensive works on weaver finches

     For weaver finch of family Estrildidae, see 598.886

.9   ***Falconiformes, Strigiformes, Caprimulgiformes**

     Including Sagittariidae

     Including secretary bird

     Class here birds of prey, raptors

     Subdivisions are added for Falconiformes, Strigiformes, Caprimulgiformes together; for Falconiformes alone

---

\>   598.92–598.96 Falconiformes

     Class comprehensive works in 598.9

.92   *Cathartidae

     Including condors, king vulture, turkey buzzard, turkey vulture

     Class here New World vultures; comprehensive works on vultures

     For Old World vultures, see 598.94

.93   *Pandionidae

     Class here osprey

*Add as instructed under 592–599

.94 *Accipitridae

  Including harriers, Old World vultures, true buzzards

  Class comprehensive works on vultures in 598.92

  See also 598.92 for turkey buzzard

.942 *Eagles

  For Haliaeetus leucocephalus, see 598.943

.942 3 *Aquila chrysaetos

  Class here golden eagle

.943 *Haliaeetus leucocephalus

  Class here bald eagle

.944 *Hawks

.945 *Kites

.96 *Falconidae

  Including caracaras, kestrels

  Class here falcons

.97 *Strigiformes

  Including Tytonidae

  Including barn owls, grass owls

  Class here Strigidae

  Class here owls

.99 *Caprimulgiformes

  Including Nyctibiidae, Podargidae

  Including frogmouths, oilbird, potoos, whippoorwill

  Class here Caprimulgidae

  Class here goatsuckers, nighthawks, nightjars

599 *Mammalia

  Class here Eutheria

  Class here mammals, placental mammals, warm-blooded vertebrates

  Class interdisciplinary works on species of domestic mammals in 636

  For Aves, see 598

  See Manual at 599

---

*Add as instructed under 592–599

SUMMARY

[.073]   Collections of living mammals

> Do not use; class in 590.73

.144   Head

> Number built according to instructions under 592–599

> Including ears, eyes, mouth, nose

> *For fangs, horns, tusks, see 599.147*

.163   Beneficial mammals

> Number built according to instructions under 592–599

> Including game mammals

> Class big game animals in 599.6; class fur-bearing animals in 599.7

[.177]   Marine mammals

> Do not use; class in 599.5

.2   *Marsupialia and Monotremata

> Class here Diprotodontia, Metatheria

> Subdivisions are added for Marsupialia and Monotremata together, for Marsupialia alone

---

>   599.22–599.27 Marsupialia

> Class comprehensive works in 599.2

>   599.22–599.25 Diprotodonta

> Class comprehensive works in 599.2

.22   *Macropodidae

> Including rat kangaroos, tree kangaroos

> Class here wallabies

---

*Add as instructed under 592–599

.222   *Macropus

> Including gray kangaroos, wallaroos

> Class here comprehensive works on kangaroos

> Class rat kangaroos, tree kangaroos in 599.22

.222 3   *Macropus rufus

> Class here red kangaroo

.23   *Australasian possums

> Including Burramyidae, Petauridae, Tarsipedidae

> Class here Phalangeroidea

> *For Macropodidae, see 599.22*

> *See also 599.276 for American opossums*

.232   *Phalangeridae

> Including brush-tailed possums, scaly-tailed possum

> Class here Phalanger

> Class here cuscuses

.24   *Vombatidae

> Class here wombats

.25   *Phascolarctidae

> Class here koala

.26   *Peramelina

> Class here Peramelidae

> Class here bandicoots

.27   *Marsupicarnivora and Paucituberculata

> Including Caenolestidae, Dasyuridae, Microbiotheriidae

> Including marsupial cats, marsupial mice, marsupial moles, marsupial rats, monito del monte, numbat, shrew opossums, Tasmanian devil, Tasmanian tiger, Tasmanian wolf, thylacine

> Subdivisions are added for Marsupicarnivora and Paucituberculata together, for Marsupicarnivora alone

.276   *Didelphidae

> Class here American opossums

> *See also 599.23 for Australasian possums*

*Add as instructed under 592–599

.29   *Monotremata

Including Ornithorhynchidae, Tachyglossidae

Including echidnas, platypus, spiny anteaters

Class here Prototheria

> **599.3–599.9 Eutheria**

Class comprehensive works in 599

.3   **Miscellaneous orders of Eutheria**

Limited to those named below

SUMMARY

599.31	**Edentata, Pholidota, Tubulidentata**
.32	**Lagomorpha**
.33	**Insectivora and related orders**
.35	**Rodentia**
.36	**Sciuridae**
.37	**Castoridae**

[.301–.309]   Standard subdivisions

Do not use; class in 599.01–599.09

.31   *Edentata, Pholidota, Tubulidentata

Including ant bear, aardvark, pangolins, scaly anteaters

Class here Xenarthra

Subdivisions are added for Edentata, Pholidota, Tubulidentata together; for Edentata alone

---

> 599.312–599.314 Edentata

Class comprehensive works in 599.31

.312   *Dasypodidae

Class here armadillos

Subdivisions are added for the family as a whole and for individual genera and species

.313   *Bradypodidae

Class here sloths

Subdivisions are added for the family as a whole and for individual genera and species

*Add as instructed under 592–599

.314   *Myrmecophagidae

         Class here comprehensive works on anteaters

         Class ant bears, scaly anteaters in 599.31

         For spiny anteaters, see 599.29

.32   *Lagomorpha

         Class here Leporidae

         Class here rabbits

         Class interdisciplinary works on domestic rabbits in 636.9322

>   599.322–599.328 Leporidae

         Class comprehensive works in 599.32

.322   *Oryctolagus

         Class here Old World rabbit

.324   *Sylvilagus

         Class here cottontails

         Subdivisions are added for the genus as a whole and for individual species

.328   *Lepus

         Class here hares, jackrabbits

         Subdivisions are added for the genus as a whole and for individual species

.329   *Ochotonidae

         Variant names: conies, pikas

         Class here Ochotona

         See also 599.68 for conies of order Hyracoidea

.33   *Insectivora and related orders

         Including Cynocephalidae, Dermoptera

         Including colugos, flying lemurs, otter shrews, solenodons, tenrecs

         Class here Lipotyphla

         Subdivisions are added for Insectivora and related orders together, for Insectivora alone

---

>   599.332–599.336 Insectivora

         Class comprehensive works in 599.33

*Add as instructed under 592–599

.332 ***Erinaceidae**

Including wood shrews

Class here hedgehogs

.332 2 ***Erinaceus**

Class here European hedgehog

Subdivisions are added for the genus as a whole and for individual species

.335 ***Talpidae and Chrysocloridae**

Class here moles

Subdivisions are added for Talpidae and Chrysocloridae together, for Talpidae alone

.336 ***Soricidae**

Class here comprehensive works on shrews

Class otter shrews in 599.33

For wood shrews, see 599.332; for elephant shrews, see 599.337; for tree shrews, see 599.338

.336 2 ***Sorex**

Class here long-tailed shrews, pigmy shrew

Subdivisions are added for the genus as a whole and for individual species

.337 ***Macroscelidea**

Variant name: Macroscelididae

Class here elephant shrews

.338 ***Scandentia**

Variant name: Tupaiidae

Class here tree shrews

.35 ***Rodentia**

Including harvest mice, jerboas, jumping mice, mole rats, swamp rats

Class here Myomorpha; Muridae covering Cricetidae, Rhizomyidae, Spalacidae

Class here mice, rats, rodents

Class results of experimental studies on internal biological processes using laboratory mice and rats in 571–573, plus notation 1935 from table under 571–572 or notation 1935 from table under 573, e.g., circulation in rats 573.11935

For Sciuridae, see 599.36; for Castoridae, see 599.37

*Add as instructed under 592–599

> 599.352–599.358 Muridae

Class comprehensive works in 599.35

.352   *Rattus

Class here black rat, brown rat, common rats, Norway rat

Subdivisions are added for the genus as a whole and for individual species

Class comprehensive works on rats in 599.35

.353   *Mus

Class here common mice, house mouse

Subdivisions are added for the genus as a whole and for individual species

Class comprehensive works on mice in 599.35

.354   *Voles

Including Arvicola

Including water voles

Class here Microtus

Class here meadow mice

.355   *Peromyscus

Variant names: deer mice, white-footed mice

.356   *Hamsters

Class here Cricetus, Mesocricetus

Class here golden hamsters

Class interdisciplinary works on domestic species of hamsters in 636.9356

.357   Miscellaneous rats of family Muridae

Limited to those named below

[.357 01–.357 09]   Standard subdivisions

Do not use; class in 599.3501–599.3509

.357 2   *Sigmodon

Class here cotton rats

.357 3   *Neotoma

Class here wood rats

*Add as instructed under 592–599

.357 9	*Muskrats
	Class here Neofiber, Ondatra
.358	Miscellaneous Muridae
	Limited to those named below
[.358 01–.358 09]	Standard subdivisions
	Do not use; class in 599.3501–599.3509
.358 2	*Lemmings
	Class here Lemmus
.358 3	*Gerbils
	Class interdisciplinary works on domestic species of gerbils in 636.93583
.358 5	*Apodemus
	Variant names: field mice, wood mice
.359	*Rodentia other than Castoridae, Muridae, Sciuridae
	Including African mole rat, agoutis, cane rats, capybaras, coypu, gundis, hutias, nutria, pacas, rock rats, spiny rats, springhaas
	Class here Caviomorpha, Hystricomorpha, Phiomorpha
.359 2	*Caviidae
	Class here Cavia
	Class here cavies, guinea pigs
	Class interdisciplinary works on domestic guinea pigs in 636.93592
.359 3	*Chinchillidae
	Class here chinchillas
	Class interdisciplinary works on chinchillas in 636.93593
.359 6	*Gliridae
	Variant name: Myoxidae
	Class here dormice
.359 7	*Porcupines
	Including Hystricidae
	Including Old World porcupines
.359 74	*Erethizontidae
	Class here New World porcupines

*Add as instructed under 592–599

.359 8	*Heteromyidae

Including kangaroo mice, pocket mice

.359 87	*Dipodomys

Class here kangaroo rats

.359 9	*Geomyidae

Class here pocket gophers

See also 599.365 for gopher of genus Spermophilus

.36	*Sciuridae

Class here squirrels

.362	*Sciurus

Class here Eurasian red squirrel, fox squirrel, gray squirrel, tree squirrels

Subdivisions are added for the genus as a whole and for individual species

.363	*Tamiasciurus

Variant names: chickarees, North American red squirrels

Class here Douglas squirrel

Subdivisions are added for the genus as a whole and for individual species

.364	*Chipmunks

Subdivisions are added for chipmunks as a whole and for individual genera and species

.365	*Ground squirrels

Including gopher, susliks

Class here Spermophilus

See also 599.3599 for pocket gophers; also 599.364 for chipmunks

.366	*Marmota

Class here groundhog, marmots, woodchuck

Subdivisions are added for the genus as a whole and for individual species

.367	*Cynomys

Class here prairie dogs

Subdivisions are added for the genus as a whole and for individual species

*Add as instructed under 592–599

.369   *Flying squirrels

    Class here Glaucomys

    Class here eastern flying squirrel

.37   *Castoridae

    Class here Castor

    Class here beavers

    Subdivisions are added for the genus as a whole and for individual species

.4   *Chiroptera

    Class here Microchiroptera

    Class here bats

.45   *Phyllostomidae

    Including neotropical fruit bats, vampire bats

.47   *Vespertilionidae

    Including big brown bats, house bats

.472   *Myotis

    Class here little brown bats

    Subdivisions are added for the genus as a whole and for individual species

.49   *Pteropodidae

    Including flying foxes

    Class here Megachiroptera

    Class here Old World fruit bats

.5   *Cetacea and Sirenia

    Class here Mysticeti, Odontoceti

    Class here baleen whales, great whales, marine mammals, toothed whales, whales

    Subdivisions are added for Cetacea and Sirenia together, for Cetacea alone

    For Pinnipedia, see 599.79

\>   599.52–599.54 Cetacea

    Class comprehensive works in 599.5

*Add as instructed under 592–599

.52	Specific Mysticeti

Including pygmy right whale

Class comprehensive works on Mysticeti in 599.5

[.520 1–.520 9]	Standard subdivisions

Do not use; class in 599.501–599.509

.522	*Eschrichtidae

Class here gray whale

.524	*Balaenopteridae

Including Bryde's whales, minke whales, sei whale

Class here Balaenoptera

Class here rorquals

For Megaptera, see 599.525

.524 6	*Balaenoptera physalus

Variant names: fin whale, finback whale

.524 8	*Balaenoptera musculus

Class here blue whale

.525	*Megaptera

Class here humpback whale

.527	*Balaenidae
.527 3	*Eubalaena

Class here right whale

.527 6	*Balaena

Variant names: bowhead whale, Greenland right whale

>	599.53–599.54 Odontoceti

Class comprehensive works in 599.5

.53	*Dolphins and porpoises

Including false killer whale, pilot whales

Class here Delphinidae

Subdivisions are added for dolphins and porpoises together, for dolphins alone

*Add as instructed under 592–599

> 599.532–599.536 Delphinidae

Class comprehensive works in 599.53

For river dolphins of family Delphinidae, see 599.538

.532 *Delphinus

Class here common dolphin

.533 *Tursiops

Class here bottle-nosed dolphins

Subdivisions are added for the genus as a whole and for individual species

.534 *Stenella

Including spinner dolphin, spotted dolphins, striped dolphin

.536 *Orcinus

Class here killer whale

.538 *River dolphins

Including Iniidae, Platanistidae, Pontoporiidae; Orcaella and Sotalia of family Delphinidae

.539 *Phocoenidae

Class here Phocoena

Class here harbor porpoises, porpoises

Subdivisions are added for the genus Phocoena as a whole and for individual species of Phocoena

.54 *Other Odontoceti

Toothed whales other than dolphins and porpoises

Class comprehensive works on Odontoceti in 599.5

For false killer whale, pilot whales, see 599.53; for killer whale, see 599.536

.542 *Delphinapterus

Variant names: beluga, white whale

Class here Monodontidae

For Monodon, see 599.543

.543 *Monodon

Class here narwhal

*Add as instructed under 592–599

.545   *Ziphiidae

Class here beaked whales

.547   *Physeteridae

Including dwarf sperm whale, pygmy sperm whale

Class here Physeter

Class here sperm whale

.55   *Sirenia

Class here Trichechidae

Class here manatees, sea cows

Subdivisions are added for the genus Trichechus and for individual species of Trichechus

.559   *Dugongidae

Class here dugong

Class Steller's sea cow in 599.559168

.6   *Ungulates

Class here hoofed mammals, comprehensive works on big game animals

Class Sirenia in 599.55; class big game hunting in 799.26

For a specific kind of nonungulate big game animal, see the kind, e.g., bears 599.78

SUMMARY

599.63	**Artiodactyla**	
.64	**Bovidae**	
.65	**Cervidae**	
.66	**Perissodactyla**	
.67	**Proboscidea**	
.68	**Hyracoidea**	

.63   *Artiodactyla

Including Tragulidae

Including chevrotains, mouse deer

Class here Ruminantia

Class here even-toed ungulates, ruminants

Class comprehensive works on Artiodactyla and Perissodactyla in 599.6

For Bovidae, see 599.64; for Cervidae, see 599.65

*Add as instructed under 592–599

.633	*Suidae

        Variant names: pigs, swine

        Including African bush pig, babirusa, giant forest hog, warthog

        Class here comprehensive works on Suiformes

          For Tayassuidae, see 599.634; for Hippopotamidae, see 599.635

.633 2	*Sus

        Including bearded pigs, Javan pig

        Class here wild boars

        Class interdisciplinary works on domestic swine in 636.4

.634	*Tayassuidae

        Class here peccaries

        Subdivisions are added for the family as a whole and for individual genera and species

.635	*Hippopotamidae

        Including pigmy hippopotamus

        Class here Hippopotamus amphibius

        Class here hippopotamuses

.636	*Camelidae
.636 2	*Camelus

        Class here camels

        Subdivisions are added for the genus as a whole and for individual species

        Class interdisciplinary works on camels in 636.295

.636 7	*Lama

        Class here guanaco, vicuña

        Class interdisciplinary works on guanaco (alpaca, llama) in 636.2966

.638	*Giraffidae

        Including okapi

        Class here giraffe

.639	*Antilocapridae

        Class here pronghorn

*Add as instructed under 592–599

.64   *Bovidae

> Including Cephalophinae
>
> Including duikers
>
> Class here antelopes
>
> *See also 599.639 for pronghorn antelope*

.642   *Bovinae

> Including buffalo, elands, four-horned antelopes
>
> *For American buffalo, see 599.643*

.642 2   *Bos

> Including banteng, gaur, yak
>
> Class here oxen
>
> Class interdisciplinary works on domestic cattle in 636.2

.642 3   *Tragelaphus

> Including bongo, bushbuck, kudus, nyalas

.643   *Bison

> Including European bison, wisent
>
> Class here American bison, American buffalo

.645   *Hippotraginae

> Including addax, hartebeests, oryx, reedbucks, roan antelope, sable antelope, waterbuck
>
> Class here Alcelaphinae

.645 9   *Connochaetes

> Variant names: gnus, wildebeests
>
> Subdivisions are added for the genus as a whole and for individual species

.646   *Antilopinae

> Including dik-diks, impala, springbok

.646 9   *Gazella

> Class here gazelles
>
> Subdivisions are added for the genus as a whole and for individual species

.647   *Caprinae

> Including chamois, saiga, serows
>
> *For Capra, see 599.648; for sheep, see 599.649*

---

*Add as instructed under 592–599

.647 5	*Oreamnos
	Class here mountain goat
.647 8	*Ovibos
	Class here muskox
.648	*Capra
	Including ibexes, turs
	Class here goats
	Class interdisciplinary works on domestic goat in 636.39
	See also 599.6475 for mountain goat
.649	*Sheep
	Including aoudad, Barbary sheep, bharals, blue sheep
	Class here Ovis
	Class interdisciplinary works on domestic sheep in 636.3
.649 7	*Ovis canadensis
	Class here bighorn sheep
.65	*Cervidae
	Including chital, muntjacs
	Class here deer
	See also 599.63 for mouse deer
.652	*Odocoileus
	Class here Virginia deer, white-tailed deer
	For Odocoileus hemionus, see 599.653
.653	*Odocoileus hemionus
	Class here mule deer
.654	*Cervus
	Including sambar
.654 2	*Cervus elaphus
	Variant names: American elk, red deer, wapiti
	See also 599.657 for elk of genus Alces
.655	*Dama
	Class here fallow deer

*Add as instructed under 592–599